68000
Assembly Language
Programming

68000 Assembly Language Programming

Second Edition

Lance A. Leventhal,
Doug Hawkins, Gerry Kane,
and William D. Cramer

Osborne **McGraw-Hill**
Berkeley, California

Osborne **McGraw-Hill**
2600 Tenth Street
Berkeley, California 94710
U.S.A.

For information on translations and book distributors outside of the U.S.A., write to Osborne **McGraw-Hill** at the above address.

68000 is a trademark of Motorola Microsystems.

68000 Assembly Language Programming, Second Edition

Copyright © 1986 by McGraw-Hill, Inc. All rights reserved. Printed in the United States of America. Except as permitted under the Copyright Act of 1976, no part of this publication may be reproduced or distributed in any form or by any means, or stored in a database or retrieval system, without the prior written permission of the publisher, with the exception that the program listings may be entered, stored, and executed in a computer system, but they may not be reproduced for publication.

1234567890 DODO 89876

ISBN 0-07-881232-1

About the Authors

Gerry Kane is co-author of several volumes of the well-known series, *An Introduction to Microcomputers*. Most recently, he authored the *CRT Controller Handbook* and the *68000 Microprocessor Handbook,* both part of the new Osborne Handbook Series. He received his B.S. degree from the United States Coast Guard Academy.

Doug Hawkins is vice president of engineering for Phoenix Digital Corporation, Phoenix, Arizona, with responsibility for the design and implementation of microprocessor-based systems for distributive plant monitoring and process control. Previously, Mr. Hawkins worked for Motorola Microsystems, the primary source for the MC68000, as manager of language systems. He received his B.S.E.E. degree from Michigan State University, and M.S.E.E. and M.B.A. degrees from Arizona State University.

Lance Leventhal is a partner in Emulative Systems Company, Inc., a San Diego-based consulting firm specializing in microprocessors and microprogramming. He is a national lecturer on microprocessors for the IEEE, the author of ten books and over sixty articles on microprocessors, and a regular contributor to such publications as *Simulation* and *Microcomputing*. He also serves as technical editor for the Society for Computer Simulation and as contributing editor for *Digital Design* magazine.

Dr. Leventhal authored the original books in this series and has just begun work on a new series, Assembly Language Subroutines. He received a B.A. degree from Washington University in St. Louis, and M.S. and Ph.D. degrees from the University of California at San Diego. He is a member of SCS, ACM, IEEE, and the IEEE Computer Society.

William D. Cramer is the co-author of *68000 Microprocessor Handbook, Second Edition,* and *MacTelecommunications.* Mr. Cramer received a B.S. in computer science and mathematics from Texas Christian University.

Contents

	Introduction	xi
Section I Fundamental Concepts		**1**
1	Introduction to Assembly Language Programming	3
2	Assemblers	9
3	MC68000 Machine Architecture	19
Section II Introductory Problems		**53**
4	Beginning Programs	59
5	Simple Program Loops	75
6	Character-Coded Data	95
7	Code Conversion	117
8	Arithmetic Problems	131
9	Tables and Lists	147
Section III Advanced Topics		**171**
10	Parameter Passing Techniques	173
11	Subroutines	177
12	Advanced MC68020 Addressing and Instructions	195
13	Connecting to Peripherals	201
14	Exception Processing	211
15	Interrupts and Other Exceptions	225
Section IV Software Development		**257**
16	Problem Definition	261
17	Program Design	275
18	Documentation	311
19	Debugging	323
20	Testing	357

Section V MC68000 Instruction Set   363
    21   Descriptions of Individual MC68000 Instructions   371

Section VI Appendices   469
    A   Alphabetic Listing of Instructions   471
    B   Numeric Listing of Instructions   475
        Index   479

Acknowledgments

A special thanks to Jeff Bork and Karyn Reott of Altos Computer Corporation for providing an Altos 3068 system for the development of all 68020 material in this book.

Introduction

68000 Assembly Language Programming, Second Edition, describes assembly language programming for the 68000 family of microprocessors—the 68008, 68010, 68012, and 68020. It assumes that you are familiar with microprocessor principles and have a basic understanding of one or more high-level programming languages. A good introductory book on microprocessors is *An Introduction to Microcomputers* by Adam Osborne (Berkeley: Osborne/ McGraw-Hill, 1980). You can find additional 68000-specific information in *68000 Microprocessor Handbook, Second Edition,* by Cramer and Kane (Berkeley: Osborne/McGraw-Hill, 1986).

We divide our discussion of assembly languages into five sections: Section I describes assembly languages in general and introduces you to the 68000 family of microprocessors. In Section II we begin writing assembler programs to solve some simple (but common) programming problems such as looping and arithmetic. In Section III we introduce you to more advanced topics, such as input/output and exception processing. Section IV presents tools for software development that are particularly appropriate to programming in assembly language. Finally, Section V enumerates the instructions available on the 68000 family of processors, paying particular attention to the unique 68020 instructions.

PRINTING AND WORDING INFORMATION

As you can see from the text on this page, this book contains both boldface and lightface type. The material in boldface type provides the most important information on a given topic; the text in lightface type expands on the topic. Therefore, depending on the level of detail you want, you may choose to read only the boldface text or both the boldface and the lightface.

This book discusses all members of the 68000 family. From a software perspective, the microprocessors are nearly identical, particularly when they are used in normal applications. However, in some of the advanced areas (particularly with 68020 instructions), certain family members differ slightly from others. We explicitly identify these differences in the text; if you don't read anything to the contrary, you may assume that a concept is valid for all family members.

I
Fundamental Concepts

The chapters in this section provide basic information on assembly language in general and the MC68000 processors in particular. Chapter 1 discusses the purpose of assembly language programming and compares it with programming in high-level languages. Chapter 2 discusses general assembler syntax and the program development sequence. Chapter 3 describes the architecture and the instruction set of the MC68000 microprocessor family.

1
Introduction to Assembly Language Programming

If you are familiar with programming in a high-level language, you've probably seen a statement similar to this one:

BALANCE = BALANCE + AMOUNT

To a programmer who uses high-level languages, this statement is self-explanatory. Unfortunately, computer design is not yet sufficiently sophisticated for a machine to understand this command directly. To execute this statement, the computer must first convert it into a form it understands; that is, into machine language. The conversion is made by means of a translation program: either a "compiler" or an "interpreter."

From the high-level language programming point of view, it doesn't matter how this translation takes place or what form the final output of the translation takes. However, to the computer executing this compiled program, the form of the output matters greatly. The output of a program compiled on an Apple Macintosh, for example, differs substantially from the output produced by compiling the same high-level program on an IBM PC. If you try to run the Macintosh version of the program on the PC, or vice versa, you will end up with a very confused computer!

MACHINE LANGUAGES

The reason for this problem is that although two computers may support the same high-level language, each may be built around a different "processor"—for example, the Macintosh is built on the Motorola MC68000, and the PC AT on the Intel 80286. Each processor has its own "architecture," or set of circuits, and its own set of primitive "instructions" for manipulating data in and around these circuits.

The basic unit of measurement commonly used in today's computers is a "switch," which can register one of two possible states, ON or OFF, at any given time. Machine instructions consist of sets of such switches. The computer responds to the condition of these switches by opening or closing electrical gates within its internal circuitry. The opening and closing of the circuits has some desired effect, such as adding one number to another.

Because switches have only two conditions, ON or OFF, it is convenient to express their values in "binary" (base 2) terms, where OFF=0 and ON=1. We can express machine instructions as sets of "binary digits" (or "bits"). One combination of bits represents one machine instruction; another combination represents a second instruction.

Programming in a high-level language is all well and good for most applications; writing an accounts-receivable business package, for example, is best accomplished through use of a high-level language. However, at some point, you need to be able to write programs aimed specifically at the machine level; for example, the compiler for the high-level language is probably written at the machine-specific level.

So how do you write programs at the machine level? Clearly, defining bit patterns for instructions becomes tedious. The preceding simple high-level program statement may translate into anywhere from 8 bits to 200 or more bits, depending on the computer being used.

One way of simplifying bit patterns is to group the bits. If you are familiar with mathematic "radices," or "bases," you know that a binary number (base 2) can be grouped evenly into an octal number (base 8) or into a hexadecimal number (base 16). Unfortunately, base 2 doesn't convert easily into base 10, the radix with which we are most famliar. Binary numbers map into octal and hexadecimal numbers, as shown in Table 1-1. From this table, you can see that a 24-bit number can be grouped into an eight-digit octal number or a six-digit hexadecimal number:

```
001 001 011 101 001 011 100 101 = 11351345   (octal)
0010 0101 1101 0010 1110 0101 = 25D2E5   (hexadecimal)
```

ASSEMBLY LANGUAGE

Using octal or hexadecimal notation simplifies the representation of bit patterns. However, many programs consist of thousands of instructions and would be extremely difficult to write even using hexadecimal notation. Further, nothing in the notation would tell you whether an instruction requests an addition, a subtraction, or some other machine function.

Assembly language serves as an intermediate step between machine-level instructions, which are directly understood by the machine, and high-level language designed to be read easily by humans. "Mnemonics," abbreviations representing the function of a machine instruction, make this possible. Programs may be written using mnemonics and then translated into the appropriate bit patterns of machine instructions. For example, the MC68000 assembly instruction

Introduction to Assembly Language Programming 5

ADD D0,D1

translates to the machine instruction

1101 0010 0100 0000.

Performing this translation by hand, while less tedious than generating bit patterns, still represents a fairly difficult task. However, a computer does repetitive translation very well. **A program for translating assembly-language programs into binary machine instructions is called, quite appropriately enough, an "assembler."**

Software developers write assemblers for a new computer on existing computers and then transfer the generated code to the new machine. In time, developers can write "utilities" (such as operating systems, assemblers, disk drivers, and printer drivers) that allow direct program development on the new computer—thus the machine actually contributes to its own maturity.

WHY ASSEMBLY LANGUAGE?

You may have noted from this discussion that an assembler works suspiciously like a high-level-language compiler. This is quite true: both convert statements readable by humans into instructions executable by a computer. There are two main differences between the assembler and the compiler, however, that deal with the formats of the statements themselves:

- Assembly-level statements address the architecture of the microprocessor directly. They often deal with storage circuits called "registers" and manipulate data at the bit level. High-level languages usually deal with data on a more abstract level as "variables" and "constants," whose internal location and bit encryption is of no importance to the programmer.
- Assembly-level statements correspond one-to-one with machine-level instructions. A high-level language statement may translate into one, two, or many machine-level instructions.

Table 1-1. Binary/Octal/Hexadecimal Conversion Table

Hexadecimal Digit	Binary Equivalent	Octal Equivalent
0	0000	0
1	0011	1
2	0010	2
3	0011	3
4	0100	4
5	0101	5
6	0110	6
7	0111	7
8	1000	10
9	1001	11
A	1010	12
B	1011	13
C	1100	14
D	1101	15
E	1110	16
F	1111	17

If you were to make a decision based on these facts alone, you would most likely choose to program in a high-level language. **And indeed, high-level languages have many positive features, including:**

- Simple formula statement. A complex mathematical formula may translate into many machine statements but can be written as a single statement in a high-level language. One of the first high-level languages, FORTRAN, was designed specifically to facilitate "formula translation."
- Block-structured code. Modern programming theory shows that the most readable and maintainable code consists of programs that are broken into "logical blocks" that perform specific tasks. High-level languages provide constructs that make block-structured code easier to write.
- Productivity. Studies show that the average programmer produces ten lines of debugged code per day. This figure holds true regardless of whether the source language is assembly or a high-level language. If one high-level statement converts to three machine-executable statements, this means that the high-level language programmer is three times as prolific as the assembly programmer.
- Level of complexity. Clearly, if the programmer must deal with hardware details, he or she must be much more technically oriented than a programmer working in a high-level language. For some tasks this technical orientation is good; however, a technical person may not be acquainted with the business processes needed to write a good data-processing package. In such a situation, the programmer has enough to worry about without the added complexity of manipulating bits inside the computer.
- Portability. As stated at the start of this chapter, high-level compilers are available for a variety of languages on a variety of machines. Most programs written on one computer will run with little or no modification on any other computer; programmers simply recompile the program using the new computer's compiler. This works because most high-level languages have "standards" that compiler writers adhere to when writing a new compiler.

  Assembly programs are machine-specific; you can't simply reassemble an 8088 program with a MC68000 assembler and expect it to run. Some attempts have been made to standardize assembly language; however, these generally result in hard-to-understand code that doesn't make efficient use of instructions or data.
- Abstract data types. Most modern high-level languages allow you to define and manipulate many data types, such as floating-point values, records and arrays (groups of simpler data types), and high-precision values. Assembly-language programs are restricted to use of the data types provided by the processor and, oftentimes, the processor supplies only 16-bit integer data.
- Readability. Most high-level languages are, to some extent, self-documenting, in that a newcomer to the programmer can read the code and get a general idea of its function. Assembly code is terse and deals in primitive instructions that may tell little about the function of the program.

High-level language programs are not without their faults, however. **Areas in which assembly-language programs may outperform their high-level counterparts include:**

- Size. In most cases, the amount of machine code produced by a high-level language

compiler exceeds the amount required to write the program in assembly language. This is because the compiler must create code general enough to work in all cases; assembly language programmers can take shortcuts because they deal directly with the machine. For example, some compilers may use memory (external to the processor) for counter variables, while an assembly program can make use of registers (internal to the processor).
- Speed. Since assembly programs deal directly with the processor, they can make use of high-speed instructions that may not be available directly through the high-level language. For example, requesting division by two from a compiled language often generates a Divide instruction, while an assembly programmer knows that a division by two can be accomplished by a Left Shift instruction, which executes much faster than a Divide instruction.
- Overhead. Since they allow for abstract data types, most high-level languages perform "typechecking" on variables, to make sure that the programmer has used the data type correctly. While typechecking can be very useful in many instances, it adds overhead in both size and speed of execution.

Advanced high-level language compilers provide for varying amounts of "optimization." Such compilers look for certain usage patterns, just as an assembly programmer might, and make substitutions of faster or more compact code. However, even the best compilers cannot produce code as efficient as that produced in assembly language.

APPLICATIONS FOR DIFFERENT LANGUAGES

As is clear from the preceding discussion, different languages lend themselves to different applications. **Applications for high-level languages include**:
- Scientific problems. Since they permit high-precision and floating-point capabilities, high-level languages allow the programmer to deal with values commonly found in scientific applications.
- Record-oriented problems. Again, since high-level languages allow the user to define records, they permit the programmer to deal with data in logical groups rather than primitive data types.
- Business applications. Many business applications require that data be moved between memory and disk storage, that data from multiple sources be combined, and that printed reports be generated. Assembly language requires far too much internal detail to produce such programs efficiently.
- Portable programs. Often, a software house may want to produce a program that will run on many different host computers. Generally, such a program can be produced from a single version of a high-level language program that is recompiled for the required host.
- Maintainability. Studies show that as much as 70% of the work on a program is done in modifying its function. Because assembly-language programs often take shortcuts, they become difficult to understand and especially difficult to modify. High-level programs, because they are easier to understand, are usually easier to modify.

- Special-purpose programs. Many languages have been designed to solve a specific type of problem. For example, a model simulation problem is best solved with a language that facilitates the use of queues and random-event generation.

Applications that require assembly-language code include:

- Input/output intensive programs. When a program is designed to move a high volume of data into and out of the computer, assembly language may be appropriate. Such programs generally need little heavy computation, and the speed gained with assembly programming often justifies its use. An example of an I/O intensive program is a "device handler," which might interface the computer to a peripheral such as a disk drive. If the disk handler cannot read incoming data fast enough, the data may be lost.
- Time-dependent applications. Certain applications require very precise timing control. For example, process control (using a computer to control peripheral devices, such as valves and sensors in a manufacturing plant) requires that events take place at specific intervals. High-level languages may sometimes add just enough overhead to cause a malfunction in the process.
- Graphics displays. Graphics programs require manipulations of "pixels," or picture elements. In most implementations, pixels correspond directly to bits (through "bit maps"). Since assembly code provides direct access to individual bits, it allows rapid generation of displays.

With the development of new medium-level languages, the choice between assembly language and a higher-level language becomes more difficult. Medium-level languages provide high-level data structures and block-oriented code, while allowing the programmer to use many machine-level instructions. An example of a medium-level language is the "C" language.

HIGH LEVEL, ASSEMBLY, OR BOTH

Clearly, the trend in program development is toward specialized high-level languages. However, there will always be a need for assembly-language programming for the specialized applications discussed earlier. Even the advent of medium-level languages will not make assembly language obsolete; some applications need to save every instruction or memory location possible, and this can be accomplished only with assembly language.

Many applications are or will become "hybrids" in their use of programming languages. After studying the executing patterns of a program written in a high-level language, a system analyst may determine that a particular piece of code is executed repeatedly; rewriting that particular piece of the program in assembly language may speed the program's execution by several orders of magnitude.

Another argument for learning assembly language is that while a high-level language routine is simpler to code and understand, inevitably a piece of code comes along that just doesn't work as you think it should. Looking at the assembly code produced by the compiler (when available) often reveals the hidden bugs in your program.

2
Assemblers

In this chapter we discuss the functions performed by assemblers. We start by defining just what an assembler does. We then describe some of the more common features of assembler "source code." Some of the material described in this chapter may seem foreign to you until you have a little assembler experience under your belt. Feel free to skim this chapter for now. You may want to come back to it after writing a few programs while working through later chapters.

FUNCTIONS OF ASSEMBLERS

As stated in Chapter 1, assemblers allow you to write machine-level programs using mnemonic commands instead of strings of bits. **However, assemblers do more than convert mnemonics to machine instructions. An instruction must perform its function on some piece of data; this datum is called an "operand."** The location of the operand is specified by the operand portion of the instruction code. The assembler must be capable of evaluating the operand field and including it as part of the machine instruction. Depending on the addressing modes allowed by the processor, this evaluation may be simple or quite complex.

Assembly programs, like high-level programs, require memory space not only for storing their instructions but also for storing variables. An assembler must be capable of defining memory storage. Ultimately, machine instructions refer to data and code stored in other locations in memory by the memory address (a binary number). However, to make the code more readable and easier to modify, assemblers let you define "labels." Labels are like variable and function names in high-level languages. The assembler translates these labels into binary memory addresses so that programs can refer to the location by its logical name rather than its physical number.

Assemblers produce "object code." In most cases, however, this object code isn't in a format that the system can load into memory and run. A **"linker" converts this object code into a load module or task image that the system can load into memory.** The linker also permits you to combine the object code of several modules into one program. This lets you keep the size of your source files to a minimum.

Assemblers let you pass along commands to the linker through "directives." Directives let you define the starting memory location of your program, the location of the first instruction of your program, sections of your program that are "read only," and many other attributes. We will discuss linkers and their associated assembler directives in more detail later in this chapter.

TYPES OF ASSEMBLERS

Assemblers come in many packages. In the optimum case, your assembler runs on the same machine for which it produces code. However, this is not always possible. New computers may not have the operating system features required to run an assembler. Some computers, particularly microprocessors, are "embedded" within other systems; a printer, for example, often has an embedded microprocessor. In such cases, program development (editing, assembling, and linking) is done on another computer and then transferred to the final host. Assemblers used for these applications are called "cross assemblers."

Another type of assembler is the "macro assembler." In addition to the primary purpose of an assembler (that is, translating mnemonics into machine instructions), these assemblers let you use "macros." Macros are another form of mnemonic. Unlike assembly mnemonics, however, macros translate into more than one machine instruction.

Macros serve a number of purposes. For example, when you use the same string of instructions several times in a program, you can avoid retyping by defining the entire string as a macro. Then, each time you want to perform this function, you can simply type in the macro name and the assembler will expand the macro into the predefined set of instructions.

ASSEMBLY LANGUAGE FORMAT

Now that we have discussed some of the features of assemblers, let's look at a typical assembly language program. (Remember, however, that not all assemblers are alike. The format of your assembler may differ slightly from that shown here.)

Assembly language, unlike many high-level languages, is line-oriented. This means that, by and large, one complete statement fits on a single line. Assembly language is further restricted in that it expects the components of the statement to lie in specific "fields" on the line. Assembly instructions are made up of three such fields: the label field, the instruction field, and the opcode field.

While some early assemblers required that you start fields in specific columns, most assemblers let you separate labels from instruction mnemonics and operands with "delimiters."

Delimiters are special characters such as blanks, tab characters, commas, and semicolons.

The assembler often assumes that a statement consists of a label (if present) always starting in column 1, followed by a delimiter, followed by the mnemonic, followed by a delimiter, followed by one or more operands. For example:

```
Label    Mnemonic   Operand
START    CLR.L      D0
```

The statement may have more than one operand; again, the operands are separated by delimiters (usually commas). For example:

```
START    ADD.L    D0,D1
```

LABELS

Let's look at the components of an assembler statement in detail, starting with labels. You use labels to assign named values to memory locations such as variables and the start of a subroutine. Writing code that refers to a variable as TOTAL makes much more sense than referring to the variable by its binary memory location. Likewise, labeling a subroutine as COSINE is infinitely clearer than calling it 000110010011000.

When the assembler encounters a new label in a program, it stores the value in a special table called a "symbol table." When it finds a reference to the label later in the assembly process, it knows that TOTAL is actually address 0010100101100110, for example, and inserts this address into the instruction.

Different assemblers have different rules for label names. In general, label names must consist of only certain characters, must be less than a certain number of characters long, and must be unique; you can't give the same label name to two locations. For example, an assembler may require that labels consist of uppercase letters and numbers and must be eight characters or less in length. In this context, START, FUNC2, and C12345 are all valid labels, while Z**2F, jki3##, and PROGRAM_NAME are illegal.

In addition to the assembler's rules for labels, some commonsense rules also apply to selecting label names. These rules include:

- Use meaningful names. "DDD" and "F$" may be legal, but they say little about the variable or code they represent.
- Don't use label names that are the same as instruction mnemonics. The assembler may permit this, but it makes the code difficult to understand.
- Make each label obviously different from all others. Labels such as SYSCOM and SYSCON may be legal, but they are easily confused.

These are recommendations, not rules. You needn't follow them, but if you don't, you may find yourself wasting time correcting needless errors.

INSTRUCTION MNEMONICS

One primary task of the assembler is to transform mnemonics into their equivalent machine-readable instructions. The assembler keeps a table of legal assembler mnemonics; when it reads a mnemonic in your source code, it looks up the instruction code in the table. The table also lists the number and type of operand associated with the mnemonic.

Instruction mnemonics are thus standard within the assembler. For the most part, you have no choice in selecting mnemonic names.

OPERANDS

Operands come in many shapes and sizes. The particular format of an operand depends on the "addressing mode." The addressing mode determines where in memory the operand is located. Common addressing modes include

- Immediate. The instruction names the operand(s) explicitly (the operand directly follows the instruction).
- Register direct. The operand resides in a special location in the processor (a register).
- Absolute. The operand resides in a memory location specified by an address following the instruction.
- Relative. The operand resides in a memory location specified by the sum of an address following the instruction and a processor register (such as the program counter).
- Indirect. The address of the operand (in memory) is specified by a processor register or an intermediate memory location.
- Indexed. The address of the operand (in memory) is specified by the sum of two processor registers (one specifying a "base" and the other specifying an "index").

MC68000-family addressing modes will be discussed further in Chapter 3.

DIRECTIVES

Directives are a special type of assembly instruction. They don't translate into machine code; rather, **they instruct the assembler on "how" to perform the assembly.** Several common assembly directives will be discussed in this section.

Data Definition

Commonly, an assembly program must define a good deal of space in the computer's memory. Such storage space may contain text, loop counters, memory "commons," tables, and temporary workspace. Typically, the assembler allows the program to set aside memory for single data items (bytes, words, longwords), text strings, arrays (homogenous groups of strings or single data items), and records (heterogenous groups of single data items, text, and arrays). In addition, most assemblers permit the programmer to "initialize" (assign values) to the defined memory locations.

Labels are often associated with data-definition directives. When the assembler encounters these directives in a program, it allocates a portion of the produced object code to the defined data (the amount of allocated code is specified by the directive). If the statement line includes a label, the assembler includes the address/label name in the symbol table. When the assembler finds a reference to this item (through an operand in an instruction statement), it inserts the corresponding address into the instruction.

Constant Definition

While assembly language permits you to specify exact values in instruction statements (with immediate addressing), common sense dictates that named values are more meaningful than numeric values. For example,

                ADD   #RECORD__SIZE,D0

is clearer than

                ADD   #120,D0

even though the assembler produces the same object code for each.

Assemblers typically let you define named constants (also known as "equates"). Whenever an assembler encounters a named constant in your source code, the assembler substitutes the numeric value before translating the line into a binary instruction.

In addition to making code more readable, constants make your code easier to modify. You might often use the same constant several times in a program. If for some reason you need to change this constant value, you can use equates to change the value at the point of definition, and all references to the equate (by name) are unchanged.

External Definition

If you have ever written a large program, you know that it is good programming practice to break the program into several logical pieces, each of which is stored in a discrete file and assembled separately. As we have said, the assembler creates a symbol table of all labeled addresses in the source. However, if a value (a function name, for example) is defined in a different source file, the assembler has no knowledge of it.

Most assemblers permit you to define "external" or "global" names. After the assembler has completed the translation of your source, it places such "unresolved references" into a second symbol table. When you link the modules of the program, the linker resolves all of the references in this symbol table.

Program Sections

In many instances, you will find it convenient to keep all of your data together, separated from all of your code. You may wish to combine together all data from each source code file. In some cases, you will want the code to be "read only" so that the system hardware will protect your program code from being written over. In other cases, you might need the code or data to begin on a specific memory address boundary.

Program sections permit you to divide your code into discrete, named segments, each of which can have separate characteristics, including read/write protection, memory-address origin, and memory alignment.

Macros

As we have said, assembly language is line-oriented. Since even simple functions may require several lines of code, your source file may grow quite large and cumbersome. **One convenient way of slimming down your program is to combine commonly used lines of code into a single macro.** Macros, like machine-instruction mnemonics, often have operand fields.

Macros are typically used to set up a call to a system routine, a routine to handle printing a string of characters, for example. A subroutine called "PRINT" may require you to provide certain parameters (address of the string, length of the string, and so on). Setting up these parameters may require several lines of code. Here is an example:

                MOVE.L   #STRING,-(SP)

```
            MOVE.W   #STRING_LENGTH,-(SP)
            JSR      PRINT
```

However, because you may make many calls to this routine, you may define a macro "PRINT_STRING" that lets you code:

```
            PRINT_STRING   #STRING,#STRING_LENGTH
```

When the assembler encounters this statement, it checks its list of defined macros and expands PRINT_STRING into the appropriate code.

Macros are a powerful tool in writing assembly language. However, each assembler has its own syntax for creating macros; we won't use macros in this book, to avoid confusion with real machine instructions. Be aware, however, that they can be a real aid in writing assembly programs.

Conditional Assembly

When writing a general program utility, or writing a function that may run in a variety of environments, you may often need to add instructions, delete instructions, or use different versions of instructions. For example, you may wish to write a program that can display data on several types of terminals, each of which requires different commands to perform the same function.

"Conditional assembly" permits you to define a constant (through use of an equate) and then generate different pieces of code based on the value of the constant. For example, you may define a constant called TERM, whose value may be NORMAL or KEYPAD. Your code may then read

```
            .if TERM=NORMAL
                    MOVE.B     #' [, D0
            .else
                    MOVE.B     #'_, D0
            .endif
```

Note here that the syntax for the conditional assembly (".if", ".else", and ".endif") will differ from assembler to assembler; these are only examples. Further, note that the decision on which line of code to generate is made at assembly time, *not* at run time.

File Inclusion

For large-scale projects, it is often necessary for everyone working on the project to use the same set of constants; also, system calls often require that you define specific constants before making the call. Most assemblers permit you to "include" library files in the assembly process.

These included files may contain constant definitions, macro definitions, and other pertinent data. The assembler treats these files as though they were physically present in your source code.

Listing Control

Most assemblers are capable of providing a variety of listings based on the results of the assembly. For example, the assembler may produce no listings at all, listings with just the source given, listings with the object given, listings including the symbol table, listings showing macro expansions, and so on. You can specify the format of the listing file by using assembler directives.

COMMENTS

While technically not required, comments contribute immeasurably to an assembly program. Comments may lie on separate lines, or they may occur after the operand field of an assembly statement. Often the comment must begin with a special character (such as a semicolon or apostrophe) so that the assembler can recognize it as a comment rather than a translatable statement. For example:

```
; Function CHECK_TEMP reads the fuel tank temperature sensors
; and calculates the temperature in Celsius.
   CHECK_TEMP:    MOVE.B    SENSOR1,D0        ; get sensor value
```

We will discuss commenting along with documentation in a later chapter, but **here are some guidelines on when and how to use comments:**

- Use comments to describe what the code is doing in the "big picture"—that is, comments should say things such as "is temperature over limit?" or "bump loop counter." Don't use comments that repeat the assembly statement: for example, "jump to START" or "increment D1."
- Avoid using abbreviations. Comments should be as descriptive as possible.
- Comment all instructions whose purpose may not be immediately clear; instructions dealing with registers rather than memory are often difficult to understand since they deal with register data rather than named memory data.
- You needn't necessarily comment every line; in some cases, a single comment may apply to several statements.
- Comment major sections of code (for example, subroutines) with several lines of comments. Don't rely solely on the comments following the instruction operand.
- Make all comments uniform in both appearance and terminology. All in-line comments should start in the same column. Don't refer to the same variable as "route distance" in one comment and "location delta" in another.
- Be especially careful to document instructions or algorithms that you found difficult to understand or write. Such code will be equally difficult for a newcomer to you code to understand. (Ignore the old adage, "It was difficult to write, so by golly it should be difficult to read!").

PROGRAM DEVELOPMENT

Now that we have described the basic functions of assemblers, let's look at how they fit into the "big scheme" of program development. **There are several steps required to create a working program. These steps include designing, editing, assembling, linking, and loading.**

DESIGN

The first thing to do when you begin to write a program is turn off your terminal. Studies have shown that a rule of thumb for projecting the time requirements for a project is 40/20/40; that is, 40% of the time is spent in design, 20% in coding, and 40% in testing and integration.

Many different methodologies are available for designing a program. We will present some of these in Section IV.

EDITING

After you have designed the program to your satisfaction, you may begin to enter source code into the computer. To do this, you need some sort of "editor." Editors come in a variety of flavors. "Character-oriented" editors are, at best, cumbersome to work with. They provide basic data entry capabilities, but often require that you move a character pointer to the position where you want to edit or insert material, and they do not automatically provide visual feedback.

On the other end of the spectrum, "full screen" editors let you treat a program as though it were printed on a long sheet of paper. This allows you to look at and edit any part of the program at any time. Such editors provide continuous visual feedback; for example, if you want to insert a character into a line, you simply move the cursor (usually, by pressing the arrow keys on the keyboard) to the point of insertion and press the desired characters. The editor puts them into the text and they appear on the screen. Often, such screen editors require that you use a specific type of terminal so that the editor can give the proper commands to control the display.

ASSEMBLY

Once you have a source file entered into the computer (and saved onto disk), you must assemble the program. As we discussed earlier, the assembler translates the source code into an "object file" containing the machine-instruction code as well as the symbol table entries of any "global" data defined in the source file.

LINKAGE

Often, a single program is made up of several modules, each of which resides in a separate source file. Also, many programs will refer to "library functions." Library functions are common utility programs that may be called from your program. In order to resolve the addresses defined as "unresolved" by the assembler, you must "link" all of the modules (and library) together.

The linker looks through all of the symbol tables of the object files. When it finds an unresolved symbol in one object file defined in another object file, it replaces the unresolved value with its true value.

In addition to resolving addresses, the linker also builds a "load module." Since the assembler is aware of only a single source module, it often produces an object module beginning at address 0. The linker must concatenate each of the object modules; to do this, it must modify all address references so that Module 1 precedes Module 2, which precedes Module 3, and so on.

Some linkers are more powerful than others. In advanced systems, the linker lets you create overlaid programs, multiuser programs, and programs that share code or data with other programs.

LOADERS

The product of the linker is a "load module." This module is almost a program; however, it needs a "loader" to move the load module from disk to memory. Typically, the load module contains some information other than the code and data produced by the assembler. This information is often called the "header," and tells the loader where to load the remainder of the module, what data and devices the program may need prior to running the program, and other system-dependent information.

Once loaded, the program is ready to run. Depending on the system, you simply tell the computer to begin execution by typing "RUN" or perhaps by entering the program name. Often, the RUN instruction tells the system to load the program into memory if it isn't already there.

ALTERNATIVES

These program development steps just outlined are required in most cases. However, in some systems, one or more of these steps may be combined. For example, some assemblers produce a loadable image; that is, they perform both the assembly and the linkage. Other systems use a "linking-loader," which performs the necessary linking at the time that the program is loaded into memory.

Both of these alternatives were common in early systems, whose programs were smaller and less modular than those of current systems. However, in these times of cheap memory and advanced software engineering techniques, only the most rudimentary programs can be conveniently produced with these tools. Most modern systems follow the basic development steps we have described.

3
MC68000 Machine Architecture

In this chapter, we describe the architecture of the MC68000 family in terms of the accessible internal components of the central processor, memory characteristics, instruction sets, and addressing modes.

THE CENTRAL PROCESSING UNIT

As its name implies, **the central processing unit, or CPU, serves as the chief component of the computing portion of the computer.** The CPU handles both functions that the user requests explicitly and functions that its own internal components and peripherals request implicitly.

The CPU performs explicit functions as directed by your program. Such functions may include arithmetic (adding two numbers together, for example), decision-making ("if...then...else" constructs), and data storage and retrieval. The CPU also handles certain types of errors generated by your programs; for example, division by zero (an illegal operation).

Besides directly executing the instructions of your programs, the CPU is also responsible for controlling the peripherals that are connected to it. In this context, such peripherals include main memory (for example, random access memory, or RAM), controllers (for example, disk-drive controllers), and support processing units (for example, floating-point processors). Whenever your program accesses one of these peripherals, the CPU must perform certain "handshaking" functions to ensure that the data transfer between itself and the peripheral follows standard rules.

Many peripherals are capable of "interrupting" normal program execution within the CPU. Such interruptions may occur when the peripheral needs to transfer some data; for example, when you press a key on the keyboard. The CPU must arbitrate interrupts between different peripherals and also determine what actions it needs to take in regard to servicing the interrupt. Typically, the CPU stops execution of the current program and begins execution of another program called an "interrupt handler routine."

CPU COMPONENTS

The CPU consists of several discrete components. These components include address registers, data registers, and status/control registers, all of which your program can access. In addition, the CPU contains many control registers that contain current instruction information, processor status information, and data buffers. Normally, your program cannot access these registers.

Typically, **an instruction will ask the CPU to take a value (from a register or memory), perform some operation on it, and then store it into a destination location (either a register or memory). The arithmetic logic unit, or ALU, is responsible for performing all such operations.**

The CPU provides pathways on which data can move between registers, external memory, and the ALU. These pathways are called "buses." CPUs have address buses (for specifying

20 68000 Assembly Language Programming

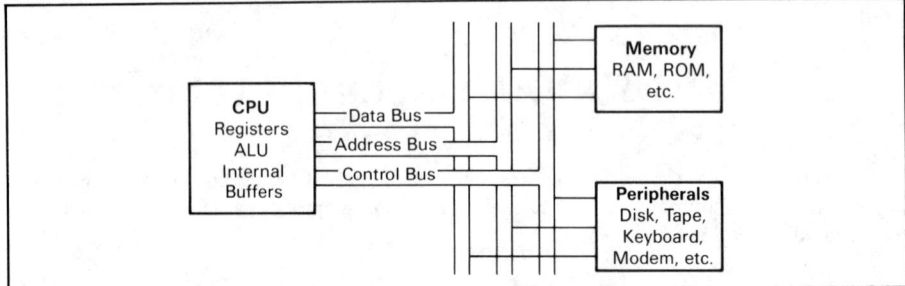

Figure 3-1. Simplified Computer System Block Diagram

memory addresses), data buses (for moving data around the CPU), and control buses (for handling data transfers and manipulating the peripherals attached to the CPU).

Figure 3-1 shows how these CPU components relate to one another.

MODES OF OPERATION

Most advanced microprocessors, like larger mainframe processors, have more than one mode of operation. **The MC68000 family of microprocessors has two modes, the user mode and the supervisor mode.** Most of the programs that you will write operate in the user mode. Operating-system functions operate in the supervisor mode.

The supervisor mode provides the operating system with special instructions that aren't necessary for normal application programs. These "privileged" instructions give the operating system access to data and registers that are associated with task scheduling and interrupt handling. **When the system includes a memory management unit, or MMU, supervisor programs may have access to all of memory.** User programs, on the other hand, have access only to the memory that contains their code and data. This limited access protects the operating system and other programs from corruption by out-of-control user programs.

The supervisor can change the CPU mode to user mode. The opposite is naturally not possible; the user cannot put the CPU into supervisor mode. **The only way for the processor to change from user mode to supervisor mode is through an exception.** Exceptions include peripheral interrupts and illegal instructions. When these occur, the processor changes to supervisor mode and begins program execution at an address typically known only by the operating system. It is virtually impossible for a user-mode program to gain access to supervisor-mode data.

Most of the programs in this book are intended to be run in user mode.

The supervisor modes of the various MC68000 family members differ in their capabilities. Their register structures also differ slightly from one another. Because of these differences, we will discuss the supervisor mode registers separately from the user mode registers.

USER MODE REGISTERS

The MC68000 processor family members have a common set of user-mode data registers, address registers, program counters, and condition code registers, as shown in Figure 3-2.

MC68000 Machine Architecture 21

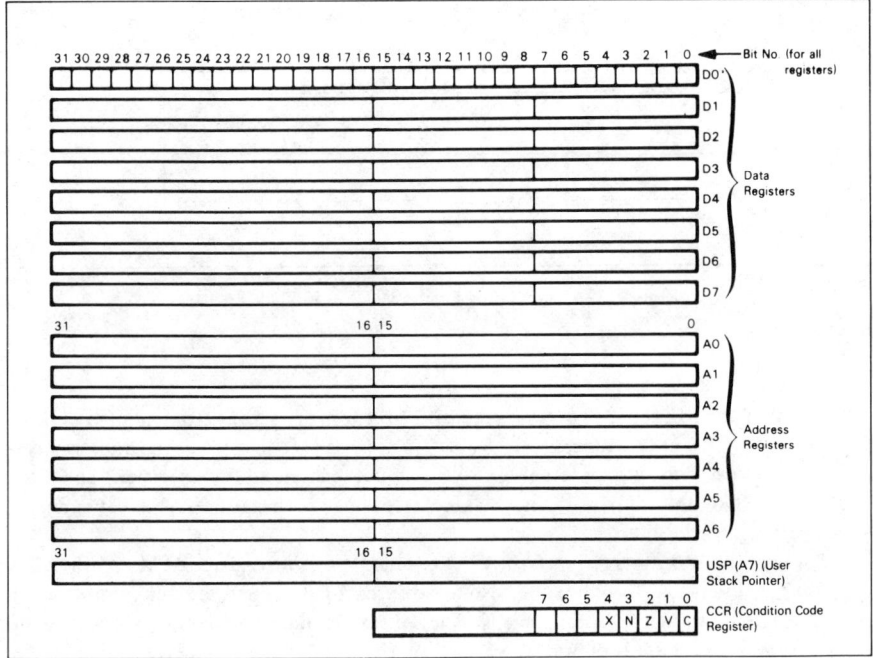

Figure 3-2. User Mode Register Set

Data Registers

The MC68000 has eight 32-bit data registers, D0 through D7. Programs use data registers to hold arithmetic values (such as sums, counters, increments, and so on), as well as "indexes" (which we will discuss later in this chapter). **Data registers can hold 1-bit values, 8-bit bytes, 16-bit words, and 32-bit long words.** It is important to note here that byte and word operations on data registers affect only the lower portion of the register. That is, a byte-sized movement into a data register affects only the least significant 8 bits of the register. The upper 24 bits are unaffected.

The various-sized operands are positioned within the data registers as shown by Figure 3-3.

Address Registers

The MC68000 has eight 32-bit address registers, A0 through A7. **Programs use these values to hold memory pointers; the registers may also contain index values.** Since they hold addresses, they are limited to storing 16-bit words and 32-bit long words (no bit or byte data). Operations that move values into an address register affect the entire 32 bits; in a word movement, the CPU "sign extends" the word into the whole 32 bits of the register (that is, it replicates bit 15 into bits 16 through 31).

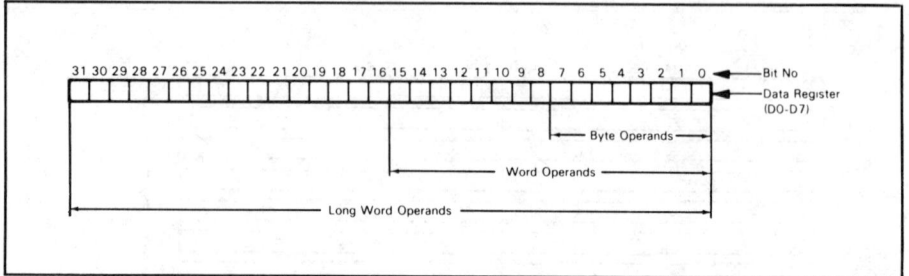

Figure 3-3. Operands Positioned Within Data Registers

Not all of the MC68000 processors permit 32-bit addresses; the actual number of bits used depends on the size of the address bus. Table 3-1 summarizes the size of the address buses on each of the processors. When fetching or writing data via an address register, the CPU uses only as much of the address register as corresponds to the address bus. It ignores any additional high-order bits.

Seven of the address registers (A0-A6) are general purpose registers. The eighth, A7, is the user stack pointer, or USP. (The supervisor mode uses A7 as a separate stack pointer, as will be discussed later in this chapter.) **A stack is a special data structure in memory whose function is to store temporary data.** It operates in a "last in, first out" ("LIFO") method; that is, the last datum "pushed" onto the stack will be the first datum "pulled" off of the stack.

The MC68000 fills a stack from high memory to low memory. For example, on a subroutine call, the processor decrements the stack pointer, pushes the program counter onto the stack, and branches to the subroutine. On return from the subroutine, the processor pulls the program counter from the stack and then increments the stack pointer. Figure 3-4 shows this operation.

Program Counter

The program counter, or PC, keeps track of the address of the next instruction to execute. Each time the CPU requires a new instruction, it reads the instruction pointed to by the PC and then increments the PC. If the instruction is more than one word long, the CPU reads the next

Table 3-1. MC68000 Family Address Buses

Processor	Bus Width	Address Space
MC68000	24	16 megabytes
MC68008	20	1 megabyte
MC68010	24	16 megabytes
MC68012	31	2 gigabytes
MC68020	32	4 gigabytes

word pointed to by the program counter.

Like the address registers, the PC is 32 bits long; however, the actual maximum address depends on the size of the address bus of the particular processor.

Condition Code Register

After completing most operations, the CPU must indicate certain results; for example, after comparing two values, the CPU must be able to indicate whether they were equal. **The user portion of the status register, or SR, contains bit-sized flags, or "condition codes," which may be true (value 1) or false (value 0); this portion of the status register is also known as the "condition code register," or CCR.**

The Carry bit (C) holds the carry from the most significant bit produced by arithmetic operations or shifts. For example, if the sum of two numbers is larger than the destination can hold, the Carry bit is set to true (1); likewise, if in a subtraction, the second number is larger than the first, the Carry bit is set to true. In this context, the bit functions as a "borrow" bit.

The Zero bit (Z) is true (1) when the operation results in a zero value. It is false (0) when the operation produces a nonzero result.

The negative bit (N) takes on the most significant bit of a result. Thus, a true (1) value means that the result was negative, and a false (0) value means the result was positive or zero.

The overflow bit (O) is true (1) when the result of an operation has a magnitude greater than can be represented by the destination and Carry bit.

The Extend bit (X) is always the same as the Carry bit.

SUPERVISOR MODE REGISTERS FOR THE MC68000 AND MC68008

The supervisor mode on the MC68000 and MC68008 processors has access to two registers in addition to the user mode registers, as shown in Figure 3-5.

Status Register

The status register for the MC68000 and MC68008 consists of the condition codes, which lie in the lower byte and are accessible by the user mode, and the upper byte, which is accessible only by the supervisor mode (the supervisor mode has access to both bytes).

The Supervisor bit, (S), specifies the execution mode of the processor. If true (1), the processor is in supervisor mode; if false (0), the processor is in user mode.

The Trace bit, (T), when true (1), specifies that the processor is operating in trace mode. In this mode, after executing an instruction, the processor automatically "traps" to a supervisor routine. The trace mode implements a single-step mode of execution. This allows a debugger program to monitor the results of an application program on an instruction-by-instruction basis.

The MC68000 processors can operate at any one of eight levels, or "priorities." The interrupt mask bits, (I0,I1,I2), form a binary number that specifies the current operation level. External devices may attempt to interrupt the processor by asserting signals on three input lines connected to the processor. When the processor receives an interrupt request, it compares the bits of the interrupt mask to the values on the interrupt lines.

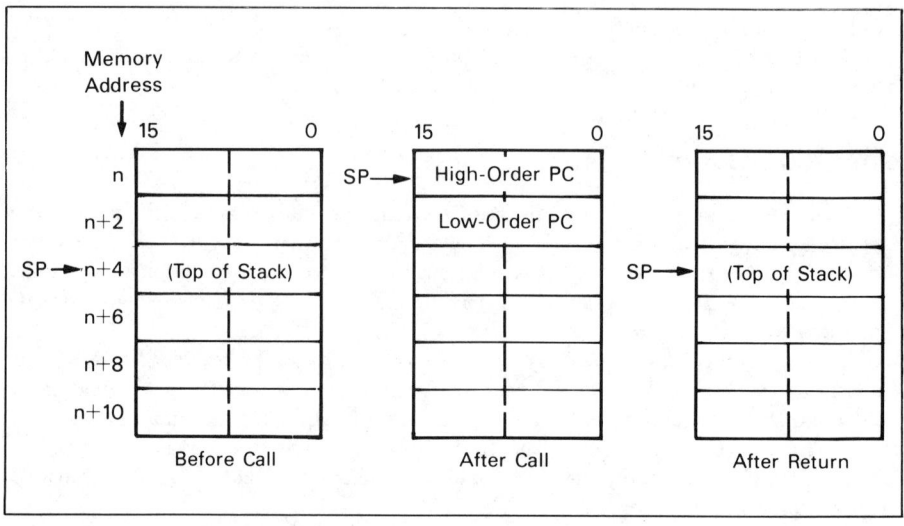

Figure 3-4. Incrementing the Stack Pointer

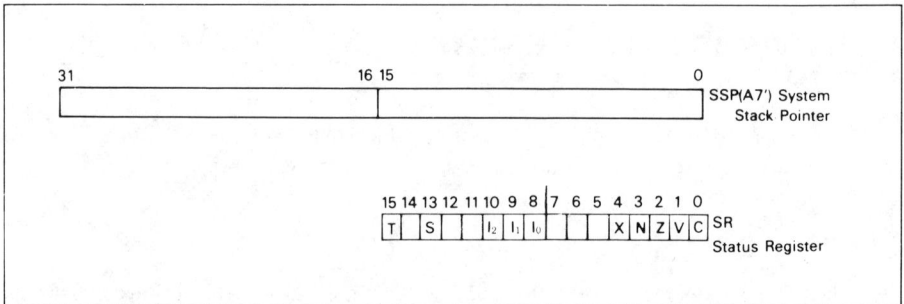

Figure 3-5. Additional Registers Available in Supervisor Mode (MC68000, MC68008)

If the CPU priority is equal to or greater than the interrupt level, the CPU ignores the interrupt (for the time being) and continues execution. Later, if and when the CPU lowers its priority, the device can interrupt the processor. If the CPU priority is less than the incoming interrupt level, the CPU responds to the interrupt request by suspending the execution of the current program and jumping to an interrupt-handler routine. When this happens, the processor raises its priority to the level indicated by the interrupt lines.

Normally, application programs run at priority 0 ($I_0=I_1=I_2=0$). This gives all peripherals the ability to interrupt the processor. Since the CPU raises its priority for interrupts, it can "prioritize" the peripherals. For example, the system clock usually has the highest priority (that is, level 7), while a terminal port may have a lower priority; say, level 4. In this instance, the clock can interrupt an applications program as well as the interrupt handler for the terminal port. The terminal-port interrupt can interrupt the applications program but cannot interrupt the clock-interrupt routine. This ensures that time-dependent functions (like the clock or disk input/output) occur without the chance of corruption.

Stack Pointer

The MC68000 and MC68008 use two stacks, the user stack and the supervisor stack. Naturally, this means that they require two stack pointers, the user stack pointer (abbreviated USP or A7) and the supervisor stack pointer (abbreviated SSP or A7'). The CPU uses the stack that matches the current mode. Since the stack selection is made internally, each mode has access only to its own stack pointer. In an assembler program, a reference to A7 (either explicitly as A7, or implicitly through a subroutine call or return) decodes to the same machine instruction; at execution time, the CPU selects the appropriate stack. The MC68000 processors include a special instruction to a supervisor mode program to access the user mode stack pointer.

SUPERVISOR MODE REGISTERS FOR THE MC68010 AND MC68012

The MC68010 and MC68012 processors both have supervisor stack pointers and status registers identical to those in the earlier models. These processors have three additional registers. The supervisor mode register set is shown in Figure 3-6.

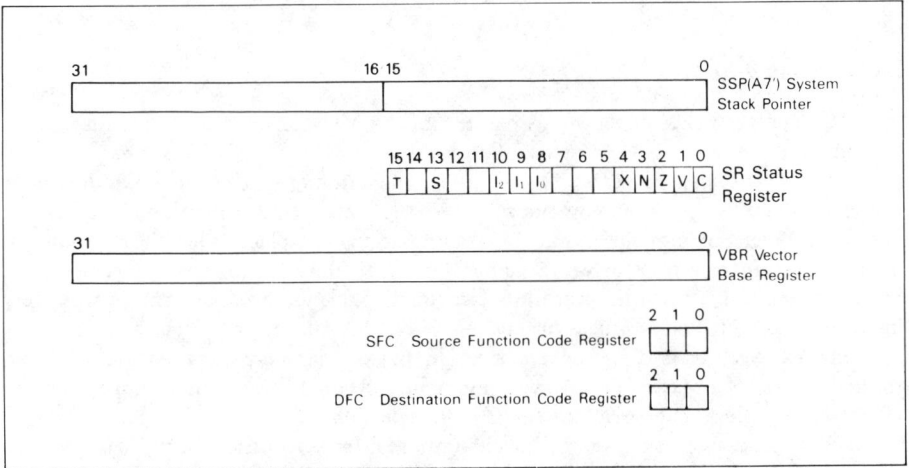

Figure 3-6. Additional Registers Available in Supervisor Mode (MC68010, MC68012)

Vector Base Register

The MC68000 processors use a specially defined block of memory called a "vector table." This table defines the starting addresses (or vectors) of interrupt handlers, illegal instruction code handlers, system-reset routines, and other operating system-oriented vectors.

In the MC68000 and MC68008, this table always starts at address 0000H. The MC68010 and MC68012 permit the operating system to redefine the starting address by use of a 32-bit vector base register, or VBR. At system reset, the vector table resides at 0000H. After reset, however, the operating system may modify this address through the VBR.

Alternate Function Code Registers

The MC68000 processors have three function code output lines (called FC0, FC1, and FC2). Whenever the processor reads or writes to memory, these function codes reflect information about the state of the processor. Specifically, they show the CPU mode (user or supervisor) and the contents of the memory accessed (instruction or data). Often, these lines are connected to the memory management unit (MMU) and permit the program to define separate memory for each CPU mode and memory-access type.

In normal execution, the processor sends well-defined data function codes. Certain instructions, however, permit the program to send out alternate codes. **The source function code register, or SFC, specifies the code for memory reads. The destination function code register, or DFC, specifies the code for memory writes.**

SUPERVISOR MODE REGISTERS FOR THE MC68020

The supervisor mode of the MC68020 offers several registers that are not available in the earlier MC68000-family processors. Some of these registers are completely new and others are redefined versions of old registers. These registers are shown in Figure 3-7.

Status Register

The supervisor byte of the status register for the MC68020 has new bit definitions in addition to those of its predecessors, as shown in Figure 3-7.

The MC68020 defines a second trace bit (T0) in addition to the one found in the earlier processors (T1). These two bits combine to allow more specific tracing than the single trace bit permitted. When the trace bits are equal to 00, no tracing takes place. When they are equal to 01, a tracing trap takes place only on a change of program flow (such as execution of a branch or subroutine call). When the trace bits are equal to 10, the processor traps after every instruction (as do the other processor models). The 11 bit value is undefined.

The MC68020 divides the supervisor mode into two submodes, master and interrupt, through the use of a Master bit, (M), which functions in conjunction with the Supervisor bit, (S). The only difference between the two is in the selection of stack pointer.

The interrupt mask bits in the MC68020 status register function identically to the mask in the other processors.

Stack Pointers

As indicated previously, **the MC68020 supervisor mode can use one of two supervisor stacks. These are called the interrupt stack pointer, or ISP (A7′), and the master stack pointer, or MSP (A7″).** When the M bit is 0, the processor uses the ISP, just as the other MC68000 processors do. When the M bit is 1, the MC68020 uses the MSP.

Having two supervisor stacks may seem redundant to you if you are new to systems programming. However, in some situations (for example, multitasking), a second supervisor stack provides a "cleaner" interface. The master stack can hold task-dependent information and provide temporary storage for operating-system routines. The interrupt stack then holds information associated with hardware interrupts.

This distinction may not be evident to you yet. For now, suffice it to say that the CPU automatically chooses which stack to use based on its current operating status (defined by the M and S bits of the status register).

Cache Control

Most programs spend the better part of execution time running in loops. While in these loops, they execute the same set of instructions over and over. Each time the processor needs to

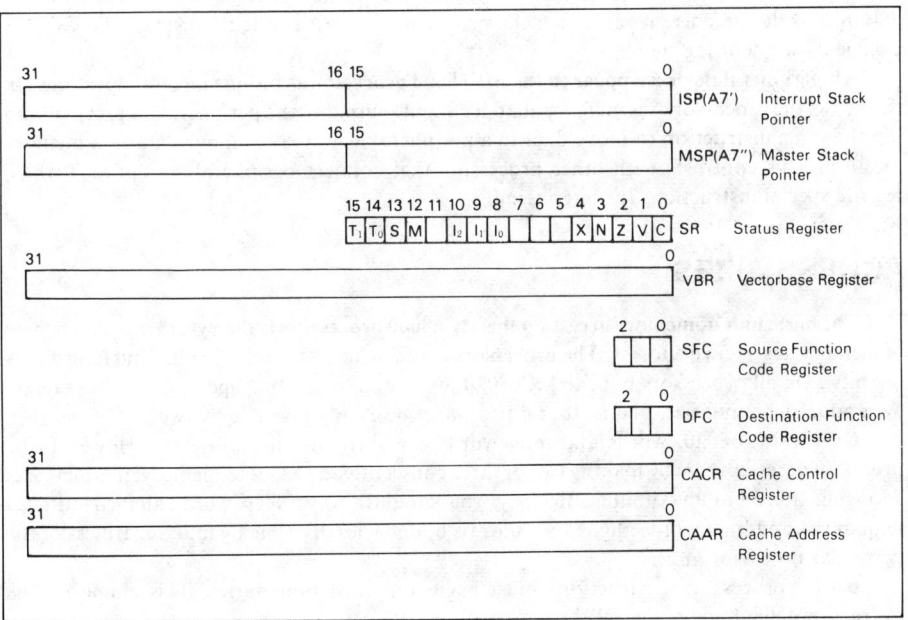

Figure 3-7. Additional Registers Available in Supervisor Mode (MC68020)

execute an instruction, it must fetch it from memory.

The MC68020 processor includes a 256-byte instruction cache, which contains the most recently executed instructions. In the case of a looping segment of code, the processor only has to fetch the instruction from memory once. It stores the instruction in the cache, displacing an instruction that hasn't been used lately. Subsequent memory requests for the instruction are canceled because the processor already has the instruction in the cache.

The operation of the instruction cache is transparent to user programs. However, running programs through the cache may not always be appropriate. Since the cache can hold only a limited number of instructions, nonlooping code may displace looping code. The supervisor mode has, therefore, the ability to enable, disable, and otherwise manipulate the cache through two registers, the cache address register, or CAAR, and the cache control register, or CACR.

MEMORY

The MC68000 memory is arranged as a single, linear, logically contiguous block of storage cells. At any given time, a program can access any point in the total address space of the system (as defined by the width of the address bus). In practice, however, the operating system uses the memory management unit to limit a program to accessing only as much memory as it needs; this may be 10K bytes, 100K bytes, or 1M byte.

This linear arrangement differs from that of some popular microprocessors, where the CPU may access memory in 64K byte segments; such microprocessors must set up segment registers that point to the starting addresses of these segments. To access an instruction or datum outside the current segments, the programmer must explicitly instruct the CPU to change its segment registers.

All peripheral devices appear to the MC68000 processor as unique memory locations. In this sense, the processor uses memory-mapped input/output to the peripherals; a program can use the same instruction to move data to a peripheral as it does to move data to a memory location. This contrasts with other processors that connect peripherals to "ports," which require special instructions for interfacing.

ACCESS SIZES

The basic unit of memory access on the MC68000 processors is the byte (8 bits). Each byte of memory has its own address. The processors may also access words (16 bits) and long words (32 bits). On all processors but the MC68020, word and long-word operands must reside on even-address boundaries; that is, the address must be evenly divisible by two.

On the MC68020, words and long words can start on odd addresses. However, the processor accesses them by making two or three consecutive accesses to memory; this increases accessing time. For maximum efficiency, you should always keep words aligned on even boundaries and long words aligned on address boundaries divisible by four, regardless of the particular processor in use.

On all processors, instructions must begin on word boundaries. This simplifies the instruction-fetch logic of the CPU.

BYTE ORDERING

The MC68000 processors store data in memory exactly as they do in registers, as shown in Figure 3-8. This implies that the most significant bit of a long word (bit 31) stored in a register

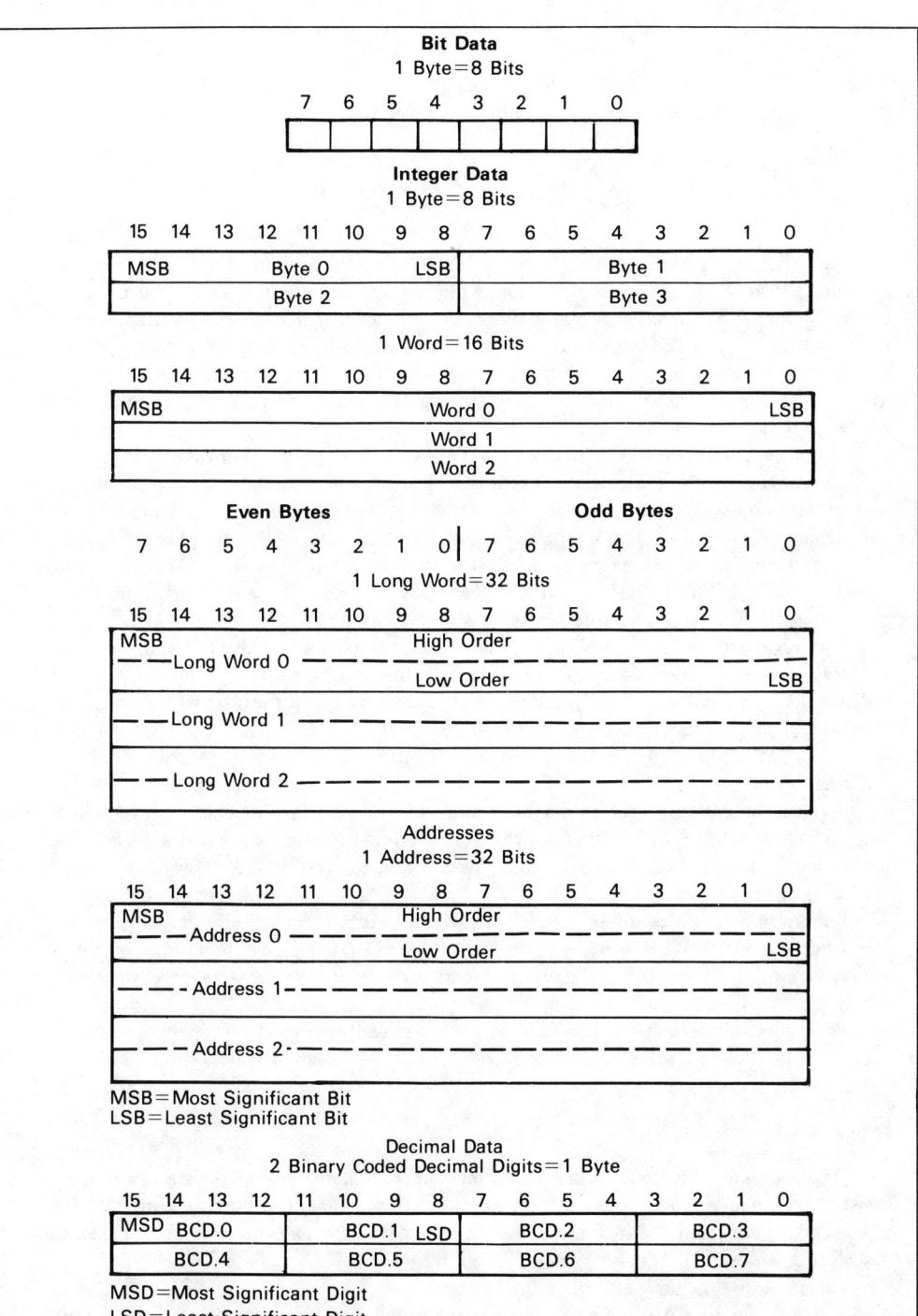

Figure 3-8. Data Organization in Memory

resides as the first bit at its address in memory. This storage setup contrasts with those of other processors, which reverse the byte order of words and long words in memory. That is, they store a word in memory so that the least significant byte resides at the address of the word and the most significant byte resides at the address plus one.

INSTRUCTION SET

The MC68000 processors have a rich instruction set that allows for data movement, arithmetic, logical testing, bit manipulation, and program flow control. The instructions are upwardly compatible in that programs written and assembled on a lower-end product, such as the MC68000, will run unaltered on an upper-end product, such as the MC68020. The opposite is not true, however; programs written for the MC68020 will not necessarily run on the MC68000. This is because there are more instructions and addressing modes available on the MC68020 than on the other processors.

The MC68000 processors' instruction sets are "regular." This means that most instructions follow the same format and may use any combination of address modes. For example, the same machine op-code may request data movement between two registers, between a register and memory, between two memory locations, or between a register and a peripheral. The only difference between the two requests lies in the operand portion of the instructions. The regularity of the MC68000 instruction set contrasts with other microprocessors, which limit many instructions to specific addressing modes.

This regularity of the instruction set has several important implications for you, the assembly-level programmer. First, it means that you needn't memorize all sorts of different instructions and formats; most instructions look the same except for the instruction mnemonic. For example, many processors have separate LOAD and STORE instructions. The MC68000 processors have only a MOVE instruction; the direction of the movement depends on the ordering of the operands.

Second, the basic instruction operates on all sizes of data. In MC68000 assembly language, the size of the operation (that is, byte, word, or long word) is specified by a suffix to the mnemonic — either .B, .W, or .L. In the machine code, the size is specified by special bits in the instruction code.

Finally, this simplification means that you needn't worry about keeping registers free for specific operations. You can use any of the eight data registers for any operation requiring a data register; you can use any of the seven general purpose address registers for an operation requiring an address register.

We will introduce each of the instructions in subsequent chapters by using them in sample programs. For now, **we will give you an overview of the MC68000 instruction set.**

DATA MOVEMENT

Data movement instructions provide for movement of data between registers, between a register and a memory location, and directly between two memory locations. The instructions allow for data movement, address movement, register data exchange, multiple register loading and storing, and stack frame linking and unlinking.

Table 3-2 lists the data-movement instructions.

A few things to note here about the data-movement instructions: First, there are no explicit stack push or pull instructions. This is in keeping with the instruction set uniformity. System stack operations use the general MOVE instruction in combination with register A7 (the stack pointer).

Second, there are no block movement instructions. On other processors, such instructions tell the CPU to move a certain number of bytes (or words or long words) starting at some address to a block of memory starting at another address. Again, in keeping with uniformity, the processor allows block movement through a combination of simple movement instructions, addressing modes, and loop instructions. We will discuss such looping in detail in Chapter 5.

Finally, the word *move* is somewhat of a misnomer here. The processor actually copies the data from one place to another. After the operation, the data resides in two places, the source and the destination. However, in keeping with convention, we will use the term *move*.

INTEGER ARITHMETIC

The MC68000 processors provide for the basic four integer arithmetic functions of add, subtract, multiply, and divide. Also provided for are aids useful in arithmetic operations for comparing two integers, zeroing an integer, negating an integer, and performing multiprecision arithmetic.

Table 3-3 summarizes the integer-arithmetic instructions.

BOOLEAN ARITHMETIC

The MC68000 processors allow for the Boolean (logical) operations of AND, OR, Exclusive OR, and NOT. Boolean arithmetic treats its operands on a true/false (or on/off) basis, in much the same way that the computer's internal circuitry does. These instructions are useful for creating and manipulating masks, testing status words, and setting bit patterns for graphics applications.

Table 3-4 summarizes the Boolean operations.

Table 3-2. Data Movement Instructions

Mnemonic	Operation
EXG	Exchange registers
LEA	Load effective address
LINK	Link and allocate stack
MOVE	Move source to destination
MOVEA	Move source to address register
MOVEC	Move control register
MOVEM	Move multiple registers
MOVEP	Move to peripheral
MOVEQ	Move short data to destination
MOVES	Move address space
PEA	Push effective address
UNLK	Unlink stack

Table 3-3. Integer Arithmetic Instructions

Mnemonic	Operation
ADD	Add source to destination
ADDA	Add source to address register
ADDI	Add immediate data to destination
ADDQ	Add short data to destination
ADDX	Add with extend bit to destination
CLR	Clear operand
CMP	Compare source to destination
CMPA	Compare source to address register
CMPI	Compare immediate data to destination
CMPM	Compare memory
CMP2*	Compare register to upper/lower bounds
DIVS	Signed divide
DIVU	Unsigned divide
DIVSL*	Long signed divide
DIVUL*	Long unsigned divide
EXT	Sign extend
EXTB	Sign extend byte
MULS	Signed multiply
MULU	Unsigned multiply
NEG	Negate
NEGX	Negate with extend
SUB	Subtract source from destination
SUBA	Subtract source from address register
SUBI	Subtract immediate from destination
SUBQ	Subtract short from destination
SUBX	Subtract with extend bit from destination

*68020 only

SHIFT AND ROTATE

The MC68000 processors permit you to shift and rotate the bits of an integer. Like Boolean operations, Shift and Rotate instructions are helpful in creating and evaluating masks. Shifts are also a handy means of performing simple multiplication and division. While the MC68000 has multiplication and division instructions, the Shift instruction operates much faster than these instruction types.

Table 3-5 summarizes the Shift and Rotate instructions.

INDIVIDUAL BIT MANIPULATION

The MC68000 permits you to test, clear, set, and logically NOT an individual bit of an operand. Such operations are useful when you need to manipulate bit flags; a single word can

MC68000 Machine Architecture **33**

Table 3-4. Boolean Instructions

Mnemonic	Operation
AND	AND source to destination
ANDI	AND immediate data to destination
EOR	Exclusive OR source to destination
EORI	Exclusive OR immediate data to destination
NOT	NOT destination
OR	OR source to destination
ORI	OR immediate data to destination
S_{cc}	Test condition codes and set operand
TST	Test operand and set condition codes

Table 3-5. Shift and Rotate Instructions

Mnemonic	Operation
ASL	Arithmetic shift left
ASR	Arithmetic shift right
LSL	Logical shift left
LSR	Logical shift right
ROL	Rotate left
ROR	Rotate right
ROXL	Rotate left with extend bit
ROXR	Rotate right with extend bit
SWAP	Swap words of a long word

contain several true/false flags.

Table 3-6 summarizes the individual bit-manipulation instructions.

BIT FIELD MANIPULATION

Besides allowing you to manipulate individual bits, the **MC68020 processor lets you manipulate strings of consecutive bits, called "fields."** These fields may be up to 32 bits in length. Using them allows you to compress your data into the minimum storage space needed for a given variable. To reach the bit field, you specify any of the MC68000 addressing modes. In addition, you must suffix the addressing mode with the start bit and the number of bits in the field.

Table 3-7 summarizes the bit field manipulation instructions.

Table 3-6. Bit Manipulation Instructions

Mnemonic	Operation
BCHG	Change bit
BCLR	Clear bit
BSET	Set bit
BTST	Test bit

Table 3-7. Bit Field Instructions

Mnemonic	Operation
BFCHG*	Change bit field
BFCLR*	Clear bit field
BFEXTS*	Extract and sign extend bit field
BFEXTU*	Extract and zero extend bit field
BFFFO*	Find first set bit in bit field
BFINS*	Insert bit field
BFSET*	Set bit field
BFTST*	Test bit field

*68020 only

BINARY-CODED DECIMAL

The MC68000 processors allow you to perform addition and subtraction on binary-coded decimal, or BCD, numbers, so they provide a simple means of manipulating numbers without first converting these numbers to binary. Binary-coded decimal notation is a form of internal coding in which decimal numbers (0-9) are stored as separate digits (as with ASCII coding), but the numbers are in 4-bit binary format. For example,

$$1234 (10) = 0001\ 0010\ 0011\ 0100\ (BCD)$$

PROGRAM FLOW CONTROL

For a program to be of much use, it must be able to test conditions and skip instructions based on results of the test. It must also be able to make calls to subroutines and return from those subroutines. **The MC68000 processors allow for several conditional and unconditional branches and subroutine calls,** as shown in Table 3-9.

Table 3-8. Binary-Coded Decimal Instructions

Mnemonic	Operation
ABCD	Add source to destination
NBCD	Negate destination
PACK*	Pack source to destination
SBCD	Subtract source from destination
UNPK*	Unpack source to destination
*68020 only	

SYSTEM CONTROL

In some instances, a user mode program needs to gain access to the supervisor mode. To do this, it may execute certain instructions that change the state of the supervisor bit (in the status word) and branch through the vector table to a special handler (usually in the operating system). The supervisor mode program must then be able to change back to user mode upon completion of the user mode program's request. Table 3-10 summarizes the instructions that affect the supervisor bit.

Table 3-9. Program Flow Instructions

Mnemonic	Operation
B_{cc}	Branch conditionally
BRA	Branch unconditionally
BSR	Branch to subroutine
CALLM*	Call module
DB_{cc}	Test, decrement, and branch
JMP	Jump to address
JSR	Jump to subroutine
NOP	No operation
RTD**	Return and deallocate stack
RTE+	Return from exception
RTM*	Return from module
RTR	Return and restore condition codes
RTS	Return from subroutine
+privileged instruction	
*68020 only	
**68010-68020 only	

Table 3-10. System Control Instructions

Mnemonic	Operation
ANDI	AND immediate to status register/condition code register
BKPT	Breakpoint trap
CHK	Trap on upper out-of-bounds operand
CHK2*	Trap on out-of-bounds operand
EORI	Exclusive OR immediate to status
ILLEGAL	Illegal instruction trap
MOVE	Move to/from status register/condition code register
MOVEC+	Move to/from control register
MOVES+	Move to/from address space
RESET+	Assert RESET line
STOP+	Stop processor
TRAP	Trap unconditionally
TRAP$_{cc}$*	Trap on condition
TRAPV	Trap on overflow

+privileged instruction
*68020 only

MULTIPROCESSOR/COPROCESSOR COMMUNICATIONS

   A **MC68000-based computer system may consist of more than one processor. Systems of this sort are called "multiprocessor systems."** In order to prevent one processor from accessing a memory location at the same time as another processor, certain instructions use a read-modify-write cycle, which gives a processor sole use of the system bus for the duration of its execution.

   In addition to its multiprocessor capabilities, the MC68020 also permits a system to include coprocessors. From the user's point of view, these coprocessors appear to be integral to the CPU. **Motorola currently supports two coprocessors: the MC68881, a high-precision, floating-point unit, and the MC68851, a memory management unit.**

   Table 3-11 lists the multiprocessor/coprocessor instructions.

ADDRESSING MODES

   As we have stated in previous sections, associated with nearly every instruction is one or more operand(s). An operand may reside in one of two places: internal to the CPU (in a register), or external to the CPU (in memory). **The addressing mode determines how the CPU will compute the "effective address" of the operand, either in a register or in memory.**

   In some addressing modes, the operand is part of the instruction itself. In other addressing

Table 3-11. Multitask/Multiprocessor Instructions

Mnemonic	Operation
CAS*	Compare and swap with operand
CAS2*	Compare and swap with operands
cpB$_{cc}$*	Branch on coprocessor condition
cpDB$_{cc}$*	Test coprocessor, decrement, and branch
cpGEN*	General coprocessor instruction
cpRESTORE*	Restore coprocessor state
cpSAVE*	Save coprocessor state
cpS$_{cc}$*	Test coprocessor condition
cpTRAP$_{cc}$*	Trap on coprocessor condition
TAS	Test and set operand
*68020 only	

modes, the effective address is a sum of several registers and displacement values determined by the operand field portion of the instruction. Some of the addressing modes are difficult to understand; we will explain why these more complex modes are useful and describe typical examples from real applications. You should try to trace these examples, since an understanding of the use of the various addressing modes is essential to writing good programs.

In our discussion of addressing modes, we will use the MOVE instruction exclusively to show how the CPU evaluates an effective address. The MOVE instruction simply moves a value from a source address to a destination address, where the first operand specifies the source and the second operand specifies the destination. We will use the dollar sign ("$") to denote hexadecimal numbers. Note that we use standard Motorola syntax for our addressing modes. Your assembler may use a slightly different syntax.

IMPLICIT ADDRESSING

Most instructions let you specify one or more operands. A few instructions, however, always work on the same operand. For example, the Return from Subroutine instruction (RTS) always fetches its operand (the return address) from the top of the stack. Similarly, the Trap on Overflow instruction (TRAPV) uses the system stack and a predefined address in the vector table. Some instructions, such as RESET and NOP, have no operands at all.

Instructions of this type use implicit addressing, since the location of their operands is determined by the instruction operation codes. Several other instructions use implicit addressing along with one of the other addressing modes. For example, a branch instruction (BRA) always affects the program counter. In addition, it requires a second explicit operand to specify the branch address.

DIRECT ADDRESSING MODES

In the direct addressing modes, the assembly instruction explicitly gives the location of the operand.

Data Register Direct

In this addressing mode, a data register contains the operand. You specify this mode by using the mnemonic Dn, where "D" means that the operand is a data register and "n" is a number from 0 to 7 that specifies the particular data register. An illustration of this follows:

Data register: | operand |

Assembler syntax: Dn

For example, D0 may contain a subtotal. You may want to perform additional arithmetic on this subtotal but keep the original value; hence, you will need to copy the value to another register. If the data registers contain the following:

register	contents
D0	10204FFF
D3	1034F88A

then after execution of the instruction

    MOVE.L   D0,D3

the registers will contain

register	contents
D0	10204FFF
D3	10204FFF

Address Register Direct

Address register direct mode is similar to data register direct, except that the register in use is an address register. You specify this mode with the mnemonic An, where "A" specifies address register and "n" is a number from 0 through 7, giving the register number. An illustration of this follows:

Address register: | operand |

Assembler syntax: An

For example, A0 may contain the base address of some table in memory. You may need to copy this address to another address register. If the address registers contain the following:

register	contents
A0	00200000
A3	0004F88A

then after execution of the instruction

    MOVE.L   A3,A0

the registers will contain

register	contents
A0	00200000
A3	00200000

Immediate

In immediate addressing, the operand is part of the instruction; the data follows the operation code in memory. In assembler code, you specify this addressing mode by preceding the operand with the "#" character; for example, #123. Optionally, you may follow the operand with a length descriptor of .B, .W, or .L. If you omit this suffix, the assembler will pick a size based on the value magnitude. An illustration of this mode follows:

```
Extension word(s):  | operand |

Assembler syntax:   #xxxx.size
```

Many times in a program you must load a register with a constant value. If the registers look like this

```
register    contents
D0          012309FF
```

then the instruction

```
MOVE.L   #$1FFFF,D0
```

results in

```
register    contents
D0          0001FFFF
```

Good programming practice dictates that the constant value be named. For example, if the value in the example was actually a bit mask for an operation, we might define a constant "STATUS__MASK" and give it the value $1FFFF. Then, our instruction might read

```
MOVE.L   #STATUS—MASK, D0
```

Absolute Addressing

In this addressing mode, the address of the operand follows the instruction word. The address may be 16 or 32 bits long. If it is only 16 bits long, then the CPU sign extends the value before using it. The assembler syntax for this mode is the address value followed optionally by .L or .W. The assembler, if it knows the value of the address, can decide whether the address should be 16 or 32 bits long. An illustration of this mode follows:

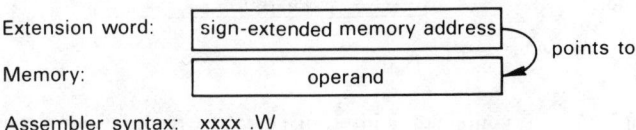

```
Extension word:    | sign-extended memory address |—┐
                                                    points to
Memory:            | operand |————————————————————┘

Assembler syntax:  xxxx .W
```

Usually you will write programs so that they are "position-independent." This means that you must treat addresses as relative to some other value (see the address register and program counter indirect modes). However, there are times that you may need to access a location by its exact value. For example, a device driver may be loaded anywhere in memory; however, it must access a port (located at a fixed address in memory) that it knows only by its physical location. A second example is the operating system's manipulation of the vector table. This table has a specific location in memory, and hence must be accessed by its physical location.

If memory looks like

address	contents
00000008	00
00000009	00
0000000A	00
0000000B	00

then the instruction

MOVE.L   #$10030,8

uses an effective destination address of 00000008 and results in

address	contents
00000008	00
00000009	01
0000000A	00
0000000B	30

Again, good programming practice dictates that you use named values instead of literal numbers, so your instruction may read

MOVE.L   #BUS_ERROR_ROUTINE, BUS_ERROR_VECTOR

REGISTER INDIRECT ADDRESSING MODES

In register indirect addressing, the operand is pointed to by an address register or the program counter. In some modes, the CPU includes additional offsets or indexes to calculate the operand in memory.

Address Register Indirect

In this addressing mode, the operand is located in memory; an address register contains the operand address. To specify this addressing mode, you enclose the address register in parentheses; for example, (A3). An illustration of this mode follows:

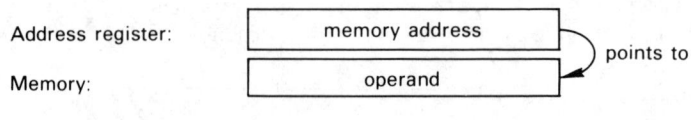

Address register:

Memory:

Assemble syntax: An

For example, A3 may contain the address of a database record where you want to move a value from D0. If the registers and memory are

register	contents	memory	contents
A0	00001000	00001000	A0
D0	1043834F	00001001	02
		00001002	3F
		00001003	00

after execution of the instruction

                  MOVE.L   D0,(A0)

the effective address for the destination is $1000 and the registers and memory will contain

register	contents	memory	contents
A0	00001000	00001000	10
D0	1043834F	00001001	43
		00001002	83
		00001003	4F

Address Register Indirect With Predecrement

In this addressing mode, as in simple address register indirect, an address register contains an address in memory. However, before determining the address of the operand, the CPU subtracts a value from the address register, leaving the actual address in memory. The value subtracted depends on the size of the operation: 1 for a byte operation, 2 for a word operation, and 4 for a long-word operation.

After the subtraction, the CPU stores the new value into the address register and uses its new value as the effective address of the operand. In an assembler statement, this mode is specified by preceding the parenthesized address register with a minus sign, as in $-$(A5). An illustration of this mode follows:

Address register:

Operand size (1, 2, or 4):

Memory:

Assembler syntax: $-$(An)

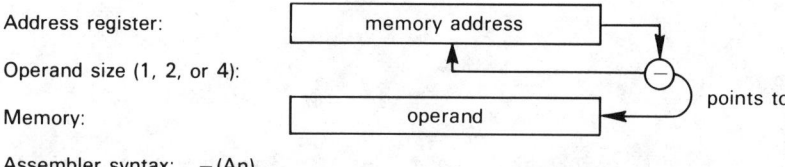

This mode is most commonly used to implement a push onto a memory stack. If registers and memory are

register	contents	memory	contents
A7	00001002	00001000	10
D0	00000143	00001001	12
		00001002	83
		00001003	4F

then the operation

                  MOVE.W   D0,$-$(A7)

uses an effective address of $1000 for the destination and leaves the registers and memory as

register	contents	memory	contents
A7	00001000	00001000	01
D0	00000143	00001001	43
		00001002	83
		00001003	4F

Address Register Indirect With Postincrement

In this addressing mode, as in the predecrement mode, an address register contains an address in memory, and the CPU modifies the address register according to the size of the operation. However, in this case, the CPU uses the value currently in the address register as the effective address of the operand. After storing this value internally, the CPU adds the operation size to the address register. The assembler syntax for this mode is the parenthesized address register followed by a plus sign, as in (A5)+. An illustration of this mode follows:

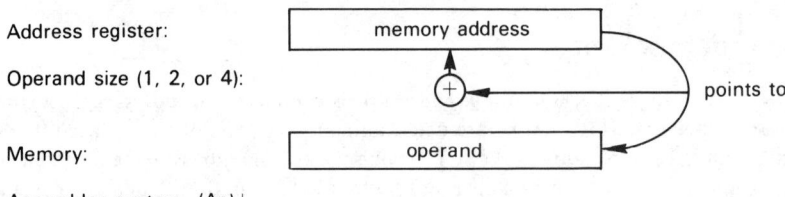

Address register:

Operand size (1, 2, or 4):

Memory:

Assembler syntax: (An)+

This mode is commonly used to move through a table or string of data. It is also used to implement a pull (also called a "pop") of data from a memory stack. If the registers and memory are

```
register    contents      memory      contents
A7          00001000      00001000    10
D0          0000FFFF      00001001    12
                          00001002    83
                          00001003    4F
```

then the operation

```
            MOVE.W        (A7)+,D0
```

uses an effective address of $1000 for the source operand and leaves the registers and memory as

```
register    contents      memory      contents
A7          00001002      00001000    01
D0          00000143      00001001    43
                          00001002    83
                          00001003    4F
```

The system does not allow a program to push or pull a single byte from the system stack (A7). If you attempt to do so, the CPU will automatically increment or decrement the stack pointer by 2 instead of 1. Since the CPU uses the system stack to store the program counter during subroutine calls, this ensures that the stack is always aligned on an even-address boundary (remember that word and long-word access to odd addresses is prohibited on the MC68000-MC68012 and is inefficient on the MC68020). User-defined stacks (using A0-A6) allow byte-sized operations.

Address Register Indirect With Displacement

In this addressing mode, the effective address of the operand is the sum of a fixed 16-bit signed "displacement" and the contents of an address register. Before the CPU adds the

MC68000 Machine Architecture 43

displacement to the value from the address register, it "sign extends" the displacement; that is, it replicates the value in bit 15 into bits 16 through 31. This allows a program to have both positive and negative displacements.

Like the other register indirect modes, the assembler syntax for this mode uses the address register enclosed in parentheses. The displacement value precedes the address register; for example, 10(A1). The value of the displacement is a constant, while the value of the address may vary during program execution. An illustration of the calculation of the effective address for this mode follows:

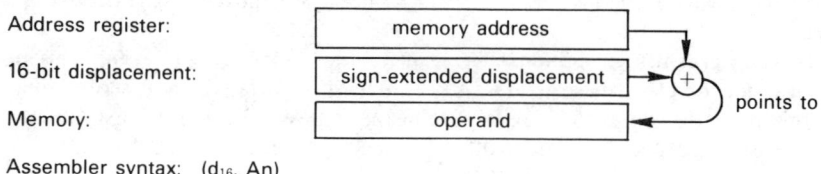

Address register:

16-bit displacement:

Memory:

Assembler syntax: (d$_{16}$, An)

This addressing mode is particularly useful for accessing an entry in a record-data structure. For example, a vehicle-information record may consist of a license number, year, color code, and serial number. To access a particular field in the record, you first load an address register so that it points to the start of the record. Now, if you know that year entry is word value offset $6 bytes from the start of the address, you can use address register indirect with displacement to access this field. If the registers and memory look like

register	contents	memory	contents
A0	00001020	00001020	31
D0	00000000	00001021	34
		00001022	35
		00001023	31
		00001024	4A
		00001025	4C
		00001026	07
		00001027	BF

then the instruction

    MOVE.W $6(A0),D0

uses an effective address of $1026 for the source and leaves memory and the registers as

register	contents	memory	contents
A0	00001020	00001020	31
D0	000007BF	00001021	34
		00001022	35
		00001023	31
		00001024	4A
		00001025	4C
		00001026	07
		00001027	BF

You seldom use numeric constants for the displacement; rather, you use symbolic constants defined through equate statements. In the preceding example, you could have defined a constant called "YEAR" and given it the value $6. Then, your assembler statement would have read

    MOVE.W   YEAR(A0),D0

This substitution makes for code that is descriptive and easy to modify. It makes absolutely no difference in the machine code produced.

Address Register Indirect With Index and Displacement

In this addressing mode, the effective address is the sum of the value in the address register, a second index register, and a signed displacement. The index register may be any of the data registers or address registers. The CPU may use either 16 or 32 bits of the index register. If only 16 bits are used, the CPU sign extends the value before adding it to the value from the address register. The displacement may be either 16 or 32 bits; again, the CPU sign extends any 16-bit value.

Indexing provides an additional degree of variation in indirect addressing. This mode is often used for complex data structures. A two-dimensional array can be described quite well with this mode; the address register may define the address of start of the first subscript; the index register may then define the offset needed to reach the entry (that is, the second subscript).

In the assembler syntax for this mode, the address register and index register are enclosed within parentheses; the address register is specified first, followed by a comma, and then by the index register specification. To specify the size of the value in the index register, you follow its name with .W or .L. The displacement precedes the parenthetical expression. For example, in the expression 20(A3,A6.L), 20 is the displacement, A3 is the address register, and A6 is the index register, while .L tells the CPU to use all 32 bits of A6.

The MC68020 processor adds further capabilities to this addressing mode. With this processor, you may specify 8-bit displacements as well as 16- and 32-bit displacements. In addition, the MC68020 allows you to "scale" the value in the index register. Scaling tells the processor to multiply the value in the index register by 1, 2, 4, or 8 before adding it to the effective address. If you have a two-dimensional array, scaling lets you use true subscripts in your index register. For example, if the array contains word entries, you might scale by 2; if it contains long-word entries, you would set the scale to 4.

The syntax for this advanced form of indexing is similar to that on the other MC68000 processors. To specify the scale of the index register, you follow it with an asterisk and the scale; for example, 10(A0,A3.L*4). The calculation of the effective address is

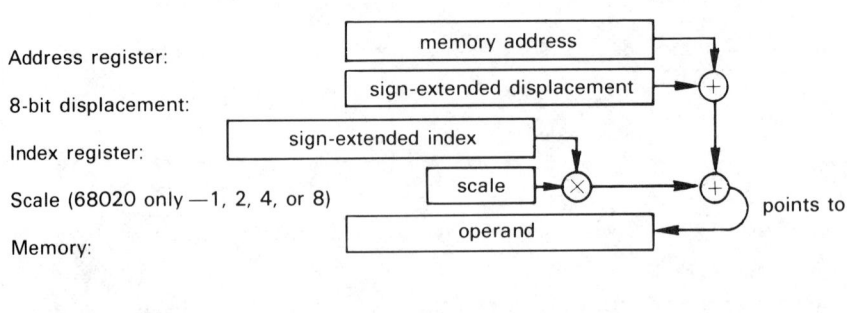

Address register:
8-bit displacement:
Index register:
Scale (68020 only — 1, 2, 4, or 8)
Memory:

Assembler syntax: (d_8,An, Xn.size)
68020:   (d_8,An, Xn.size*scale)

If you have defined a two-dimensional table starting at address 1000, which was four rows (0-3) by five columns (0-4) and contained byte values, then to access the element at (2,2), you would load an address register with $A (row number 2, times the number of columns per row, 5) and an index register with the column number, 12. If the registers and memory look like

register	contents	memory	contents
A0	0000000A	0000100A	C3
D0	00000002	0000100B	A4
D1	00000000	0000100C	25

then the instruction

    MOVE.B $1000(A0,D0),D1

uses an effective source address of $100C ($1000 + $A + $2) and leaves the registers and memory as

register	contents	memory	contents
A0	0000000A	0000100A	C3
D0	00000002	00000002	A4
D1	00000025	00000025	25

If you were using the MC68020, and the table contained long words rather than bytes, then to access the element at (2,3), you would load the address register with $28 (row 2 times 5 columns per row times 4 bytes per entry) and an index register with the column number (3). If memory and the registers look like

register	contents	memory	contents
A0	00000028	00001034	C3
A3	00000003	00001035	A4
D1	FFFFFFFE	00001036	25
		00001037	30

then the instruction

    MOVE.L   D1,$1000(A0,A3.L*4)

will result in an effective destination address of $1034 ($28 + 3*4) and yield

register	contents	memory	contents
A0	00000028	00001034	FF
A3	00000003	00001035	FF
D1	FFFFFFFE	00001036	FF
		00001037	FE

Program Counter Indirect With Displacement

This addressing mode functions identically to address register indirect with displacement, except that the effective address is a displacement from the current contents of the program counter instead of an address register. The PC value used is the address of the operand word portion of the instruction. The displacement in this mode is a 16-bit signed value. To signify this mode, you enclose the displacement and the PC mnemonic in parentheses, for example, 10(PC).

The calculation of the effective address is

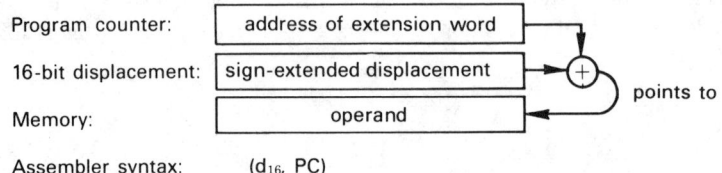

Assembler syntax: (d_{16}, PC)

If the registers and memory look like

register	contents	memory	contents
PC	00001020	00001000	05
D0	00000000	00001001	43

then the instruction

                  MOVE.B   (-$22,PC),D0

uses an effective address of $1000 ($1022 + -$22), which results in

register	contents	memory	contents
PC	00001024	00001000	05
D0	00000005	00001001	43

Usually you use a label name as the displacement; for example, (HEAD,PC). At assembly time (or at link time, depending on the system), the system evaluates the value of the label (that is, its address) and calculates the relative displacement from the instruction's location.

Program Counter Indirect With Index And Displacement

In this mode, as with the indexed/displaced mode using an address register, the effective address of the operand is the sum of a register (in this case, the program counter), the value of the displacement, and the value in the index register. As with the former version, the displacement may be 16 or 32 bits long (or, on the MC68020, 8 bits long), and the index register may be a data or address register whose value is 16 or 32 bits long (and may be scaled on the MC68020).

To signify this mode, you enclose the mnemonic PC and the index register name in parentheses and precede this expression with the displacement value; for example, (10,PC,D0). The calculation of the effective address is

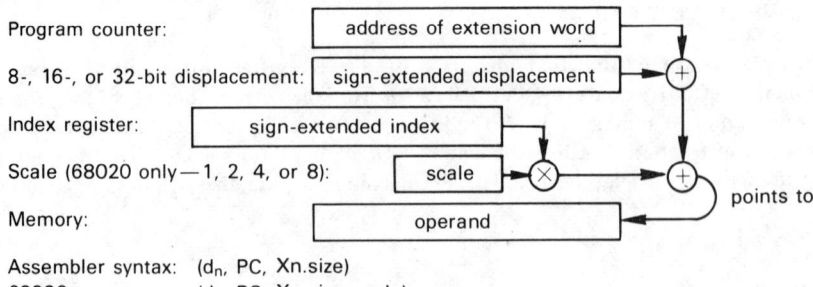

Assembler syntax: (d_n, PC, Xn.size)
68020:   (d_n, PC, Xn.size*scale)

MC68000 Machine Architecture 47

This mode is useful for accessing an array of data using position-independent code. For example, if you have a table of bytes, labeled "TABLE," which starts at address $1000, then if the registers and memory look like

register	contents	memory	contents
PC	00001024	00001000	05
D0	00000002	00001001	43
D1	00000000	00001002	FF
		00001003	FC

then the instruction

        MOVE.B   (TABLE,PC,D0), D1

uses an effective address of $1002 ($1026 − $26 + $2) and results in

register	contents	memory	contents
PC	00001028	00001000	05
D0	00000002	00001001	43
D1	000000FF	00001002	FF
		00001003	FC

MEMORY INDIRECT MODES

In the memory indirect addressing modes, the processor must evaluate two effective addresses before coming up with the operand. Unlike the register indirect modes, where a register points to the operand, in this mode a location in memory points to the operand. **The memory indirect modes are available only on the MC68020 processor.**

Memory Indirect Postindexed

In this mode, the CPU must use five values in order to come up with the effective address of the operand: the contents of an address register, a 16- or 32-bit base displacement, the value in an intermediate memory location, the scaled value from an index register, and a second 16- or 32-bit outer displacement.

Both displacement values, as well as the index register, are sign extended if necessary. The address register, displacements, and index register are all optional; you may use any or all of them to specify your operand. The assembler syntax for this mode encloses the base displacement and address register in square brackets, followed by the index register and scale, followed by the outer displacement, with the whole expression enclosed in parentheses; for example, ([$10,A0],D0.L*4,$20). If you want to omit one of the entries, leave it blank; for example, ([,A0],D1*4,) leaves both of the displacements out of the calculation.

The calculation of the effective address is as follows.

48   68000 Assembly Language Programming

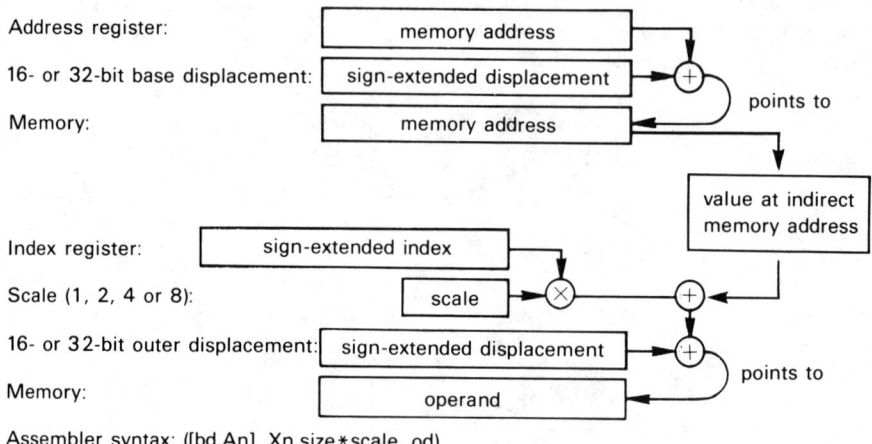

Assembler syntax: ([bd,An], Xn.size*scale, od)

Typically, you won't use all of the potential fields in the effective address calculation. However, for the sake of demonstration, if the registers and memory look like

register	contents	memory	contents
A0	00001000	00001010	00
D0	00000002	00001011	00
D1	0000FFCC	00001012	20
		00001013	00
		0000200A	FF
		0000200B	CC

then the instruction

>   MOVE.W   ([$10,A0],D0*2,$6), D1

uses an effective address of $200A ($10 + $1000 gives the intermediate address of $1010. This address contains the value $2000 to which the outer displacement of $6 and the scaled index value of 2*2 are added.) This results in

register	contents	memory	contents
A0	00001000	00001010	00
D0	00000002	00001011	00
D1	0000FFCC	00001012	20
		00001013	00
		0000200A	FF
		0000200B	CC

You will normally use named values for the displacements.

Memory Indirect Preindexed

This mode uses the same values in determining the effective address of the operand as does the postindexed version. The difference between the two modes is in the order of the evaluation. The postindexed version added the scaled index value to the value at the intermediate address; the preindexed version uses the scaled index value as part of the calculation to get the intermediate address. An illustration of this mode follows.

MC68000 Machine Architecture

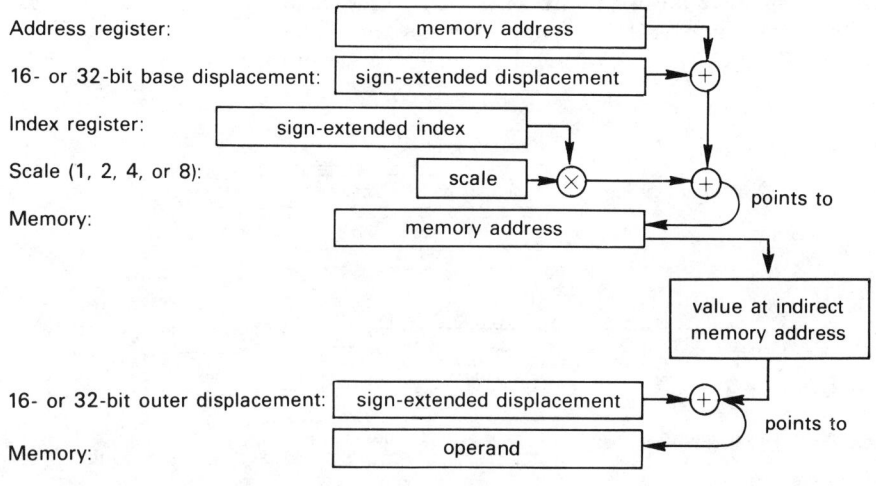

Address register:
16- or 32-bit base displacement:
Index register:
Scale (1, 2, 4, or 8):
Memory:

16- or 32-bit outer displacement:
Memory:

Assembler syntax: ([bd,An,Xn.size*scale], od)

If the registers and memory look like

register	contents	memory	contents
A0	00001000	00001014	00
D0	00000002	00001015	00
D1	0000F000	00001016	20
		00001017	00
		00002006	FF
		00002007	CC

then the instruction

MOVE.W   ([$10,A0,D0*2],$6), D1

uses an effective address of $2006 for the source operand. ($10 + $1000 + 2*2 gives $1014, the address of the intermediate address. $1014 contains the value $2000, to which the outer displacement of $6 is added.) This gives

register	contents	memory	contents
A0	00001000	00001014	00
D0	00000002	00001015	00
D1	0000FFCC	00001016	20
		00001017	00
		00002006	FF
		00002007	CC

Program Counter Memory Indirect With Postindex

In this addressing mode, like the other memory indirect modes, the CPU uses an intermediate memory location to determine the actual address of the operand. In this case, however, rather than using an address register, the CPU uses the current value of the PC (when

it is pointing to the extension word following the op-code word). The assembler syntax is similar, with substitution of the program counter mnemonic for the address register name; for example, ([$10,PC],D0*2,$20). The calculation of the effective address is

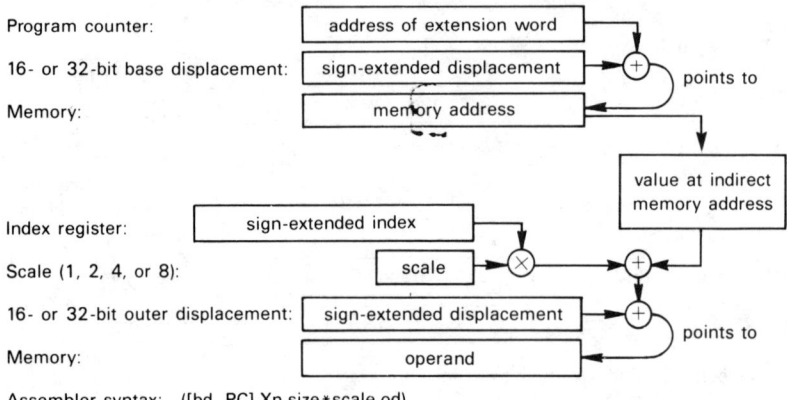

Assembler syntax: ([bd, PC],Xn.size*scale,od)

If you have a table of pointers labeled PTRS that begins at $1000, and if the registers and memory look like

register	contents	memory	contents
PC	00001020	00001000	00
D0	00000002	00001001	00
D1	00000000	00001002	20
		00001003	00
		00002012	FF

then the instruction

                   MOVE.B   ([PTRS,PC],D0*1,$10), D1

affects address $2012. ($1022 + −$22 gives the intermediate address $1000. $1000 contains the value $2000, to which the CPU adds the index register value of $2 and the outer displacement value of $10.). This yields

register	contents	memory	contents
PC	00001028	00001000	00
D0	00000002	00001001	00
D1	000000FF	00001002	20
		00001003	00
		00002010	FF

Program Counter Memory Indirect With Preindex

Like the previous addressing mode, the CPU uses the value from an intermediate memory location (pointed to, in part, by the PC) to reach the operand. However, instead of adding the index register to the intermediate value, in this mode the CPU includes the index register in finding the address of the intermediate value. The assembler syntax is similar to address register memory indirect; for example, ([$10,PC,D0*2],$20). The calculation of the effective address is

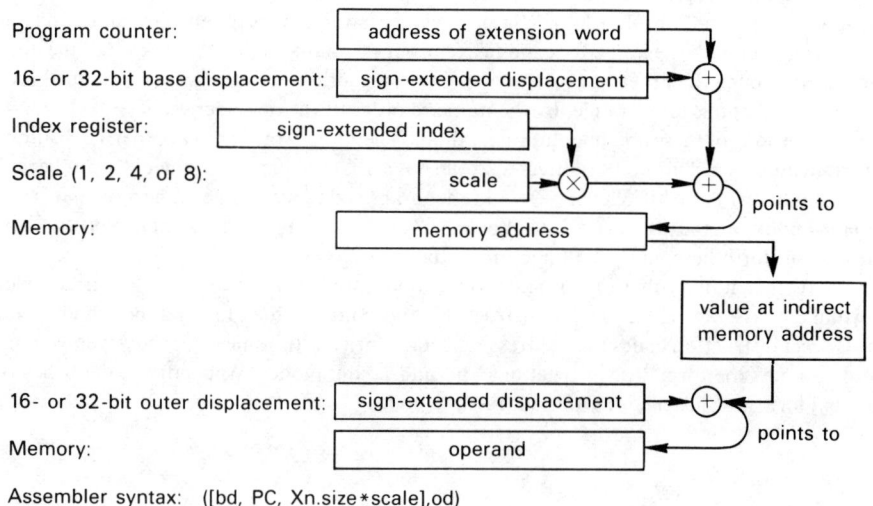

Assembler syntax: ([bd, PC, Xn.size*scale],od)

If you have a table of pointers labeled PTRS that begins at $1000, and if the registers and memory look like

register	contents	memory	contents
PC	00001020	00001004	00
D0	00000001	00001005	00
D1	00000001	00001006	20
		00001007	00
		00002010	FF

then the instruction

    MOVE.B   D1, ([PTRS,PC,D0*4],$10)

affects address $2010. ($1022 + -$22 + $2 gives the intermediate address of $1002, which contains the value $2000. To this value, the CPU adds the outer displacement value of $10.) This yields

register	contents	memory	contents
PC	00001028	00001004	00
D0	00000001	00001005	00
D1	00000001	00001006	20
		00001007	00
		00002010	FF

CONCLUSION

Various documentation sources describe the architecture, instruction set, and addressing modes of the MC68000 family from differing points of view. For example, some documentation separates the 16-bit version of absolute addressing from the 32-bit version, calling the modes "absolute short" and "absolute long." Some documentation groups the absolute short and long modes together with the immediate mode as "program counter relative modes." Some documentation groups the processor instructions in groups other than the way we grouped them here in this chapter; for example, by the numeric order of the op-code.

While none of these documentation methods is better or worse than another, each aims at a certain audience. This book is directed at the novice assembly programmer. As you become more familiar with the MC68000, we would encourage you to read some of the more hardware-oriented books on the processors; such books will give you a slightly different perspective from the one put forth here on the architecture of the device.

A further note: some of the addressing modes and instructions may seem complex. Fortunately, assemblers know what instructions and syntax to look for, and they can generate the correct instruction codes and addressing details for you. In some cases, however, you may need to know the format of instructions and addressing modes; Appendix A describes the internal format of instructions and addressing modes.

II
Introductory Problems

The only way to learn assembly language is to work with it. The chapters of Section II contain examples of simple programs that perform common programming chores. You should read each example carefully and try to execute the programs on a MC68000-based computer. Work the problems at the end of each chapter and run the resulting programs to ensure that you understand the material.

GENERAL FORMAT OF EXAMPLES

Each program example contains the following parts:

- A title that describes the general problem.
- A statement of purpose that describes the task that the program performs as well as the variables (memory) required to perform that task.
- A sample problem with data and results.
- A flowchart (if the program logic is complex).
- An assembler listing of the program (showing the source as well as the generated hexadecimal code).
- A discussion of the finer points of the program.

For ease of reference, we have named each of the program examples according to their occurrence in the chapter, as follows:

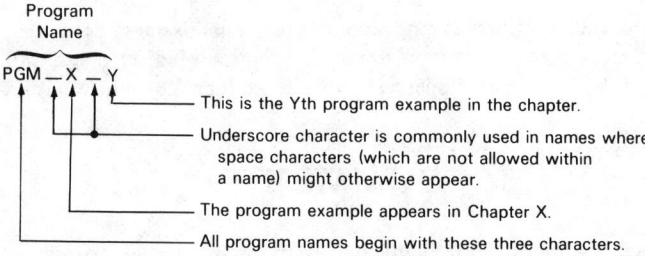

By this convention,

PGM_6_3,

names the third program example in Chapter 6.

This convention is useful for our purpose of clearly naming sample programs. You might want to store the programs in disk files of the same name. However, we don't want to give you the impression that you should use such naming conventions in real-life applications. Clearly, a name like COSINE has more meaning in a large application than does an internally coded name like

$$\text{MOD\_1\_A.}$$

Always use meaningful names for your programs and modules.

NOTATION CONVENTIONS

Many companies offer MC68000-based systems and products. Since we don't know which of these products you have at your disposal, we chose to write our sample programs in a generic format. We use only the simplest of assembler directives, labels, and radices, so that you can concentrate on learning MC68000 assembly language. We aim our notation at the simplest of systems. If your system is more powerful, we encourage you to experiment with its advanced features.

NAMES AND LABELS

All variables, constants, and labels consist of one to eight characters, the first of which must be an uppercase letter. The characters that follow that initial character may be uppercase letters, or numbers, or the special characters ., $, or _. Labels start in column 1 of the program line. Each label is separated from the remainder of the line by either a colon or a space.

Your system may permit you to use longer names than we use and allow "local" labels. Both concepts are useful, and if your system permits, we encourage you to experiment with them.

MNEMONICS

We use the standard Motorola mnemonics throughout this book. Because many operators can operate on various sizes of data, the size of the operator is indicated by a suffix of .B (byte), .W (word), or .L (long). We use uppercase letters for all operator mnemonics.

COMMENTS

Comments may appear on the same line as an assembler statement or on lines of their own. In-line comments must follow the assembler statement and are separated from that statement by one or more spaces. For comments appearing alone on a line, we start the line with an asterisk in column 1 of that line.

Your system may require you to use special characters to indicate the start of comments, such as a semicolon (;) or a slash (/). Consult your assembler manual for its requirements.

CONSTANTS AND RADICES

Differing circumstances often call for different formats for constant data. For example, if a constant represented an ASCII character, we would want to use that character rather than a hexadecimal number. Similarly, we might want to use the binary radix to represent a bit mask. We will use the following convention for representing data and constants:

- **Decimal.** A number with no prefix or suffix. For example:

    12345

- **Hexadecimal.** A number prefixed with a dollar sign. For example:

    $1234

- **Binary.** A number (all 0s and 1s) prefixed with a percent sign. For example:

    %00101001

- **ASCII.** A character or string of characters enclosed in single or double quotes. For example:

    "Test #0"

EXPRESSIONS

Most assemblers permit you to use certain logical and arithmetic operators in constant expressions. The assembler will evaluate the expression and insert the appropriate constant value into the object code. The operators our assembly programs will use are

```
 +    addition
 −    subtraction
 *    multiplication
 /    division
>>    shift right
<<    shift left
 &    logical AND
 !    logical OR
 ~    logical NOT
<..>  parenthetical expression
```

Note, however, that you can only combine constants in these expressions. Also note that expressions must result in values of 32 or fewer bits.

DIRECTIVES

Our assembly programs will use only the most simple directives so you can pay more attention to the MC68000 instructions. The directives we use include

DC Define data. This directive defines a location in memory and initializes that data with some constant value. To indicate the size of the memory location reserved for the data, you suffix the DC mnemonic with .B, .W, or .L. For example:

    FILE__CNT: DC.B 4

defines a byte in memory (labeled FINECNT) and initializes it with the value 4. You can also initialize several consecutive locations in memory with a single DC instruction. For example:

```
POWER_10:  DC.W    1, 10, 100, 1000, 10000
```

defines five words in memory. The first word, 1, has the memory label POWER_10. The most common use of this directive is to initialize strings of text. For example,

```
ERR_MSS: DC.B    "File not found—create?"
```

defines 25 consecutive bytes in memory and initializes them to the given characters.

DS Define storage. The directive lets you define one or more units of memory (but leaves them uninitialized). As with DC, you specify the size of the data by suffixing the mnemonic. You specify the repetition of the unit as an operand to the DS mnemonic. For example:

```
COUNTER: DS.L    1
```

defines one long word of memory and gives it the label COUNTER.

```
OUTBUF: DS.B    20
```

defines 20 bytes of memory, labeling the first as OUTBUF.

EQU Equate. This directive equates a constant value to a constant name. For example:

```
BUFF_CNT EQU 10
```

defines a constant called BUFF_CNT and gives it the value of 10.

ORG Origin. This directive defines the origin, or starting address, of a block of code or data. When the assembler produces object code, it will use this value as the basis for evaluating label addresses and offsets.

END End of program. This directive signals the end of the assembly program.

Note that each of the directives has one or more arguments or operands. These operands can be literal constants, named constants, or program/code labels. In the example

```
BUF_SIZE EQU  10
BUFFER   DS.B BUF_SIZE
BUF_PTR  DC.L BUFFER
```

the assembler allocates 10 bytes of data, which it labels BUFFER. It then allocates one long word labeled BUF_PTR, which it initializes to the address of BUFFER.

PROGRAM FORMAT

We will use a standard format for presenting each of our sample programs. For example:

```
          00006000      DATA      EQU      $6000
          00004000      PROGRAM   EQU      $4000

          00006000                ORG      DATA
006000    00000002      VALUE     DS.W     1        VALUE TO TRANSFER
006002    00000002      RESULT    DS.W     1        STORAGE FOR TRANSFERRED DATA

          00004000                ORG      PROGRAM

004000    30386000      PGM_4_1   MOVE.W   VALUE,D0    GET DATA TO BE MOVED
004004    31C06002                MOVE.W   D0,RESULT   SAVE DATA

004008    4E75                    RTS

                                  END      PGM_4_1
```

Note several things about this listing:

- We define the starting locations of the code and data segments in equates and then use the ORG directive to pass this information along to the assembler. The numbers in the far left column represent the addresses of the code and data.
- The second column of numbers represents the hexadecimal code for the command given by the source line. For directives, this data may be address, constant, or data values. For MC68000 instructions, this data is the object code produced by the instruction operator and operand(s).
- The third column and those columns to the right represent the source code. This is the data that you will type into your computer (via its editor).

RUNNING THE PROGRAMS

In our examples, the last executable statement is always a Return from Subroutine (RTS) instruction. Depending on your computer and operating system, this may or may not be an appropriate way to end your program. You might prefer to end the program with a STOP instruction or with a call to the operating system, which will signal it that you want to return control to its monitor. This is machine- and operating-system dependent; you must look through your system's manuals to find the system call and syntax.

If your system includes a machine-level debugger, we urge you to use it. Such debuggers allow you to single-step interactively through a program; that is, they let you execute instructions one at a time. After the computer has executed an instruction, the debugger lets you examine memory and the registers. You therefore have a valuable tool for learning how instructions execute.

4
Beginning Programs

This chapter contains some very elementary programs. They will introduce some fundamental features of the MC68000. In addition, these programs demonstrate some primitive tasks that are common to assembly language programs for many different applications.

PROGRAM EXAMPLES

4-1. 16-BIT DATA TRANSFER

Purpose: Move the contents of one 16-bit variable VALUE at location 6000 to another 16-bit variable RESULT at location 6002.

Sample Problem:

    Input: VALUE-(6000)=2E56
    Output: RESULT-(6002)=2E56

Program 4-1:

```
               00006000        DATA      EQU     $6000
               00004000        PROGRAM   EQU     $4000

               00006000                  ORG     DATA
006000  00000002        VALUE     DS.W    1               VALUE TO TRANSFER
006002  00000002        RESULT    DS.W    1               STORAGE FOR TRANSFERRED DATA

               00004000                  ORG     PROGRAM

004000  30386000        PGM_4_1   MOVE.W  VALUE,D0        GET DATA TO BE MOVED
004004  31C06002                  MOVE.W  D0,RESULT       SAVE DATA

004008  4E75                      RTS

                                  END     PGM_4_1
```

This program solves the problem in two simple steps. The first instruction loads data register D0 with the 16-bit value in location VALUE. The next instruction saves the 16-bit contents of data register D0 in location RESULT.

Remember — if you want to try this program with some sample data, *you* must first load the data that is to be transferred into the variable VALUE at memory location 6000. If your system does not allow this, use the Define Constant directive.

During the execution of this program, only the least significant 16 bits of the 32-bit data register D0 are affected. The most significant 16 bits are not modified, since both instructions specified an operation size of word (16 bits) by using the '.W' instruction suffix. If a data transfer of one byte (8 bits) or one long word (32 bits) is desired, a size suffix of '.B' or '.L', respectively, should be used.

The MC68000 combines three classes of instruction provided by most microprocessors — load register, store register, and transfer between registers — into a single class of instructions — MOVE. Using a register as the source operand (first operand) with a MOVE instruction is similar to a typical microprocessor's store register operation. Using a register specified as a destination operand with the MOVE instruction is similar to a typical microprocessor's load register operation. Using internal registers to provide both the source and destination operands with a MOVE instruction accomplishes the same function as a typical microprocessor's register transfer instruction.

When you use the MOVE instruction to accomplish the LOAD, STORE, or TRANSFER function, it generally affects the status flags in the status register. The execution of most MOVE instructions sets or clears the Negative (N) and Zero (Z) flags depending on the value moved, while clearing the Overflow (V) and Carry (C) flags. The Extend (X) flag is not affected.

In addition to moving data between registers, and between registers and memory, the MOVE instruction can also be used to move data between two memory locations. As a result, the two MOVE instructions in PGM 4-1 can be replaced by the single instruction:

MOVE.W VALUE, RESULT

This version of the MOVE instruction moves the 16-bit word contained in memory location VALUE to memory location RESULT without utilizing any of the data or address registers. The status register is still affected.

If you examine the instruction set of the MC68000 you will see that a number of other instructions are capable of operating on memory in this same manner.

4-2. ONE'S COMPLEMENT

Purpose: Form the bitwise complement of the contents of the 16-bit variable VALUE at location 6000.

Sample Problem:

        Input: VALUE-(6000)=7F3E
       Output: VALUE-(6000)=80C1

Program 4-2:

```
       00006000        DATA      EQU       $6000
       00004000        PROGRAM   EQU       $4000

       00006000                  ORG       DATA
006000 00000002        VALUE     DS.W      1                 VALUE TO BE COMPLEMENTED

       00004000                  ORG       PROGRAM

004000 30386000        PGM_4_2   MOVE.W    VALUE,D0          FETCH VALUE
004004 4640                      NOT.W     D0                LOGICAL COMPLEMENT OF VALUE
004006 31C06000                  MOVE.W    D0,VALUE          STORE COMPLEMENTED RESULT

00400A 4E75                      RTS

                                 END       PGM_4_2
```

This program solves the problem in three steps. The first instruction moves the contents of location VALUE into data register D0. The next instruction takes the logical complement of data register D0. Finally, in the third instruction the result of the logical complement is stored in VALUE.

Note that any data register may be referenced in any instruction that uses data registers. (The same is true of address registers although you must pay special attention to register A7 which the processor uses as the stack pointer.) Thus, in the MOVE instruction we've just illustrated, any of the eight data registers could have been used.

The two MOVE instructions in this program, like those in Program 4-1, demonstrate two of the MC68000's addressing modes. The data reference to VALUE as either a source or destination operand is an example of absolute addressing. In absolute addressing the address for the data being referenced is contained in the extension word(s) following the operation word of the instruction. As shown in the assembly listing, the address (6000) corresponding to VALUE is found in the extension word for the MOVE instructions.

Since the address of VALUE requires only one extension word, the MC68000 refers to this form of absolute addressing as short absolute. Addresses in the ranges from 00000000 to 00007FFF and FFFF8000 to FFFFFFFF may be referenced using short absolute addressing. This range may appear somewhat different than expected, but it is consistent with the MC68000's treatment of 16-bit addresses and address displacements which are always sign-extended to 32 bits. This technique of addressing memory allows the system designer to organize his or her memory map so as to permit the usage of efficient short absolute addressing for both memory and peripheral device references. One way of achieving this would be to organize random access memory (RAM) starting at address 0 and peripheral devices in the upper 64K memory bytes.

Another form of absolute addressing is long absolute. This form is similar to short absolute except that two extension words are required to reference the data. Therefore to reduce your program size, you should strive to keep your frequently referenced variables in the short absolute addressing range.

Most programs in this book use short absolute addressing. Try modifying the value of DATA to a value outside the short absolute addressing range such as 9000_{16}. What happens to the generated object code? To ensure that the assembler generates the short absolute form whenever possible, you should try to define all data references prior to their use. Try moving the two assembler psuedo-instructions ORG DATA and VALUE DS.W 1 to the end of the program. Note the resulting object code.

The other addressing mode used in all instructions in Program 4-2 is data register direct. In this mode, the contents of the data register are directly affected. The contents are either loaded, modified, or stored as specified by the instruction.

The MOVE instruction allows any of the processor's 14 different addressing modes to be used to specify the source operand. However, the destination operand must be specified using addressing modes which reference memory locations that are "alterable." Thus you cannot use program counter relative or immediate addressing modes since such memory locations may be located in nonalterable, read-only memory.

If you want to perform a MOVE-type instruction with an address register as the destination, the MOVEA instruction must be used. The MOVEA instruction performs the same function as the MOVE instruction, but it does not affect the status register. Motorola's MC68000 assemblers allow you to specify an address register as the destination operand in a MOVE instruction. However, in this case the assembler actually generates the machine code for a MOVEA instruction; thus the status flags are unchanged.

Program 4-2 is another example where a single instruction may replace two or more instructions. The three instructions in this program may be replaced by the single instruction:

                        NOT.W VALUE

With this instruction, the contents of the variable VALUE are complemented without using the data or address registers. The operation is performed directly on the designated memory location VALUE.

4-3. 16-BIT ADDITION

Purpose: Add the contents of the 16-bit variable VALUE1 at location 6000 to the contents of the 16-bit variable VALUE2 at location 6002 and place the result in the 16-bit variable RESULT at location 6004.

Sample Problem:
```
         Input:  VALUE1-(6000)=10F5
                 VALUE2-(6002)=2621
         Output: RESULT-(6004)=3716
```

Program 4-3a:
```
         00006000       DATA      EQU    $6000
         00004000       PROGRAM   EQU    $4000

         00006000                 ORG    DATA
006000   00000002       VALUE1    DS.W   1           FIRST VALUE
006002   00000002       VALUE2    DS.W   1           SECOND VALUE
006004   00000002       RESULT    DS.W   1           16 BIT STORAGE FOR ADDITION RESULT
```

Beginning Programs   63

```
            00004000              ORG     PROGRAM
004000 30386000    PGM_4_3A MOVE.W   VALUE1,D0        GET FIRST VALUE
004004 D0786002             ADD.W    VALUE2,D0        ADD SECOND VALUE TO FIRST VALUE
004008 31C06004             MOVE.W   D0,RESULT        STORE RESULT OF ADDITION

00400C 4E75                 RTS

                            END      PGM_4_3A
```

The ADD instruction in this program is another example of a two-operand instruction. However, unlike the MOVE instruction, this instruction's second operand not only represents the instruction's destination but also is operated upon to calculate the result. The format

SOURCE Operation DESTINATION → DESTINATION

is common to many of the MC68000's instructions.

We should note at this point that the MC68000 processor provides an external 16-bit data bus for data accesses to memory. Internally, however, the processor also supports 8- and 32-bit data operations. Therefore, the ADD instruction, just like the MOVE and most other MC68000 instructions, permits data operations on all three data sizes. By simply changing the .W suffix to .B or .L anywhere in the programs we have shown, the programs would be converted to 8-bit or 32-bit addition programs.

As we noted in Program 4-1, the MC68000 allows many instructions to have both operands in memory. You should note, however, that this capability is not available with all instructions; for example, the ADD instruction only allows the source or destination operand to reference memory. Thus you could not add the contents of one memory location directly to the contents of another memory location.

As with any microprocessor, there are many instruction sequences you can execute with the MC68000 which will solve the same problem. Program 4-3*b*, for example, is a modification of Program 4-3*a* and uses address register indirect addressing instead of absolute short addressing. If you use address register indirect addressing, the address of the actual operand may not (need not) be known until execution time.

Program 4-3b:

```
            00006000        DATA     EQU      $6000
            00004000        PROGRAM  EQU      $4000


            00006000                 ORG      DATA
006000 00000002    VALUE1   DS.W     1                FIRST VALUE
006002 00000002    VALUE2   DS.W     1                SECOND VALUE
006004 00000002    RESULT   DS.W     1                16 BIT STORAGE FOR ADDITION RESULT

            00004000                 ORG      PROGRAM
004000 207C00006000 PGM_4_3B MOVEA.L  #VALUE1,A0       INITIALIZE A0 WITH ADDRESS OF VALUE
004006 3010                  MOVE.W   (A0),D0          GET FIRST VALUE IN D0
004008 D1FC00000002          ADDA.L   #2,A0            INCREMENT ADDRESS REGISTER A0 BY 2
00400E D050                  ADD.W    (A0),D0          ADD SECOND VALUE TO FIRST VALUE
004010 D1FC00000002          ADDA.L   #2,A0            INCREMENT A0 BY 2 AGAIN
004016 3080                  MOVE.W   D0,(A0)          STORE RESULT OF ADDITION

004018 4E75                  RTS

                             END      PGM_4_3B
```

The MOVEA instruction introduces two addressing modes — immediate and address register direct, which we have not used previously. Immediate addressing lets you define a data constant and include that constant in the instruction's associated

64 68000 Assembly Language Programming

object code. Motorola assembler format identifies immediate addressing with a pound sign (#) preceding the data constant. The size of the data constant varies depending on the instruction. Immediate addressing is extremely useful when small data constants must be referenced.

The second addressing mode — address register direct — is similar to data register direct except the address register is affected instead of the data register. Only word or long word references are permitted with address direct. When word size operands are used to modify an address register, the 16-bit operand is always sign-extended to 32 bits.

Program 4-3b also demonstrates the use of address register indirect addressing. In this mode the address of the operand is contained in the specified 32-bit address register. Since an extension word is not required, the address register indirect mode of addressing is more memory-efficient than absolute addressing. Because of the need to set up the address register, several references must be made to a particular data item before this mode really becomes more memory-efficient.

Another advantage of this addressing mode is its faster execution time as compared to absolute addressing. This improvement occurs because the address extension word(s) does not have to be fetched from memory prior to the actual data references.

A final advantage is the flexibility provided by having the reference address in an address register instead of fixed as part of the instruction. This flexibility allows the same code to be used for more than one address. Thus if you wanted to add the values contained in consecutive variables VALUE3 and VALUE4, you could simply change the contents of A0.

4-4. SHIFT LEFT ONE BIT

Purpose: Shift the contents of the 16-bit variable VALUE at location 6000 to the left one bit. Store the result back in VALUE.

Sample Problem:

```
      Input:  VALUE-(6000)=57B6 0101 0111 1011 0110₂
     Output:  VALUE-(6000)=AF6C 1010 1111 0110 1100₂
```

Program 4-4:

```
       00006000       DATA     EQU      $6000
       00004000       PROGRAM  EQU      $4000

       00006000                ORG      DATA
006000 00000002       VALUE    DS.W     1                VALUE TO BE SHIFTED LEFT

       00004000                ORG      PROGRAM

004000 30386000       PGM_4_4  MOVE.W   VALUE,D0         GET VALUE TO BE SHIFTED
004004 E348                    LSL.W    #1,D0            SHIFT LEFT LOGICALLY ONE BIT
004006 31C06000                MOVE.W   D0,VALUE         STORE SHIFTED RESULT

00400A 4E75                    RTS

                               END      PGM_4_4
```

The LSL instruction is used to perform a logical shift left. Using the operand format of the LSL instruction shown in Program 4-4, a data register can be shifted from 1 to 8 bits on either a byte, word or long word basis. Another form of the LSL instruction allows a shift count (modulo 64) to be specified in another data register. A final form of the LSL instruction, which uses only one operand, allows the contents of a memory location to be shifted one bit to the left without the use of a data register.

Except for different status register results, the following sequences all could replace the instruction LSL #1, D0, and produce the same results in D0:

```
MOVE    #1,D1
LSL     D1,D0

LSL     VALUE
MOVE    VALUE,D0

ROL     #1,D0
BCLR    #0,D0

ADD     D0,D0
```

How many others can you find? Which of those presented will execute the fastest?

4-5. BYTE DISASSEMBLY

Purpose: Divide the least significant byte of the 8-bit variable VALUE at location 6000 into two 4-bit nibbles and store one nibble in each byte of 16-bit variable RESULT at location 6002. The low-order four bits of the byte will be stored in the low-order four bits of the least significant byte of RESULT. The high-order four bits of the byte will be stored in the low-order four bits of the most significant byte of RESULT.

Sample Problem:

```
        Input:  VALUE-(6000)=5F
        Output: RESULT-(6002)=050F
```

Program 4-5a:

```
       00006000        DATA     EQU     $6000
       00004000        PROGRAM  EQU     $4000

       00006000                 ORG     DATA
       0000000F        MASK     EQU     $000F
006000 00000001        VALUE    DS.B    1               MASK FOR LOWER NIBBLE
006001 00000001                 DS.B    1               BYTE TO BE DISASSEMBLED
006002 00000002        RESULT   DS.W    1               ALIGN RESULT ON WORD BOUNDARY
                                                        STORAGE FOR DISASSEMBLED BYTE

       00004000                 ORG     PROGRAM

004000 10386000        PGM_4_5A MOVE.B  VALUE,D0        GET BYTE TO BE DISASSEMBLED
004004 0200000F                 AND.B   #MASK,D0        ISOLATE LOWER NIBBLE OF BYTE
004008 11C06003                 MOVE.B  D0,RESULT+1     SAVE LOWER ORDER NIBBLE
00400C 10386000                 MOVE.B  VALUE,D0        GET BYTE TO BE DISASSEMBLED
004010 E808                     LSR.B   #4,D0           ISOLATE HIGH NIBBLE
004012 11C06002                 MOVE.B  D0,RESULT       SAVE HIGH ORDER NIBBLE

004016 4E75                     RTS
                                END     PGM_4_5
```

This is an example of byte manipulation. The MC68000 allows most instructions which operate on words also to operate on bytes. Thus, by using the .B suffix, all the instructions in Program 4-5a perform byte operations.

Remember that the MOVE instruction, in addition to performing register-to-memory and memory-to-register transfers also performs register-to-register transfers. This use of the MOVE instruction is quite frequent.

66 68000 Assembly Language Programming

Generally, it is more efficient in terms of program memory usage and execution time to minimize references to memory. Program 4-5b is a modification of the above problem which demonstrates this.

Program 4-5b:

```
         00006000      DATA    EQU     $6000
         00004000      PROGRAM EQU     $4000

         00006000              ORG     DATA
006000   00000001      VALUE   DS.B    1           BYTE TO BE DISASSEMBLED
006001   00000001              DS.B    1           ALIGN RESULT ON WORD BOUNDARY
006002   00000002      RESULT  DS.W    1           STORAGE FOR DISASSEMBLED BYTE

         00004000              ORG     PROGRAM
004000   4240          PGM_4_5B CLR.W  D0          CLEAR DATA REGISTER D0(0:15)
004002   10386000              MOVE.B VALUE,D0     BYTE TO BE DISASSEMBLED IN D0(0:7)
004006   E958                  ROL.W  #4,D0        MOVE BYTE TO D0(4:11)
004008   E808                  LSR.B  #4,D0        SHIFT D0(4:7) TO D0(0:3)
00400A   31C06002              MOVE.W D0,RESULT    STORE DISASSEMBLED BYTE

00400E   4E75                  RTS

                               END     PGM_4_5B
```

The CLR.W instruction is required to clear the least significant 16 bits of data register D0. Only the least significant byte of D0 is affected by the byte transfer from VALUE. The ROL instruction rotates the least significant word of D0 such that the high-order nibble of VALUE is in the second byte of D0. Could the ROXL instruction be used in place of the ROL instruction?

Although the MC68000 allows manipulation of various data sizes, you must take care when you define a program's data. All of the processor's instructions, when making memory references to 16-bit or 32-bit data, assume the least significant bit of the memory address to be zero — that is, an even address. For this reason, an additional byte of memory storage is required to align the variable RESULT on an even address (6002_{16}) instead of at the next available memory location which would be 6001_{16}. Would the results of Program 4-5a have been the same if the memory addresses associated with RESULT had been 6001_{16}? What about Program 4-5b?

4-6. FIND THE LARGER OF TWO NUMBERS

Purpose: Find the larger of two 32-bit variables VALUE1 (at location 6000) and VALUE2 (at location 6004). Place the results in the variable RESULT at location 6008. Assume the values are unsigned.

Sample Problems:

```
    a.  Input:  VALUE1 - (6000) = 12345678
                VALUE2 - (6004) = 87654321
        Output: RESULT - (6008) = 87654321
    b.  Input:  VALUE1 - (6000) = 12345678
                VALUE2 - (6004) = 0ABCDEF1
        Output: RESULT - (6008) = 12345678
```

Program 4-6:

```
       00006000         DATA     EQU     $6000
       00004000         PROGRAM  EQU     $4000

       00006000                  ORG     DATA
006000 00000004         VALUE1   DS.L    1              FIRST VALUE
006004 00000004         VALUE2   DS.L    1              SECOND VALUE
006008 00000004         RESULT   DS.L    1              RESERVE LONG WORD STORAGE

       00004000                  ORG     PROGRAM
004000 4CF800036000     PGM_4_6  MOVEM.L VALUE1,D0/D1   LOAD VALUES TO BE COMPARED
004006 B280                      CMP.L   D0,D1          COMPARE 32 BIT VALUES
004008 62000004                  BHI     STORE          IF VALUE2 >= VALUE1 THEN GOTO STORE
00400C 2200                      MOVE.L  D0,D1          ...ELSE D1 = VALUE1
00400E 21C16008         STORE    MOVE.L  D1,RESULT      STORE LARGER VALUE

004012 4E75                      RTS

                                 END     PGM_4_6
```

The MOVE Multiple instruction, MOVEM, used in Program 4-6, lets us transfer the contents of selected address/data registers to or from a block of consecutive memory locations. In Program 4-6, D0 and D1 are loaded via the MOVEM instruction with the contents of the variables VALUE1 and VALUE2, respectively.

While you can specify which registers are to be selected with the MOVEM instruction, the order in which the register contents are transferred is not subject to your control. The transfer order is always data register D0 (or the lowest data register number you have specified) through data register D7 (or the highest data register you have specified) and then address registers A0 through A7 (once again, with the same limitations). The only exception to this sequence occurs when you use the predecrement addressing mode; in this case, the order is just the reverse of that which we have described. For details on the register specification and sequence, refer to the description of the MOVEM instruction in Chapter 22.

The Compare instruction, CMP, in Program 4-6 sets the status register flags as if the source, D0, were subtracted from the destination, D1. The order of the operands is the same as the operands in the subtract instruction, SUB.

The conditional transfer instruction BHI transfers control to the statement labeled FINI if the unsigned contents of D1 are greater than or equal to the contents of D0. Otherwise, the next instruction, (MOVE.L D0,D1) is executed. At STORE, register D1 will always contain the larger of the two values.

The BHI instruction is one of fourteen conditional branch instructions. To change the program to operate on signed numbers, simply change the BHI to BGE:

```
                CMP.L   D0,D1
                BGE     STORE
```

You can use the following table to determine which conditionals to use when performing signed and unsigned comparisons:

Compare Condition	Signed	Unsigned
greater than or equal	BGE	BCC
greater than	BGT	BHI
equal	BEQ	BEQ
not equal	BNE	BNE
less than or equal	BLE	BLS
less than	BLT	BCS

Note that the same instructions are used for signed and unsigned addition, subtraction, or comparison; however, the comparison operations are different.

The branch conditionally instructions are an example of program counter relative addressing. In other words, if the branch condition is satisfied, control will be transferred to an address relative to the current value of the program counter. The MC68000 permits two sizes of relative displacement, either 8-bit or 16-bit. Since the displacement is a two's complement byte displacement, and the displacement is from the program counter after it has been incremented, the branch instructions permit a maximum backward reference of either 126 or 32766 bytes, or a maximum forward reference of either 128 or 32768 bytes.

Dealing with compares and branches is an important part of programming the MC68000. Don't confuse the sense of the CMP instruction. **After a compare, the relation tested is:**

DESTINATION condition **SOURCE**.

For example, if the condition is "less than," then you test for destination less than source. Become familiar with all of the conditions and their meanings. Unsigned compares are very useful when comparing two addresses.

4-7. 64-BIT ADDITION

Purpose: Add the contents of two 64-bit variables VALUE1 (at location 6000) and VALUE2 (at location 6008). Store the result in RESULT (at location 6010).

Sample Problem:

```
      Input:  VALUE1 -  (6000) = 12A2
                        (6002) = E640   12A2E640F210123
                        (6004) = F210
                        (6006) = 0123
              VALUE2 -  (6008) = 0010
                        (600A) = 19BF   001019BF40023F51
                        (600C) = 4002
                        (600E) = 3F51
      Output: RESULT -  (6010) = 12B3
                        (6012) = 0000   12B3000032124074
                        (6014) = 3212
                        (6016) = 4074
```

Program 4-7:

```
          00006000         DATA     EQU      $6000
          00004000         PROGRAM  EQU      $4000

          00006000                  ORG      DATA
006000    00000008         VALUE1   DS.L     2           FIRST VALUE
006008    00000008         VALUE2   DS.L     2           SECOND VALUE
006010    00000008         RESULT   DS.L     2           RESERVE 64 BITS FOR RESULT

          00004000                  ORG      PROGRAM

004000    4CF8000F6000 PGM_4_7     MOVEM.L  VALUE1,D0-D3   D0-D1 := VALUE1 AND D2-D3 := VALUE2
004006    D283                     ADD.L    D3,D1          ADD LEAST SIGNIFICANT LONG WORD
004008    D182                     ADDX.L   D2,D0          ADD MOST SIG. LONG WORD WITH EXTEND
00400A    48F800036010             MOVEM.L  D0-D1,RESULT   STORE 64 BIT ADDITION RESULT

004010    4E75                     RTS

                                   END      PGM_4_7
```

The usefulness of the Move Multiple (MOVEM) instruction is again demonstrated in this 128-bit transfer to data registers D0 through D3. The status register flags are not affected by the transfer. Both the Carry and Extend flags are affected by the ADD instruction. The condition of the Extend flag is used in the ADDX (Add with Extend) instruction to include in the addition the carry from the previous 32-bit addition operation.

4-8. TABLE OF FACTORIALS

Purpose: Calculate the factorial of the 8-bit variable VALUE at location 6010 from a table of factorials FTABLE which occupies memory locations 6000 through 600F. Store result in the 16-bit variable RESULT at location 6012. Assume VALUE has a value between 0 and 7.

Sample Problem:

Input: FTABLE-
(6000) = 0000 0! = 1_{10}
(6002) = 0001 1! = 1_{10}
(6004) = 0002 2! = 2_{10}
(6006) = 0006 3! = 6_{10}
(6008) = 0018 4! = 24_{10}
(600A) = 0078 5! = 120_{10}
(600C) = 02D0 6! = 720_{10}
(600E) = 13B0 7! = 5040_{10}
VALUE - (6010) = 05
Output: RESULT - (6012) = 0078 5! = 120_{10}

Program 4-8a:

```
        00006000    DATA    EQU     $6000
        00004000    PROGRAM EQU     $4000

        00006000            ORG     DATA
                    *  TABLE OF FACTORIALS
006000 0001         FTABLE  DC      1               0! := 1
006002 0001                 DC      1               1! := 1
006004 0002                 DC      2               2! := 2
006006 0006                 DC      6               3! := 6
006008 0018                 DC      24              4! := 24
00600A 0078                 DC      120             5! := 120
00600C 02D0                 DC      720             6! := 720
00600E 13B0                 DC      5040            7! := 5040

006010 00000001     VALUE   DS.B    1               DETERMINE FACTORIAL FOR THIS VALUE
006011 00000001             DS.B    1               ALIGNMENT STORAGE
006012 00000002     RESULT  DS.W    1               RESULT OF FACTORIAL

       00004000             ORG     PROGRAM

004000 4240         PGM_4_8A CLR.W  D0              D0(0:15) := 0
004002 10386010             MOVE.B VALUE,D0         GET VALUE
004006 D000                 ADD.B  D0,D0            D0(0:7) := 2 * VALUE
004008 307C6000             MOVEA.W #FTABLE,A0      INITIALIZE POINTER TO FACTORIAL TABLE
00400C 31F000006012         MOVE.W 0(A0,D0),RESULT  STORE FACTORIAL RESULT

004012 4E75                 RTS
                            END    PGM_4_8A
```

The approach to this table lookup problem, as implemented in Program 4-8*a*, demonstrates the use of the address register indirect addressing mode with index. The first two instructions, CLR and MOVE, load the index register D0 with the contents of

VALUE. The CLR instruction is required since the data size of VALUE is byte and the index register size used in this addressing mode is either word or long word. The MC68000 allows either a data register or an address register to be used as the index register.

The Move Address (MOVEA) instruction initializes address register A0 with the address of the factorial table. All 32 bits of the address register are affected by the move regardless of the instruction's data size. When the data size is word, as in Program 4-8a, the source operand is sign-extended to 32 bits.

The actual calculation of the entry in the table is determined by the first operand of the MOVE.W instruction. The long word contents of address register A0 are added to the sign-extended word contents of data register D0 to form the effective address used to address the table entry. When D0 is used in this manner, it is referred to as an index register. As in most MC68000 addressing modes, the usage of an address or data register in determining the effective address does not alter the contents of the register. The direct, postincrement, and predecrement addressing modes are exceptions to this rule.

The address register indirect with index mode permits either the 16-bit or 32-bit contents of the index register to be used in the calculation of the effective address. The size of the index register to be used is specified by the size suffix of the index register operand specification. As in the specification of the instruction size, the default suffix is '.W' or word. Why can't the suffix .L be used for index register D0 in Program 4-8a?

In addition to allowing the effective address to be determined by the contents of the address and index registers, the address register indirect with index mode also permits a small displacement. The displacement field allows for an 8-bit value. However, like the 16-bit index, this displacement is sign-extended. Thus, displacements of from -126 bytes to $+129$ bytes are possible.

Program 4-8b:

```
            00006000        DATA      EQU       $6000
            00004000        PROGRAM   EQU       $4000

            00006000                  ORG       DATA
                        *   TABLE OF FACTORIALS

006000 0001         FTABLE    DC        1                  0! := 1
006002 0001                   DC        1                  1! := 1
006004 0002                   DC        2                  2! := 2
006006 0006                   DC        6                  3! := 6
006008 0018                   DC        24                 4! := 24
00600A 0078                   DC        120                5! := 120
00600C 02D0                   DC        720                6! := 720
00600E 13B0                   DC        5040               7! := 5040

006010 00000001     VALUE     DS.B      1                  DETERMINE FACTORIAL FOR THIS VALUE
006011 00000001               DS.B      1                  ALIGNMENT STORAGE
006012 00000002     RESULT    DS.W      1                  RESULT OF FACTORIAL

            00004000                  ORG       PROGRAM

004000 4240         PGM_4_8B  CLR.W     D0                 D0(0:15) := 0
004002 10386010               MOVE.B    VALUE,D0           GET VALUE
004006 D000                   ADD.B     D0,D0              D0(0:7) := 2 * VALUE
004008 3040                   MOVEA.W   D0,A0              MOVE TABLE OFFSET TO ADDRESS REG.
00400A 31E860006012            MOVE.W    FTABLE(A0),RESULT  STORE FACTORIAL RESULT

004010 4E75                   RTS

                              END       PGM_4_8B
```

Program 4-8b performs the same function as Program 4-8a except it demonstrates the use of another addressing mode — it uses address register indirect with displacement addressing. In this addressing mode, the effective address of the operand is the sum of the address register and the sign-extended 16-bit displacement. The displacement is stored in the extension word following the instruction in program memory.

In Program 4-8b, the "displacement" is actually the base of the table, while the address register is the offset into the table. It is very important to remember that the 16-bit displacement is sign-extended when used. Therefore, if FTABLE had been located at any address of 8000_{16} or higher, the sign extension of bit 15 (=1) would cause an address of $FF8000_{16}$ through $FFFFFF_{16}$ to be loaded as the table base address. Thus, for example, Program 4-8b would not work if FTABLE were located at address 015000_{16}. This method of using the "displacement" as a base address is only useful in the address range of $0-7FFF_{16}$ or $FF8000_{16}$ through $FFFFFF_{16}$.

Program 4-8b usage of address register indirect with displacement addressing is not a typical example of this addressing mode. Generally, the address register will contain the address of a table or data structure while the displacement will represent a fixed offset from the base of the table or structure.

PROBLEMS

4-1. 64-BIT DATA TRANSFER

Purpose: Move the contents of memory locations 6000 through 6006 to locations 6800 through 6806.

Sample Problem:

```
Input:   (6000) = 3E2A
         (6002) = 42A1
         (6004) = 21F2
         (6006) = 60A0
Output:  (6800) = 3E2A
         (6802) = 42A1
         (6804) = 21F2
         (6806) = 60A0
```

4-2. 16-BIT SUBTRACTION

Purpose: Subtract the contents of the 16-bit variable VALUE1 at location 6000 from the contents of the 16-bit variable VALUE2 at location 6002 and store the result back in VALUE1.

Sample Problem:

```
Input:   VALUE1 - (6000) = 3977
         VALUE2 - (6002) = 2182
Output:  VALUE1 - (6000) = 17F5
```

4-3. SHIFT RIGHT THREE BITS

Purpose: Shift the contents of the 16-bit variable VALUE1 at location 6000 right three bits. Clear the three most significant bit positions.

Sample Problem:

a. Input: VALUE1 - (6000) = 415D
    Output: VALUE1 - (6000) = 082B

b. Input: VALUE1 - (6000) = C15D
    Output: VALUE1 - (6000) = 182B

4-4. WORD ASSEMBLY

Purpose: Combine the low four bits of each of the four consecutive bytes beginning at location 6000 into one 16-bit word. The value at 6000 goes into the most significant nibble of the result; the value at 6003 becomes the least significant nibble. Store the result in location 6004.

Sample Problems:

Input: (6000) = 0C
        (6001) = 02
        (6002) = 06
        (6003) = 09
Output: (6004) = C269

4-5. FIND SMALLEST OF THREE NUMBERS

Purpose: Locations 6000, 6002, and 6004 each contain an unsigned number. Store the smallest of these numbers in location 6006.

Sample Problem:

Input: (6000) = 9125
        (6002) = 102C
        (6004) = 7040
Output: (6006) = 102C

4-6. SUM OF SQUARES

Purpose: Calculate the squares of the contents of word VALUE1 at location 6000 and word VALUE2 at 6002 and add them together. Place the result into the long word RESULT at location 6004. Use signed arithmetic.

Sample Problem:

Input: VALUE1 - (6000) = 0007
        VALUE2 - (6002) = 0032
Output: RESULT - (6004) = 000009F5

That is, $7^2 + 50^2 = 49 + 2500 = 2549$ (decimal)
$7^2 + 32^2 = 31 + 9C4 = 9F5$ (hexadecimal)

Sample Answer:

```
MOVE.W   VALUE1,D0
MULS.W   VALUE1,D0
MOVE.W   VALUE2,D1
MULS.W   VALUE2,D1
ADD.L    D0,D1
MOVE.L   D1,RESULT
```

4-7. SHIFT LEFT VARIABLE NUMBER OF BITS

Purpose: Shift the contents of the word VALUE at memory location 6000 left. The number of positions to shift is contained in the word COUNT at memory location 6002. Assume that the shift count is less than 32. The low-order bits should be cleared.

Sample Problems:

```
a.  Input:   (6000) = 182B
             (6002) = 0003     shift left 3 positions
    Output:  (6000) = C158

b.  Input:   (6000) = 182B
             (6002) = 0010     shift left 16 positions
    Output:  (6000) = 0000
```

Sample Answer:

```
MOVEM.W   VALUE,D0/D1
LSL.W     D1,D0
MOVE.W    D0,VALUE
```

5
Simple Program Loops

The program loop is the basic structure that forces the CPU to repeat a sequence of instructions. Loops have four sections:

1. **The initialization section,** which establishes the starting values of counters, pointers, and other variables.
2. **The processing section,** where the actual data manipulation occurs. This is the section that does the work.
3. **The loop control section,** which updates counters and pointers for the next iteration.
4. **The concluding section,** that may be needed to analyze and store the results.

The computer performs Sections 1 and 4 only once, while it may perform Sections 2 and 3 many times. Therefore, the execution time of the loop depends mainly on the execution time of Sections 2 and 3. Those sections should execute as quickly as possible, while the execution times of Sections 1 and 4 have less effect on overall program speed.

Figure 5-1 and 5-2 contain two alternative flowcharts for a typical program loop. Following the flowchart in Figure 5-1 results in the computer always executing the processing section at least once. On the other hand, the computer may not execute the processing section in Figure 5-2 at all. The order of operations in Figure 5-1 is more natural, but the order in Figure 5-2 is often more efficient and eliminates the problem of the computer going through the processing sequence once even where there is no data for it to handle.

The computer can use the loop structure to process large sets of data (usually called "arrays"). The simplest way to use one sequence of instructions to handle an array of data is to have the program increment a register (usually an index register or

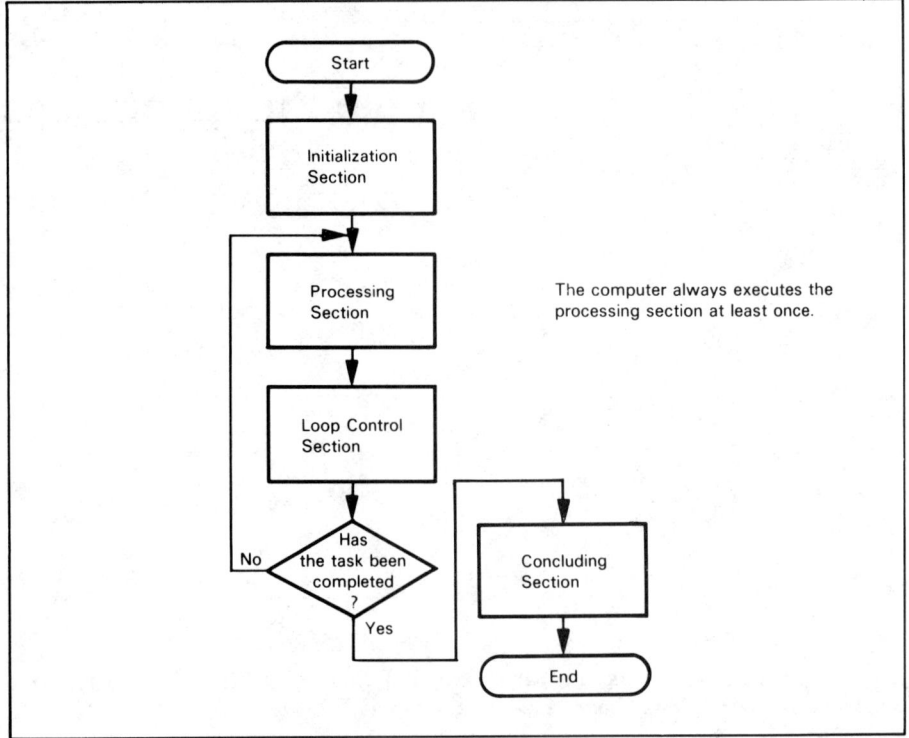

Figure 5-1. Flowchart of a Program Loop

stack pointer) after each iteration. Then the register will contain the address of the next element in the array when the computer repeats the sequence of instructions. The computer can then handle arrays of any length with a single program.

Register indirect addressing is the key to processing arrays with the MC68000 microprocessor, since that mode allows you to vary the actual address of the data (the "effective address") by changing the contents of a register. In the absolute addressing modes, the instruction completely determines the effective address; that address is therefore fixed if program memory is read-only.

The MC68000's autoincrementing mode is particularly convenient for processing arrays since it automatically updates the address register for the next iteration. No additional instruction is necessary. You can even have an automatic increment by 2 or 4 if the array contains 16-bit or 32-bit data or addresses.

Although our examples show the processing of arrays with autoincrementing (adding 1, 2, or 4 after each iteration), **the procedure is equally valid with autodecrementing** (subtracting 1, 2, or 4 before each iteration). Many programmers find moving backward through an array somewhat awkward and difficult to follow, but it is more efficient in many situations. The computer obviously does not know backward from forward. **The programmer, however, must remember that the MC68000 increments an address register after using it but decrements an address register before using it.** This

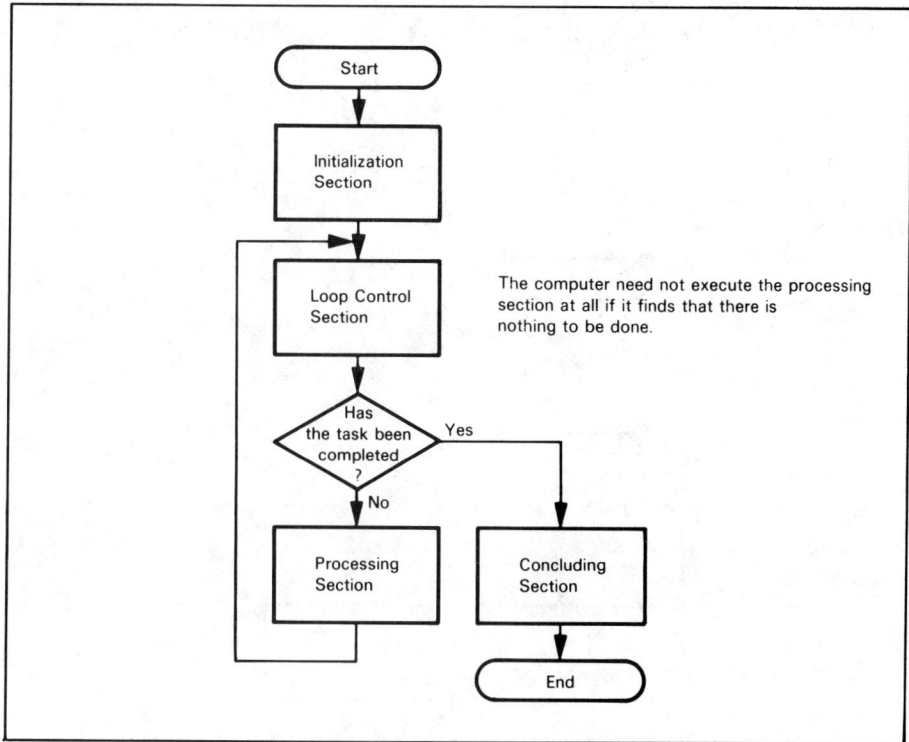

Figure 5-2. An Alternative for a Program Loop

difference affects initialization as follows:

1. When moving forward through an array (autoincrementing), start the address register at the lowest address occupied by the array.
2. When moving backward through an array (autodecrementing), start the address register one step (1, 2, or 4) beyond the highest address occupied by the array.

PROGRAM EXAMPLES

5-1. 16-BIT SUM OF DATA

Purpose: Calculate the sum of a series of numbers. The length of the series (in words) is defined by the variable LENGTH at location 6000. The starting address of the series is contained in the long-word variable START at location 6002. Store the sum in the variable TOTAL at location 6006. Assume that the sum is a 16-bit number so that you can ignore carries.

Sample Problem:

```
Input:  LENGTH  -  (6000)  =  0003
        START   -  (6002)  =  00005000
                   (5000)  =  2040
                   (5002)  =  1C22
                   (5004)  =  0242
Output: TOTAL   -  (6006)  =  (5000) + (5002) + (5004)
                           =  2040 + 1C22 + 0242
                           =  3EA4
```

Flowchart 5-1:

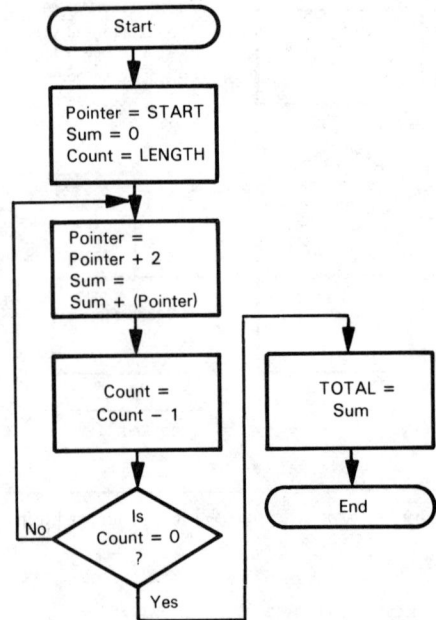

Program 5-1a:

```
               00006000              DATA     EQU      $6000
               00004000              PROGRAM  EQU      $4000

               00006000                       ORG      DATA
006000 00000002                      LENGTH   DS.W     1          NUMBER OF DATA ELEMENTS
006002 00000004                      START    DS.L     1          ADDRESS OF DATA ELEMENTS
006006 00000002                      TOTAL    DS.W     1          SUM OF DATA ELEMENTS

               00004000                       ORG      PROGRAM

004000 20786002                      PGM_5_1A MOVEA.L  START,A0   INITIALIZE POINTER REGISTER
004004 7000                                   MOVEQ    #0,D0      INITIALIZE SUM TO ZERO
004006 32386000                               MOVE.W   LENGTH,D1  INITIALIZE ELEMENT COUNT

00400A D058                          LOOP     ADD.W    (A0)+,D0   SUM NEXT ELEMENT
00400C 5341                                   SUBQ.W   #1,D1      UPDATE ELEMENT COUNT
00400E 66FA                                   BNE      LOOP       IF COUNT NOT ZERO THEN GOTO LOOP

004010 31C06006                               MOVE.W   D0,TOTAL   STORE SUMMATION

004014 4E75                                   RTS

                                              END      PGM_5_1A
```

The initialization section of the program consists of the first three instructions, which set the data pointer, sum, and counter to the appropriate initial values. In this program we encounter the first example of parameter passing where the parameters include an address (the contents of START) along with such parameters as size or count (LENGTH) which we have encountered in previous programs. The first MOVE instruction in the program loads the beginning address (from location START) of the data elements into address register A0. Once again we will defer a detailed discussion of parameter passing until Chapters 10 and 11; at this point, you must simply ensure that the required starting address is in the long word at location 6002 prior to attempting to execute this program.

Frequently in programming, you must initialize a data register with a small data value as we have done in Program 5-1a. For values in the range -128 to $+127$, you should use the MOVEQ instruction. The MOVEQ instruction encodes the value within the instruction word, thus eliminating an additional operand word that would otherwise be needed to define the initial value. You should note that the MOVEQ instruction, unlike most other MC68000 instructions, only has a data size of long word. We could have used the CLR instruction to initialize the sum to zero; both the MOVEQ and CLR instructions require the same number of bytes and microprocessor cycles. In what cases is the use of the CLR instruction preferred?

The processing section of Program 5-1a consists of the single instruction ADD.W (A0)+,D0 which adds the contents of the memory location addressed by address register A0 to the contents of data register D0. This instruction does all the real work of the program and is the first example of the address register indirect with postincrement mode of addressing. You probably noticed that the program contained no explicit instruction to update the address register to the next word in the series. Instead, the address register is implicitly updated by execution of the ADD instruction. Thus, this instruction is also part of the loop control section. In the postincrement addressing mode, the processor increments the contents of the address register after the address register has been used to determine the effective address of the data references. The contents of the address register are incremented by either 1, 2, or 4 depending on the size of the data being referenced. An increment of 1 is used for byte references, 2 for word references and 4 for long word references. Thus, the instruction ADD.W (A0)+,D0 results in the contents of address register A0 being incremented by 2. This addressing mode is extremely useful when you are performing operations on data tables.

The loop control section of the program consists of the single instruction SUBQ.W, since the instruction ADD.W (A0)+,D0 updates the pointer automatically. The SUBQ instruction decrements the counter that keeps track of the number of iterations the processor has left to perform. The Subtract Quick (SUBQ) instruction is another instruction which you'll find useful in reducing the size of your programs. Like the MOVEQ instruction, SUBQ allows the encoding of small data values within a single instruction word. Unlike the MOVEQ instruction, SUBQ only allows data values in the range from 1 to 8. However, you can use the SUBQ instruction to operate on byte, word or long word data and SUBQ can be used to operate on memory directly, or on any address register as well as a data register.

The instruction BNE causes a branch if the Zero (Z) flag is reset (that is, if the result of decrementing D1 *was not* zero). The offset part of the BNE instruction is a two's complement number, determined by the distance between the destination and the instruction. In this case, the distance is from memory location 4010 (the address of the BNE instruction+2) to memory location 400A (the destination). So the offset (using two's complement arithmetic) is:

$$\begin{array}{r} 400A \\ -(400E+2) \\ \hline \end{array} = \begin{array}{r} 400A \\ +BFF0 \\ \hline FFFA \end{array}$$

The offset of $FA corresponds to a negative six (−6) bytes which is the number of bytes to the label LOOP from the location of the branch instruction plus two. This single byte sign-extended form of the branch instruction allows offsets in the range −63 words to +64 words from the location of the branch instruction. The address range is described in words rather than bytes since all MC68000 instructions must start on a word boundary and have sizes which are word multiples. Another form of the branch instruction allows a 16-bit sign-extended offset, thus providing a branching range of −16383 words to +16384 words. When you use this form, an additional operand word is required.

If the Zero flag is 1 (that is, if the result of decrementing D1 *was* zero), the processor continues its normal sequence. Thus the result of executing BNE is:

PC = LOOP if the result of decrementing D1 is zero
     (PC) + 2 if the result of decrementing D1 is zero

The extra 2, as usual, comes from the two bytes occupied by the BNE instruction itself. This is true for either form of the branch instruction since the PC is incremented by two in either case, before adding the offset. With the 16-bit offset, the PC is incremented by another two if the branch is not taken. The result is the same for both the 8-bit and the 16-bit offset; the instruction following the conditional branch will be executed if the test fails.

Most programmers make computer loops count down rather than up so that they can use the setting of the Zero flag as an exit condition. Remember that the Zero flag is 1 if the most recent result was zero and 0 if that result was not zero. Try rewriting the program so that it loads register D1 with zero initially and increments it after each iteration. Which approach is more efficient?

Program 5-1a executes correctly for all initial values unless the number of elements is zero. This problem is solved by modifying Program 5-1a to include a specific check for this condition prior to the loop processing as shown in Program 5-1b.

Program 5-1b:

```
               00006000       DATA      EQU    $6000
               00004000       PROGRAM   EQU    $4000

               00006000                 ORG    DATA
006000 00000002                LENGTH   DS.W   1          NUMBER OF DATA ELEMENTS
006002 00000004                START    DS.L   1          ADDRESS OF DATA ELEMENTS
006006 00000002                TOTAL    DS.W   1          SUM OF DATA ELEMENTS

               00004000                 ORG    PROGRAM

004000 20786002                PGM_5_1B MOVEA.L START,A0  INITIALIZE POINTER REGISTER
004004 7000                             MOVEQ   #0,D0     INITIALIZE SUM TO ZERO
004006 32386000                         MOVE.W  LENGTH,D1 INITIALIZE ELEMENT COUNT

00400A 6706                             BEQ.S   DONE      IF LENGTH = 0 THEN DONE
```

Simple Program Loops

```
00400C  D058        LOOP      ADD.W    (A0)+,D0      SUM NEXT ELEMENT
00400E  5341                  SUBQ.W   #1,D1         UPDATE ELEMENT COUNT
004010  66FA                  BNE      LOOP          IF COUNT NOT ZERO THEN GOTO LOOP

004012  31C06006    DONE      MOVE.W   D0,TOTAL      STORE SUMMATION

004016  4E75                  RTS

                              END      PGM_5_1B
```

In this program, the single instruction BEQ is used to check for number of elements equal to zero, and it will cause the program's flow of control to be transferred to DONE if there are no numbers in the series. You may have noticed that the BEQ branch instruction had a suffix of ".S". This suffix is used by the assembler to determine which offset form of the branch instruction should be used. This suffix is only necessary when the label in the operand field is a forward reference and the assembler default is the long offset form.

The order in which the processor executes instructions is often very important. In Program 5-1*b,* BEQ must come immediately after the MOVE.W LENGTH,D1 instruction; otherwise, an intervening instruction might change the Zero flag. Similarly, the SUBQ instruction must be followed immediately by the BNE instruction.

5-2. 32-BIT SUM OF DATA

Purpose: Calculate the sum of a series of unsigned 16-bit numbers. The length of the series (in words) is defined by the variable LENGTH at location 6000. The starting address of the series is contained in the long-word variable START at location 6002. Store the sum in the long word (32-bit) variable TOTAL at location 6006. Take carries into account.

Sample Problem:

```
        Input:   LENGTH  -  (6000)  =  0003
                 START   -  (6002)  =  00005000
                            (5000)  =  2040
                            (5002)  =  1C22
                            (5004)  =  E242
        Output:  TOTAL   -  (6006)  =  (5000)+(5002)+(5004)
                                    =  2040 + 1C22 + E242
                                    =  00011EA4
```

Program 5-2a:

```
            00006000        DATA       EQU     $6000
            00004000        PROGRAM    EQU     $4000

            00006000                   ORG     DATA
006000      00000002        LENGTH     DS.W    1            NUMBER OF DATA ELEMENTS
006002      00000004        START      DS.L    1            ADDRESS OF DATA ELEMENTS
006006      00000004        TOTAL      DS.L    1            SUM OF DATA ELEMENTS
            00010000        CARRYBIT   EQU     $10000       CARRY BIT VALUE

            00004000                   ORG     PROGRAM

004000      20786002        PGM_5_2A   MOVEA.L START,A0     INITIALIZE POINTER REGISTER
004004      7000                       MOVEQ   #0,D0        INITIALIZE SUM TO ZERO
004006      32386000                   MOVE.W  LENGTH,D1    INITIALIZE ELEMENT COUNT

00400A      670E                       BEQ.S   DONE         IF LENGTH = 0 THEN DONE
```

```
00400C  D058            LOOP      ADD.W   (A0)+,D0       SUM NEXT ELEMENT
00400E  6406                      BCC.S   LOOPTEST       IF CARRY = 0 THEN GOTO LOOPTEST

004010  068000010000              ADDI.L  #CARRYBIT,D0   ...ELSE ADD 16-BIT CARRY

004016  5341            LOOPTEST  SUBQ.W  #1,D1          UPDATE ELEMENT COUNT
004018  66F2                      BNE     LOOP           IF COUNT NOT ZERO THEN GOTO LOOP

00401A  21C06006        DONE      MOVE.L  D0,TOTAL       STORE SUMMATION

00401E  4E75                      RTS
                                  END     PGM_5_2A
```

Flowchart 5-2:

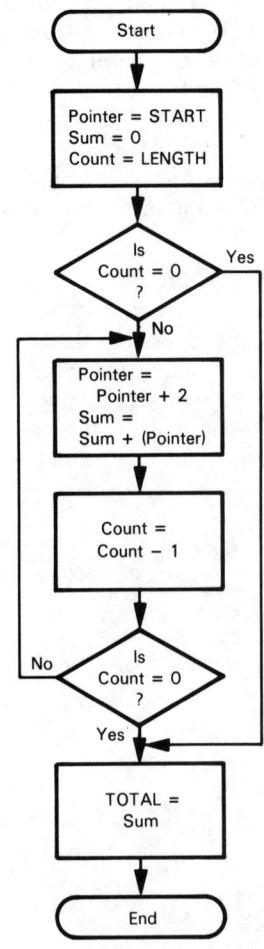

This program differs only slightly from the 16-bit addition program. Since a 32-bit sum is to be generated, we must now handle the carry generated by the ADD instruction. The two new instructions (BCC and ADDI) test for the carry during addition and add the carry bit back into the sum when a carry occurs.

Simple Program Loops 83

The instruction BCC causes a jump to memory location LOOPTEST if the Carry (C) flag = 0. Thus, if there is no carry from the 16-bit addition, the program jumps around the statement that increments the most significant 16 bits of the sum. The relative offset for BCC LOOPTEST is:

$$\begin{array}{r} 4016 \\ -(400E+2) \end{array} = \begin{array}{r} 4016 \\ -4010 \\ \hline 06 \end{array}$$

The relative offset for BNE LOOP is:

$$\begin{array}{r} 400C \\ -(4018+2) \end{array} = \begin{array}{r} 400C \\ -401A \\ \hline -0E \end{array} = FFF2$$

The relative offset for BEQ.S DONE is:

$$\begin{array}{r} 401A \\ -(400A+2) \end{array} = \begin{array}{r} 401A \\ -400C \\ \hline 0E \end{array}$$

The long word form of the ADD instruction might simplify this program. However, since the series consists of 16-bit values we must do some extra work to make these values into long words. Program 5-2b accomplishes this.

Program 5-2b:

```
           00006000      DATA     EQU       $6000
           00004000      PROGRAM  EQU       $4000

           00006000               ORG       DATA
006000 00000002          LENGTH   DS.W      1          NUMBER OF DATA ELEMENTS
006002 00000004          START    DS.L      1          ADDRESS OF DATA ELEMENTS
006006 00000004          TOTAL    DS.L      1          SUM OF DATA ELEMENTS

           00004000               ORG       PROGRAM

004000 20786002          PGM_5_2B MOVEA.L   START,A0   INITIALIZE POINTER REGISTER
004004 7000                       MOVEQ     #0,D0      INITIALIZE SUM TO ZERO
004006 2400                       MOVE.L    D0,D2      CLEAR TEMPORARY REGISTER
004008 32386000                   MOVE.W    LENGTH,D1  INITIALIZE ELEMENT COUNT

00400C 6708                       BEQ.S     DONE       IF LENGTH = 0 THEN DONE

00400E 3418            LOOP       MOVE.W    (A0)+,D2   D2[15-0] := DATA ELEMENT
004010 D082                       ADD.L     D2,D0      ADD DATA ELEMENT TO SUM
004012 5341                       SUBQ.W    #1,D1      UPDATE ELEMENT COUNT
004014 66F8                       BNE       LOOP       IF COUNT NOT ZERO THEN GOTO LOOP

004016 21C06006         DONE      MOVE.L    D0,TOTAL   STORE SUMMATION

00401A 4E75                       RTS

                                  END       PGM_5_2B
```

We clear the most significant 16-bits of register D2 during the initialization section; since these bits will never change, we don't need to clear them each time through the loop. The 16-bit values from memory are then loaded into the low-order 16 bits of D2 and then a long add (ADD.L) is used to add the 32-bit contents of D2 to register D0.

84 68000 Assembly Language Programming

Because the purpose said the values were unsigned numbers, the high-order 16 bits will always be zero.

Note that we need not check for carry in the loop processing section since, with a 32-bit operation, any carry from the low-order 16 bits will automatically be propagated into the high-order portion of D0. The changes in the loop processing section reduced the number of instructions in the loop and perhaps make the program easier to understand. The number of bytes in the loop is also reduced. However, does this make the loop execute faster? The processing section in Program 5-2a takes 18 or 36 cycles:

```
ADD     8 cycles
BCC    10 cycles (12 if branch not taken)
ADDI.L (16) cycles (not always executed)
       18 (36) cycles (if BCC.S used – 18 (32) cycles)
```

The second version takes 16 cycles:

```
MOVE    8 cycles
ADD.L  (8) cycles
       16 cycles
```

The second version is both smaller and faster. However, you may not always find this to be the case. A single more powerful instruction may take longer to execute than two or more simpler instructions that perform the same task. Can you find an example of this?

5-3. NUMBER OF NEGATIVE ELEMENTS

Purpose: Determine the number of negative elements in a series of signed 16-bit numbers. Negative elements are identified by a 1 in the most significant bit position (bit 15). The length of the series is defined by the variable LENGTH at location 6000. The starting address of the series is defined by the long word variable START at location 6002. Store the number of negative elements in the variable TOTAL at location 6006.

Sample Problem:

```
Input:  LENGTH - (6000) = 0003
        START  - (6002) = 00005000
                 (5000) = F1DC
                 (5002) = 7E0A
                 (5004) = 824B
Output: TOTAL  - (6006) = 0002, since memory locations 5000 and
                         5004 contain negative numbers
```

Program 5-3:

```
       00006000           DATA     EQU      $6000
       00004000           PROGRAM  EQU      $4000

       00006000                    ORG      DATA
006000 00000002           LENGTH   DS.W     1          NUMBER OF DATA ELEMENTS
006002 00000004           START    DS.L     1          ADDRESS OF DATA ELEMENTS
006006 00000002           TOTAL    DS.W     1          SUM OF DATA ELEMENTS

       00004000                    ORG      PROGRAM

004000 20786002           PGM_5_3  MOVEA.L  START,A0   INITIALIZE POINTER REGISTER
004004 7000                        MOVEQ    #0,D0      NNEG := 0
004006 32386000                    MOVE.W   LENGTH,D1  INITIALIZE ELEMENT COUNT
```

```
00400A  670A                    BEQ.S     DONE          IF LENGTH = 0 THEN DONE
00400C  4A58          LOOP      TST.W     (A0)+         TEST DATA ELEMENT
00400E  6A02                    BPL.S     LOOPTEST      IF  > 0 THEN GOTO LOOPTEST
004010  5240                    ADDQ.W    #1,D0            ...ELSE NNEG := NNEG + 1
004012  5341          LOOPTEST  SUBQ.W    #1,D1         UPDATE ELEMENT COUNT
004014  66F6                    BNE       LOOP          IF COUNT NOT ZERO THEN GOTO LOOP
004016  31C06006      DONE      MOVE.W    D0,TOTAL      STORE NUMBER OF NEGATIVE ELEMENTS
00401A  4E75                    RTS
                                END       PGM_5_3
```

Flowchart 5-3:

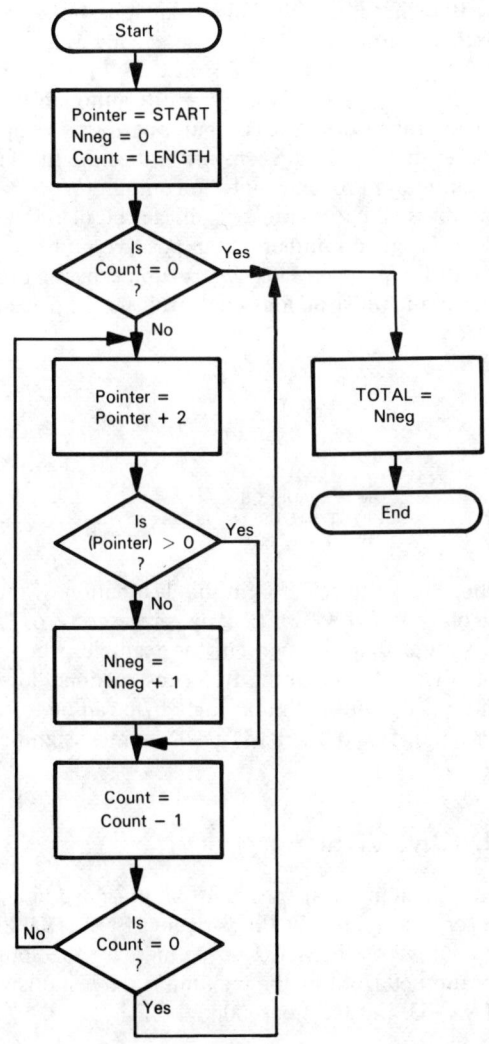

The TST instruction is used to determine if the next element in the series is a negative number. TST compares the operand with zero and sets the status flags accordingly. Thus, the operation of the TST instruction is essentially equivalent to:

SUBQ #0,(A0)+

Why should you use TST instead of SUBQ in cases like this? Because it provides clearer documentation.

While testing the operand, TST sets the Negative (N) and Zero (Z) flags according to the results of the comparison. The Carry (C) and Overflow (V) flags are always reset to zero.

The Negative (N) flag simply reflects the value of bit 15 of the most recent result. If you are using signed numbers, bit 15 is, in fact, the sign (0 for positive, 1 for negative); the mnemonics for Branch if Plus (BPL) and Branch if Minus (BMI) assume that you are using signed numbers. However, you can use equally well bit 15 for other purposes, such as the status of peripherals or other 1-bit data. In these cases you can still test bit 15 with BMI (bit 15 = 1) or BPL (bit 15 = 0); although the mnemonics no longer make sense, the operations work. The computer performs its operations without considering whether the user thinks they are sensible or meaningful. The interpretation of the results is the programmer's problem, not the computer's.

Negative signed numbers all have a most significant bit of 1 and thus are actually larger, when considered as unsigned numbers, than positive numbers.

In Program 5-3, the BPL (Branch if Plus) instruction causes a branch if the Negative flag is 0. Which other branch instructions could you use in place of BPL?

We could also replace:

TST (A0)+
BPL LOOPTEST

with

MOVE (A0)+,D3
BTST #15,D3
BEQ LOOPTEST

The BTST instruction tests a specific bit in the destination. If the bit is zero, the Zero (Z) flag is set; if the bit is one, the Zero (Z) flag is reset to zero. This instruction is most useful in testing bits other than the sign bit; for example, when you need to test the status of a peripheral device. Although the BTST instruction allows you to directly test the contents of memory, only bits within a single byte can be tested in this mode. How could you rewrite Program 5-3 so that BTST tests the most significant byte of a 16-bit element in memory?

5-4. FIND MAXIMUM VALUE

Purpose: Find the largest element in a series of 16-bit unsigned binary numbers. The length of the series is defined by the variable LENGTH at location 6000 and the starting address of the series is defined by the long word variable START at location 6002. Store the maximum (largest unsigned element) in the value MAXNUM at location 6006.

Sample Problem:

Input: LENGTH - (6000) = 0004
       START - (6002) = 00005000
                (5000) = A48E
                (5002) = 71AC
                (5004) = 34F1
                (5006) = E57A
Output: MAXNUM - (6006) = E57A, since this is the largest of the four unsigned numbers.

Flowchart: 5-4a:

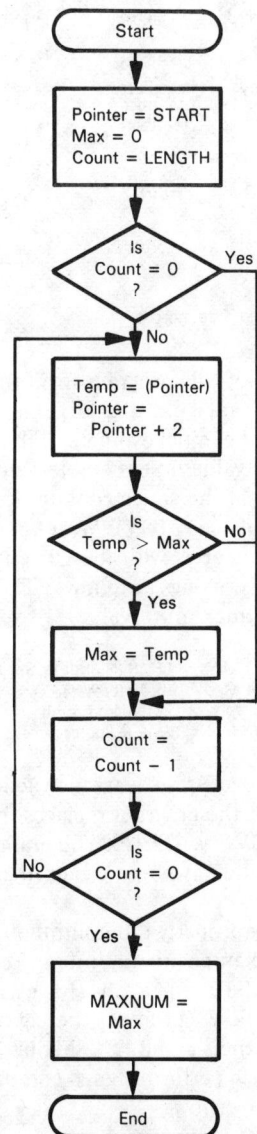

Program 5-4a:

```
           00006000           DATA       EQU      $6000
           00004000           PROGRAM    EQU      $4000

           00006000                      ORG      DATA
006000     00000002           LENGTH     DS.W     1            NUMBER OF DATA ELEMENTS
006002     00000004           START      DS.L     1            ADDRESS OF DATA ELEMENTS
006006     00000002           MAXNUM     DS.W     1            MAXIMUM NUMBER IN SERIES

           00004000                      ORG      PROGRAM

004000     20786002           PGM_5_4A   MOVEA.L  START,A0     INITIALIZE POINTER REGISTER
004004     7000                          MOVEQ    #0,D0        MAX := 0
004006     32386000                      MOVE.W   LENGTH,D1    INITIALIZE ELEMENT COUNT

00400A     670C                          BEQ.S    DONE         IF LENGTH = 0 THEN DONE

00400C     3418               LOOP       MOVE.W   (A0)+,D2     TEMP := NEXT DATA ELEMENT
00400E     B042                          CMP.W    D2,D0        COMPARE TEMP WITH MAX, "MAX-TEMP" !
004010     6402                          BCC.S    LOOPTEST     IF MAX > OR = TEMP GOTO LOOPTEST

004012     3002                          MOVE.W   D2,D0        ...ELSE NEW MAX, MAX := TEMP

004014     5341               LOOPTEST   SUBQ.W   #1,D1         UPDATE ELEMENT COUNT
004016     66F4                          BNE      LOOP         IF COUNT NOT ZERO THEN GOTO LOOP

004018     31C06006           DONE       MOVE.W   D0,MAXNUM    STORE MAXIMUM NUMBER IN SERIES

00401C     4E75                          RTS

                                         END      PGM_5_4A
```

The first three instructions of this program form the initialization section.

In this program we take advantage of the fact that zero is the smallest unsigned binary number. If you make zero the initial estimate of the maximum, then the program will set the maximum to a larger value unless all elements in the array are zeros. The maximum will also be set to zero if the series contains no elements.

The two instruction sequence MOVE.W (A0)+,D2 and CMP.W D2,D0 compares the next element in the series with the current maximum value. The CMP instruction affects the Carry and Zero flags as follows (TEMP is the value of the current element and MAX is the current maximum value):

>   Carry = 0 if MAX > TEMP (Higher or Same)
>   Carry = 1 if MAX < TEMP (Lower)
>   Zero = 0 if MAX = TEMP (Not Equal)
>   Zero = 1 if MAX = TEMP (Equal)

The program uses the branch BCC (Carry Clear) instruction which tests both the Carry and Zero flags. If either flag is set, the program replaces the maximum with the current element using the instruction MOVE.W D2,D0. The branch instruction BHI could have been used instead of BCC and would have been easier to understand. Why is BCC a better choice of branch instructions?

The program does not work properly if the numbers are signed, because negative numbers all appear to be larger than positive numbers. You must use the Sign (Negative) flag instead of the Carry in the comparison. However, you must also consider the fact that two's complement overflow can affect the sign; that is, the magnitude of a signed result could overflow into the sign bit. The MC68000 has special instructions — BGT, BGE, BLE and BLT — which perform signed comparison branches and automatically handle two's complement overflow.

As we have seen before, the MC68000 allows for some operations to be performed directly on memory without requiring the use of an additional data register. Program 5-4b uses this feature to eliminate the MOVE.W (A0)+,D2 instruction in Program 5-4a.

Program 5-4b:

```
              00006000     DATA      EQU    $6000
              00004000     PROGRAM   EQU    $4000

              00006000               ORG    DATA
006000 00000002            LENGTH    DS.W   1          NUMBER OF DATA ELEMENTS
006002 00000004            START     DS.L   1          ADDRESS OF DATA ELEMENTS
006006 00000002            MAXNUM    DS.W   1          MAXIMUM NUMBER IN SERIES

              00004000               ORG    PROGRAM

004000 20786002            PGM_5_4B  MOVEA.L START,A0  INITIALIZE POINTER REGISTER
004004 7000                          MOVEQ   #0,D0     MAX := 0
004006 32386000                      MOVE.W  LENGTH,D1 INITIALIZE ELEMENT COUNT

00400A 670C                          BEQ.S   DONE      IF LENGTH = 0 THEN DONE

00400C B058              LOOP        CMP.W   (A0)+,D0  COMPARE DATA ELEMENT WITH MAX
00400E 6404                          BCC.S   LOOPTEST  IF MAX > OR = ELEMENT GOTO LOOPTEST

004010 3028FFFE                      MOVE.W  -2(A0),D0 ...ELSE NEW MAX, MAX := ELEMENT

004014 5341              LOOPTEST    SUBQ.W  #1,D1     UPDATE ELEMENT COUNT
004016 66F4                          BNE     LOOP      IF COUNT NOT ZERO THEN GOTO LOOP

004018 31C06006          DONE        MOVE.W  D0,MAXNUM STORE MAXIMUM NUMBER IN SERIES

00401C 4E75                          RTS

                                     END     PGM_5_4B
```

Although the CMP.W (A0)+,D0 instruction appears to simplify this program, it does cause one slight problem — it increments register A0 while performing the compare. Now, when updating the maximum value, the new maximum is no longer in any data register or pointed to by any address register. The address register indirect with displacement addressing mode can be used to overcome this problem. By using a displacement of -2, we essentially back the pointer up to the element we just compared. The effective address for the instruction MOVE -2(A0),D0 is calculated as follows:

Effective Address of -2(A0) = (A0) -2

The contents of register A0 are not changed by this calculation.

At first glance CMP.W (A0)+,D0 may appear not to optimize the loop processing since the loop processing of Program 5-4b requires the same number of words as Program 5-4a. However, the execution cycles for program 5-4a are 17 or 20 cycles:

```
              MOVE   8     cycles
              CMP    4     cycles
              BCC    5     cycles (4 if branch not taken)
              MOVE  (4)    cycles (not always executed)
                    ——
                    17     (20) cycles
```

compared to 13 or 24 cycles for Program 5-4b:

```
              CMP    8     cycles
              BCC    5     cycles (4 if branch not taken)
              MOVE  (12)   cycles (not always executed)
                    ——
                    13     (24) cycles
```

90 68000 Assembly Language Programming

Although both programs require the same number of loop cycles to update the maximum, the second program is slightly more efficient when no update is required.

5-5. NORMALIZE A BINARY NUMBER

Purpose: Shift a 32-bit binary number until the most significant bit of the number is 1. The address of the number is defined by the long word variable NUMBER at location 6000. Store the normalized number (shifted number) in the variable NORMNUM at location 6004. Store the number of left shifts required in the byte variable SHIFTNUM at location 6008. If the number is zero, clear both variables NORMNUM and SHIFTNUM.

The processing is just like converting a number to a scientific notation; for example:

$$0.0057 \quad 5.7 \times 10^{-3}$$

Sample Problems:

a. Input: NUMBER - (6000) = 00005000
                    (5000) = 30001000
   Output: NORMNUM - (6004) = C0004000
           SHIFTNUM - (6008) = 02

b. Input: NUMBER - (6000) = 00005000
                    (5000) = 00000001
   Output: NORMNUM - (6004) = 80000000
           SHIFTNUM - (6008) = 1F

c. Input: NUMBER - (6000) = 00005000
                    (5000) = 00000000
   Output: NORMNUM - (6004) = 00000000
           SHIFTNUM - (6008) = 00

d. Input: NUMBER - (6000) = 00005000
                    (5000) = C1234567
   Output: NORMNUM - (6004) = C1234567
           SHIFTNUM - (6008) = 00

Program 5-5:

```
       00006000          DATA     EQU      $6000
       00004000          PROGRAM  EQU      $4000

       00006000                   ORG      DATA
006000 00000004          NUMBER   DS.L     1          ADDRESS OF NUMBER TO BE NORMALIZED
006004 00000004          NORMNUM  DS.L     1          NORMALIZED NUMBER
006008 00000001          SHIFTNUM DS.B     1          NUMBER OF SHIFT REQUIRED TO NORMALIZE

       00004000                   ORG      PROGRAM
004000 7000              PGM_5_5  MOVEQ    #0,D0      INITIALIZE SHIFT COUNT
004002 20786000                   MOVEA.L  NUMBER,A0  GET ADDRESS OF NUMBER TO NORMALIZE
004006 2210                       MOVE.L   (A0),D1    GET NUMBER TO BE NORMALIZED
004008 6F06                       BLE.S    DONE       IF ZERO OR NORMALIZED THEN DONE

00400A 5240              JUSTIFY  ADDQ.W   #1,D0      INCREMENT SHIFT COUNT
00400C E389                       LSL.L    #1,D1      SHIFT NUMBER 1 BIT TO THE LEFT
00400E 6AFA                       BPL      JUSTIFY    AGAIN IF MSB = 0

004010 11C06008          DONE     MOVE.B   D0,SHIFTNUM  STORE SHIFT COUNT
004014 21C16004                   MOVE.L   D1,NORM      STORE NORMALIZED NUMBER

004018 4E75                       RTS

                                  END      PGM_5_5
```

Flowchart 5-5:

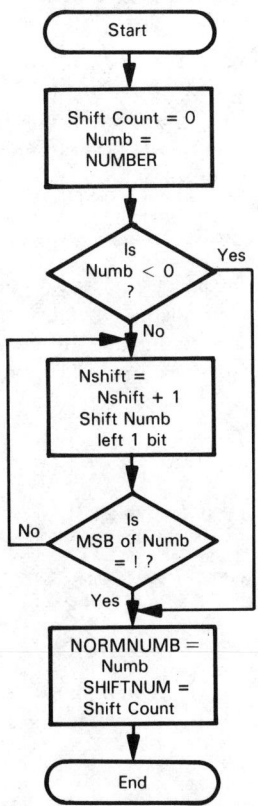

The BLE instruction performs both the test for number being zero and being already justified. The status conditions for the branch are set during the MOVE instruction which loads the number into data register D0. BLE causes a branch to DONE if the Zero flag is 1. If the number is already normalized, the most significant bit will be 1 and the Negative flag will be set by the MOVE. In this case, BLE causes a branch to DONE if the Negative flag is 1. Why can BLE be used to perform this last test, since the state of the Overflow (V) flag must also be taken into consideration when you use the BLE instruction?

LSL.L #1,D0 (Logical Shift Left Long) shifts the contents of the specified data register D0 left one bit and clears the least significant bit. The most significant bit ends up in the Carry flag and the old Carry value is lost. This use of LSL is equivalent to adding D0 to itself; the result is, of course, twice the original number.

BPL causes a branch to JUSTIFY if the Negative flag is 0. This condition may mean that the result was a positive number, or it may just mean that the most significant bit of the result was 0; the microprocessor simply performs the operation; only the programmer can provide the interpretation. Since the LSL instruction affects the state of the Carry flag, how could you modify this program to use BCC (Branch if Carry Clear) instead of BPL?

PROBLEMS

5-1. CHECKSUM OF DATA

Purpose: Calculate the checksum of a series of 8-bit numbers. The length of the series is defined by the variable LENGTH at location 6000. The starting address of the series is contained in the long-word variable START at location 6002. Store the checksum in the variable CHECKSUM at location 6006. The checksum is formed by Exclusive-ORing all the numbers in the list.

Note: Checksums are often used by paper tape and cassette systems to ensure that data has been correctly read. A checksum calculated when reading the data is compared to a checksum that is stored with the data on the tape. If the two checksums do not agree, the system will usually indicate an error, or automatically read the data again.

Sample Problem:

```
Input:   LENGTH   - (6000) = 0003
         START    - (6002) = 00005000
                    (5000) = 28
                    (5001) = 55
                    (5002) = 26
Output:  CHECKSUM - (6006) = (5000) ⊕ (5001) ⊕ (5002)
                          = 28 ⊕ 55 ⊕ 26
                          =   01101000
                          = ⊕ 01010101
                            ──────────
                              01111101
                          = ⊕ 00100110
                            ──────────
                              01011011
                          = 5B
```

5-2. NUMBER OF ZERO, POSITIVE, AND NEGATIVE NUMBERS

Purpose: Determine the number of zero, positive (most significant bit zero, but entire number not zero), and negative (most significant bit 1) elements in a series of signed 16-bit numbers. The length of the series is defined by the variable LENGTH at location 6000 and the starting address is defined by the contents of the long word variable START at location 6002. Place the number of negative elements in variable NUMNEG at location 6006, the number of zero elements in variable NUMZERO at location 6008, and the number of positive elements in variable NUMPOS at location 600A.

Sample Problem:

```
Input:  LENGTH - (6000) = 0006
        START  - (6002) = 00005000
                 (5000) = 7602
                 (5002) = 8D48
                 (5004) = 2120
                 (5006) = 0000
                 (5008) = E605
                 (500A) = 0004
```

Output: 2 negative, 1 zero, 3 positive, so
```
       NUMNEG  - (6006) = 0002
       NUMZERO - (6008) = 0001
       NUMPOS  - (600A) = 0003
```

5-3. FIND MINIMUM

Purpose: Find the smallest element in a series of unsigned byte data. The length of the series is defined by the variable LENGTH at location 6000 and the starting address of the series is contained in the long-word variable START at location 6002. Store the minimum byte value in the variable NUMMIN at location 6006.

Sample Problem:
```
Input:  LENGTH - (6000) = 0005
        START  - (6002) = 00005000
                 (5000) = 65
                 (5001) = 79
                 (5002) = 15
                 (5003) = E3
                 (5004) = 72
Output: NUMMIN - (6006) = 15, since this is the smallest
                          of five unsigned numbers.
```

5-4. COUNT 1 BITS

Purpose: Determine the number of bits which are one in the 16-bit variable NUM at location 6000, and store the result in the variable NUMBITS at location 6002.

Sample Problem:
```
Input:  NUM    -(6000) = B794 = 1011011110010100
Output: NUMBITS - (6002) = 09
```

5-5. FIND ELEMENT WITH MOST 1 BITS

Purpose: Determine which element in a series of 16-bit numbers has the largest number of bits that are one. The length of the series is defined by the variable LENGTH at location 6000 and the starting address of the series is contained in the long-word variable START at location 6002. Store the value with the most 1 bits in the variable NUM at location 6006. If two or more elements have the same number of 1 bits, use the value of the earliest element in the series.

Sample Problem:
```
Input:  LENGTH - (6000) = 0005
        START  - (6002) = 00005000
                 (5000) = 6779 = 0110011101111001
                 (5002) = 15E3 = 0001010111100011
                 (5004) = 68F2 = 0110100011110010
                 (5006) = 8700 = 1000011100000000
                 (5008) = 592A = 0101100100101010
Output: NUM    - (6006) = 6779, since this element is the first element
                          in the series to have ten bits = 1.
```

6
Character-Coded Data

Microprocessors often handle data which represents printed characters rather than numeric quantities. Not only do keyboards, teletypewriters, communications devices, displays, and computer terminals expect or provide character-coded data, but many instruments, test systems, and controllers also require data in this form. ASCII (American Standard Code for Information Interchange) is the most commonly used code; others include Baudot (telegraph) and EBCDIC (Extended Binary-Coded-Decimal Interchange Code).

Throughout this book, we will assume all of our character-coded data to be seven-bit ASCII, as shown in Table 6-1; the character code occupies the low-order seven bits of the byte, and the most significant bit of the byte holds a 0 or a parity bit.

HANDLING DATA IN ASCII

Here are some principles to remember in handling ASCII-coded data:

1. **The codes for the numbers and letters form ordered sequences.** Since the ASCII codes for the numbers 0 through 9 are 30_{16} through 39_{16}, you can convert a decimal digit to the equivalent ASCII characters (and ASCII to decimal) by means of a simple additive factor: 30_{16} = ASCII 0. Since the codes for the upper-case letters (41_{16} through $5A_{16}$) are ordered alphabetically, you can alphabetize strings by sorting them according to their numerical values.
2. **The computer does not distinguish between printing and non-printing characters.** Only the I/O devices make that distinction.
3. **An ASCII I/O device handles data only in ASCII.** For example, if you want an ASCII printer to print the digit 7, you must send it 37_{16} as the data; 07_{16} is the bell character. Similarly, if an operator presses the 9 key on an ASCII keyboard, the input data will be 39_{16}; 09_{16} is the horizontal tab character.

Table 6-1. Hexadecimal ASCII Character Codes

MSBs / LSBs	0	1	2	3	4	5	6	7	Control Characters			
0	NUL	DLE	SP	0	@	P	`	p	NUL	Null	DC1	Device control 1
1	SOH	DC1	!	1	A	Q	a	q	SOH	Start of heading	DC2	Device control 2
2	STX	DC2	"	2	B	R	b	r	STX	Start of text	DC3	Device control 3
3	ETX	DC3	#	3	C	S	c	s	ETX	End of text	DC4	Device control 4
4	EOT	DC4	$	4	D	T	d	t	EOT	End of transmission	NAK	Negative acknowledge
5	ENQ	NAK	%	5	E	U	e	u	ENQ	Enquiry	SYN	Synchronous idle
6	ACK	SYN	&	6	F	V	f	v	ACK	Acknowledge	ETB	End of transmission block
7	BEL	ETB	'	7	G	W	g	w	BEL	Bell, or alarm	CAN	Cancel
8	BS	CAN	(	8	H	X	h	x	BS	Backspace	EM	End of medium
9	HT	EM	)	9	I	Y	i	y	HT	Horizontal tabulation	SUB	Substitute
A	LF	SUB	*	:	J	Z	j	z	LF	Line feed	ESC	Escape
B	VT	ESC	+	;	K	[	k	{	VT	Vertical tabulation	FS	File separator
C	FF	FS	,	<	L	\	l			FF	Form feed	GS	Group separator
D	CR	GS	-	=	M	]	m	}	CR	Carriage return	RS	Record separator
E	SO	RS	.	>	N	^	n	~	SO	Shift out	US	Unit separator
F	SI	US	/	?	O	_	o	DEL	SI	Shift in	SP	Space
									DLE	Data link escape	DEL	Delete

4. **Many ASCII devices do not use the entire character set.** For example, devices may ignore many control characters and may not print lower-case letters.

5. **ASCII control characters often have widely varying interpretations.** Each ASCII device typically uses control characters in a special way to provide features such as cursor control on a CRT, and to allow software control of characteristics such as rate of data transmission, print width, and line length.

6. **Some widely used ASCII control characters are:**

   $0A_{16}$ line feed (LF)
   $0D_{16}$ carriage return (CR)
   08_{16} backspace
   $7F_{16}$ rubout or delete character (DEL)

7. **Each ASCII character occupies eight bits.** This allows a large character set but is wasteful when only a few characters are actually being used. If, for example, the data consists entirely of decimal numbers, the ASCII format (allowing one digit per byte) requires twice as much storage, communications capacity, and processing time as does the BCD format (allowing two digits per byte).

Most assembly languages have features that make character-coded data easy to handle. In Motorola's assembly language, quotation marks around a character indicate the character's ASCII value. For example,

                     MOVE.B # 'A',D0

is the same as

                     MOVE.B # $41,D0

The first form is preferable for several reasons. It increases the readability of the instruction; it also avoids errors that may result from looking up a value in a table. The program does not depend on ASCII as the character set, since the assembler handles the conversion using whatever code has been designed into it.

PROGRAM EXAMPLES

6-1. LENGTH OF A STRING OF CHARACTERS

Purpose: Determine the length of a string of characters. The starting address is contained in the 32-bit variable START at location 6000. The end of the string is marked by an ASCII carriage return character ($0D_{16}$). Place the length of the string (excluding the carriage return) in the variable LENGTH at location 6004.

Sample Problems:

```
    a.  Input:   START   —   (6000) = 00005000
                             (5000) = 0D
        Output:  LENGTH  —   (6004) = 0000
    b.  Input:   START   —   (6000) = 00005000
                             (5000) = 4D   'M'
                             (5001) = 43   'C'
                             (5002) = 36   '6'
                             (5003) = 38   '8'
                             (5004) = 30   '0'
                             (5005) = 30   '0'
                             (5006) = 30   '0'
                             (5007) = 0D   CR
        Output:  LENGTH  —   (6004) = 07
```

Flowchart 6-1a:

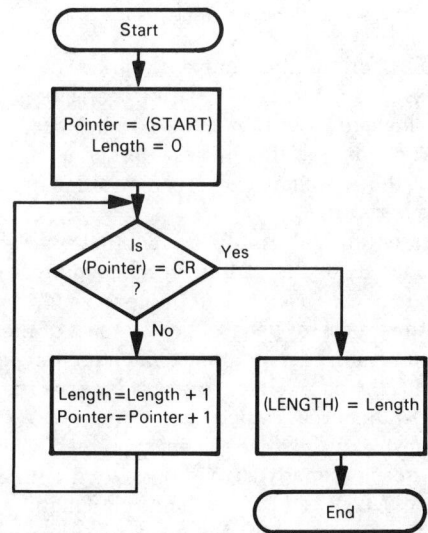

Program 6-1a:

```
         00006000        DATA     EQU    $6000
         00004000        PROGRAM  EQU    $4000

         00006000                 ORG    DATA
006000   00000004        START    DS.L   1          ADDRESS OF STRING
006004   00000002        LENGTH   DS.W   1          NUMBER OF CHARACTERS IN STRING
```

```
          0000000D    CR         EQU       $0D              ASCII VALUE FOR CARRIAGE RETURN
          00004000               ORG       PROGRAM
004000 20786000       PGM_6_1A   MOVEA.L   START,A0         POINTER TO START OF STRING
004004 7000                      MOVEQ     #0,D0            INITIALIZE LENGTH COUNTER
004006 0C18000D       LOOP       CMPI.B    #CR,(A0)+        IS CURRENT CHAR A CARRIAGE RETURN?
00400A 6704                      BEQ.S     DONE             IF YES THEN DONE
00400C 5240                      ADDQ.W    #1,D0            ...ELSE INCREMENT LENGTH COUNTER
00400E 60F6                      BRA       LOOP             CONTINUE SCAN
004010 31C06004       DONE       MOVE.W    D0,LENGTH        SAVE STRING LENGTH
004014 4E75                      RTS
                                 END       PGM_6_1A
```

As far as the processor is concerned, the carriage return (CR) is just another ASCII code ($0D_{16}$). The fact that the carriage return can cause an output device to perform a control function rather than print a symbol does not affect the processor. The processor simply treats $0D_{16}$ as a value that is to be searched for.

The search is performed using the compare instruction CMPI. This instruction sets the flags as if the immediate operand, the carriage return ($0D_{16}$) character, had been subtracted from the destination operand. The destination operand (the next character in the string) is not affected. In this program the CMPI instruction affects the Zero (Z) flag as follows:

        Z = 1 if the character in the string is a carriage return.
        Z = 0 if it is not a carriage return.

In addition to performing the compare, the CMPI instruction also uses the postincrementing address mode to update the string character pointer. Thus, a portion of the loop control processing shown in Flowchart 6-1a has been completed. Normally, combining several instructions like this makes a program more efficient. However, how would the results of the flowchart and program differ if you also needed to save the pointer to the carriage return?

The postincrementing address mode is another variation of the MC68000 address register indirect modes. Like the address register indirect mode, the contents of the specified address registers are used to determine the address of operand. However after the data reference, the processor updates the contents of the register by incrementing it by the size associated with the data reference. Incrementing is by one, two, or four bytes depending on whether the data reference size is byte, word, or long word, respectively. The only exception to this occurs when address register A7 (the stack pointer) is used and the data size is byte. In this case the stack pointer is incremented by two bytes to ensure that the pointer is properly aligned on a word boundary.

The instruction ADDQ adds 1 to the string length counter in data register D0. This counter was initialized to zero before the loop began by the MOVEQ #0,D0 instruction. You must remember to initalize variables before using them in a loop; failure to do so is a common programming error.

By rearranging the logic and changing the initial conditions, you can shorten the program and decrease the execution time. If we rearrange the flowchart so that the program increments the string length before it checks for the carriage return, only one branch instruction is needed instead of two.

Program 6-1b:

```
         00006000    DATA     EQU      $6000
         00004000    PROGRAM  EQU      $4000

         00006000             ORG      DATA
006000   00000004    START    DS.L     1          ADDRESS OF STRING
006004   00000002    LENGTH   DS.W     1          NUMBER OF CHARACTERS IN STRING

         0000000D    CR       EQU      $0D        ASCII VALUE FOR CARRIAGE RETURN

         00004000             ORG      PROGRAM

004000   20786000    PGM_6_1B MOVEA.L  START,A0   POINTER TO START OF STRING
004004   70FF                 MOVEQ    #-1,D0     INITIALIZE LENGTH COUNT
004006   720D                 MOVEQ    #CR,D1     INITIALIZE WITH ASCII VALUE OF CR

004008   5240        LOOP     ADDQ.W   #1,D0      INCREMENT LENGTH COUNT
00400A   B218                 CMP.B    (A0)+,D1   IS CURRENT CHAR A CARRIAGE RETURN?
00400C   66FA                 BNE      LOOP       IF NO THEN CONTINUE SCAN

00400E   31C06004             MOVE.W   D0,LENGTH  ...ELSE DONE, SAVE LENGTH COUNT

004012   4E75                 RTS

                              END      PGM_6_1B
```

Flowchart 6-1b:

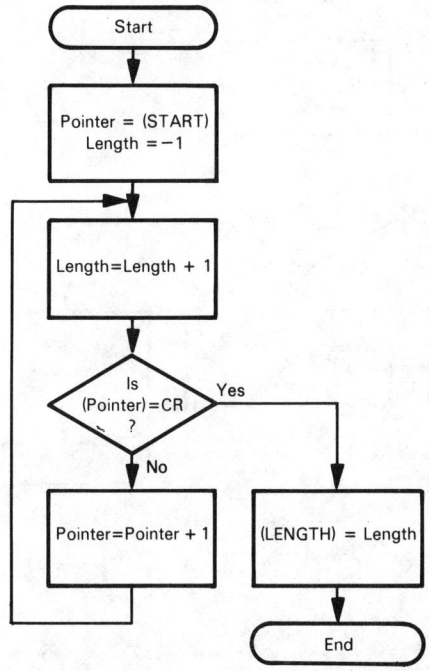

As you can see in Program 6-1b, incrementing the string length at the beginning of the loop rather than at the end allows elimination of one of the branch instructions. We have made another less obvious change in the loop of Program 6-1b that further decreases execution time of the loop: we have used data register direct addressing for the source operand of the Compare instruction instead of using immediate data as we did in Program 6-1a. This change reduces the object code for the Compare instruction

100 68000 Assembly Language Programming

by two bytes and saves the microprocessor from loading the ASCII value for carriage return each time through the loop. In general, eliminating the use of the immediate operands within loops can improve the loop efficiency. The family of "quick" instructions such as MOVEQ and ADDQ is an exception to this general rule. You should also note that the use of immediate operands does provide for better program documentation.

Neither of the preceding programs has loops which terminate by decrementing a counter to zero or by incrementing a counter to reach a maximum value. In fact, the processor will simply continue examining characters until it finds a carriage return. Obviously, this will create a problem if the string, because of an error or an omission, does not contain a carriage return. It is good programming practice to place a maximum count in a loop like this even though it does not appear to be necessary. What would happen if the example programs were used on a string which does not contain a carriage return? Program 6-1c corrects this problem.

Flowchart 6-1c

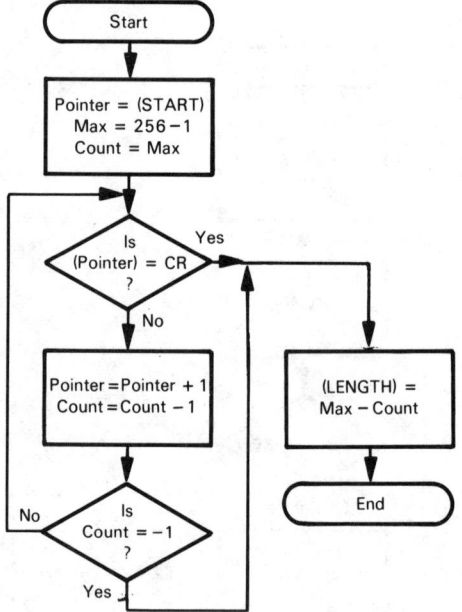

Program 6-1c:

```
               00006000        DATA      EQU       $6000
               00004000        PROGRAM   EQU       $4000

               00006000                  ORG       DATA
006000 00000004 START           DS.L      1                   ADDRESS OF STRING
006004 00000002 LENGTH          DS.W      1                   NUMBER OF CHARACTERS IN STRING

               0000000D         CR        EQU       $0D       ASCII VALUE FOR CARRIAGE RETURN

               00004000                   ORG       PROGRAM

004000 20786000 PGM_6_1C MOVEA.L START,A0                     POINTER TO START OF STRING
```

```
004004  74FF              MOVEQ    #256-1,D2      INITIALIZE MAX STRING LENGTH = 256
004006  3002              MOVE.W   D2,D0          LENGTH COUNT := MAX STRING LENGTH
004008  720D              MOVEQ    #CR,D1         INITIALIZE WITH ASCII VALUE OF CR
                        * SCAN STRING FOR CARRIAGE RETURN. STOP SCAN WHEN
                        * CARRIAGE RETURN FOUND OR 256 CHARACTERS SCANNED.
00400A  B218       LOOP   CMP.B    (A0)+,D1       IS CURRENT CHAR A CARRIAGE RETURN?
00400C  57C8FFFC          DBEQ     D0,LOOP        IF NO AND NOT END OF STRING - CONT.
004010  9440              SUB.W    D0,D2          DETERMINE STRING LENGTH
004012  31C26004          MOVE.W   D2,LENGTH      SAVE STRING LENGTH
004016  4E75              RTS
                          END      PGM_6_1C
```

This program makes use of one of the Test Condition, Decrement and Branch instructions, DBcc. This set of instructions can be very useful in loop or array processing. The DBcc instructions have the form

DBcc Dn, < label >

and perform the following steps:

1. If the condition being tested is satisfied, control passes to the instruction following the DBcc.
2. If the condition is not satisfied then
    a. The *lower 16-bits* of the specified data register are decremented by one.
    b. If the result is a −1, control passes to the instruction following the DBcc.
    c. If the result is not −1, control is transferred to the specified branch location. The location must be within a sign-extended 16-bit displacement from the current PC value.

The conditional tests allowed by the DBcc instructions are identical to the tests allowed by the Bcc instructions except that DBcc also permits the conditions "never true" or "false" (F) and "always true" (T). The Motorola MC68000 assembler allows DBRA as well as DBF.

With the DBEQ instruction, the two instruction sequences CMP and DBEQ will scan a string with a maximum length of 256 bytes for a carriage return character. The scan will terminate either when a carriage return is found or when the entire 256 character string has been searched. You will note that in either termination, the instruction immediately following the DBEQ will always be executed. In this program the same calculation will be performed regardless of the cause of termination. However, in some programs you may want to perform different operations based on which condition caused the termination. When this is necessary, you can follow the DBcc instruction with an appropriate Bcc branch instruction to transfer control to the program associated with the conditional test that caused termination.

When using the DBcc instructions, you must be careful to properly initialize data counters. In Program 6-1c, the counter was initialized to 256−1 (255), since **the loop terminates when the counter reaches −1, not zero.** The operand form 256−1 instead of 255 was used in order to more clearly document this initialization condition.

After the loop terminates, the counter does not contain the length of the string: we must calculate the string length by subtracting the counter contents from the maximum string length minus 1. (Remember the termination condition!)

6-2. FIND FIRST NON-BLANK CHARACTER

Purpose: Search a string of ASCII characters for a non-blank character. The starting address of the string is contained in the 32-bit variable START at location 6000. Store the address of the first non-blank character in the 32-bit variable POINTER at location 6004. A blank character is the same as a space and the ASCII code for this character is 20_{16}.

Sample Problems:

```
a.  Input:   START   —  (6000) = 00005000
                        (5000) = 37   '7'
    Output:  POINTER  —  (6004) = 00005000
b.  Input:   START   —  (6000) = 5000
                        (5000) = 20   blank
                        (5001) = 20   blank
                        (5002) = 20   blank
                        (5003) = 46   'F'
                        (5004) = 20   blank
    Output:  POINTER  —  (6004) = 00005003, since the previous
                        memory locations all contained blanks.
```

Flowchart 6-2:

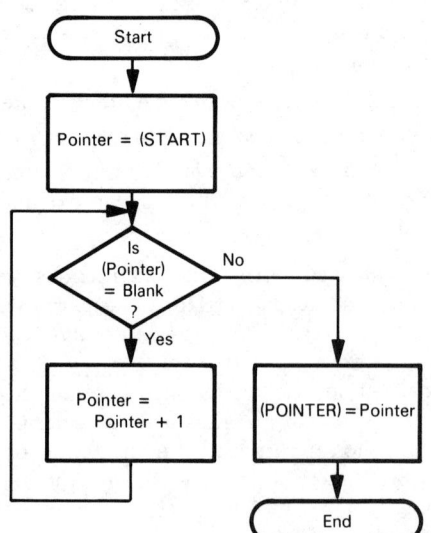

Program 6-2:

```
              00006000      DATA     EQU      $6000
              00004000      PROGRAM  EQU      $4000

              00006000               ORG      DATA
006000 00000004               START    DS.L     1           ADDRESS OF STRING
006004 00000004               POINTER  DS.L     1           ADDRESS OF FIRST NON-BLANK

              00000020      BLANK    EQU.B    ' '          ACSII VALUE FOR BLANK/SPACE

              00004000               ORG      PROGRAM

004000 20786000      PGM_6_2  MOVEA.L  START,A0    POINTER TO START OF STRING
004004 7220                   MOVEQ    #BLANK,D1   INITIALIZE WITH ASCII VALUE FOR ' '

004006 B218          LOOP     CMP.B    (A0)+,D1    IS CURRENT CHAR A BLANK?
```

```
004008  67FC            BEQ     LOOP            IF YES THEN CONTINUE SCAN
00400A  5388            SUBQ.L  #1,A0           ..ELSE ADJUST POINTER TO CURRENT CHAR
00400C  21C86004        MOVEA.L A0,POINTER      SAVE ADDRESS OF FIRST NON-BLANK

004010  4E75            RTS
                        END     PGM_6_2
```

Note the use of the apostrophes (') or single quotation marks before and after the ASCII character. You can place a single ASCII character in an MC68000 assembly language program by preceding it and following it with an apostrophe (') as in the EQU statements. The EQU is not a MC68000 instruction but rather an assembly language directive which assigns the expression in the operand field to the label in the label field. The .B suffix is required to put the ASCII code in the low-order byte; otherwise the assembler puts the ASCII value in the high-order byte of a 16-bit value and fills out the 16-bit value with zero bits.

You can place a string of ASCII characters in memory by using the DC (Define Constant) directive of the MC68000 assembler. Like the EQU directive, the string is placed within apostrophes in the DC's operand field. If an apostrophe is contained within the string, the apostrophe must be preceded by another apostrophe. Examples of some string definitions are:

```
                        DC      'ABCD'   Defines string ABCD
                        DC      'IT''S'  Defines string IT'S
```

Each ASCII character requires eight bits of storage, as compared to four bits for a BCD digit. Therefore, ASCII is a relatively inefficient format in which to store or transmit numerical data.

Looking for spaces in strings is a common task in microprocessor applications. Programs often reduce storage requirements by removing spaces that serve to increase readability or fit data in particular formats. Storing and transmitting extra space characters obviously can waste memory, communications capacity, and processor time. However, operators find it easier to enter data and programs when the computer accepts extra spaces; the entry is then said to be in free format rather than fixed format. One use for microcomputers is to convert data and commands between the forms that are easy for people to handle and the forms that are most efficient for computers and communication systems.

The autoincrement addressing mode used in the CMP (A0)+,D1 instruction provides us with a fast and simple way to step to the next character. However, once we have found the first non-blank character, we must remember that the pointer has already been incremented past the address we want to save. We must therefore explicitly subtract the increment of 1 with the instruction SUBQ #1,A0. This instruction would not be necessary if we were working backwards instead of forward, since the MC68000 autodecrements *before* using the address. However, as we noted earlier, if you use autodecrementing you must use a starting address that is one beyond the end of the string.

6-3. REPLACE LEADING ZEROS WITH BLANKS

Purpose: Edit a string of ASCII decimal characters by replacing all leading zeros with blanks. The starting address of the string is contained in the long-word variable START at location 6000. The first two bytes of the string represent the length of the string in bytes. The actual string of characters starts in the third byte.

104 68000 Assembly Language Programming

    a.   Input: START   —   (6000) = 00005000
                                       (5000) = 0002   Length of the string in bytes
                                       (5002) = 36   '6'
                                       (5003) = 39   '9'

The program leaves the string unchanged, since the leading digit is not zero.

    b.   Input: START   —   (6000) = 00005000
                                       (5000) = 0008
                                       (5002) = 30   '0'
                                       (5003) = 30   '0'
                                       (5004) = 38   '8'

                                       (5002) = 20   Space
                                       (5003) = 20   Space
                                       (5004) = 38   '8'

The program replaces the two leading zeros with ASCII spaces. The printed result would be ' 8...' instead of '008...'.

Flowchart 6-3:

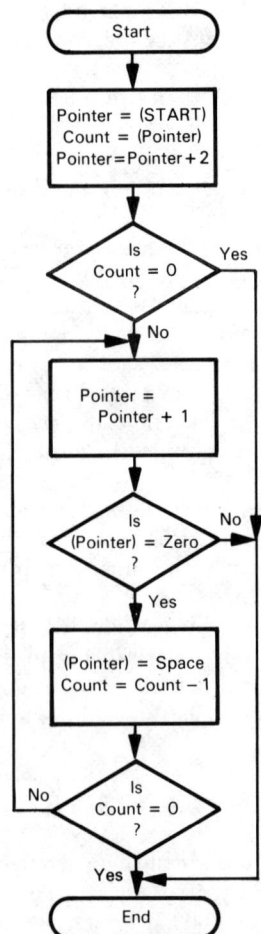

Program 6-3:

```
             00006000        DATA      EQU       $6000
             00004000        PROGRAM   EQU       $4000

             00006000                  ORG       DATA
006000       00000004        START     DS.L      1                ADDRESS OF STRING

             00000030        CHAR_0    EQU.B     '0'              ASCII VALUE FOR ZERO
             00000020        BLANK     EQU.B     ' '              ASCII VALUE FOR BLANK/SPACE

             00004000                  ORG       PROGRAM

004000  20786000             PGM_6_3   MOVEA.L   START,A0         POINTER TO START OF STRING
004004  7030                           MOVEQ     #CHAR_0,D0       INITIALIZE WITH ASCII ZERO
004006  7220                           MOVEQ     #BLANK,D1        INITIALIZE WITH ASCII BLANK
004008  3418                           MOVE.W    (A0)+,D2         STRING LENGTH TO D2
00400A  670E                           BEQ.S     DONE             IF LENGTH = 0 THEN DONE
00400C  5342                           SUBQ.W    #1,D2            ADJUST STRING COUNTER FOR DBRA

00400E  B018                 LOOP      CMP.B     (A0)+,D0         IS CURRENT CHAR A ZERO?
004010  6608                           BNE.S     DONE             IF NO THEN DONE

004012  1141FFFF                       MOVE.B    D1,-1(A0)        REPLACE ZERO BY BLANK IN CURR CHAR
004016  51CAFFF6                       DBRA      D2,LOOP          STOP SCAN IF ALL CHAR = '0'

        0000401A             DONE      EQU       *                DONE

00401A  4E75                           RTS
                                       END       PGM_6_3
```

The string storage format with the length of the string immediately preceding the actual string is quite frequently used in microprocessor applications. With this format the length is known; thus you don't have to scan for a carriage return and can easily move strings in memory.

Editing strings of decimal digits to improve their appearance is a common task in microprocessor programs. Typical procedures include the removal of leading zeros, justification, the addition of signs (+ or −), delimiters or symbols for units (such as $, %, or #), and rounding. **Programs should print numbers in the form that the user wants and expects;** results like "0006", "$27.34382", or "135000000" are annoying and difficult to interpret.

This loop has two exits — one if the processor finds a non-zero digit and the other if it scans the entire string. In an actual application, you would have to be careful to leave one zero if all the digits in the string are zero. How would you modify the program to do this?

We have assumed that all the digits in the string are in ASCII; that is, the digits used are 30_{16} through 39_{16} rather than the binary representation of the numbers 0 to 9. Converting a digit from BCD to ASCII is simply a matter of adding 30_{16} (ASCII zero), while converting from ASCII to decimal involves subtracting the same number.

The instruction MOVE.B D1,−1(A0) places an ASCII space (20_{16}) in a memory location that previously contained an ASCII zero. Address register indirect addressing with a displacement of −1 is used to make up for the +1 that was added to register A0 by the CMP.B (A0)+,D0 instruction.

The DBRA instruction ensures that the program does not continue beyond the end of the string. DBRA is a form of the DBcc instruction for which the conditional test is never true. DBRA, or its equivalent form DBF, is functionally equal to the instruction sequence:

```
                    SUBI.W  #1,D2
                    BNE     LOOP
```

106   68000 Assembly Language Programming

The DBRA instruction thus always causes a branch back to LOOP unless the entire string has been processed (D2 = −1).

6-4. ADD EVEN PARITY TO ASCII CHARACTERS

Purpose: Add even parity to a string of 7-bit ASCII characters. The starting address of the string is contained in the long word START at location 6000. The first word of the string represents the string length in bytes. The actual string of characters starts in the third byte. The parity bit is the most significant bit of a byte; for even parity the bit is set to 1 if that makes the total number of 1 bits in the byte an even number; otherwise it is set to 0. In either case the final number of 1 bits is even.

Sample Problem:

```
Input:   START    — (6000) = 00005000
                    (5000) = 0006      string length
                    (5002) = 31        0011 0001
                    (5003) = 32        0011 0010
                    (5004) = 33        0011 0011
                    (5005) = 34        0011 0100
                    (5006) = 35        0011 0101
                    (5007) = 36        0011 0110
Output:             (5002) = B1        1011 0001
                    (5003) = B2        1011 0010
                    (5004) = 33        0011 0011
                    (5005) = B4        1011 0100
                    (5006) = 35        0011 0101
                    (5007) = 36        0011 0110
```

Program 6-4:

```
               00006000    DATA      EQU       $6000
               00004000    PROGRAM   EQU       $4000

               00006000              ORG       DATA
006000 00000004 START     DS.L      1                     ADDRESS OF STRING

               00004000              ORG       PROGRAM

004000 20786000 PGM_6_4   MOVEA.L   START,A0              POINTER TO START OF STRING
004004 3418               MOVE.W    (A0)+,D2              STRING LENGTH TO D2
004006 6720               BEQ.S     DONE                  IF LENGTH = 0 THEN DONE
004008 5342               SUBQ.W    #1,D2                 ADJUST STRING COUNTER FOR DBRA
00400A 7600               MOVEQ     #0,D3                 CONSTANT ZERO FOR ADDX INSTRUCTION

               0000400C    MAIN_LOOP EQU       *
00400C 1218               MOVE.B    (A0)+,D1              GET CURRENT CHARACTER
00400E 7000               MOVEQ     #0,D0                 CLEAR BIT COUNTER

               00004010    PARITY_LOOP EQU     *
004010 E309               LSL.B     #1,D1                 SHIFT MSB OF CHAR INTO C & X-BITS
004012 D103               ADDX.B    D3,D0                 ADD X-BIT TO BIT COUNT
004014 4A01               TST.B     D1                    TEST IF ALL BITS = 1 COUNTED
004016 66F8               BNE       PARITY_LOOP           IF NO THEN CONTINUE COUNTING

004018 08000000           BTST.B    #0,D0                 ...ELSE CHECK FOR ODD PARITY
00401C 6706               BEQ.S     NEXT_CHAR             IF EVEN THEN PROCESS NEXT CHAR

00401E 08E80007FFFF       BSET.B    #7,-1(A0)             ...ELSE SET PARITY BIT

               00004024    NEXT_CHAR EQU       *
004024 51CAFFE6           DBRA      D2,MAIN_LOOP          CONTINUE IF CHAR LEFT IN STRING

               00004028    DONE      EQU       *
004028 4E75               RTS                             STRING NOW HAS EVEN PARITY
                          END       PGM_6_4
```

Character-Coded Data 107

Flowchart 6-4:

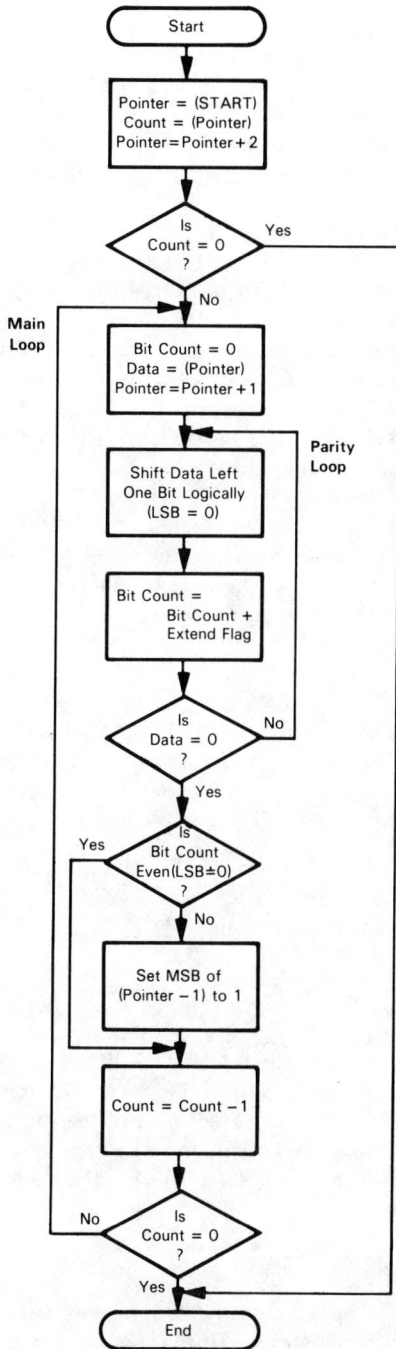

Parity provides a simple means of checking for errors on noisy communications lines. If the transmitter sends parity along with the actual data, the receiver can then check for correct parity of the data that it receives. If the parity is not correct, the receiver can request retransmission of the data. If there is a single bit in error, the parity will be incorrect, since the number of 1 bits in the data will clearly change from even to odd or odd to even. However, two bit errors will just as obviously result in the same parity as the original data. Thus we say that **parity detects single but not double bit errors.** Of course, single bit errors are usually more common than are double bit errors, so the test is still useful.

A more serious problem with **parity** is that it **provides no way to correct errors.** An error in any bit position will produce the same change in parity, so the receiver cannot determine which bit is wrong. **More advanced coding techniques provide for error correction as well as error detection.** Parity, however, is easy to calculate and adequate in situations in which retransmission of data is tolerable.

The procedure for calculating parity is to count the number of 1 bits in each byte of data. If that number is odd and even parity is desired, the program sets the most significant bit (MSB) of the data byte to 1 to make the parity even. One of the advantages of the 7-bit ASCII code is that it leaves the most significant bit available for parity; the 8-bit EBCDIC code does not.

The LSL instruction clears the least significant bit of the data register or memory location that it is shifting. Therefore, **a series of LSL instructions will eventually result in a zero value, regardless of the original data.** (Try it!) The bit counting procedure in the example program does not use a counter for termination since it stops as soon as all the remaining data bits are zero. This procedure is simple and reduces execution time in most cases.

Note that Program 6-4 assumes that the most significant bit (the parity bit) of each 8-bit data byte being processed is set to 0 at the outset; if this bit were initially set to 1, then Program 6-4 would generate odd parity instead of even.

In addition to clearing the least significant bit of the data byte, the LSL instruction affects the Carry (C) and Extend (X) flags as follows:

C=X=1 if MSB of data = 1 prior to shift
C=X=0 if MSB of data = 0 prior to shift

The state of the Extend flag is used in the ADDX.B D3,D0 instruction which has the same affect as:

D0=D0+D3+X=D0+0+X=D0+X

Thus the number of 1 bits in the byte is counted in register D0.

Like the other Add instructions, ADDX affects the status flags, so the TST instruction is used to determine if the LSL instruction cleared the data register. TST.B D1 compares the contents of the low-order byte of register D1 with zero and sets the status flags accordingly without modifying the data register contents. The TST instruction is thus an optimized form of the Compare Immediate instruction CMPI #0, D1.

Bit Manipulation Instructions

The MC68000 allows operations on individual bits within a *single byte or long word*. The Bit Clear (BCLR) instruction is used to clear a single bit. Bit Change (BCHG) is used to change the state of a specified bit. The Bit Set (BSET) instruction is used to set a specific bit to 1. Finally, you may use the Bit Test (BTST) instruction to test the state of a single bit without altering its state. All of these bit operation instructions perform an implicit Bit Test (BTST) instruction prior to operating on the specified bit.

6-5. PATTERN MATCH

Purpose: Compare two strings of ASCII characters to see if they are the same. The starting addresses of the strings are contained in the long word variables START1 at location 6000 and START2 at location 6004. The first byte of each string contains the string length (in bytes) and is followed by the string. If the two strings match, clear the variable MATCH at location 6008; otherwise set its value to -1 (all ones = $FFFF_{16}$).

Sample Problems:

a. Input: START1 — (6000) = 00005000
   START2 — (6004) = 00005400
   (5000) = 03
   (5001) = 43 'C'
   (5002) = 41 'A'
   (5003) = 54 'T'
   (5400) = 03
   (5401) = 43 'C'
   (5402) = 41 'A'
   (5403) = 54 'T'
   Output: MATCH — (6008) = 0000   0, since the strings match

b. Input: START1 — (6000) = 00005000
   START2 — (6008) = 00005400
   (5000) = 03
   (5001) = 43 'C'
   (5002) = 41 'A'
   (5003) = 54 'T'
   (5400) = 03
   (5401) = 52 'R'
   (5402) = 41 'A'
   (5403) = 54 'T'
   Output: MATCH — (6008) = FFFF -1, since the first characters differ

c. Input: START1 — (6000) = 00005000
   START2 — (6004) = 00005400
   (5000) = 03
   (5400) = 04
   Output: MATCH — (6008) = FFFF -1, since the strings are not the same length

Note: the matching process ends as soon as we find a difference. The rest of the string is not examined.

Flowchart 6-5a:

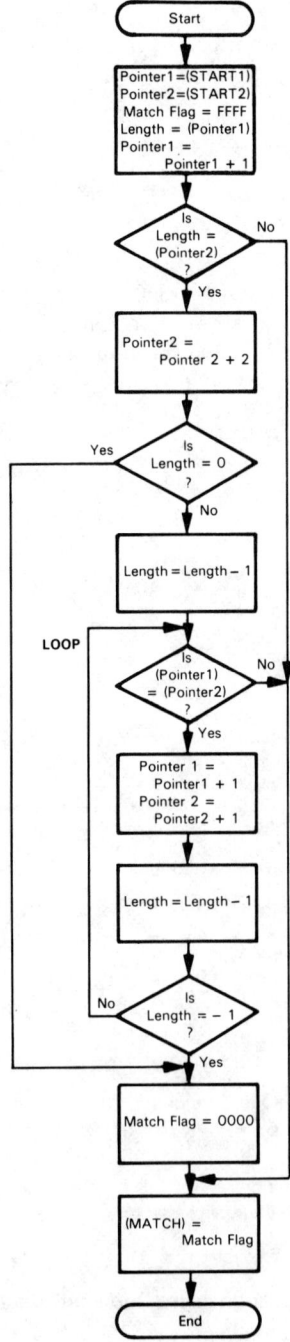

Program 6-5a:

```
              00006000    DATA     EQU    $6000
              00004000    PROGRAM  EQU    $4000

              00006000             ORG    DATA
006000 00000004    START1  DS.L   1       ADDRESS OF FIRST STRING
006004 00000004    START2  DS.L   1       ADDRESS OF SECOND STRING
006008 00000002    MATCH   DS.W   1       MATCH FLAG

              00004000             ORG    PROGRAM

004000 20786000    PGM_6_5A MOVEA.L START1,A0   POINTER TO FIRST STRING
004004 22786004             MOVEA.L START2,A1   POINTER TO SECOND STRING
004008 72FF                 MOVEQ   #-1,D1      ASSUME NO MATCH
00400A 7000                 MOVEQ   #0,D0       LENGTH COUNTER := 0
00400C 1018                 MOVE.B  (A0)+,D0    INITIALIZE LENGTH COUNTER
00400E B019                 CMP.B   (A1)+,D0    STRING LENGTHS EQUAL?
004010 6610                 BNE.S   DONE        IF NOT = THEN NO MATCH

004012 4A00                 TST.B   D0          STRING LENGTHS = 0?
004014 670A                 BEQ.S   SAME        IF = 0 THEN STRINGS MATCH

004016 5340                 SUBQ.W  #1,D0       ADJUST COUNTER FOR DBNE

004018 B308       LOOP      CMPM.B  (A0)+,(A1)+ COMPARE CURRENT STRING ELEMENTS
00401A 56C8FFFC             DBNE    D0,LOOP     IF MATCH AND NOT END OF STRING-CONT

00401E 6602                 BNE.S   DONE        IF NO MATCH AND END THEN DONE

004020 4641       SAME      NOT.W   D1          STRING MATCH

004022 31C16008   DONE      MOVE.W  D1,MATCH    SAVE MATCH STATE

004026 4E75                 RTS

                            END     PGM_6_5A
```

Matching strings of ASCII characters is an essential part of recognizing names or commands, identifying variables or operation codes in assemblers and compilers, accessing named files, and many other tasks.

The MOVEQ #−1,D1 instruction has the effect of assuming there will be no match. If a match is found, the match flag is cleared by using the NOT.W D1 instruction which complements the state of each bit in the destination operand; thus a zero bit becomes 1 and a one bit becomes 0. Had we not initialized the match flag in this way, the end of the program would have been more complicated:

```
                BNE     DONE
     SAME:      MOVE    #-1, MATCH
                BRA     DONE
     FINI:      MOVE    #0, MATCH
     DONE:      RTS
```

Assuming a result is true until proven false, or false until proven true, is a common technique that simplifies many programs.

The Compare Memory instruction CMPM allows data in memory to be compared directly without first moving one of the data elements into a data register. The CMPM instruction is extremely useful and efficient in performing string comparisons. Note that only the postincrementing address mode can be used with this instruction to specify the operands. Of course, this is exactly the mode that is most useful for comparing strings since the addresses are automatically incremented to point to the next elements to be compared.

When control is passed to the instruction following the DBNE instruction, we know that either a match did not occur on a given pair of string elements, or that the two strings are identical. The BNE instruction is used to determine which condition caused

112 68000 Assembly Language Programming

the exit from DBNE. The correct execution of the BNE instruction depends on the fact that the DBNE instruction does not affect the status flags.

Why must the instruction MOVEQ #0,D0 be used prior to loading the lower byte of D0 with the string length?

This program is much more complicated than it need be. We can treat the length bytes of the strings as if they were part of the string. If the lengths are unequal, the strings are unequal.

Flowchart 6-5b:

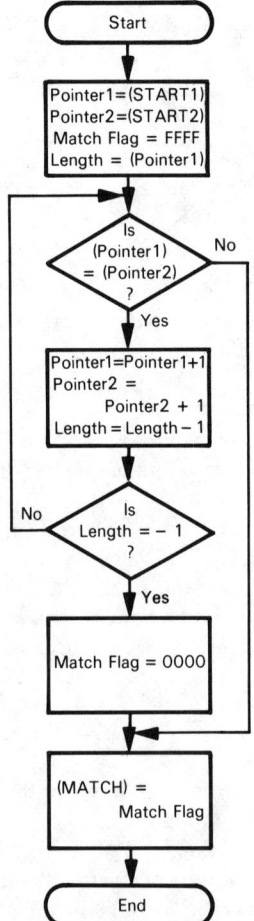

Program 6-5b:

```
                00006000    DATA     EQU    $6000
                00004000    PROGRAM  EQU    $4000


                00006000             ORG    DATA
006000 00000004             START1   DS.L   1           ADDRESS OF FIRST STRING
006004 00000004             START2   DS.L   1           ADDRESS OF SECOND STRING
```

```
006008  00000002          MATCH    DS.W     1                    MATCH FLAG
        00004000                   ORG      PROGRAM
004000  20786000  PGM_6_5B         MOVEA.L  START1,A0            POINTER TO FIRST STRING
004004  22786004                   MOVEA.L  START2,A1            POINTER TO SECOND STRING
004008  72FF                       MOVEQ    #-1,D1               ASSUME NO MATCH
00400A  7000                       MOVEQ    #0,D0                LENGTH COUNTER := 0
00400C  1010                       MOVE.B   (A0),D0              INITIALIZE LENGTH COUNTER
00400E  B308      LOOP             CMPM.B   (A0)+,(A1)+          COMPARE CURRENT STRING ELEMENTS
004010  56C8FFFC                   DBNE     D0,LOOP              IF MATCH AND NOT END OF STRING-CONT
004014  6602                       BNE.S    DONE                 IF NO MATCH AND END THEN DONE
004016  4641      SAME             NOT.W    D1                   STRING MATCH
004018  31C16008  DONE             MOVE.W   D1,MATCH             SAVE MATCH STATE
00401C  4E75                       RTS
                                   END      PGM_6_5B
```

If the string lengths are unequal, the program will terminate after the first iteration. Why can we use the string length as a loop counter without first decrementing it by 1?

PROBLEMS

6-1. LENGTH OF A TELETYPEWRITER MESSAGE

Purpose: Determine the length of an ASCII message. All characters are 7-bit ASCII with MSB=0. The string of characters in which the message is embedded has a starting address which is contained in the variable START at location 6000. The message itself starts with an ASCII STX character (02_{16}) and ends with ETX (03_{16}). Save the length of the message (the number of characters between the STX and the ETX but including neither) in the variable LENGTH at location 6004.

Sample Problem:

```
Input:   START    — (6000) = 00005000
                    (5000) = 02  STX
                    (5001) = 47  'G'
                    (5002) = 4F  'O'
                    (5003) = 03  ETX
Output:  LENGTH   — (6004) = 02, since there are two
                             characters between the STX in
                             location 5000 and ETX in
                             location 5003.
```

6-2. FIND LAST NON-BLANK CHARACTER

Purpose: Search a string of ASCII characters for the last non-blank character. Starting address of the string is contained in the variable START at location 6000 and the string ends with a carriage return character ($0D_{16}$). Place the address of the last non-blank character in the variable ADDRESS at location 6004.

Sample Problems:

a. Input: START   —   (6000) = 00005000
                          (5000) = 37   '7'
                          (5001) = 0D   CR
   Output: ADDRESS —   (6004) = 5000

Since the last (and only) non-blank character is in memory location 5000.

b. Input: START   —   (6000) = 5000
                          (5000) = 41   'A'
                          (5001) = 20   SP
                          (5002) = 48   'H'
                          (5003) = 41   'A'
                          (5004) = 54   'T'
                          (5005) = 20   SP
                          (5006) = 20   SP
                          (5007) = 0D   CR
   Output: ADDRESS —   (6004) = 5004

6-3. TRUNCATE DECIMAL STRING TO INTEGER FORM

Purpose: Edit a string of ASCII decimal characters by replacing all digits to the right of the decimal point with ASCII blanks (20_{16}). The starting address of the string is contained in the variable START at location 6000 and the string is assumed to consist entirely of ASCII-coded decimal digits and a possible decimal point ($2E_{16}$). The length of the string is stored in the variable LENGTH at location 6004. If no decimal point appears in the string, assume that the decimal point is at the far right.

Sample Problems:

a. Input: START   —   (6000) = 00005000
            LENGTH   —   (6004) = 0004   Length of string
                          (5000) = 37   '7'
                          (5001) = 2E   '.'
                          (5002) = 38   '8'
                          (5003) = 31   '1'
   Output: (5000) = 37   '7'
                          (5001) = 2E   '.'
                          (5002) = 20   SP
                          (5003) = 20   SP

b. Input: START   —   (6000) = 00005000
            LENGTH   —   (6004) = 0003   Length of string
                          (5000) = 36   '6'
                          (5001) = 37   '7'
                          (5002) = 31   '1'

   Output: Unchanged, as number is assumed to be 671.

6-4. CHECK EVEN PARITY AND ASCII CHARACTERS

Purpose: Check for even parity in a string of ASCII characters. A string's starting address is contained in the variable START at location 6000. The first byte of the string is its length which is followed by the string itself. If the parity of all the characters in the string is correct, clear the variable PARITY at location 6004; otherwise, place all ones ($FFFF_{16}$) into PARITY.

Sample Problems:

a. Input: START — (6000) = 00005000
(5000) = 03   Length of string
(5001) = B1 = 1011   0001
(5002) = B2 = 1011   0010
(5003) = 33 = 0011   0011
Output: PARITY — (6004) = 0000, since all the characters have even parity.

b. Input: START — (6000) = 5000
(5000) = 03   Length of string
(5001) = B1 1011   0001
(5002) = B6 1011   0110
(5003) = 33 0011   0011
Output: PARITY — (6004) = FFFF, since the character in memory location 5002 does not have even parity.

6-5. STRING COMPARISON

Purpose: Compare two strings of ASCII characters to see which is larger (that is, which follows the other in alphabetical ordering). Both strings have the same length as defined by the variable LENGTH at location 6000. The strings' starting addresses are defined by the variables START1 at location 6002 and START at location 6006. If the string defined by START1 is greater than or equal to the other string, clear the variable GREATER at location 600A; otherwise, set GREATER to all ones ($FFFF_{16}$).

Sample Problems:

a. Input: LENGTH — (6000) = 0003   Length at each string
START1 — (6002) = 00005000
START — (6006) = 00005400

(5000) = 43   'C'
(5001) = 41   'A'
(5002) = 54   'T'

(5400) = 42   'B'
(5401) = 41   'A'
(5402) = 54   'T'

Output: GREATER — (600A) = 0000, since CAT is "larger" than BAT.

b. Input: LENGTH — (6000) = 0003   Length at each string
START1 — (6002) = 00005000
START — (6006) = 00005400

(5000) = 43   'C'
(5001) = 41   'A'
(5002) = 54   'T'

(5400) = 43   'C'
(5401) = 41   'A'
(5402) = 54   'T'

Output: GREATER — (600A) = 0000, since CAT is not "larger" than CAT.

c. Input: LENGTH — (6000) = 0003   Length of each string
         START1 — (6002) = 00005000
         START — (6006) = 00005400
                  (5000) = 43 'C'
                  (5001) = 41 'A'
                  (5002) = 54 'T'
                  (5400) = 43 'C'
                  (5401) = 55 'U'
                  (5402) = 54 'T'
   Output: GREATER — (600A) = FFFF, since CUT is 'larger' than CAT

7
Code Conversion

Code conversion is a continual problem in microcomputer applications. Peripherals provide data in ASCII, BCD, or various special codes. The microcomputer must convert the data into some standard form for processing. Output devices may require data in ASCII, BCD, seven-segment, or other codes. Therefore, the microcomputer must convert the results to the proper form after it completes the processing.

There are several ways to approach code conversion:

1. **Some conversions can easily be handled by algorithms involving arithmetic or logical functions.** The program may, however, have to handle special cases separately.
2. **More complex conversions can be handled with lookup tables.** The lookup table method requires little programming and is easy to apply. However, the table may occupy a large amount of memory if the range of input values is large.
3. **Hardware is readily available for some conversion tasks.** Typical examples are decoders for BCD to seven-segment conversion and Universal Asynchronous Receiver/Transmitters (UARTs) for conversion between parallel (ASCII) and serial (teletypewriter) formats.

In most applications, the program should do as much as possible of the code conversion work. This approach reduces parts counts and power dissipation, saves board space, and increases reliability. Furthermore, most code conversions are easy to program and require little execution time.

PROGRAM EXAMPLES

7-1. HEXADECIMAL TO ASCII

Purpose: Convert the contents of the variable DIGIT at location 6000 to an ASCII character representing the hexadecimal value of the variable. DIGIT contains a single hexadecimal digit (the four most significant bits are zero). Store the ASCII character in the variable CHAR at location 6001.

Sample Problems:

   a. Input: DIGIT - (6000) = 0C
      Output: CHAR - (6001) = 43 'C'
   b. Input: DIGIT - (6000) = 06
      Output: CHAR - (6001) = 36 '6'

Flowchart 7-1:

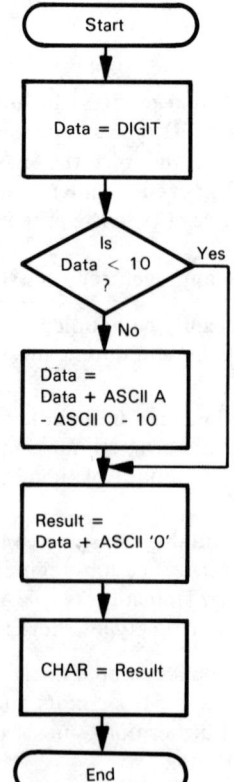

Code Conversion 119

Program 7-1:

```
          00006000      DATA      EQU       $6000
          00004000      PROGRAM   EQU       $4000

          00006000      DIGIT     EQU       $6000          ADDRESS OF DIGIT
          00006001      CHAR      EQU       $6001          ADDRESS OF CHAR

          00004000                ORG       PROGRAM
004000 10386000         PGM_7_1   MOVE.B    DIGIT,D0       GET HEX-DIGIT
004004 0C00000A                   CMP.B     #10,D0         IS DIGIT < 10?
004008 6D02                       BLT.S     ADD_0          IF YES THEN ADD '0' ONLY

00400A 5E00                       ADD.B     #'A'-'0'-10,D0 ...ELSE ADD OFFSET FOR 'A'-'F' ALSO

00400C 06000030        ADD_0     ADD.B     #'0',D0        CONVERT TO ASCII
004010 11C06001                   MOVE.B    D0,CHAR        STORE ASCII DIGIT

004014 4E75                       RTS
                                  END       PGM_7_1
```

The basic idea of this program is to add ASCII 0 (30_{16}) to all the hexadecimal digits. This addition converts the digits 0 through 9 to ASCII correctly. However, the letters A through F do not follow immediately after the digit 9 in the ASCII code; instead, there is a break between the ASCII code for 9 (39_{16}) and the ASCII code for A (41_{16}), so that **the conversion must add a further constant to the values greater than 9** (A, B, C, D, E, and F) to account for the break. The first ADD instruction does this by adding 'A' − '0' − 10 to data register D0. Can you explain why the extra factor for letter digits has the value 'A' − '0' − 10? Note that this value is small enough to fit into the 3-bit data field of an ADDQ instruction. The assembler discovers this and automatically generates the ADDQ object code (even though the instruction mnemonic does not indicate this). How can you force the assembler to create the object code for ADDI?

We have used the ASCII forms for the addition factors in the source program; a single quotation mark (apostrophe) before and after a character indicates the ASCII equivalent. We have also left the offset for the letters as an arithmetic expression to make its meaning as clear as possible. The extra assembly time is a small price to pay for the great increase in clarity. A routine like this is necessary in many applications; for example, monitor programs must convert hexadecimal digits to their ASCII equivalents in order to display the contents of memory locations in hexadecimal on an ASCII printer or CRT display.

7-2. DECIMAL TO SEVEN-SEGMENT

Purpose: Convert the contents of the variable DIGIT at location 6000 to a seven-segment code and store in the variable CODE at location 6001. If DIGIT does not contain a single decimal digit, clear CODE.

Figure 7-1 illustrates the seven-segment display and our representation of it as a binary code. The segments are usually assigned the letters a through g as shown in Figure 7-1. We have organized the seven-segment code as shown: segment g is in bit position 6, segment f in bit position 5, and so on. Bit position 7 is always zero. The segment names are standard, but the assignment of segments to bit positions is arbitrary; in actual applications, this assignment is a hardware function.

The table in Figure 7-1 is a typical example of those used to convert decimal numbers to seven-segment code; it assumes positive logic, that is, 1 = on and 0 = off. Note that the table uses 7D for 6 rather than the alternative 7C (top bar off) to avoid confusion with lower-case b, and 6F for 9 rather than 67 (bottom bar off) for symmetry with the 6.

Sample Problems:

    a. Input: DIGIT - (6000) = 03
        Output: CODE - (6001) = 4F
    b. Input: DIGIT - (6000) = 28
        Output: CODE - (6001) = 00
    c. Input: DIGIT - (6000) = 0A
        Output: :CODE - (6001) = 00

Flowchart 7-2:

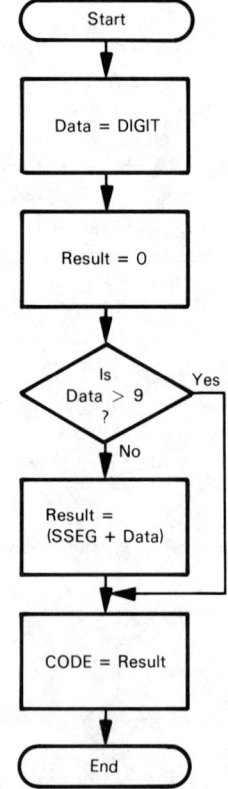

Note that the addition of base address (SSEG) and index (Data) produces the address that contains the answer.

Code Conversion   121

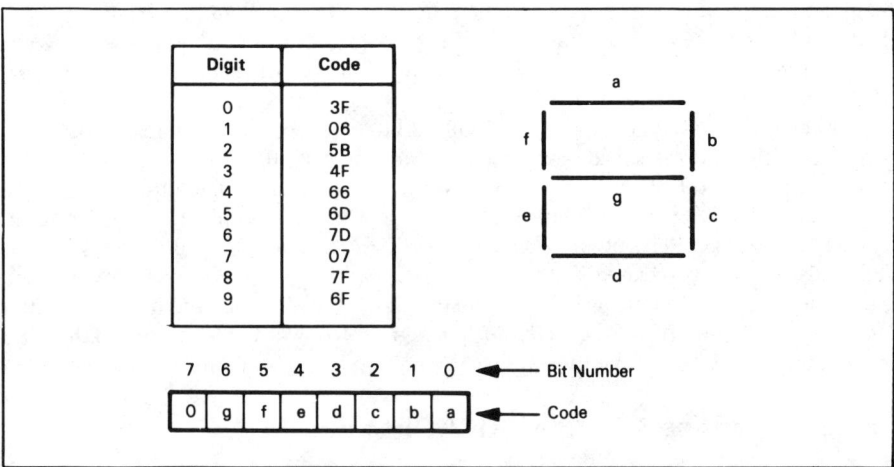

Figure 7-1. Seven-Segment Arrangement

Program 7-2:

```
           00006000         DATA     EQU     $6000
           00004000         PROGRAM  EQU     $4000

           00006000                  ORG     DATA
006000 00000001             DIGIT    DS.B    1                         DIGIT
006001 00000001             CODE     DS.B    1                         BCD CODE
006002 3F                   SSEG     DC.B    $3F,$06,$5B,$4F,$66,$6D,$7D,$07,$7F,$6F CONVERSION TABLE

           00004000                  ORG     PROGRAM
004000 207C00006002 PGM_7_2          MOVEA.L #SSEG,A0                  POINTER TO CONVERSION TABLE
004006 4201                          CLR.B   D1
004008 10386000                      MOVE.B  DIGIT,D0                  GET DIGIT
00400C 0C000009                      CMP.B   #9,D0                     VALID DIGIT?
004010 6206                          BHI.S   DONE                      IF NOT VALID THEN CLEAR RESULT

004012 4880                          EXT.W   D0                        MAKE INDEX BYTE LOOK LIKE A WORD
004014 12300000                      MOVE.B  0(A0,D0),D1               GET SEVEN-SEGMENT CODE FROM TABLE

004018 11C16001    DONE              MOVE.B  D1,CODE                   SAVE BCD CODE

00401C 4E75                          RTS

                                     END     PGM_7_2
```

The Clear instruction (CLR), like the MOVEQ + instruction, can be used to clear all 32 bits of a data register and requires only one instruction word. However, CLR, unlike MOVEQ +, can also be used to clear just the lower byte or word of a data register. (In this program, we use CLR.B D1 to clear the least significant 8 bits of D1). In addition, we can clear a memory location directly with CLR. Why does the MC68000 have several means of clearing memory or registers?

The program calculates the memory address of the seven-segment code by adding an index — the digit to be converted — to the base address of the seven-segment code table. This procedure is known as a "table lookup." The addition does not require any explicit instructions, since the processor performs it automatically as part of the calculation of the effective address in the indexed addressing mode. Since all 32 bits of the address register are used in this indexing addition, we can place the table anywhere in memory.

When indexed addressing is used, all 32 bits of the primary address register are involved in the address calculation, but only the least significant word of the specified index register (or offset register) is used. In the program, the offset into the table is a byte value and loading this byte offset into a data register affects only the least significant 8 bits of the register. The other 24 bits of the register are not affected. Bits 8-15 of the data register must be cleared in order for the register to be used as an index register. This is accomplished by using the EXT instruction which extends the most significant bit (MSB) of the byte or word data in the data register to a word or long word. If the MSB is 0, all bits to the left of the data are cleared; if the bit is 1, all bits are set to one.

Using the Define Constant (DC) Directive

The assembler directive DC (Define Constant) places constant byte-length data in program memory. Such data may include tables, headings, error messages, prompting messages, format characters, threshold values, and mathematical constants. The optional label attached to a DC pseudo-operation is assigned the value of the address in which the assembler places the first byte of data.

The assembler assigns the data from the DC directive to consecutive memory addresses, with no changes other than numerical conversions. One DC directive can fill many bytes of memory; all the programmer must do is separate the entries with commas.

Tables are a simple, fast, and convenient approach to code conversion problems that are more complex than our hexadecimal-to-ASCII example. The required lookup tables simply contain all the possible results organized by input value; that is, the first entry is the code for input value zero and so on.

Seven-segment displays provide recognizable forms of the decimal digits and a few letters and other characters. They are relatively inexpensive and easy to handle with microprocessors. However, many people find seven-segment coded digits somewhat difficult to read. Their widespread use in calculators and watches has made them more familiar.

7-3. ASCII TO DECIMAL

Purpose: Convert the contents of the variable CHAR at location 6000 from an ASCII character to a decimal digit and store the result in the variable DIGIT at location 6001. If the contents of CHAR are not the ASCII representation of a decimal digit, set the contents of DIGIT to FF_{16}.

Sample Problems:

    a. Input: CHAR - (6000) = 37 '7'
          Output: DIGIT - (6001) = 07

    b. Input: CHAR - (6000) = 55   'U' (an invalid code, since it is not an ASCII decimal digit)

          Output: DIGIT - (6001) = FF

Code Conversion

Flowchart 7-3:

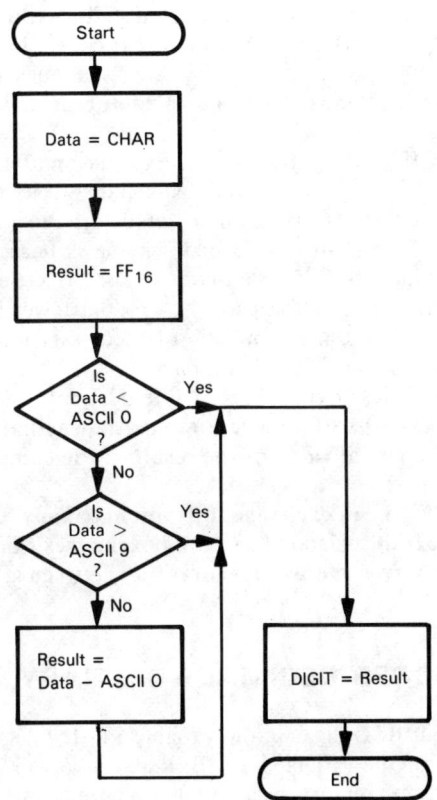

Program 7-3:

```
          00006000    DATA     EQU    $6000
          00004000    PROGRAM  EQU    $4000

          00006001    DIGIT    EQU    $6001            ADDRESS OF DIGIT
          00006000    CHAR     EQU    $6000            ADDRESS OF CHAR

          00004000             ORG    PROGRAM

004000 72FF          PGM_7_3  MOVEQ  #-1,D1           SET ERROR FLAG
004002 10386000               MOVE.B CHAR,D0          GET CHARACTER
004006 04000030               SUB.B  #'0',D0          IS CHARACTER BELOW ASCII ZERO?
00400A 6508                   BCS.S  DONE             IF YES THEN NOT A DIGIT

00400C 0C000009               CMP.B  #9,D0            IS CHARACTER ABOVE ASCII NINE?
004010 6202                   BHI.S  DONE             IF YES THEN NOT A DIGIT

004012 C141                   EXG    D0,D1            GET NUMBER VALUE OF CHARACTER

004014 11C16001      DONE     MOVE.B D1,DIGIT         SAVE DIGIT OR ERROR FLAG

004018 4E75                   RTS

                              END    PGM_7_3
```

This program handles ASCII-coded characters just like ordinary numbers. Since ASCII assigns an ordered sequence of codes to the decimal digits, **we can identify an ASCII character as a digit by determining if it falls within the proper range of numerical values.** We could use the order of ASCII codes similarly to determine if a character is in a particular group of letters or symbols, such as A through F. **This approach assumes detailed knowledge of a particular code and would not necessarily be valid for other codes.**

Subtracting ASCII 0 (30_{16}) from any ASCII decimal digit gives the decimal value of that digit. An ASCII character is a decimal digit if its value lies between 30_{16} and 39_{16} (including the endpoints). How would you determine if an ASCII character is a valid hexadecimal digit? ASCII-to-decimal conversion is necessary in applications in which decimal data is entered from an ASCII device such as a teletypewriter or terminal.

The program performs one comparison — to the lower limit — with an actual subtraction (SUB '0',D0) since the subtraction is necessary for the ASCII-to-decimal conversion. It performs the other comparison with an implied subtraction (CMP.B#9,D0) to avoid destroying the possible decimal digit in data register D0. **Implied subtractions (CMP) are far more common than actual subtractions (SUB) in programs, since the numerical value of the result of the comparison is often not of interest.**

The instruction EXG can exchange the contents of any 32-bit register with the contents of any other 32-bit register. Long word exchanges can be made between any two data registers, any two address registers, or between a data register and an address register.

7-4. BINARY-CODED DECIMAL TO BINARY

Purpose: Convert four BCD digits in the variable STRING at location 6000 to a binary number in the variable NUMBER at location 6004. The most significant BCD digit is in memory location 6000. There is one BCD digit in each byte of STRING.

Sample Problems:

```
        a.  Input:   STRING -  (6000) = 02
                               (6001) = 09
                               (6002) = 07
                               (6003) = 01
            Output:  NUMBER -  (6004) = 0B9B₁₆ = 2971₁₀
        b.  Input:   STRING -  (6000) = 09
                               (6001) = 07
                               (6002) = 00
                               (6003) = 02
            Output:  NUMBER -  (6004) = 25E6₁₆ = 9702₁₀
```

Program 7-4a:

```
00006000        DATA      EQU    $6000
00004000        PROGRAM   EQU    $4000

00006000        STRING    EQU    $6000           ADDRESS OF FOUR DIGIT BCD STRING
00006004        RESULT    EQU    $6004           ADDRESS OF RESULT

00004000                  ORG    PROGRAM
```

```
004000 307C6000    PGM_7_4A  MOVEA.W  #STRING,A0   POINTER TO FIRST BCD DIGIT
004004 7003                  MOVEQ    #4-1,D0      NUMBER OF DIGITS(-1) TO PROCESS
004006 4281                  CLR.L    D1           CLEAR FINAL RESULT - D1
004008 4282                  CLR.L    D2           CLEAR DIGIT REGISTER
00400A 6008                  BRA.S    NOMULT       SKIP MULTIPLY FIRST TIME

00400C D241        LOOP      ADD.W    D1,D1        2X
00400E 3601                  MOVE.W   D1,D3
004010 E54B                  LSL.W    #2,D3        8X = 2X * 4
004012 D243                  ADD.W    D3,D1        10X = 8X + 2X

004014 1418        NOMULT    MOVE.B   (A0)+,D2     NEXT BCD DIGIT,(D2[15-8] UNCHANGED)
004016 D242                  ADD.W    D2,D1        ADD NEXT DIGIT
004018 51C8FFF2              DBRA     D0,LOOP      CONTINUE PROCESSING IF STILL DIGITS

00401C 31C16004              MOVE.W   D1,RESULT    STORE RESULT

004020 4E75                  RTS

                             END      PGM_7_4A
```

Flowchart 7-4a:

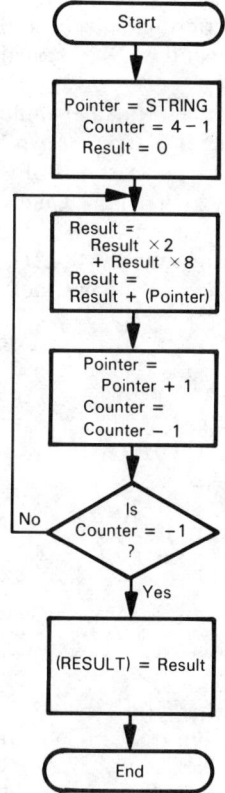

Program 7-4a multiplies each intermediate result by 10 using the formula $10x = 8x + 2x$. Multiplying by 2 requires one logical shift left (LSL), and multiplying by 8 requires three such shifts.

BCD entries are converted to binary in order to take advantage of the inherent binary operators provided by the processor. In addition, a binary representation requires less storage than the equivalent BCD form. However, in some cases, the program time and space required for conversion may affect some of the advantages of binary storage and arithmetic.

Program 7-4a uses a word length ADD to add the BCD digit to the accumulated result in register D1. Had we used ADD.B D2,D1, the program would not have worked for all values. Consider the value 0257. Before adding the lowest digit, D1 would contain 0250_{10} or $00FA_{16}$. Adding 7 to the low byte of D1 yields FA + 07 = 01, and the high byte is still 0. Since we cannot directly add a byte value to a word value, we chose to load the value into a data register prior to the addition. Why don't we have to perform an extend operation prior to the addition?

This program skips the first multiply, since we know the initial value of D2 is 0. However, if we eliminated the branch instructions, we'd still get the same result.

There are often several ways to perform a function using assembly language instructions. In this program, we used the ADD instruction to shift a value left one place since this is the fastest means of performing this operation in the MC68000. Two ADD instructions would also be faster than the LSL instruction but would require two additional bytes of storage.

We could also use one of the MC68000 multiply instructions. The multiply instructions perform a multiplication operation on two 16-bit operands to produce a 32-bit result in one of the data registers. At least one of the 16-bit operands must be in a data register. The MC68000 allows for both signed and unsigned multiplication. If signed multiplication (MULS) is used, operands are treated as signed values and the result is signed. For unsigned multiplication (MULU), all values are unsigned. In program 7-4b, we have modified program 7-4a to use the MULU instruction instead of the ADD and shift (LSL) instructions:

Program 7-4b:

```
            00006000     DATA      EQU    $6000
            00004000     PROGRAM   EQU    $4000

            00006000     STRING    EQU    $6000         ADDRESS OF FOUR DIGIT BDC STRING
            00006004     CODE      EQU    $6004         ADDRESS OF RESULT

            00004000               ORG    PROGRAM


004000 307C6000  PGM_7_4B MOVEA.W  #STRING,A0     POINTER TO FIRST BCD DIGIT
004004 7003               MOVEQ    #4-1,D0        NUMBER OF DIGITS(-1) TO PROCESS
004006 4281               CLR.L    D1             CLEAR FINAL RESULT - D1
004008 4282               CLR.L    D2             CLEAR DIGIT REGISTER
00400A 6004               BRA.S    NOMULT         SKIP MULTIPLY FIRST TIME

00400C C2FC000A  LOOP     MULU.W   #10,D1         D1 = D1 * 10

004010 1418      NOMULT   MOVE.B   (A0)+,D2       NEXT BCD DIGIT(D2[15-8] UNCHANGED)
004012 D242               ADD.W    D2,D1          ADD NEXT DIGIT
004014 51C8FFF6           DBRA     D0,LOOP        CONTINUE PROCESSING IF STILL DIGITS

004018 31C16004           MOVE.W   D1,CODE        STORE RESULT

00401C 4E75               RTS

                          END      PGM_7_4B
```

7-5. BINARY NUMBER TO ASCII STRING

Purpose: Convert the 16-bit binary number in the variable NUMBER at memory location 6000 into 16 ASCII characters (either ASCII 0 or ASCII 1). Store the ASCII characters in the 16-character string variable STRING located at memory location 6002.

Sample Problem:

```
     Input:  NUMBER - (6000) = 31D2 = 0011 0001 1101 0010
     Output: STRING - (6002) = 30  '0'
                      (6003) = 30  '0'
                      (6004) = 31  '1'
                      (6005) = 31  '1'
                      (6006) = 30  '0'
                      (6007) = 30  '0'
                      (6008) = 30  '0'
                      (6009) = 31  '1'
                      (600A) = 31  '1'
                      (600B) = 31  '1'
                      (600C) = 30  '0'
                      (600D) = 31  '1'
                      (600E) = 30  '0'
                      (600F) = 30  '0'
                      (6010) = 31  '1'
                      (6011) = 30  '0'
```

Program 7-5:

```
       00006000            DATA     EQU     $6000
       00004000            PROGRAM  EQU     $4000

       00006000            NUMBER   EQU     $6000              ADDRESS OF 16 BIT NUMBER
       00006002            STRING   EQU     $6002              ADDRESS OF EQUIVALENT ASCII STRING

       00004000                     ORG     PROGRAM
004000 207C00006012 PGM_7_5         MOVEA.L #STRING+16,A0      POINTER TO END OF STRING(+1)
004006 700F                         MOVEQ   #15,D0             LOOP COUNT(-1)
004008 123C0030                     MOVE.B  #'0',D1
00400C 34386000                     MOVE.W  NUMBER,D2          GET NUMERIC DATA

004010 1101         LOOP            MOVE.B  D1,-(A0)           ASSUME CURRENT LSB IS ZERO
004012 E25A                         ROR.W   #1,D2              TEST CURRENT LSB
004014 6404                         BCC.S   LOOPEND            IF ZERO THEN TRY NEXT BIT

004016 06100001                     ADDI.B  #1,(A0)            CHANGE ASCII '0' TO ASCII '1'

00401A 51C8FFF4     LOOPEND         DBRA    D0,LOOP            PROCESS ALL BITS

00401E 4E75                         RTS
                                    END     PGM_7_5
```

The ASCII digits form a sequence so ASCII 1 = ASCII 0 + 1. The ADD instruction can be used to directly increment the contents of a memory location. As a result, no explicit instructions are required to load the data from memory into a register or to store the result back into memory. Nor are any registers disturbed.

Note that the string pointer, A0, starts at the end of the string +1 (6002+16_{10}) and is decremented at the beginning of each step. When accessing data in this manner, note that the end-of-the-string address is actually the address of the first byte not in the string. For example, the byte at 6002 + 16_{10} is not in the string of ASCII digits. Finally, note that 6002 + 16_{10} is more easily identified with a 16-byte string than 6002 + 15_{10}.

Binary-to-ASCII conversion is necessary if numbers are to be printed in binary on an ASCII device. Binary outputs are helpful in debugging and testing when each bit has a separate meaning; typical examples are inputs from a set of panel switches or outputs to a set of LEDs. If the programmer can only obtain the value in some other number system (such as octal or hexadecimal), he or she must perform an error-prone hand conversion to check the bits.

Flowchart 7-5:

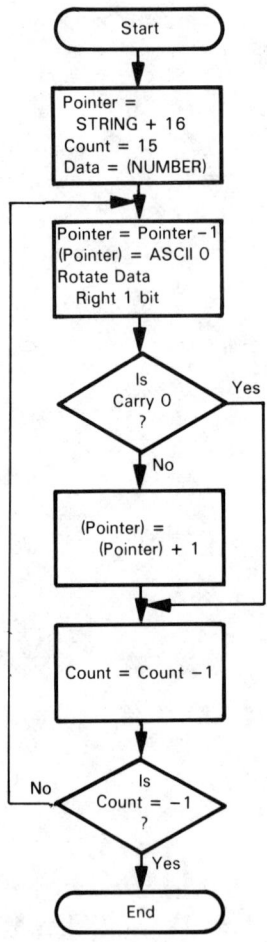

PROBLEMS

7-1. ASCII TO HEXADECIMAL

Purpose: Convert the contents of the variable A DIGIT at memory location 6000 from an ASCII character to a hexadecimal digit and store the result in the variable H DIGIT at memory location 6001. Assume that A DIGIT contains the ASCII representation of a hexadecimal digit (7 bits with MSB=0).

Sample Problems:

a. Input: A DIGIT - (6000) = 43 'C'
   Output: H DIGIT - (6001) = 0C
b. Input: A DIGIT - (6000) = 36 '6'
   Output: H DIGIT - (6001) = 06

7-2. SEVEN-SEGMENT TO DECIMAL

Purpose: Convert the contents of the variable CODE at memory location 6000 from a seven-segment code to a decimal number and store the result in the variable NUMBER at location 6001. If CODE does not contain a valid seven-segment code, set NUMBER to FF_{16}. Use the seven-segment table given in Figure 7-1 and try to match codes.

Sample Problems:

a. Input: CODE - (6000) = 4F
   Output: NUMBER - (6001) = 03
b. Input: CODE - (6000) = 28
   Output: NUMBER - (6001) = FF

7-3. DECIMAL TO ASCII

Purpose: Convert the contents of the variable DIGIT at memory location 6000 from a decimal digit to an ASCII character and store the result in the variable CHAR at memory location 6001. If the number in DIGIT is not a decimal digit, set the contents of CHAR to an ASCII space (20_{16}).

Sample Problems:

a. Input: DIGIT - (6000) = 07
   Output: CHAR - (6001) = 37 '7'
b. Input: DIGIT - (6000) = 55
   Output: CHAR - (6001) = 20 space

7-4. BINARY TO BCD

Purpose: Convert the contents of the variable NUMBER at memory location 6000 to four BCD digits in the variable STRING at location 6002 (most significant digit in 6002). The 16-bit number in NUMBER is unsigned and less than 10,000.

Sample Problem:

```
 Input:  NUMBER -  (6000) = 1C52   (7250 decimal)
Output:  STRING -  (6002) = 07
                   (6003) = 02
                   (6004) = 05
                   (6005) = 00
```

7-5. ASCII STRING TO BINARY NUMBER

Purpose: Convert the eight ASCII characters in the variable STRING starting at location 6000 to an 8-bit binary number in the variable NUMBER at location 6008 (the most significant bit-character is in location 6000). Clear the byte variable ERROR at location 6009 if all the ASCII characters are either ASCII 1 or ASCII 0; otherwise set ERROR to all ones (FF_{16}).

Sample Problems:

```
a.   Input:  STRING -  (6000) = 31   '1'
                       (6001) = 31   '1'
                       (6002) = 30   '0'
                       (6003) = 31   '1'
                       (6004) = 30   '0'
                       (6005) = 30   '0'
                       (6006) = 31   '1'
                       (6007) = 30   '0'
    Output:  NUMBER -  (6008) = D2
                       (6009) = 0

b.   Input:  Same as (a)
             above
             except
                       (6005) = 37   '7'
    Output:  ERROR -   (6009) = FF
```

REFERENCES

Other BCD-to-binary conversion methods are discussed in M.L. Roginsky and J.A. Tabb, "Microprocessor Algorithms Make BCD-Binary Conversions Super-fast," *EDN*, January 5, 1977, pp. 46-50, and in J.B. Peatman, *Microcomputer-based Design*, New York: McGraw-Hill, 1977, pp. 400-06.

8
Arithmetic Problems

MULTIPLE-WORD AND DECIMAL ARITHMETIC

Much of the arithmetic in some microprocessor applications consists of multiple-word binary or decimal manipulations. A decimal correction (decimal adjust) or some other means for performing decimal arithmetic is frequently the only arithmetic instruction provided besides basic addition and subtraction. When this is the case, you must implement other arithmetic operations with sequences of instruction. The MC68000, however, provides both signed and unsigned multiply and divide instructions for 16-bit binary arithmetic, as well as decimal addition and subtraction instructions.

The MC68000 provides for both signed and unsigned binary arithmetic. Signed numbers are represented in two's complement form. This means that the operations of addition and subtraction are the same whether the numbers are signed or unsigned. Different instructions are needed for signed and unsigned multiplication and division, but not for addition and subtraction. Try some examples to convince yourself this is true.

Multiple-precision binary arithmetic requires simple repetitions of the basic instructions. The Extend bit transfers information between words. It is set when an addition results in a carry or a subtraction results in a borrow. Add with Extend and Subtract with Extend use this information from the previous arithmetic operation. You must be careful to clear the Extend bit before operating on the first words. (Obviously there is no carry into or borrow from the least significant bits.)

Decimal arithmetic is a common enough task for microprocessors that most have special instructions for this purpose. These instructions may either perform decimal operations directly or correct the results of binary operations to the proper decimal form. Decimal arithmetic is essential in such applications as point-of-sale terminals, check processors, order entry systems, and banking terminals. The MC68000 provides instructions for decimal addition and subtraction. Since the MC68000 performs decimal arithmetic directly, there is no need for a decimal adjust instruction such as is found in many other microprocessors.

You can implement decimal multiplication and division as series of additions and subtractions, respectively. Extra storage must be reserved for results, since a multiplication produces a result twice as long as the operands. A division contracts the length of the result. Multiplications and divisions are time-consuming when done in software because of the repeated operations that are necessary.

PROGRAM EXAMPLES

8-1. 64-BIT BINARY ADDITION

Purpose: Add two four-word (64-bit) binary numbers. The first number is the 64-bit variable NUM1 and occupies memory locations 6000 through 6007, the second is the 64-bit variable NUM2 and occupies locations 6200 through 6207. Place the sum in NUM1 at locations 6000 through 6007.

Sample Problem:

```
       Input:  NUM1  —  (6000) = 6A4D
                        (6002) = ED05   6A4DED05A9376414₁₆ is the
                        (6004) = A937   first number
                        (6006) = 6414
               NUM2  —  (6200) = 56C8
                        (6202) = 46E6   56C846E676C84AEA₁₆ is the
                        (6204) = 76C8   second number
                        (6206) = 4AEA
       Output: NUM1  —  (6000) = C116
                        (6002) = 33EC   C11633EC1FFFAEFE₁₆ is sum
                        (6004) = 1FFF
                        (6006) = AEFE
```

Program 8-1a:

```
       00006000         DATA     EQU     $6000
       00004000         PROGRAM  EQU     $4000

       00006000         NUM1      EQU     $6000         ADDR. OF 1:ST 64-BIT BINARY NUMBER
       00006200         NUM2      EQU     $6200         ADDR. OF 2:ND 64 BIT BINARY NUMBER
       00000008         BYTECOUNT EQU     $8            NUMBER OF BYTES TO ADD

       00004000                   ORG     PROGRAM

004000 207C00006008 PGM_8_1A      MOVEA.L #NUM1+BYTECOUNT,A0  ADDRESS BEYOND END OF FIRST NUMBER
004006 227C00006208               MOVEA.L #NUM2+BYTECOUNT,A1  ADDRESS BEYOND END OF SECOND NUMBER
00400C 44FC0000                   MOVE    #0,CCR              CLEAR EXTEND FLAG(AND OTHER FLAGS)
004010 7407                       MOVEQ   #BYTECOUNT-1,D2     LOOPCOUNTER, ADJUSTED FOR DBRA
```

```
004012  1020         LOOP    MOVE.B  -(A0),D0
004014  1221                 MOVE.B  -(A1),D1
004016  D101                 ADDX.B  D1,D0           D0[0-7]:= D0[0-7] + D1[0-7] + (EXT)
004018  1080                 MOVE.B  D0,(A0)         STORE RESULT
00401A  51CAFFF6             DBRA    D2,LOOP         CONTINUE

00401E  4E75                 RTS

                             END     PGM_8_1A
```

Flowchart 8-1:

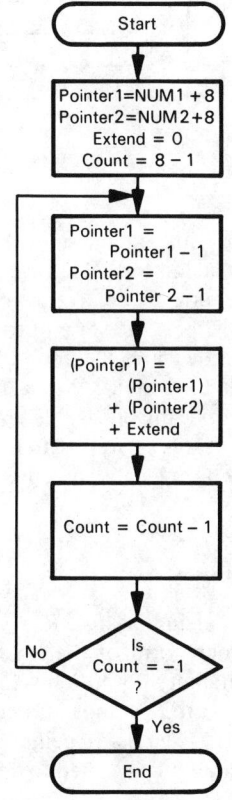

Clearing and Setting Flags

The instruction MOVE TO CCR sets *all the condition codes* in the processor's status register according to the contents of the source operand. Although the source operand is always a 16-bit word, only the least significant byte is used to set the condition codes. Therefore MOVE #0,CCR clears all the conditions (Negative, Zero, Overflow, Carry and Extend). This instruction is used to clear the Extend flag in preparation for the first ADDX instruction.

MOVE TO CCR is not the only instruction which can explicitly modify the contents of condition codes. The immediate instructions ANDI, EORI, and ORI can also be used to selectively clear, complement, and set individual condition codes. For example, by using the instruction ANDI #$EF,CCR we could clear only the Extend flag without modifying the other condition codes. The format for the immediate operand when modifying condition codes is:

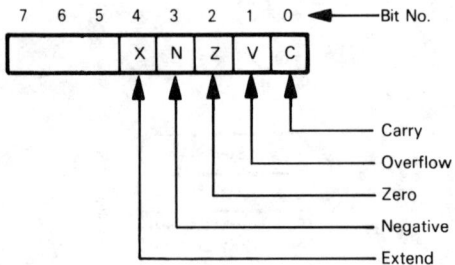

Add with Extend

The ADDX instruction, Add with Extend, adds the contents of the two registers. If the Extend flag is set, then 1 is added to the sum. Besides performing the addition, ADDX sets the Extend flag appropriately for future operations. Note that no other instruction in this program's loop affects the state of the Extend flag.

The Extend flag is similar to the Carry flag found in most other microprocessors. The MC68000 has both a Carry and Extend flag. As a general rule, the Carry flag is set if a carry occurs out of the most significant bit of the result for addition or if a borrow occurs during subtraction; otherwise it is cleared. The Extend flag is generally set to the same state as the Carry flag, except during data movement, when the state of the Extend flag is not affected.

Adding Memory Operands

A quicker and more elegant version of this addition program is shown in Program 8-1*b*. This program uses the second form of the Add with Extend instruction, the powerful MC68000 memory-to-memory form. This format requires the use of two address registers which point to the two operands in memory. The address registers are *decremented* according to the operand size *prior* to being used to fetch the operands. Note that the ADD with Extend instruction may be used to operate on 8-, 16-, or 32-bit data.

Program 8-1b:

```
          00006000     DATA       EQU      $6000
          00004000     PROGRAM    EQU      $4000

          00006000     NUM1       EQU      $6000        ADDR. OF 1:ST 64-BIT BINARY NUMBER
          00006200     NUM2       EQU      $6200        ADDR. OF 2:ND 64-BIT BINARY NUMBER

          00004000                ORG      PROGRAM

004000    207C00006008 PGM_8_1B   MOVEA.L  #NUM1+8,A0   ADDRESS BEYOND END OF 64-BIT NUMBER
004006    227C00006208            MOVEA.L  #NUM2+8,A1   ADDRESS BEYOND END OF SECOND NUMBER
00400C    44FC0000                MOVE     #0,CCR       CLEAR EXTEND FLAG(AND OTHER FLAGS)

004010    D189                    ADDX.L   -(A1),-(A0)  ADD LOWER LONG WORDS,RESULT IN NUM1
004012    D189                    ADDX.L   -(A1),-(A0)  ADD HIGHER LONG WORDS, RES IN NUM1

004014    4E75                    RTS

                                  END      PGM_8_1B
```

In addition to the Add with Extend (ADDX) instruction, the MC68000 also supports binary addition with the ADD instruction. ADD is similar to ADDX except that the state of the Extend flag is not used in the addition operation. The ADD instruction also requires at least one of its operands to be in a data register. How could we modify Program 8-1a to use the ADD instruction instead of ADDX?

Decimal Precision in Binary Representation

Storing data in a binary format as opposed to decimal requires less memory. For example, **ten bits correspond to approximately three decimal digits** since $2^{10} = 1024$. **So you can calculate the approximate number of bits required to give a certain accuracy in decimal digits from the formula:**

$$\text{Number of bits} \approx (10/3) \times \text{Number of decimal digits}$$

Thus, twelve decimal digit accuracy requires:

$$12 \times 10/3 = 40 \text{ bits}$$

8-2. DECIMAL ADDITION

Purpose: Add two multiple-byte packed BCD numbers. The length of the numbers (in bytes) is defined by the variable LENGTH at location 6000. The first number (most significant bits first) is contained in the variable BCDNUM1 at location 6001. The second number is contained in the variable BCDNUM2 at location 6101. The sum replaces the number at BCDNUM1. Each byte of the BCD numbers contains two decimal digits.

Sample Problem:

```
Input:   LENGTH   —  (6000) = 04    Number of bytes in each number
         BCDNUM1  —  (6001) = 36
                     (6002) = 70    36701985 is first number
                     (6003) = 19
                     (6004) = 85
         BCDNUM2  —  (6101) = 12
                     (6102) = 66    12663459 is second number
                     (6103) = 34
                     (6104) = 59
Output:  BCDNUM1  —  (6001) = 49
                     (6002) = 36    49365444 is decimal sum
                     (6003) = 54
                     (6004) = 44

That is,  36701985
        + 12663459
          --------
          49365444
```

Program 8-2a:

```
00006000        DATA      EQU    $6000
00004000        PROGRAM   EQU    $4000

00006000        LENGTH    EQU    $6000         LENGTH OF BCD NUMBER IN BYTES
00006001        BCDNUM1   EQU    $6001         ADDRESS OF FIRST BCD NUMBER
00006101        BCDNUM2   EQU    $6101         ADDRESS OF SECOND BCD NUMBER
```

136 68000 Assembly Language Programming

```
              00004000                    ORG     PROGRAM
004000  4242               PGM_8_2A  CLR.W   D2
004002  14386000                     MOVE.B  LENGTH,D2
004006  3442                         MOVE.W  D2,A2          A2[0-31] = BYTES IN BCD NUMBER
004008  41EA6001                     LEA     BCDNUM1(A2),A0 POINTS BEYOND END OF BCDNUM1
00400C  43EA6101                     LEA     BCDNUM2(A2),A1 POINTS BEYOND END OF BCDNUM2

004010  5342                         SUBQ    #1,D2          ADJUST LENGTH FOR LOOP TERMINATION
004012  44FC0000                     MOVE    #0,CCR         CLEAR EXTEND FLAG FOR ABCD

004016  C109               LOOP      ABCD.B  -(A1),-(A0)    BCD ADDITION WITH EXTEND
004018  51CAFFFC                     DBRA    D2,LOOP        CONTINUE

00401C  4E75                         RTS

                                     END     PGM_8_2A
```

Flowchart 8-2:

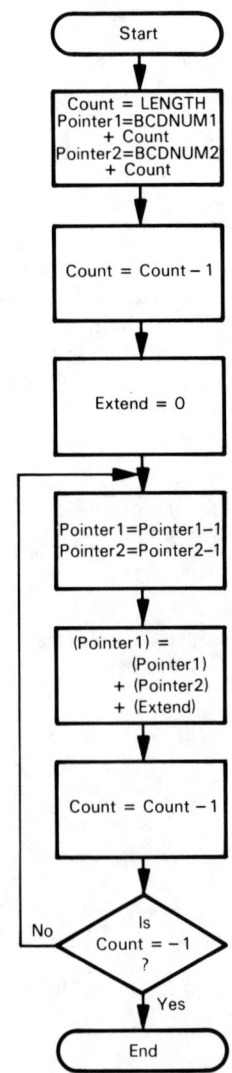

Arithmetic Problems **137**

The MC68000, unlike most microprocessors, implements decimal addition in a single instruction ABCD, Add Decimal with Extend. Like the ADDX instruction, ABCD performs addition using the state of the Extend flag. However, the addition is performed using binary-coded decimal arithmetic. This eliminates the need for the typical decimal adjust instruction such as the DAA instruction on Motorola's 6809 microprocessor. The MC68000 also provides a decimal subtraction instruction, SBCD.

Program 8-2 uses the Load Effective Address, LEA, instruction to calculate the address of the decimal number's last byte plus one. This instruction calculates an effective address in the normal way, but then simply places that address in the specified address register rather than using it to transfer data. The effective address is available for later use and need not be recalculated.

We should note that use of the register indirect with displacement mode of addressing with the LEA instruction results in some restrictions being placed on Program 8-2a: since the displacement (BCDNUM1) that is part of the operand can only be 16-bits in length, the full addressing space of the processor cannot be utilized. We can make Program 8-1b more general purpose so that it can utilize the full addressing space, although this will require several additional instructions. Program 8-2b provides this more general solution.

Program 8-2b:

```
              00006000      DATA     EQU    $6000
              00004000      PROGRAM  EQU    $4000

              00006000      LENGTH   EQU    $6000           LENGTH OF BCD NUMBER IN BYTES
              00006001      BCDNUM1  EQU    $6001           ADDRESS OF FIRST BCD NUMBER
              00006101      BCDNUM2  EQU    $6101           ADDRESS OF SECOND BCD NUMBER

              00004000               ORG    PROGRAM
004000 4242            PGM_8_2B CLR     D2
004002 14386000                 MOVE.B  LENGTH,D2
004006 207C00006001             MOVEA.L #BCDNUM1,A0        POINTER TO START OF BCDNUM1
00400C 227C00006101             MOVEA.L #BCDNUM2,A1        POINTER TO START OF BCDNUM2
004012 41F02000                 LEA     0(A0,D2.W),A0      ADJUST TO POINT BEYOND END OF VALUE
004016 43F12000                 LEA     0(A1,D2.W),A1      ADJUST TO POINT BEYOND END OF VALUE

00401A 5342                     SUBQ.W  #1,D2              ADJUST LENGTH FOR LOOP TERMINATION
00401C 44FC0000                 MOVE    #0,CCR             CLEAR EXTEND FLAG FOR ABCD

004020 C109           LOOP      ABCD.B  -(A1),-(A0)        BCD ADDITION WITH EXTEND
004022 51CAFFFC                 DBRA    D2,LOOP            CONTINUE

004026 4E75                     RTS

                                END     PGM_8_2B
```

The procedure used in both of these programs can add decimal (BCD) numbers of any length (up to 131,072 digits!). Since each decimal digit requires four bits, twelve digit precision requires

$$12 \times 4 = 48 \text{ bits}$$

as compared to 40 bits using binary addition. This is six bytes instead of five, a 20% increase.

Note that if we replaced the ABCD instruction in Program 8-2a or 8-2b with an ADDX instruction, these programs would provide a more general solution to the binary addition problem presented in Program 8-1.

8-3. 16-BIT BINARY MULTIPLICATION

Purpose: Multiply the 16-bit unsigned number in the variable NUM1 at location 6000 by the 16-bit unsigned binary number in the variable NUM2 at location 6002. Place the 32-bit result in the long word variable RESULT at location 6004 with the 16 most significant bits of the result in location 6004 and the 16 least significant bits in location 6006.

Sample Problems:

a. Input: NUM1 — (6000) = 0003
NUM2 — (6002) = 0005
Output: RESULT — (6004) = 0000
(6006) = 000F
or in decimal, 3 × 5 = 15

b. Input: NUM1 — (6000) = 706F
NUM2 — (6002) = 0161
Output: RESULT — (6004) = 009B
(6006) = 090F
or in decimal, 28783 × 353 = 10160399

Program 8-3a:

```
        00006000        DATA    EQU     $6000
        00004000        PROGRAM EQU     $4000

        00006000                ORG     DATA
006000  00000002        NUM1    DS.W    1               16-BIT MULTIPLICAND
006002  00000002        NUM2    DS.W    1               16-BIT MULTIPLIER
006004  00000004        RESULT  DS.L    1               32-BIT MULTIPLICATION RESULT

        00004000                ORG     PROGRAM
004000  30386000        PGM_8_3A MOVE.W NUM1,D0         MULTIPLICAND
004004  C0F86002                 MULU   NUM2,D0         UNSIGNED MULTIPLICATION
004008  21C06004                 MOVE.L D0,RESULT       STORE 32-BIT MULTIPLICATION RESULTS

00400C  4E75                    RTS

                                END     PGM_8_3A
```

The MC68000 supports signed, as well as unsigned, binary multiplication or division. To multiply two signed 16-bit binary numbers, you simply replace MULU with MULS, the Signed Multiply instruction.

Besides its obvious uses in, for example, point-of-sale terminals, multiplication is also a key part of many mathematical algorithms. The speed at which a processor can perform multiplication determines its usefulness in process control, adaptive control, signal detection, and signal analysis.

Multidimensional Arrays

Another common use of multiplication is in locating elements in multidimensional arrays. For example, if we have an array of sensor readings organized by remote station number and sensor number, we can refer to the reading from the seventh sensor at station number 5 as R(5,7), where R is the name of the entire array. The usual method of storing such an array is to start at address RBASE with R(0,0) and continue with R(0,1), etc. If there are three stations (0, 1, and 2) and four sensors at each station (0, 1, 2, and 3), we keep the readings in the following memory locations:

Memory Location	Reading
RBASE	R(0,0)
RBASE + 1	R(0,1)
RBASE + 2	R(0,2)
RBASE + 3	R(0,3)
RBASE + 4	R(1,0)
RBASE + 5	R(1,1)
RBASE + 6	R(1,2)
RBASE + 7	R(1,3)
RBASE + 8	R(2,0)
RBASE + 9	R(2,1)
RBASE + 10	R(2,2)
RBASE + 11	R(2,3)

In general, if we know the station number I and the sensor number J, the reading R(I,J) is located at address

RBASE + (N × I) + J

where N is the number of sensors at each station. Thus, locating a particular reading in order to update it, display it, or perform some mathemetical operations on it requires a multiplication. For example, the operator might want an instrument to print the current reading of sensor O3 at station O2. To find that reading, the processor must calculate the address

RBASE + (4 × 2) + 3 = RBASE + 11

Even more multiplications are necessary if the array has more dimensions. For example, we might organize the sensors by station number, position in the X direction, and position in the Y direction. (Each station thus has sensors at regular positions on a two-dimensional surface.) Now we can describe a reading R(2,3,1), which refers to the reading of the sensor at station O2, X position O3, and Y position O1. We can add even more dimensions, such as vertical position, type of sensor, or time of reading. Each added dimension means that the processor must perform more multiplications to locate elements in the essentially one-dimensional memory.

A Binary Multiplication Algorithm

It is interesting to look at a binary multiplication routine for two reasons: first, we can compare the execution time of the routine with the MULU or MULS instruction; and second, some other microprocessors don't have multiply instructions and understanding multiplication is important.

You can perform multiplication on a computer in the same way that you do long multiplication by hand. Since the numbers are binary, you will only multiply by 0 or 1; multiplying by zero obviously give zero as a result, while multiplying by one produces the same number you started with (the multiplicand). So each step in binary multiplication can be reduced to the following operation: if the current bit in the multiplier is 1, add the multiplicand to the partial product.

The only remaining problem is to ensure that you line everything up correctly each time. The following operations perform this task.

1. Shift the multiplier left one bit so that the bit to be examined is placed in the Carry.
2. Shift the product left one bit so that the next addition is lined up correctly.

To keep things simple, we will multiply two 8-bit values to produce a 16-bit result.

Step 1 - Initialization

    Product = 0
    Counter = 8

Step 2 - Shift Product so as to line up properly

    Product = 2 × Product (LSB = 0)

Step 3 - Shift Multiplier so bit goes to Carry

    Multiplier = 2 × Multiplier

Step 4 - Add Multiplicand to Product if Carry is 1

    If Carry = 1, Product = Product + Multiplicand

Step 5 - Decrement Counter and check for zero

    Counter = Counter − 1
    If Counter > 0 go to Step 2

Assuming the multiplier is 61_{16} and the multiplicand is $6F_{16}$, the algorithm works as follows.

Initialization:

    Product   0000 = 0000000000000000_2
    Multiplier   61 = 01100001_2
    Multiplicand   6F = 01101111_2
    Counter   08

After first iteration of steps 2-5:

    Product   0000 = 0000000000000000_2
    Multiplier   C2 = 11000010_2
    Multiplicand   6F = 01101111_2
    Counter   07
    Carry from
      Multiplier   0

After second iteration:

    Product   006F = 0000000001101111_2
    Multiplier   84 = 10000100_2
    Multiplicand   6F = 01101111_2
    Counter   06
    Carry from
      Multiplier   1

After third iteration:

    Product   014D = 0000000101001101_2
    Multiplier   08 = 00001000_2
    Multiplicand   6F = 01101111_2
    Counter   05
    Carry from
      Multiplier   1

After fourth iteration:

Product	029A	=	0000001010011010_2
Multiplier	10	=	00010000_2
Multiplicand	6F	=	01101111_2
Counter	04		
Carry from Multiplier	0		

After fifth iteration:

Product	0534	=	0000010100110100_2
Multiplier	20	=	00100000_2
Multiplicand	6F	=	01101111_2
Counter	03		
Carry from Multiplier	0		

After sixth iteration:

Product	0A68	=	0000101001101000_2
Multiplier	40	=	01000000_2
Multiplicand	6F	=	01101111_2
Counter	02		
Carry from Multiplier	0		

After seventh iteration:

Product	14D0	=	0001010011010000_2
Multiplier	80	=	10000000_2
Multiplicand	6F	=	01101111_2
Counter	01		
Carry from Multiplier	0		

After eighth iteration:

Product	2A0F	=	0010101000001111_2
Multiplier	00	=	00000000_2
Multiplicand	6F	=	01101111_2
Counter	00		
Carry from Multiplier	1		

Program 8-3b:

```
          00006000          DATA      EQU     $6000
          00004000          PROGRAM   EQU     $4000

          00006000                    ORG     DATA
006000    00000002          NUM1      DS      1           16-BIT MULTIPLICAND
006002    00000002          NUM2      DS      1           16-BIT MULTIPLIER
006004    00000004          RESULT    DS.L    1           32-BIT MULTIPLICATION RESULT

          00004000                    ORG     PROGRAM
004000    4280              PGM_8_3B  CLR.L   D0          CLEAR 32-BIT PRODUCT
004002    2200                        MOVE.L  D0,D1       UPPER WORD MUST BE CLEAR FOR ADD.L
004004    32386000                    MOVE.W  NUM1,D1     16-BIT MULTIPLICAND
004008    34386002                    MOVE.W  NUM2,D2     16-BIT MULTIPLIER
00400C    760F                        MOVEQ   #16-1,D3    LOOP COUNT := 16 (-1 FOR DBRA)

00400E    D080              LOOP      ADD.L   D0,D0       SHIFT PRODUCT LEFT 1 BIT
004010    D442                        ADD.W   D2,D2       SHIFT MULTIPLIER LEFT 1 BIT
004012    6402                        BCC.S   STEP        IF MULTIPLIER[15] WAS 1

004014    D081                        ADD.L   D1,D0       ...THEN ADD MULTIPLICAND
```

```
004016 51CBFFF6      STEP    DBRA    D3,LOOP         ...ELSE CONTINUE
00401A 21C06004              MOVE.L  D0,RESULT       STORE RESULT

00401E 4E75                  RTS

                             END     PGM_8_3B
```

Flowchart 8-3b:

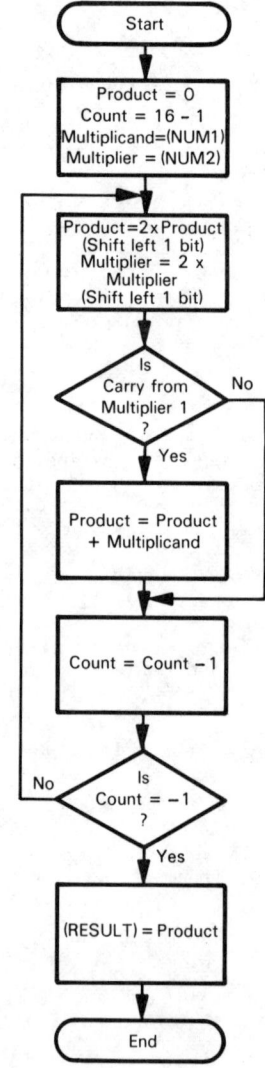

This program performs the same 16-bit multiplication operation as Program 8-3a. If you count clock cycles for the two versions, you will find the expected results: the MULU version takes less than 109 cycles while the long version (Program 8-3b) takes 58 cycles outside the loop, and $516 + 6n$ (n = number of 1 bits in multiplier) cycles inside the loop.

8-4. 32-BIT BINARY DIVIDE

Purpose: Divide the 32-bit unsigned number in variable NUM1 at location 6000 by the 16-bit unsigned binary number in variable NUM2 at location 6004. Place the 16-bit remainder in the variable REMAINDER at location 6006 and the 16-bit quotient in the variable QUOTIENT at location 6008.

Sample Problem:

```
        Input:     NUM1       —    (6000) = 0074
                                   (6002) = CBB1  32-bit dividend
                   NUM2       —    (6004) = 0141  16-bit divisor
        Output:    REMAINDER  —    (6006) = 004C
                   QUOTIENT   —    (6008) = 5D25
                                   or in decimal, 7654321 321 = 23845 with
                                   remainder of 76
```

Program 8-4:

```
        00006000        DATA    EQU     $6000
        00004000        PROGRAM EQU     $4000

        00006000                ORG     DATA
006000  00000004        NUM1    DS.L    1               32-BIT DIVIDEND
006004  00000002        NUM2    DS.W    1               16-BIT DIVISOR
006006  00000002        REMAIND DS.W    1               16-BIT REMAINDER
006008  00000002        QUOTIENT DS.W   1               16-BIT QUOTIENT

        00004000                ORG     PROGRAM

004000  20386000        PGM_8_4 MOVE.L  NUM1,D0         32 BIT DIVIDEND
004004  80F86004                DIVU    NUM2,D0         UNSIGNED DIVIDE - NUM1/NUM2
004008  21C06006                MOVE.L  D0,REMAIND      STORE RESULTS-REMAINDER & QUOTIENT

00400C  4E75                    RTS
                                END     PGM_8_4
```

The MC68000 provides two instructions (DIVU and DIVS) which perform a divide operation using a 32-bit binary dividend and a 16-bit binary divisor. The operation results in a 16-bit binary quotient as well as a 16-bit binary remainder. The DIVU instruction should be used for unsigned arithmetic, while the DIVS instruction is used with signed numbers. When performing a signed divide, the sign of the remainder will be the same as the sign of the dividend. The sign of the quotient is positive if both operands have the same sign and negative if they have different signs. Both instructions place the remainder in the 16 most significant bits of the destination data register while the quotient is placed in the 16 least significant bits of the destination data register.

Two special conditions can occur when executing either of the Divide instruction. First, if the divisor equals zero, the processor will cause a zero divide trap. (A description of traps and of trap processing will be delayed until Chapter 15.) Secondly, the microprocessor may detect an overflow condition. In this case, the Overflow (V) bit in the status register will be set and the operands will be unaffected.

PROBLEMS

8-1. MULTIPLE PRECISION BINARY SUBTRACTION

Purpose: Subtract one multiple-word number from another. The length in words of both numbers is in the variable LENGTH at location 6000. The numbers themselves are stored (most significant bits first) in the variables NUM1 and NUM2 at locations 6002 and 6102, respectively. Subtract the number in NUM2 from the one in NUM1. Store the difference in NUM1.

Sample Problem:

```
Input:    LENGTH  —  (6000) = 0003
          NUM1    —  (6002) = 2F5B
                     (6004) = 47C3
                     (6006) = 306C
          NUM2    —  (6102) = 14DF
                     (6104) = 85B8
                     (6106) = 03BC
Output:   NUM1    —  (6002) = 1A7B
                     (6004) = C20B
                     (6006) = 2CB0
```

```
That is:    2F5B47C3306C
          − 14DF85B803BC
            1A7BC20B2CB0
```

8-2. DECIMAL SUBTRACTION

Purpose: Subtract one multiple-byte packed decimal (BCD) number from another. The length in bytes of both numbers is in the byte variable LENGTH at location 6000. The numbers themselves (most significant digits first) are in the variables NUM1 and NUM2 at locations 6001 and 6101, respectively. Subtract the number contained in NUM2 from the one starting in NUM1. Store the difference in NUM1.

Sample Problem:

```
Input:    LENGTH  —  (6000) = 04
          NUM1    —  (6001) = 36
                     (6002) = 70
                     (6003) = 19
                     (6004) = 85
          NUM2    —  (6101) = 12
                     (6102) = 66
                     (6103) = 34
                     (6104) = 59
Output:   NUM1    —  (6001) = 24
                     (6002) = 03
                     (6003) = 85
                     (6004) = 26
```

```
That is:    36701985
          − 12663459
            24038526
```

8-3. 32-BIT BY 32-BIT MULTIPLY

Purpose: Multiply the 32-bit value in the variable NUM1 which begins in memory location 6000 (high-order) by the 32-bit value in variable NUM2 at location 6004. Do the multiply twice: first use the MULU instruction and place the results in the 64-bit variable PROD1 starting at location 6008; then use a shift and add method as illustrated in Program 8-3b and place the result in the 64-bit variable PROD2 starting at location 6010.

Sample Problem:

```
Input:    NUM1   —   (6000) = 0024
                     (6002) = 68AC
          NUM2   —   (6004) = 0328
                     (6006) = 1088
Output:   PROD1  —   (6008) = 0000
                     (600A) = 72EC
                     (600C) = BBC2
                     (600E) = 5B60
          PROD2  —   (6010) = 0000
                     (6012) = 72EC
                     (6014) = B8C2
                     (6016) = 5B60
```

REFERENCES

Other methods for implementing multiplication, division, and other arithmetic tasks are discussed in:

Ali, Z. "Know the LSI Hardware Tradeoffs of Digital Signal Processors," *Electronic Design,* June 21, 1979, pp. 66-71.

Geist, D. J. "MOS Processor Picks up Speed with Bipolar Multipliers," *Electronics,* July 7, 1977, pp. 113-15.

Kolodzinski, A. and D. Wainland. "Multiplying with a Microcomputer," *Electronic Design,* January 18, 1978, pp. 78-83.

Mor, S. "An 8 x 8 Multiplier and 8-Bit Microprocessor Perform 16 x 16-Bit Multiplication,"*EDN,* November 5, 1979, pp. 147-52.

Tao, T. F. et al. "Applications of Microprocessors in Control Problems," Proceedings of the 1977 Joint Automatic Control Conference, San Francisco, Ca., June 22-24, 1977.

Waser, S. "State-of-the-Art in High-Speed Arithmetic Integrated Circuits," *Computer Design,* July 1978, pp. 67-75.

Waser, S. and A. Peterson. "Medium-Speed Multipliers Trim Cost, Shrink Bandwidth in Speech Transmission," *Electronic Design,* February 1, 1979, pp. 58-65.

Weissberger, A. J. and T. Toal. "Tough Mathematical Tasks are Child's Play for Number Cruncher," *Electronics,* February 17, 1977, pp. 102-07.

9
Tables and Lists

Tables and lists are two of the basic data structures used with all computers. We have already seen tables used to perform code conversions and arithmetic. Tables may also be used to identify or respond to commands and instructions, provide access to files or records, define the meaning of keys or switches, and choose among alternate programs. Lists are usually less structured than tables. **Lists may record tasks that the processor must perform, messages or data that the processor must record, or conditions that have changed or should be monitored.** Tables are a simple way of making decisions or solving problems, since no computations or logical functions are necessary. The task, then, is reduced to organizing the table so that the proper entry is easy to find. Lists allow the execution of sequences of tasks, the preparation of sets of results, and the construction of interrelated data (or data bases). Problems include how to add elements to a list and remove elements from it.

PROGRAM EXAMPLES

9-1. ADD ENTRY TO LIST

Purpose: Add the contents of the word variable ITEM at memory location 6000 to a list if it is not already present in the list. The list is comprised of word elements and the starting address of the list is in the long-word variable LIST at memory location 6002. The first word of the list contains the list's length in words.

Sample Problems:

a. Input: ITEM — (6000) = 16B2
            LIST — (6002) = 00005000   List's address
                    (5000) = 0004   Length of list
                    (5002) = 5376
                    (5004) = 7618
                    (5006) = 138A
                    (5008) = 21DC
    Output: (5000) = 0005   Length of list
                      .
                      .
                      .
                    (500A) = 16B2

b. Input: ITEM — (6000) = 16B2
            LIST — (6002) = 00005000
                    (5000) = 0003
                    (5002) = 5376
                    (5004) = 16B2
                    (5006) = 7431
    Output: No change to list, since the item is already in the list at location 5004.

Flowchart 9-1a:

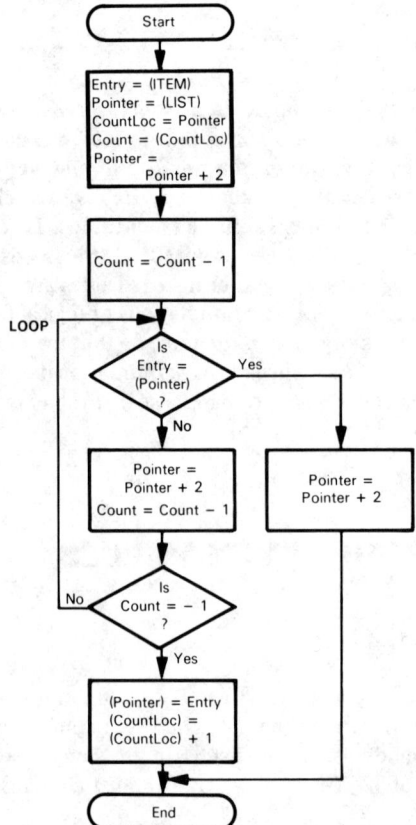

Program 9-1a:

```
          00006000      DATA      EQU       $6000
          00004000      PROGRAM   EQU       $4000

          00006000      ITEM      EQU       $6000           SEARCH ITEM
          00006002      LIST      EQU       $6002           POINTER TO START OF LIST

          00004000                ORG       PROGRAM
004000 30386000         PGM_9_1A  MOVE.W    ITEM,D0         GET SEARCH ITEM
004004 20786002                   MOVEA.L   LIST,A0         A0 - POINTER TO LIST
004008 2248                       MOVEA.L   A0,A1           SAVE POINTER TO LIST COUNT
00400A 3218                       MOVE.W    (A0)+,D1        D1.W - NUMBER OF ELEMENTS IN LIST
00400C 5341                       SUBQ.W    #1,D1           ADJUST FOR DBEQ

00400E B058             LOOP      CMP.W     (A0)+,D0        TEST NEXT ELEMENT FOR MATCH
004010 57C9FFFC                   DBEQ      D1,LOOP         CONTINUE UNTIL MATCH OR LIST END
004014 6704                       BEQ.S     DONE            IF MATCH THEN DONE

004016 3080                       MOVE.W    D0,(A0)         ...ELSE ADD ELEMENT TO LIST
004018 5251                       ADDQ.W    #1,(A1)         INCREMENT LIST COUNT

00401A 4E75             DONE      RTS
                                  END       PGM_9_1A
```

In this program, we use the autoincrement mode of addressing to access the list indirectly via register A0. When we move the length of the list to register D1, the pointer in A0 was also autoincremented so that it points to the first item in the list when LOOP is begun. When we exit from the loop due to no match being found, the pointer will have already been incremented to point to the location beyond the last item currently in the list; thus we don't have to adjust the pointer in order to add the new entry to the end of the list. You should compare this program to Program 5-4*b* to clarify those situations that require pointers to be adjusted and those that do not.

Clearly, the method of adding elements used in this program is very inefficient if the list is long. We could improve the procedure by limiting the search to part of the list or by ordering the list. We could limit the search by using the entry to get a starting point in the list. This method is called *hashing,* and is much like selecting a starting page in a dictionary or directory on the basis of the first letter in an entry.[1] We could order the list by numerical value. The search could end when the list values went beyond the entry (larger or smaller, depending on the ordering technique used). A new entry would have to be inserted properly, and all the other entries would have to be moved down in the list.

The program could be restructured to use two tables. One table could provide a starting point in the other table; for example, the search point could be based on the most or least significant 4-bit digit in the entry.

The program does not work if the length of the list is zero. (What happens?) We could avoid this problem by checking the length initially. The initialization procedure and other program changes required are shown in Program 9-1*b*.

Program 9-1b:

```
          00006000      DATA      EQU       $6000
          00004000      PROGRAM   EQU       $4000

          00006000      ITEM      EQU       $6000           SEARCH ITEM
          00006002      LIST      EQU       $6002           POINTER TO START OF LIST

          00004000                ORG       PROGRAM
```

150 68000 Assembly Language Programming

```
004000 30386000    PGM_9_1B MOVE.W   ITEM,D0        GET SEARCH OBJECT
004004 20786002             MOVEA.L  LIST,A0        A0 - POINTER TO LIST
004008 2248                 MOVEA.L  A0,A1          SAVE POINTER TO LIST COUNT
00400A 3218                 MOVE.W   (A0)+,D1       D1.W - NUMBER OF ELEMENTS IN LIST
00400C 670A                 BEQ.S    INSERT         IF LENGTH = 0 THEN INSERT ITEM

00400E 5341                 SUBQ.W   #1,D1          ADJUST FOR DBEQ

004010 B058       LOOP      CMP.W    (A0)+,D0       TEST NEXT ELEMENT FOR MATCH
004012 57C9FFFC             DBEQ     D1,LOOP        CONTINUE UNTIL MATCH OR LIST END
004016 6704                 BEQ.S    DONE           IF MATCH THEN DONE

004018 3080       INSERT    MOVE.W   D0,(A0)        ELSE ADD ELEMENT TO LIST
00401A 5251                 ADDQ.W   #1,(A1)        INCREMENT LIST COUNT

00401C 4E75       DONE      RTS
                            END      PGM_9_1B
```

If the length of the list is zero, it means that there are currently no elements in the list. Therefore, the element in ITEM cannot be in the list and must be inserted (as the first element of the list).

9-2. CHECK AN ORDERED LIST

Purpose: Check the contents of the word variable ITEM at memory location 6000 to see if it is in an ordered list. The list consists of 16-bit unsigned binary numbers in increasing order. The address of the first element in the list is in the variable LIST at location 6004. The first entry in the list is the list's length in words. If the contents of ITEM are in the list, place the index of its entry in the variable INDEX at 6002; otherwise, set INDEX to $FFFF_{16}$.

Sample Problems:

```
a.    Input:   ITEM —   (6000) = 5376
               LIST —   (6004) = 00005000
                        (5000) = 0004         List's length
                        (5002) = 138A
                        (5004) = 21DC
                        (5006) = 5376
                        (5008) = 8613
      Output:  INDEX —  (6002) = 0004, since the search item is at
                                        location 5006 = (5002+0004).
b.    Input:   ITEM —   (6000) = 46B2
               LIST —   (6004) = 00005000
                        (5000) = 0002
                        (5002) = 138A
                        (5004) = 71DC
      Output:  INDEX —  (6002) = FFFF, since the search item is
                                       not in the list.
```

Flowchart 9-2a:

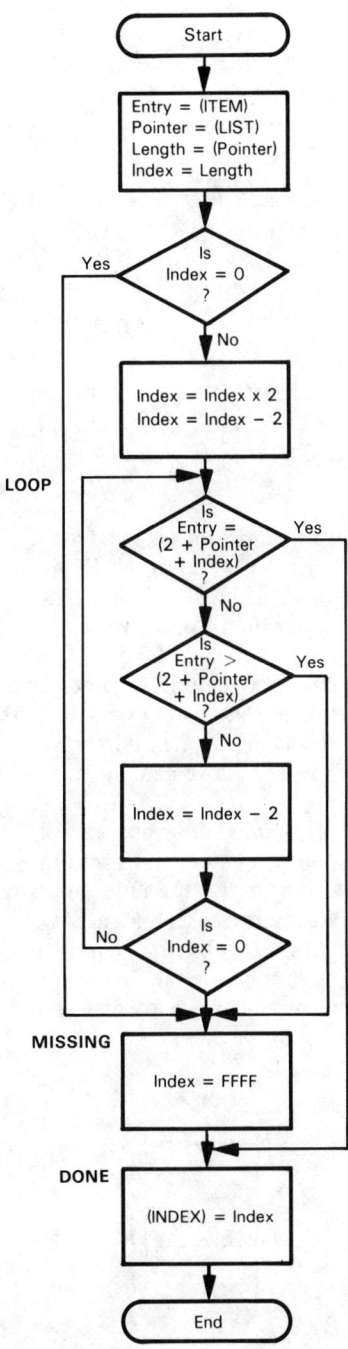

Program 9-2a:

```
           00006000       DATA     EQU      $6000
           00004000       PROGRAM  EQU      $4000

           00006000       ITEM     EQU      $6000
           00006002       INDEX    EQU      $6002
           00006004       LIST     EQU      $6004

           00004000                ORG      PROGRAM

004000 30386000  PGM_9_2A MOVE.W   ITEM,D0          GET SEARCH OBJECT
004004 20786004           MOVEA.L  LIST,A0          GET START ADDRESS OF LIST
004008 7200               MOVEQ    #0,D1            CLEAR THE ELEMENT COUNT
00400A 3210               MOVE.W   (A0),D1          GET THE ELEMENT COUNT
00400C 6710               BEQ.S    MISSING          IF LENGTH = 0,OBJECT IS NOT IN LIST

00400E D241               ADD.W    D1,D1            EACH ELEMENT CONSISTS OF TWO BYTES
004010 5541               SUBQ.W   #2,D1            INDEX RANGE = 0 - (LENGTH*2 - 2) !

004012 B0701002  LOOP     CMP.W    2(A0,D1.W),D0    SEARCH FROM END OF LIST TO START
004016 6708               BEQ.S    DONE             OBJECT IS IN LIST, D1 HOLDS INDEX
004018 6204               BHI.S    MISSING          LIST ELEM. SMALLER, OBJ NOT IN LIST
00401A 5541               SUBQ.W   #2,D1            INDEX FOR NEXT SMALLER ELEMENT
00401C 64F4               BCC      LOOP             INDEX >= 0 - CONTINUE

00401E 72FF     MISSING   MOVEQ    #$FF,D1          "NOT FOUND"-INDEX

004020 31C16002 DONE      MOVE.W   D1,INDEX         SAVE INDEX

004024 4E75               RTS

                          END      PGM_9_2A
```

The searching process of this program takes advantage of the fact that the elements are ordered. We begin the search with the last element in this list which will also be the largest. Once we find an element smaller than the entry, the search is over, since subsequent elements will be even smaller. You may want to try an example to convince yourself that the procedure works.

As in the previous problem, any method of choosing a good starting point will speed up the search. One such method starts in the middle of the list, determines which half of the list the entry is in, then divides the half into halves, and so on. This method is called a binary search since it divides the remaining part of the list into halves each time.[2,3]

Program 9-2a works if the length is zero since we test for zero length when forming the word index. Note the addressing mode used with the CMP.W instruction in the loop. This is a good example of how to use the indexed addressing with displacement mode. Address register A0 points to the "base" of a data structure, which in this case is an ordered list with the list's length being the first element in the list. The displacement is used to address a substructure, in this case the first number in the list. Register D1 is used as an index register to dynamically access the objects within the list. This addressing method can be illustrated as follows:

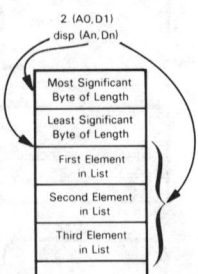

Tables and Lists **153**

Remember that the displacement is interpreted as a two's complement number: it is possible to have a negative displacement. The size of the displacement is eight bits, and since the displacement is sign-extended, this allows for displacements in the range -128 bytes to $+127$ bytes.

The effective address is calculated by adding the sign-extended displacement to the *32-bit* contents of the address register and the index register. The value in the index register is treated as a signed number. If you define the index register size to be word, as we have done in this program with D1, the value in the index register is sign-extended to 32 bits for the effective address calculation. The actual contents of the index register are not, however, affected by the address calculation.

Because the index register may contain a negative number, the final effective address may be before or after the base address in the address register.

Note that an unsigned comparison, BHI, is used in this program. In the sample problems, a comparison using GT will not work correctly since the last entry in the list, 8613, has its sign bit set. Unsigned compares are particularly useful when dealing with addresses, which are always unsigned.

The two branch instructions (BEQ.S and BHI.S) in this program can be replaced by a single branch instruction which will speed up execution of the loop. Program 9-2*b* is the resultant program:

Program 9-2b:

```
               00006000      DATA     EQU     $6000
               00004000      PROGRAM  EQU     $4000

               00006000      ITEM     EQU     $6000
               00006002      INDEX    EQU     $6002
               00006004      LIST     EQU     $6004

               00004000               ORG     PROGRAM
004000 30386000 PGM_9_2B MOVE.W   ITEM,D0          GET SEARCH OBJECT
004004 20786004          MOVEA.L  LIST,A0          GET START ADDRESS OF LIST
004008 7200              MOVEQ    #0,D1            CLEAR THE ELEMENT COUNT
00400A 3210              MOVE.W   (A0),D1          GET THE ELEMENT COUNT
00400C 6710              BEQ.S    MISSING          IF LENGTH = 0,OBJECT IS NOT IN LIST

00400E D241              ADD.W    D1,D1            EACH ELEMENT CONSISTS OF TWO BYTES
004010 5541              SUBQ.W   #2,D1            INDEX RANGE = 0 - (LENGTH*2 - 2) !

004012 B0701002 LOOP     CMP.W    2(A0,D1.W),D0    SEARCH FROM END OF LIST TO START
004016 6404              BCC.S    LPEXIT           DONE IF FOUND OR ITEM > LIST ELEM.
004018 5541              SUBQ.W   #2,D1            INDEX FOR NEXT SMALLER ELEMENT
00401A 64F6              BCC      LOOP             INDEX >= 0  - CONTINUE

00401C 6702     LPEXIT   BEQ.S    DONE             OBJECT IS IN LIST, D1 HOLDS INDEX

00401E 72FF     MISSING  MOVEQ    #$FF,D1          "NOT FOUND"-INDEX

004020 31C16002 DONE     MOVE.W   D1,INDEX         SAVE INDEX

004024 4E75              RTS

                         END      PGM_9_2B
```

In this program, the first branch instruction in the loop transfers control to LPEXIT if the entry is equal to or greater than the list element being compared. There is one dangerous aspect that has been introduced in this program, however. Take a look at the

154 68000 Assembly Language Programming

BEQ instruction at LPEXIT. There are two different ways in which the program can arrive at this instruction:

1. the BCC.S LPEXIT instruction in the loop can cause a branch to LPEXIT and in this case the status flags are set according to the result of the CMP.W instruction in the loop.
2. if all elements in the list have been tested without finding the entry item, then the loop is exhausted and the instruction immediately following BCC LOOP is executed. In this case, the status flags are set according to the results of the SUBQ instruction in the loop.

Thus, the BEQ instruction at LPEXIT tests the status flags that have been set by one of two possible instructions. You must be very careful to ensure that there are not conflicting conditions which will give you unexpected results and errors that are very difficult to find. The surest way to avoid errors is to make up a table to see what happens for all possible situations. Such a table for Program 9-2*b* would look like this:

		N	Z	V	C	
After CMP.W	item < (list)	?	0	?	1	These should cause exit from the loop. Use BCC to exit.
	item = (list)	0	1	0	0	
	item > (list)	?	0	?	0	
After SUBQ	D1 ≥ 0	?	?	?	0	This should cause loop to terminate. Use BCC to loop.
	D1 = −2	1	0	0	1	

As you can see from this table, the Z flag will always be 0 when the loop is exhausted. Thus, when the BEQ instruction at LPEXIT is executed following the BCC LOOP instruction, the branch to DONE will not be taken.

It is possible to speed up this program a bit more. Since the fastest loop in this case is the one that makes use of a CMP instruction with predecrement and the DBcc instruction, it may be worth the effort to write a program based on this construction. The changes required are shown in Program 9-2*c*.

Program 9-2c:

```
        00006000        DATA     EQU     $6000
        00004000        PROGRAM  EQU     $4000

        00006000        ITEM     EQU     $6000
        00006002        INDEX    EQU     $6002
        00006004        LIST     EQU     $6004

        00004000                 ORG     PROGRAM

004000  20786004       PGM_9_2C MOVEA.L LIST,A0         GET START ADDRESS OF LIST
004004  3210                    MOVE.W  (A0),D1         GET THE ELEMENT COUNT
004006  6718                    BEQ.S   MISSING         IF LENGTH = 0,OBJECT IS NOT IN LIST

004008  5341                    SUBQ.W  #1,D1           ADJUST FOR DBCC AND INDEX RANGE
00400A  3401                    MOVE.W  D1,D2           D2 IS THE LOOP COUNTER

00400C  D241                    ADD.W   D1,D1           EACH ELEMENT CONSISTS OF TWO BYTES
00400E  5441                    ADDQ.W  #2,D1           ADJUST FOR 1:ST PREDECREMENT IN LOP
004010  41F01002                LEA     2(A0,D1.W),A0   POINTER BEYOND END OF LIST

004014  30386000                MOVE.W  ITEM,D0         GET SEARCH OBJECT

004018  B060           LOOP     CMP.W   -(A0),D0        SEARCH FROM END OF LIST
00401A  54CAFFFC                DBCC    D2,LOOP         TEST NEXT IF ELEM>OBJ AND ELEM LEFT
00401E  6704                    BEQ.S   MATCHING        OBJECT IS IN LIST, D2 HAS INDEX
```

```
004020 74FF          MISSING MOVEQ   #$FF,D2         "NOT FOUND"-INDEX
004022 6002                  BRA.S   DONE

004024 D442          MATCHING ADD.W  D2,D2           ADJUST INDEX TO WORD SIZE
004026 31C26002      DONE    MOVE.W  D2,INDEX        SAVE IT

00402A 4E75                  RTS

                              END    PGM_9_2C
```

Flowchart 9-2c:

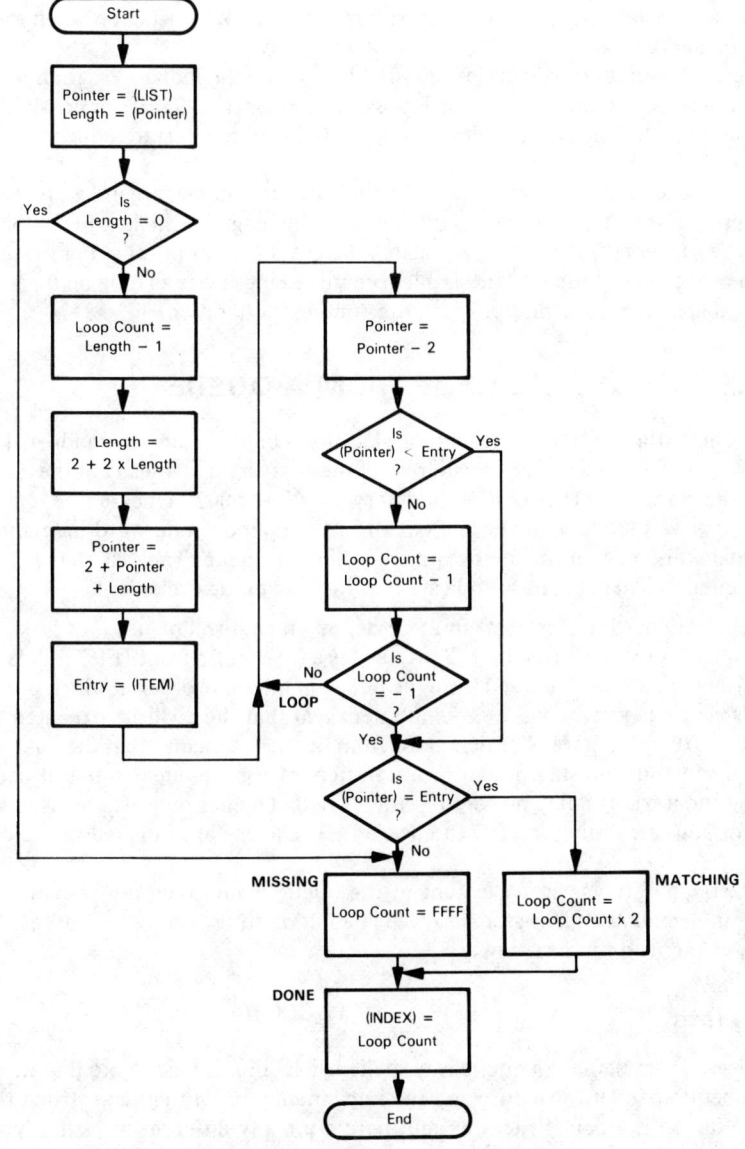

Besides changing the loop in the program, we have made some subtle changes to the initialization portion. First of all, note that we do not get the search object (entry) until we have first checked for length equal zero. There is no need to get the entry until we are sure that we have to perform a search.

The LEA instruction is used in this program to construct the address of the first element in the data structure in the same way as in Programs 9-2a and 9-2b, but in this case we form the starting address before we enter the loop.

Also note that Program 9-2c avoids the problem with the status flag that we discussed following Program 9-2b. Since the DBcc instruction does not affect the Condition codes, they are still set according to the result of the CMP.W instruction when the loop is exhausted and we can feel free to test in any way we want.

If you compare the clock cycles required to execute the loop in Program 9-2c you will see that it is more than twice as fast as the one in Program 9-2a. If it is possible that a loop may be executed many times, it is often worth the extra effort to reduce the execution time of the loop.

The average execution time of this simple search technique, regardless of which of the three programs you use, increases linearly with the length of the list. In comparison, the average execution time for a binary search increases logarithmically. For example, if the length of the list is doubled, the simple technique takes twice as long on the average while the binary search method only requires one extra iteration.

9-3. REMOVE AN ELEMENT FROM A QUEUE

Purpose: The variable QUEUE at memory location 6000 contains the address for the head of a queue. Save the address of the first element (head) of the queue in the variable POINTER at memory location 6002. Update the queue to remove the element. Each element in the queue is one word long and contains the address of the next element in the queue. The last element in the queue contains zero to indicate that there is no next element.

Queues are used to store data in the order in which it will be used, or tasks in the order in which they will be executed. The queue is a first-in, first-out (FIFO) data structure; that is, elements are removed from the queue in the same order in which they were entered. Operating systems place tasks in queues so that they will be executed in the proper order. I/O drivers transfer data to or from queues to ensure that the data will be transmitted or handled in the proper order. Buffers may be queued so that it becomes easy to find the next available buffer in a storage pool. Queues may also be used to link requests for storage, timing, or I/O to ensure that requests are satisfied in the correct order.

In real applications, each element in the queue would typically contain a large amount of information and/or storage space in addition to providing the address which links each element to the next one.

Linked Lists

One way to implement a queue is to make use of a linked list. Note that there is a difference between a data structure and the implementation of that data structure. For example, a queue is a data structure, and there are many different ways that you can implement a queue. However, the basic function of the queue (first-in, first-out) is always the same regardless of the way in which you implement this data structure.

The basic principle of a linked list is that each entry in the list contains the address to the next entry in the list, in addition to any data that may be found in a particular element. This can be illustrated as follows:

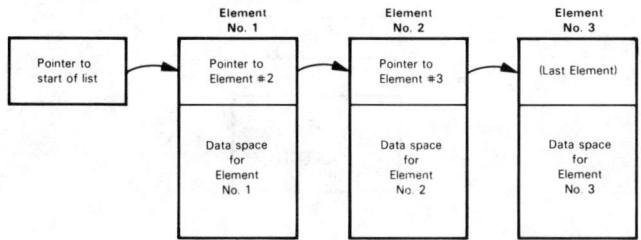

One advantage of this technique is that the elements in the list do not have to be stored sequentially in memory, since each entry contains the address pointing to the next entry. To change the order of two elements in a linked list, all you have to do is move the pointers — the data associated with each element need not be moved. Thus, to remove the first element in a queue we simply move a couple of pointers and the task is done; we don't have to move a single bit of data, just addresses. Linked lists require extra storage as compared to sequential lists, but elements are far easier to add, delete, or insert.

Sample Problems:

a.   Input: QUEUE — (6000) = 00006020   Address of first element in queue
                                  (6020) = 00006060   First element in queue
                                  (6060) = 000060A0
                                  (60A0) = 00000000   Last element in queue
    Output: QUEUE — (6000) = 00006060   Address of new first element in queue

             POINTER — (6004) = 00006020   Address of element removed from queue

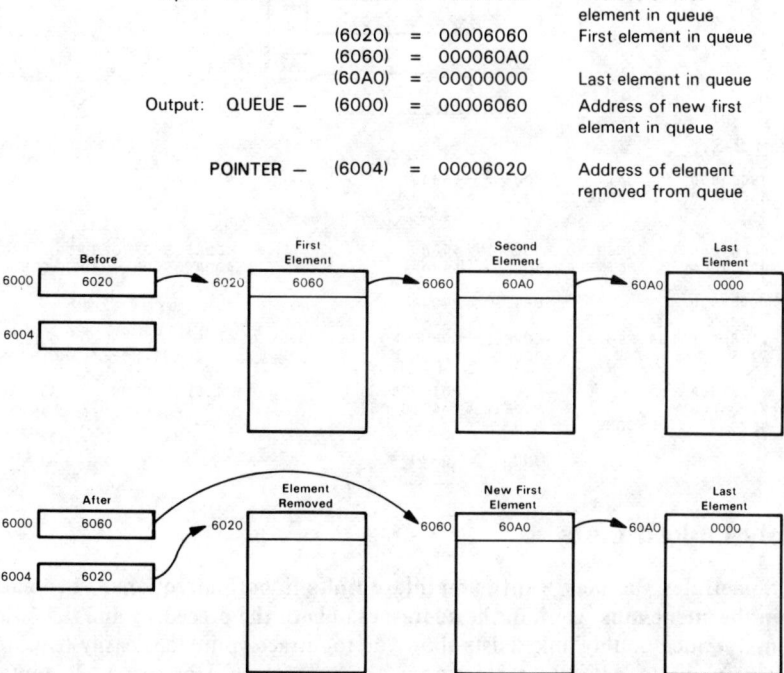

158 68000 Assembly Language Programming

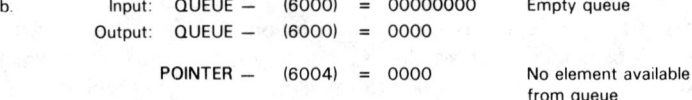
b. Input: QUEUE — (6000) = 00000000   Empty queue
    Output: QUEUE — (6000) = 0000
            POINTER — (6004) = 0000   No element available
                                         from queue

Flowchart 9-3:

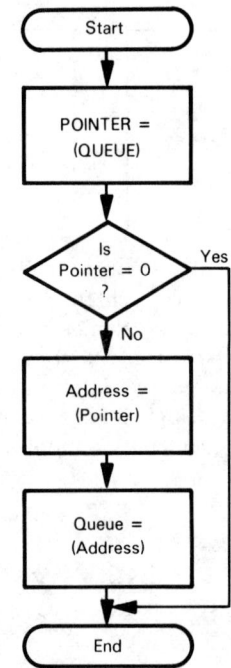

Program 9-3:

```
         00006000      DATA     EQU    $6000
         00004000      PROGRAM  EQU    $4000

         00006000      QUEUE    EQU    $6000              ADDRESS OF QUEUE HEAD
         00006004      POINTER  EQU    $6004              ADDRESS OF FORMER QUEUE HEAD

         00004000               ORG    PROGRAM

004000 21F860006004  PGM_9_3   MOVE.L  QUEUE,POINTER      SAVE OLD HEAD OF QUEUE
004006 6708                    BEQ.S   DONE               IF QUEUE EMPTY THEN DONE

004008 20786004                MOVE.L  POINTER,A0         ...ELSE REMOVE FIRST ELEMENT
00400C 21D06000                MOVE.L  (A0),QUEUE         AND REPLACE WITH SECOND
004010 4E75        DONE        RTS

                               END     PGM_9_3
```

Doubly Linked Lists

Sometimes you may want to maintain links in both directions. Then each element in the queue must contain the addresses of both the preceding and the following elements.[4,5] Such doubly linked lists allow you to retrace your steps easily (e.g., repeating the previous task if an error occurs in the current one) or access elements from either end (e.g., allowing you to remove or change the last two elements without having to go through the entire queue). **The data structure may then be used in either a first-in, first-out manner or in a last-in, first-out manner, depending on whether new elements are added to the head or to the tail.**

Empty Queue

If there are no elements in the queue, the program clears POINTER at location 6004. A program that requests an element from the queue must check this memory location to see if its request has been satisfied (i.e., if there was anything in the queue). Can you suggest other ways to indicate to the requesting program whether the queue is empty?

Another way of implementing a queue is as a list in sequential memory positions. The MC68000 architecture is well suited to manipulation of such queues. You can use any pair of address registers (A0 − A6) and the postincrement or predecrement mode of addressing to implement the queue. If the queue is to go from low to high memory, then the postincrement addressing mode is used, and if the queue goes from high to low memory, the predecrement mode would be used. For example, a queue going from low memory to high memory could be implemented using address registers A0 and A1 as shown in the following illustration:

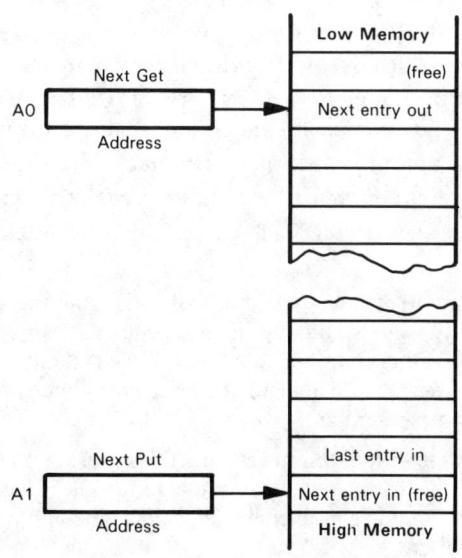

A0 points to the first or oldest entry in the queue while A1 points to the location where the next or newest entry in the queue will be made. If you use the postdecrement mode of addressing when accessing this queue, then A0 will always hold the next "get" address and register A1 will always hold the next "put" address for the queue.

Stack Operations

Another form of data structure similar to the queue is the stack: a stack is a last-in first-out (LIFO) list. Most microprocessors provide special push and pull instructions to manipulate stacks. In the MC68000, however, you can simply use the powerful MOVE instructions with predecrement or postincrement addressing to manipulate stacks.

You can implement a stack using a single address register in the predecrement or postincrement addressing mode. In fact, the processor itself uses address register A7 to maintain special system and user stacks. We will discuss the processor's use of these stacks further in Chapter 10.

Using Data Structures

The various indexed and indirect addressing modes allow us to use data structures in a very flexible way. If, for example, an address register contains the starting address of a block of information, we can refer to elements in the block with constant offsets.

How would we use such data structures? For example, we might want a piece of test equipment to execute a series of tests as specified by the operator. Using entries from a control panel, we will make up a queue of blocks of information, one for each test that the operator will eventually want to run. Each block of information contains:

1. The starting address of the next block (or 0 if there is no next block).
2. The starting address of the test program.
3. The address of the input device (e.g., keyboard, card reader, or communications line) from which data will be read during the test.
4. The address of the output device (e.g., printer, CRT terminal, or communications line) to which the results will be sent as the test is run.
5. The number of times the test will be repeated.
6. The starting address of the data area to be used for storing temporary data.
7. A flag that indicates whether failing a test should preclude continuing to the next test.

Clearly the block could contain even more information if there were more options for the operator to specify while setting up the test sequence. Note that some elements in the block contain data, others contain addresses, while still others may be 1-bit flags.

Consider what we mean by flexibility in this example. Some of the procedures that the operator can easily implement are:

1. Run the same test with different sets of I/O devices. A trial run might use data from a local keyboard and send the results to the CRT, while a production run might use data from a remote communications line and produce a permanent record on a printer.
2. Execute tests in any order, just by changing the order in the queue.
3. Place temporary data in an area where it can easily be displayed or retrieved by a debugging program.
4. Make alternative decisions as to whether tests should be continued, errors reported, or procedures repeated. Here again, trial or debugging runs may use one option, while production runs use another.

5. Delete or insert tests merely by changing the links which connect a test to its successor. The operator can thus correct errors or make changes without reentering the entire list of tests.

For example, assume that the operator enters the sequence TEST 1, TEST 2, TEST 4, and TEST 5, accidentally omitting TEST 3. The blocks are linked as follows:

Block 1 (for TEST 1) contains the starting address for block 2 (for TEST 2).

Block 2 (for TEST 2) contains the starting address for block 3 (for TEST 4).

Block 3 (for TEST 4) contains the starting address for block 4 (for TEST 5).

Block 4 (for TEST 5) contains a link address of zero to indicate that it is the last block.

To insert TEST 3 between TEST 2 and TEST 4 merely involves the following changes:

Block 2 (for TEST 2) must now contain the starting address for block 5 (for TEST 3).

Block 5 (for TEST 3) must contain the starting address for block 3 (for TEST 4).

No other changes are necessary and no blocks have to be moved. Note how much simpler it is to insert or delete using linked lists than to use lists that are stored in consecutive memory locations. There is no problem of moving elements up or down to remove or create empty spaces.

9-4. 8-BIT SORT

Purpose: Sort a list of unsigned binary 8-bit numbers into descending order. The address of the start of the list is in the variable LIST at memory location 6000. The first entry in the list is the number of remaining elements in the list — that is, the length of the list beyond this first entry. Thus, the list has 255 or fewer elements.

Sample Problem:

Input:	LIST —	(6000)	=	00005000	Address of beginning of list
		(5000)	=	06	Number of elements in list
		(5001)	=	2A	First element in list
		(5002)	=	B5	
		(5003)	=	60	
		(5004)	=	3F	
		(5005)	=	D1	
		(5006)	=	19	
Output:	LIST —	(6000)	=	00005000	
		(5000)	=	06	
		(5001)	=	D1	Largest element in list
		(5002)	=	B5	
		(5003)	=	60	
		(5004)	=	3F	
		(5005)	=	2A	
		(5006)	=	19	Smallest element in list

Simple Sorting Algorithm

A simple sorting technique works as follows:

Step 1. Clear a flag named EXCHANGE.

Step 2. Examine each consecutive pair of numbers in the list. If any are out of order, exchange them and set EXCHANGE.

Step 3. If EXCHANGE is set after the entire list has been examined, return to Step 1.

EXCHANGE will be set if any consecutive pair of numbers is found out of order. Therefore, if EXCHANGE is clear at the end of a pass through the entire list, the list is in proper order.

This sorting method is referred to as a "bubble sort." It is an easy algorithm to implement. However, it is slow; other sorting techniques should be considered when sorting long lists where speed is important.[6-8]

The technique operates as follows in a simple case. Let us assume that we want to sort a list into descending order; the list has four elements — 12, 03, 15, 08.

1st Iteration:

    Step 1. EXCHANGE = 0

    Step 2. Final order of the array is:
        12
        15
        08
        03
    since the second pair (03, 15) is exchanged and so is the third pair (03, 08).
    EXCHANGE = 1

2nd Iteration:

    Step 1. EXCHANGE = 0

    Step 2. Final order of the array is:
        15
        12
        08
        03
    since the first pair (12, 15) is exchanged.
    EXCHANGE = 1

3rd Iteration:

    Step 1. EXCHANGE = 0

    Step 2. The elements are already in order, so no exchanges are necessary and EXCHANGE remains 0.

This approach always requires one extra iteration to ensure that the elements are in the proper order. No exchanges are performed in the last iteration, so it does not really accomplish anything. **Tracing through the examples shows that many of the comparisons are wasted and even repetitive. Thus the method could be improved** greatly, particularly if the number of elements is in the thousands or millions, as it commonly is in large data processing applications. New sorting techniques are an important area of current research.[9]

Flowchart 9-4:

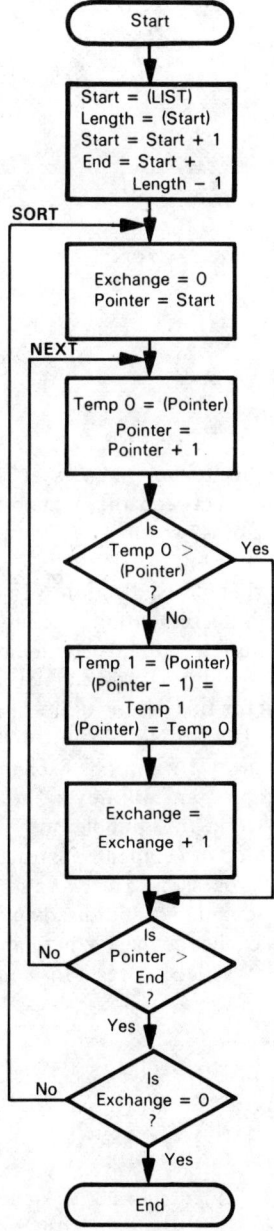

Program 9-4a:

```
               00006000    DATA       EQU       $6000
               00004000    PROGRAM    EQU       $4000

               00006000    LIST       EQU       $6000         ADDRESS TO START OF LIST

               00004000               ORG       PROGRAM

004000 20786000            PGM_9_4A   MOVEA.L   LIST,A0       POINTER TO START OF LIST
004004 4240                           CLR.W     D0
004006 1018                           MOVE.B    (A0)+,D0      LENGTH OF LIST
004008 43F000FF                       LEA       -1(A0,D0.W),A1 POINTER TO LAST LIST ELEMENT

00400C 4241     SORT                  CLR.W     D1            COUNTER FOR EXCHANGES
00400E 2448                           MOVEA.L   A0,A2         POINTER TO START OF LIST

004010 101A     NEXT                  MOVE.B    (A2)+,D0      GET NEXT ELEMENT
004012 B012                           CMP.B     (A2),D0       COMPARE IT WITH FOLLOWING ELEMENT
004014 640A                           BCC.S     NSWITCH       IF PREVIOUS ELEMENT >= THEN DO NEXT

004016 1212                           MOVE.B    (A2),D1       ...ELSE EXCHANGE ELEMENTS
004018 1541FFFF                       MOVE.B    D1,-1(A2)
00401C 1480                           MOVE.B    D0,(A2)
00401E 5241                           ADDQ.W    #1,D1         INCREMENT EXCHANGE COUNT

004020 B3CA     NSWITCH                CMPA.L   A2,A1         END OF LIST
004022 62EC                           BHI       NEXT          IF NOT THEN LOOK AT NEXT ELEMENT
004024 4A41                           TST.W     D1            EXCHANGE OCCURRED?
004026 66E4                           BNE       SORT          YES, CONTINUE SORT
004028 4E75                           RTS

                                      END       PGM_9_4A
```

The program must reduce the end pointer A1 by 1 because the last element has no successor. The final comparison is between the next to last element and the last element. Before starting each sorting pass, we must be careful to reinitialize the pointer and the Exchange flag.

Previous examples in this chapter used counters to control loops. In this example we compare addresses. This avoids decrementing a counter on each step. It is interesting to note what happens if there are fewer than two elements in the list. Although the results are not as tragic as they would be if we used counters, the results are incorrect nevertheless. Actually, checking for this case is quite simple. We simply insert BRA.S NSWITCH before the statement labeled NEXT.

Two equal elements in the array must not be exchanged; if they are, the exchange will occur on every pass and the program will never end.

There are many ways to code this bubble sort program using the MC68000 instruction set. The memory-to-memory compare instruction can be used to reduce the program's size and improve loop processing. This variation, as well as others, are shown in Program 9-4*b*. What are the advantages and disadvantages of using the bit operate instructions to set the program's exchange flag? What happens if you don't test for zero elements in the list? Remember that DBRA tests for counter value = −1.

Program 9-4b:

```
               00006000    DATA       EQU       $6000
               00004000    PROGRAM    EQU       $4000

               00006000    LIST       EQU       $6000         START OF LIST

               00004000               ORG       PROGRAM

004000 20786000            PGM_9_4B   MOVEA.L   LIST,A0       POINTER TO LIST LENGTH
004004 4280                           CLR.L     D0            CLEAR ALL 32 BITS OF D0
```

```
004006 1018              MOVE.B  (A0)+,D0        LENGTH OF LIST
004008 6724              BEQ.S   DONE            IF LENGTH = 0 THEN DONE
00400A 43E80001          LEA.L   1(A0),A1        POINTER TO SECOND ELEMENT
00400E 08810000          BCLR.B  #0,D1           EXCHANGE FLAG := 0
004012 5340              SUBQ.W  #1,D0           ADJUST COUNTER FOR DBCC INSTRUCTION
004014 600E              BRA.S   NSWITCH         CHECK FOR ONLY 1 ENTRY

004016 B308      NEXT    CMPM.B  (A0)+,(A1)+     COMPARE ADJACENT ENTRIES
004018 630A              BLS.S   NSWITCH         IF FIRST <= SECOND THEN NO SWITCH
00401A 1420              MOVE.B  -(A0),D2        EXCHANGE
00401C 10E1              MOVE.B  -(A1),(A0)+     ... ENTRIES
00401E 12C2              MOVE.B  D2,(A1)+
004020 08C10000          BSET.B  #0,D1           SET EXCHANGE FLAG

004024 51C8FFF0  NSWITCH DBRA    D0,NEXT         COMPARE ALL ENTRIES
004028 08010000          BTST.B  #0,D1           EXCHANGE FLAG SET?
00402C 66D2              BNE     PGM_9_4B        IF YES THEN REPEAT TESTING

00402E 4E75      DONE    RTS

                         END     PGM_9_4B
```

There have been entire books written on sorting and searching, so a discussion of sorting methods would be beyond our scope. However, there is one variation that should be considered. At the end of every step, we know that the smallest element is at the end of the list. Therefore the number of pairs we need to compare decreases by one each step. (Try a few examples to convince yourself this is true. Do you see how the method gets its name?) What changes to the program would take advantage of this?

9-5. USING AN ORDERED JUMP TABLE

Purpose: Use the contents of the variable INDEX at location 6000 as an index to a jump table starting at TABLE (location 6002). Each entry in the jump table contains a 16-bit address. The program should transfer control to the address with the appropriate index; that is, if the index is 6, the program jumps to address entry number 6 in the table. (Note that we start counting with entry number 0, the zeroth element in the table.)

Sample Problem:

```
        INDEX —   (6000)  = 0002
        TABLE —   (6002)  = 4740    Zeroth element in jump table
                  (6004)  = 47A6
                  (6006)  = 47D0
                  (6008)  = 4620
                  (600A)  = 4854    Fourth element in jump table
```

Result: (PC) = 0047D0 since that is entry number 2 (starting from zero) in the jump table. The next instruction to be executed will be the one located at that address.

Flowchart 9-5:

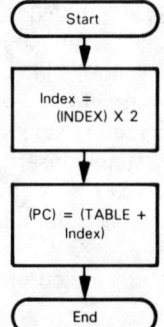

The last box in the flowchart results in a transfer of control to the address obtained from the table. No ending block is necessary. Such transfers do not bother the processor at all, but you may want to add special notes to your flowchart and program documentation so that the sequence does not appear to be a "dead-end street" to the reader.

Program 9-5a:

```
         00006000      DATA    EQU     $6000
         00004000      PROGRAM EQU     $4000

         00006000      INDEX   EQU     $6000           INDEX INTO TABLE
         00006002      TABLE   EQU     $6002           START OF TABLE

         00004000              ORG     PROGRAM
004000 30786000       PGM_9_5A MOVEA.W INDEX,A0        GET TABLE INDEX
004004 D0C8                    ADDA.W  A0,A0           ADJUST INDEX FOR WORD OFFSET
004006 32686002                MOVEA.W TABLE(A0),A1    GET ADDRESS FROM TABLE
00400A 4ED1                    JMP     (A1)            TRANSFER TO ADDRESS
                               END     PGM_9_5A
```

When you run this program, be sure to place some executable code (such as a TRAP instruction) at each address to which control could be transferred. Otherwise the processor will be executing random code and you will have no way to tell which branch was taken.

Jump Tables

Jump tables are very useful in situations where the processor must select one of several routines for execution. Such situations arise in decoding commands (entered, for example, from a control keyboard), selecting test programs, choosing alternative methods or units, or selecting an I/O configuration. For example, a four-position switch on the front of an instrument or test system may select among the remote, self-test, automatic, or manual modes of operation. The processor reads the switch and selects the appropriate routine from a jump table. References 10 and 11 contain additional examples of the use of jump tables.

The jump table thus replaces a whole series of compare and jump operations. The program is compact, efficient and easily changed or extended.

The index into the jump table must be multiplied by 2 to give the correct word offset since each entry in the table is a 16-bit address occupying two bytes of memory. This assumes that the addresses in the table are short absolute references. What else does the program assume in regard to the length of the jump table?

If addresses in the table could reference anywhere in the processor's 16-megabyte address space, then each entry would require at least three bytes. By using entries of five bytes, this case could be handled by simply inserting an additional ADDA instruction and modifying the MOVE.W TABLE(A0),A1 to a MOVE.L instruction. However, you will encounter difficulties if you try to place the jump table in 9-5a at addresses greater than 7FFF. Why?

Program 9-5*b* illustrates another method of implementing the jump table using indexed addressing.

Program 9-5b:

```
         00006000     DATA       EQU    $6000
         00004000     PROGRAM    EQU    $4000

         00006000     INDEX      EQU    $6000           INDEX INTO JUMP TABLE
         00006002     TABLE      EQU    $6002           START OF JUMP TABLE

         00004000                ORG    PROGRAM
004000   207C00006002 PGM_9_5B   MOVEA.L #TABLE,A0      GET TABLE ADDRESS
004006   30386000                MOVE.W  INDEX,D0       GET TABLE INDEX
00400A   E540                    ASL.W   #2,D0          ADJUST FOR 4 BYTE ENTRY
00400C   22700000                MOVEA.L 0(A0,D0.W),A1  GET ADDRESS FROM JUMP TABLE
004010   4ED1                    JMP     (A1)

                                 END     PGM_9_5B
```

In both of these programs, the instruction JMP (A1) is an indirect jump which transfers the contents of register A1 to the program counter. This instruction sometimes causes confusion because of the "level of indirection." To clarify this, compare the action of JMP (A1) with MOVEA (A1),A0. In the case of JMP (A1), the program counter receives the value held in A1. In the MOVEA (A1),A0 instruction, A0 receives the value pointed to by A1.

This is an apparent inconsistency in the assembly language syntax. It can be resolved by reading the instruction JMP (A1) as:

"Jump to the location pointed to by A1."

What would happen if we had replaced the last two instructions in Program 9-5*a* with JMP TABLE(A0)?

How could you modify Program 9-5*b* to accept the address of the table in the variable TABLE, instead of the beginning of the table itself?

PROBLEMS

9-1. REMOVE ENTRY FROM LIST

Purpose: Remove the value in the variable ITEM at memory location 6000 from a list if the value is present. The address of the list is in the variable LIST at location 6002. The first entry in the list is the number (in words) of elements remaining in the list. Move entries below the one removed up one position and reduce the length of the list by 1.

Sample Problems:

a. Input: ITEM — (6000) = D010   Entry to be removed
          LIST — (6002) = 00005000 Address of list
                 (5000) = 0004   Length of list
                 (5002) = C121   First element in list
                 (5004) = A346
                 (5006) = 3A64
                 (5008) = 6C20

Result: No change to list since the entry is not in the list.

b. Input: ITEM — (6000) = D010   Entry to be removed
           LIST —   (6002) = 00005000 Address of list
                    (5000) = 0004   Length of list
                    (5002) = C121   First element in list
                    (5004) = D010
                    (5006) = 3A64
                    (5008) = 6C20

    Result: (5000) = 0003   Length of list reduced by 1
                    (5002) = C121
                    (5004) = 3A64   Other elements in list
                    (5006) = 6C20   moved up one position

9-2. ADD ENTRY TO ORDERED LIST

Purpose: Insert the value in the variable ITEM at location 6000 into an ordered list if it is not already there. The address of the list is in the variable LIST at location 6002. The first entry in the list is the list's length in words. The list itself consists of unsigned binary numbers in increasing order. Place the new entry in the correct position in the list, adjust the elements below it down, and increase the length of the list by 1.

Sample Problems:

a. Input: ITEM — (6000) = 7010   Entry to be added to list
           LIST —   (6002) = 00005000 Address of list
                    (5000) = 0004   Length of list
                    (5002) = 0037   First element in list
                    (5004) = 5322
                    (5006) = A101
                    (5008) = C203

    Result: (5000) = 005   Length of list increased
                    (5002) = 0037   by 1
                    (5004) = 5322
                    (5006) = 7010   New entry
                    (5008) = A101   Other elements moved
                    (500A) = C203   down one position

b. Input: ITEM — (6000) = 7010   Entry to be added to list
           LIST —   (6002) = 00005000 Address of list
                    (5000) = 0004   Length of list
                    (5002) = 0037   First element in list
                    (5004) = 5322
                    (5006) = 7010
                    (5008) = C203

    Result: No change in the list since entry is already in the list.

9-3. ADD ELEMENT TO QUEUE

Purpose: Add the value in the variable ITEM at memory location 6000 to a queue. The address of the first element in the queue is in the variable QUEUE at location 6002. Each element in the queue contains either the address of the next element in the queue or zero if there is no next element. The new element is placed at the end (tail) of the queue; the new element's address will be in the element that *was* at the end of the queue. The new element will contain zero to indicate that it is now the end of the queue.

Sample Problem:

```
Input:   ITEM —    (6000)  =  000060A0
         QUEUE —   (6002)  =  00006020    Pointer to head of queue
                   (6020)  =  00006030
                   (6030)  =  0000        Last element in queue

Result:  QUEUE —   (6002)  =  00006020
                   (6020)  =  00006030
                   (6030)  =  000060A0    Old last element points
                                          to new last element
                   (60A0)  =  0000        New last element
```

How would you add an element to the queue if memory location 6006 contained the address of the tail of the queue (the last element)? Remember to update this end-of-queue pointer.

9-4. 4-BYTE SORT

Purpose: Sort a list of 4-byte entries into descending order. The first three bytes in each entry are an unsigned key with the first byte being the most significant. The fourth byte is additional information and should not be used to determine the sort order, but should be moved along with its key. The number of entries in the list is defined by the word variable LENGTH at location 6000. The list itself begins at location 6002 (LIST).

Sample Problem:

```
Input:   LENGTH —  (6000)  =  0004    4 entries in list
         LIST —    (6002)  =  41      Beginning of first entry key
                   (6003)  =  42
                   (6004)  =  43      End of first entry key
                   (6005)  =  07      First entry additional
                                      information

                   (6006)  =  4A      Beginning of second entry
                   (6007)  =  4B
                   (6008)  =  4C
                   (6009)  =  13

                   (600A)  =  4A      Beginning of third entry
                   (600B)  =  4B
                   (600C)  =  41
                   (600D)  =  37

                   (600E)  =  44      Beginning of fourth entry
                   (600F)  =  4B
                   (6010)  =  41
                   (6011)  =  3F

Result:  LIST —    (6002)  =  4A
                   (6003)  =  4B
                   (6004)  =  4C
                   (6005)  =  13      End of first entry
                   (6006)  =  4A
                   (6007)  =  4B
                   (6008)  =  41
                   (6009)  =  37      End of second entry
                   (600A)  =  44
                   (600B)  =  4B
                   (600C)  =  41
                   (600D)  =  3F      End of third entry
                   (600E)  =  41
                   (600F)  =  42
                   (6010)  =  43
                   (6011)  =  07      End of last entry
```

The data in the unsorted entries are 'ABC',$07; 'JKL',$13; 'JKA',$37; 'DKA',$3F.

9-5. USING A JUMP TABLE WITH A KEY

Purpose: Use the value in the variable INDEX at memory location 6000 as a key to a jump table (TABLE) starting at location 6002. Each entry in the jump table contains a 16-bit identifier followed by a 32-bit address to which the program should transfer control if the key is equal to that identifier.

Sample Problem:

```
Input:  INDEX — (6000) = 4142
        TABLE — (6002) = 4348       First key
                (6004) = 00004900   First transfer address
                (6008) = 4142       Second entry
                (600A) = 00004940
                (600E) = 4558       Third entry
                (6010) = 00004A20

Result: (PC) — 004940 since that address corresponds to
               key value 4142.
```

REFERENCES

1. J. Hemenway and E. Teja. "EDN Software Tutorial: Hash Coding," *EDN,* September 20, 1979, pp. 108-10.
2. D. Knuth. *The Art of Computer Programming, Volume III: Searching and Sorting.* Reading, Mass.: Addison-Wesley, 1978.
3. D. Knuth. "Algorithms," *Scientific American,* April 1977, pp. 63-80.
4. K. J. Thurber and P. C. Patton. *Data Structures and Computer Architecture.* Lexington Mass.: Lexington Books, 1977.
5. J. Hemenway and E. Teja. "Data Structures — Part 1," *EDN,* March 5, 1979, pp. 89-92; "Data Structures — Part 2," *EDN,* May 5, 1979, pp. 113-16.
6. See Reference 2.
7. B. W. Kernighan and P. J. Plauger. *The Elements of Programming Style.* New York: McGraw-Hill, 1978.
8. K. A. Schember and J. R. Rumsey. "Minimal Storage Sorting and Searching Techniques for RAM Applications," *Computer,* June 1977, pp. 92-100.
9. "Sorting 30 Times Faster with DPS," *Datamation,* February 1978, pp. 200-03.
10. L. A. Leventhal. "Cut Your Processor's Computation Time," *Electronic Design,* August 16, 1977, pp. 82-89.
11. J. B. Peatman. *Microcomputer-Based Design.* New York: McGraw-Hill, 1977, Chapter 7.

III
Advanced Topics

The following chapters discuss more advanced areas of assembly language programming. Chapters 10 and 11 deal with subroutines, an important aspect of all levels of programming. Chapter 12 describes some of the advanced features found on the MC68020. In Chapter 13, we cover many basic principles of connecting the MC68000 to peripherals. Chapters 14 and 15 describe interrupts and exception processing; Chapter 14 provides an overview of all family members, while Chapter 15 concentrates on the MC68000.

10
Parameter Passing Techniques

None of the examples that we have shown thus far is a typical program that would stand by itself. Most real programs perform a series of tasks, many of which may be used a number of times or be common to other programs.

SUBROUTINES

The standard method of producing programs which can be used in this manner is to write subroutines that perform particular tasks. The resulting sequences of instructions can be written once, tested once, and then used repeatedly.

In order to be really useful, a subroutine must be general. For example, a subroutine that can perform only a specialized task, such as looking for a particular letter in an input string of fixed length, will not be very useful. If, on the other hand, the subroutine can look for any letter, in strings of any length, it will be far more helpful.

In order to provide subroutines with this flexibility, it is necessary to provide them with the ability to receive various kinds of information. We call data or addresses that we provide the subroutine *parameters*. An important part of writing subroutines is providing for transferring the parameters to the subroutine. This process is called Parameter Passing.

GENERAL PARAMETER PASSING TECHNIQUES

There are three general approaches to passing parameters:

1. Place the parameters in registers.
2. Place the parameters immediately after the subroutine call in program memory.
3. Transfer the parameters and results on the hardware stack.

The registers often provide a fast, convenient way of passing parameters and returning results. The limitations of this method are that it cannot be expanded beyond the number of available registers; it often results in unforeseen side effects; and it lacks generality.

The trade-off here is between fast execution time and a more general approach. Such a trade-off is common in computer applications at all levels. General approaches are easy to learn and consistent; they can be automated through the use of macros. On the other hand, approaches that take advantage of the specific features of a particular task require less time and memory. The choice of one approach over the other depends on your application, but you should take the general approach (saving programming time and simplifying documentation and maintenance) unless time or memory constraints force you to do otherwise.

Passing Parameters In Registers

The first and simplest method of passing parameters to a subroutine is via the registers. After calling a subroutine, the calling program can load memory addresses, counters, and other data into registers. For example, suppose a subroutine operates on two data buffers of equal length. The subroutine might specify that the length of the two data buffers be in the register D0 while the two data buffer beginning addresses are in the registers A0 and A1. The calling program would then call the subroutine as follows:

```
        MOVE.W   #BUFL,D0         LENGTH OF BUFFER IN D0
        MOVEA.L  BUFA,A0          BUFFER A BEGINNING ADDRESS IN A0
        MOVEA.L  BUFB,A1          BUFFER B BEGINNING ADDRESS IN A1
        JSR      SUBR             CALL SUBROUTINE
```

Using this method of parameter passing, the subroutine can simply assume that the parameters are there. Results can also be returned in registers, or the addresses of locations for results can be passed as parameters via the registers. Of course, this technique is limited by the number of registers available. Such MC68000 features as register indirect addressing, indexed addressing, the ability to use any address register as a stack pointer, and the LEA instruction provide far more powerful and more general ways of passing parameters.

Passing Parameters In Program Memory

Parameters that are to be passed to a subroutine can also be placed directly after the subroutine call. The subroutine must then modify the return address at the top of the stack in addition to fetching the parameters. Using this technique, our example would be modified as follows:

```
        JSR     SUBR
        DC.W    BUFL            BUFFER LENGTH
        DC.L    BUFA            BUFFER A STARTING ADDRESS
        DC.L    BUFB            BUFFER B STARTING ADDRESS
```

The subroutine saves prior contents of CPU registers, then loads parameters and adjusts the return address as follows:

```
SUBR    MOVEM.L D0/A0-A2,-(A7)  SUBROUTINE USES D0,A0,A1,A2
        MOVEA.L 16(A7),A2       RETURN ADDRESS POINTS TO BUFL
        MOVE.W  (A2)+,D0        BUFL TO D0
        MOVEA.L (A2)+,A0        BUFA TO A0
        MOVEA.L (A2)+,A1        BUFB TO A1
        MOVEA.L A2,16(A7)       ADJUST RETURN ADDRESS
```

The constant 16 is to adjust for the change in A7 when the four registers D0, A0, A1, and A2 are saved on the stack.

This parameter passing technique has the advantage of being easy to read. It has, however, the disadvantage of requiring parameters to be fixed when the program is written. A modification which allows parameters to vary uses an address pointer following the subroutine call. The pointer addresses an area of data memory where the parameters are actually found. This may be illustrated as follows:

```
        JSR     SUBR
        DC.L    PLIST           BEGINNING ADDRESS OF PARAMETERS
PLIST   DC.W    BUFL
        DC.L    BUFA
        DC.L    BUFB

SUBR    MOVEM.L D0/A0-A2,-(A7)  SUBROUTINE USES D0,A0,A1,A2
        MOVEA.L 16(A7),A1       RETURN ADDRESS POINTS TO PLIST
        MOVEA.L (A1)+,A2        GET ADDRESS OF PARAMETER LIST
        MOVEA.L A1,16(A7)       ... AND UPDATE RETURN ADDRESS
        MOVE.L  (A2)+,D0        BUFL IN D0
        MOVE.L  (A2)+,A0        BUFA IN A0
        MOVEA.L (A2)+,A1        BUFB IN A1
```

Parameters held in a separate area of memory are frequently referred to as a "parameter block." In the illustration above, we stored the beginning address for a three word parameter block after the JSR. The address of the parameter block could also be passed to the subroutine as follows:

```
        MOVE.L  #PLIST,-(A7)    PUSH ADDRESS OF PARAMETER BLOCK
        JSR     SUBR
```

The subroutine would fetch parameters as follows:

```
SUBR    MOVEM.L D0/A0-A2,-(A7)  SUBROUTINE USES D0,A0,A1,A2
        MOVEA.L 20(A7),A2       GET PARAMETER ADDRESS
        MOVE.W  (A2)+,D0        BUFL IN D0
        MOVEA.L (A2)+,A0        BUFA IN A0
        MOVEA.L (A2)+,A1        BUFB IN A1
```

No adjustment of the stack pointer is required when this method is used.

Results can be returned by storing them in the same parameter block, or addresses for storing results can also be passed as parameters.

Passing Parameters On The Stack

Another common method of passing parameters to a subroutine is to push the parameters onto the stack. Using this parameter passing technique, the subroutine call illustrated above would occur as follows:

```
        MOVE.W   #BUFL,-(A7)     PUSH BUFFER LENGTH
        MOVEA.L  BUFA,-(A7)      PUSH TWO BUFFER STARTING ADDRESSES
        MOVEA.L  BUFB,-(A7)      ... ONTO STACK
        JSR      SUBR
```

The subroutine must begin by loading parameters into CPU registers as follows:

```
SUBR    MOVEM.L  D0/A0/A1,-(A7)  SAVE PRIOR REGISTER CONTENTS
        MOVEA.L  12(A7),A1       BUFFER B STARTING ADDRESS IN A1
        MOVEA.L  16(A7),A0       BUFFER A STARTING ADDRESS IN A0
        MOVE.W   20(A7),D0       BUFFER LENGTH IN D0
```

In this approach, all parameters are passed and results are returned on the stack.

The MC68000 stack grows downward (toward lower addresses). This occurs because elements are pushed onto the stack using the predecrement address mode. The use of the predecrement mode causes the stack pointer to always contain the address of the last occupied location, rather than the next empty one as on some other microprocessors, such as the 6800. This implies that you must initialize the stack pointer to a value higher than the largest address in the stack area.

When passing parameters on the stack, the programmer must implement this approach as follows:

1. Decrement the system stack pointer to make room for parameters on the system stack, and store them using offsets from the stack pointer; or simply push the parameters on the stack.
2. Access the parameters by means of offsets from the system stack pointer, remembering that JSR places the return address at the top of the stack.
3. Store the results on the stack by means of offsets from the systems stack pointer.
4. Clean up the stack before or after returning from the subroutine, so that the parameters are removed and the results are handled appropriately.

TYPES OF PARAMETERS

Regardless of our approach to passing parameters, we can specify the parameters in a variety of ways. For example, we can:

1. Place the actual values in the parameter list. This method is sometimes referred to as call-by-value, since only the values of the parameters are of concern.
2. Place the addresses of the parameters in the parameter list. This method is sometimes referred to as call-by-name, since we are concerned with the locations of the parameters as well as their values.

11
Subroutines

Most microprocessors have special instructions for transferring control to subroutines and restoring control to the main program. We often refer to the special instruction that transfers control to a subroutine as Call, Jump-to-Subroutine, Jump-and-Mark Place, or Jump-and-Link. The special instruction that restores control to the main program is usually called Return.

On the MC68000 microprocessor, the Jump-to-Subroutine (JSR) or Branch-to-Subroutine (BSR) instructions save the old value of the program counter on the stack before placing the starting address of the subroutine in the program counter; the Return-from-Subroutine (RTS) instruction gets the old value from the stack and puts it back in the program counter. The effect is to transfer program control, first to the subroutine and then back to the main program. Clearly, the subroutine may itself transfer control to a subroutine, and so on.

TYPES OF SUBROUTINES

Sometimes a subroutine must have special characteristics. **A subroutine is relocatable if it can be placed anywhere in memory.** You can use such a subroutine easily, regardless of other programs or the arrangement of the memory. **A relocating loader is necessary to place the program in memory properly; the loader will start the program after other programs and will add the starting address or relocation constant to all addresses in the program. Position independent code does not require a relocating loader — all program addresses are expressed relative to the program counter's current value. Data addresses are held in registers at all times.** We will discuss the writing of position independent code later in this chapter.

A subroutine is reentrant if it can be interrupted and called by the interrupting program and still give the correct results for both the interrupting and interrupted

programs. Reentrancy is important for standard subroutines in an interrupt-based system. Otherwise the interrupt service routines cannot use the standard subroutines without causing errors. Microprocessor subroutines are easy to make reentrant since the Call instruction uses the stack and use of the stack is automatically reentrant. The only remaining requirement is that the subroutine use only the registers and the stack rather than fixed memory locations for temporary storage.

A subroutine is recursive if it calls itself. Such a subroutine clearly must also be reentrant.

SUBROUTINE DOCUMENTATION

Most programs consist of a main program and several subroutines. This is advantageous because you can use proven routines when available and you can debug and test the other subroutines properly and remember their exact effects on registers and memory locations.

Subroutine listings must provide enough information that users need not examine the subroutine's internal structure. Among necessary specifications are:

- A description of the purpose of the subroutine
- A list of input and output parameters
- Registers and memory locations used
- A sample case, perhaps including a sample calling sequence

The subroutine will be easy to use if you follow these guidelines.

PROGRAM EXAMPLES

Examples in this chapter assume that the stack and stack pointer have already been initialized. Instructions that load an address into the stack pointer or clear the stack prior to use are not shown. If you wish to establish your own stack area, remember to save any prior stack pointer and to restore it in order to produce a proper return at the end of your program. Since the MC68000 allows any address register to be used as a stack pointer, it is better to use a stack for your needs and not change the system stack pointer (A7).

The MC68000 has no special instructions to load or save the current stack value. Instead you use the MOVEA instruction to alter the stack register as shown in the following program.

```
          00006000      DATA      EQU     $6000
          00004000      PROGRAM   EQU     $4000

          00006000      PSTACK    EQU     DATA
          00008000      STACK     EQU     $8000

          00004600      MAIN      EQU     $4600

          00004000                ORG     PROGRAM
004000 21CF6000                   MOVEA.L A7,PSTACK            SAVE PRIOR STACK
```

```
004004 2E7C00008000        MOVEA.L  #STACK,A7        SET UP OUR STACK
00400A 4EB84600            JSR      MAIN
00400E 2E785000            MOVEA.L  PSTACK,A7        RESTORE PRIOR STACK

004012 4E75                RTS
                           END
```

The program illustrated above saves the prior stack pointer, sets up the main program's stack pointer, and then calls the main program. The stack base for the main program is then 8000. When the main program has completed execution, it can execute an RTS to transfer control to the setup routine, which restores the prior stack pointer and then returns control to the prior program.

11-1. CONVERTING HEXADECIMAL TO ASCII

Purpose: Convert the contents of data register D0 from a hexadecimal digit to an ASCII character. Assume that the original contents of data register D0 are less than 16.

Sample Problems:

```
a.      Input:   D0   =  0C
        Result:  D0   =  43   'C'
b.      Input:   D0   =  06
        Result:  D0   =  36   '6'
```

The JSR instruction saves the program counter (the address of the instruction following the JSR) on the system stack and then places the subroutine starting address in the program counter. The procedure is:

Step 1. Decrement the stack pointer by 4.
Step 2. Save the program counter in the top word of the stack.
Step 3. Place the subroutine start address in the program counter.

For program 11-1, the following occurs as a result of executing the JSR instruction:

```
Before JSR
PC = 004604
A7 = 7FFC

After executing the JSR
PC      = 00460E
A7      = 7FF8
(7FF8)  = 00004608
```

The stack pointer is always adjusted by four since all addresses are stored on the stack as 32-bit values, even if the return addresses can be referenced with short absolute addressing. Since the processor has fetched the entire JSR instruction, the program counter has been incremented to address the instruction following the JSR. This is the address that is saved as a 32-bit value on the stack.

The JSR instruction is similar to the JMP instruction except that JSR "remembers" where it came from. In this regard, the JSR instruction can call any-

180 68000 Assembly Language Programming

where in memory. Like the JMP and its related instruction BRA, JSR has a relationship with the BSR instruction. BSR, like JSR, is used to call a subroutine and place the return address on the stack. However, the addressing modes of BSR are similar to the BRA instruction in that only instructions within an 8-bit or 16-bit displacement may be referenced by BSR.

The RTS instruction reverses the process:

Step 1. Place the value on the top of the stack in the program counter.

Step 2. Increment the stack pointer by 4.

For 11-1 the RTS instruction then causes the following to occur:

```
           Before RTS
                         PC    = 00461A
                         A7    = 7FF8
                      (7FF8)   = 00004608
```

Flowchart 11-1:

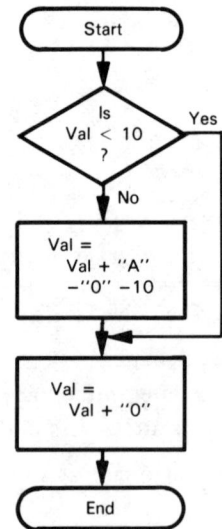

The calling program gets the data from the variable HDIGIT at memory location 6000, calls the conversion subroutine, and stores the result in the variable ACHAR at memory location 6001.

Program 11-1:

```
              00006000       DATA      EQU    $6000
              00004600       PROGRAM   EQU    $4600

              00006000                 ORG    DATA

006000 00000001              HDIGIT    DS.B   1              HEX DIGIT TO BE CONVERTED
006001 00000001              ACHAR     DS.B   1              CONVERTED ASCII CHARACTER

              00004600                 ORG    PROGRAM
```

```
004600 10386000         MAIN      MOVE.B  HDIGIT,D0          GET DATA: RANGE IS 00 - 0F
004604 4EB8460E                   JSR     HEXDIGIT           CONVERT TO ASCII CHARACTER
004608 11C06001                   MOVE.B  D0,ACHAR
00460C 4E75                       RTS

                                * SUBROUTINE HEXDIGIT
                                *
                                * PURPOSE: HEXDIGIT CONVERTS A HEXADECIMAL DIGIT TO AN ASCII CHARACTER
                                *
                                * INITIAL CONDITIONS:    D0.B CONTAINS VALUE IN RANGE 00 - 0F
                                *
                                * FINAL CONDITIONS:      D0.B CONTAINS AN ASCII CHARACTER IN THE
                                *                        RANGE '0'-'9' OR 'A' - 'F'
                                *
                                * REGISTERS CHANGED:     D0 ONLY
                                *
                                * SAMPLE CASE:           INITIAL CONDITIONS: D0.B = 6
                                *                        FINAL CONDITIONS:   D0.B = 36 ('6')
                                *
00460E 0C00000A         HEXDIGIT  CMP.B   #$0A,D0            DECIMAL DIGIT OR HEX LETTER?
004612 6D02                       BLT.S   ADDZ               IF DIGIT GOTO ADDZ
004614 5E00                       ADD.B   #'A'-'0'-$0A,D0    OFFSET FOR LETTERS
004616 06000030         ADDZ      ADD.B   #'0',D0            CONVERT TO ASCII

00461A 4E75                       RTS
                                  END     HEXDIGIT
```

After executing RTS
PC = 004608
A7 = 7FFC

The MC68000 always increments the stack pointer after pulling data from the stack, so the procedure is the same as in the postincrement addressing mode. RTS balances the JSR or BSR. The action of the RTS instruction, however, is simply to take the top four bytes in the stack and place them in the program counter. The programmer must be certain that these four bytes contain a legitimate return address — the processor does not examine them.

This subroutine has a single parameter and produces a single result. A data register is the obvious place to put both the parameter and the result.

The calling program consists of three steps:

- Placing the data into the data register.
- Calling the subroutine.
- Storing the result.

The overall initialization program must also load the stack pointer with the appropriate address.

This program is reentrant since it uses no data memory, and it is relocatable since the address ADDZ is referenced relative to the program counter. Using BSR (Branch to Subroutine) instead of JSR (Jump to Subroutine) would make the calling program relocatable as well.

The JSR instruction results in the execution of four or five instructions, taking either 44 or 48 clock cycles. A subroutine call may take a long time even though it appears to be only a single instruction in the program. Calling a routine always involves some overhead, since both the JSR and the BSR instructions take time. In fact, a JSR takes 10 clock cycles longer than the corresponding JMP (with the same addressing mode) because JSR must save the current program counter in the stack. RTS takes 16 clock cycles.

11-2. HEX WORD TO ASCII STRING

Purpose: Convert the value in the variable NUMBER at memory location 6000 to four ASCII hex digits in the four-byte array STRING starting at memory location 6002. Perform the task using a subroutine with the hex value and the string address as parameters.

Sample Problem:

```
        Input:    NUMBER    (6000) = 4CD0
        Results:  STRING    (6002) = 34    '4'
                            (6003) = 43    'C'
                            (6004) = 44    'D'
                            (6005) = 30    '0'
```

Program 11-2:

```
        00006000        DATA     EQU     $6000
        00004600        PROGRAM  EQU     $4600

        00006000                 ORG     DATA
006000  00000002        NUMBER   DS.W    1              NUMBER TO BE CONVERTED TO ASCII HEX
006002  00000004        STRING   DS.B    4              CHARACTER STRING FOR ASCII HEX DIGI

        00004600                 ORG     PROGRAM
004600  2F3C00006002    MAIN     MOVE.L  #STRING,-(A7)  PUSH ADDRESS OF STRING ON STACK
004606  3F386000                 MOVE.W  NUMBER,-(A7)   PUSH 16 BIT NUMBER TO BE CONVERTED
00460A  4EB84610                 JSR     BINHEX         BINARY TO ASCII/HEX

00460E  4E75                     RTS

                        *  SUBROUTINE BINHEX
                        *
                        *  PURPOSE: CONVERT A 16 BIT VALUE TO 4 ASCII HEX DIGITS
                        *
                        *  INITIAL CONDITIONS:   THE FIRST PARAMETER ON THE STACK IS THE
                        *                        VALUE; THE SECOND PARAMETER IS THE
                        *                        ADDRESS OF THE STRING TO BE BUILT
                        *
                        *  FINAL CONDITIONS:     THE HEX STRING OCCUPIES 4 SUCCESSIVE
                        *                        BYTES BEGINNING WITH THE ADDRESS PASSED
                        *                        AS THE SECOND PARAMETER
                        *
                        *  REGISTER USAGE:       NO REGISTERS ARE AFFECTED
                        *
                        *  SAMPLE CASE:          INITIAL CONDITIONS: 4CD0 AT TOP OF STACK,
                        *                                            THEN 00006002
                        *                        FINAL CONDITIONS:   THE STRING '4CD0' IN ASCII
                        *                                            OCCUPIES MEMORY 6002-5

004610  48E7E080        BINHEX   MOVEM.L D0-D2/A0,-(A7)  SAVE REGISTERS USED IN BINHEX
004614  7203                     MOVEQ   #3,D1           LOOP COUNTER:= 4-1
004616  342F0014                 MOVE.W  16+4(A7),D2     GET VALUE
00461A  206F0016                 MOVEA.L 16+6(A7),A0     GET STRING ADDRESS
00461E  D1FC00000004             ADDA.L  #4,A0           ADJUST POINTER PAST END OF STRING

004624  1002            LOOP     MOVE.B  D2,D0
004626  0200000F                 ANDI.B  #$0F,D0         GET LOW NIBBLE
00462A  4EB84646                 JSR     HEXDIGIT        CONVERT TO ASCII CHARCTER
00462E  1100                     MOVE.B  D0,-(A0)        SAVE ASCII DIGIT
004630  E84A                     LSR.W   #4,D2           SHIFT D2 TO GET NEXT NIBBLE
004632  51C9FFF0                 DBRA    D1,LOOP         REPEAT FOR ALL 4 DIGITS

004636  4CDF0107                 MOVEM.L (A7)+,D0-D2/A0  RESTORE INITIAL REGISTER VALUES
00463A  2F570006                 MOVE.L  (A7),6(A7)      MOVE RETURN ADDRESS DOWN
00463E  DFFC00000006             ADDA.L  #6,A7           ADJUST STACK POINTER TO RETURN ADDR
```

```
004644  4E75                    RTS


004646  0C00000A    HEXDIGIT CMP.B   #$0A,D0          DECIMAL DIGIT OR HEX LETTER ?
00464A  6D02                 BLT.S   ADDZ             IF DIGIT GOTO ADDZ
00464C  5E00                 ADD.B   #'A'-'0'-$0A,D0  OFFSET FOR LETTERS
00464E  06000030    ADDZ     ADD.B   #'0',D0          CONVERT TO ASCII

004652  4E75                 RTS

                             END     BINHEX
```

This program demonstrates another method of passing parameters. Instead of passing the two parameters in registers, the parameters are passed on the stack. Therefore, upon entry to the subroutine, the stack would look like this:

Address Parameter	(32 bits)
Hex Digit Parameter	(16 bits)
Return Address	(32 bits) System Stack Pointer (A7)

The system stack pointer (A7) usually operates like any other register. However, since all word and long word references must be aligned on a word boundary, the MC68000 takes special precautions to ensure proper alignment. Thus, **all data pushed or pulled from the system stack is word-aligned — even byte data.** In the case of byte data, the data is stored in the high-order (most significant) byte of the word, the lower order (least significant) byte is left unchanged.

Unlike our first subroutine example, BINHEX modifies the contents of data and address registers other than those which are used to pass subroutine results. In some cases, the unexpected modification of registers by a subroutine may cause unpredictable results in the calling program. **It is good programming practice to define which registers are being affected by the execution of the subroutine.** This has been done for subroutine BINHEX in its introductory description block.

A common practice used to prevent any inadvertent effects due to modification of the registers is to save all registers used in a subroutine and to restore them upon subroutine exit. **The Move Multiple (MOVEM) instruction provides an efficient means of saving or restoring registers. Whenever two or more index registers (address or data register) are to be saved or restored, it is always more memory-efficient to use MOVEM.** In terms of execution performance, it is *generally* better to use MOVEM when saving two or more index registers and when restoring three or more. The order in which index registers are transferred via MOVEM is dependent upon the effective address mode. If the effective address is the postincrement mode, the registers are stored starting with data register 0 through data register 7, then address register 0 to address register 7. If the effective address is the predecrement mode, the registers are loaded in the reverse order starting with address register 7. Therefore, after the execution of the first MOVEM instruction in BINHEX, the system stack will be as follows:

Address Parameter	(32 bits)
Hex Digit Parameter	(16 bits)
Return Address	(32 bits)
A0	(32 bits)
D2	(32 bits)
D1	(32 bits)
D0 (32 bits)	System Stack Pointer (A7)

The parameters are not passed in registers; they must be retrieved from the system stack. We must take care in retrieving the parameters from the stack, because other elements have been pushed onto the stack. The MOVEM instruction pushed 16 bytes onto the stack while JSR pushed the 4-byte return address (0000460E in our example). The MOVE.W 16+4(A7),A0 is used to load A0 with the 32-bit string address. The order of these two instructions makes no difference since the system stack register is not affected.

Both these MOVE instructions are examples of address register indirect with displacement addressing. This addressing mode is similar to the program counter with displacement mode used by the branch instruction, but it has two main differences. First, an address register is used instead of the program counter. And second, only a 16-bit displacement is allowed although it is still sign-extended. In program 11-2 the system stack pointer contains $7FFC upon MAIN entry. Thus the address referenced in the first MOVE is:

```
(A7) + 16 + 4
= $7FE2 + 16 + 4
= $7FF6 (the address of the digit value)
```

Prior to returning control back to program MAIN, the system stack must be restored. First, the saved registers are pulled by MOVEM (A7)+,D0-D2/A0. At this point we could return to MAIN by using an RTS instruction since the return address is on top of the system stack. However, this would leave the parameters still on the stack and the calling program would have to adjust the stack. This adjustment would have to be performed after each subroutine call to BINHEX. Instead, the system stack is adjusted in BINHEX by the instruction sequence:

```
MOVE.L (A7),6(A7)
ADDA 06,A7
```

Using the memory-to-memory move capability, the return address is stored at the system stack entry previously occupied by the address parameter. The system stack is then modified to point to this new return address entry. The same results could be obtained faster by substituting the instruction LEA 6(A7),A7 for the ADDA instruction. A picture of the stack before and after the MOVE and ADDA instructions is:

```
Before:
(A7) → 7FF2 — 0000460E (return address)
       7FF6 — 4CD0 (value parameter)
       7FF8 — 00006002 (address parameter)
After:
       7FF2 — 0000460E
       7FF6 — 4CD0
(A7) → 7FF8 — 0000460E (return address)
```

If results were to be returned on the stack, a different adjustment would be made.

This subroutine is both reentrant and position-independent since it uses no fixed memory addresses and only relative branches.

The BSR and JSR instructions allow the nesting of subroutines, since subsequent subroutine calls will place their return addresses further down the stack. No addresses are ever lost and the RTS instruction always returns control to the instruction just after the most recent BSR and JSR.

Subroutines **185**

11-3. 64 BIT ADDITION

Purpose: Add two 64-bit (4-word) values and return the results in data registers D0 and D1. D0 shall contain the most significant word of the result.

Sample Problem:

	Input:	Value 1	—	$0420147AEB529CB8
		Value 2	—	$3020EB8520473118
	Result:	D0	—	34410000
		D1	—	0B99CDD0

Program 11-3a:

```
        00006000        DATA      EQU     $6000
        00004600        PROGRAM   EQU     $4600

        00006000                  ORG     DATA

        00004600                  ORG     PROGRAM

004600  4EB84616        MAIN      JSR     ADD64               64 BIT ADDITION
004604  00000001                  DC.L    $1,$12345678        FIRST PARAMETER
00460C  00000001                  DC.L    $1,$12345           SECOND PARAMETER
004614  4E75                      RTS

                        *  SUBROUTINE ADD64
                        *
                        *  PURPOSE              ADD TWO 64 BIT VALUES
                        *
                        *  INITIAL CONDITIONS:  THE TWO PARAMETER VALUES ARE PASSED
                        *                       IMMEDIATELY FOLLOWING THE SUBROUTINE CALL
                        *
                        *  FINAL CONDITIONS:    THE SUM OF THE TWO 64 BIT PARAMETERS
                        *                       IS RETURNED IN D0.L AND D1.L. THE EXTEND
                        *                       CONDITION CODE = 1 IF OVERFLOW, ELSE = 0
                        *
                        *  REGISTER USAGE       NO REGISTERS ARE AFFECTED EXCEPT D0 AND D1
                        *
                        *  SAMPLE CASE          INITIAL CONDITIONS: 1ST PARAMETER = $112345678
                        *                                           2ND PARAMETER = $100012345
                        *                       FINAL CONDITIONS    D0.L = $00000002
                        *                                           D1.L = $123579BD
                        *                                           CC.X = 0
                        *
                        *

004616  48E73080        ADD64     MOVEM.L D2-D3/A0,-(A7)      SAVE D2,D3 AND A0
00461A  206F000C                  MOVEA.L 12(A7),A0           A0 - ADDRESS OF FIRST PARAMETER
00461E  4CD8000F                  MOVEM.L (A0)+,D0-D3         D0-D1 = FIRST VALUE, D2-D3 = SECOND

004622  D283                      ADD.L   D3,D1               ADD LEAST SIGNIFICANT WORD
004624  D182                      ADDX.L  D2,D0               ADD MOST SIGNIFICANT 16 BIT WITH EX

004626  4CDF010C                  MOVEM.L (A7)+,D2-D3/A0      RESTORE D2,D3 AND A0
00462A  40E7                      MOVE.W  SR,-(A7)            SAVE EXTEND FLAG
00462C  06AF00000010
        0002                      ADDI.L  #16,2(A7)           ADJUST RETURN ADDRESS
004634  4E77                      RTR     .                   RETURN AND RESTORE EXTEND FLAG

                                  END     ADD64
```

In Program 11-3a the parameters for the subroutine ADD64 are passed immediately following the subroutine call. Upon entry to ADD64, the address of this parameter block may be found on top of the system stack, since it is the return address for the JSR instruction. The MOVEA.L instruction loads address register A0 with this parameter block address. The displacement of 12 in this instruction is necessary because of the three 32-bit registers pushed onto the system stack.

The actual addition process is quite simple and was demonstrated in Chapter 8. Prior to returning to the calling program, MAIN, the return address must be adjusted since it points to the address following the JSR. An adjustment of 16 bytes is necessary to jump around the two 8-byte parameters. This adjustment is performed via the ADDI instruction on the return address without first having to move it into a register. The system stack (before and after the ADDI instruction) is pictured as follows:

Before:
    (A7) (7FF6) = Status Register (16 bits)
           (7FF8) = 4604

After:
    (A7) (7FF6) = Status Register
           (7FF8) = 4614

After the addition to adjust the stack pointer, the status register is pushed onto the stack in order to preserve the condition codes. This allows the calling program to test for overflow or carry as a result of the 64-bit addition. Such a test would normally be performed by a "branch conditional" instruction following the JSR or the JSR parameter list. In this instance the condition codes had to be saved since their state could have been changed by the ADDI. To accomplish this the MC68000 provides a special return instruction: RTR (return and restore condition codes). RTR pulls *both* the condition codes and the return address from the stack. The supervisor portion of the status register is not affected by this instruction. The RTR instruction can be extremely useful when error conditions from subroutines are indicated by the condition codes.

Generally you may assume that a subroutine call changes the condition codes unless it is specifically stated otherwise. If the main program needed the old condition codes (for checking later), it could have saved them on the system stack using MOVE SR,−(A7) before calling the subroutine. It would then be able to restore them afterwards using MOVE (A7)+,CCR.

This program lacks some generality since the values associated with the parameters are passed following the call. For example, if the program were placed in read-only memory the parameters could not be modified. To overcome this problem, the addresses of the parameters could have been passed instead of their values.

Program 11-3b shows how we might modify the program to pass addresses instead of values.

Program 11-3b:

```
               00006000    DATA      EQU    $6000
               00004600    PROGRAM   EQU    $4600

               00006000              ORG    DATA

006000 00000008  VALUE1    DS.L   2            FIRST 64-BIT VALUE
006008 00000008  VALUE2    DS.L   2            SECOND 64-BIT VALUE

               00004600              ORG    PROGRAM

004600 4EB8460E  MAIN      JSR    ADD64        64 BIT ADDITION
004604 00006000            DC.L   VALUE1       ADDRESS OF FIRST PARAMETER
004608 00006008            DC.L   VALUE2       ADDRESS OF SECOND PARAMETER
00460C 4E75                RTS
```

```
*  SUBROUTINE ADD64
*
*  PURPOSE:              ADD TWO 64 BIT VALUES
*
*  INITIAL CONDITIONS    THE TWO PARAMETERVALUES ARE PASSED
*                        IMMEDIATELY FOLLOWING THE SUBROUTINE CALL
*
*  FINAL CONDITIONS      THE SUM OF THE TWO 64 BIT PARAMETERS
*                        IS RETURNED IN D0.L AND D1.L. THE EXTEND
*                        CONDITION CODE = 1 IF OVERFLOW, ELSE = 0
*
*  REGISTER USAGE:       NO REGISTERS ARE AFFECTED EXCEPT D0 AND D1
*
*  SAMPLE CASE:          INITIAL CONDITIONS: 1ST PARAMETER = $00006000
*                                            2ND PARAMETER = $00006004
*                                            ($6000) = $0420147AEB529CB8
*                                            ($6004) = $3020EB8520473118
*
*                        FINAL CONDITIONS:   D0.L = $34410000
*                                            D1.L = $0B99CDD0
*                                            CC.X = 0
*
```

```
00460E  48E730C0  ADD64   MOVEM.L  D2-D3/A0-A1,-(A7)   SAVE D2,D3,A0 AND A1
004612  206F0010          MOVEA.L  16(A7),A0           A0 - ADDRESS OF PARAMETER BLOCK

004616  2258              MOVEA.L  (A0)+,A1            A1 - FIRST PARAMETER ADDRESS
004618  20290000          MOVE.L   0(A1),D0            MOST SIGNIFICANT WORD OF FIRST VALUE
00461C  22290004          MOVE.L   4(A1),D1            .. AND LEAST SIGNIFICANT

004620  2258              MOVEA.L  (A0)+,A1            A1 - SECOND PARAMETER ADDRESS
004622  24290000          MOVE.L   0(A1),D2            MOST SIGNIFICANT WORD OF SECOND VALUE
004626  26290004          MOVE.L   4(A1),D3            ... AND LEAST SIGNIFICANT

00462A  2F480010          MOVEA.L  A0,16(A7)           UPDATE RETURN ADDRESS
00462E  D283              ADD.L    D3,D1               ADD LEAST SIGNIFICANT WORD
004630  D182              ADDX.L   D2,D0               ADD MOST SIGNIFICANT WORD

004632  4CDF030C          MOVEM.L  (A7)+,D2-D3/A0-A1   RESTORE USED REGISTERS

004636  4E75              RTS
                          END      ADD64
```

The initial instructions in 11-3*b* are essentially the same as those found in 11-3*a*. However, once the address of the parameter block is determined (MOVE.L 16(A7),A0), another instruction must be performed to obtain the parameter values:

```
MOVEA.L  (A0)+,A1     Get address of parameter
MOVE.L   0(A1),D0     Get value
MOVE.L   4(A1),D1     ...of parameter
```

The use of the predecrement mode in fetching the parameter addresses also aids in updating the return address. After the two MOVE.L (A0)+,A1 instructions, A0 contains the correct return address which is used to modify the return address on the system stack: (MOVEA.L A0,16(A7)). This means of updating the return address eliminates the ADDI instruction and therefore the need to push the condition codes onto the system stack.

11-4. FACTORIAL OF A NUMBER

Purpose: Determine the factorial of the number in the variable NUMB at memory location 6000. Store the result in the variable FNUMB at memory location 6002. Assume the number is less than nine but greater than zero.

188 68000 Assembly Language Programming

Sample Problems:

a.   Input: NUMB–(6000)   =   0002

      Result: FNUMB–(6002)   =   0002

b.   Input: NUMB–(6000)   =   0005

      Result: FNUMB–(6002)   = $0078(120_{10})$

Flowchart:

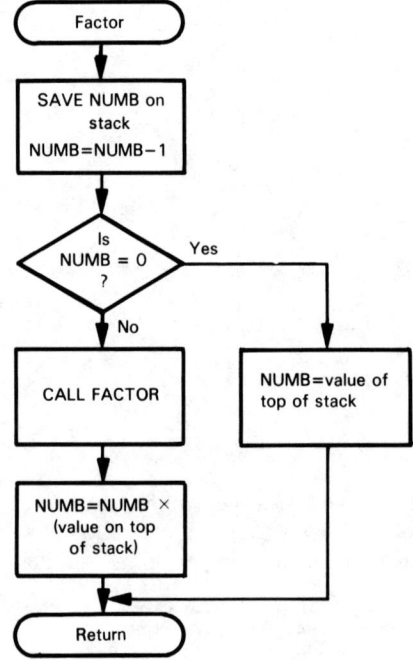

Program 11-4a:

```
          00006000      DATA      EQU       $6000
          00004600      PROGRAM   EQU       $4600

          00006000                ORG       DATA

006000 00000002         NUMB      DS.W      1              NUMBER
006002 00000002         F_NUMB    DS.W      1              FACTORIAL OF NUMBER

          00004600                ORG       PROGRAM

004600 30386000         MAIN      MOVE.W    NUMB,D0        GET NUMBER
004604 6106                       BSR.S     FACTOR         FIND FACTORIAL
004606 31C06002                   MOVE.W    D0,F_NUMB      STORE FACTORIAL

00460A 4E75                       RTS
```

```
* SUBROUTINE FACTOR
* PURPOSE:              DETERMINE THE FACTORIAL OF A GIVEN NUMBER
*
* INITIAL CONDITIONS: D0.W = NUMBER WHOSE FACTORIAL IS TO BE
*                     DETERMINED. D0.W > 0 AND < 9
*
* FINAL CONDITIONS:   D0.W = FACTORIAL OF INPUT NUMBER
*
* REGISTER USAGE:     NO REGISTERS EXCEPT D0 AFFECTED
*
* SAMPLE CASE:        INITIAL CONDITIONS: D0.W = 5
*                     FINAL CONDITIONS  : D0.W = 120
*
00460C 3F00       FACTOR   MOVE.W  D0,-(A7)      PUSH CURRENT NUMBER TO STACK
00460E 5340                SUBQ.W  #1,D0         DECREMENT NUMBER
004610 6604                BNE.S   F_CONT        NOT END OF FACTORIAL PROCESS

004612 301F                MOVE.W  (A7)+,D0      FACTORIAL:= 1
004614 6004                BRA.S   RETURN

004616 61F4       F_CONT   BSR     FACTOR
004618 C0DF                MULU    (A7)+,D0      FACTORIAL: = N * (N-1)

00461A 4E75       RETURN   RTS

                           END     FACTOR
```

This subroutine is reentrant since it does not use any fixed data storage area. Instead, all temporary data is allocated space on the stack. In addition, this subroutine is recursive because it invokes itself via the BSR FACTOR instruction.

Recursive subroutines are a special case of subroutine nesting. Like any other subroutine call using a BSR or JSR instruction, the return address is placed on top of the stack. In this case, the processor does not care if identical return addresses appear at the top of the stack.

Subroutine FACTOR is a simple example of a recursive routine because it is easy to see that FACTOR calls itself. However, a subroutine can still be recursive if a routine it calls eventually invokes the calling subroutine. For example, FACTOR would still be recursive if:

```
        F CONT:    BSR FACTOR
                   MULU (A7)+,D0
```

were replaced with:

```
        F CONT:    BSR MULTIPLY
```

where MULTIPLY was a subroutine like:

```
        MULTIPLY:  BSR FACTOR
                   MULU (A7)+,D0
                   RTS
```

Like any subroutine which uses the stack for temporary storage, FACTOR *must* ensure that no data is left on the stack prior to the execution of return. Both the MOVE.W (A7)+,D0 and MULU (A7)+,D0 instructions ensure that the stack is properly restored.

In many instances, you may not be sure of the exact state of the stack prior to return. This could be especially true if you practice good programming techniques and use only one exit or return statement per program (as in subroutine FACTOR). More important, the execution of a subroutine frequently will not save temporary data on

the stack in an orderly manner. For these reasons, the MC68000 has implemented the LINK and UNLK instructions.

Subroutine FACTOR has been rewritten in Program 11-4b using LINK and UNLK. With the aid of the LINK instruction, we are able to dynamically reserve up to 32,768 bytes of storage on the stack, as well as set up a pointer to the top of the reserved area. In addition, the LINK instruction saves the current value of the pointer.

Program 11-4b:

```
                00006000    DATA    EQU     $6000
                00004600    PROGRAM EQU     $4600

                00006000            ORG     DATA

006000 00000002 NUMB        DS.W    1                       NUMBER
006002 00000002 F_NUMB      DS.W    1                       FACTORIAL OF NUMBER

                00004600            ORG     PROGRAM

004600 30386000 MAIN        MOVE.W  NUMB,D0                 GET NUMBER
004604 6106                 BSR.S   FACTOR                  FIND FACTORIAL
004606 31C06002             MOVE.W  D0,F_NUMB               STORE FACTORIAL

00460A 4E75                 RTS

                * SUBROUTINE FACTOR
                * PURPOSE:            DETERMINE THE FACTORIAL OF A GIVEN NUMBER
                *
                * INITIAL CONDITIONS: D0.W = NUMBER WHOSE FACTORIAL IS TO BE
                *                     DETERMINED. D0.W > 0 AND < 9
                *
                * FINAL CONDITIONS:   D0.W = FACTORIAL OF INPUT NUMBER
                *
                * REGISTER USAGE:     NO REGISTERS EXCEPT D0 AFFECTED
                *
                * SAMPLE CASE:        INITIAL CONDITIONS: D0.W = 5
                *                     FINAL CONDITIONS  : D0.W = 120
                *

00460C 4E50FFFE FACTOR      LINK    A0,#-2                  ALLOCATE TEMPORARY STACK STORAGE
004610 3140FFFE             MOVE.W  D0,-2(A0)               SAVE NUMBER
004614 5340                 SUBQ.W  #1,D0                   DECREMENT NUMBER
004616 6604                 BNE.S   F_CONT                  NOT END OF FACTORIAL PROCESS

004618 7001                 MOVEQ   #1,D0                   FACTORIAL := 1
00461A 6006                 BRA.S   RETURN                  RETURN TO CALLING ROUTINE

00461C 61EE    F_CONT       BSR     FACTOR                  CONTINUE FACTORIAL PROCESS
00461E C0E8FFFE             MULU    -2(A0),D0               FACTORIAL:= N * (N-1)

004622 4E58    RETURN       UNLK    A0                      FREE TEMPORARY STORAGE

004624 4E75                 RTS

                             END    FACTOR
```

In Program 11-4b, the instruction LINK A0,-2 has the following effect:

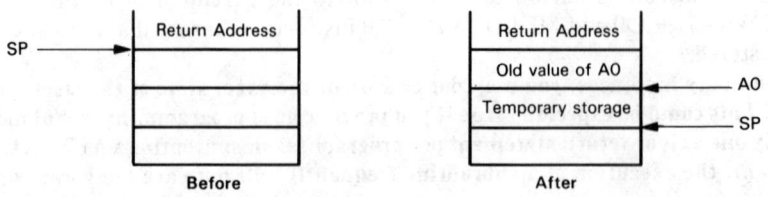

The UNLK instruction reverses the results of the LINK instruction, thus restoring the stack and address registers.

When using these two instructions, remember that the displacement for data storage is a negative displacement, since the stack expands toward low address memory. Offsets to the pointer register should also be negative, since the address register points to the top of the temporary data area.

PROBLEMS

Write both a calling program for the sample problem and at least one properly documented subroutine for each problem.

11-1. ASCII Hex to Binary

Purpose: Convert the least significant eight bits in data register D0 from the ASCII representation of a hexadecimal digit to the 4-bit binary representation of the digit. Place the result back into D0.

Sample Problems:

a.	Input:	D0	=	43	'C'
	Result:	D0	=	0C	
b.	Input:	D0	=	36	'6'
	Result:	D0	=	06	

11-2. ASCII Hex String to Binary Word

Purpose: Convert the four ASCII characters in the variable STRING starting in memory location 6002 into a 16-bit binary value. Store the value in the variable VALUE at memory location 6000. Write a subroutine that takes the string address from the stack and returns the value on the stack.

Sample Problem:

Input:	STRING –	(6002)	=	42	'B'
		(6003)	=	32	'1'
		(6004)	=	46	'F'
		(6005)	=	30	'0'
Result:	VALUE –	(6000)	=	B1F0	

11-3. Test for Alphabetic Character

Purpose: If the ASCII character in the variable CHAR at memory location 6000 is an alphabetic (upper- or lower-case), set the variable FLAG at memory location 6001 to FF_{16}; otherwise set FLAG to 0. Write a subroutine that finds its parameter in a register and returns its result using the condition code flags.

Sample Problems:

a.	Input:	CHAR – (6000)	=	47 'G'
	Results:			
		FLAG – (6001)	=	FF
b.	Input:	CHAR – (6000)	=	36 '6'
	Results:	FLAG – (6001)	=	00
c.	Input:	CHAR – (6000)	=	6A 'j'
	Results:			
		FLAG – (6001)	=	FF

11-4. Scan to Next Nonalphabetic

Purpose: The variable STRING at memory location 6000 contains the address of an ASCII string. Place the address of the first nonalphabetic character in this string in the variable ADDRESS at memory location 6002. Write a subroutine that takes the string address from a register and returns the result in the same register.

Sample Problems:

a.	Input:	STRING – (6000)	=	6100
		(6100)	=	43 'C'
		(6101)	=	61 'a'
		(6102)	=	74 't'
		(6103)	=	0D CR
	Result:	ADDRESS – (6002)	=	6103
b.	Input:	STRING – (6000)	=	6100
		(6100)	=	32 '2'
		(6101)	=	50 'P'
		(6102)	=	49 'I'
		(6103)	=	0D CR
	Result:	ADDRESS – (6002)	=	6100

11-5. Check Even Parity

Purpose: The variable LENGTH at memory location 6001 contains the length in bytes of a string variable STRING that begins at location 6002. If each byte in the string has even parity, set the variable FLAG at location 6000 to 0; if one or more bytes have odd parity, set FLAG to FF_{16}. Write a subroutine that obtains length and location from the stack and returns its result on the stack.

Sample Problems:

a.	Input:	LENGTH – (6001)	=	3
		STRING – (6002)	=	47
		(6003)	=	AF
		(6004)	=	18
	Result:	FLAG – (6000)	=	00
b.	Input:	LENGTH – (6001)	=	3
		STRING – (6002)	=	47
		(6003)	=	AF
		(6004)	=	19
	Result:	FLAG – (6000)	=	FF, since 19 = 00011001 has odd parity

11-6. Compare Two Strings

Purpose: Write a subroutine, and a main program that tests it, to compare two ASCII strings. The first byte in each string is its length. Return the information in the condition codes; i.e., the S flag will be set if the first string is lexically less than (prior to) the second, the Z flag will be set if the strings are equal, no flags are set if the second is prior to the first. Note that ABCD is lexically greater than ABC.

12
Advanced MC68020 Addressing And Instructions

The MC68000 processor line is **upwardly compatible**; that is, any program written for a lower-end model, such as the MC68008, will run on an upper-end product, such as the MC68020. In addition to supporting the instructions and addressing modes of lower-end products, the MC68020 also supports several new instructions and addressing modes not found on the lower-end processors. This chapter highlights many of these added features.

PROGRAM EXAMPLES

12-1. SCALED INDEXES

The MC68020 processor allows you to specify a scale factor when you use indexed addressing. This addressing method is particularly useful when you need to access arrays. With the processors MC68000 through MC68012, you might use code, as shown in Program 12-1A.

Purpose: Move the contents of the 32-bit variable VAL1 into the long word array ARRAY (subscripted from 0-99) at the element indicated by the word variable SUBSCR.

Sample Problem:

```
        Input:   ARRAY[10]  (6040) = 0
                 SUBSCR     (6250) = 10
                 VAL1       (6252) = 179224

        Output:  ARRAY[10]  (6040) = 179224
```

Program 12-1A:

```
        00006000        DATA      EQU    $6000
        00004000        PROGRAM1  EQU    $4000
        00005000        PROGRAM2  EQU    $5000

        00006000                  ORG    DATA
006000  00000000        ARRAY     DS.L   100          ARRAY
006250  0000000A        SUBSCR    DC.W   10           SUBSCRIPT
006252  00179224        VAL1      DC.L   $179224      NEW VALUE

        00004000                  ORG    PROGRAM1
004000  207C00006000    PGM_12_1A MOVEA.L ARRAY, A0
004006  303900006250              MOVE.W  SUBSCR, D0
00400C  E540                      ASL.W   #2, D0
00400E  21B900006252              MOVE.L  VAL1, (A0, D0.W)
004004  4E75                      RTS
```

195

196 68000 Assembly Language Programming

With the MC68020's scaled indexing, you can eliminate the Shift instruction. Since you are dealing with an array of long words, you can specify a scale of 4, as indicated by Program 12-1B.

Program 12-1B:

```
       00006000           DATA       EQU      $6000
       00004000           PROGRAM1   EQU      $4000
       00005000           PROGRAM2   EQU      $5000

       00006000                      ORG      DATA
006000 00000000           ARRAY      DS.L     100        ARRAY
006250 0000000A           SUBSCR     DC.W     10         SUBSCRIPT
006252 00179224           VAL1       DC.L     $179224    NEW VALUE

       00005000                      ORG      PROGRAM2
005000 207C00006000       PGM_12_1B  MOVEA.L  ARRAY, A0
005006 30390000006250                MOVE.W   SUBSCR, D0
00500C 21B900006252                  MOVE.L   VAL1, (A0, D0.W*4)
005012 4E75                          RTS
```

12-2. MEMORY INDIRECT ADDRESSING

Normal address register indirect addressing provides you with a means of pointing to data. **Memory indirect expands on that concept and allows a value in memory to point to data.** While the full syntax of the memory indirect addressing mode allows pre- or postindexing, two displacements, and an address register all to contribute to the final data address, you more commonly will use only one or two of these features at a time.

A common application for memory indirect addressing is for a function table. **A function table contains the addresses of various functions.** Typically, a program requests one of the functions through a user menu, message number, or token number. For example, you may present the user with a menu of six entries and tell him or her to enter a number from 1 to 6. By using memory indirect addressing you can directly call a function from the function table. This process is shown in Program 12-2.

Purpose: Call the function listed in FUNC__TBL as indicated by the variable SELECT (valued 1=6). For simplicity, the functions will move a value into D5; FUNC__1 will load a 1, FUNC__2 will load a 2, and so on.

Sample Problem:

```
        Input:   FUNC_TBL (6000)   = 00005000
                          (6004)   = 00005200
                          (6008)   = 00005400
                          (600C)   = 00005600
                          (6010)   = 00005750
                          (6014)   = 00005A00
                 SELECT   (6018)   = 3
                 D5                = 0

        Output:  D5                = 3
```

Program 12-2:

```
       00006000           DATA       EQU      $6000
       00004000           PROGRAM1   EQU      $4000
```

```
            00006000                        ORG        DATA
006000                  FUNC_TBL            DC.L       FUNC_1
006004                                      DC.L       FUNC_2
006008                                      DC.L       FUNC_3
00600C                                      DC.L       FUNC_4
006010                                      DC.L       FUNC_5
006014                                      DC.L       FUNC_6
006018                  SELECT              DC.W       3

            00004000                        ORG        PROGRAM
004000  303900006018    PGM_12_2            MOVE.W     SELECT, D0
004006  5340                                SUBQ.W     #1, D0
004008  4EB005B100006000                    JSR        ([FUNC_TBL, ZA0, D0.W*4])
004010  4E75                                RTS
004012  3A3C0001        FUNC_1              MOVE.W     #1, D5
004016  4E75                                RTS
004018  3A3C0002        FUNC_2              MOVE.W     #2, D5
00401C  4E75                                RTS
00401E  3A3C0003        FUNC_3              MOVE.W     #3, D5
004022  4E75                                RTS
004024  3A3C0004        FUNC_4              MOVE.W     #4, D5
004028  4E75                                RTS
00402A  3A3C0005        FUNC_5              MOVE.W     #5, D5
00402E  4E75                                RTS
```

If the user selected menu item 3, the program would convert this value to 2 (the subscript entry into CMDTBL). The program then calls FUNC3 indirectly; using CMDTBL's address plus the scaled index in D0, which loads D5 with a 3.

Note that the ZA0 term appears in the effective address. This tells the assembler to omit the address register contribution to the effective address. Also note that we omitted the outer displacement; by default, the assembler knew to omit this term. These conventions are assembler-dependent; consult your assembler documentation for specific details on how to omit optional terms.

12-3. BIT FIELD INSTRUCTIONS

Bit fields represent a new data type for the MC68000 family. They allow you to group a series of bits together as a single entity, without regard to byte alignment. This grouping allows you to pack your data more tightly—a useful tool if you work with large data bases or data communications.

MC68020 bit fields range from a single bit up to 32 bits in length. The processor understands bit fields in terms of starting byte, offset from that byte, and field width. The standard assembler syntax for this is

base_byte{offset:width}

You may specify the base_byte using almost any of the standard addressing modes. The offset can be any value from 8000 0000 to 7FFF FFFF. When you use a data register for the base byte, the offset is naturally limited to 32. Width can be a value from 1 to 32.

Since bit fields have no formal byte boundaries, the way that the starting address and offset combine to form the starting bit is unlike the way that normal byte, word, and long words align. Instead of counting from the least significant bit to the most significant bit, the offset starts counting from the most significant bit.

Bit field offset	2 3 4 5 6 7	8 9 19 11 12 13 14 15	16 17 18 19 20 21 22 23	24 25 26 27 28 29 30 31
Byte offset	5 4 3 2 1 0	7 6 5 4 3 2 1 0	7 6 5 4 3 2 1 0	7 6 5 4 3 2 1 0
Address	1000	1001	1002	1003

As you can see, the bit specified by the notation 1000{25:3} corresponds to memory address 1003, bits 4, 5, and 6.

At first inspection, this may seem like an awkward method to get to the start of a bit field. However, since the point of bit fields is to construct a tightly packed record, you normally will have several fields stored adjacently. The byte boundaries within the set of bit fields are irrelevant; your only concern as far as byte boundaries go is the total size of the bit-field data.

Let's look at a common application for bit fields. Often in computer applications, you need to insert a "time tag" along with some transaction data. For example, if you are writing a program for an automatic teller machine, you might keep an audit of all transactions done through the machine. Associated with each audit record may be the user's ID number, the teller ID, the transaction performed, and the time and date.

You can choose to use a long word for the user ID and short words for the teller ID and transaction type. These sizes should be sufficient regardless of the ultimate size of the data base (allowing for expansion). The time and date information is different, however, in that these entries are fixed in size; there will never be more than 60 seconds in a minute, and so on.

If you only need to store a few dozen records a day, you might go ahead and use bytes for the hour, minute, second, month, day, and year. However, if you need to store a few thousand records each day, the storage requirements for your audit trail may make the data base unmanageably large. If you can somehow cut down on the size of the time/date tag, you can keep the data base size under control.

There are two common solutions to this problem. The first is to convert the time and date data into an offset (in seconds) from some arbitrary point in the recent past. A long word can contain the number of seconds for more than 100 years, so this is a viable alternative. However, to convert between a count in seconds and a real time and date requires substantial CPU time.

The second alternative for storing the time/date tag makes use of bit fields. Since each element of the time/date tag has a fixed maximum, you can compact the binary values of the tag into a single long word entry.

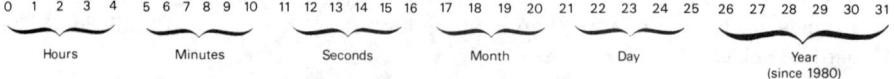

If you were using any of the other MC68000-family processors, converting between these bit fields and the expanded version of the time and date would require a series of masking and shifting. With the MC68020's bit-field manipulation instructions, you can insert and extract the time/date information from the bit fields with a few simple instructions. Program 12-3A packs a table of time/date information into a long word; Program 12-3B unpacks a long word of time/date information back into tabular format.

Advanced MC68020 Addressing and Instructions 199

Purpose: Convert the time/date information stored in the byte buffer TIMDAT into a single long word TIMTAG.

Sample Problem:

Input:	TIMDAT	(6000)	= 13 hours
		(6001)	= 52 minutes
		(6002)	= 19 seconds
		(6003)	= 3 month
		(6004)	= 18 day
		(6005)	= 6 year (since 1980)
Output:	TIMTAG	(6006)	= 514A40C5

Program 12-3A:

```
        00006000           DATA       EQU       $6000
        00004000           PROGRAM1   EQU       $4000
        00005000           PROGRAM2   EQU       $5000

        00006000                      ORG       DATA
006000  0000000D           TIMDAT     DC.B      13              HOURS
006001  00000034                      DC.B      52              MINUTES
006002  00000013                      DC.B      19              SECONDS
006003  00000003                      DC.B      3               MONTHS
006004  00000012                      DC.B      18              DAYS
006005  00000006                      DC.B      6               YEARS (SINCE 1980)
006006  00000000           TIMTAG     DC.L      0               PACKED TIME TAG

        00004000                      ORG       PROGRAM1
004000  207C00006000       PGM_12_3A  MOVEA.L   TIMDAT, A0      ADDRESS OF UNPACKED TIME/DATE
004006  227C00006006                  MOVEA.L   TIMTAG, A1      ADDRESS OF PACKED TIME/DATE
00400C  2018                          MOVE.B    (A0)+, D0       PACK HOURS
00400E  EFD10005                      BFINS     D0, (A1){0:5}
004012  2018                          MOVE.B    (A0)+, D0       PACK MINUTES
004014  EFD10146                      BFINS     D0, (A1){5:6}
004018  2018                          MOVE.B    (A0)+, D0       PACK SECONDS
00401A  EFD102C6                      BFINS     D0, (A1){11:6}
00401E  2018                          MOVE.B    (A0)+, D0       PACK MONTHS
004020  EFD10444                      BFINS     D0, (A1){17:4}
004024  2018                          MOVE.B    (A0)+, D0       PACK DAYS
004026  EFD10545                      BFINS     D0, (A1){21:5}
00402A  2018                          MOVE.B    (A0)+, D0       PACK YEARS
00402C  EFD10686                      BFINS     D0, (A1){26:6}
004030  4E75                          RTS
```

Purpose: Convert the packed long word at TIMTAG into its time and date components and store this information into the byte table at TIMDAT.

Sample Problem:

Input:	TIMTAG	(6006)	= 514A40C5
Output:	TIMDAT	(6000)	= 13 hours
		(6001)	= 52 minutes
		(6002)	= 19 seconds
		(6003)	= 3 month
		(6004)	= 18 day
		(6005)	= 6 year (since 1980)

Program 12-3B:

```
                00006000        DATA            EQU     $6000
                00004000        PROGRAM1        EQU     $4000
                00005000        PROGRAM2        EQU     $5000

                00006000                        ORG     DATA
006000 0000000D                 TIMDAT          DC.B    13              HOURS
006001 00000034                                 DC.B    52              MINUTES
006002 00000013                                 DC.B    19              SECONDS
006003 00000003                                 DC.B    3               MONTHS
006004 00000012                                 DC.B    18              DAYS
006005 00000006                                 DC.B    6               YEARS (SINCE 1980)
006006 00000000                 TIMTAG          DC.L    0               PACKED TIME TAG

                                                ORG     PROGRAM2
005000 207C00006000             PGM_12_3B       MOVEA.L TIMDAT, A0      ADDRESS OF UNPACKED TIME/DATE
005006 227C00006006                             MOVEA.L TIMTAG, A1      ADDRESS OF PACKED TIME/DATE
00500E E9D10005                                 BFEXTU  (A1){0:5}, D0   EXTRACT HOURS
005012 10C0                                     MOVE.B  D0, (A0)+
005014 E9D10146                                 BFEXTU  (A1){5:6}, D0   EXTRACT MINUTES
005018 10C0                                     MOVE.B  D0, (A0)+
00501A E9D102C6                                 BFEXTU  (A1){11:6}, D0  EXTRACT SECONDS
00501E 10C0                                     MOVE.B  D0, (A0)+
005020 E9D10444                                 BFEXTU  (A1){17:4}, D0  EXTRACT MONTHS
005024 10C0                                     MOVE.B  D0, (A0)+
005026 E9D10545                                 BFEXTU  (A1){21:5}, D0  EXTRACT DAYS
00502A 10C0                                     MOVE.B  D0, (A0)+
00502C E9D10686                                 BFEXTU  (A1){26:6}, D0  EXTRACT YEARS
005030 10C0                                     MOVE.B  D0, (A0)+
005032 4E75                                     RTS
```

CONCLUSION

This chapter introduced some of the advanced features of the MC68020 processor. We could not give examples of all of the new instructions and addressing modes. However, we hope we have presented enough examples to show you where to begin.

13
Connecting to Peripherals

Thus far in our programming examples, we have highlighted the internal workings of the processor. Our programs work on data stored in memory and return the result of the computation to some other location in memory.

This type of programming is, of course, not truly representative of real-life computing needs. **A computer system, as you know, consists not only of the CPU but also of displays, disk drives, keyboards, printers, and other "peripheral" devices. This chapter deals with the basics of how the CPU and these peripherals interact.**

TYPES OF PERIPHERALS

The term *peripheral* applies to a broad range of devices. These devices may be large or small; they may be contained in the same cabinet as the CPU or they may be located in another building. They may consist of a complex system of circuitry or they may consist of a single chip. **For our needs, consider a peripheral to be any part of the computer system other than the CPU.**

STORAGE DEVICES

The CPU has space for only a limited amount of storage in its registers. Storage devices provide a means of holding data while you use the CPU registers for other data.

On-Line Memory

The storage device that you are probably most familiar with is the on-line memory in the form of random access memory, or RAM. RAM offers short-term storage for our data and programs. The word *random* tells you that you can access any part of memory without regard to the location of the previous or next access. **On-line memory on the MC68000 systems is byte-addressable;** that is, each byte has its own address and can be accessed individually.

There are many varieties of system memories (for example, static random access memory, SRAM, and read-only memory, ROM). They all interface closely, both physically and electrically, to the CPU. Like the CPU, the system memories consist of integrated circuits of the same type as those that make up the CPU. **The connection between the CPU and memory is the system bus.**

For the CPU to fetch and store data between itself and memory, it applies a low voltage to the lines on the bus; memory, in turn, interprets the voltages as requests for fetches or storage of data. The delay between the CPU request and the memory response is minimal; depending on the system configuration, the CPU may need to wait only an instant for memory to respond, or, in the optimal system, not at all.

Off-Line Storage

In the ideal system, the on-line memory supplies all of the storage needs. In reality, however, this is not the case. Even though the price of memory keeps dropping while the storage capacity of individual chips keeps rising, some applications require more data than can be economically or physically put into the system.

A second problem exists with relying solely on on-line memory: it requires constant power in order to keep its internal circuitry from forgetting its contents. If power should for some reason fail (for example, if you turn off the computer), the computer will forget what it was doing.

To handle this situation, **computer systems incorporate various off-line storage devices.** Such devices include hard disks, floppy disks, and magnetic tape. By using technologies different from those employed by on-line memory, these devices can store data more densely than on-line memory can. The trade-off, however, is that the CPU can't access individual bytes stored on off-line memory as it can with on-line memory. It must read blocks of data (typically 256, 512, or 1024 bytes at a time) from the off-line storage device into on-line memory and then search for the appropriate byte.

In addition to the time overhead required to read in blocks of data, these devices also introduce a mechanical delay. While access to the on-line memory meant dealing only with electrical signaling (very fast), off-line devices require certain mechanical actions to read or write a block of data. For example, when your data is stored at the end of a magnetic tape, for the CPU to access that data, the tape drive must unwind the tape before it can find the data.

To combat the problem of storing data for long periods, the off-line storage devices use technologies to store the data that don't require constant electrical power. Because the electrical and mechanical methods used by these devices differ from those making up the circuitry of the CPU (and on-line memory), the CPU cannot directly access the data via the system bus; it must work through some translator. This requirement adds access overhead as well as circuit complexity.

COMMUNICATIONS DEVICES

Along with its storage requirements, the CPU must have some means for the user to enter data and see the results of the CPU's computations. Devices that give the user this ability include video terminals, keyboards, and printers, as well as some more exotic devices such as mice, joysticks, plotters, and analog/digital converters.

As we said earlier, the CPU and its on-line memory use specific voltages to communicate with each other. To keep power consumption and heat to a minimum, these voltages are typically very low. For the sake of speed, the transitions between a binary 1 and a binary 0 occur quickly, as shown in the following:

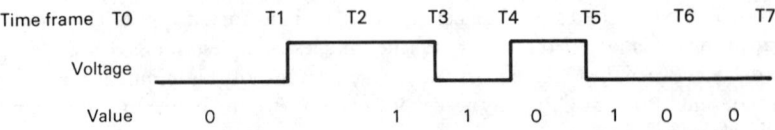

These voltage levels and signal speeds require that the CPU and memory reside close to each other, within an enclosure that protects the signals from outside interference (such as radio and television signals, radiation from fluorescent light bulbs, and so on). Special wiring on printed circuit boards ensures that the signal level doesn't drop as it would with the different resistance and capacitance of ordinary wire.

Our input and output devices however, may reside some distance away from the actual computer enclosure — in a different room, on a different floor, or even in a different city. If we were to simply connect the system bus to the terminal or printer via a cable, by the time the electrical signals reached the other end of the cable, they might look like this:

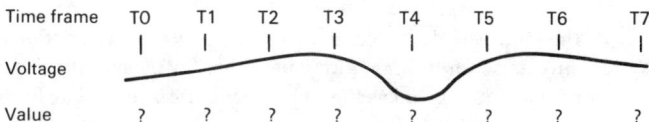

It isn't practical to build a network of enclosed printed circuit boards between the computer and its peripherals, so the next best thing to do is to use some signaling convention that is less affected than these boards by radiation and other interference. As when you use off-line storage devices, you must pay a price for this convenience. To prevent the intrinsic capacitance of the wire and the outside radiation of the environment from ruining signals, you must make the transitions between binary 1s and 0s much more pronounced.

To do this, you must slow down the transitions. The VMEbus (a common system bus used within MC68000-based systems) transmits data at up to 10 million bits per second over each of its 32 data lines (for a net of 320 million bits per second). Data traveling to a terminal typically travels at speeds no greater than 9600 bits per second — and its cable has only one data line!

CPU SUPPORT PERIPHERALS

In addition to communicating with peripherals outside of the computer enclosure, the CPU must also interface with circuitry that supports the functions of the CPU. Such support peripherals include timers (for programming delays as well as maintaining the system time), special-purpose processors (such as units that perform floating-point arithmetic), and memory management units (which control memory accesses in multiuser systems).

These support chips generally work at the same voltages as do the CPU and on-line memory. Problems arise in that while these support chips are "intelligent," they need direction from the CPU as to how they should work.

CPU — PERIPHERAL INTERFACE

We have discussed several types of peripherals and the problems associated with connecting the CPU with them. In summary, these are the problems:

- Peripherals may be slower than the CPU
- Peripherals may use different internal electrical technologies
- Peripherals may need instructions on how to do their work
- Peripherals may use different basic storage sizes (for example, blocks instead bytes).

Computer designers have overcome these interface problems by creating special circuits, often known as "device controllers." Often, these circuits fit on a single integrated circuit chip.

Device controllers form a two-sided interface that connects the CPU to the dissimilar peripheral, as shown:

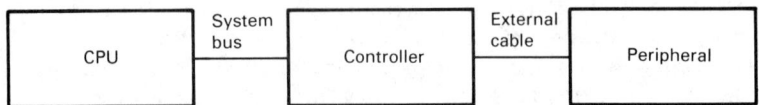

On one side of the interface, device controllers operate at the well-defined signal levels found on the system bus, as do on-line memories and other CPU support chips. On the other side of the device controller, the signal levels and protocols are appropriate for the particular attached peripheral.

Device controllers typically have one or more registers. Depending on the function of the controller and on the complexity of the peripheral it interfaces, there may be only a few registers or there may be 100 or more. These registers differ from the address and data registers found in the CPU in that they are generally highly specialized.

Often, a single bit within these registers may control or show the status of a particular aspect of the peripheral. Such registers are called "control" registers and "status" registers, respectively. So that the CPU can pass data between itself and the peripheral, the controller usually has one or more "data" registers.

Since the device controller chips have the same electrical characteristics as does the CPU, and since the registers are sized like memory (that is, in bytes, or in some cases, in words or long words), the controller attaches directly to the system bus. To the CPU, the controller appears at some specific address in memory, just as if it were standard RAM. This means that the CPU can use regular MOVE instructions to read and write to the controller.

In most systems, the designers dedicate a certain portion of the address space to correspond to device controllers. For example, addresses $00000000 to $007FFFFF may be RAM; addresses $00800000 to $80000FFF may correspond to the various device controllers in the system. This simplifies the system-control circuitry and lessens the chance that you will inadvertently try to use device-controller addresses as normal address space.

Figure 13-1 shows the registers associated with a primitive parallel-printer controller and how they relate to the CPU/printer interface. While this controller is oversimplified compared to one you would find in a real application, it does help describe how a controller works.

The function of the data register may be obvious to you: through it the CPU passes characters to the printer for printing. The control register passes commands from the CPU to the printer. In our illustration case, we have two control bits: the data ready bit and the interrupt enable bit. When the CPU sets the data ready bit, the printer knows that the data lines contain valid data. (We will discuss the meaning of the interrupt enable bit later.) The status register has just one bit that shows whether the printer is ready to print a character.

The scenario for printing a character is as follows:

1. The CPU checks the printer ready bit in the status register.
2. If the printer is ready (if the ready bit is "true"), the CPU loads the data register with a character.
3. The CPU signals the printer by setting the data ready bit. In the meantime, the device controller has already copied the data onto the data lines. When the CPU sets the data ready bit, the controller raises a "true" signal on the data ready line.

Connecting to Peripherals 205

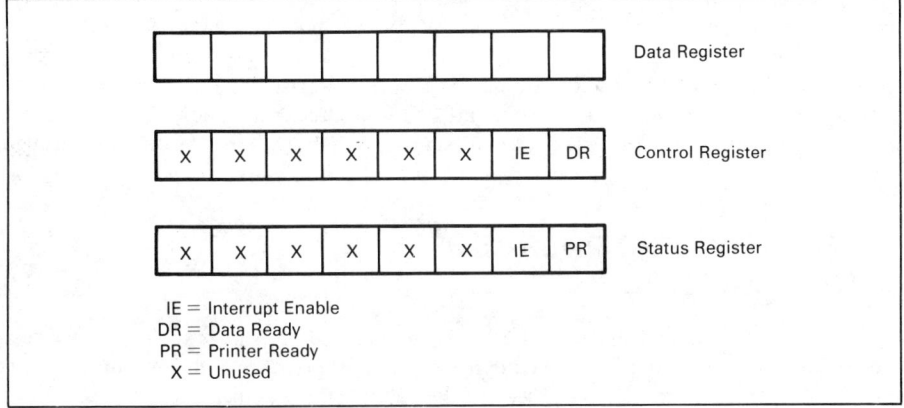

Figure 13-1. Printer Controller Registers

4. The printer, sensing that the data ready line has become true, reads the data lines and begins processing the character (doing whatever printers do in order to print a character). So that the CPU doesn't try to send another character while the printer is still thinking about the first, the printer sends a "false" signal on the printer ready line.
5. If the CPU wants to send another character, it repeats the procedure from step 1.

The program performs the interface chores described in the preceding print example.

Program

Purpose: Print a string of characters starting at PRT__STRING. The string ends in a NULL character (ASCII code 0).

Sample Problem:

```
                           Input:   PRT__STRING (6000) = "Text 0"
                           Output:  (on the printer)

       00006000     DATA       EQU    $6000
       00004000     PROGRAM    EQU    $4000
       00800000     PTR_DATA   EQU    $800000
       00800001     PTR_CTRL   EQU    $800001
       00800002     PTR_STAT   EQU    $800002
       00000001     DATA_RDY   EQU    0
       00000001     PTR_RDY    EQU    0
       00000002     INT_ENB    EQU    1

       00006000                ORG           DATA
006000 5465787400  PTR_STRING  DC.B          "Text\0"        DATA TO PRINT

       00004000                ORG           PROGRAM
004000 207C00006000 PGM_13_1   MOVEA.L       #PRT_STRING, A0 GET ADDRESS OF STRING
004006 4A10         LOOP       TST.B         (A0)            END OF STRING?
004008 67000022                BEQ           DONE            IF SO, THEN DONE
00400C 0C3900010000 TST_STAT   CMP.B         PTR_STAT, #PTR_RDY PRINTER READY TO PRINT
       6000
004014 6600FFEA                BNE           TST_STAT        IF NOT, KEEP CHECKING
004018 13D800800000            MOVE.B        (A0)+, PTR_DATA LOAD DATA REGISTER
00401E 13FC00010080            MOVE.B        #DATA_RDY, PTR_CTRL INFORM PRINTER
       0000
004026 6000FFDE                BR            LOOP            AND CONTINUE ...
00402A 4E75         DONE       RTS
```

Accesses to all types of device controllers, whether they be printer interfaces, disk interfaces, or floating-point units, work similarly to our example, in that the device controllers all have status, control, and data registers. Particular devices vary from one another according to their functions; most devices require more of each type of register than does the device in the example and have many status- and control-bit definitions. In all cases, however, each register has a specific address (defined by the system designers), which is accessed by the CPU through MOVE instructions.

ALTERNATIVE PERIPHERAL ACCESS METHODS

The program shows one means of accessing a device controller. As you'll note, **we kept testing the status register until the printer indicated that it was ready for another character. This method of I/O is called "polled I/O,"** because the CPU continually checks, or polls, the device to see if it is ready.

As you might guess, **if someone has left the printer off-line (or powered off or unplugged from the system), the CPU will loop indefinitely,** waiting for the printer to say that it is ready. If you are in a single-user environment (that is, if your computer supports only one user at a time), this may not seem too important; you'll realize right away that something is wrong because the printer isn't printing.

However, if your system supports several simultaneous users, you will soon make enemies among your fellow users because no one can work while your program is in this tight loop. Moreover, your program may need to monitor the status of several devices at the same time, particularly if you are using a real-time system. You may lose valuable information from another device (say, a temperature sensor) because you are waiting on the printer.

To handle this problem, **most processors (including the MC68000 and its associated device controllers) support two alternate means of accessing peripherals; "interrupts" and "direct memory access" (DMA).**

Interrupts

As you know, a telephone has a ringing mechanism to alert you to incoming calls. If it were not so, you would be forced to pick up the receiver continually to check whether anyone was on the other end. This clearly would pose a great inconvenience!

This constant checking of the telephone is analogous to using polled I/O. While in theory it works, in most cases it proves to be, at best, cumbersome. Fortunately, **most CPUs and device controllers (including the MC68000 and its associated controllers) have a mechanism similar to the bell on a telephone, called the "interrupt".**

A device that supports interrupts can be configured (through the control register) to send a special signal to the CPU when it encounters certain conditions. In our printer example, the printer ready state is one such condition. When the CPU receives this signal, it knows it should stop whatever it is doing because some device in the system wants its attention.

As you will recall from our discussions in Chapter 3, the MC68000 dedicates a 1024-byte block of memory as the "vector table." Certain entries in this table are reserved for "interrupt vectors." When a device sends the interrupt signal to the CPU, the CPU responds by sending an "acknowledged" signal to the device. The device then loads a vector number onto the system bus.

This vector number corresponds to an entry in the vector table. Prior to enabling the device controller, your program must have loaded this vector with the address of an "interrupt handler." The CPU reads the vector number sent to it by the device, looks up the vector and its corresponding handler address, and jumps to the interrupt handler subroutine.

The interrupt handler subroutine then performs some processing with the device. In the example of the printer, the handler might load the controller data register with the next character to print. When it has completed what it has to do, it executes a special Return from Exception instruction (RTE), and the CPU can continue with the program that it was executing prior to the interrupt.

Program:

Purpose: Print a null-terminated string of characters starting at PRT__STRING. The interrupt vector for the printer is number 64 (address $100).

Sample problem:

Input: PRT__STRING = "Text \0"
Output: (on the printer)

```
                00006000      DATA         EQU      $6000
                00004000      PROGRAM      EQU      $4000
                00800000      PTR_DATA     EQU      $800000
                00800001      PTR_CTRL     EQU      $800001
                00800002      PTR_STAT     EQU      $800002
                00000001      DATA_RDY     EQU      0
                00000001      PTR_RDY      EQU      0
                00000002      INT_ENB      EQU      2
                00000100      PTR_VEC      EQU      64

                00006000                   ORG      DATA
006000 00000000               NXT_CHAR     DS.L     1                  POINTER TO NEXT CHAR
006004 00000000               DONE_FLAG    DS.L     1                  POINTER TO DONE FLAG
006008 5465787400             STRING       DC.B     "Text\0"           STRING TO PRINT
00600D 00                     COMPLETE     DS.B     1                  COMPLETION FLAG

                00004000                   ORG      PROGRAM
004000 2F3C0000600D PGM_13_2               MOVE.L   #COMPLETE, -(SP)   PUSH ADDRESS OF COMPLETION FLAG
004006 2F3C00006008                        MOVE.L   #STRING, -(SP)     PUSH ADDRESS OF STRING
00400C 4EBD00004020                        JSR      PRINT              SETUP PRINT
004012 508F                                ADDQ.L   #8, SP             CLEAN STACK
004014 4A790000600D WAITFOR                TST.B    COMPLETE           WAIT TILL PRINT COMPLETE
00401A 6700FFF8                            BEQ      WAITFOR
00401E 4E75                                RTS

004020 23FC00004048 PRINT                  MOVE.L   #PRT_XRPT, PRT_VEC SET UP VECTOR TABLE ENTRY
       00000100
00402A 23EF00040000                        MOVE.L   4(SP), NXT_CHAR    GET ADDRESS OF STRING
       6000
004032 206F0008                            MOVE.L   8(SP), A0          GET ADDRESS OF DONE FLAG
004036 4210                                CLR.B    (A0)               INITIALIZE DONE FLAG TO FALSE
004038 23C800006004                        MOVE.L   A0, DONE_FLAG      SAVE ADDRESS OF DONE FLAG
```

```
00403E 08F900010080            BSET       #INT_ENB, PTR_CTRL   ENABLE INTERRUPTS
       0001
004046 4E75                    RTS

004048 2F08           PRT_XRPT MOVE.L     A0, -(SP)            SAVE OFF A0
00404A 207900006000            MOVE.L     NXT_CHAR, A0         GET POINTER TO NEXT CHAR
004050 13D800080000            MOVE.B     (A0)+, PTR_DATA      MOVE CHAR TO DATA REGISTER
004056 08F900000080            BSET       #DATA_RDY, PTR_CTRL  INFORM PRINTER ABOUT NEW DATA
       0001
00405E 23C800006000            MOVE.L     A0, NXT_CHAR         SAVE NEW STRING POINTER
004064 4A10                    TST.B      (A0)                 IS NEW CHAR A NULL?
004066 66000012                BNE        WRAPUP               IF NOT, THEN WRAPUP
00406A 08B900010080            BCLR       #INT_ENB, PTR_CTRL   IF NULL, THEN DISABLE INTERRUPTS
       0001
004072 207900006004            MOVE.L     DONE_FLAG, A0        GET USER'S DONE FLAG
004078 4610                    NOT.B      (A0)                 SET DONE FLAG TO -1
00407A 205F           WRAPUP   MOVE.L     (SP)+, A0            RESTORE A0
00407C 4E73                    RTE
```

Direct Memory Access

Direct memory access, or DMA, gives us another alternative to polled I/O. While DMA isn't a complete substitute for polled I/O or even interrupt-driven I/O, it does let you move **data without using the CPU for every transfer.**

The CPU often uses DMA when it performs DMA disk reads and writes. As we stated earlier in this chapter, disks store their data in blocks. Whether we use polled I/O or interrupt-driven I/O, the CPU must explicitly move data into or out of the disk device data register. DMA lets us tell the device to read a block or more of data from the disk and store it starting at some particular address in on-line memory. While the device is handling this block transfer, the CPU is free to execute other sections of your program or other programs in the system.

A device controller that supports DMA must have a bit more intelligence than one that does not. Internally, it must check its various status bits and maintain a memory pointer that shows where to read or write the data. Typically, a program interfacing a DMA device must tell the device:

1. The starting memory address where the data should go or come from,
2. The function you want it to perform (for example, a disk read from disk block #100), and
3. The number of bytes or words to transfer.

Once the device is set up, your program tells it to perform the function. For a read, the device waits for the ready signal from the peripheral, receives a byte or word from the peripheral, stores the data into memory, increments its memory pointer, and decrements its transfer count. When the device has completed transferring the requested number of bytes, it sets appropriate status bits in its status register (and usually sends an interrupt signal to the CPU). While the device was handling the transfer, the CPU was executing some other piece of related or unrelated code.

DMA relieves the CPU (and programmer) of the burden of repetitive data movement. Also, while few devices move data faster than the CPU, if several high-speed devices are present in the system, the CPU may not be able to keep up with all of them, and hence runs the risk of losing data. DMA lessens, if not removes, the chance of this happening.

CONCLUSION

We have only touched on the surface of the interesting task of interfacing peripherals with the CPU. Pursuing the topic in further detail, however, is difficult because of the wide variety of devices available.

For the purposes of learning assembly language, be comforted in knowing that even the most primitive operating systems usually provide you with device handlers. By using subroutine calls to the system, we can effectively move data in and out of the computer system without regard to the particular status and control bits for a particular device.

14
Exception Processing

In the last chapter, we introduced the concept of interrupt-driven I/O and said that it fell under the broad category of exception processing. Many seemingly unrelated topics fall into the category of exception processing, including instruction executions, hardware configurations, operating systems, and array boundary checking. The common factor in all of these exceptions is in how the CPU responds when they occur.

In this chapter, we will discuss other types of exception processing and go into greater detail about how the processor handles various exceptions. Toward the end of the chapter, we will discuss a concept closely related to exception processing: virtual memory.

The various members of the MC68000 family differ from one another in the ways they handle exception processing. Fortunately, all exception processing is handled at the supervisor level; if you are writing user-level programs, you needn't worry about the differences in the processors. In fact, if you are content with user-level programming, you may choose to skip this chapter entirely; your programs will function quite well without your having to know the details of exception processing, because the operating system takes care of it for you. However, if you are writing operating-system programs, the information in this chapter is a necessity.

THE EXCEPTION VECTOR TABLE

In Chapter 13, we learned that an interrupting device controller sends a vector number to the CPU. The CPU, in turn, transfers control to the address stored in the vector table slot specified by the vector number. The vector table contains more than just interrupt-handler addresses; it contains addresses of handler routines for all types of exceptions. Whenever the CPU must handle an exception, it fetches the address of the appropriate handler from the exception vector table.

There is nothing special about the vector table itself; it resides in regular memory, and you must load its contents just as you would load any other data structure. If you are using the MC68010, MC68012, or MC68020, you can even change the starting address of the table from its default base of $00000000 to anywhere in memory, via the vector base register (VBR).

Table 14-1 shows the various assignments of the slots of the exception vector table. Some slot locations have well-defined definitions, for example, the bus error exception. Other slots are user-defined, for example, device interrupts. Still other slots are labeled as "reserved"; Motorola may use these in future MC68000 products.

Depending on what your system's configuration is, not all of the slots will be of use to you; for example, the floating-point exception slots are relevant only if you have a computer with an MC68020 central processor and an MC68881 floating-point coprocessor.

Under some advanced operating systems, users are prevented, through hardware and software means, from accessing the exception vector table; clearly, randomly loading data into the vector table can cause system failure or lost data. In these systems, the operating system takes responsibility for initializing the vectors and handling the exception processing.

If your system limits your access to the exception vector table, you may not be able to try

Table 14-1. Exception Table Assignments

Vector Number	Offset	Assignment
0	000	Reset: Initial interrupt stack pointer
1	004	Reset: Initial program counter
2	008	Bus error
3	00C	Address error
4	010	Illegal instruction
5	014	Divide by zero
6	018	CHK, CHK2 instruction
7	01C	cpTRAPcc, TRAPcc, TRAPV instruction
8	020	Privilege violation
9	024	Trace
10	028	A-line emulator
11	02C	F-line emulator
12	030	Reserved
13	034	Coprocessor protocol violation
14	038	Format error
15	03C	Unitialized interrupt
16-23	040-05C	Reserved
24	060	Spurious interrupt
25	064	Autovector (level 1)
26	068	Autovector (level 2)
27	06C	Autovector (level 3)
28	070	Autovector (level 4)
29	074	Autovector (level 5)
30	078	Autovector (level 6)
31	07C	Autovector (level 7)
32-47	080-0BC	TRAP #0-15
48	0C0	FPCP Branch or set on unordered condition
49	0C4	FPCP Inexact result
50	0C8	FPCP Divide by zero
51	0CC	FPCP Underflow
52	0D0	FPCP Operand error
53	0D4	FPCP Overflow
54	0D8	FPCP Signaling NAN
55	0DC	Reserved
56	0E0	PMMU configuration
57	0E4	PMMU illegal operation
58	0E8	PMMU access level
59-63	0EC-0FC	Reserved
64-255	100-3FC	User defined vectors

FPCP=floating point coprocessor
PMMU=paged memory management unit

out everything we talk about in this chapter. Do check, however, in your system's manuals. Usually, the system designers leave enough "hooks" in the system so that you can write your own exception handlers.

TYPES OF EXCEPTIONS

Exceptions fall into two broad categories: exceptions that originate from within the CPU and those that come from outside the CPU. Interrupts are an example of the latter. The external exceptions include

- Interrupts
- Bus errors
- System reset.

Exceptions may originate internally also, coming from the execution of certain instructions. Some instructions always produce exceptions. Other instructions may cause an exception if they are executed incorrectly. The internal exceptions include

- Odd addressing errors
- Illegal instructions (invalid op-codes)
- Illegal operations (such as divide by zero)
- Invalid use of a coprocessor
- Execution tracing
- Privilege violations.

When one exception occurs while another exception is still pending, the CPU arbitrates according to the priorities, as shown in Table 14-2.

EXCEPTION PROCESSING SEQUENCES

All of the various exceptions cause the CPU to follow a basic pattern of execution on all of the MC68000 processors. However, the specific details of a particular exception on a particular processor vary enough that we will discuss each type of exception separately, noting when one processor functions differently from another.

The general pattern followed by the CPU when starting exception processing is

1. Copy the status register to a temporary internal register.
2. Set the supervisor bit and clear the trace bit(s) in the status register (depending on what the current machine mode is, they may already be in this state).
3. Fetch the appropriate exception handler address from the vector table. Depending on what the exception type is, the CPU will either know intrinsically what vector location to use, or, in the case of interrupts, it will ask the peripheral for the vector number.
4. Depending on the exception and processor type, push additional internal information onto the stack.
5. Push the old version of the status register onto the supervisor stack.
6. Push the current program counter value onto the supervisor stack.
7. Begin execution in the exception handler program.

After the exception handler completes what it has to do, it may take one of two actions. If the exception was the result of an error (hardware failure or serious programming error), the exception handler may transfer control to the operating system, which will take further action

Table 14-2. Exception Priorities

Group/Priority	Characteristics
0.0 Reset	Aborts all processing (does not save old contents)
1.0 Address error	Suspends processing (saves old contents)
1.1 Bus error	
2.0 BKPT, CALLM, CHK, CHK2, cp Mid instruction, cpProtocol violation, cpTRAPcc, Divide by zero, RTE, RTM, TRAP, TRAPV	Exception processing is part of instruction execution
3.0 Illegal instruction, F-line, A-line, privilege violation, cp preinstruction	Exception processing begins before instruction is executed
4.0 cp post instruction	Exception processing begins when current instruction or previous exception processing is completed
4.1 Trace	
4.2 Interrupt	

(such as aborting your program and returning you to the monitor). If the exception was not due to a fatal error, but rather part of normal processing (as in the case of an interrupt), the exception handler executes a special instruction, RTE (Return from Exception). This instruction tells the CPU to

1. Pull the old program counter address from the supervisor stack and return it to the program counter register.
2. Pull the old status value from the supervisor stack and return it to the status register.
3. Pull any other stacked information back into the internal registers from which it was copied.
4. Continue execution at the point where the program was interrupted.

STACK FRAMES

We said that the CPU pushes certain information onto the supervisor stack at the beginning of the exception. Depending on which CPU and exception type are involved, the amount of this information may vary from 3 words of data to as many as 90 words. **The data structure on the stack is called the "stack frame."** The MC68000 and MC68008 use two unnamed stack frames, while the MC68010, MC68012, and MC68020 use stack frames that are named according to a format field included in the stacked data.

Figures 14-1 through 14-9 show the various types of stack frames. For now, just take a glance at these different stack frames. We will tell you which ones are used with which exceptions later in this chapter.

INSTRUCTION TRAPS

Instruction traps occur when your program executes certain instructions. Your program can request exception processing explicitly through the TRAP instruction. Often, the operating system provides you with some standard functions, such as input and output services, timing services, and intertask communications. Typically, these are implemented through TRAPs.

Certain other instructions cause exception processing when you attempt to execute those instructions incorrectly. For example, if you attempt to divide by zero (which would result in an undefined quotient), the CPU considers the action reason to perform exception processing. Instructions that may cause exception processing (in some instances) include TRAPV, CHK, CHK2, DIVS, DIVU, CALLM, and RTM. Your processor may not include all of these instructions.

On the MC68000 and the MC68008, the processor builds a three-word stack frame, as shown in Figure 14-1. On the MC68010 and the MC68012, the processor builds a four-word stack frame (called "format $0"), as shown in Figure 14-3. On the MC68020, a TRAP instruction causes a format $0 stack frame (Figure 14-3), while all other instruction exceptions push a format $2 stack frame (Figure 14-5).

ILLEGAL/UNIMPLEMENTED INSTRUCTIONS

As we pointed out, MC68000 instructions are one word long (plus any additional operands). Since a word is 16 bits, this gives a potential of 2^{16} (65536) instructions. The processor, however, implements far fewer instructions than this—something on the order of 300 to 500 instructions (60 or so basic instructions, with variations due to addressing modes). Clearly, **this leaves many instruction combinations undefined.**

The MC68000 makes a distinction between illegal and undefined instructions. By definition, **all instruction codes that have the binary patterns 1010 and 1111 in their high bits are defined as "unimplemented" instructions rather** than illegal instructions. These instructions

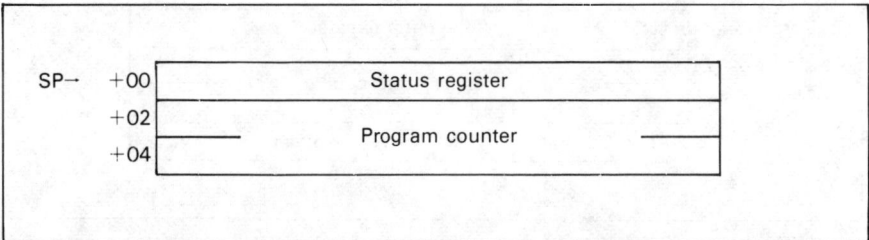

Figure 14-1. 68000/68008 Short Stack Frame

(known as "A-line" and "F-line," respectively) allow you to create new instructions that are not in the standard MC68000 instruction set; for example, floating-point instructions.

Whenever you execute an unimplemented instruction, the CPU vectors through the A-line or F-line vector-table entry. For illegal instructions, the CPU vectors through the illegal instruction vector. The MC68000 and MC68008 both create a three-word stack frame (Figure 14-1). The other processors create a four-word format $0 stack frame (Figure 14-3).

The exception handler can then perform whatever steps it needs to emulate or reject the instruction. Since the stack contains the address of the faulting instruction, the emulation routine knows where to look for the instruction code and operands. When it has completed its emulation, it then modifies the stacked program counter so that it points to the next instruction past the emulated instruction and returns control to the user program.

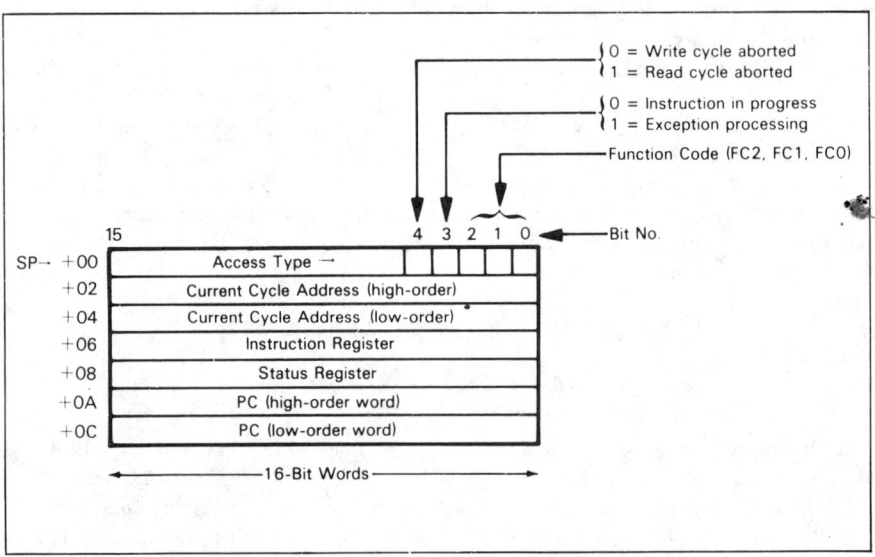

Figure 14-2. 68000/68008 Bus and Address Error Stack Frame

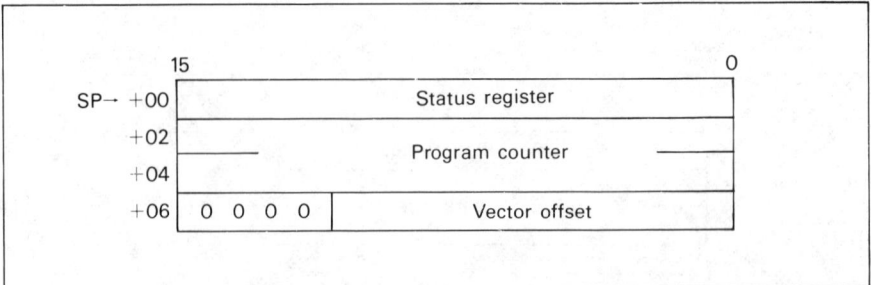

Figure 14-3. Format $0 Stack Frame

Exception Processing 217

The MC68020 processor carries this process a step further. Since it can interface to a coprocessor (such as the MC68881 floating-point processor), it considers all F-line instructions as potential coprocessor instructions. After deciding that it cannot execute the instruction by itself, it looks for any attached coprocessor that may execute the instruction. If the MC68020 finds a coprocessor, that coprocessor will execute the instruction; the CPU does not perform the exception. If no coprocessor responds, the CPU traps through the F-line vector.

ADDRESS ERRORS

All instructions must lie on word (even-byte) boundaries. Also, on all processors except the MC68020, word and long-word operands must also lie on even-byte boundaries. If your program attempts one of these illegal memory accesses, the CPU traps through the address error vector. The MC68000 and MC68008 create a seven-word stack frame (Figure 14-2), the MC68010 and MC68012 build a format $8 stack frame (Figure 14-6), and the MC68020 builds a format $A stack frame (Figure 14-8).

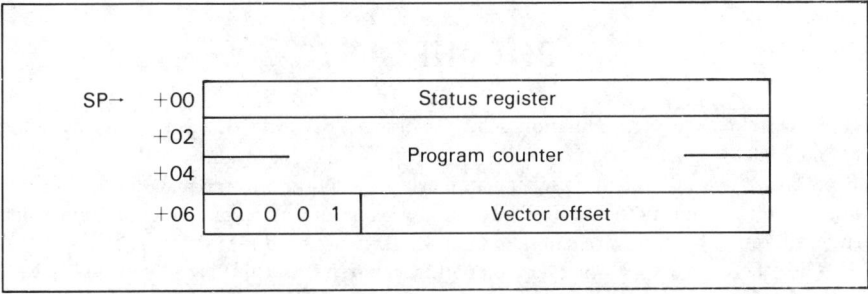

Figure 14-4. Format $1 Stack Frame

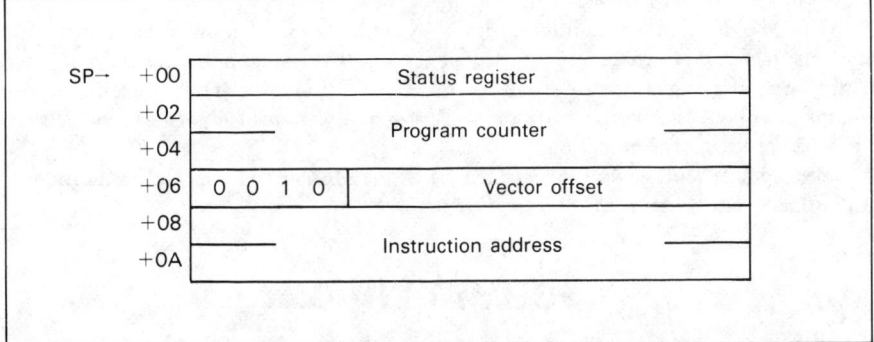

Figure 14-5. Format $2 Stack Frame

TRACING

Recall from Chapter 3 that the MC68000 status register has a bit defined as the trace bit (the MC68020 has trace two bits). When tracing is enabled (that is, when this bit is set), the CPU executes an instruction. Then, before executing the next instruction, it traps through the trace vector to an exception handler. When the CPU begins exception handling, it automatically disables the trace bit so that the exception handler can run unhindered.

The MC68020 gives you a more selective form of tracing, since you can configure it (by the right combination of trace bits) to trace after every instruction or else trace only after executing a change of flow instruction, such as a branch, jump, or subroutine call.

The MC68000 and MC68008 use the three-word stack frame (Figure 14-1). The MC68010 and MC68012 use the format $0 stack frame (Figure 14-3). The MC68020 uses the format $2 stack frame (Figure 14-5).

With the proper exception handler, tracing can provide a means of debugging programs. The exception handler can be written to accept commands from the keyboard, display registers and data, and return back to your program. This isn't the only way to implement a debugger, however; other methods involve insertion of instructions (for example, a TRAP) into your program. Using this method, you can execute many instructions before entering the exception handler.

BREAKPOINTS

In certain hardware-emulation schemes, it may be useful for you to notify external hardware that the CPU has reached a certain point in a program. On the MC68000 and MC68008, you can do this by inserting an illegal instruction into the program and installing hardware that monitors the address bus lines, waiting for an access to the illegal instruction vector address. The hardware can then take whatever action it sees fit.

The other processors, however, don't allow you to follow this procedure since they allow you to redefine the vector table base address (through the vector base register, VBR). **These processors define a special instruction group called "breakpoint" instructions (codes $4848 through $484F). When the CPU attempts to execute these instructions, it traps through the illegal instruction vector but also issues a special signal over the bus called a "breakpoint bus cycle,"** which external hardware can look for.

The MC68020 offers additional flexibility with the breakpoint instructions. After it attempts to execute the breakpoint instruction, it sends the breakpoint bus cycle. If external hardware chooses, it may load a new instruction into the processor. If this happens, processing continues without the exception occurring; if the hardware instead signals a bus error, the MC68020 processes the exception.

Breakpoints represent a sophisticated use of the MC68000. In normal applications, you will probably never use them.

FORMAT ERROR

The MC68020 has three instructions that perform error checking on stack-frame data. These instructions are Call Module (CALLM), Return from Module (RTM), and Coprocessor

Restore (cpRESTORE). These instructions, when executed, expect the stack frame to contain certain descriptors and format numbers; if an error exists, the CPU will trap through the format error exception vector using a format $0 stack frame (Figure 14-3).

INTERRUPTS

We have already discussed interrupts in some detail. **What we will cover in the following paragraphs is what the processor does when it receives an interrupt.**

The CPU can run at any of eight levels, as defined by the interrupt mask in the status register. Interrupts are also prioritized; the interrupting device indicates its priority by raising a signal on one or more of three interrupt-request lines.

If the value of the interrupt mask is less than the value on the interrupt-request lines, the CPU begins service on the interrupt. If the value of the interrupt mask is greater than or equal to the value on the interrupt request lines, the CPU ignores the request. A special case occurs when the interrupt request lines are all set. This is called a "nonmaskable" interrupt, and the CPU will service the interrupt regardless of the state of its interrupt mask.

Unlike other exception types where the vector number is determined by the particular exception, with interrupts the requesting device specifies the vector number. It may do so in one of two ways: explicitly, by giving the processor a vector number, or implicitly, by using "autovectoring."

When the CPU is ready to service the interrupt, it sets its interrupt mask (in the status register) to the value of the interrupt request lines. It then sends a special signal, called "interrupt acknowledge," to all devices. The interrupting device may then load a vector number onto the data bus. In some cases, you can program the device to provide a specific vector number; in other cases, external circuitry associated with the device determines the vector number.

In some simple computer systems, there may be only a few devices capable of interrupting the CPU. In such cases, it may be undesirable to build external circuitry for providing the vector number. To handle this case, the MC68000 processors provide autovectoring. After the CPU acknowledges the device, the device may signal the CPU to use one of eight vectors reserved in the vector table for autovectoring. The CPU then chooses one of these eight based on the priority of the interrupt lines.

A special case arises when no device responds to the interrupt-acknowledge signal. In this case, the CPU traps through the "spurious interrupt" vector. Another special case arises when a device with a programmable vector interrupts the CPU, but the operating system has not yet programmed its vector number. In this case, the device produces a special vector number and the CPU traps through the uninitialized vector.

After obtaining a vector number, the CPU creates a stack frame on the supervisor stack. The MC68000 and MC60008 create a three-word stack frame, as shown in Figure 14-1. The MC68010 and M68012 create a format $0 stack frame, as shown in Figure 14-3. If it is interrupted between main processor instructions, the MC68020 also creates a format $0 stack frame; if it is interrupted while a coprocessor is executing an instruction, the CPU creates a format $9 stack frame (Figure 14-7).

Recall, too, that the MC68020 has two supervisor bits: the S bit, present in all family members, and the M bit, found only on this processor. If the M bit is set, the CPU builds the stack frame on the master stack; it also builds a "throwaway" stack frame (format $1, Figure 14-4) on the interrupt stack.

BUS ERRORS AND VIRTUAL MEMORY

Whenever the CPU reads or writes to memory, it expects memory to respond with a "transfer acknowledged" signal. If, however, the memory referenced does not exist, it cannot acknowledge the transfer. Typically, a system will make use of a programmable clock that starts at the beginning of the memory cycle. If, after a certain time period, the addressed memory does not respond, the clock will "time out" and generate a bus error signal to the CPU. In systems that include a memory management unit (MMU), the MMU will verify that the addressed

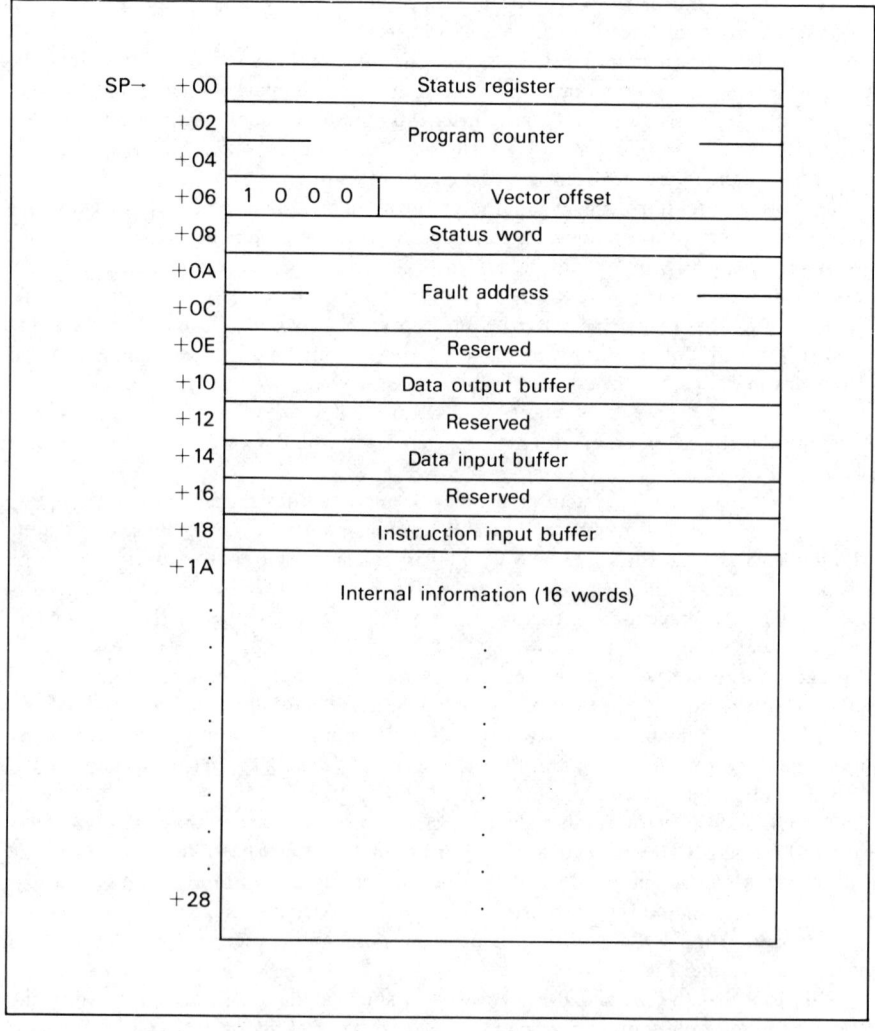

Figure 14-6. Format $8 Stack Frame

memory exists. If it does not exist, the MMU will generate the bus error signal to the CPU.

On the MC68000 and MC68008, upon receipt of the bus error signal, the processor will build a seven-word stack frame on supervisor stack (Figure 14-2) and trap through the bus error vector.

The MC68010, MC68012, and MC68020 implement "virtual memory." In a virtual memory system, a program can access more memory than is physically present in the system; the data may reside in memory or on disk. When external hardware signals the bus error, these processors save additional data onto the stack frame. This data includes certain internal CPU registers and other information that permit it to continue execution of an instruction after the bus error has been corrected.

The MC68010 and MC68012 create a format $8 stack frame (Figure 14-6). The MC68020 creates one of two stack frames; either a format $A stack frame (Figure 14-8), if the bus error occurred during an instruction fetch, or a format $B stack frame (Figure 14-9), if the bus error occurred during instruction execution.

After trapping through the bus error vector, if the system does not implement virtual memory, the operating system takes normal steps to notify the user of the error. However, if the system permits virtual memory, the operating system determines whether the requested memory resides on disk. If it does, the operating system can swap old data back out to disk and read in new data. After the data has been brought into memory, the CPU can restore the stacked data and pick up execution of the instruction where it left off.

Virtual memory is useful in large (many user) systems. It is also useful when dealing with a large data set since it allows you to deal with the data base as though it was memory resident. Also, since the disk I/O for swapping pages in and out of memory is hidden from your program (it's handled by the operating system) if you get more memory for your computer at some later point, your program remains unchanged.

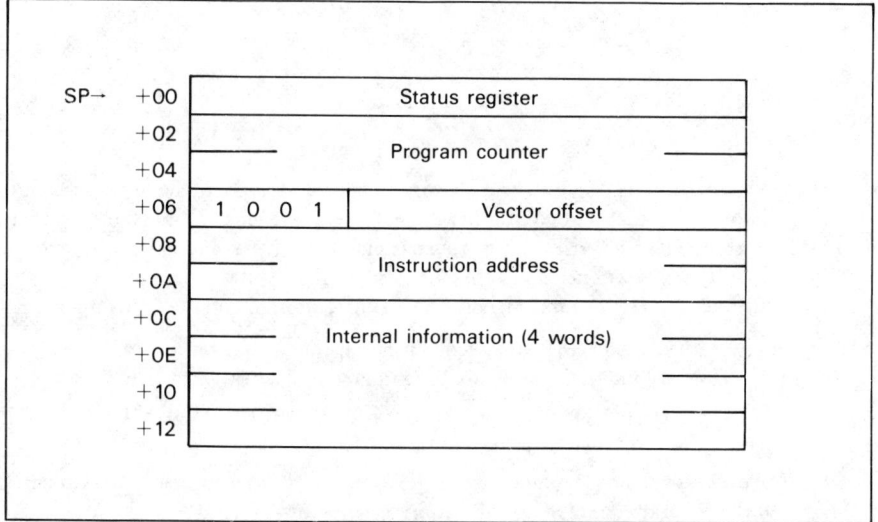

Figure 14-7. Format $9 Stack Frame

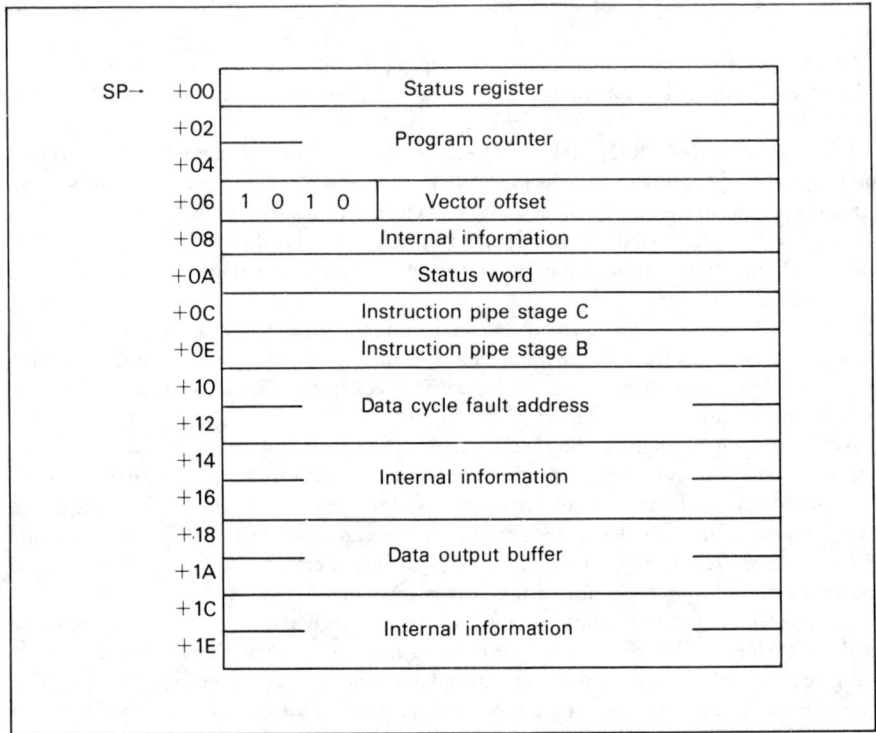

Figure 14-8. Format $A Stack Frame

RESET

The reset exception is unique among the various exception types in that it does not bother to save any information on the stack. In this context, "reset" refers to a hardware reset rather than execution of the RESET instruction. Your system probably has a reset switch somewhere on it, or else reset may be connected to the on/off switch.

When an external reset occurs, current processing is aborted and the following happens:

1. In the status register, the supervisor bit is set, the master bit is cleared (MC68020 only), the trace bit(s) is cleared, and the interrupt mask is set to level 7.
2. The vector base register is set to $0000 (MC68010-MC68020 only).
3. The cache control register is cleared (MC68020 only).
4. The processor loads the supervisor stack pointer with the address at vector entry 0, and the program counter with the address at vector entry 1.
5. The processors assert signals to the peripherals to reset themselves.

Exception Processing **223**

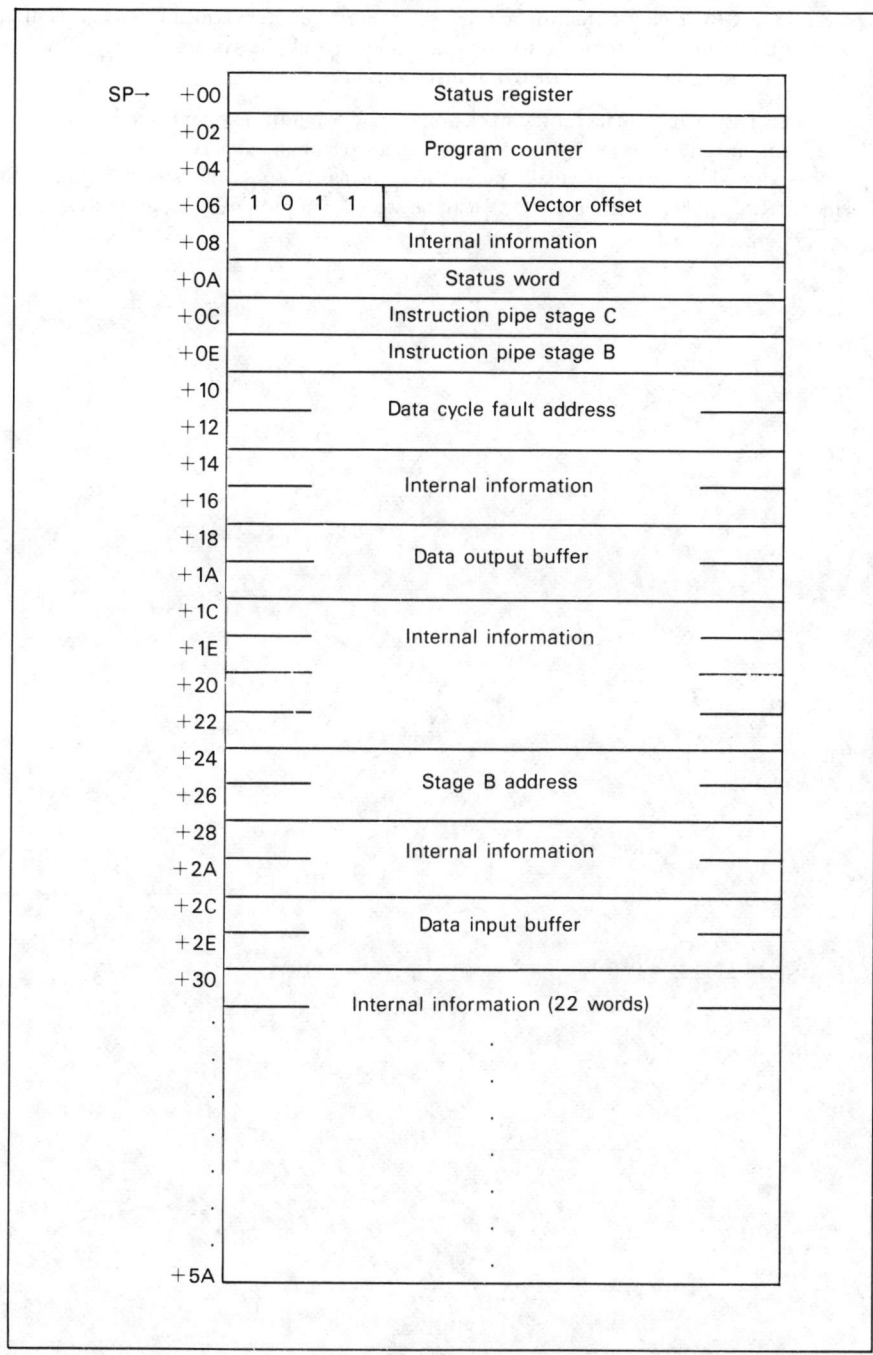

Figure 14-9. Format $B Stack Frame

6. The CPU begins execution at the new program counter. Typically, code is contained in a read only memory (ROM) that "bootstraps" the system (that is, it reads the operating system from disk into memory).

Note: The vector fetches for the stack pointer and program counter occur in what is called "supervisor program space," while normal fetches occur in "supervisor data space." This permits external hardware to break up memory. Normal vectors can reside in regular system memory (RAM), while the reset vectors can be stored in a physically separate ROM.

15
Interrupts And Other Exceptions

The previous chapter presented an overview of exception processing for the MC68000 family. This chapter explores the same subject in greater detail, concentrating on the most common family member, the MC68000 itself. While some of this material may seem redundant, exceptions play such an important role in MC68000-based systems that we feel they merit the level of detail included here.

Interrupts are inputs that the CPU examines as part of each instruction cycle. These inputs allow the CPU to react to asynchronous events more efficiently than by polling devices. The use of interrupts generally involves more hardware than does ordinary (programmed) I/O, but interrupts provide a faster and more direct response.[1]

In the MC68000, interrupts are but one category of events described as *exceptions*. Although this nomenclature is not used in other microprocessors, it is rather appropriate with the MC68000 since the number and types of events that can initiate *exception processing* extend well beyond the typical external interrupt requests. Nonetheless, before proceeding to describe the complete exception processing system provided by MC68000, let us discuss some general characteristics and considerations of interrupts since these are the most commonly encountered exceptions.

Why use interrupts? **Interrupts allow events such as alarms, power failure, the passage of a certain amount of time, and peripherals having data or being ready to accept data to get the immediate attention of the CPU. The program does not have to examine (poll) every potential source, nor need the programmer worry about the system missing events.**

An interrupt system is like the bell on a telephone — it rings when a call comes in so that you don't have to pick up the receiver occasionally to see if someone is on the line. The CPU can go about its normal business (and get a lot more done). When something happens, the interrupt alerts the CPU and forces it to service the input before resuming normal operations. Of course, this simple description becomes more complicated (just like a telephone switchboard) when there are many interrupts of varying importance and when there are tasks that cannot be interrupted.

CHARACTERISTICS OF INTERRUPT SYSTEMS

The implementation of interrupt systems varies greatly. Among the questions that characterize a particular system are:
1. How many interrupt inputs are there?
2. How does the CPU respond to an interrupt?
3. How does the CPU determine the source of an interrupt if the number of sources exceeds the number of inputs?
4. Can the CPU differentiate between important and unimportant interrupts?
5. How and when is the interrupt system enabled and disabled?

There are many different answers to these questions. The aim of all the implementations, however, is to have the CPU respond rapidly to interrupts and resume normal activity afterwards.

The number of interrupt inputs on the CPU chip determines the number of different responses that the CPU can produce without any additional hardware or software. Each input can produce a different internal response.

The ultimate response of the CPU to an interrupt must be to transfer control to the correct interrupt service routine and to save the current value of the program counter. The CPU must therefore execute the equivalent of a Jump-to-Subroutine or Call instruction with the beginning of the interrupt service routine as its address. This action will save the return address in the stack and transfer control to the interrupt service routine. The amount of external hardware required to produce this response varies greatly. Some CPUs internally generate the instruction and the address; others require external hardware to form them. The CPU can generate a different instruction or address only for each different input.

Polling and Vectoring

If the number of interrupting devices exceeds the number of inputs, the CPU will need extra hardware or software to identify the source of the interrupt. In the simplest case, the software can be a polling routine which checks the status of the devices that may be interrupting. The only advantage of such a system over normal polling is that the CPU knows that at least one device is active. **The alternative solution is for additional hardware to provide a unique data input (or "vector") for each source.** The two alternatives can be mixed; the vectors can identify groups of inputs from which the CPU can identify a particular one by polling.

Priority

An interrupt system that can differentiate between important and unimportant interrupts is called a "priority interrupt system." Internal hardware can provide as many priority levels as there are inputs. External hardware can provide additional levels through the use of a priority register and comparator. The external hardware does not allow the interrupt to reach the CPU unless its priority is higher than the contents of the priority register. A priority interrupt system may need a special way to handle low priority interrupts that may be ignored for long periods of time.

Enabling and Disabling

Most interrupt systems can be enabled or disabled. In fact, most CPUs automatically disable interrupts when a RESET is performed (so the startup routine can initialize the interrupt system) and when they accept an interrupt (so that another interrupt will not interrupt the same service routine). The programmer may wish to disable interrupts while preparing or processing data, performing a timing loop, or executing a multibyte operation.

An interrupt that cannot be disabled (sometimes called a "nonmaskable interrupt") may be useful to warn of power failure, an event that obviously must take precedence over all other activities.

Disadvantages of Interrupts

The advantages of interrupts are obvious, but there are also disadvantages. These include:

1. Interrupt systems may require a large amount of extra hardware.
2. Interrupts still require data transfers under program control through the CPU. There is no speed advantage as there is with DMA.
3. Interrupts are random inputs, which make debugging and testing difficult. Errors may occur sporadically, and therefore may be very hard to locate and correct.[2]
4. Interrupts may involve a large amount of overhead if many registers must be saved and the source must be determined by polling.

THE MC68000 EXCEPTION PROCESSING SYSTEM

The MC68000 provides extensive exception processing logic including a very complete set of external interrupts as well as internally initiated exceptions upon detection of various faults, traps, and so on.

OPERATING MODES

Before proceeding to describe the exception processing system, let us discuss the operating modes of the MC68000, since these affect exception processing. As we mentioned previously, **the MC68000 can operate in either a supervisor mode or a user mode. When the MC68000 is reset** using the RESET input, it starts operating in the supervisor mode. **The processor operates in supervisor mode until one of the following instructions is executed:** Return from Exception **(RTE),** Move to status register **(MOVE word to SR),** AND Immediate to status register **(ANDI word to SR),** and Exclusive OR Immediate to status register **(EORI word to SR).** None of these instructions automatically causes the transition to the user mode of operation — rather, they are capable of changing the state of the S-bit in the status register. **If one of these instructions resets the S-bit, the MC68000 will begin operating in the user mode.**

228 68000 Assembly Language Programming

Once the MC68000 is operating in the user mode, the only thing that can cause a transition back to the supervisor mode is an exception. All initial exception processing is performed in supervisor mode regardless of the current setting of the S-bit of the status register at the time of the exceptions. When the exception processing has been completed, the Return from Exception (RTE) instruction allows return to the User mode.

A number of instructions, designated as "privileged," are reserved for the supervisor mode. An attempt to execute one of these instructions in the user mode results in a "privilege violation" which is one type of exception. We will discuss these instructions and the privilege violation response later in this chapter.

EXCEPTION TYPES

The response of the MC68000 to the various types of exceptions is similar. Before we describe this response, let us look at the sources of exceptions since they go well beyond those provided by other microprocessors.

Exceptions originate in a variety of ways which can be divided into two general categories:

1. **Internally generated exceptions** that result from the execution of certain instructions, or from internally detected errors.
2. **Externally generated exceptions** which include bus errors, reset, and interrupt requests.

Internally Generated Exceptions

The internally generated exceptions to which the MC68000 responds can be further subdivided into three categories: internally detected errors, instruction traps, and the trace function.

The following are the internally detected errors which will cause the MC68000 to initiate exception processing:

1. **Addressing errors.** Any attempt by the MC68000 attempts to access word data, long word data, or an instruction at an odd address is an address error, since all such accesses must be on even address boundaries.
2. **Privilege violations.** Again, some instructions are reserved for use only in the supervisor mode. Exception processing will be initiated if you attempt to execute any of the following instructions when in the User mode: STOP, RESET, RTE, MOVE to SR, AND (word) Immediate to SR, EOR (word) Immediate to SR, OR (word) Immediate to SR, MOVE USP.
3. **Illegal and unimplemented opcodes.** If an instruction is fetched whose bit pattern is not one of the defined instruction bit patterns for the MC68000, exception processing will be initiated. Two bit patterns are defined as unimplemented rather than illegal; if bits 15-12 are 1010 or 1111, these are treated as unimplemented instruction opcodes. If these opcodes are fetched, special exception processing is initiated which can allow you to simulate unimplemented instructions in your own software.

Instruction traps are exceptions which are caused by the execution of instruc-

tions in your program. There is a standard **TRAP instruction** which is similar to the Z8000 System Call instruction. **There are four other instructions — TRAPV, CHK, DIVS, and DIVU — which will cause exception processing to be initiated** if certain conditions, such as arithmetic overflows or divide by zero, are detected.

The third type of internally generated exception occurs when the MC68000 is operating with the trace function. If the T-bit in the Status register is set, exception processing will be performed after each instruction. The Trace function is used for program debugging since you can analyze, by stepping through the program, the results of each instruction's execution.

Externally Generated Exceptions

There are three different types of externally generated exceptions:

1. **Bus errors.** When the BERR signal is asserted by external logic (and the processor is not halted), exception processing is initiated.
2. **Reset.** When the RESET signal is asserted by external logic, exception processing is initiated.
3. **Interrupt request.** This is the most familiar form of exception processing and is initiated by external logic via the three interrupt request lines (IPL0, IPL1, and IPL2).

Exception Priorities

The different types of exceptions have different priorities, and processing of an exception depends on its priority. The following table lists the types of exceptions according to their relative priorities, and also defines when processing of each type begins.

Group	Priority	Exception Source	Exception Processing Response
0	Highest	Reset Bus Error Address Error	Abort current cycle, then process exception
1		Trace Interrupt Request Illegal/Unimplemented Opcode Privilege Violation	Complete current instruction, then process exception
2	Lowest	TRAP, TRAPV CHK Divide-by-zero	Instruction execution initiates exception processing

The highest priority types of exceptions are Reset, Bus Error, and Address Error. Any of these exceptions will cause immediate termination of the current instruction, even within a bus cycle. The next group of exceptions — trace, interrupt requests, illegal/unimplemented instructions, and privilege violations — allow completion of the current instruction before initiating exception processing. Note that interrupt requests include an additional prioritization which we will discuss later. The lowest priority of exceptions are those that are caused by trap-type instructions. These instructions can initiate exception processing as part of their formal execution. All of the instruction trap exceptions have equal priority since it is impossible for two instructions to be executed at the same time.

Exception Vector Table

Central to the MC68000 exception processing sequence is a vector table that occupies 1024 bytes (512 sixteen-bit words) of memory. This table occupies memory addresses 000000_{16} through $0003FF_{16}$. **Figure 15-1 illustrates the exception vector table.** The table is organized as 256 four-byte vectors. Each vector is a 32-bit address which will be loaded into the program counter as part of the exception processing sequence.

As you can see, a number of the vector table entries serve the defined types of exceptions which we have discussed. Other entries of the vector table are reserved for use by Motorola and should not be used by your program if compatibility with future Motorola software and hardware is desired. The first 64 exception vectors have predefined uses; this leaves 192 vectors available to user defined external interrupt requests — this should be more than enough for most applications. (Of course, in this case, "user" means the microcomputer designer, not the assembly language programmer.) However, the first 64 vector locations are not protected by the MC68000; thus they can be used by external interrupts if a system requires it.

EXCEPTION PROCESSING SEQUENCES

The general sequence of events performed by the MC68000 in response to an exception is the same regardless of the source of the exception. There are, however, some differences. Let us begin by examining the response to internally generated exceptions.

Internally Generated Exception Processing

If exception processing is initiated as a result of either the trace function, a TRAP instruction, an illegal or unimplemented opcode, or a privilege violation, the following steps occur:

1. The status register contents are copied into an internal register.
2. The S-bit in the status register is set, thus placing the MC68000 in the supervisor mode of operation.
3. The T-bit in the status register is reset to disable tracing to allow for continuous execution of the interrupt service routine when debugging using TRACE.
4. The program counter contents are pushed onto the supervisor stack.
5. The previously copied status register contents are pushed onto the supervisor stack.
6. The new program counter contents are taken from the appropriate location in the interrupt vector table.

Interrupts and Other Exceptions   231

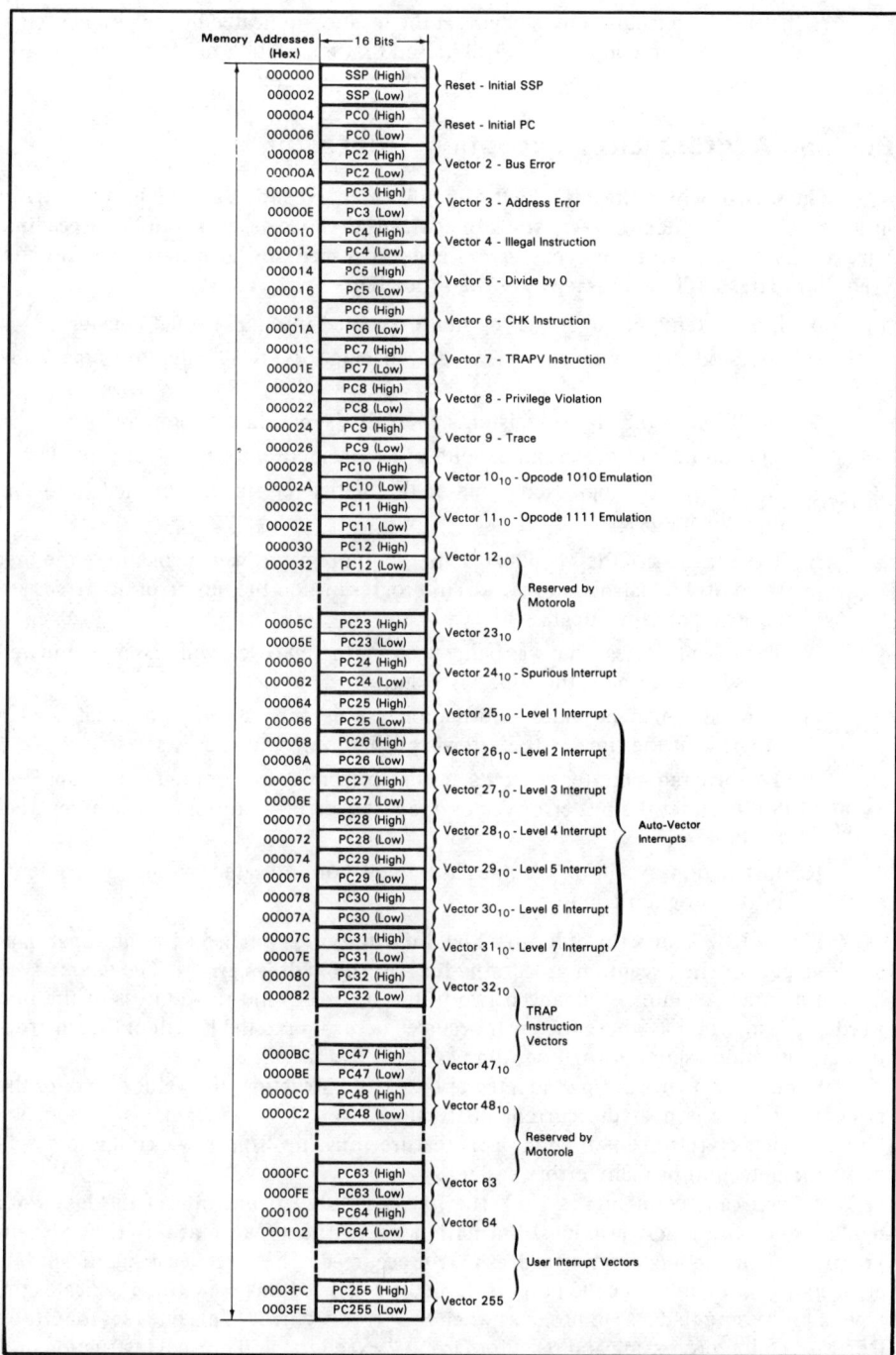

Figure 15-1. Exception Vector Table

7. Instruction execution then begins at the location indicated by the new contents of the program counter; this will be the first instruction of the exception processing program you have provided for that particular type of exception.

Bus and Address Error Exception Processing

The way in which the MC68000 responds to an exception caused by a bus error or address error includes several steps in addition to those described in the preceding paragraphs. First, either of these errors causes immediate termination of the bus cycle in progress. The next steps are the following:

1. The contents of the status register are copied into an internal register.
2. The S-bit in the status register is set, placing the MC68000 in the supervisor mode.
3. The T-bit in the status register is reset to disable trace operations.
4. The contents of the program counter are pushed onto the supervisor stack.
5. The previously copied contents of the status register are pushed onto the supervisor stack.
6. The contents of the MC68000's instruction register, which constitute the first word of the instruction that was in progress when the bus error occurred, are pushed onto the supervisor stack.
7. The 32-bit address that was being used for the bus cycle which was terminated is also pushed onto the supervisor stack.
8. A word which provides information as the the type of cycle that was in progress at the time of the error is pushed onto the supervisor stack.
9. The program counter contents are taken from the appropriate interrupt vector — either the bus error vector or address error vector of the exception vector table.
10. Instruction execution resumes at the location indicated by the new contents of the program counter.

Figure 15-2 shows the order in which information is pushed onto the supervisor stack as part of the exception processing for bus and address errors. The value saved for the program counter is advanced two to ten bytes beyond the address of the first word of the instruction where the error occurred according to the length of that instruction and its addressing information, if any.

If the error occurs during the fetch of the next instruction, the value saved for the program counter is near the current instruction, even if the current instruction is a jump, branch or return instruction. This feature, missing from most computers, will make the detection of many errors easier.

As you can see in Figure 15-2, **the five least significant bits of the last word pushed onto the stack provide information as to the type of access that was in progress when the bus error or address error occurred.** The three least significant bits are a copy of the function code outputs during the aborted bus cycle. Bit 3 indicates the type of processing that was in progress when the error occurred. This bit is set for Group 0 or 1 exception processing and reset for Group 2 exception and normal instruction processing (see the exception priority table shown earlier). Bit 4 indicates whether a read

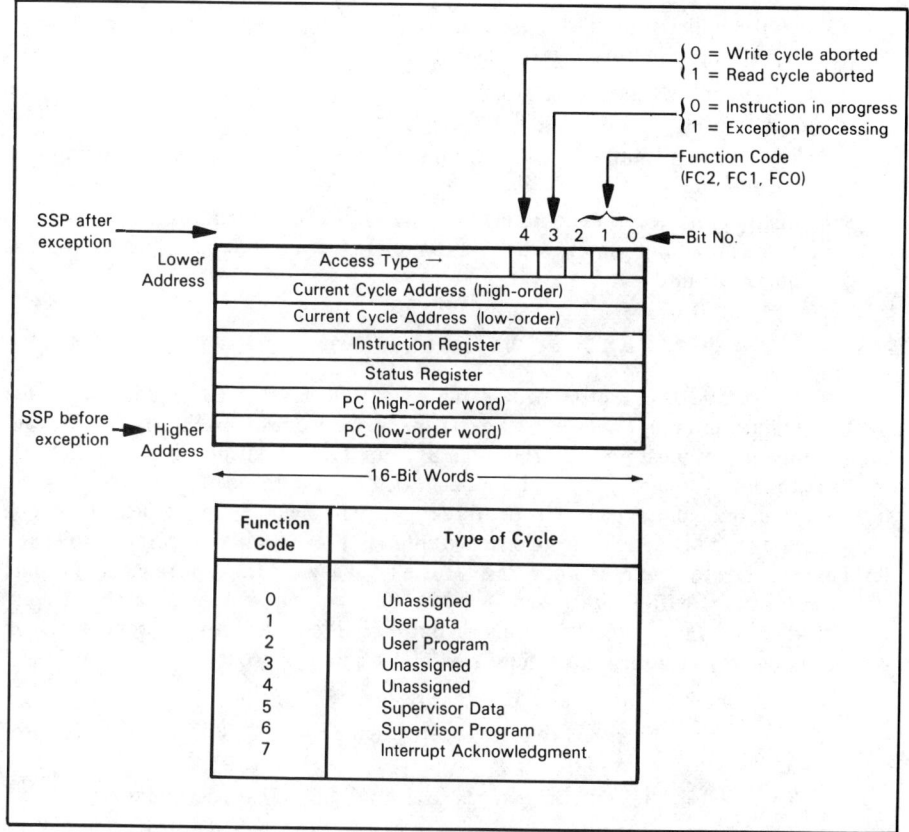

Figure 15-2. System Stack After Bus Error or Address Error Exception

(bit 4 set) or write (bit 4 reset) cycle was in progress when the error occurred. If an error occurs during the exception processing of a preceding bus error, address error, or reset operation, the MC68000 will enter the Halt state and remain there.

All of the information that is pushed onto the supervisor stack as part of the bus and address error exception processing sequence is intended to aid you in analyzing possible sources of the error. Either of these errors implies a serious system failure and it is not likely that you will be able to return to normal program execution.

Reset Exception Processing

An external reset causes a special type of exception processing. After an external RESET has been signalled the following steps occur:

1. The S-bit in the status register is set, placing the MC68000 in the supervisor mode.
2. The T-bit in the status register is reset to disable the trace function.

3. All three interrupt mask bits in the status register are set, thus specifying the interrupt priority mask at level seven.
4. The supervisor stack pointer is loaded with the contents of the first four bytes of memory (addresses 000000-000003).
5. The program counter is loaded from the next four bytes of memory (addresses 00004-00007).
6. Instruction execution commences at the address indicated by the new contents of the program counter, which should reference your power-up/reset initialization program.

Interrupt Request Exception Processing

The last type of exception processing we will discuss is the sequence initiated by the standard interrupt request. **An external device requests an interrupt by encoding an interrupt request level on the interrupt inputs.** The MC68000 compares these inputs to the interrupt mask bits in the status register. If the encoded priority level is less than or equal to the one specified by the three-bit mask, the interrupt request will not be recognized by the MC68000. **If the encoded interrupt level is higher priority than the level established by the interrupt mask (or if a level seven interrupt request is input) then the interrupt will be processed.** The MC68000 responds to the allowed interrupt request as soon as it completes the instruction execution currently in progress. **Upon completion of the current instruction, the following steps occur:**

1. The contents of the status register are saved internally.
2. The S-bit in the status register is set, placing the MC68000 in the supervisor mode.
3. The T-bit in the status register is reset to disable the trace function.
4. The interrupt mask bits in the status register are changed to the level of the interrupt request that is encoded on the interrupt inputs. This allows the current interrupt to be processed without being interrupted by lower priority events or events at the same level.
5. The MC68000 then performs an interrupt acknowledgement bus cycle. This cycle serves two functions; first, the processor lets the requesting device know that its interrupt request is being serviced, and second, the processor fetches an exception vector byte from the requesting device. After the vector byte has been read from the interupting device, the MC68000 proceeds with the following exception processing steps.
6. The contents of the program counter are pushed onto the supervisor stack.
7. The contents of the previously saved status register are pushed onto the supervisor stack.
8. The program counter is loaded with four bytes of data from the appropriate location in the exception vector table as defined by the exception vector byte.

After the program counter has been loaded with the new value from the exception vector table, instruction execution commences at the location indicated by the new contents of the program counter; this will be the first instruction of your interrupt processing routine for the particular device requesting the interrupt.

Autovector Interrupt Response

A variation on interrupt request processing is the autovector response. If you refer back to Figure 15-1, you will see that seven vector locations are provided in the exception vector table for autovectors, corresponding to the seven interrupt priority levels. These vectors will be used if the device requesting an interrupt responds to the interrupt acknowledge bus cycle by asserting the Valid Peripheral Address (VPA) signal to the CPU instead of supplying a byte of vector data. The processor will then use the autovector from the exception vector table which corresponds to the interrupt level to obtain a new program counter value. This autovector response was provided specifically to emulate the interrupt sequence expected by 6800 family peripheral devices. Of course a non-6800 family device in the system could also exploit this autovector capability should it be advantageous.

PROGRAM EXAMPLE

15-1. STARTUP

Purpose: Power up the computer and wait for a PIA interrupt to occur before starting actual operation.

When power is applied to an MC68000 system, the processor is reset and starts its initialization process. On RESET, the processor is placed in supervisor state and the interrupt priority mask is set to inhibit all interrupts except level seven. The supervisor stack pointer is loaded with the first two words of the reset exception vector at memory location 0. The program counter is loaded with the next two words from low memory and execution then starts at the instruction whose address is contained in the program counter.

Flowchart:

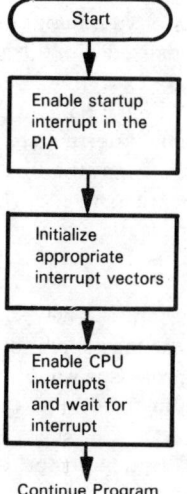

Program 15-1:

```
                00004000        POWER:     EQU    $4000
                00004600        SERVICE:   EQU    $4600
                00005100        STACK:     EQU    $5100
                00006000        DATA:      EQU    $6000

                0003FF40        PIADDA:    EQU    $3FF40       DATA DIRECTION REGISTER A
                0003FF40        PIADA:     EQU    $3FF40       DATA REGISTER A
                0003FF44        PIACA:     EQU    $3FF44       CONTROL REGISTER A
                00000005        PIA_EN:    EQU    $05          PIA INTERRUPT ENABLE
                00002000        IMSK0:     EQU    $2000        SUPERVISOR/INTERRUPT LEVEL 0
                00000064        SVECTOR:   EQU    $64          ADDRESS OF INTERRUPT VECTOR

                00000000                   ORG    0
000000          00005100                   DC.L   STACK        ADDRESS OF STACK
000004          00004000                   DC.L   PGM15_1      ADDRESS OF RESET PROGRAM

                00004000                   ORG    POWER

004000          13FC0005
                0003FF44    PGM15_1:       MOVE.B #PIA_EN,PIACA  ENABLE INTERRUPT FROM STARTUP PIA
004008          21FC00004600
                0064                       MOVE.L #STARTUP,SVECTOR  INITIALIZE PIA VECTOR
004010          4E722000                   STOP   #IMSK0       ENABLE INTERRUPTS AND WAIT FOR INTE

                *       STARTUP INTERRUPT SERVICE ROUTINE

                00004600                   ORG    SERVICE
004600          4A390003FF40 STARTUP:      TST.B  PIADA        CLEAR STARTUP INTERRUPT
004606          4E73                       RTE                 RETURN TO INTERRUPTED ROUTINE

                                           END    PGM15_1
```

If this program is stored in Read Only Memory (ROM) or Programmable ROM (PROM), when a power on RESET occurs, the supervisor stack will be loaded with 5100 and the program counter with 4000, the address of the startup program. The status register will have its supervisor and interrupt level bits set. Once these three registers have been set up, program execution commences at location 4000 just as in the examples in previous chapters.

Unlike other exception vectors, the reset vector must be in ROM or PROM. The same is true for the initial program to be executed. You must ensure that valid RAM and ROM addresses are referenced by the stack pointer and program counter entries in the reset vector.

All other exception vectors may be located in either RAM or ROM. The design of your system determines which is best for you. In our example, the exception vectors are in RAM. Therefore, they must be initialized with the addresses of the associated service routines prior to the occurrence of any exception.

The instruction MOVE.L #STARTUP,SVECTOR initializes the exception vector associated with the PIA. In our example, interrupts from the PIA are of low priority and have been assigned a priority of level 1. Since the PIA (and also the ACIA) do not support vector numbers, their interrupts are handled by the MC68000's autovectoring. As shown in Figure 15-1, the autovectors start at address 64. Address 64 is the location of Level 1 autovector interrupts and this is the vector in which we store the address of our service routine.

If you forget to initialize an exception vector, the processor will still use the contents of the vector to determine the starting address of the exception handler. However, this address will be invalid and the processor would continue execution at this invalid address. **You must initialize exception vectors, just as you initialize certain program data before use.**

In addition to setting up the exception vector, the program's only other action is to enable the interrupt from the startup PIA. The program enables that interrupt by setting bit 0 of the PIA control register and then enabling processor interrupts.

Finally, the program is ready to wait for the start-up interrupt. Instead of waiting for the interrupt by executing an endless loop such as jump-to-self (LOOP: JMP LOOP), the instruction STOP could be executed. STOP causes the processor to stop executing instructions and wait for an interrupt or exception (TRACE or RESET). The STOP instruction also allows you to change the processor's interrupt level, since the data word following the STOP is loaded into the status register. In order to allow interrupts, the interrupt level must be changed from level 7 (set during RESET) to level 0 (one level less than the startup PIA's level 1). Priority level 0 allows the processor to recognize interrupts at any level. The data word must also have the bit corresponding to the status register's Supervisor Mode (S) bit set.

The STOP instruction is one of the few MC68000 instructions which can only be executed in supervisor mode. If executed in user mode, a privilege violation exception will occur. (Generally, instructions which attempt to change the processor's interrupt level, supervisor/user state, or user stack pointer are privileged instructions.)

When an interrupt is generated from the PIA, the exception process is initiated. First, the contents of the full status register are saved on top of the supervisor stack followed by the contents of the program counter. The program counter is pointing to the next instruction to be executed, in this example the address of the instruction following the STOP instruction. The processor is set to supervisor state and the priority interrupt level is set to the level of the interrupt being processed. Next the processor fetches the address of the interrupt handler from the associated interrupt vector. Since we are expecting an autovector level 1 interrupt, the associated vector is located at address 64.

Upon entry to the interrupt service routine at location STARTUP, the priority level will be 1 and the processor will be in supervisor mode. Since the priority level has now changed, other interrupts of level 1 priority will be masked from interrupting the processor. What would happen if the STOP instruction had set the priority level to 1?

The service routine clears the startup interrupt by reading the appropriate PIA data register. This operation is necessary, even though no data transfer is required. Otherwise the startup interrupt would remain active and would interrupt again as soon as level 1 interrupts were reenabled.

The TST instruction is used to clear the interrupt since it does not modify any registers except the condition code register. **The exception process does not save any data or address registers. If the exception service routine needs to use any registers, they must be saved upon entry and restored upon exit from the routine.**

RTE restores control to the interrupted program sequence at the instruction following the STOP. As part of the restoration process, the supervisor/user state and interrupt priority level are reset to their states prior to the interrupt by pulling the previously copied status register contents from the stack. Next, the previous value of the program counter is pulled from the stack and loaded into the program counter. No other registers except the program counter and status register are modified by RTE. Like STOP, RTE is a privileged instruction and can only be executed in supervisor state.

This program assumes that there are no other level 1 interrupts being generated. If other level 1 interrupts can occur, a polling routine would have to be added to the interrupt handler and the main program would have to be modified. How would you do this?

15-2. A KEYBOARD INTERRUPT

Purpose: The main program clears the variable FLAG at memory location 6000 and waits for a keyboard interrupt. The interrupt service routine sets FLAG to 1 and places the data from the keyboard in the variable KEY at memory location 6001.

Sample Problem:

```
         Keyboard data = 43
Result:  FLAG - (6000) = 01   Flag indicating new
                              keyboard data
         KEY - (6001) = 43    Keyboard data
```

Flowchart:

Main Program:

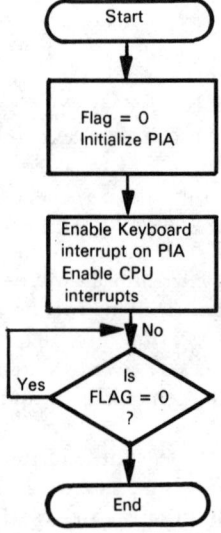

Interrupt Service Routine:

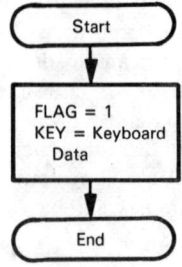

Program 15-2a:

```
                00004000     PROGRAM:    EQU     $4000
                00004600     INT_25:     EQU     $4600
                00006000     DATA:       EQU     $6000

                0003FF40     PIADDA:     EQU     $3FF40          DATA DIRECTION REGISTER A
                0003FF40     PIADA:      EQU     $3FF40          DATA REGISTER A
                0003FF44     PIACA:      EQU     $3FF44          CONTROL REGISTER A
                00000005     PIA_EN:     EQU     $05             PIA INTERRUPT ENABLE
                00002000     IMSK0:      EQU     $2000           SUPERVISOR/INTERRUPT LEVEL 0

                00006000                 ORG     DATA
006000          00000001     FLAG:       DS.B    1               DATA READY FLAG
006001          00000001     KEY:        DS.B    1               INPUT KEY DATA

                00004000                 ORG     PROGRAM

004000          42386000     PGM15_2A:   CLR.B   FLAG            CLEAR DATA READY FLAG
004004          42390003FF44             CLR.B   PIACA           ADDRESS DATA DIRECTION REGISTER
00400A          42390003FF40             CLR.B   PIADDA          MAKE ALL DATA LINES INPUTS
004010          13FC0005
                0003FF44                 MOVE.B  #PIA_EN,PIACA   ENABLE INTERRUPT FROM KEYBOARD PIA
004018          46FC2000                 MOVE    #IMSK0,SR       ENABLE ALL INTERRUPTS
00401C          4A386000     WTRDY:      TST.B   FLAG            IS THERE DATA FROM THE KEYBOARD
004020          67FA                     BEQ     WTRDY           NO, WAIT

004022          4E75                     RTS

                             *   INTERRUPT SERVICE ROUTINE

                00004600                 ORG     INT_25

004600          11FC00016000             MOVE.B  #1,FLAG         SET DATA READY FLAG
004606          11F90003FF40
                6001                     MOVE.B  PIADA,KEY       SAVE KEYBOARD DATA
00460E          4E73                     RTE                     RETURN TO INTERRUPTED ROUTINE

                                         END     PGM15_2A
```

You must initialize the PIA completely before enabling interrupts. This includes establishing the directions of ports and control lines and determining the transitions to be recognized on input strobes.

The main program clears the Data Ready flag (FLAG) and then simply waits for the interrupt service routine to set it. The main program and the service routine communicate through two fixed memory addresses:

The variable FLAG indicates whether new data has been received from the keyboard.

The variable KEY is a single-location data buffer used to hold the value received from the keyboard.

Note the similarity between the Data Ready flag in memory and the status bit in the control register of the keyboard PIA. The program does not have to test bit 7 of the PIA control register, because there is a direct hardware (interrupt) connection between that bit and the CPU. Of course, we have also assumed that the keyboard is the only source of interrupts.

Unlike our previous example, we don't use the privileged instruction STOP. Instead, we monitor the variable FLAG to determine when an interrupt has occurred. Remember, however, that the STOP instruction, besides waiting for an interrupt to occur, also sets the desired interrupt priority level in the status register. In program 15-2a, we use the MOVE to Status Register instruction (MOVE #IMSK0,SR) to set the desired interrupt level. The data word ($2000 in this program) following the instruction opcode word defines the new interrupt priority level. Note that this instruction also defines the state of all condition codes in the status register. The MOVE to Status Register instruction is a privileged instruction.

Sometimes you may want to temporarily accept interrupts of a lower level than are

240 68000 Assembly Language Programming

currently being permitted by the status register interrupt mask. If you do this, you would probably want to save the current interrupt mask before enabling lower level interrupts. You could then restore the previous mask after the lower level interrupts have been processed. The MOVE from Status Register instruction can be used to save the current interrupt mask (along with the rest of the status register contents) and it is not a privileged instruction.

Remember that upon entry to the interrupt service routine, the interrupt mask in the status register has already been set automatically by the CPU to the level associated with the interrupt being processed. This inhibits additional interrupts at this level or lower. Only interrupts of a higher level can interrupt the CPU.

The RTE instruction at the end of the service routine transfers control back to the main program. If you want to transfer control somewhere else (perhaps to an error routine), you can change the program counter in the supervisor stack using the methods outlined earlier. RTE also restores the interrupt priority mask to the level that existed prior to the interrupt.

We do not use the registers to pass parameters and results. If we were to change the register values, we could interfere with the execution of the main program. In most applications, the main program is using the registers and random changes will cause havoc. At the very least, changing the registers lacks generality, since modifications to the main program surely could result in the use of registers that are currently available.

The service routine does not have to explicitly reenable the interrupts. The reason is that RTE automatically restores the old status register with the priority level in its original state. In fact, you will have to change the priority level on the stack if you do not want the interrupts to be reenabled to their prior levels.

You can save and restore other data (such as the contents of a memory location) by using the stack. This method can be expanded indefinitely (as long as there is RAM available for the stack), since nested service routines will not destroy the data saved by earlier routines.

Filling a Buffer via Interrupts

An alternative approach would be for the interrupt service routine to set FLAG only after receiving an entire line of text (such as a string of characters ending with a carriage return). Here we use FLAG as an end-of-line flag and memory locations 6002 and 6003 as a buffer pointer, POINTER. We will assume that the buffer starts in memory location 6004.

Program 15-2b:

```
        00004000          PROGRAM:  EQU    $4000
        00004600          INT_25:   EQU    $4600
        00006000          DATA:     EQU    $6000

        0003FF40          PIADDA:   EQU    $3FF40      DATA DIRECTION REGISTER A
        0003FF40          PIADA:    EQU    $3FF40      DATA REGISTER A
        0003FF44          PIACA:    EQU    $3FF44      CONTROL REGISTER A
        00000005          PIA_EN:   EQU    $05         PIA INTERRUPT ENABLE
        00002000          IMSK0:    EQU    $2000       SUPERVISOR/INTERRUPT LEVEL 0
        0000000D          CR:       EQU    $0D         CARRIAGE RETURN

        00006000                    ORG    DATA
006000  00000001          FLAG:     DS.B   1           END OF LINE FLAG
```

```
006001    00000001                    DS.B    1
006002    00000002    POINTER:        DS.W    1               POINTER TO BUFFER END + 1.
006004    00000050    BUFFER:         DS.B    80              INPUT BUFFER

          00004000                    ORG     PROGRAM

004000    42386000    PGM15_2B:       CLR.B   FLAG            CLEAR DATA READY FLAG
004004    31FC60046002                MOVE.W  #BUFFER,POINTER INITIALIZE POINTER
00400A    42390003FF44                CLR.B   PIACA           ADDRESS DATA DIRECTION REGISTER
004010    42390003FF40                CLR.B   PIADDA          MAKE ALL DATA LINES INPUTS
004016    13FC0005
          0003FF44                    MOVE.B  #PIA_EN,PIACA   ENABLE INTERRUPT FROM KEYBOARD PIA
00401E    46FC2000                    MOVE    #IMSK0,SR       ENABLE ALL INTERRUPTS
004022    4A386000    WTRDY:          TST.B   FLAG            HAS A LINE BEEN RECEIVED FROM KEYBO
004026    67FA                        BEQ     WTRDY           NO, WAIT

004028    4E75                        RTS

                      * INTERRUPT SERVICE ROUTINE

          00004600                    ORG     INT_25

004600    2F08                        MOVE.L  A0,-(SP)        PUSH A0 ON SUPERVISOR STACK
004602    30786002                    MOVE.W  POINTER,A0      GET POINTER TO NEXT BUFFER ENTRY
004606    10F90003FF40                MOVE.B  PIADA,(A0)+     SAVE KEY DATA IN BUFFER
00460C    0C28000DFFF                 CMPI.B  #CR,-1(A0)      IS KEY INPUT A CARRIAGE RETURN?
004612    6606                        BNE.S   DONE            NO, RETURN
004614    11FC00016000                MOVE.B  #1,FLAG         SET END OF LINE FLAG
00461A    31C86002    DONE:           MOVE.W  A0,POINTER      UPDATE BUFFER POINTER
00461E    205F                        MOVE.L  (SP)+,A0        RESTORE REGISTER A0
004620    4E73                        RTE                     RETURN TO INTERRUPTED ROUTINE

                                      END     PGM15_2B
```

This program fills a buffer starting at memory location 6004 until it receives a carriage return character (CR). POINTER holds the current buffer pointer. The interrupt service routine increments that pointer (with autoincrementing) after each use.

In a real application, the CPU could perform other tasks between interrupts. It could, for example, edit, move, or transmit a line from one buffer while the interrupt service routine was filling another buffer. This is the double buffering approach. The main program only has to ensure that the interrupt service routine doesn't run out of buffers.

An alternative approach would be for FLAG to contain a counter rather than a flag. The contents of that location would then indicate to the main program how many bytes of data had been received. The main program would then know how many characters were in the buffer without counting them. It could even deal with the buffer whenever a certain number of new data bytes were in it. The service routine would simply increment the counter as well as the buffer pointer as part of each input operation.

Interrupt service routines are invoked randomly because of the nature of interrupts. Therefore, you can't know which registers the interrupt program may have been using. **To prevent accidental modification of registers that may be in use by an interrupted program, you should always save and restore the contents of all registers used by the interrupt service routine.** The MOVEM instruction, which we have previously discussed, provides a simple means of saving and restoring registers.

15-3. A PRINTER INTERRUPT

Purpose: The main program clears a variable FLAG at memory location 6000 and waits for a ready interrupt from a printer. This interrupt service routine sets FLAG to 1 and sends the contents of the variable CHAR at memory location 6001 to the printer.

242 68000 Assembly Language Programming

Sample Problem:

                CHAR - (6001) = 51
      Result: FLAG - (6000) = 01   Flag indicating last data item
                                     has been sent

Printer receives a 51_{16} (ASCII Q) when it is ready.

Flowchart:

Main Program:

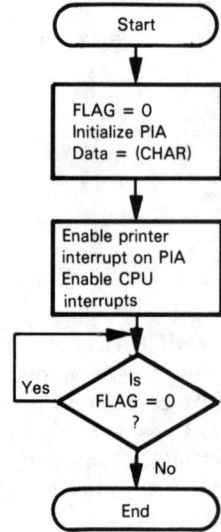

Interrupt Service Routine:

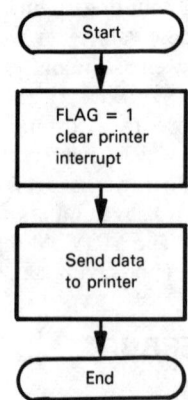

Program 15-3a:

```
00004000          PROGRAM:   EQU      $4000
00004600          INT_25:    EQU      $4600
```

Interrupts and Other Exceptions 243

```
             00006000      DATA:       EQU       $6000

             0003FF40      PIADDA:     EQU       $3FF40       DATA DIRECTION REGISTER A
             000000FF      DLOUT:      EQU       $FF          PIA DATA LINES AS OUTPUTS
             0003FF40      PIADA:      EQU       $3FF40       DATA REGISTER A
             0003FF44      PIACA:      EQU       $3FF44       CONTROL REGISTER A
             00000005      PIA_EN:     EQU       $05          PIA INTERRUPT ENABLE
             00002000      IMSK0:      EQU       $2000        SUPERVISOR/INTERRUPT LEVEL 0

             00006000                  ORG       DATA
006000       00000001      FLAG:       DS.B      1            DATA ACCEPT FLAG
006001       00000001      CHAR:       DS.B      1            PRINTER OUTPUT DATA

             00004000                  ORG       PROGRAM
004000       42386000      PGM15_3A:   CLR.B     FLAG         CLEAR DATA ACCEPT FLAG
004004       42390003FF44              CLR.B     PIACA        ADDRESS DATA DIRECTION REGISTER
00400A       13FC00FF
004012       13FC0005                  MOVE.B    #DLOUT,PIADDA MAKE ALL DATA LINES OUTPUTS
             0003FF40
             0003FF44                  MOVE.B    #PIA_EN,PIACA ENABLE INTERRUPT FROM PRINTER PIA
00401A       46FC2000                  MOVE      #IMSK0,SR    ENABLE ALL INTERRUPTS
00401E       44386000      WTACK:      TST.B     FLAG         HAS DATA BEEN OUTPUTTED TO PRINTER?
004022       67FA                      BEQ       WTACK        NO, WAIT

004024       4E75                      RTS

                           *   INTERRUPT SERVICE ROUTINE

             00004600                  ORG       INT_25
004600       11FC00016000              MOVE.B    #1,FLAG      SET DATA ACCEPT FLAG
004606       4A390003FF40              TST.B     PIADA        CLEAR PRINTER INTERRUPT
00460C       13F86001
             0003FF40                  MOVE.B    CHAR,PIADA   OUTPUT DATA TO PRINTER
004614       4E73                      RTE                    RETURN TO INTERRUPTED ROUTINE
                                       END       PGM15_3A
```

The only differences from the keyboard interrupt routines are the meaning of the flag, the direction of the data transfer, and the need for the instruction TST.B PIADA to clear bit 7 of the PIA control register. Remember that an input operation automatically clears that bit, but an output operation does not.

Here a cleared FLAG indicates that the CPU has data available that has not yet been sent to the printer. When the interrupt service routine sets the flag, the main program knows the data has been sent. The flag acts as an acknowledgment from the printer or a data accepted indicator.

Remember that you may find it necessary to place a read at the start of the main program to clear stray interrupts. MOVE.B PIADA,D0 or TST.B PIADA will do the job, as long as you place it after the instruction that addresses the data register but before the instruction that enables CPU interrupts.

Emptying a Buffer with Interrupts

As in the keyboard example, **we could have the interrupt service routine set the Data Accepted flag after it sends the printer an entire line of data** ending with a carriage return. Here again we use FLAG as an end-of-line flag and memory locations 6002 and 6003 as a buffer pointer. We will assume that the buffer starts in memory location 6004.

Program 15-3b:
Main Program:

```
00004000      PROGRAM:    EQU       $4000
00004600      INT_25:     EQU       $4600
00006000      DATA:       EQU       $6000
```

```
                0003FF40        PIADDA:     EQU     $3FF40          DATA DIRECTION REGISTER A
                000000FF        DLOUT:      EQU     $FF             DATA LINES AS ALL OUTPUTS
                0003FF40        PIADA:      EQU     $3FF40          DATA REGISTER A
                0003FF44        PIACA:      EQU     $3FF44          CONTROL REGISTER A
                00000005        PIA_EN:     EQU     $05             PIA INTERRUPT ENABLE
                00002000        IMSK0:      EQU     $2000           SUPERVISOR/INTERRUPT LEVEL 0
                0000000D        CR:         EQU     $0D             CARRIAGE RETURN

                00006000                    ORG             DATA
006000          00000001        FLAG:       DS.B    1               END OF LINE FLAG
006001          00000001                    DS.B    1
006002          00000002        POINTER:    DS.W    1               POINTER TO BUFFER END + 1
006004          00000050        BUFFER:     DS.B    80              INPUT BUFFER

                00004000                    ORG             PROGRAM

004000          42386000        PGM15_3B:   CLR.B   FLAG            CLEAR END OF LINE FLAG
004004          31FC60046002                MOVE.W  #BUFFER,POINTER INITIALIZE POINTER
00400A          42390003FF44                CLR.B   PIACA           ADDRESS DATA DIRECTION REGISTER
004010          13FC00FF
                0003FF40                    MOVE.B  #DLOUT,PIADDA   MAKE ALL DATA LINES OUTPUTS
004018          13FC0005
                0003FF44                    MOVE.B  #PIA_EN,PIACA   ENABLE INTERRUPT FROM PRINTER PIA
004020          46FC2000                    MOVE    #IMSK0,SR       ENABLE ALL INTERRUPTS
004024          4A386000        WTEOL:      TST.B   FLAG            HAS ALL OF LINE BEEN PRINTED?
004028          67FA                        BEQ     WTEOL           NO, WAIT

00402A          4E75                        RTS

                                *   INTERRUPT SERVICE ROUTINE

                00004600                    ORG             INT_25

004600          2F08                        MOVE.L  A0,-(SP)        PUSH A0 ON SUPERVISOR STACK
004602          4A390003FF40                TST.B   PIADA           CLEAR PRINTER INTERRUPT
004608          30786002                    MOVE.W  POINTER,A0      GET POINTER TO NEXT BUFFER ENTRY
00460C          13D80003FF40                MOVE.B  (A0)+,PIADA     SEND NEXT CHARACTER TO PRINTER
004612          0C28000DFFFF                CMPI.B  #CR,-1(A0)      WAS LAST CHARACTER A CARRIAGE RETURN
004618          6606                        BNE.S   DONE            NO, RETURN
00461A          11FC00016000                MOVE.B  #1,FLAG         SET END OF LINE FLAG
004620          31C86002        DONE:       MOVE.W  A0,POINTER      UPDATE BUFFER POINTER
004624          205F                        MOVE.L  (SP)+,A0        RESTORE REGISTER A0
004626          4E73                        RTE                     RETURN TO INTERRUPTED ROUTINE

                                            END             PGM15_3B
```

We could use double buffering to allow I/O and processing to occur independently without ever halting the CPU to wait for the printer.

Fixed-Length Buffer

Still another approach uses FLAG as a buffer counter. For example, the following program waits for 20 characters to be sent to the printer.

Program 15-3c:

```
                00004000        PROGRAM:    EQU     $4000
                00004600        INT_25:     EQU     $4600
                00006000        DATA:       EQU     $6000

                0003FF40        PIADDA:     EQU     $3FF40          DATA DIRECTION REGISTER A
                000000FF        DLOUT:      EQU     $FF             DATA LINES AS ALL OUTPUTS
                0003FF40        PIADA:      EQU     $3FF40          DATA REGISTER A
                0003FF44        PIACA:      EQU     $3FF44          CONTROL REGISTER A
                00000005        PIA_EN:     EQU     $05             PIA INTERRUPT ENABLE
                00002000        IMSK0:      EQU     $2000           SUPERVISOR/INTERRUPT LEVEL 0
                0000000D        CR:         EQU     $0D             CARRIAGE RETURN

                00006000                    ORG             DATA
006000          00000001        FLAG:       DS.B    1               BUFFER COUNTER
006001          00000001                    DS.B    1
006002          00000002        POINTER:    DS.W    1               POINTER TO BUFFER END + 1
006004          00000050        BUFFER:     DS.B    80              INPUT BUFFER

                00004000                    ORG             PROGRAM

004000          42386000        PGM15_3C:   CLR.B   FLAG            CLEAR BUFFER COUNTER
004004          31FC60046002                MOVE.W  #BUFFER,POINTER INITIALIZE POINTER
```

```
00400A    42390003FF44              CLR.B    PIACA                ADDRESS DATA DIRECTION REGISTER
004010    13FC00FF
          0003FF40                  MOVE.B   #DLOUT,PIADDA        MAKE ALL DATA LINES OUTPUTS
004018    13FC0005
          0003FF44                  MOVE.B   #PIA_EN,PIACA        ENABLE INTERRUPT FROM PRINTER PIA
004020    46FC2000                  MOVE     #IMSK0,SR            ENABLE ALL INTERRUPTS
004024    0C3800146000  WTEOL:      CMP.B    #20,FLAG             HAVE 20 CHARACTERS BEEN SENT?
00402A    66F8                      BNE      WTEOL                NO, WAIT

00402C    4E75                      RTS
                                *   INTERRUPT SERVICE ROUTINE
          00004600                  ORG      INT_25
004600    2F08                      MOVE.L   A0,-(SP)             PUSH A0 ON SUPERVISOR STACK
004602    4A390003FF40              TST.B    PIADA                CLEAR PRINTER INTERRUPT
004608    30786002                  MOVE.W   POINTER,A0           GET POINTER TO NEXT BUFFER ENTRY
00460C    13D80003FF40              MOVE.B   (A0)+,PIADDA         SEND NEXT CHARACTER TO PRINTER
004612    0C28000DFFFF              CMPI.B   #CR,-(A0)            WAS LAST CHARACTER A CARRIAGE RETURN
004618    6604                      BNE.S    DONE                 NO,RETURN
00461A    52786000                  ADDQ     #1,FLAG              INCREMENT BUFFER COUNTER
00461E    31C86002      DONE:       MOVE.W   A0,POINTER           UPDATE BUFFER POINTER
004622    205F                      MOVE.L   A0,POINTER           RESTORE REGISTOR A0
004624    4E73                      RTE                           RETURN TO INTERRUPTED ROUTINE
                                    END      PGM15_3C
```

15-4. A REAL-TIME CLOCK INTERRUPT

Purpose: The computer waits for an interrupt from a real-time clock.

Real-Time Clock

A real-time clock simply provides a regular series of pulses. The interval between the pulses can be used as a time reference. **Real-time clock interrupts can be counted to give any multiple of the basic time interval.** A real-time clock can be produced by dividing down the CPU clock, by using a timer like the 6840 device or the one included in the 6846 multifunction support device, or by using external sources such as the AC line frequency.

Note the tradeoffs involved in determining the frequency of the real-time clock. A high frequency (say 10 kHz) allows the creation of a wide range of time intervals of high accuracy. On the other hand, the overhead involved in counting real-time clock interrupts may be considerable. **The choice of frequency depends on the precision and timing requirements of your application. The clock may, of course, consist partly of hardware; a counter may count high frequency pulses and interrupt the processor only occasionally. A program will have to read the counter to measure time to high accuracy.**

One problem is synchronizing operations with the real-time clock. Clearly, there will be some effect on the precision of the timing interval if the CPU starts the measurement randomly during a clock period, rather than exactly at the beginning. Some ways to synchronize operations are:

1. **Start the CPU and clock together.** RESET or a startup interrupt can start the clock as well as the CPU.
2. **Allow the CPU to start and stop the clock under program control.**
3. **Use a high-frequency clock** so that an error of less than one clock period will be small.

246 68000 Assembly Language Programming

4. Line up the clock (by waiting for an edge or interrupt) **before starting the measurement.**

A real-time clock interrupt should have very high priority, since the precision of the timing intervals will be affected by any delay in servicing the interrupt. **The usual practice is to make the real-time clock the highest priority interrupt except for power failure.** The clock interrupt service routine is generally kept extremely short so that it does not interfere with other CPU activities.

In the following programs we assume a clock has been connected to a PIA interrupt. An interrupt will occur once each clock cycle.

15-4a. Wait for Real-Time Clock

Program 15-4a:

```
           00004000      PROGRAM:   EQU      $4000
           00004600      INT_26:    EQU      $4600
           00006000      DATA:      EQU      $6000

           0003FF40      TPIADA:    EQU      $3FF40        DATA REGISTER A FOR TIMER PIA
           0003FF44      TPIACA:    EQU      $3FF44        CONTROL REGISTER A FOR TIMER PIA
           00000005      PIA_EN:    EQU      $05           PIA INTERRUPT ENABLE
           00002000      IMSK0:     EQU      $2000         SUPERVISOR/INTERRUPT LEVEL 0

           00006000                 ORG      DATA
006000     00000001      COUNTER:   DS.B     1             TIMER COUNTER

           00004000                 ORG      PROGRAM
004000     42386000      PGM15_4A:  CLR.B    COUNTER       CLEAR TIMER COUNTER
004004     13FC0005
             0003FF44               MOVE.B   #PIA_EN,TPIACA ENABLE INTERRUPT FROM TIMER PIA
00400C     46FC2000                 MOVE     #IMSK0,SR     ENABLE ALL INTERRUPTS
004010     4A386000      TWAIT:     TST.B    COUNTER       HAS TIMER COUNTER BEEN INCREMENTED?
004014     67FA                     BEQ      TWAIT         NO, WAIT
004016     4E75                     RTS

                            *  TIMER INTERRUPT SERVICE ROUTINE

           00004600                 ORG      INT_26
004600     4A390003FF40             TST.B    TPIADA        CLEAR TIMER INTERRUPT
004606     52386000                 ADDQ.B   #1,COUNTER    INCREMENT TIMER COUNTER
00460A     4E73                     RTE                    RETURN TO INTERRUPTED ROUTINE

                                    END      PGM15_4A
```

The variable COUNTER at memory location 6000 contains the clock counter.

If bit 1 of the PIA control register is 0, the interrupt will occur on the high-to-low (falling) edge of the clock. If that bit is 1, the interrupt will occur on the low-to-high (rising) edge of the clock.

The interrupt service routine must explicitly clear bit 7 of the PIA control register since no data transfer is necessary.

You could still use the PIA data port as long as you did not accidentally clear the status bit from the real-time clock before it was recognized. This would be no problem if the port were used for output to a simple peripheral (such as a set of LEDs), since output operations do not affect the status bits anyway.

Clearly, **we can easily extend this routine to handle more counts and provide greater precision by using more memory locations for the clock counter** and a different test in the main program.

15-4b. Wait for 10 Clock Interrupts

Program 15-4b:

```
          00004000      PROGRAM:         EQU     $4000
          00004600      INT_26:          EQU     $4600
          00006000      DATA:            EQU     $6000

          0003FF40      TPIADA:          EQU     $3FF40         DATA REGISTER A FOR TIMER PIA
          0003FF44      TPIACA:          EQU     $3FF44         CONTROL REGISTER A FOR TIMER PIA
          00000005      PIA_EN:          EQU     $05            PIA INTERRUPT ENABLE
          00002000      IMSK0:           EQU     $2000          SUPERVISOR/INTERRUPT LEVEL 0
          0000000A      TDELAY:          EQU     10             TIMER DELAY

          00006000                       ORG     DATA
006000    00000001      COUNTER:         DS.B    1              TIMER COUNTER

          00004000                       ORG     PROGRAM
004000    42386000      PGM15_4B: CLR.B                         CLEAR TIMER COUNTER
004004    13FC0005
              0003FF44                   MOVE.B  #PIA_EN,TPIACA ENABLE INTERRUPT FROM TIMER PIA
00400C    46FC2000                       MOVE    #IMSK0,SR      ENABLE ALL INTERRUPTS
004010    103C000A                       MOVE.B  #TDELAY,D0     TIMER COUNT DELAY
004014    B0386000      TWAIT:           CMP.B   COUNTER,D0     HAS DESIRED DELAY BEEN ACHIEVED?
004018    67FA                           BEQ     TWAIT          NO, WAIT

00401A    4E75                           RTS

                        *   TIMER INTERRUPT SERVICE ROUTINE

          00004600                       ORG     INT_26
004600    4A390003FF40                   TST.B   TPIADA         CLEAR TIMER INTERRUPT
004606    52386000                       ADDQ.B  #1,COUNTER     INCREMENT TIMER COUNTER
00460A    4E73                           RTE                    RETURN TO INTERRUPTED ROUTINE

                                         END     PGM15_4B
```

15-4c. Maintaining Real Time

A more realistic real-time clock interrupt routine could keep track of the passage of time using several memory locations. For example, the following routine uses addresses 6000 through 6003 to maintain clock time as follows:

  6000 - hundredths of seconds
  6001 - seconds
  6002 - minutes
  6003 - hours

We assume that a 100Hz input provides the regular source of interrupts.

Program 15-4c:

```
          00004000      PROGRAM:         EQU     $4000
          00004600      INT_26:          EQU     $4600
          00006000      DATA:            EQU     $6000

          0003FF40      TPIADA:          EQU     $3FF40         DATA REGISTER A FOR TIMER PIA
          0003FF44      TPIACA:          EQU     $3FF44         CONTROL REGISTER A FOR TIMER PIA
          00000005      PIA_EN:          EQU     $05            PIA INTERRUPT ENABLE
          00002000      IMSK0:           EQU     $2000          SUPERVISOR/INTERRUPT LEVEL 0
          0000001E      TDELAY:          EQU     30             300 DELAY (DELAY MUST BE < 1 SECOND.

          00006000                       ORG     DATA
006000    00000001      HUNDSEC:         DS.B    1              HUNDREDTHS OF SECONDS
006001    00000001      SECONDS:         DS.B    1              SECONDS
006002    00000001      MINUTES:         DS.B    1              MINUTES
006003    00000001      HOURS:           DS.B    1              HOURS

          00004000                       ORG     PROGRAM
```

```
004000      13FC0005
            0003FF44    PGM15_4C:  MOVE.B     #PIA_EN,TPIACA      ENABLE INTERRUPT FROM TIMER PIA
004008      46FC2000               MOVE       #IMSK0,SR           ENABLE ALL INTERRUPTS
00400C      10386000               MOVE.B     HUNDSEC,D0          GET CURRENT HUNDREDTHS OF SECOND TI
004010      0600001E               ADDI.B     #TDELAY,D0          ADD DELAY TIME
004014      0C000064               CMPI.B     #100,D0             MOD 100
004018      65000006               BCS        TWAIT
00401C      04000064               SUBI.B     #100,D0
004020      B0386000    TWAIT:     CMP.B      HUNDSEC,D0          HAS DESIRED DELAY BEEN ACHIEVED?
004024      67FA                   BEQ        TWAIT               NO, WAIT

004026      4E75                   RTS
                                * TIMER INTERRUPT SERVICE ROUTINE
            00004600               ORG        INT_26
004600      48E78000               MOVEM.L    D0,-(SP)            SAVE D0
004604      4A390003FF40           TST.B      TPIADA              CLEAR TIMER INTERRUPT
00460A      52386000               ADDQ.B     #1,HUNDSEC          UPDATE HUNDREDTHS OF SECONDS
00460E      103C0064               MOVE.B     #100,D0
004612      B0386000               CMP.B      HUNDSEC,D0          IS THERE A CARRY FROM HUNDREDTHS?
004616      6628                   BNE.S      TDONE               NO, DONE
004618      42386000               CLR.B      HUNDSEC             YES, CLEAR HUNDREDTHS OF SECONDS
00461C      52386001               ADDQ.B     #1,SECONDS          UPDATE SECONDS
004620      103C003C               MOVE.B     #60,D0
004624      B0386001               CMP.B      SECONDS,D0          IS THERE A CARRY TO MINUTES
004628      6616                   BNE.S      TDONE               NO, DONE
00462A      42386001               CLR.B      SECONDS             YES, CLEAR SECONDS
004632      B0386002               CPM.B      MINUTES,D0          IS THERE A CARRY TO HOURS
004636      6608                   BNE.S      TDONE               NO, DONE
004638      42386001               CLR.B      MINUTES             YES, MAKE MINUTES ZERO
00463C      52386003               ADDQ.B     #1, HOURS           UPDATE HOURS
00462E      52386002               ADDQ.B     #1,MINUTES          UPDATE MINUTES
004640      4CDF0001    TDONE:     MOVEM.L    (SP)+,D0            RESTORE D0
004644      4E73                   RTE                            RETURN TO INTERRUPTED ROUTINE

                                   END        PGM15_4C
```

The main program produces a delay of 300 milliseconds. The longest delay that can be handled by this routine is 990 milliseconds. How would you modify this program to handle longer delays?

This approach is the same one you would take if you had to let something cook for 20 minutes. You must determine the current time by reading your watch (the counter), calculate the target time by adding 20 (mod 60, so 20 minutes past 6:50 is 7:10), and wait for your watch to reach the target time. Notice that if the delay is less than one hour, you can ignore the hour hand and wait until the minute hand comes around to ten minutes after the hour. This is the method the program uses. (If your watch doesn't have hands, just wait until the minutes numbers display 10.)

Change the program so it produces a 20 minute delay (an obvious requirement for a microprocessor-controlled microwave oven).

Of course, the program could perform other tasks and only check the elapsed time occasionally. How would you produce a delay of seven seconds? of three minutes? Many applications do not require long delays to be highly accurate; for example, the operator of a microwave oven does not care if intervals in minutes are off by a few seconds.

Sometimes you may want to keep time either as BCD digits or as ASCII characters. How would you revise the last interrupt service routine to handle these alternatives?

Assuming that the clock PIA generates level 2 interrupts, its interrupts are then handled by the level 2 autovector at address 68. If the MC68000 has its interrupt priority mask set at level 0 and simultaneous interrupts are received from both the clock PIA

Interrupts and Other Exceptions **249**

Flowchart 15-4c:

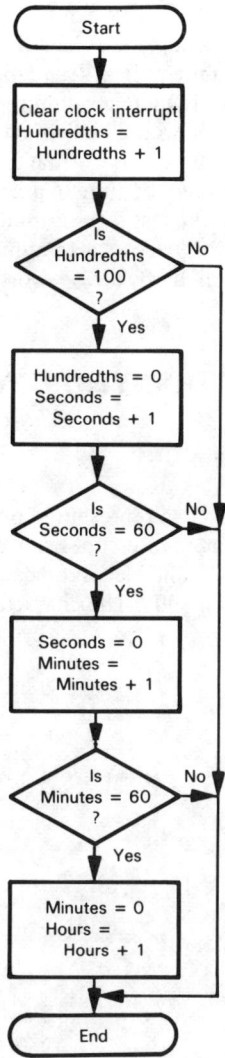

and the printer PIA in example 15-3, here is what happens. Since the printer PIA generates a level 1 interrupt, the clock PIA is serviced first. The interrupt from the printer PIA would be inhibited until the priority mask was reset to zero. If the printer interrupt occurs first and service of this interrupt has begun, this service would be interrupted by the occurrence of a clock PIA interrupt. After the clock service routine has been completed, control would be returned to the printer service routine at the point where it was interrupted.

High-Frequency Clock

Even a high-frequency real-time clock can be handled without much processor intervention. The usual method is to have the clock increment a set of counters which then interrupt the processor at a much lower frequency. For example, the input frequency could be 1 MHz; that input frequency would then be passed through 3 decimal counters and the output of the last one would be tied to the PIA. The PIA would recive a single clock pulse for every 1000 input pulses (that is, when the 3 decimal counters overflow). The processor can determine the time to greater precision than 1 ms by reading the counters, since they contain the less significant digits. As usual, some additional hardware (counters and input ports) is necessary to reduce the burden on the CPU. This is a typical tradeoff; the additional hardware is worthwhile only if the application requires precise timing.

15-5. A TELETYPEWRITER INTERRUPT

15-5a. ACIA Interrupt Routine

Purpose: The main program clears a flag represented by the variable FLAG at memory location 6000 and waits for an interrupt from a 6850 ACIA. The interrupt service routine sets FLAG to 1 and places the data from the ACIA in the variable CHAR at memory location 6001. The characters are 7 bits in length with odd parity and 2 stop bits.

Program 15-5a:

```
                00004000      PROGRAM:    EQU     $4000
                00004600      INT_25:     EQU     $4600
                00006000      DATA:       EQU     $6000

                0003FF01      ACIACR:     EQU     $3FF01          ACIA CONTROL REGISTER
                000EFF03      ACIADR:     EQU     $EFF03          ACIA DATA REGISTER
                000000C5      AMODE:      EQU     $C5             ACIA OPERATING MODE
                00000003      MRESET:     EQU     $03             ACIA MASTER RESET
                00002000      IMSK0:      EQU     $2000           SUPERVISOR/INTERRUPT LEVEL 0

                00006000                  ORG     DATA
006000          00000001      FLAG:       DS.B    1               DATA ACCEPT FLAG
006001          00000001      CHAR:       DS.B    1               CHARACTER FROM TTY

                00004000                  ORG     PROGRAM
004000          42386000      PGM15_5A:   CLR.B   FLAG            CLEAR DATA ACCEPT FLAG
004004          13FC0003
                0003FF01                  MOVE.B  #MRSET,ACIACR   MASTER RESET ACIA
00400C          13FC00C5
                0003FF01                  MOVE.B  #AMODE,ACIACR   ENABLE ACIA INTERRUPT/SET MODE
004014          46FC2000                  MOVE    #IMSK0,SR       ENABLE ALL INTERRUPTS
004018          4A386000      WAIT:       TST.B   FLAG            IS THERE DATA FROM ACIA?
00401C          67FA                      BEQ     WAIT            NO, WAIT
00401E          4E75                      RTS

                                *   INTERRUPT SERVICE ROUTINE

                00004600                  ORG     INT_25
004600          11FC00016000              MOVE.B  #1,FLAG         SET DATA ACCEPT FLAG
004606          11F9000EFF03
                6001                      MOVE.B  ACIADR,CHAR     SAVE TTY CHARACTER INPUT
00460E          4E73                      RTE                     RETURN TO INTERRUPTED ROUTINE
00460E          4E73                      RTE                     RETURN TO INTERRUPTED ROUTINE
                                          END     PGM15_5A
```

Since the 6850 ACIA has no RESET input, a master reset (setting control register

bits 0 and 1 to one simultaneously) is necessary before the ACIA is initialized.
We then initialize the bits in the ACIA control register as follows:

Bit 7 = 1 to enable the receiver interrupt
Bit 6 = 1 and Bit 5 = 0 to disable the transmitter
    interrupt
Bit 4 = 0, Bit 3 = 0, and Bit 2 = 1 to select 7-bit
    data with odd parity and two stop bits
Bit 1 = 0 and Bit 0 = 1 to select the divide by 16
    clock mode (a 1760 Hz clock must be supplied for a
    110 Baud data rate).

To determine if a particular 6850 ACIA is the source of an interrupt, the program must examine the interrupt request bit (bit 7 of the status register) in each ACIA. To differentiate between receiver and transmitter interrupts, the program must examine the Receive Data Register Full bit (bit 0 of the status register). Either reading the receive data register or writing into the transmit data register clears the ACIA's interrupt request bit.

15-5b. PIA Start Bit Interrupt

Teletypewriter data can also be received with a PIA. In this case, the serial input line from the teletypewriter is connected to both data bit 7 and control line 1 of the PIA.

Purpose: The main program clears a flag represented by the variable FLAG at memory location 6000 and waits for a teletypewriter interrupt. The interrupt service routine sets FLAG to 1 and places the data from the teletypewriter in the variable CHAR at memory location 6001.

Program 15-5b:

```
                00004000        PROGRAM:   EQU     $4000
                00004600        INT_25:    EQU     $4600
                00006000        DATA:      EQU     $6000
                00004800        TTYRCV:    EQU     $4800

                0003FF40        PIADDA:    EQU     $3FF40      DATA DIRECTION REGISTER A
                00000000        DATIN:     EQU     $0          PIA DATA LINES AS INPUTS
                0003FF40        PIADA:     EQU     $3FF40      DATA REGISTER A
                0003FF44        PIACA:     EQU     $3FF44      CONTROL REGISTER A
                00000005        PIA_EN:    EQU     $05         PIA INTERRUPT ENABLE
                00000004        PIA_DIS:   EQU     $04         PIA INTERRUPT DISABLE
                00002000        IMSK0:     EQU     $2000       SUPERVISOR/INTERRUPT LEVEL 0

                00006000                   ORG     DATA
006000          00000001        FLAG:      DS.B    1           DATA ACCEPT FLAG
006001          00000001        CHAR:      DS.B    1           CHARACTER INPUT FROM TTY

                00004000                   ORG     PROGRAM
004000          42386000        PGM15_5B:  CLR.B   FLAG        CLEAR DATA ACCEPT FLAG
004004          42390003FF44               CLR.B   PIACA       ADDRESS DATA DIRECTION REGISTER
00400A          13FC0000
                0003FF40                   MOVE.B  #DATIN,PIADDA  MAKE ALL DATA LINES INPUTS
004012          13FC0005
                0003FF44                   MOVE.B  #PIA_EN,PIACA  ENABLE INTERRUPT FROM TTY PIA
00401A          46FC2000                   MOVE    #IMSK0,SR   ENABLE ALL INTERRUPTS
00401E          4A386000        WAIT:      TST.B   FLAG        HAS START BIT BEEN RECEIVED?
004022          67FA                       BEQ     WAIT        NO, WAIT
004024          4EB84800                   JSR     TTYRCV      YES, FETCH DATA FROM TTY
004028          11C06001                   MOVE.B  D0,CHAR     SAVE TTY INPUT CHARACTER

00402C          4E75                       RTS

                                *   INTERRUPT SERVICE ROUTINE
```

252 68000 Assembly Language Programming

```
                00004600            ORG     INT_25
004600  11FC00016000        MOVE.B  #1,FLAG         SET DATA ACCEPT FLAG
004606  4A390003FF40        TST.B   PIADA           CLEAR START BIT INTERRUPT
00460C  13FC0004
        0003FF44            MOVE.B  #PIA_DIS,PIACA  DISABLE START BIT INTERRUPT
004614  4E73                RTE                     RETURN TO INTERRUPTED ROUTINE
                            END     PGM15_5B
```

Subroutine TTYRCV called by Program 15-5b is similar to the teletypewriter receive routine shown in Chapter 13, example 9, except that we have assumed a version that leaves the data in data register D0. The edge used to cause the interrupt is very important here. The transition from the normal '1' (MARK) state to the '0' (SPACE) state must cause the interrupt, since this transition signifies the start of the transmission. No '0' to '1' transition will occur until a non-zero data bit is received.

The service routine must disable the PIA interrupt, since otherwise each '1' to '0' transition in the character will cause an interrupt. Note that reading the data bits will clear any status flags set by the ignored transitions. Of course, the program must reenable the PIA interrupt (by setting bit 0 of the control register) to allow receipt of the next character, but this should be done after the current character has been read.

15-6. A Supervisor Call

Purpose: Allowing programs in the user state to access utility routines in the supervisor state.

In the design of systems which include monitors or operating systems, it is good programming practice to make utility routines out of frequently used sequences of instructions. These routines may provide simple functions such as determining time-of-day or they may provide much more complex functions such as memory management in a multi-user system or logical input/output on a disk-based system. The two-state architecture of the MC68000 prevents application programs in the user state from performing certain privileged instructions which are reserved for operation in the supervisor state. In future systems which may provide memory management, programs in the user state may be restricted to using memory only within their own limited address space.

In cases where user state programs must communicate with a monitor or operating system in the supervisor state, you can use the TRAP instructions. Execution of a TRAP instruction causes a processor exception and exception processing is performed in much the same manner as interrupt processing. Programs 15-6a and 15-6b show typical uses of the TRAP instruction.

Program 15-6a:

```
                00004000            PROGRAM: EQU    $4000
                00004400            TTYIN:   EQU    $4400
                00004500            PRINT:   EQU    $4500
                00004600            TRAP1:   EQU    $4600
                00005100            USTACK:  EQU    $5100
                00006000            DATA:    EQU    $6000

                00000084            ORG      $84                  TRAP 1 VECTOR
000084          00004600            DC.L     TRAP1

                00006000            ORG      DATA

006000          00000050   BUFFER:  DS.B     80                   INPUT/OUTPUT BUFFER

                00004000            ORG      PROGRAM
```

Interrupts and Other Exceptions 253

```
                    *  PROGRAM IN USER STATE
004000    3C7C6000   PGM156A:  MOVE.W    #BUFFER,A6
004004    4E41                 TRAP      #1               POINTER TO INPUT/OUTPUT BUFFER
004006    0001                 DC.W      1                MONITOR CALL
004008    4E41                 TRAP      #1               TO READ ONE TTY LINE
00400A    0002                 DC.W      2                MONITOR CALL
00400C    4E75                 RTS                        TO WRITE ONE PRINTER LINE

                    *  TRAP 1 HANDLER
          00004600            ORG       TRAP1
004600    48E7FFFE             MOVEM.L   D0-D7/A0-A6,-(SP)
004604    2A6F003E             MOVE.L    60+2(SP),A5      SAVE ALL USER REGISTERS
004608    48ED0002             LEA.L     2(A5),A5         RETURN ADDRESS
00460C    2F4D003E             MOVE.L    A5,60+2(SP)      ADDRESS OF INSTRUCTION AFTER TRAP
004610    0C6D0001FFFE         CMP.W     #1,-2(A5)        UPDATE STACK VALUE
004616    6606                 BNE.S     PRINTER          READ MONITOR CALL?
004618    4EB84400             JSR       TTYIN            NO, PRINTER CALL
00461C    6004                 BRA.S     DONE             READ ONE LINE FROM TTY
00461E    4EB84500   PRINTER:  JSR       PRINT
004622    4CDF7FFF   DONE:     MOVEM.L   (SP)+,D0-D7/A0-A6   OUTPUT ONE LINE TO PRINTER
004626    4E73                 RTE                        RESTORE USER REGISTERS
                                                          RETURN TO USER PROGRAM
                               END       PGM15 6A
```

Each of the processor's two states has its own stack pointer (address register A7). When the MC68000 is reset, all references to address register A7 use the supervisor stack pointer. The supervisor stack pointer is used until the s-bit in the status register is cleared, and the user state is entered. While in the user state, A7 references the user stack pointer.

Program 15-6a demonstrates a typical instruction sequence used to read and write from a TTY device using a monitor such as Motorola's MAC^{s}BUG.™ The sequence uses the TRAP #1 instruction to perform a call to supervisor function. In this example, address register A6 is used as an input parameter to the function and it points to the TTY input/output buffer. A second parameter to the function is contained in the word immediately following the TRAP instruction. This parameter indicates whether an input or output function is requested. A detailed description of parameter passing is contained in Chapter 10.

As discussed in the beginning of this chapter, the exception processing of the TRAP instruction causes the current processor program counter and status register to be pushed on the supervisor stack. The trap number, 1 in this example, is used to determine the appropriate TRAP vector much as the interrupt vector number is used to calculate the address of the interrupt vector. Since the TRAP vectors start at address $80, the vector for TRAP #1 is located at

$$\$80 + 1 * 4 = \$84$$

The long word address at location $84 contains the starting address of the TRAP #1 processing routine at location $4600. Again, like interrupt processing, initial exception processing is performed in supervisor mode.

Since only the status register and program counter are saved as part of the exception process, the exception handler must save any register which it uses. These registers must be restored prior to returning to the instruction following the exception. In the event that control may not immediately be returned to the application program causing the exception, you may also want to save the user stack register. The instruction MOVE USP,An can be used to accomplish this operation. On completion of processing, a MOVE An,USP is used to restore the user stack pointer. Both instructions are privileged instructions and necessary for systems with more than one task.

254 68000 Assembly Language Programming

Upon completion of exception processing by the exception handler, control must be returned to the instruction following the instruction which caused the exception. This is accomplished by using the RTE instruction which restores the previously saved status register and program counter from the supervisor stack. Since RTE affects the supervisor portion of the status register, it is a privileged instruction.

A variation of program 15-6a is shown in 15-6b. This variation uses two different TRAP instructions and therefore two exception handlers. Normally, we think of using the TRAP instructions while in user mode to communicate with functions in supervisor mode. However, the TRAP instructions may be used while in supervisor mode.

Program 15-6b:

```
              00004000      PROGRAM:  EQU       $4000
              00004400      TTYIN:    EQU       $4400
              00004500      PRINT:    EQU       $4500
              00004600      TRAPHDLR: EQU       $4600
              00005100      USTACK:   EQU       $5100
              00006000      DATA:     EQU       $6000

              00000084                ORG       $84                    TRAP 1/2 VECTOR
000084        00004600                DC.L      TRAP1
000088        0000460A                DC.L      TRAP2

              00006000                ORG       DATA
006000        00000050      BUFFER:   DS.B      80                     INPUT/OUTPUT BUFFER

              00004000                ORG       PROGRAM
                            *   PROGRAM IN USER STATE
004000        3E7C5100      PGM15_6B: MOVEA.W   #USTACK,A7             INITIALIZE USER STACK
004004        3C7C6000                MOVE.W    #BUFFER,A6             POINTER TO INPUT/OUTPUT BUFFER
004008        4E41                    TRAP      #1                     MONITOR CALL TO READ ONE TTY LINE
00400A        4E42                    TRAP      #2                     MONITOR CALL TO PRINT ONE LINE
00400C        4E75                    RTS

                            *   TRAP 1 AND 2 HANDLERS
              00004600                ORG       TRAPHDLR
004600        48E7FFFE      TRAP1:    MOVEM.L   D0-D7/A0-A6,-(SP)      SAVE ALL USER REGISTERS
004604        4EB84400                JSR       TTYIN                  READ ONE LINE FROM TTY
004608        6008                    BRA.S     RETURN
00460A        48E7FFFE      TRAP2:    MOVEM.L   D0-D7/A0-A6,-(SP)      SAVE ALL USER REGISTERS
00460E        4EB84500                JSR       PRINT                  OUTPUT ONE LINE TO PRINTER
004612        4CDF7FFF      RETURN:   MOVEM.L   (SP)+,D0-D7/A0-A6      RESTORE USER REGISTERS
004616        4E73                    RTE                              RETURN TO USER PROGRAM

                                      END       PGM15_6B
```

15-7. ENTERING USER MODE

Purpose: Establishing programs in user mode.

Program 15-7:

```
              00004800      RESET:    EQU       $4800
              00005100      STACK:    EQU       $5100
              00005300      USTACK:   EQU       $5300
              00000000      USER:     EQU       $0                     USER STATE/PRIORITY LEVEL 0
              00004000      USERPGM:  EQU       $4000                  USER PROGRAM

              00000000                ORG       0
000000        00005100                DC.L      STACK                  ADDRESS OF STACK
000004        00004800                DC.L      PGM15                  ADDRESS OF RESET PROGRAM

              00004800                ORG       RESET
004800        307C5300      PGM15:    MOVE.A W  #USTACK,A0             ADDRESS OF USER STACK
```

```
004804    4E60           MOVE.L    A0,USP         INITIALIZE USER STACK
004806    46FC0000       MOVE.W    #USER,SR       SET TO USER MODE
00480A    4EF84000       JMP       USERPGM        JUMP TO USER PROGRAM
                         END       PGM15
```

As mentioned previously, the MC68000 is initialized to operate in supervisor mode. To enter user mode, the Supervisor flag (S-bit) in the status register must be reset. This can be accomplished by any instruction which affects the Supervisor flag such as MOVE to SR, ANDI to SR, EORI to SR or RTE. With the MOVE, ANDI or EORI instructions, only the status register is affected and the instruction following the MOVE, ANDI or EORI is executed next in the user mode. The RTE instruction allows you to switch to user mode at a given address.

MORE GENERAL SERVICE ROUTINES[8]

More general interrupt service routine that are part of a complete interrupt-driven system must handle the following tasks:

1. **Saving any needed data on the stack so that interrupted programs can resume correctly.** The MC68000 saves only the program counter and the status register on the supervisor stack during its response to an interrupt. Therefore, your interrupt service routines must save and restore any additional registers they use.
2. **Restoring data and registers before executing RTE** and returning control to interrupted programs.
3. **Polling of all devices associated with a given interrupt** when more than one device can cause the interrupt. This is generally the case for devices which use autovectoring.
4. **Enabling and disabling interrupts appropriately.** Remember that the CPU automatically disables interrupts of the same or lower level as that of the interrupt just accepted.

REFERENCES

1. A, Osborne. *An Introduction to Microcomputers: Volume 1 — Basic Concepts.* Berkeley: Osborne/McGraw-Hill, 1980, Chapter 5.
2. R. L. Baldridge. "Interrupts Add Power, Complexity to Microcomputer Software Design," *EDN,* August 5, 1977, pp. 67-73.
3. R. Morris. "6800 Routine Supervises Service Requests," *EDN,* October 5, 1979, pp. 73-81.

4. I. P. Breikss. "Nonmaskable Interrupt Saves Processor Register Contents," *Electronics,* July 21, 1977, p. 104.
5. A. Osborne. *An Introduction to Microcomputers: Volume 2 — Some Real Microprocessors.* Berkeley: Osborne/McGraw-Hill, 1980, pp. 9-71 through 9-77.
6. R. Grappel. "Technique Avoids Interrupt Dangers," *EDN,* May 5, 1979, p. 88.
7. G. Horner. "Online Control of a Laboratory Instrument by a Timesharing Computer," *Computer Design,* February 1980, pp. 90-106.
8. For further discussion and some real-life examples of designing systems with interrupt, see the following:

    S. C. Baunach. "An Example of an M6800-based GPIB Interface," *EDN,* September 20, 1977, pp. 125-28.

    L. E. Cannon and P. S. Kreager. "Using a Microprocessor: a Real-Life Application, Part 2 — Software," *Computer Design,* October 1975, pp. 81-89.

    D. Fullager et al. "Interfacing Data Converters and Microprocessors," *Electronics,* December 8, 1976, pp. 81-9.

    S. A. Hill. "Multiprocess Control Interface Makes Remote MP Command Possible," *EDN,* February 5, 1976, pp. 87-9.

    Holderby. "Designing a Microprocessor-based Terminal for Factory Data Collection," *Computer Design,* March 1977, pp. 81-8.

    A. Lange. "OPTACON Interface permits the Blind to 'Read' Digital Instruments," *EDN,* February 5, 1976, pp. 84-6.

    J. D. Logan and P. S. Kreager. "Using a Microprocessor: a Real-Life Application, Part 1 — Hardware," *Computer Design,* September 1975, pp. 69-77.

    A. Moore and M. Eidson. "Printer Control," Application Note available from Motorola Semiconductor Products, Phoenix, Ariz.

    M. C. Mulder and P. P. Fasang. "A Microprocessor Controlled Substation Alarm Logger," IECI '78 Proceedings — Industrial Applications of Microprocessors, March 20-22, 1978, pp. 2-6.

    P. J. Zsombar-Murray et al. "Microprocessor Based Frequency Response Analyzer," IECI '78 Proceedings — Industrial Applications of Microprocessors, March 20-22, 1978, pp. 36-44.

The Proceedings of the IEEE's Industrial Electronics and Control Instrumentation Group's Annual Meeting on "Industrial Applications of Microprocessors" contain many interesting articles. Volumes (starting with 1975) are available from IEEE Service Center, CP Department, 445 Hoes Lane, Piscataway, N. J. 08854.

IV
Software Development

The previous chapters have described how to write short assembly language programs. While this is an important topic, it is only a small part of software development. Although writing assembly language programs is a major task for the beginner, it soon becomes simple. By now you should be familiar with standard methods for programming in assembly language on the MC68000 microprocessor. **The next six chapters will describe how to formulate tasks as programs and how to combine short programs to form a working system.**

THE STAGES OF SOFTWARE DEVELOPMENT

Software development consists of many stages. **Figure IV-1 is a flowchart of the software development process.** Its stages are:

- Problem definition
- Program design
- Coding
- Debugging
- Testing
- Documentation
- Maintenance and redesign

Each of these stages is important in the construction of a working system. Coding, the writing of programs in a form that the computer understands, is only one stage in a long process.

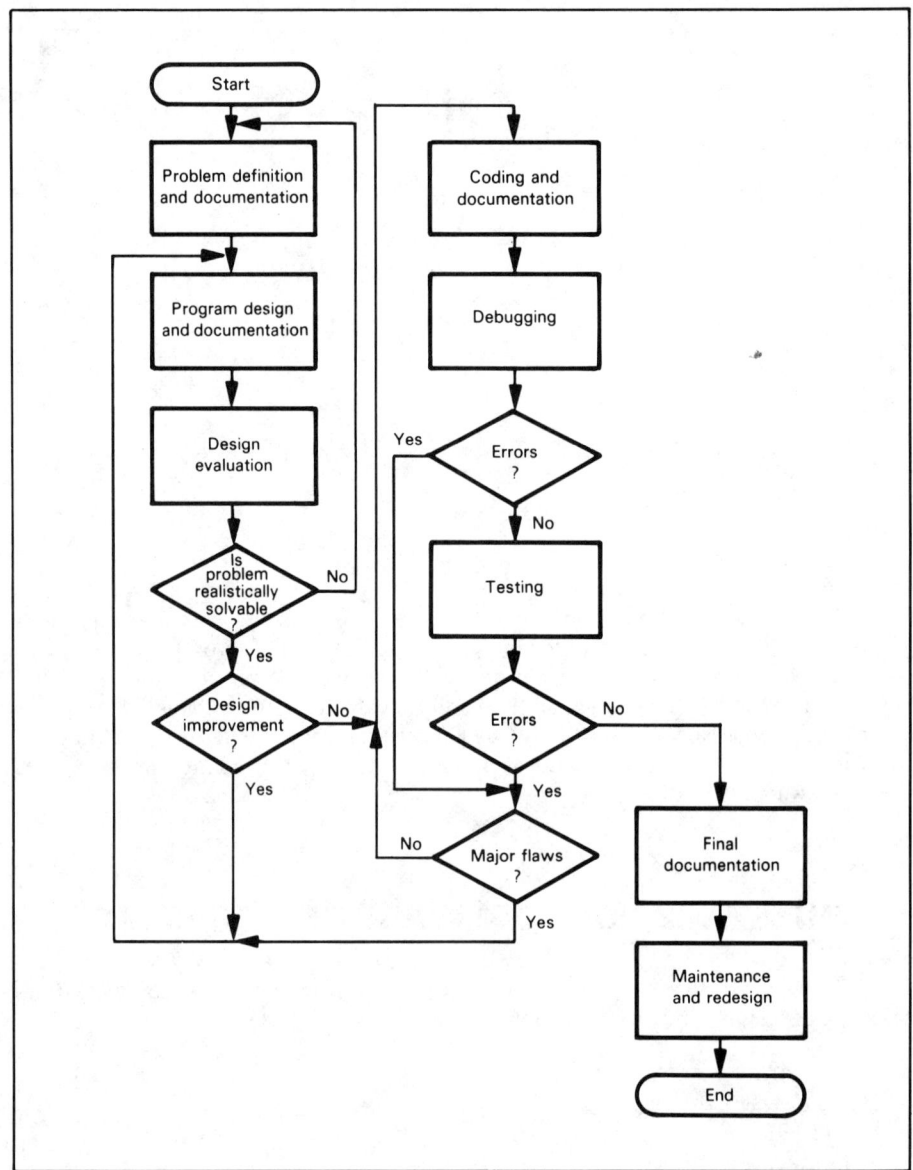

Figure IV-1. Flowchart of Software Development

RELATIVE IMPORTANCE OF CODING

Coding is usually the easiest stage to define and perform. The rules for writing computer programs are easy to learn. They vary somewhat from computer to computer, but the basic techniques remain the same. Few software projects run into trouble because of coding; indeed, coding is not the most time-consuming part of software development. Experts estimate that a programmer can write one to ten fully debugged and documented statements per day. Clearly, the mere coding of one to ten statements is hardly a full day's effort. On most software projects, coding occupies less than 25% of the programmer's time.

MEASURING PROGRESS IN OTHER STAGES

Measuring progress in other stages is difficult. You can say that half of the program has been written, but you can hardly say that half of the errors have been removed or half of the problem has been defined. Timetables for such stages as program design, debugging, and testing are difficult to produce. Many days or weeks of effort may result in no clear progress. Furthermore, an incomplete job in one stage may result in tremendous problems later. For example, poor problem definition or program design can make debugging and testing very difficult. Time saved in one stage may be spent many times over in later stages.

DEFINITION OF THE STAGES

Problem Definition

Problem definition is the formulation of the requirements that the task places on the computer. For example, what is necessary to make a computer control a tool, run a series of electrical tests, or handle communications between a central controller and a remote instrument? Problem definition requires that you determine the forms and rates of inputs and outputs, the amount and speed of processing that is needed, and the types of possible errors and their handling. Problem definition takes a vague idea of building a computer-controlled system and defines the tasks and requirements for the computer.

Program Design

Program design is the outline of the computer program that will meet the requirements. In the design stage, the tasks are described in a way that can easily be converted into a program. **Among the useful techniques in this stage are flowcharting, structured programming, modular programming, and top-down design.**

Coding

Coding is the writing of the program in a form that the computer can either directly understand or translate. The form may be machine language, assembly language, or a high-level language.

Debugging

Debugging, also called program verification, **is making the program perform according to the design.** In this stage, you use such tools as breakpoints, traces, simulators, logic analyzers, and in-circuit emulators. The end of the debugging stage is hard to define, since you never know when you have found the last error.

Testing

Testing, also referred to as program validation, **is ensuring that the program performs the overall system tasks correctly.** The designer uses simulators, exercisers, and statistical techniques to measure the program's performance. This stage is like quality control for hardware.

Documentation

Documentation is the description of the program in the proper form for users and maintenance personnel. Documentation also allows the designer to develop a program library so that subsequent tasks will be far simpler. Flowcharts, comments, memory maps, and library forms are some of the tools used in documentation.

Maintenance and Redesign

Maintenance and redesign are the servicing, improvement, and extension of the program. Clearly, the designer must be ready to handle field problems in computer-based equipment. Special diagnostic modes or programs and other maintenance tools may be required. Upgrading or extension of the program may be necessary to meet new requirements or handle new tasks.

16
Problem Definition

Typical microprocessor tasks require a lot of definition. For example, what must a program do to control a scale, a cash register, or a signal generator? Clearly, we have a long way to go just to define the tasks involved.

INPUTS

How do we start the definition? The obvious place to begin is with the inputs. **We should begin by listing all the inputs that the computer may receive in this application.**
Examples of inputs are:

- Data blocks from transmission lines
- Status words from peripherals
- Data from A/D converters

Then we may ask the following questions about each input:

1. What is its form; that is, what signals will the computer actually receive?
2. When is the input available and how does the processor know it is available? Does the processor have to request the input with a strobe signal? Does the input provide its own clock?
3. How long is it available?
4. How often does it change, and how does the processor know that it has changed?
5. Does the input consist of a sequence or block of data? Is the order important?
6. What should be done if the data contains errors? These may include transmission errors, incorrect data, sequencing errors, extra data, etc.
7. Is the input related to other inputs or outputs?

OUTPUTS

The next step to define is the output. **We must list all the outputs that the computer must produce.** Examples of outputs include:

- Data blocks to transmission lines
- Control words to peripherals
- Data to D/A converters

Then we may ask the following questions about each output:

1. What is its form; that is, what signals must the computer produce?
2. When must it be available, and how does the peripheral know it is available?
3. How long must it be available?
4. How often must it change, and how does the peripheral know that it has changed?
5. Is there a sequence of outputs?
6. What should be done to avoid transmission errors or to sense and recover from peripheral failures?
7. How is the output related to other inputs and outputs?

PROCESSING SECTION

Between the reading of input data and the sending of output results is the processing section. Here **we must determine exactly how the computer must process the input data.** The questions are:

1. What is the basic procedure (algorithm) for transforming input data into output results?
2. What time constraints exist? These may include data rates.
3. What memory constraints exist? Do we have limits on the amount of program memory or data memory, or on the size of buffers?
4. What standard programs or tables must be used? What are their requirements?
5. What special cases exist, and how should the program handle them?
6. How accurate must the results be?
7. How should the program handle processing errors or special conditions such as overflow, underflow, or loss of significance?

ERROR HANDLING

An important factor in many applications is the handling of errors. Clearly, the designer must make provisions for recovering from common errors and for diagnosing malfunctions. **Among the questions that the designer must ask at the definition stage are:**

1. What errors could occur?
2. Which errors are most likely? If a person operates the system, human error is the most common. Following human errors, communications or transmission errors are more common than mechanical, electrical, mathematical, or processor errors.
3. Which errors will not be immediately obvious to the system? A special problem is the occurrence of errors that the system or operator may not recognize as incorrect.
4. How can the system recover from errors with a minimum loss of time and data and yet be aware that an error has occurred?
5. Which errors or malfunctions cause the same system behavior? How can these errors or malfunctions be distinguished for diagnostic purposes?
6. Which errors involve special system procedures? For example, do parity errors require retransmission of data?

Another question is: How can the field technician systematically find the source of malfunctions without being an expert? Built-in test programs, special diagnostics, or signature analysis can help.[1]

HUMAN FACTORS/OPERATOR INTERACTION

Many microprocessor-based systems involve human interaction. **Human factors must be considered throughout the development process for such systems. Among the questions that the designer must ask are:**

1. What input procedures are most natural for the human operator?
2. Can the operator easily determine how to begin, continue and end the input operations?
3. How is the operator informed of procedural errors and equipment malfunctions?
4. What errors is the operator most likely to make?
5. How does the operator know that data has been entered correctly?
6. Are displays in a form that the operator can easily read and understand?
7. Is the response of the system adequate for the operator?
8. Is the system easy for the operator to use?
9. Are there guiding features for an inexperienced operator?
10. Are there shortcuts and reasonable options for the experienced operator?
11. Can the operator always determine or reset the state of the system after interruptions or distractions?

Building a system for people to use is difficult. The microprocessor can make the system more powerful, more flexible, and more responsive. However, **the designer** still **must add the human touches that can greatly increase the usefulness and attractiveness of the system and the productivity of the human operator.**[2]

The processor, of course, has no intrinsic preference in situations involving human characteristics or cultural choices. The processor does not prefer left-to-right over right-to-left, forward over backward, increasing order over decreasing order, or decimal numbers over other number systems. Nor does the processor recognize the operator's preference for simplicity, consistency, compatibility with previous experience, and "logical" order of operations. The processor never gets distracted, disoriented, confused, or bored. The designer must allow for all these considerations in the design and development of interactive systems.

EXAMPLES

DEFINING A SWITCH AND LIGHT SYSTEM

Figure 16-1 shows a simple system in which the input is from a single SPST switch and the output is to a single LED display. In response to a switch closure, the processor turns the display on for one second. This system should be easy to define.

Switch Input

Let us first examine the input and answer each of the questions previously presented:

1. The input is a single bit, which may be either '0' (switch closed) or '1' (switch open).
2. The input is always available and need not be requested.
3. The input is available for at least several milliseconds after the closure.
4. The input will seldom change more than once every few seconds. The processor has to handle only the bounce in the switch. The processor must monitor the switch to determine when it is closed.
5. There is no sequence of inputs.
6. The obvious input errors are switch failure, failure in the input circuitry, and the operator attempting to close the switch again before a sufficient amount of time has elapsed. We will discusss the handling of these errors later.
7. The input does not depend on any other inputs or outputs.

Light Output

The next requirement in defining the system is to examine the output. The answers to our questions are:

1. The output is a single bit, which is '0' to turn the display on, '1' to turn it off.
2. There are no time constraints on the output. The peripheral does not need to be informed of the availability of data.

Problem Definition

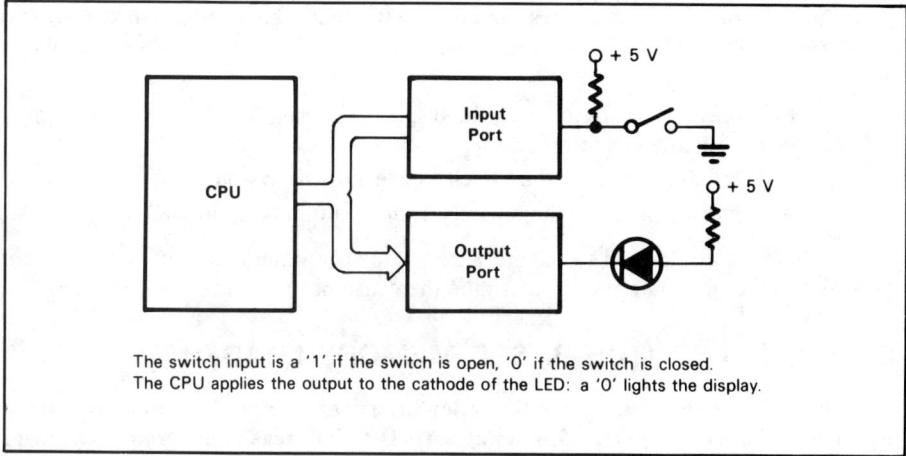

Figure 16-1. The Switch and Light System

3. If the display is an LED, the data need be available for only a few milliseconds at a pulse rate of about 100 times per second. The observer will see a continuously lit display.
4. The data must change (go off) after one second.
5. There is no sequence of outputs.
6. The possible output errors are display failure and failure in the output circuitry.
7. The output depends only on the switch input and time.

Processing

The processing section is extremely simple. As soon as the switch input becomes a logic '0', the CPU turns the light on (a logic '0') for one second. No time or memory constraints exist.

Error Handling

Let us now look at the possible errors and malfunctions. These are:

- Another switch closure before one second has elapsed
- Switch failure
- Display failure
- Computer failure

Surely the first error is the most likely. The simplest solution is for the processor to ignore switch closures until one second has elapsed. This brief unresponsive period will hardly be noticeable to the human operator. Furthermore, ignoring the switch during this period means that no debouncing circuitry or software is necessary, since the system will not react to the bounce anyway.

Clearly, the last three failures can produce unpredictable results. The display may stay on, stay off, or change state randomly. Some possible ways to isolate the failures would be:

- Lamp-test hardware to check the display; i.e., a button that turns the light on independently of the processor
- A direct connection to the switch to check its operation
- A diagnostic program that exercises the input and output circuits

If both the display and switch are working, the computer is at fault. A field technician with proper equipment can determine the cause of the failure.

DEFINING A SWITCH-BASED MEMORY LOADER

Figure 16-2 shows a system that allows the user to enter data into any memory location in a microcomputer. One input port, DPORT, reads data from eight toggle switches. The other input port, CPORT, is used to read control information. There are four momentary switches: High Address, Mid Address, Low Address and Data. The output is the value of the last completed entry from the data switches; eight LEDs are used for the display.

The system will also, of course, require resistors, buffers, and drivers.

Inputs

The characteristics of the switches are the same as in the previous example. To simplify the debouncing procedure and force the operator to release the buttons, we have the system respond only after a button is released; this is a common technique that reduces wear on the switches as well, since the operator is less tempted to press a button repeatedly. In this system **there is a distinct sequence of inputs, as follows:**

1. The operator must set the data switches according to the eight most significant bits of an address, then
2. press and release the High Address button. The high address bits will appear on the lights, and the program will interpret the data as the high byte of the address (bits A23-A16).
3. Then the operator must set the data switches with the value of the middle byte of the address (bits A15-A8) and
4. press and release the Mid Address button. The middle address bits will appear on the lights, and the program will consider the data to be the middle byte of the address.
5. Then the operator must set the data switches with the value of the least significant byte of the address bits (A7-A0) and
6. press and releast the Low Address button. The low address bits will appear on the lights, and the program will consider the data to be the low byte of the address.
7. Finally, the operator must set the desired data into the data switches and
8. press and release the Data button. The display will now show the data, and the program stores the data in memory at the previously entered address.

Problem Definition **267**

The operator may repeat the process to enter an entire program. Clearly, even in this simplified situation, we will have many possible sequences to consider. How do we cope with erroneous sequences and make the system easy to use?

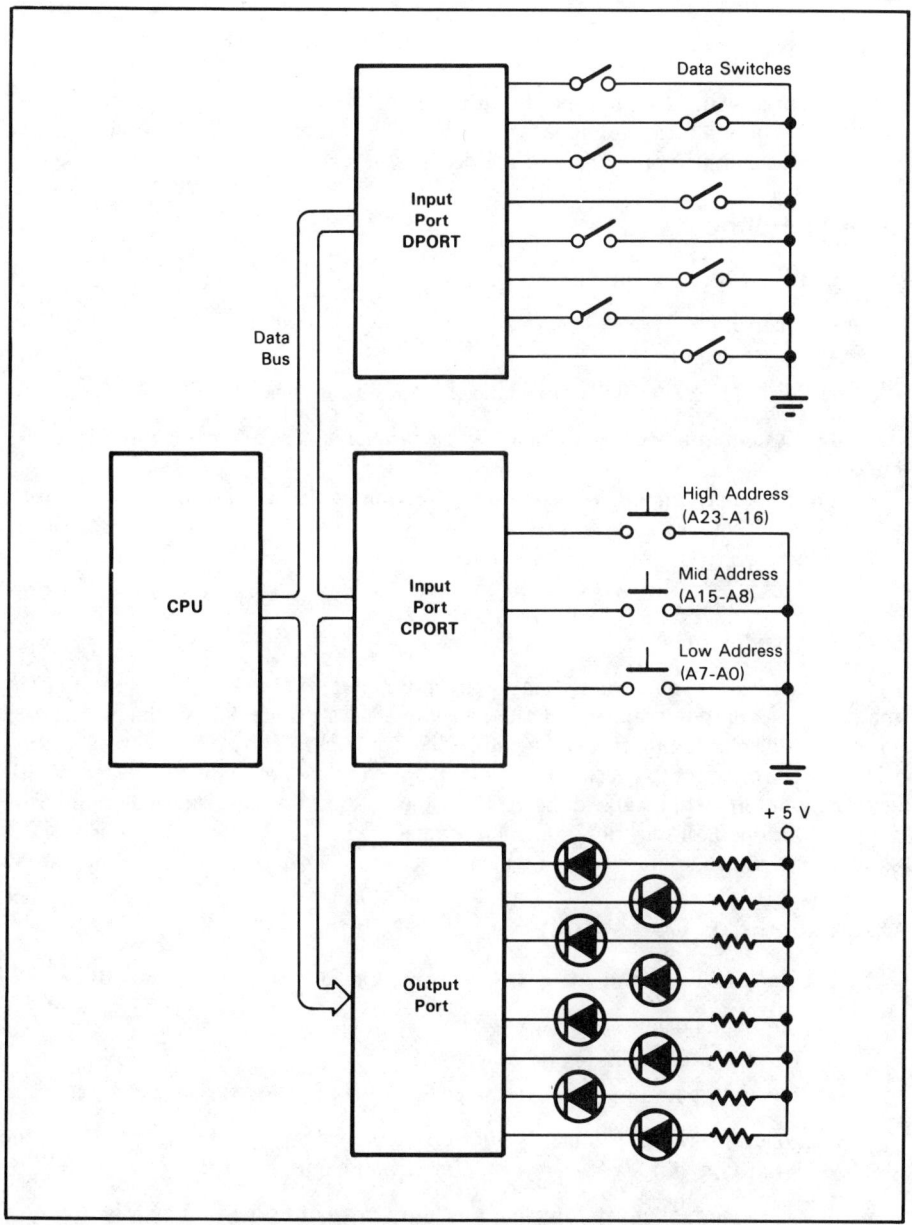

Figure 16-2. The Switch-Based Memory Loader

Output

Output is no problem. After each input, the program sends to the displays the complement (since the displays are active-low) of the input bits. The output data remains the same until the next input operation.

Processing

The processing section remains quite simple. There are no time or memory constraints. The program can debounce the switches by waiting for a few milliseconds, and must provide complemented data to the displays.

Error Handling

The most likely errors are operator mistakes. These include:

- Incorrect entries
- Incorrect order
- Incomplete entries; for example, forgetting the data

The system must be able to handle these problems in a reasonable way, since they are certain to occur in actual operation.

The designer must also consider the effects of equipment failure. Just as before, the possible difficulties are:

- Switch failure
- Display failure
- Computer failure

In this system, however, we must pay more attention to how these failures affect the system. A computer failure will cause a complete system breakdown that will be easy to detect. A display failure may not be immediately noticeable; here a Lamp Test feature will allow the operator to check the operation. Note that we would like to test each LED separately, in order to diagnose the case in which output lines are shorted together. In addition, the operator may not immediately detect switch failure; however, the operator should soon notice it and establish which switch is faulty by a process of elimination.

Operator Error Correction

Let us look at **some of the possible operator errors.** Typical errors **will be:**

- Erroneous data
- Wrong order of entries or switches
- Trying to go on to the next entry without completing the current one

The operator will presumably notice erroneous data as soon as it appears on the displays. **What is a viable recovery procedure? Some options are:**

1. The operator must complete the entry procedure; i.e., enter Mid Address, Low Address and Data if the error occurs in the High Address. Clearly, this

procedure is wasteful and annoying.
2. The operator may restart the entry process by returning to the high address entry steps. This solution is useful if the error was in the High Address, but forces the operator to re-enter earlier data if the error was in the Mid Address, Low Address or Data stage.
3. The operator may enter any part of the sequence at any time simply by setting the Data switches with the desired data and pressing the corresponding button. This procedure allows the operator to make corrections at any point in the sequence.

This type of procedure should always be preferred over one that does not allow immediate error correction, has a variety of concluding steps, or enters data into the system without allowing the operator a final check. Any added complication in hardware or software will be justified in increased operator efficiency. You should always prefer to let the microcomputer do the tedious work and recognize arbitrary sequences; it never gets tired and never forgets the operating procedures.

A further helpful feature would be status lights that would define the meaning of the display. Four status lights, marked "High Address," "Mid Address," "Low Address," and "Data," would let the operator know what had been entered without having to remember which button was pressed. The processor would have to monitor the sequence, but the added complication in software would simplify the operator's task. Clearly, four separate sets of displays plus the ability to examine a memory location would be even more helpful to the operator.

We should note that, although we have emphasized human interaction, machine or system interaction has many of the same characteristics. The microprocessor should do the work. If complicating the microprocessor's task makes error recovery simple and the causes of failure obvious, the entire system will work better and be easier to maintain. Note that you should not wait until after the software has been completed to consider system use and maintenance; instead, you should include these factors in the problem definition stage.

DEFINING A VERIFICATION TERMINAL

Figure 16-3 is a block diagram of a simple credit-verification terminal. One input port derives data from a keyboard (see Figure 16-4); the other input port accepts verification data from a transmission line. One output port sends data to a set of displays (see Figure 16-5); another sends the credit card number to the central computer. A third output port turns on one light whenever the terminal is ready to accept an inquiry, and another light when the operator sends the information. The "busy" light is turned off when the terminal receives a response. Clearly, the input and output of data will be more complex than in the previous case, although the processing is still simple.

Additional displays may be useful to emphasize the meaning of the response. Many terminals use a green light for "Yes," a red light for "No," and a yellow light for "Consult Store Manager." Note that these lights will still have to be clearly marked with their meanings to allow for a color-blind operator.

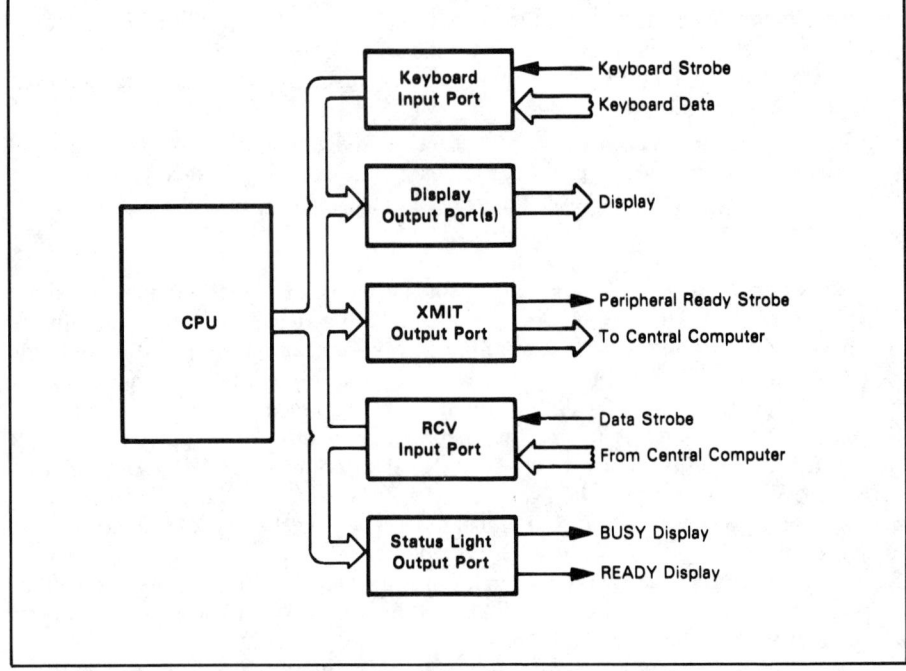

Figure 16-3. Block Diagram of a Verification Terminal

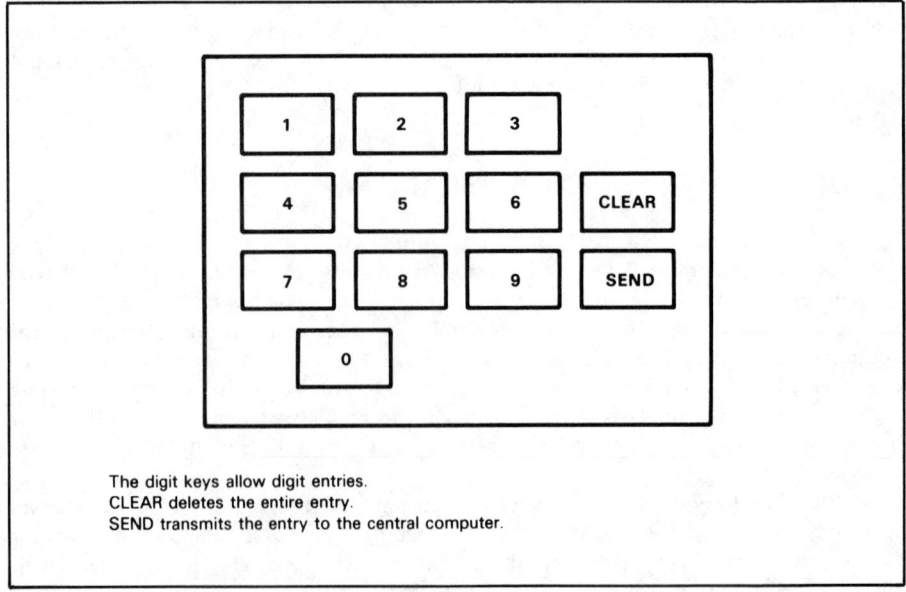

The digit keys allow digit entries.
CLEAR deletes the entire entry.
SEND transmits the entry to the central computer.

Figure 16-4. Verification Terminal Keyboard

Problem Definition

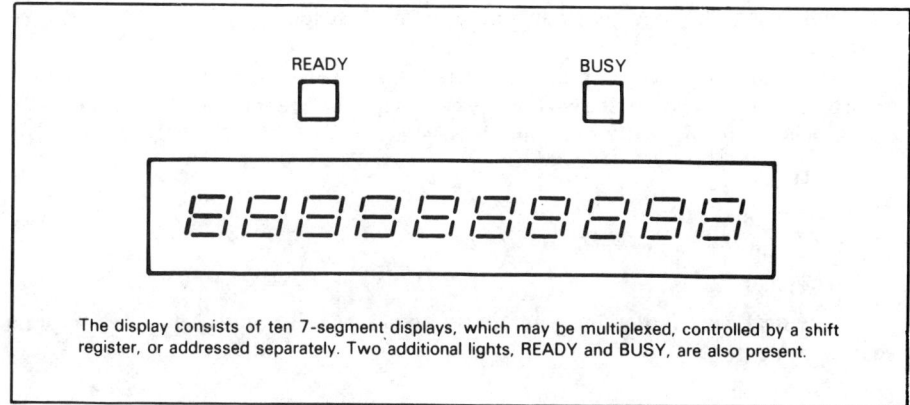

Figure 16-5. Verification Terminal Display

Inputs

Let us first look at the keyboard input. This is, of course, different from the switch input, since the CPU must have some way of distinguishing new data. **We will assume that each key closure provides a unique hexadecimal code (we can code each of the 12 keys into one digit) and a strobe. The program will have to recognize the strobe and fetch the hexadecimal number that identifies the key.** There is a time constraint, since the program cannot miss any data or strobes. The constraint is not serious, since keyboard entries will be at least several milliseconds apart.

The transmission input similarly consists of a series of characters, each identified by a strobe (perhaps from a UART). The program will have to recognize each strobe and fetch the character. The data being sent across the transmission lines is usually organized into messages. A possible message format is:

- Introductory characters, or header
- Terminal destination address
- Coded yes or no
- Ending characters, or trailer

The terminal will check the header, read the destination address, and see if the message is intended for it. If the message is for the terminal, the terminal accepts the data. The address could be (and often is) hard-wired into the terminal so that the terminal receives only messages intended for it. This approach simplifies the software at the cost of some flexibility.

Outputs

The output is also more complex than in the earlier examples. **If the displays are multiplexed, the processor must not only send the data to the display port but must also direct the data to a particular display.** We will need either a separate control port or a counter and decoder to handle this. Note that hardware blanking controls can blank leading zeros as long as the first digit in a multi-digit number is never zero. Software can also handle this task. Time constraints include the pulse length and frequency required to produce a continuous display for the operator.

The communications output will consist of a series of characters with a particular format. The program will also have to consider the time required between characters. A possible format for the output message is:

- Header
- Terminal address
- Credit card number
- Trailer

A central communication computer may poll the terminals, checking for data **ready to be sent.**

Processing

The processing in this system involves many new tasks, such as:

- Identifying the control keys by number and performing the proper actions
- Adding the header, terminal address, and trailer to the outgoing message
- Recognizing the header and trailer in the returning message
- Checking the incoming terminal address

Note that none of the tasks involves any complex arithmetic or any serious time or memory constraints.

Error Handling

The number of possible errors in this system is, of course, much larger than in the earlier examples. Let us first consider the possible operator errors. These include:

- Entering the credit card number incorrectly
- Trying to send an incomplete credit card number
- Trying to send another number while the central computer is processing one
- Clearing nonexistent entries

Some of these errors can be handled easily by organizing the program correctly. For example, the program should not accept the Send key until the credit card number has been completely entered, and it should ignore any additional keyboard entries until the response comes back from the central computer. Note that the operator will know that the entry has not been sent, since the Busy light will not go on. The operator will also know when the keyboard has been locked out (the program is ignoring keyboard entries), since entries will not appear on the display and the Ready light will be off.

Correcting Keyboard Errors

Incorrect entries are an obvious problem. **If the operator recognizes an error, he or she can use the Clear key to make corrections. The operator would probably find it more convenient to have two Clear keys, one that cleared the most recent key and one** that cleared the entire entry. This would allow both for the situation in which the operator recognizes the error immediately and for the situation in which the operator recognizes the error late in the procedure. **The operator should be able to correct errors immediately and have to repeat as few keys as possible. The operator will, however, make a certain number of errors without recognizing them. Most credit card numbers include a self-checking digit; the terminal could check the number before permitting it to be sent to the central computer.** This step would save the central computer from wasting processing time checking the number.

This requires, however, that the terminal have some way of informing the operator of the error, perhaps by flashing one of the displays or by providing some other special indicator that the operator is sure to notice.

Still another problem is how the operator knows that an entry has been lost or processed incorrectly. Some terminals simply unlock after a maximum time delay. The operator notes that the Busy light has gone off without an answer being received. The operator is then expected to try the entry again. After one or two further attempts, the operator should report the failure to supervisory personnel.

Many equipment failures are also possible. Besides the displays, keyboard, and processor, there now exist the problems of communications errors or failures and central computer failures.

Correcting Transmission Errors

The data transmission will probably have to include error checking and correcting procedures. Some possibilities are:

1. Parity provides an error detection facility but no correction mechanism. The receiver will need some way of requesting retransmission, and the sender will have to save a copy of the data until proper reception is acknowledged. Parity is, however, very simple to implement.
2. Short messages may use more elaborate schemes. For example, the yes/no response to the terminal could be coded to provide error detection and correction capability.
3. An acknowledgement and a limited number of retries could trigger an indicator that would inform the operator of a communications failure (inability to transfer a message without errors) or central computer failure (no response within a certain period of time). Such a scheme, along with the Lamp Test, would allow simple failure diagnosis.

A communications or central computer failure indicator should also "unlock" the terminal, that is, allow it to accept another entry. This is necessary if the terminal will not accept entries while a verification is in progress. **The terminal may also unlock after a certain maximum time delay. Certain entries could be reserved for diagnostics;** i.e., certain credit card numbers could be used to check the internal operation of the terminal and test the displays.

REVIEW

Problem definition is as important a part of software development as it is of any other engineering task. Note that it does not require any programming or knowledge of the computer; rather, it is based on an understanding of the system and sound engineering judgment. Microprocessors offer flexibility and local intelligence that the designer can use to provide a wide range of features.

Problem definition is independent of any particular computer, computer language, or development system. It should, however, provide guidelines as to what type or speed of computer the application will require and what kind of hardware/software tradeoffs the designer can make. The problem definition stage should not even depend on whether a computer is used, although a knowledge of the capabilities of the computer can help the designer in suggesting possible implementations of procedures.

REFERENCES

1. D. R. Ballard. "Designing Fail-Safe Microprocessor Systems," *Electronics*, January 4, 1979, pp. 139-43.

   "A Designer's Guide to Signature Analysis," Hewlett-Packard Application Note 222, Hewlett-Packard, Inc, Palo Alto, CA, 1977.

   Donn, E. S. and M. D. Lippman. "Efficient and Effective Microcomputer Testing Requires Careful Preplanning," *EDN*, February 20, 1979, pp. 97-107 (includes self-test examples for 6502).

   Gordon, G. and H. Nadig. "Hexadecimal Signatures Identify Troublespots in Microprocessor Systems," *Electronics*, March 3, 1977, pp. 89-96.

   Neil, M. and R. Goodner. "Designing a Serviceman's Needs into Microprocessor-Based Systems," *Electronics*, March 1, 1979, pp. 122-28.

   Schweber, W. and L. Pearce. "Software Signature Analysis Identifies and Checks PROMs," *EDN*, November 5, 1978, pp. 79-81.

   Srini, V. P. "Fault Diagnosis of Microprocessor Systems," *Computer*, January 1977, pp. 60-65.

2. For a brief discussion of human factors considerations, see G. Morris. "Make Your Next Instrument Design Emphasize User Needs and Wants," *EDN*, October 20, 1978, pp. 100-05.

17
Program Design

Program design is the stage in which the problem definition is formulated as a program. If the program is small and simple, this stage may involve little more than the writing of a one-page flowchart. If the program is larger or more complex, the designer should consider more elaborate methods.

We will discuss flowcharting, modular programming, structured programming, and top-down design. We will try to indicate the reasoning behind these methods, and their advantages and disadvantages. We will not, however, advocate any particular method since there is no evidence that one method is always superior to all others. You should remember that the goal is to produce a good working system, not to follow religiously the tenets of one methodology or another.

BASIC PRINCIPLES

All the methodologies are based on common principles, many of which apply to any kind of design. Among these principles are:

1. **Proceed in small steps.** Do not try to do too much at one time.
2. **Divide large jobs into small, logically separate tasks.** Make the sub-tasks as independent of one another as possible, so that they can be tested separately and so that changes can be made in one without affecting the others.
3. **Keep the flow of control simple** to make programs easy to follow and errors easy to locate and correct.
4. **Use pictorial or graphic design descriptions** as much as possible. They are easier to visualize than word descriptions. This is the great advantage of flowcharts.

5. **Emphasize clarity and simplicity at first.** You can improve performance (if necessary) once the system is working.
6. **Proceed in a thorough and systematic manner.** Use checklists and standard procedures.
7. **Do not tempt fate. Either do not use methods that you are not sure of, or use them very carefully. Watch for situations that might cause confusion,** and clarify them as soon as possible.
8. Keep in mind that **the system must be debugged, tested and maintained. Plan for these later stages.**
9. **Use simple and consistent terminology and methods.** Repetitiveness is no fault in program design, nor is complexity a virtue.
10. **Have your design completely formulated before you start coding.** Resist the temptation to start writing down instructions: it makes no more sense than making parts lists or laying out circuit boards before you know exactly what will be in the system.
11. Be particularly careful of factors that may change. **Make the implementation of likely changes as simple as possible.**
12. **Keep the overall task in mind.** Build a total framework in which individual pieces can be defined and tested. Do not leave the entire system integration to the end.
13. If the data is complex or there are numerous relationships between data items, **you must organize your data just as carefully as you organize your program. We will briefly discuss the design of data structures at the end of this chapter.**

FLOWCHARTING

Flowcharting is certainly the best known of all program design methods. Programming textbooks describe how programmers first write complete flowcharts and then start writing the actual program. In fact, few programmers have ever worked this way, and flowcharting has often been more of a joke or a nuisance to programmers than a design method. We will try to describe both the advantages and disadvantages of flowcharts, and show the place of this technique in program design.

ADVANTAGES OF FLOWCHARTING

The basic advantage of the flowchart is that it is a pictorial representation. People find such representations much more meaningful than written descriptions. The designer can visualize the whole system and see the relationships of the various parts. Logical errors and inconsistencies often stand out instead of being hidden in a printed page. At its best, the flowchart is a picture of the entire system.

Some specific advantages of flowcharts are:

1. Standard symbols exist (see Figure 17-1) so that flowcharting forms are widely recognized.

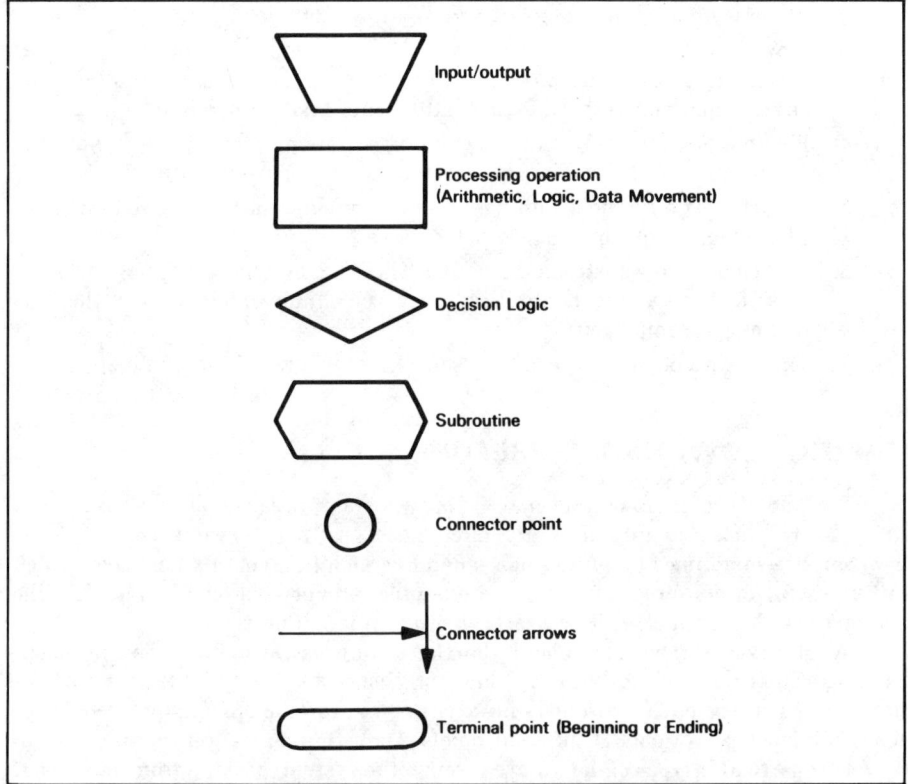

Figure 17-1. Standard Flowchart Symbols

2. Flowcharts can be understood by someone without a programming background.
3. Flowcharts can be used to divide the entire project into sub-tasks. The flowchart can then be examined to measure overall progress.
4. Flowcharts show the sequence of operations and can therefore aid in locating the source of errors.
5. Flowcharting is widely used in other areas besides programming.
6. There are many tools available to aid in flowcharting, including programmer's templates and automated drawing packages.

DISADVANTAGES OF FLOWCHARTING

These advantages are all important. There is no question that flowcharting will continue to be widely used. But **we should note some disadvantages of flowcharting as a program design method:**

1. Flowcharts are difficult to design, draw, or change in all except the simplest situations.

2. There is no easy way to debug or test a flowchart.
3. Flowcharts tend to become cluttered. Designers find it difficult to balance between the amount of detail needed to make the flowchart useful and the amount that makes the flowchart little better that a program listing.
4. Flowcharts show only the program organization. They do not show the organization of the data or the structure of the input/output modules.
5. Flowcharts do not help with hardware or timing problems or give hints as to where these problems might occur.
6. Flowcharts allow unstructured design. There are no rules governing the numbers of entries and exits, the number or type of interconnections, or the logic that may be employed.
7. There is no obvious way to represent the simple repetition of a loop.

MAKING FLOWCHARTS USEFUL

The most useful flowcharts may ignore program variables and ask questions directly. Of course, compromises are often necessary here. **Two versions of the flowchart are sometimes helpful — one general version in layman's language, which will be useful to non-programmers, and one programmer's version in terms of the program variables, which will be useful to other programmers.**

A third type of flowchart, a data flowchart, may also be helpful. This flowchart serves as a cross-reference for the other flowcharts, since it shows how the program handles a particular type of data. Ordinary flowcharts show how the program proceeds, handling different types of data at different points. **Data flowcharts, on the other hand, show how particular types of data move through the system, passing from one part of the program to another.** Such flowcharts are very useful in debugging and maintenance, since errors most often show up as a particular type of data being handled incorrectly.

Thus **flowcharting is a helpful technique that you should not try to extend too far. Flowcharts are useful as program documentation, since they have standard forms and are comprehensible to non-programmers.** As a design tool, **however,** flowcharts cannot provide much more than a starting outline; **the programmer cannot debug a detailed flowchart** and the flowchart is often more difficult to design than the program itself.

EXAMPLES

Flowcharting the Switch and Light System

This simple task, in which a single switch turns on a light for one second, is easy to flowchart. In fact, such tasks are typical examples for flowcharting books, although they form a small part of most systems. The data structure here is so simple that it can be safely ignored.

Figure 17-2 is the flowchart. There is little difficulty in deciding on the amount of detail required. The flowchart gives a straightforward picture of the procedure, which anyone could understand.

Program Design 279

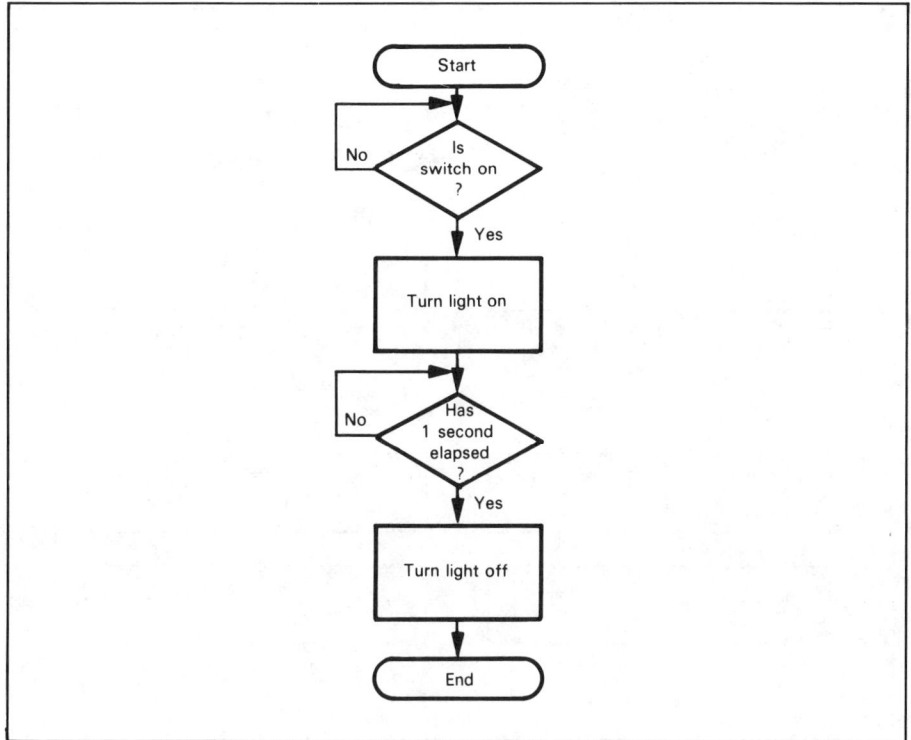

Figure 17-2. Flowchart of One-Second Response to a Switch

Flowcharting the Switch-Based Memory Loader

This system (see Figure 16-2) is considerably more complex than the previous example, and involves many more decisions. **The flowchart (see Figure 17-3) is more difficult to draw and is not as straightforward as the previous example.** In this example, we face the problem that there is no way to debug or test the flowchart.

The flowchart in Figure 17-3 includes the improvements we suggested as part of the problem definition. Clearly, this flowchart is beginning to get cluttered and lose its advantages over a written description. Adding other features that define the meaning of the entry with status lights and allow the operator to check entries after completion would make the flowchart even more complex. Drawing the complete flowchart from scratch could quickly become a formidable task. However, once the program has been written, the flowchart is useful as documentation.

Flowcharting the Verification Terminal

In this application (see Figures 16-3 through 16-5) the flowchart will be even more complex than in the switch-based memory loader case. Here, **the best idea is to flowchart sections separately so that the flowcharts remain manageable.** However, the presence of data structures (as in the multi-digit display and the messages) will make the gap between flowchart and program much wider.

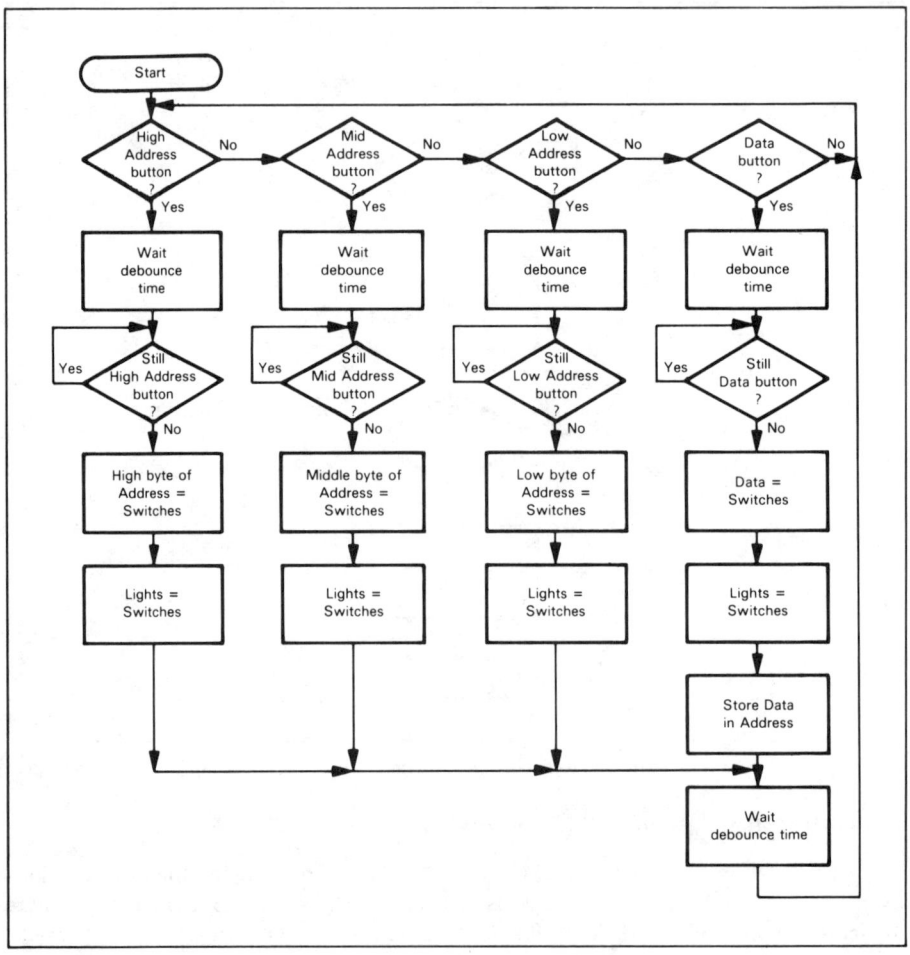

Figure 17-3. Flowchart of a Switch-Based Memory Loader

Let us look at some of the sections. **Figure 17-4 shows the keyboard entry process for the digit keys.** The program must fetch the data after each strobe and place the digit into the display array if there is room for it. If there are already ten digits in the array, the program simply ignores the entry.

The actual program will have to handle the displays at the same time. Note that either software or hardware must de-activate the keyboard strobe after the processor reads a digit.

Figure 17-5 adds the Send key. This key, of course, is optional. The terminal could just send the data as soon as the operator enters a complete number. However, that procedure would not give the operator a chance to check the entire entry. The flowchart with the Send key is more complex because there are two alternatives.

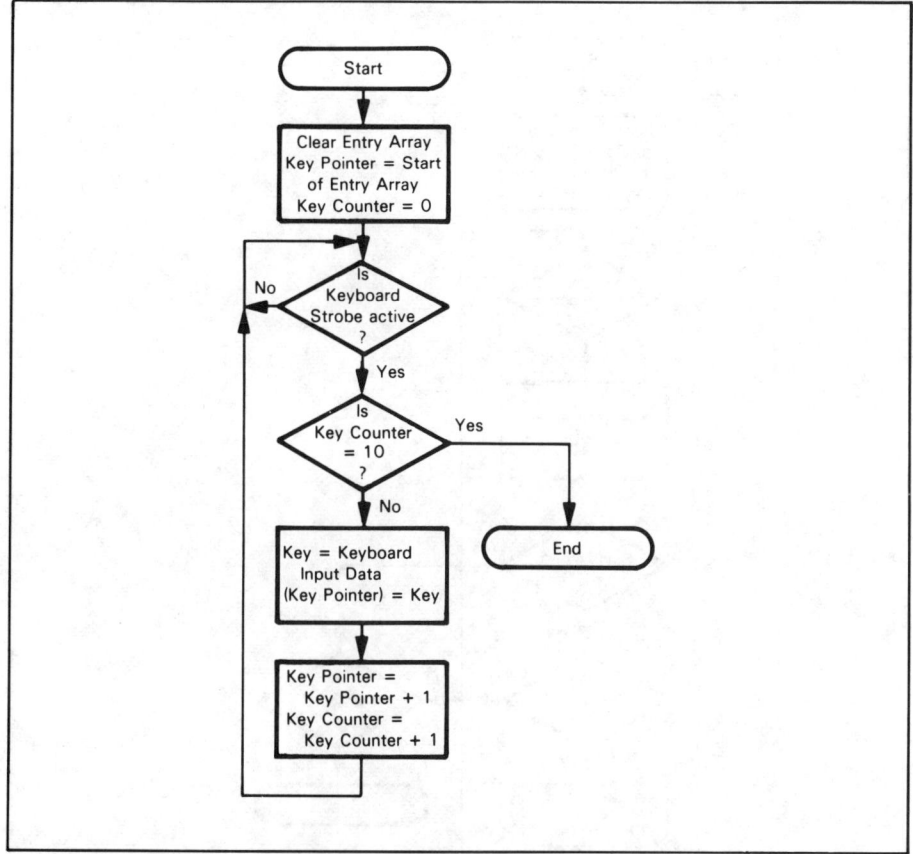

Figure 17-4. Flowchart of Keyboard Entry Process

1. If the operator has not entered ten digits, the program must ignore the Send key and place any other key into the entry.
2. If the operator has entered ten digits, the program must respond to the Send key by transferring control to the Send routine; and ignore all other keys.

Note that the flowchart has become much more difficult to organize and to follow. There is also no obvious way to check the flowchart.

Figure 17-6 shows the flowchart of the keyboard entry process with all the function keys. In this example, the flow of control is not simple. Clearly, some written description is necessary. The organization and layout of complex flowcharts requires careful planning. We have followed the process of adding features to the flowchart one at a time, but this still results in a large amount of redrawing. Again we should remember that throughout the keyboard entry process, the program must also refresh the displays if they are multiplexed and not controlled by shift registers or other hardware.

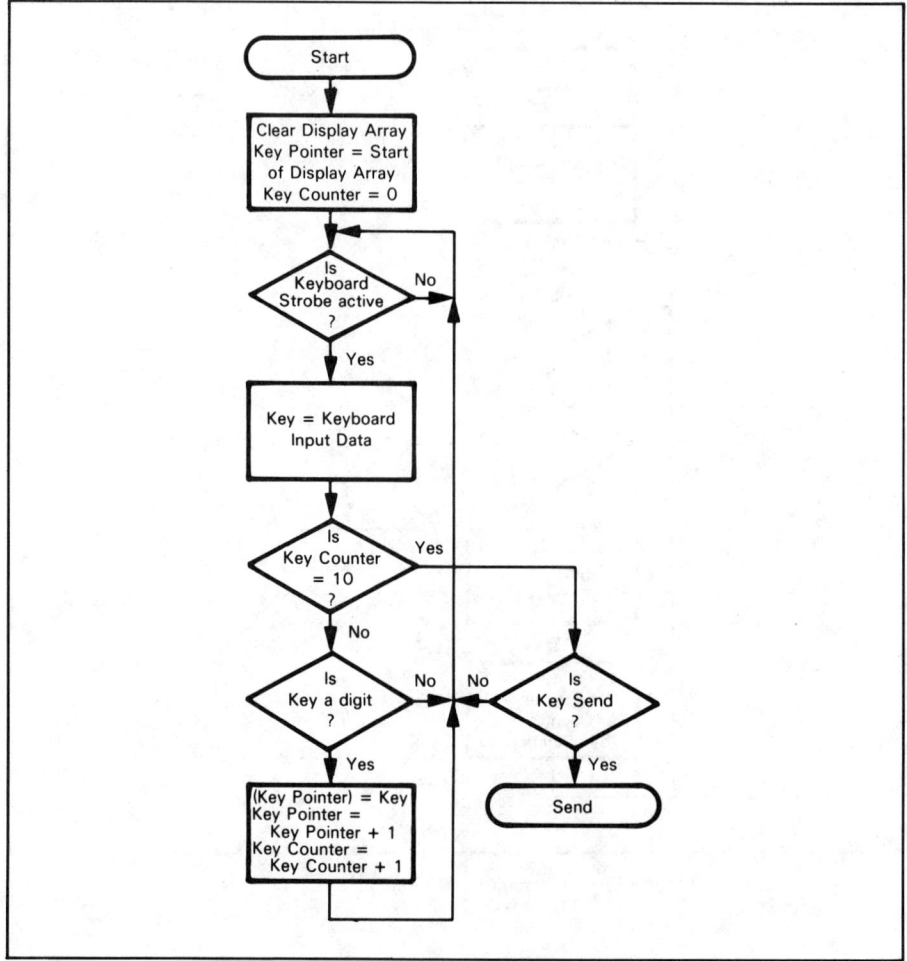

Figure 17-5. Flowchart of Entry Process With Send Key

Figure 17-7 is the flowchart of a receive routine. We assume that the serial/parallel conversion and error checking are done in hardware (e.g., by a UART). The processor must:

1. Look for the header. (We assume that it is a single character.)
2. Read the destination address (we assume that it is three characters long) and see if the message is meant for this terminal; i.e., if the three characters agree with the terminal address.
3. Wait for the trailer character.

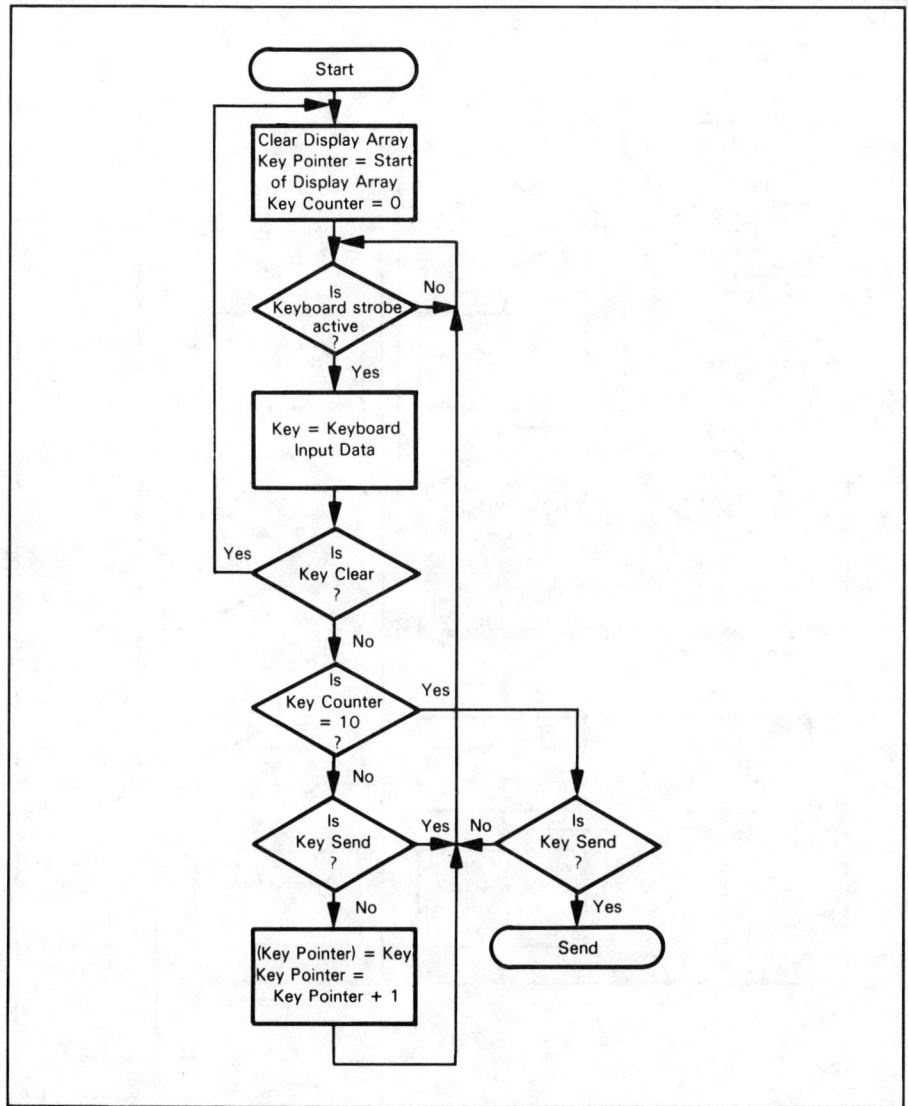

Figure 17-6. Flowchart of Keyboard Entry Process With Function Keys

4. If the message is meant for the terminal, turn off the Busy light and go to Display Answer routine.
5. In the event of any errors, request retransmission by going to the appropriate RTRANS routine.

This routine involves a large number of decisions, and the flowchart is neither simple nor obvious.

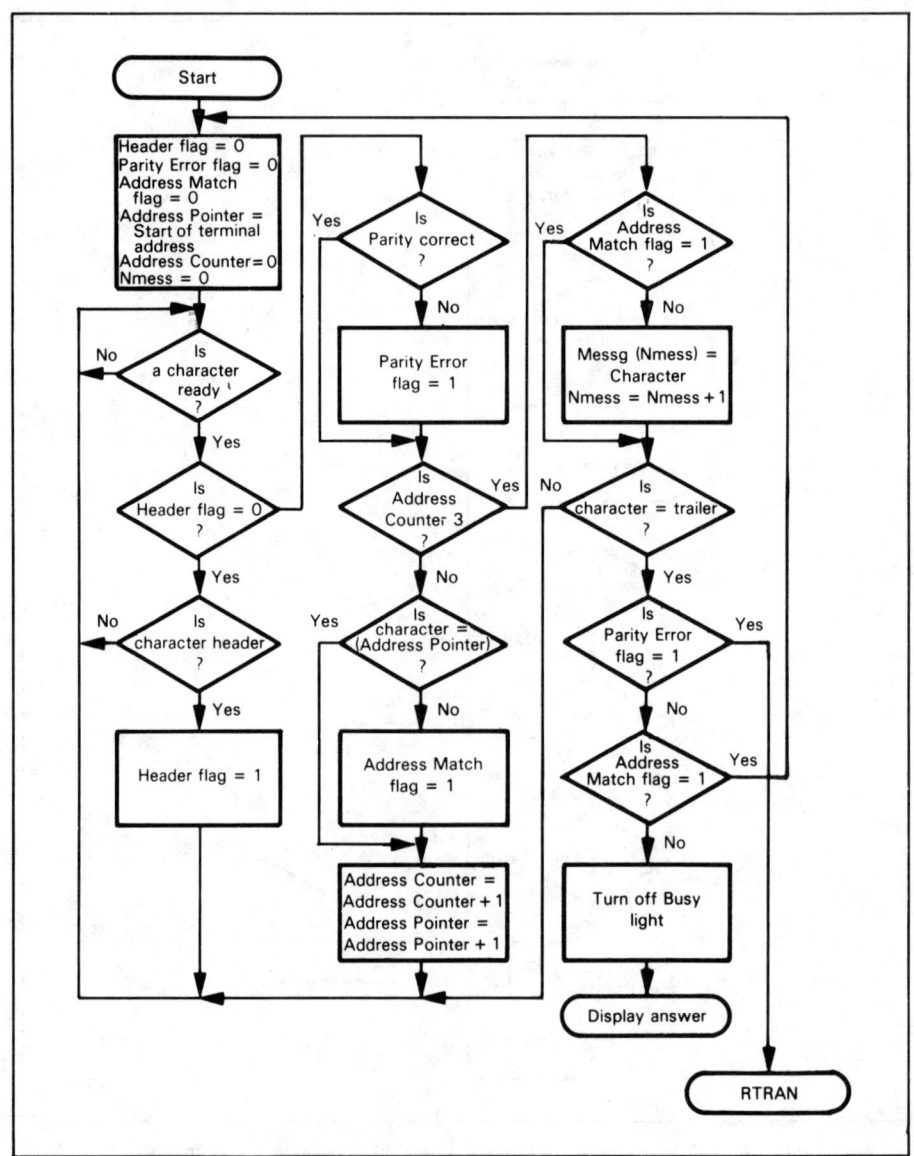

Figure 17-7. Flowchart of Receive Routine

Clearly, we have come a long way from the simple flowchart (Figure 17-2) of the first example. A complete set of flowcharts for the transaction terminal would be **a major task.** It would consist of several interrelated charts with complex logic, and would require a large amount of effort. Such an effort would be just as difficult as writing a preliminary program, and not as useful, since you could not check the flowcharts on the computer.

MODULAR PROGRAMMING

Once programs become large and complex, flowcharting is no longer a satisfactory design tool. However, the problem definition and the flowchart can help you divide the program into reasonable sub-tasks. **The division of the entire program into sub-tasks or modules is called "modular programming."** Clearly, most of the programs we presented in earlier chapters would typically be modules in a large program. **The problems that the designer faces in modular programming are how to divide the program into modules and how to put the modules together.**

ADVANTAGES OF MODULAR PROGRAMMING

The advantages of modular programming are obvious:

1. A single module is easier to write, debug, and test than an entire program.
2. A module is likely to be useful in many places and in other programs, particularly if it is reasonably general and performs a common task. You can build a library of standard modules.
3. Modular programming allows the programmer to divide tasks and use previously written programs.
4. Changes can be incorporated into one module rather than into the entire system.
5. Errors can often be isolated and then attributed to a single module.
6. Modular programming helps with project management, since it results in obvious goals and milestones.

DISADVANTAGES OF MODULAR PROGRAMMING

The idea of modular programming is so simple that its disadvantages are often ignored. These include:

1. Fitting the modules together can be a major problem, particularly if different people write the modules.
2. Modules require very careful documentation, since they may affect other parts of the program, such as data structures used by all the modules.
3. Testing and debugging modules separately is difficult, since other modules may produce the data used by the module being debugged and still other modules may use the results. You may have to write special programs (called "drivers") just to produce sample data and test the programs. These drivers require extra programming effort that adds nothing to the system.
4. Programs may be very difficult to modularize. If you modularize the program poorly, integration will be very difficult, since almost all errors and changes will involve several modules.
5. Modular programs often require extra time and memory, since the separate modules may repeat functions.

Therefore, while modular programming is certainly an improvement over trying to write the entire program from scratch, it does have some disadvantages as well.

Important considerations include restricting the amount of information shared by modules, limiting design decisions that are subject to change to a single module, and restricting the access of one module to another.[1]

PRINCIPLES OF MODULARIZATION

An obvious problem is that there are no proven, systematic methods for modularizing programs. We should mention the following principles:[2]

1. Modules that reference common data should be parts of the same overall module.
2. Two modules in which the first uses or depends on the second, but not the reverse, should be separate.
3. A module that is used by more than one other module should be part of a different overall module than the others.
4. Two modules in which the first is used by many other modules and the second is used by only a few other modules should be separate.
5. Two modules whose frequencies of usage are significantly different should be part of different modules.
6. The structure or organization of related data should be hidden within a single module.

If a program is difficult to modularize, you may need to redefine the tasks that are involved. Too many special cases or too many variables that require special handling are typical signs of inadequate problem definition.

EXAMPLES

Modularizing the Switch and Light System

This simple program can be divided into two modules:

Module 1 waits for the switch to be turned on and turns the light on in response.

Module 2 provides the one-second delay.

Module 1 is likely to be specific to the system, since it will depend on how the switch and light are attached. Module 2 will be generally useful, since many tasks require delays. Clearly, it would be advantageous to have a standard delay module that could provide delays of varying lengths. The module will require careful documentation so that you will know how to specify the length of the delay, how to call the module, and what registers and memory locations the module affects.

A general version of Module 1 would be far less useful, since it would have to deal with different types and connections of switches and lights.

You would probably find it simpler to write a module for a particular configuration of switches and lights rather than try to use a standard routine. Note the difference between this situation and Module 2.

Modularizing the Switch-Based Memory Loader

The switch-based memory loader is difficult to modularize, since all the programming tasks depend on the hardware configuration and the tasks are so simple that modules hardly seem worthwhile. The flowchart in Figure 17-3 suggests that one module might be the one that waits for the operator to press one of the four pushbuttons.

Some other modules might be:

- A delay module that provides the delay required to debounce the switches
- A switch and display module that reads the data from the switches and sends it to the displays
- A Lamp Test module

Highly system-dependent modules such as the last two are unlikely to be generally useful. This example is not one in which modular programming offers great advantages.

Modularizing the Verification Terminal

The **verification terminal,** on the other hand, lends itself very well to modular programming. The entire system **can easily be divided into three main modules:**

- **Keyboard and display module**
- **Data transmission module**
- **Data reception module**

A general keyboard and display module could handle many keyboard- and display-based systems. The sub-modules would perform such tasks as:

- Recognizing a new keyboard entry and fetching the data
- Clearing the array in response to a Clear Key
- Entering digits into storage
- Looking for the terminator or Send key
- Displaying the digits

Although the key interpretations and the number of digits will vary, the basic entry, data storage, and data display processes will be the same for many programs. Such function keys as Clear would also be standard. Clearly, **the designer must consider which modules will be useful in other applications, and pay careful attention to those modules.**

The data transmission module could also be divided into such sub-modules as:

1. Adding the header character.
2. Transmitting characters as the output line can handle them.
3. Generating delay times between bits or characters.
4. Adding the trailer character.
5. Checking for transmission failures; i.e., no acknowledgement, or inability to transmit without errors.

The data reception module could include sub-modules which:

1. Look for the header character.
2. Check the message destination address against the terminal address.
3. Store and interpret the message.
4. Look for the trailer character.
5. Generate bit or character delays.

INFORMATION HIDING PRINCIPLE

Note here how important it is that each design decision (such as the bit rate, message format, or error-checking procedure) be implemented in only one module. A change in any of these decisions will then require changes only to that single module. The other modules should be written so that they are totally unaware of the values chosen or the methods used in the implementing module. **An important concept here is the "information-hiding principle,"[3] whereby modules share only information that is absolutely essential to getting the task done. Other information is hidden within a single module.**

Error handling is a typical situation in which information should be hidden. When a module detects a lethal error, it should not try to recover; instead, it should inform the calling module of the error status and allow that module to decide how to proceed. The reason is that the lower level module often lacks sufficient information to establish recovery procedures. For example, suppose that the lower level module is one that accepts numeric input from a user. This module expects a string of numeric digits terminated by a carriage return. Entry of a non-numeric character causes the module to terminate abnormally. Since the module does not know the context (i.e. is the numeric string an operand, a lone number, an I/O unit number, or the length of a file?), it cannot decide how to handle an error. If the module always followed a single error recovery procedure, it would lose its generality and only be usable in those situations where that procedure was required.

REVIEW OF MODULAR PROGRAMMING

Modular programming can be very helpful if you abide by the following rules:

1. **Use modules of 20 to 50 lines.** Shorter modules are usually a waste of time, while longer modules are seldom general and may be difficult to integrate.
2. **Make modules reasonably general.** Differentiate between common features like ASCII code or asynchronous transmission formats, which will be the same for many applications, and key identifications, number of displays, or number of characters in a message, which are likely to be unique to a particular application. Make the changing of the latter parameters simple. Major changes like different character codes should be handled by separate modules.
3. **Take extra time on modules** like delays, display handlers, keyboard handlers, etc. **that will be useful in other projects or in many different places in the present program.**

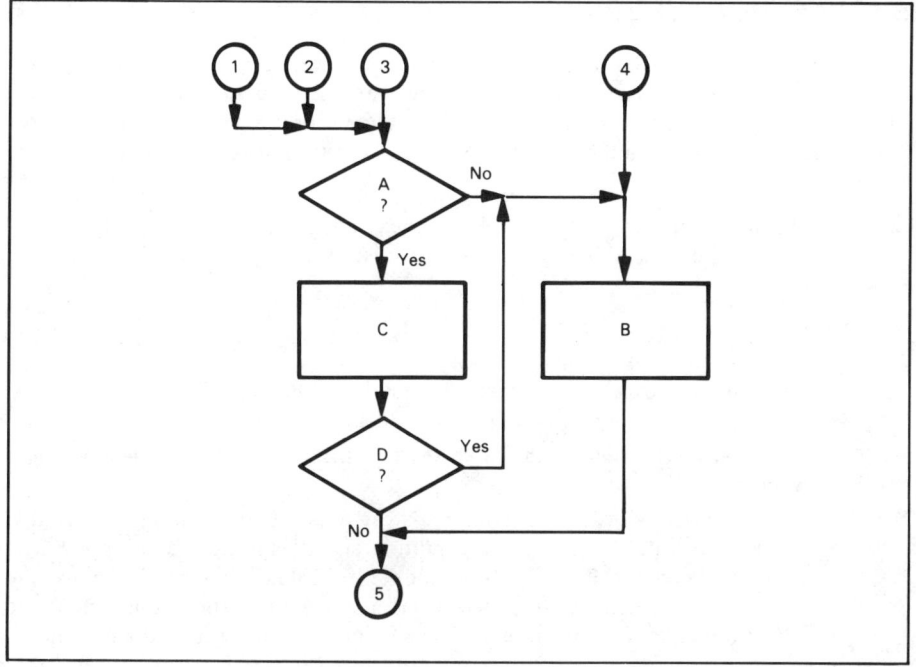

Figure 17-8. Flowchart of an Unstructured Program

4. **Make modules independent of each other.** Restrict the flow of information between modules and implement each design in a single module.
5. **Do not modularize simple tasks** that are already easy to implement.

STRUCTURED PROGRAMMING

How do you keep modules distinct and stop them from interacting? How do you write a program that has a clear sequence of operations so that you can isolate and correct errors? One answer is to use the methods known as "structured programming," whereby each part of the program consists of elements from a limited set of structures and each structure has a single entry and a single exit.

Figure 17-8 shows a flowchart of an unstructured program. **If an error occurs in Module B, we have five possible sources for that error.** Not only must we check each sequence, but we also have to make sure that corrections do not affect any sequences. The usual result is that debugging becomes like wrestling an octopus. Every time you think the situation is under control, there is another loose tentacle somewhere.

BASIC STRUCTURES

The solution is to **establish a clear sequence of operations so that you can isolate errors. Such a sequence uses single-entry, single-exit structures.** A program consists of a sequence of structures; it may be a single statement or it may consist of structures that are nested within each other to any level of complexity. **The required structures are listed below.**

1. **An ordinary sequence;** that is, a linear structure in which programs are executed consecutively. If the sequence is:

    P1
    P2
    P3

    the computer executes P1 first, P2 second, and P3 third. P1, P2, and P3 may be single statements or complex programs.

2. **A conditional structure in which the execution of a program depends on a condition.**

    There are many possible conditional structures, but a common one is "if C then P1 else P2" where C is a condition and P1 and P2 are programs. The computer executes P1 if C is true, and P2 if C is false. Figure 17-9 shows the logic of this structure. Note that it has a single entry and a single exit; the computer cannot enter or leave P1 or P2 other than through the structure.

3. **A loop structure in which a program is repeated until (or as long as) a condition holds.**

    There are many possible loop structures. A common one (called a "do-while" structure) is "while C do P," where C is a condition and P is a program. The computer continually checks C and then executes P as long as C is true.

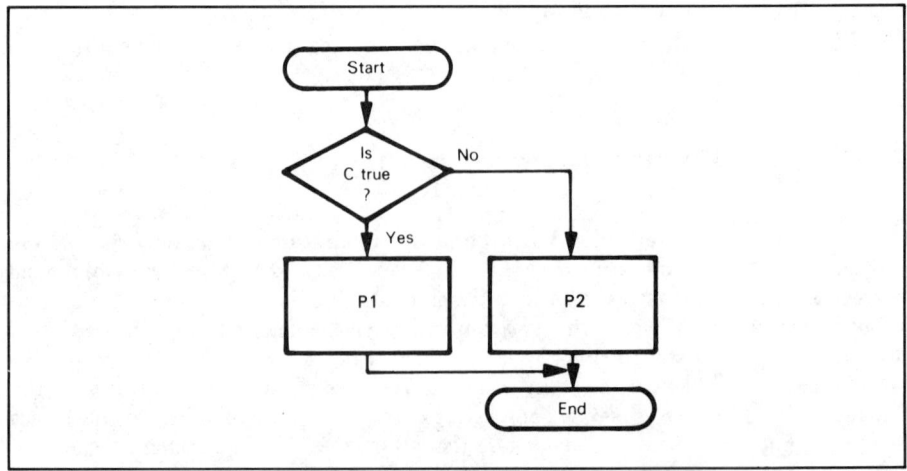

Figure 17-9. Flowchart of the If-Then-Else Structure

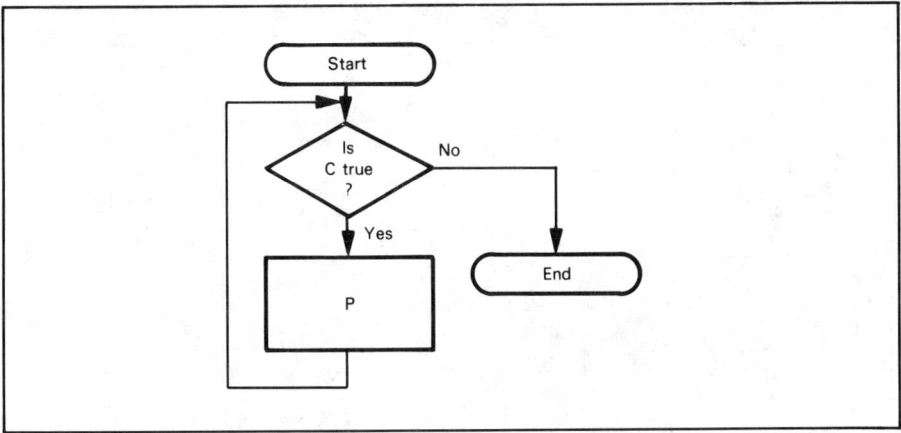

Figure 17-10. Flowchart of the Do-While Structure

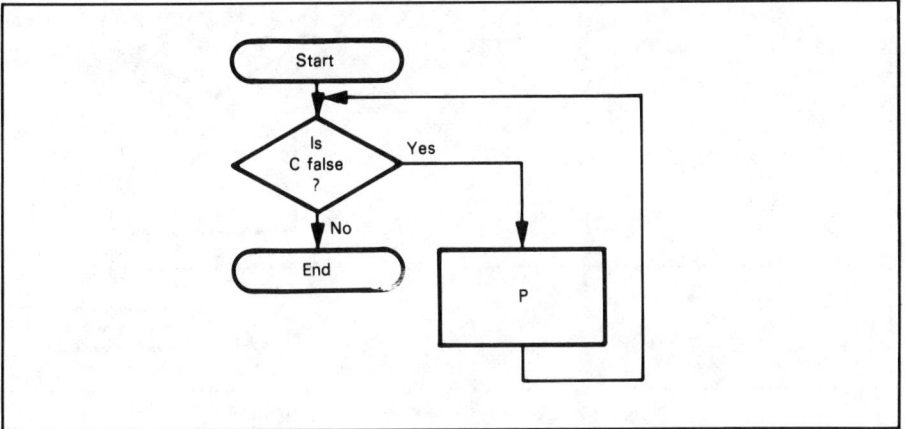

Figure 17-11. Flowchart of the Do-Until Structure

An obvious alternative is "until C do P" in which the computer continually checks C and then executes P as long as C is false. Figures 17-10 and 17-11 show the logic of these alternatives. Both have a single entry and a single exit. The computer will not execute P at all if C is originally in the exit state; thus P is not executed at least once automatically as it is in a FORTRAN DO loop. Alternative structures like "do P while C" or "repeat P until C" produce the FORTRAN implementation in which the computer checks the condition after executing the program (remember Figures 5-1 and 5-2). This approach is often more efficient, but we will use only the form in Figure 17-10 to simplify the discussion. Most high-level structured languages allow all four alternatives to provide flexibility. In most cases, the program P must eventually force C into the exit state; if it does not, the computer will execute P endlessly (the

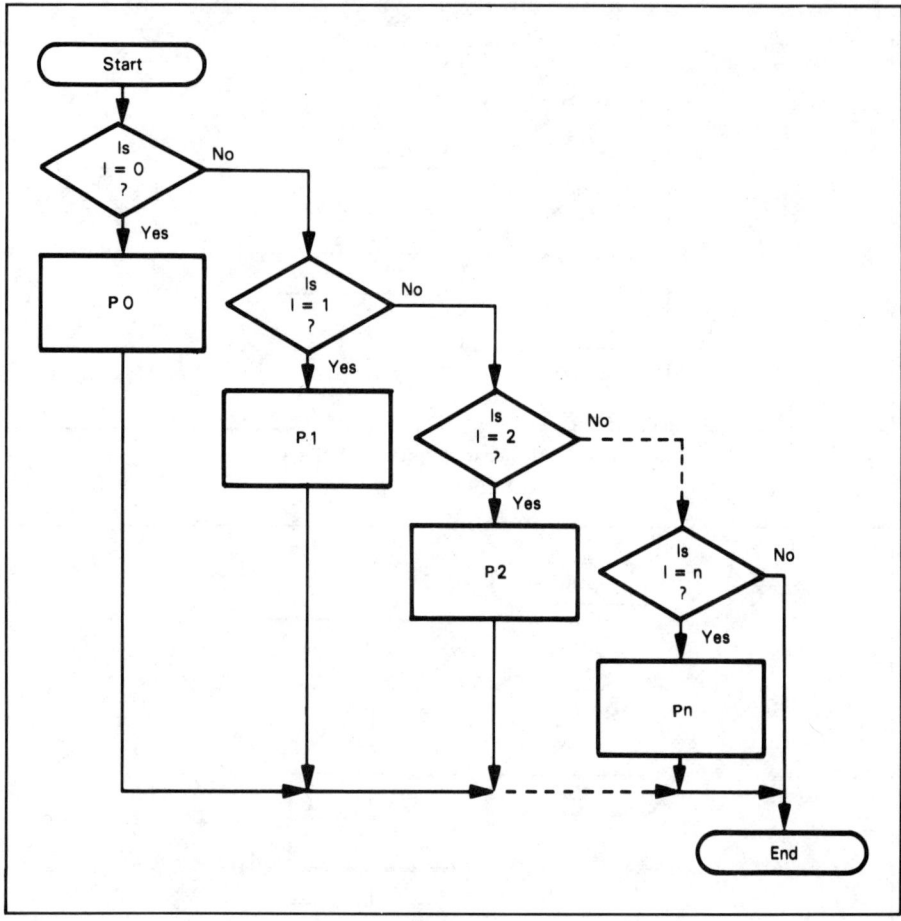

Figure 17-12. Flowchart of the Case Structure

so-called DO FOREVER structure) as it must if P is the overall control program for an instrument, computer peripheral, test system, or electronic game.

4. **A case structure.** Although it is not a primitive structure like our first three, the case structure is so common that it merits a special description. The case structure is "case I of P0, P1, ... , Pn," where I is an index and P0, P1, ... , Pn are programs. The computer executes program P0 if I is 0, P1 if I is 1, and so on; it executes only one of the n programs. If I is greater than n (the number of programs in the case statement) or after execution of one of the programs, the computer then executes the next sequential statement as shown in Figure 17-12. Obviously, we could implement a case structure as a series of conditional structures, much as we could implement a jump table as a series of conditional branches. However, the alternative implementations are long, awkward, and difficult to expand.

FEATURES AND EXAMPLES OF STRUCTURES

Note the following features of structured programming:

1. **Only the three basic structures, and possibly a small number of auxiliary structures, are permitted.** Variations of the conditional and loop structures may be allowed.
2. **Structures may be nested to any level of complexity** since any structure can, in turn, contain any of the structures.
3. **Each structure has a single entry and a single exit.**

Some examples of the conditional structure illustrated in Figure 17-9 are:

1. **P2 included:**

    ```
    IF X > 0 THEN NPOS = NPOS + 1
       ELSE NNEG = NNEG + 1
    ```

Both P1 and P2 are single statements.

2. **P2 omitted:**

    ```
    IF X = 0 THEN Y = 1/X
    ```

Here no action is taken if C (X · 0) is false. P2 and "else" can be omitted in this case.

Some examples of the loop structure illustrated in Figure 17-10 are:

1. **Form the sum of integers from 1 to N.**

    ```
    I = 0
    SUM = 0
    DO WHILE I < N
       I = I + 1
       SUM = SUM + I
    END
    ```

The computer executes the loop as long as $I < N$. If $N = 0$, the program within the "do-while" is not executed at all.

2. **Count characters in an array SENTENCE until you find an ASCII period.**

    ```
    NCHAR = 0
    DO WHILE SENTENCE(NCHAR) ≠ PERIOD
       NCHAR = NCHAR + 1
    END
    ```

The computer executes the loop as long as the character in SENTENCE is not an ASCII period. The count is zero if the first character is a period.

ADVANTAGES OF STRUCTURED PROGRAMMING

The advantages of structured programming are:

1. The sequence of operations is simple to trace. This allows you to test and debug programs easily.
2. The number of structures is limited and the terminology is standardized.
3. The structures can easily be made into modules.
4. Theoreticians have proved that the given set of structures is complete; that is, all programs can be written in terms of the three structures.

5. The structured version of a program is partly self-documenting and fairly easy to read.
6. Structured programs are easy to describe with program outlines.
7. Structured programming has been shown in practice to increase programmer productivity.

Structured programming basically forces much more discipline on the programmer than does modular programming. The result is more systematic and better organized programs.

DISADVANTAGES OF STRUCTURED PROGRAMMING

The disadvantages of structured programming are:

1. Only a few high-level languages (e.g., PL/M, Pascal) will directly accept the structures. The programmer therefore has to go through an extra translation stage to convert the structures to assembly language code. The structured version of the program, however, is often useful as documentation.
2. Structured programs often execute more slowly and use more memory than unstructured programs.
3. Limiting the structures to the three basic forms makes some tasks very awkward to perform. The completeness of the structures only means that all programs can be implemented with them; it does not mean that a given program can be implemented efficiently or conveniently.
4. The standard structures are often quite confusing: e.g., nested "if-then-else" structures may be very difficult to read, since there may be no clear indication of where the inner structures end. A series of nested "do-while" loops can also be difficult to read.
5. Structured programs consider only the sequence of program operations, not the flow of data. Therefore, the structures may handle data awkwardly.
6. Few programmers are accustomed to structured programming. Many find the standard structures awkward and restrictive.

WHEN TO USE STRUCTURED PROGRAMMING

We are neither advocating nor discouraging the use of structured programming. It is one way of systematizing program design. In general, structured programming is most useful in the following situations:

- Larger programs, perhaps exceeding 1000 instructions.
- Applications in which memory usage is not critical.
- Low-volume applications where software development costs, particularly testing and debugging, are important factors.
- Applications involving string manipulation, process control, or other algorithms rather than simple bit manipulations.

In the future, we expect the cost of memory to decrease, the average size of microprocessor programs to increase, and the cost of software development to increase. Therefore, methods like structured programming, which decrease software development costs for larger programs but use more memory, will become more valuable.

Just because structured programming concepts are usually expressed in high-level languages does not mean that structured programming is not applicable to assembly language programming. On the contrary, **the assembly language programmer, with the total freedom of expression that assembly level programming allows, needs the structuring concept provided by structured programming. Creating modules with single entry and exit points, using simple control structures and keeping the complexity of each module minimal increases the productivity of the assembly language programmer.**

EXAMPLES

Structured Program for the Switch and Light System

The structured version of this example is:

```
SWITCH = OFF
DO WHILE SWITCH = OFF
  READ SWITCH
  END
LIGHT = ON
DELAY 1
LIGHT = OFF
```

ON and OFF must have the proper definitions for the switch and light. We assume that DELAY is a module that provides a delay given by its parameter in seconds.

A statement in a structured program may actually be a subroutine. However, in order to conform to the rules of structured programming, the subroutine cannot have any exits other than the one that returns control to the main program.

Since "do-while" checks the condition before executing the loop, we set the variable SWITCH to OFF before starting. The structured program is straightforward, readable, and easy to check by hand. However, it would probably require somewhat more memory than an unstructured program, which would not have to initialize SWITCH and could combine the reading and checking procedures.

Structured Program for the Switch-Based Memory Loader

The switch-based memory loader is a more complex structured programming problem. We may implement the flowchart of Figure 17-3 as follows (a * indicates a comment, and we use "begin" and "end" around a conditionally executed program that consists of more than one line):

```
*
*CLEAR ADDRESS INITIALLY SO ITS STARTING VALUE IS ZERO
*
HIADDRESS = 0
MIDADDRESS = 0
LOADDRESS = 0
*
*CONTINUOUSLY EXAMINE THE SWITCHES AND LOAD DATA INTO MEMORY
```

```
::   NOTE THAT "DO FOREVER" IS JUST "DO WHILE" WITH NO CONDITION
::
DO FOREVER
::
::TEST HIGH ADDRESS BUTTON. IF IT IS BEING PRESSED, DEBOUNCE IT
::  AND WAIT FOR THE OPERATOR TO RELEASE IT. THEN ENTER HIGH
::  ADDRESS FROM THE SWITCHES AND SHOW IT ON THE LIGHTS
::
    IF HIGHADDRBUTTON = 0 THEN
        BEGIN
            DO WHILE HIADDRBUTTON = 0
                DELAY (DEBOUNCE TIME)
                END
            HIADDRESS = SWITCHES
            LIGHTS = SWITCHES
        END
::TEST MID ADDRESS BUTTON. IF IT IS BEING PRESSED, DEBOUNCE IT
::  AND WAIT FOR THE OPERATOR TO RELEASE IT. THEN ENTER MID
::  ADDRESS FROM THE SWITCHES AND SHOW IT ON THE LIGHTS
::
    IF MIDADDRBUTTON .= 0 THEN
        BEGIN
            DO WHILE MIDADDRBUTTON - 0
                DELAY (DEBOUNCE TIME)
                END
            MIDADDRESS = SWITCHES
            LIGHTS = SWITCHES
        END
::TEST LOW ADDRESS BUTTON. IF IT IS BEING PRESSED, DEBOUNCE IT AND
::  WAIT FOR THE OPERATOR TO RELEASE IT. THEN ENTER LOW ADDRESS
::  FROM THE SWITCHES AND SHOW IT ON THE LIGHTS
::
    IF LOADDRBUTTON = 0 THEN
        BEGIN
            DO WHILE LOADDRBUTTON = 0
                DELAY (DEBOUNCE TIME)
                END
            LOADDRESS = SWITCHES
            LIGHTS = SWITCHES
        END
::
::TEST DATA BUTTON. IF IT IS BEING PRESSED, DEBOUNCE IT AND WAIT
::  FOR THE OPERATOR TO RELEASE IT. THEN ENTER DATA FROM THE
::  SWITCHES, SHOW IT ON THE LIGHTS, AND STORE IT IN MEMORY AT
::  (HIGH ADDRESS, MID ADDRESS, LOW ADDRESS)
::
    IF DATABUTTON = 0 THEN
        BEGIN
            DO WHILE DATABUTTON = 0
                DELAY (DEBOUNCE TIME)
                END
            DATA = SWITCHES
            LIGHTS = SWITCHES
            (HIADDRESS, MIDADRESS, LOADDRESS) = DATA
        END
::
::WAIT THE DEBOUNCING TIME BEFORE EXAMINING THE BUTTONS AGAIN.
::  THIS DELAY DEBOUNCES THE RELEASE FOR SURE
::
    DELAY (DEBOUNCE TIME)
END
::
::THE LAST END ABOVE TERMINATES THE
::  DO FOREVER LOOP
::
```

Structured programs are not easy to write, but they can give a great deal of insight into the overall program logic. You can check the logic of the structured program by hand before writing any actual code.

Structured Program for the Verification Terminal

Let us look at the keyboard entry for the transaction terminal. We will assume that the display array is ENTRY, the keyboard strobe is KEYSTROBE, and the keyboard data is KEYIN. **The structured program without the function keys is:**

```
NKEYS = 10
::
::CLEAR ENTRY TO START
::
  DO WHILE NKEYS > 0
    NKEYS = NKEYS - 1
    ENTRY(NKEYS) = 0
  END
::
::FETCH A COMPLETE ENTRY FROM KEYBOARD
::
  DO WHILE NKEYS < 10
    IF KEYSTROBE = ACTIVE THEN
      BEGIN
        KEYSTROBE = INACTIVE
        ENTRY(NKEYS) = KEYIN
        NKEYS = NKEYS + 1
      END
  END
```

Adding the SEND key means that the program must ignore extra digits after it has a complete entry, and must ignore the SEND key until it has a complete entry. The structured program is:

```
NKEYS = 10
::
::CLEAR ENTRY TO START
::
  DO WHILE NKEYS > 0
    NKEYS = NKEYS - 1
    ENTRY(NKEYS) = 0
  END
::
::WAIT FOR COMPLETE ENTRY FOLLOWED BY SEND KEY
::
  DO WHILE KEY ≠ SEND OR NKEYS ≠ 10
    IF KEYSTROBE = ACTIVE THEN
      BEGIN
        KEYSTROBE = INACTIVE
        KEY = KEYIN
        IF NKEYS ≠ 10 AND KEY ≠ SEND THEN
          BEGIN
            ENTRY(NKEYS) = KEY
            NKEYS = NKEYS + 1
          END
      END
  END
```

Note the following features of this structured program.

1. The second if-then is nested within the first one, since the keys are only entered after a strobe is recognized. If the second if-then were on the same level as the first, a single key could fill the entry, since its value would be entered into the array during each iteration of the do-while loop.
2. KEY need not be defined initially, since NKEYS is set to zero as part of the clearing of the entry.

Adding the CLEAR key allows the program to clear the entry originally by

simulating the pressing of CLEAR; i.e., by setting NKEYS to 10 and KEY to CLEAR before starting. The structured program must also only clear digits that have previously been filled. **The new structured program is:**

```
;
; SIMULATE COMPLETE CLEARING
;
NKEYS = 10
KEY = CLEAR
;
;WAIT FOR COMPLETE ENTRY AND SEND KEY
;
DO WHILE KEY = SEND OR NKEYS = 10
;
;CLEAR WHOLE ENTRY IF CLEAR KEY STRUCK
;
    IF KEY = CLEAR THEN
        BEGIN
            KEY = 0
            DO WHILE NKEYS > 0
                NKEYS = NKEYS - 1
                ENTRY(NKEYS) = 0
                END
            END
;
;GET DIGIT IF ENTRY INCOMPLETE
;
    IF KEYSTROBE = ACTIVE THEN
        BEGIN
            KEYSTROBE = INACTIVE
            KEY = KEYIN
            IF KEY < 10 AND NKEYS ≠ 10 THEN
                BEGIN
                    ENTRY(NKEYS) = KEY
                    NKEYS = NKEYS + 1
                    END
                END
        END
END
```

Note that the program resets KEY to zero after clearing the array, so that the operation is not repeated.

We can similarly build a structured program for the receive routine. An initial program could just look for the header and trailer characters. We will assume that RSTB is the indicator that a character is ready. **The structured program is:**

```
;
;CLEAR HEADER FLAG TO START
;
HFLAG = 0
;
;WAIT FOR HEADER AND TRAILER
;
DO WHILE HFLAG = 0 OR CHAR ≠ TRAILER
;
;GET CHARACTER IF READY. LOOK FOR HEADER
;
    IF RSTB = ACTIVE THEN
        BEGIN
            RSTB = INACTIVE
            CHAR = INPUT
            IF CHAR = HEADER THEN HFLAG = 1
            END
END
```

Now we can add the section that checks the message address against the three digits in TERMINAL ADDRESS (TERMADDR). If any of the corresponding digits are not equal, the ADDRESS MATCH flag (ADDRMATCH) is set to 1.

```
;
;CLEAR HEADER FLAG, ADDRESS MATCH FLAG, ADDRESS COUNTER TO START
;
HFLAG = 0
ADDRMATCH = 0
ADDRCTR = 0
```

```
::
::WAIT FOR HEADER, DESTINATION ADDRESS, AND TRAILER
::
DO WHILE HFLAG = 0 OR CHAR = TRAILER OR ADDRCTR = 3
   ::
   ::GET CHARACTER IF READY
   ::
      IF RSTB = ACTIVE THEN
         BEGIN
            RSTB = INACTIVE
            CHAR = INPUT
         END
   ::
   ::CHECK FOR TERMINAL ADDRESS AND HEADER
   ::
      IF HFLAG = 1 AND ADDRCTR = 3 THEN
         BEGIN
            IF CHAR = TERMADDR(ADDRCTR) THEN ADDRMATCH = 1
            ADDRCTR = ADDRCTR + 1
         END
      IF CHAR = HEADER THEN HFLAG = 1
END
```

The program must now wait for a header, a three-digit identification code, and a trailer. You must be careful of what happens during the iteration when the program finds the header, and of what happens if an erroneous identification code character is the same as the trailer.

A further addition can store the message in MESSG. NMESS is the number of characters in the message; if it is not zero at the end, the program knows that the terminal has received a valid message. We have not tried to minimize the logic expressions in this program.

```
::
::CLEAR FLAGS, COUNTERS TO START
::
HFLAG = 0
ADDRMATCH = 0
ADDRCTR = 0
NMESS = 0
::
::WAIT FOR HEADER, DESTINATION ADDRESS, AND TRAILER
::
DO WHILE HFLAG = 0 OR CHAR = TRAILER OR ADDRCTR ≠ 3
   ::
   ::GET CHARACTER IF READY
   ::
      IF RSTB = ACTIVE THEN
         BEGIN
            RSTB = INACTIVE
            CHAR = INPUT
         END
   ::
   ::READ MESSAGE IF DESTINATION ADDRESS = TERMINAL ADDRESS
   ::
      IF HFLAG = 1 AND ADDRCTR = 3 THEN
         IF ADDRMATCH = 0 AND CHAR ≠ TRAILER THEN
            BEGIN
               MESSG(NMESS) = CHAR
               NMESS = NMESS + 1
            END
   ::
   ::CHECK FOR TERMINAL ADDRESS
   ::
      IF HFLAG = 1 AND ADDRCTR ≠ 3 THEN
         BEGIN
            IF CHAR = TERMADDR(ADDRCTR) THEN ADDRMATCH = 1
            ADDRCTR = ADDRCTR + 1
         END
   ::
   ::LOOK FOR HEADER
   ::
      IF CHAR = HEADER THEN HFLAG = 1
END
```

The program checks for the identification code only if it found a header during a previous iteration. It accepts the message only if it has previously found a header and a complete, matching destination address. The program must work properly during the iterations when it finds the header, the trailer and the last digit of the destination address. It must not try to match the header with the terminal address or place the trailer or the final digit of the destination address in the message. **You might try adding the rest of the logic from the flowchart (Figure 17-7) to the structured program. Note that the order of operations is often critical. You must be sure that the program does not complete one phase and start the next one during the same iteration.**

REVIEW OF STRUCTURED PROGRAMMING

Structured programming brings discipline to program design. It forces you to limit the types of structures you use and the sequence of operations. It provides single-entry, single-exit structures, which you can check for logical accuracy. Structured programming often makes the designer aware of inconsistencies or possible combinations of inputs. Structured programming is not a cure-all, but it does bring some order into a process that can be chaotic. The structured program should also aid in debugging, testing, and documentation.

Structured programming is not simple. The programmer must not only define the problem adequately, but must also work through the logic carefully. This is tedious and difficult, but it results in a clearly written, working program.

Terminators

The particular structures we have presented are not ideal and are often awkward. In addition, it can be difficult to determine where one structure ends and another begins, particularly if they are nested. Theorists may provide better structures in the future, or designers may wish to add some of their own. A terminator for each structure seems necessary, since indenting does not always clarify the situation. "End" is a logical terminator for the "do-while" loop. There is no obvious terminator, however, for the "if-then-else" statement; some theorists have suggested "endif" or "fi" ("if" backwards), but these are both awkward and detract from the readability of the program.

RULES FOR STRUCTURED PROGRAMMING

We suggest the following rules for applying structured programming:

1. **Begin by writing a basic flowchart** to help define the logic of the program.
2. **Start with the "sequential," "if-then-else," and "do-while" structures.** They are known to be a complete set, i.e., any program can be written in terms of these structures.
3. **Indent each level** a few spaces from the previous level, so that you will know which statements belong where.
4. **Use terminators for each structure:** e.g., "end" for the "do-while" and "endif" or "fi" for the "if-then-else." The terminators plus the indentation should make the program reasonably clear.

5. **Emphasize simplicity and readability.** Leave lots of spaces, use meaningful names, and make expressions as clear as possible. Do not try to minimize the logic at the cost of clarity.
6. **Comment the program** in an organized manner.
7. **Check the logic.** Try all the extreme cases or special conditions and a few sample cases. Any logical errors you find at this level will not plague you later.

TOP-DOWN DESIGN

The remaining problem is how to check and integrate modules or structures. Certainly we want to divide a large task into sub-tasks. But how do we check the sub-tasks in isolation and put them together? The standard procedure, called "bottom-up design," requires extra work in testing and debugging and leaves the entire integration task to the end. What we need is a method that allows testing and debugging in the actual program environment and modularizes system integration.

This method is "top-down design." Here we start by writing the overall supervisor program. We replace the undefined sub-programs by program "stubs," temporary programs that may either record the entry, provide the answer to a selected test problem, or do nothing. We then test the supervisor program to see that its logic is correct.

We proceed by expanding the stubs. Each stub will often contain sub-tasks, which we will temporarily represent as stubs. **This process of expansion, debugging, and testing continues until all the stubs are replaced by working programs.** Note that testing and integration occur at each level, rather than all at the end. No special driver or data generation programs are necessary. We get a clear idea of exactly where we are in the design. **Top-down design assumes modular programming, and is compatible with structured programming as well.**

DISADVANTAGES OF TOP-DOWN DESIGN

The disadvantages of top-down design are:

1. The overall design may not mesh well with system hardware.
2. It may not take good advantage of existing software.
3. Stubs may be difficult to write, particularly if they must work correctly in several different places.
4. Top-down design may not result in generally useful modules.
5. Errors at the top level can have catastrophic effects, whereas errors in bottom-up design are usually limited to a particular module.

In large programming projects, top-down design has been shown to greatly improve programmer productivity. However, almost all of these projects have used some bottom-up design in cases where the top-down method would have resulted in a large amount of extra work.

Top-down design is a useful tool that should not be followed to extremes. It provides the same discipline for system testing and integration that structured programming provides for module design. The method, however, has more general applicability, since it does not assume the use of programmed logic. However, top-down design may not result in the most efficient implementation.

EXAMPLES

Top-Down Design of Switch and Light System

The first structured programming example actually demonstrates top-down design as well. The program was:

```
SWITCH = OFF
DO WHILE SWITCH = OFF
   READ SWITCH
END
LIGHT = ON
DELAY 1
LIGHT = OFF
```

These statements are really stubs, since none of them is fully defined. For example, what does READ SWITCH mean? If the switch were one bit of input port SPORT, it really means:

```
SWITCH = SPORT AND SMASK
```

where SMASK has a '1' bit in the appropriate position. The masking may, of course, be implemented with a Bit Test instruction.

Similarly, DELAY 1 actually means (if the processor itself provides the delay):

```
REG = COUNT
DO WHILE REG ≠ 0
   REG = REG - 1
END
```

COUNT is the appropriate number to provide a one-second delay. **The expanded version of the program is:**

```
SWITCH = 0
DO WHILE SWITCH = 0
   SWITCH = SPORT AND MASK
END
LIGHT = ON
REF = COUNT
DO WHILE REG = 0
   REG = REG - 1
END
LIGHT - NOT(LIGHT)
```

Certainly this program is more explicit, and could more easily be translated into actual instructions or statements.

Top-Down Design of the Switch-Based Memory Loader

This example is more complex than the first example, so we must proceed systematically. Here again, **the structured program contains stubs.**

For example, if the HIGH ADDRESS button is one bit of input port CPORT, "if HIADDRBUTTON=0" really means:

1. Input from CPORT
2. Logical AND with HAMASK

where HAMASK has a '1' in the appropriate bit position and '0's elsewhere. Similarly the condition "if DATABUTTON=0" really means:

1. Input from CPORT
2. Logical AND with DAMASK

So, the initial stubs could just assume that no buttons are being pressed:

```
HIADDRBUTTON = 1
MIDADDRBUTTON = 1
LOADDRBUTTON = 1
DATABUTTON = 1
```

A run of the supervisor program should show that it takes the implied "else" path through the "if-then-else" structures, and never reads the switches. Similarly, if the stub were:

```
HIADDRBUTTON = 0
```

the supervisor program should stay in the "do while HIADDRBUTTON=0" loop waiting for the button to be released. These simple runs check the overall logic.

Now we can expand each stub and see if the expansion produces a reasonable overall result. Note how debugging and testing proceed in a straightforward and modular manner. We expand the HIADDRBUTTON=0 stub to:

```
READ CPORT
HIADDRBUTTON = (CPORT) AND HAMASK
```

The program should wait for the HIGH ADDRESS button to be released. The program should then display the values of the switches on the lights. This run checks for the proper response to the HIGH ADDRESS button.

We then expand the MID ADDRESS button module to:

```
READ CPORT
MIDADDRBUTTON = (CPORT) AND MAMASK
```

When the MID ADDRESS button is released, the program should display the value of the switches on the lights. This run checks for the proper response to the MID ADDRESS button.

We then expand the LOW ADDRESS button module to:

```
READ CPORT
LOADDRBUTTON = (CPORT) AND LAMASK
```

When the LOW ADDRESS button is released, the program should display the values of the switches on the lights. This run checks for the proper response to the LOW ADDRESS button.

Similarly, we can expand the DATA button module and check for the proper response to that button. The entire program will then have been tested.

When all the stubs have been expanded, the coding, debugging, and testing stages will all be complete. Of course, we must know exactly what results each stub should produce. However, many logical errors will become obvious at each level without any further expansion.

304 68000 Assembly Language Programming

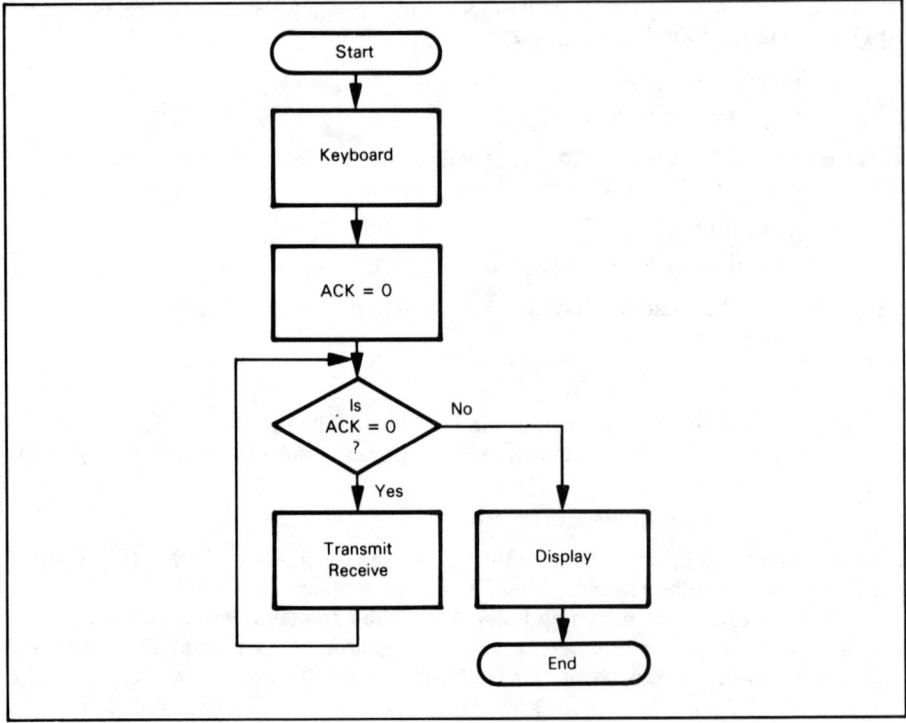

Figure 17-13. Initial Flowchart of Transaction Terminal

Top-Down Design of Verification Terminal

This example, of course, will have more levels of detail. **We could start with the following program** (see Figure 17-13 for a flowchart):

```
KEYBOARD
ACK = 0
DO WHILE ACK = 0
    TRANSMIT
    RECEIVE
END
DISPLAY
```

Here, **KEYBOARD, TRANSMIT, RECEIVE, and DISPLAY are program stubs that will be expanded later.** KEYBOARD, for example, could simply place a ten-digit verified number into the appropriate buffer.

The next stage of expansion could produce the following program for KEYBOARD (see Figure 17-14):

```
VER = 0
DO WHILE VER = 0
    COMPLETE = 0
    DO WHILE COMPLETE = 0
        KEYIN
        KEYDS
    END
    VERIFY
END
```

Program Design **305**

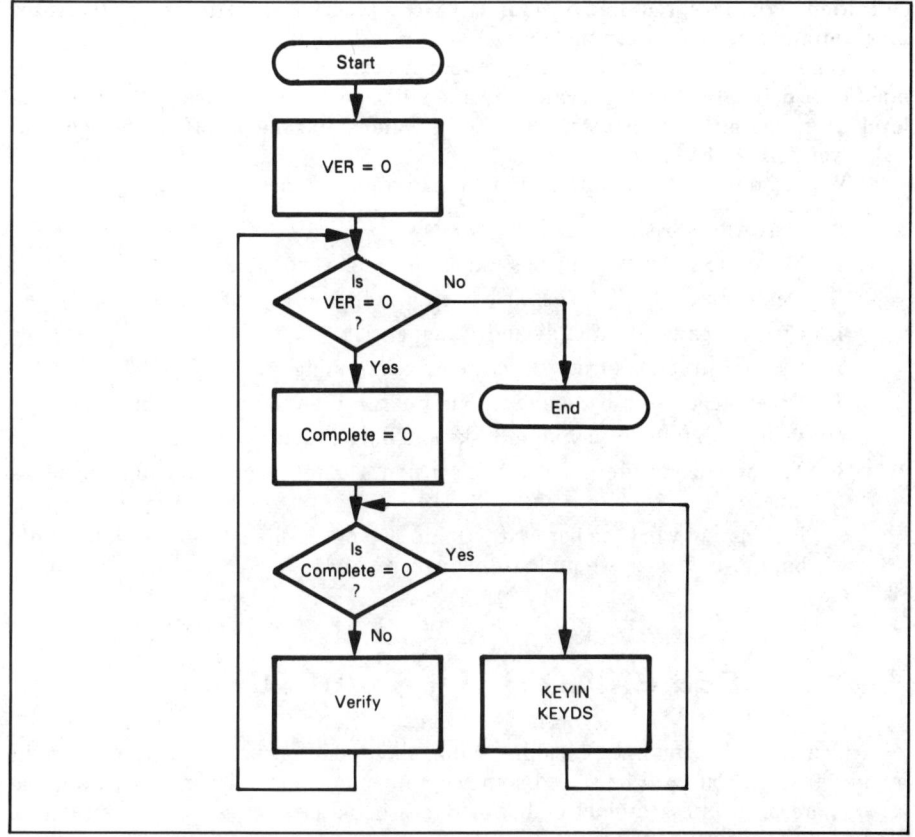

Figure 17-14. Flowchart for Expanded KEYBOARD Routine

Here VER=0 means that an entry has not been verified; COMPLETE=0 means that the entry is incomplete. KEYIN and KEYDS are the keyboard input and display routines respectively. VERIFY checks the entry. A stub for KEYIN would simply place a random entry (from a random number table or generator) into the buffer and set COMPLETE to 1.

We would continue by similarly expanding, debugging, and testing TRANSMIT, RECEIVE, and DISPLAY. Note that you should expand each program by one level so that you do not perform the integration of an entire program at any one time. You must use your judgment in defining levels. Too small a step wastes time, while too large a step gets you back to the problems of system integration that top-down design is supposed to solve.

REVIEW OF TOP-DOWN DESIGN

Top-down design brings discipline to the testing and integration stages of program design. It provides a systematic method for expanding a flowchart or problem definition to the level required to actually write a program. Together with structured programming, it forms a complete set of design techniques.

Like structured programming, top-down design is not simple. The designer must have defined the problem carefully and must work systematically through each level. Here again the methodology may seem tedious, but the payoff can be substantial if you follow the rules.

We recommend the following approach to top-down design:

1. Start with a basic flowchart.
2. Make the stubs as complete and as separate as possible.
3. Define precisely all the possible outcomes from each stub and select a test set.
4. Check each level carefully and systematically.
5. Use the structures from structured programming.
6. Expand each stub by one level. Do not try to do too much in one step.
7. Watch carefully for common tasks and data structures.
8. Test and debug after each stub expansion. Do not try to do an entire level at a time.
9. Be aware of what the hardware can do. Do not hesitate to stop and do a little bottom-up design where that seems necessary.

DESIGNING DATA STRUCTURES

Beginning programmers seldom think about data structures. They generally assume that the data will be stored somewhere in the computer's memory, much as records are piled into a cabinet or books into a bookcase. Designing data structures seems as far fetched as establishing a complete card catalog for one's books or records; few people take organization to such lengths.

But the fact is that **most computer-based systems involve a surprisingly large amount of data processing.** Numerical algorithms assume that the processor can easily find the element in the next row or next column of an array. Editor programs assume that the processor can easily find the next character, the previous line, a particular string of characters, or the starting point of an entire paragraph or page. An operator interface for a piece of test equipment may assume that the processor can easily find a particular command or data entry and move it from one place to another. **Imagine how difficult the following tasks would be to implement if the data is simply scattered through memory or organized in a long, linear array:**

1. The operator of a machine tool wants to insert two extra cutting steps between steps 14 and 15 of a 40-step pattern.
2. The operator of a chemical processing plant wants to see the last ten values of the temperature at the inlet to tank 05.
3. An accounting clerk wants to enter a new account into an alphabetical list.

The processor may spend most of its time finding the data, moving from one data item to the next, and organizing the data.

SELECTING DATA STRUCTURES

Obviously, we cannot provide a complete description of data structures here.[4,5] Just as clearly, **the design of data structures has great influence on the design of programs if the data is complex.** We will briefly mention the following considerations in selecting data structures:

1. **How are the data items related?** Closely related items should be accessible from each other, since such accesses will be frequent.
2. **What kind of operations will be performed on the data?** Simple linear structures are adequate if the data is always handled in a single, fixed order. However, more complex structures are essential if the tasks involve operations such as searching, editing, or sorting.
3. **Can standard structures be used?** Methods are readily available for handling structures such as queues, stacks, and linked lists. Other arrangements will require special programming.
4. **What kind of access is necessary?** Clearly we need more structure if we must find elements that are identified by a number or a relative position, rather than just the first or last entries. We must organize the data to make the accesses as rapid as possible.

REVIEW OF PROBLEM DEFINITION AND PROGRAM DESIGN

You should note that we have spent two entire chapters without mentioning any specific microprocessor or assembly language, and without writing a single line of actual code. However, you should now know a lot more about the examples than you would if we had just asked you to write the programs at the start. **Although we often think of the writing of computer instructions as a key part of software development, it is actually one of the easiest stages.**

Once you have written a few programs, coding will become simple. You will soon learn the instruction set, recognize which instructions are really useful, and remember the common sequences that make up the largest part of most programs. **You will then find that many of the other stages of software development remain difficult and have few clear rules.**

We have suggested some ways to systematize the important early stages. In the problem definition stage, you must define all the characteristics of the system — its inputs, outputs, processing, time and memory constraints, and error handling. **You must particularly consider how the system will interact with the larger system of which it is a part, and whether that larger system includes electrical equipment, mechanical equipment, or a human operator. You must start at this stage to make the system easy to use and maintain.**

In the program design stage, several techniques can help you to systematically specify and document the logic of your program. Modular programming forces you to divide the total program into small, distinct modules. Structured programming provides a systematic way of defining the logic of those modules, while top-down design is a systematic method for integrating and testing them. Of course, no one can compel you to follow all of these techniques; they are, in fact, guidelines more than anything else. But they do provide a unified aproach to design, and you should consider them a basis on which to develop your own approach.

REFERENCES

1. D. L. Parnas (see the references below) has been a leader in the area of modular programming.
2. Collected by B. W. Unger (see reference below).
3. Formulated by D. L. Parnas.
4. K. J. Thurber. and P. C. Patton. *Data Structures and Computer Architecture*, Lexington Books, Lexington, Mass., 1977.
5. K. S. Shankar. "Data Structures, Types, and Abstractions," *Computer*, April 1980, pp. 67-77.

The following references provide additional information on problem definition and program design:

Chapin, N. *Flowcharts,* Auerbach, Princeton, N. J., 1971.

Dalton, W. F. "Design Microcomputer Software like Other Systems — Systematically," *Electronics,* January 19, 1978, pp. 97-101.

Dijkstra, E. W. *A Discipline of Programming,* Prentice-Hall, Englewood Cliffs, N. J., 1976.

Halstead, M. H. *Elements of Software Science,* American Elsevier, New York, 1977.

Hughes, J. K. and J. I. Michtom. *A Structured Approach to Programming,* Prentice-Hall, Englewood Cliffs, N. J., 1977.

Morgan, D. E. and D. J. Taylor. "A Survey of Methods for Achieving Reliable Software," *Computer,* February 1977, pp. 44-52.

Myers, W. "The Need for Software Engineering," *Computer,* February 1978, pp. 12-25.

Parnas, D. L. "On the Criteria to be Used in Decomposing Systems into Modules," *Communications of the ACM,* December 1972, pp. 1053-58.

Parnas, D. L. "A Technique for the Specification of Software Modules with Examples," *Communications of the ACM,* May 1973, pp. 330-336.

Phister, M. Jr. *Data Processing Technology and Economics,* Santa Monica Publishing Co., Santa Monica, Ca., 1976.

Schneider, V. "Prediction of Software Effort and Project Duration — Four New Formulas," *SIGPLAN Notices,* June 1978, pp. 49-59.

Schneiderman, B. et al. "Experimental Investigations of the Utility of Detailed Flowcharts in Programming," *Communications of the ACM,* June 1977, pp. 373-381.

Tausworthe, R. C. *Standardized Development of Computer Software.* Prentice-Hall: Englewood Cliffs, N. J., 1977 (Part 1); 1979 (Part 2).

Unger, B. W. "Programming Languages for Computer System Simulation," *Simulation,* April 1978, pp. 101-10.

Wirth, N. *Algorithms + Data Structures = Programs.* Prentice-Hall: Englewood Cliffs, N. J., 1976.

Wirth, N. *Systematic Programming: an Introduction.* Prentice-Hall: Englewood Cliffs, N. J., 1973.

Yourdon, E. U. *Techniques of Program Structure and Design.* Prentice-Hall: Englewood Cliffs, N. J., 1975.

18
Documentation

Software development must yield more than just a working program. A software product must also include the documentation that allows it to be used, maintained, and extended. Adequate documentation is helpful during program debugging and testing, and essential in the later stages of the program's life cycle.

SELF-DOCUMENTING PROGRAMS

Although no program is ever completely self-documenting, some of the rules that we mentioned earlier can help. These include:
- Clear, simple structure with as few transfers of control (jumps) as possible
- Use of meaningful names and labels
- Use of names instead of literal numbers for I/O devices, parameters, numerical factors, subroutine addresses, branch destinations, etc.
- Emphasis on simplicity rather than on minor savings in memory usage, execution time, or typing

For example, the following program sends a character to a teletypewriter:

```
            MOVEQ    -1,D0
            MOVE.B   $6000,D0
            MOVEQ    #10,D2

            BCLR.B   #7,0(A0)
   SNDBIT   BSR      DELAY9_1
            ROR.W    #1,D0
            BCS.S    SNDONE

            BCLR.B   #7,0(A0)
            BRA.S    NEXT

   SNDONE   BSET.B   #7,0(A0)
   NEXT     DBRA     D2,SNDBIT

            RTS
            END
```

CHOOSING USEFUL NAMES

Even without comments we can improve the program as follows:

```
PROGRAM  EQU    $4000
DATA     EQU    $6000

PIADA    EQU    $00                    OFFSET DATA REGISTER A

TTYBIT   EQU    $07                    TTY CONNECTED TO BIT 7
CHRBIT   EQU    $08                    NUMBER OF DATA BITS IN CHARACTER
STPBIT   EQU    $02                    NUMBER OF STOPBITS TO TRANSMIT

TTYOUT   MOVEQ  -1,D0                  FORM STOP BITS
         MOVE.B CHAR,D0                GET TTY OUTPUT DATA
         MOVEQ  #1+CHRBIT+STPBIT-1,D2  BIT COUNT ADJUSTED FOR DBRA

         BCLR.B #TTYBIT,PIADA(A0)      SEND START BIT
SNDBIT   BSR    DELAY9_1               WAIT 1 BIT TIME
         ROR.W  #1,D0                  CARRY = NEXT DATA BIT
         BCS.S  SNDONE                 IF DATA = 1 THEN SEND A ONE

         BCLR.B #TTYBIT,PIADA(A0)      SEND '0' AS DATA BIT
         BRA.S  NEXT

SNDONE   BSET.B #TTYBIT,PIADA(A0)      SEND '1' AS DATA BIT
NEXT     DBRA   D2,SNDBIT              CONTINUE UNTIL ALL DATA BITS SENT

         RTS
         END
```

This program is undoubtedly easier to understand than the earlier version. **Even without further documentation, you could probably guess at the function of the program and the meanings of most of the variables.** Other documentation techniques cannot substitute for self-documentation.

Some further notes on choosing names:

1. **Use the obvious name** when it is available, like TTY or CRT for output devices, START or RESET for addresses, DELAY or SORT for subroutines, COUNT or LENGTH for data.
2. **Avoid acronyms** like S16BA for SORT 16-BIT ARRAY. These seldom mean anything to anybody.
3. **Use full words** or close to full words when possible, like DONE, PRINT, SEND, etc.
4. **Keep the names** as **distinct** as possible. Avoid names that look alike, such as TEMPI and TEMP1, or those that resemble operation codes or other built-in names.

COMMENTS

Comments are a simple form in which to provide additional documentation. However, few programs (even those used as examples in books) have effective comments. **You should consider the following guidelines for good comments:**

1. **Don't explain the internal effects of the instruction.** Instead, explain the purpose of the instruction in the program. Comments like

```
         SUBQ.W #1,D0                  D0 := D0 - 1
```

do not help the reader understand the program. A more useful comment is

```
SUBQ.W  #1,D0              LINE NUMBER := LINE NUMBER - 1
```

Remember that the standard manuals contain descriptions of how the processor executes its instructions. The comments should explain what tasks the program is performing and what methods it is using.

2. **Make the comments as clear as possible.** Do not use abbreviations or acronyms unless they are well known (like ASCII, PIA, or UART) or standard (like "num" for number, "ms" for millisecond, etc.). Avoid comments like

```
SUBQ.W  #1,D0              L N := L N - 1
```

or

```
SUBQ.W  #1,D0              DEC. LN BY 1
```

The extra typing required to enter meaningful comments is certainly worthwhile.

3. **Comment every important or obscure point.** Be particularly careful to mark operations that may not have obvious functions, such as

```
MOVEA.L (A0),A0            GET ADDRESS TO NEXT ELEMENT IN QUEUE
```

or

```
ANDI.B  #$FE,PIADA(A0)     TURN OFF LED INDICATOR
```

Clearly, I/O operations often require extensive comments. If you're not exactly sure what an instruction does, or if you have to think about it, add a clarifying comment. The comment will save you time later and will be helpful in documentation.

4. **Don't comment the obvious.** A comment on each line makes it difficult to find the important points. Standard instructions like

```
DBRA    D1,LOOP
```

need not be marked unless you're doing something special. One comment will often suffice for several lines, as in

```
CLR.B   PIACA(A0)          INITIALIZE A SIDE
MOVE.B  #A_DATDIR,PIADDA(A0)
MOVE.B  #A_CNTRL,PIACA(A0)
```

or

```
MOVE.B  (A0)+,D0           EXCHANGE MOST SIGNIFICANT AND
MOVE.B  (A0),-(A0)         .. LEAST SIGNIFICANT BYTES
MOVE.B  D0,1(A0)
```

5. **Place comments on the lines to which they refer or at the start of a sequence.**

6. **Keep your comments up-to-date.** If you change the program, change the comments.

7. **Use standard forms and terms** in commenting. Don't worry about repetition. Varied names for the same things are confusing, even if the variations are just COUNT and COUNTER, START and BEGIN, DISPLAY and LEDS, or PANEL and SWITCHES. You gain nothing from inconsistency. Minor varia-

tions may be obvious to you now, but may not be clear later; others will get confused immediately.

8. **Make comments mingled with instructions brief.** Leave a complete explanation to header comments and other documentation. Otherwise the program gets lost in the comments and you may have a hard time even finding the actual instructions.
9. **Keep improving your comments.** If you come to one that you cannot read or understand, take the time to change it. If you find that the listing is getting crowded, add some blank lines. The comments won't improve themselves; in fact, they will just become worse as you leave the task behind and forget exactly what you did.
10. **Use comments to place a heading in front of every major section, subsection, or subroutine.** The heading should describe the functions of the code that follows it; it should include information about the algorithm employed, the inputs and outputs, and any incidental effects that may be produced.
11. **If you modify a working program, use comments to describe the modifications that you made and identify the date and author of the revision.** This information should go both at the front of the program (so a user can easily tell one version from another) and at the points where changes were actually made.

Remember, **comments are important. Good ones will save you time and effort.** Put some work into comments and try to make them effective.

EXAMPLES

18-1. COMMENTING A TELETYPEWRITER OUTPUT ROUTINE

The basic program is:

```
                MOVEQ   -1,D0
                MOVE.B  $6000,D0
                MOVEQ   #10,D2

                BCLR.B  #7,0(A0)
        SNDBIT  BSR     DELAY9_1
                ROR.W   #1,D0
                BCS.S   SNDONE

                BCLR.B  #7,0(A0)
                BRA.S   NEXT

        SNDONE  BSET.B  #7,0(A0)
        NEXT    DBRA    D2,SNDBIT

                RTS
                END
```

Commenting the important points and adding names for numbers gives:

```
                *      TELETYPEWRITER OUTPUT
                *      THIS PROGRAM SENDS THE CHARACTER IN LOCATION CHAR
                *      TO THE TELETYPE AT THE ADDRESS IN REGISTER A0

PROGRAM   EQU    $4000
DATA      EQU    $6000

PIADA     EQU    $00                   OFFSET FOR DATA REGISTER A OF PIA

TTYBIT    EQU    $07                   TTY CONNECTED TO BIT 7
CHRBIT    EQU    $08                   NUMBER OF DATA BITS IN CHARACTER
STPBIT    EQU    $02                   NUMBER OF STOPBITS TO TRANSMIT

          ORG    DATA

CHAR      DS.B   1                     TTY OUTPUT CHARACTER

          ORG    PROGRAM

TTYOUT    MOVEQ  -1,D0                 FORM STOP BITS
          MOVE.B CHAR,D0               GET TTY OUTPUT DATA
          MOVEQ  #1+CHRBIT+STPBIT-1,D2 BIT COUNT ADJUSTED FOR DBRA

          BCLR.B #TTYBIT,PIADA(A0)     SEND START BIT
SNDBIT    BSR    DELAY9_1              WAIT 1 BIT TIME
          ROR.W  #1,D0                 CARRY = NEXT DATA BIT
          BCS.S  SNDONE                IF DATA = 1 THEN SEND A ONE

          BCLR.B #TTYBIT,PIADA(A0)     SEND '0' AS DATA BIT
          BRA.S  NEXT

SNDONE    BSET.B #TTYBIT,PIADA(A0)     SEND '1' AS DATA BIT
NEXT      DBRA   D2,SNDBIT             CONTINUE UNTIL ALL DATA BITS SENT

          RTS
          END
```

Changing the Program

Note how easily we could change this program so that it would transfer a whole string of data, starting at the address in location CHRSTR and ending with an 03 character (ASCII ETX).

```
                    *
                    *     PROGRAM    TTYOUT
                    *
                    *     TELETYPEWRITER OUTPUT
                    *
                    *     THIS PROGRAM SENDS A STRING TO A
                    *     TELETYPEWRITER
                    *
                    *     TO USE THIS PROGRAM:
                    *
                    *           CHRSTR          PUT ADDRESS OF STRING IN
                    *                           THIS LOCATION
                    *           A0              PUT ADDRESS OF TELETYPEWRITER
                    *                           DEVICE IN REGISTER A0
                    *           ETX             END STRING WITH AN ASCII
                    *                           ETX CHARACTER
                    *
00004000            PROGRAM   EQU    $4000
00006000            DATA      EQU    $6000

00000000            PIADA     EQU    $00        OFFSET FOR DATA REGISTER A OF PIA

00000007            TTYBIT    EQU    $07        TTY CONNECTED TO BIT 7
00000008            CHRBIT    EQU    $08        NUMBER OF DATA BITS IN CHARACTER
00000002            STPBIT    EQU    $02        NUMBER OF STOPBITS TO TRANSMIT
00000003            ENDMARK   EQU    $03        ASCII ETX MARKS END OF OUTPUT STRIN

00006000                      ORG    DATA
```

```
006000 00000001        CHRSTR DS.B    1                    TTY OUTPUT CHARACTERSTRING
       00004000               ORG     PROGRAM
004000 227C00006000 TTYOUT    MOVEA.L #CHRSTR,A1           GET ADDRESS OF OUTPUT STRING
004006 70FF         OUTCHR    MOVEQ   -1,D0                FORM STOP BITS
004008 1019                   MOVE.B  (A1)+,D0             GET TTY OUTPUT DATA
00400A 0C000003               CMPI.B  #ENDMARK,D0          IS IT END OF STRING
00400E 6724                   BEQ.S   DONE                 ..THEN DONE
004010 740A                   MOVEQ   #1+CHRBIT+STPBIT-1,D2 BIT COUNT ADJUSTED FOR DBRA
004012 08A800070000           BCLR.B  #TTYBIT,PIADA(A0)    SEND START BIT
004018 6100BFE6     SNDBIT    BSR     DELAY9_1             WAIT 1 BIT TIME
00401C E258                   ROR.W   #1,D0                CARRY = NEXT DATA BIT
00401E 6508                   BCS.S   SNDONE               IF DATA = 1 THEN SEND A ONE
004020 08A800070000           BCLR.B  #TTYBIT,PIADA(A0)    SEND '0' AS DATA BIT
004026 6006                   BRA.S   NEXT
004028 08E800070000 SNDONE    BSET.B  #TTYBIT,PIADA(A0)    SEND '1' AS DATA BIT
00402E 51CAFFE8     NEXT      DBRA    D2,SNDBIT            CONTINUE UNTIL ALL DATA BITS SENT
004032 60D2                   BRA     OUTCHR               CONTINUE UNTIL ALL CHARACTERS SENT
004034 4E75         DONE      RTS
```

Good comments will help you change a program to meet new requirements. For example, try changing the last program so that it:

- Starts each message with ASCII STX (02) followed by a two-digit identification code stored in memory location IDCODE.
- Adds no start or stop bits.
- Waits 1 ms between bits.
- Transmits 40 characters, starting with the one located at the address in DPTR.
- Ends each message with two consecutive ASCII ETXs (03).

18-2. COMMENTING A MULTIPLE-PRECISION ADDITION ROUTINE

The basic program is:

```
            ORG     $4000
            MOVE.L  #$6008,A0
            MOVE.L  #$6208,A1
            MOVE    #0,CCR
            MOVEQ   #7,D2
   LOOP     MOVE.B  -(A0),D0
            MOVE.B  -(A1),D1
            ADDX.B  D1,D0
            MOVE.B  D0,(A0)
            DBRA    D2,LOOP
            RTS
            END
```

Important Points

First, comment the important points. These are typically initializations, data fetches, and processing operations. Don't bother with standard sequences like updating pointers and counters. Remember that **names are clearer than numbers, so use them freely.**

The new version of the program is:

```
*       MULTIPRECISION ADDITION
*
*       THIS PROGRAM ADDS TWO NUMBERS STORED
*       AT LOCATIONS NUM1 AND NUM2 AND
*       STORES THE RESULT IN LOCATION NUM1
*
*       THE NUMBERS MUST BE EIGHT BYTES LONG
*       (OR CHANGE BYTECOUNT)

PROGRAM   EQU     $4000

NUM1      EQU     $6000
NUM2      EQU     $6200
BYTECOUNT EQU     $8

          ORG     PROGRAM

          MOVEA.L #NUM1+BYTECOUNT,A0    ADDRESS BEYOND END OF FIRST NUMBER
          MOVEA.L #NUM2+BYTECOUNT,A1    ADDRESS BEYOND END OF SECOND NUMBER
          MOVE    #0,CCR
          MOVEQ   #BYTECOUNT-1,D2
LOOP      MOVE.B  -(A0),D0              GET BYTES TO ADD, START WITH
          MOVE.B  -(A1),D1              LEAST SIGNIFICANT BYTES
          ADDX.B  D1,D0                 ADD THEM WITH CARRY
          MOVE.B  D0,(A0)               STORE RESULT IN NUM1
          DBRA    D2,LOOP

          RTS
```

Obscure Functions

Second, look for instructions that may not have obvious functions and explain their purposes with comments. Here, the purpose of MOVE #0,CCR is to clear the Extend flag (and other flags) before adding the least significant bytes.

```
*       MULTIPRECISION ADDITION
*
*       THIS PROGRAM ADDS TWO NUMBERS STORED
*       AT LOCATIONS NUM1 AND NUM2 AND
*       STORES THE RESULT IN LOCATION NUM1
*
*       THE NUMBERS MUST BE EIGHT BYTES LONG
*       (OR CHANGE BYTECOUNT)

PROGRAM   EQU     $4000

NUM1      EQU     $6000                 ADDRESS OF FIRST BINARY NUMBER
NUM2      EQU     $6200                 ADDRESS OF SECOND BINARY NUMBER
BYTECOUNT EQU     $8                    NUMBER OF BYTES TO ADD

          ORG     PROGRAM

          MOVEA.L #NUM1+BYTECOUNT,A0    ADDRESS BEYOND END OF FIRST NUMBER
          MOVEA.L #NUM2+BYTECOUNT,A1    ADDRESS BEYOND END OF SECOND NUMBER
          MOVE    #0,CCR                CLEAR EXTEND FLAG (AND OTHER FLAGS)
          MOVEQ   #BYTECOUNT-1,D2       LOOP COUNTER ADJUSTED FOR DBRA
LOOP      MOVE.B  -(A0),D0              GET BYTES TO ADD, START WITH
          MOVE.B  -(A1),D1              LEAST SIGNIFICANT BYTES
          ADDX.B  D1,D0                 ADD THEM WITH CARRY
          MOVE.B  D0,(A0)               STORE RESULT IN NUM1
          DBRA    D2,LOOP

          RTS
```

Questions for Commenting

Third, ask yourself whether the comments tell you what you would need to know to use the program; for example:

1. Where is the program entered? Are there alternative entry points?
2. What parameters are necessary? How and in what form must they be supplied?
3. What operations does the program perform?
4. From where does it get the data?
5. Where does it store the results?
6. What special cases does it consider?
7. What does the program do about errors?
8. How does it exit?

Some questions may be irrelevant and some answers may be obvious. Make sure, however, that you wouldn't have to dissect the program to answer the important questions. Remember also that too much explanation may be an obstacle to using the program. Are there any changes you would like to see in the listing? If so, make them — you are the one who has to decide if the commenting is adequate and reasonable.

FLOWCHARTS AS DOCUMENTATION

We have already described the use of flowcharts as a design tool in Chapter 17. Flowcharts are also useful in documentation, particularly if:

- They are not cluttered or too detailed.
- Their decision points are explained and marked clearly.
- They include all branches.
- They correspond to the actual program listings.

Flowcharts are helpful if they give you an overall picture of the program. They are not helpful if they are just as difficult to read as the program listing.

STRUCTURED PROGRAMS AS DOCUMENTATION

A **structured program can serve as documentation** for an assembly language program if:

- You describe the purpose of each section in the comments.
- You make it clear which statements are included in each conditional or loop structure by using indentation and ending markers.
- You make the total structure as simple as possible.
- You use a consistent, well-defined language.

The structured program can help you check the logic or improve it. Furthermore, since the structured program is machine-independent, it can also help you implement the same task on another computer.

MEMORY MAPS

A memory map is simply a list of all the memory assignments in a program. The map allows you to determine the amount of memory needed, the locations of data or subroutines, and the parts of memory not allocated. The map is a handy reference for finding storage locations and entry points and for dividing memory between different routines or programmers. The map will also give you easy access to data and subroutines if you need them in later extensions or in maintenance. **Sometimes a graphical map is more helpful than a listing.**

A typical map is:

Program Memory

Address	Routine	Purpose
E000 - E1FF	RDKBD	Interrupt Service Routine for Keyboard
E200 - E240	BRKPT	Breakpoint Routine Entered Via Software Interrupt
E241 - E250	DELAY	Generalized Delay Program
E251 - E270	DSPLY	Control Program for Operator Displays
E271 - E3EF	SUPER	Main Supervisor Program
0000 - 03FF		Interrupt and Reset Vectors

Data Memory

Address	Name	Purpose
1000	NKEYS	Number of Keys Pressed by Operator
1001 - 1002	KBPTR	Keyboard Buffer Pointer
1003 - 1041	KBUFFR	Keyboard Buffer
1042 - 1050	DBUFFR	Display Buffer
1051 - 106F	TEMP	Miscellaneous Temporary Storage
1070 - 10FF	STACK	Hardware Stack

The map may also list additional entry points and include a specific description of the unused parts of memory.

PARAMETER AND DEFINITION LISTS

Parameter and definition lists at the start of the main program and each subroutine make understanding and changing the program far simpler. The following rules can help.

1. **Separate data locations, I/O units, parameters, definitions, and fixed memory addresses.**
2. **Arrange lists alphabetically when possible, with a description of each entry.**
3. **Give each parameter that might change a name and include it in the lists.** Such parameters may include time constants, inputs or codes corresponding to particular keys or functions, control or masking patterns, starting or ending characters, thresholds, etc.
4. **List fixed memory addresses separately.** These may include reset and interrupt service addresses, the starting address of the program memory areas, stack areas, etc.

5. **Give each port used by an I/O device a name,** even though devices may share ports in the current system. The separation will make it easier for you to expand or change the I/O section.

A typical list of definitions is:

```
::
:: MEMORY SYSTEM CONSTANTS
::
IRQ_1LEV  EQU     $21000          LEVEL 1 INTERRUPT SERVICE ROUTINE
IRQ_2LEV  EQU     $210AB          LEVEL 2 INTERRUPT SERVICE ROUTINE
IRQ_7LEV  EQU     $22000          LEVEL 7 INTERRUPT SERVICE ROUTINE
MEMORY    EQU     $0              STARTING ADDRESS FOR MEMORY
SSTKPNT   EQU     $F000           INITIAL SUPERVISOR STACK POINTER
USTKPNT   EQU     $E000           INITIAL USER STACK POINTER
::
:: I/O UNITS
::
PIA1      EQU     $3FF40          BASE ADDRESS PIA 1
PIA2      EQU     $3FF41          BASE ADDRESS PIA 2
ACIA1     EQU     $3FF01          BASE ADDRESS ACIA 1
ACIA2     EQU     $3FF21          BASE ADDRESS ACIA 2
::
:: I/O UNITS OFFSETS
::
PIADDA    EQU     $0              OFFSET FOR DATA DIRECTION REGISTER A
PIADA     EQU     $0              OFFSET FOR DATA REGISTER A
PIACA     EQU     $4              OFFSET FOR CONTROL REGISTER A
::
:: DATA STORAGE
::
          ORG     RAM
NUMROWS   DS.B    1               NUMBER OF ROWS ON INPUT KEYBOARD
NUMCOL    DS.B    1               NUMBER OF COLUMNS ON INPUT KEYBOARD
INPUTBUF  DS.L    1               ADDRESS TO INPUT BUFFER
OUTBUF    DS.L    1               ADDRESS TO OUTPUT BUFFER
TEMP      DS.L    $10             TEMPORARY DATA BUFFER
::
:: PARAMETERS
::
BOUNCE1   EQU     $2              BOUNCE TIME IN MS FOR KEYBOARD
OPEN      EQU     $0F             INPUT PATTERN WHEN NO KEYS ARE CLOSED
DISDLY    EQU     $01             PULSE LENGTH FOR DISPLAYS IN MS
::
:: DEFINITIONS
::
ALLHI     EQU     $FF             ALL ONES INPUT
STCON     EQU     $80             OUTPUT FOR START OF CONVERSION PULSE
```

Of course, the **data storage entries may not always be in alphabetical order,** since the designer may order these differently for various reasons.

LIBRARY ROUTINES

Standard documentation of subroutines helps you build a library of programs that are easy to use. If you describe each subroutine with a standard form, anyone can see at a glance what the routines do and how to use them. You should organize the forms carefully, defining them, for example, by processor, language, and type of program. Remember, without proper documentation and organization, using the library may be more difficult than writing programs from scratch. If you are going to use subroutines from a library or other outside source, you must know all their effects in order to debug your overall program.

STANDARD PROGRAM LIBRARY FORMS

Among the information that you will need in the standard form is:
- Purpose of the program
- Processor used
- Language used
- Parameters required and how they are passed to the subroutine
- Results produced and how they are passed to the calling program
- Number of bytes of memory used
- Number of clock cycles required. This number may be an average or a typical figure, or it may vary widely. Actual execution time will, of course, depend on the processor clock rate and the memory cycle time.
- Registers affected
- Flags affected
- A typical example
- Error handling
- Special cases
- Documented program listing

If the program is complex, the standard library form should also include a general flowchart or a structured outline of the program. As we have mentioned before, a library program is most likely to be useful if it performs a single function in a general manner.

TOTAL DOCUMENTATION

Complete documentation of microprocessor software will include all or most of the elements that we have mentioned.

DOCUMENTATION PACKAGE

The total documentation package may involve:
- General flowcharts
- A written description of the program
- A list of all parameters and definitions
- A memory map
- A documented listing of the program
- A description of the test plan and test results

The documentation may also include:
- Program flowcharts
- Data flowcharts
- Structured programs

Even this package is sufficient only for non-production software. **Production software also requires the following documents:**
- Program Logic Manual
- User's Guide
- Maintenance Manual

Program Logic Manual

The program logic manual expands the written explanation provided wih the software. It should explain the system's design goals, algorithms, and tradeoffs, assuming a reader who is competent technically but lacks detailed knowledge of the program. It should provide a step-by-step guide to the operations of the program and it should explain the data structures and their manipulation.

User's Guide

The user's guide is the most important single piece of documentation. No matter how well designed the system may be, it will not be useful if no one can understand its operations or take advantage of its features. **The user's guide should explain system features and their use, provide frequent examples that clarify the text, and give tested step-by-step directions. The writing of user's guides requires care and objectivity, since the writer must be able to take an outsider's point of view.**

One problem in writing user's guides is the need to avoid overwhelming the beginner or taxing the patience of the experienced user. Two separate versions can help overcome this problem. **A guide for the beginner can explain the most common features of the program with the aid of simple examples and detailed discussions. A guide for the experienced user can provide more extensive descriptions of features and fewer examples.** Remember that the beginner needs help getting started, whereas the experienced user wants organized reference material.

Maintenance Manual

The maintenance manual is designed for the programmer who has to modify the system. It **should explain the procedures for any changes or expansion that have been designed into the program.**

IMPORTANCE OF DOCUMENTATION

Documentation should not be taken lightly or left to the last minute. Good documentation, combined with proper programming practices, is not only an important part of the final product but can also make development simpler, faster, and more productive. **The designer should make consistent and thorough documentation part of every stage of software development.**

19
Debugging

As we noted at the beginning of this section, debugging and testing are among the most time-consuming stages of software development. **Even though such methods as modular programming, structured programming and top-down design can simplify programs and reduce the frequency of errors, debugging and testing are still difficult** because they are so poorly defined. The selection of an adequate set of test data is seldom a clear or scientific process. Finding errors sometimes seems like a game of pin the tail on the donkey, except that the donkey is moving and the programmer must position the tail by remote control. Few tasks are as frustrating as debugging programs.

This chapter will first describe the tools available to aid in debugging. It will then discuss basic debugging procedures, describe the common types of errors, and present some examples of program debugging. The next chapter will describe how to select test data and test programs.

We will describe only the purposes of most debugging tools. There is little standardization in this area and we cannot discuss all the available products. The examples show the uses, advantages, and limitations of some common tools.

Debugging tools have two major functions. One is to pin the error down to a short section of the program; the other is to provide more detailed information about what the computer is doing than is provided by normal runs, and so make the source of the error obvious. Current debugging tools do not find and correct errors by themselves; you must know enough about what is happening to recognize and correct the error when the debugging tools zero in on it and show its effects in detail.

SIMPLE DEBUGGING TOOLS

The most common simple debugging tools are:
- A breakpoint facility
- A single-step facility
- A trace facility
- A register dump program
- A memory dump program

BREAKPOINT

A breakpoint is a place at which the program will automatically halt or wait so that the user can examine the current status of the system. A program will not continue until the user orders its resumption. Breakpoints allow you either to check or pass over an entire section of a program. To see if an initialization routine is correct, you can place a breakpoint at the end of it and run the program. You can then check memory locations and registers to see if the entire section is correct. However, note that if the section is not correct, you must still pinpoint the error, either with earlier breakpoints or with a single-step mode.

Breakpoints often use the exception processing system (see Chapter 15). You can use any of the 16 trap vectors to act as a breakpoint. Any of the 7 interrupt levels can also be used by external equipment to cause breakpoints. A breakpoint will usually cause a special program to be executed; for example, it might automatically print the contents of specified registers or wait for the user to enter a command.

Inserting Breakpoints

The simplest and best way to insert a breakpoint in a program is to replace the first word of an instruction with a trap instruction. When the trap instruction is executed, program control is transferred to a breakpoint routine specified via a trap vector, the processor is forced into supervisor mode, and the program counter and status register contents are saved.

Don't forget that the value saved for the program counter points to the instruction after the one which caused the trap. If you want the actual breakpoint address displayed, or if you want the program to resume correctly after restoring the original instruction, you will have to subtract two from the stored program counter value. The simplest way to accomplish this would be to execute the instruction SUBQ.L #2,−2(A7). Note that this method assumes that the supervisor stack pointer still points to the data saved at the time of the trap.

Figure 19-1 shows a simple breakpoint routine with its trap vector and a call to the breakpoint routine. This routine causes an endless loop, and the only way to terminate the loop is with a reset or an interrupt.

Setting and Clearing Breakpoints

**Many monitors have facilities for automatically inserting (setting) and remov-

```
*EXCEPTION VECTORS
            ORG 0
            .
            DS.L    BRKPT               TRAP 0 = BREAKPOINT
            .
*
* USER PROGRAM
*
            ORG $4000
PGM14_2     MOVEA.L #ACIA,A0            ADDRESS OF ACIA
            .
            TRAP    #0                  BREAKPOINT HERE
            .
            .
*
* BREAKPOINT HANDLER
*
            ORG $10000
BRKPT       BRA BRKPT                   WAIT IN PLACE
            .
            .
```

Figure 19-1. A Simple Breakpoint Routine

ing (clearing) **breakpoints based on one of the TRAP instructions.** Such breakpoints do not affect the timing of the program until one of them is executed. However, you obviously cannot replace instructions that are in ROM or PROM. **Other monitors implement breakpoints by actually checking the address lines or the program counter in hardware or in software.** This method allows the user to set breakpoints on addresses in ROM or PROM, but it may affect system timing if the address must be checked in software. A more powerful facility would allow the user to enter an address to which the processor would transfer control. Another possibility would be a return dependent on a switch as in the following example.

```
BRKPT       BTST #7,PIADR               WAIT FOR SWITCH IN BIT 7 TO CLOSE
            BNE  BRKPT
            RTE
```

Of course, other PIA data or control lines could also be used. Remember that RTE automatically reenables interrupts. If a PIA interrupt is used, the service routine must read the PIA data register to clear the interrupt status bit.

Precautions in Using Breakpoints

When you use breakpoints (whether manually or through monitor facilities), remember the following precautions:

1. **Only set breakpoints at addresses that contain operation codes.** Replacing data or parts of addresses with Trap instructions can result in chaos.

2. **Interpret the results carefully.** Remember that the computer has not yet executed the instruction that was replaced.
3. **Check all conditions before resuming the program.** You may have to change the program counter, correct the contents of registers or memory locations, clear breakpoints that are no longer necessary, and set new breakpoints. Methods for resuming programs vary greatly, so consult your microcomputer's user's guide. Be particularly careful never to resume a program in the middle of an instruction (that is, at an address that does not contain an operation code) or in the middle of an I/O or timing operation (e.g., sending data to a teletypewriter) that cannot logically be resumed after a delay.

REGISTER DUMP

A register dump is a facility that lists the contents of all, or some selected subset, of the processor's registers. A register dump routine is very often a part of a breakpoint handling routine and the debug program that controls the trace facility.

A useful register dump program will let you specify which registers, and even which portion of selected registers, to display. Since the MC68000 allows operations on portions of registers (byte or word operations) it will often be useful to display, for example, just the least significant byte of a register. Similarly, if you are only interested in the contents of a few data registers, it would be most useful simply to display the contents of those registers rather than the contents of all 16 data and address registers. **Figure 19-2 shows the results of a typical register dump program.**

There are a couple of things we must keep in mind when we write a register dump program. **First, if we want the program counter contents to be displayed, it is usually possible to find the PC contents somewhere on the stack.** However, you have to know how many exceptions and/or subroutine calls may have intervened before the register dump program, since they may have stored additional items on the stack.

Secondly, stack pointer A7 may cause problems if you don't keep track of whether the processor is in the user or supervisor state. Here are some rules to remember:

- In the user state, the user stack pointer is in A7 and it is impossible to reach the supervisor stack pointer.
- In the supervisor state, the supervisor stack pointer is in A7 and you can reach the user stack pointer with the help of the MOVE USP,An instruction.

Thirdly, remember that a subroutine call stores just a program counter value on the stack while an exception (trap, interrupt, and so on) **stores the program counter content and the status register contents.**

Lastly, if you are in the user state and save the status register contents somewhere, don't attempt to restore the entire status register; that is a privileged instruction. It will be sufficient to restore the condition code part of the status register with a MOVE to CCR instruction. Alternately, you can use the RTR instruction which automatically restores the condition code portion of the status register.

Figure 19-3 shows a flowchart of the register dump program REGDUMP. In this program, we assume that the subroutines PRT8HEX and PRT4HEX convert and

Debugging **327**

```
D0=3FD56709  D1=100002  D2=2430  D4=3C  A0=00014000  A1=6000  A7=00056421
```

Figure 19-2. Results of a Typical MC68000 Register Dump

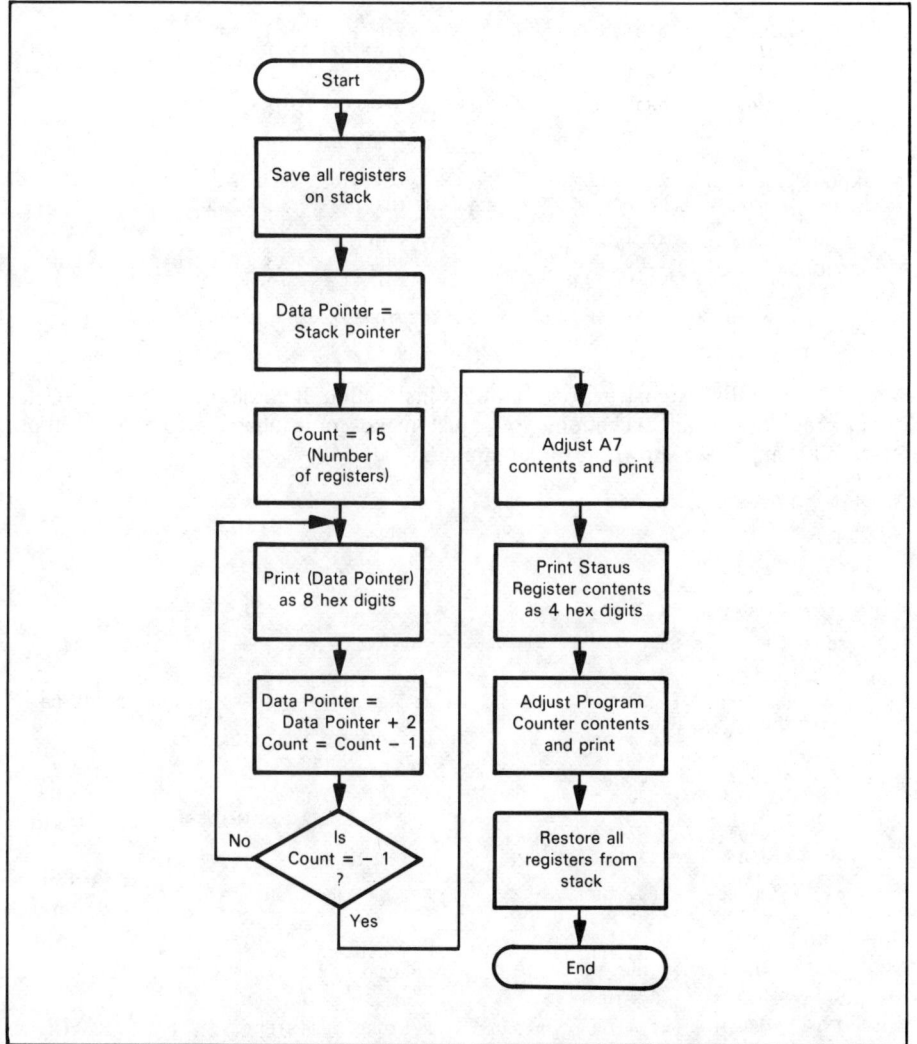

Figure 19-3. Flowchart of a Register Dump Program

print 32 or 16 bits of register D0 as hex digits on the system printer. We also assume that the register dump routine is called by a **BSR** or **JSR** instruction and that the system is in the user state.

```
*
*REGISTER DUMP PROGRAM
*
        PROGRAM  EQU      $4000
                 ORG      PROGRAM

        REGDUMP  MOVE.W   SR,-(A7)              SAVE STATUS REGISTER
                 MOVEM.L  D0-D7/A0-A7,-(A7)     SAVE REST OF REGISTERS

                 MOVEA.L  A7,A0                 A0 IS LOCAL STACKPOINTER
                 MOVEQ    #15-1,D4              15 REGISTERS TO PRINT-ADJUST FOR DB

        LOOP     MOVE.L   (A0)+,D0              GET PUSHED REGISTER
                 BSR      PRT8HEX               AND PRINT IT
                 DBRA     D4,LOOP

                 MOVE.L   (A0)+,D0              GET STACKPOINTER
                 ADDI.L   #6,D0                 ADJUST TO VALUE BEFORE CALL
                 BSR      PRT8HEX               PRINT IT

                 MOVE.W   (A0)+,D0              GET STATUS WORD
                 BSR      PRT4HEX               PRINT IT

                 MOVE.L   (A0)+,D0              GET OLD PC
                 SUBI.L   #2,D0                 ADJUST IT TO VALUE BEFORE CALL
                 BSR      PRT8HEX               PRINT IT

                 MOVEM.L  (A7)+,D0-D7/A0-A7     RESTORE REGISTERS

                 RTR      RETURN                AND RESTORE THE CONDITION CODES
```

Note that the last instruction is an **RTR** instruction. If you want to call the register dump program via an exception, you must make some changes to this program. Required changes are shown in the program SYSDUMP.

```
*
*REGISTER DUMP AFTER TRAP OR EXCEPTION
*
        PROGRAM  EQU      $4000

                 ORG      PROGRAM

        SYSDUMP  MOVEM.L  D0-D7/A0-A6,-(A7)     SAVE REGISTERS ON SUPERVISOR STACK

                 MOVEA.L  A7,A0                 A0 IS LOCAL STACKPOINTER
                 MOVEQ    #15-1,D4              15 REGISTERS TO PRINT-ADJUST FOR DB.

        LOOP     MOVE.L   (A0)+,D0              GET PUSHED REGISTER
                 BSR      PRT8HEX               AND PRINT IT
                 DBRA     D4,LOOP

                 MOVE.L   USP,A1                GET USER STACKPOINTER
                 MOVE.L   A1,D0
                 BSR      PRT8HEX               PRINT IT

                 MOVE.W   (A0)+,D0              GET STATUS WORD
                 BSR      PRT4HEX               PRINT IT

                 MOVE.L   (A0)+,D0              GET OLD PC
                 SUBI.L   #2,D0                 ADJUST IT TO VALUE BEFORE CALL
                 BSR      PRT8HEX               PRINT IT

                 MOVEM.L  (A7)+,D0-D7/A0-A6     RESTORE REGISTERS

                 RTE      RETURN                AND RESTORE THE CONDITION CODES
```

Make sure you understand the difference between the instructions RTE, RTR, and RTS. Which of them is privileged and why?

SINGLE-STEP

A single-step facility allows you to execute a program one instruction or one memory cycle at a time. After each step you might display some register or memory contents. Usually, single-stepping is associated with some external circuitry which monitors the output lines of the processor. The MC68000, however, provides internal circuitry to accomplish single-stepping via its trace logic.

TRACE

The trace facility allows you to see intermediate results since you can determine the status of the processor's registers after each instruction is executed. A simple trace usually lets you step through your program instruction by instruction and prints all the registers after each instruction is executed. A more useful **trace facility might allow you to execute several instructions before stopping and permit you to specify how much information you want each time you stop.** It might also allow you to print the contents of memory locations you specify. This will result in a reduced volume of information and means that you must decide what you need before instituting the trace, but it should give you the information that is most useful.

Simple instruction tracing may provide you with very detailed information about what happens inside the processor. This information should be sufficient to identify such errors as jump and branch instructions with incorrect conditions and/or destinations, omitted or incorrect addresses, incorrect operation codes, and improper data values.

You must keep in mind, however, **that a single-step trace slows the processor far below its normal speed.** Thus, you cannot check delay loops or I/O operations in real time. Nor can a single-step trace help you find timing errors or errors in the interrupt or DMA systems. In fact, the single-step mode typically operates at less than one millionth of normal processor speed. To single-step through one second of real processor time would require more than ten days. **The single-step trace mode, therefore, is useful only to check the logic of short sequences of instructions.**

The MC68000 has a built-in trace facility not often found on microprocessors. Bit 15 in the status register can be set to force the processor into the trace state. In this state, an exception is forced after each instruction, thus allowing a debug program to have control over program execution. **In the trace mode, it essentially looks as though we had inserted breakpoints (trap instructions) after every instruction.**

The exception processing for the trace operation follows the same general pattern as for the processing of a trap instruction. The contents of the program counter and status register are saved, and control is transferred to the address stored in the trace exception vector which is #9, at memory address 24_{16}.

If you want to implement a very simple trace facility on your MC68000 system, just place the address of the register dump program (SYSDUMP), described previously, in address 24_{16} (the trace exception vector location).

```
        ORG     $24
        DC.L    SYSDUMP
```

Then set bit 15 in the status register, using one of the instructions that operate on the status register, and start your program. You will get all of the processor's registers (except the supervisor stack pointer) printed after each instruction is executed. Once again, for a more detailed discussion of exception processing, refer to Chapter 15. Note that the program counter printout resulting from SYSDUMP would have to be modified. How would you modify it?

This trace routine will provide you with an enormous amount of information. If you improve on it, or if you have a good trace program already, here is some advice to keep in mind:

1. **Decide what you need before executing the trace.** Otherwise you will not know what to do with the results.
2. **Start by tracing only one or two variables and printing the results infrequently.** This will give you less information to analyze at one time.
3. **Use breakpoints to limit the extent of the trace.** Turn tracing on or off at the breakpoints.
4. **Use whatever facility your computer has to mark the output.** Otherwise you will end up with pages of unidentified numbers and you will spend most of your time just figuring out what they are.
5. **Be careful when you specify that only a portion of a register is to be displayed** (if your trace allows this option). Remember that phenomena like sign-extensions can cause problems that you won't see if you don't display the contents of the entire register.

MEMORY DUMP

A memory dump is a program that lists the contents of memory on an output device (such as a printer). This is a more efficient way of examining data arrays or entire programs than just looking at single locations. However, very large memory dumps are not useful (except to supply scrap paper) because of the sheer mass of information that they produce. They may also take a long time to execute on a slow printer. **Small dumps may,** however, **provide the programmer with a reasonable amount of information that can be examined as a unit. Regular repetitions of data patterns or offsets of entire arrays are easily spotted in a dump.**

A general dump program is often rather difficult to write. Make sure that the ending memory address is not smaller than the starting memory address. A larger starting memory address might be treated as an error, or it may cause no output.

Since the speed of the memory dump depends on the speed of the output device, the efficiency of the routine seldom matters. **The following program will ignore cases where the starting address is larger than the ending address, and will handle memory blocks of any length.**

```
                        ::
                        :: THIS PROGRAM PRINTS A PIECE OF MEMORY CONTENTS ON THE
                        :: SYSTEM PRINTER.
                        ::
00004000                PROGRAM   EQU    $4000
00006000                DATA      EQU    $6000

 00006000                         ORG    DATA
```

Debugging 331

```
006000  00000004      START     DS.L    1
006004  00000004      END       DS.L    1

        00004000                ORG     PROGRAM

004000  20786000      MEMDUMP   MOVEA.L START,A0    GET START ADDRESS
004004  22786004                MOVEA.L END,A1      GET THE END ADDRESS

004008  B1C9          LOOP      CMPA.L  A1,A0       IF END > START
00400A  6208                    BHI.S   DONE        ..THEN DONE
00400C  2018                    MOVE.L  (A0)+,D0    ..ELSE GET DATA, INCREMENT START
00400E  61000006                BSR     PRT8HEX     AND PRINT DATA
004012  60F4                    BRA     LOOP

004014  4E75          DONE      RTS
```

A typical result of this memory dump program is shown in Figure 19-4. Note that since we are printing long words, we may print a maximum of three bytes beyond the specified ending address. To illustrate this, try START = 6000, END = 6004.

This memory dump routine correctly handles the case in which the starting and ending locations are the same (try it!). You will have to interpret the results carefully if the dump area includes the stack, since the dump subroutine itself uses the stack. The PRT8HEX subroutine may also change memory and stack locations.

Obviously, these results may sometimes be hard to interpret. They don't tell you which addresses are involved and the results are not output in a very satisfying format. **Figure 19-5 shows a better format that gives you the addresses involved and makes it easier to distinguish between bytes, words, and long words.**

If you are working a lot with ASCII strings, then it will be useful to get the ASCII characters corresponding to the memory locations as shown in Figure 19-6. This is a common and useful format. It will, for example, immediately show you if some unprintable character is intermixed in the string. Thus, if we happen to get a byte with a

```
                    48415353
                    45204D41
                    44452054
                    48495320
                    44554D50
```

Figure 19-4. Results of an Unformatted Memory Dump

```
005000  43 48 41 4C   4D 45 52 53   20 53 57 45   44 45 4E 20
```

Figure 19-5. Results of a Formatted Memory Dump

```
005000   54 48 45 20 4D 45 4D 4F 52 59 20 44 55 4D 50 20    THE.MEMORY.DUMP
```

Figure 19-6. Results of a Memory Dump with ASCII Characters

```
005000   54 48 45 20 4D 45 4D 15 4F 52 59 20 44 55 4D 50    THE.MEM.ORY.DUMP
```

Figure 19-7. Results of an ASCII Memory Dump with Unprintable Character

value 15_{16} between M and O in MEMORY the dump would appear as shown in Figure 19-7. A dump program which just shows you printable characters wouldn't have revealed this extra character.

Try to rewrite the memory dump program so that it produces a memory dump that shows you the address and the hexadecimal form as well as the ASCII characters contained in memory.

MORE ADVANCED DEBUGGING TOOLS

The more advanced debugging tools that are most widely used are:
- Simulator programs to check program logic
- Logic analyzers to check signals and timing

Many variations of both these tools exist, and we will discuss only the standard features.

Software Simulator

The simulator is the computer equivalent of a pencil-and-paper computer. It **is a computer program that goes through the operating cycle of a computer, keeping track of the contents of all the registers, flags, and memory locations.** We could, of course, do this by hand, but it would require a large effort and close attention to the exact effects of each instruction. The simulator program never gets tired or confused, never forgets an instruction or register, and does not run out of paper.

Typical simulator features include:
- **A breakpoint facility.** Usually, breakpoints can be set to occur after a particular number of cycles have been executed; when a memory location or one of a set

of memory locations is referenced; when the contents of a location or one of a set of locations is altered, or on other conditions.
- **Register and memory dump facilities** that display the contents of memory locations, registers, and I/O ports.
- **A trace facility** that prints the contents of particular registers or memory locations whenever the program changes or uses them.
- **A load facility** that allows you to set initial register and/or memory location contents, or change them during the simulation.

Some simulators can simulate input/output, interrupts, and even DMA. **The simulator has many advantages:**

1. It can provide a complete description of the status of the computer, since the simulator program is not restricted by microprocessor chip pinout limitations or other characteristics of the underlying circuitry.
2. It can provide breakpoints, dumps, traces, and other facilities, without using any of the simulated processor's memory space or control system. These facilities will therefore not interfere with the user program.
3. Programs, starting points, and other conditions are easy to change.
4. All the facilities of a large computer, including peripherals and software, are available to the microprocessor designer.

On the other hand, the simulator is limited by its software base and its separation from the real microcomputer. The major limitations are:

1. The simulator cannot cope with timing problems, since it operates at less than real-time execution speed. The simulator is usually quite slow. Reproducing one second of actual processor time may require hours of computer time.
2. The simulator cannot model the input/output section exactly since it cannot represent external hardware or interfaces accurately.

The simulator represents the software side of debugging; it has the typical advantages and limitations of a wholly software-based approach. The simulator can provide insight into program logic and other software problems, but often cannot help with timing, I/O, and hardware problems.

Logic Analyzer

The logic, or microprocessor, analyzer is the hardware solution to debugging. **Basically, the analyzer is a parallel digital version of the standard oscilloscope.** The analyzer displays information in binary, hexadecimal, or mnemonic form on a CRT, and has a variety of triggering events, thresholds, and inputs. Most analyzers also have a memory so that they can display the past contents of the microcomputer busses.

The standard procedure is to set a triggering event, such as the occurrence of a particular address on the address bus or instruction on the data bus. For example, one might trigger the analyzer if the microcomputer tries to store data in a particular address, or execute an input or output instruction. One may then look at the sequence of events that preceded the breakpoint. **Common problems you can find in this way include short noise spikes (or glitches), incorrect signal sequences, overlapping waveforms,**

- **Number of input lines.** At least 40 are necessary to monitor a 16-bit data bus and a 24-bit address bus. Still more are necessary for control signals, clocks, and other important inputs.
- **Amount of memory.** Each previous state that is saved will occupy several bytes of memory.
- **Maximum frequency.** It must be several MHz to handle the fastest processors.
- **Minimum signal width** (important for catching glitches).
- **Type and number of triggering events allowed.** Important features are pre- and post-trigger delays; these allow the user to display events occurring before or after the trigger event.
- **Methods of connecting to the microcomputer.** This may require a rather complex interface.
- **Number of display channels.**
- **Binary, hexadecimal, or mnemonic displays.**
- **Display formats.**
- **Signal hold time requirements.**
- **Probe capacitance.**
- **Single or dual thresholds.**

All of these factors are important in comparing different logic and microprocessor analyzers, since these instruments are new and unstandardized. A tremendous variety of products is already available and this variety will become even greater in the future.[1]

Logic analyzers, of course, **are necessary only for systems with complex timing. Simple applications with low-speed peripherals have few hardware problems that a designer cannot handle with a standard oscilloscope.**

DEBUGGING WITH CHECKLISTS

No one can hope to check an entire program by hand; however, certain trouble spots can be checked. **You can use systematic hand checking to find a large number of errors without resorting to any debugging tools.**

The question is where to place the effort. The answer is on points that can be handled with either a yes-no answer or a simple arithmetic calculation. Do not do complex arithmetic, follow all status flags, or try every conceivable case. Limit your hand-checking to matters that can be settled easily. Leave the complex problems to be solved with the aid of debugging tools. But proceed systematically; build your checklist, and make sure that the program performs all basic operations correctly.

The first step is to compare the flowchart or other program documentation with the actual code. Make sure that everything which appears in one also appears in the other. A simple checklist will do the job. It is easy to omit an entire branch or a processing section.

Next concentrate on the program loops. Make sure that all registers and memory locations used inside the loops are initialized correctly. This is a common source of errors; once again, a simple checklist will suffice.

Now look at each conditional branch. Select a sample case that should produce a branch and one that should not; try both of them. Is the branch correct or reversed? If the branch involves checking whether a number is above or below a threshold, try the equality case. Does the correct branch occur? Make sure that your choice is consistent with the problem definition.

Look at the loops as a whole. Try the first and last iterations by hand; these are often troublesome special cases. What happens if the number of iterations is zero; e.g., there is no data or the table has no elements? Does the program fall through correctly? Programs will often perform one iteration unnecessarily, or, even worse, decrement counters past zero before checking them. Check for other trivial cases where there is nothing for the program to do.

Check off everything down to the last statement. Don't optimistically assume that the first error is the only one in the program. Hand-checking will allow you to get the maximum benefit from debugging runs, since you will get rid of many simple errors ahead of time.

Hand-Checking Questions

Here is a quick review of the hand-checking questions:

1. Does the program include everything that was designed into it (and vice versa for documentation purposes)?
2. Are all registers and memory locations initialized before they are used inside loops?
3. Are all conditional branches logically correct?
4. Do all loops start and end properly?
5. Are equality cases handled correctly?
6. Are trivial cases handled correctly?

LOOKING FOR ERRORS

Of course, despite all these precautions (or if you skip over some of them), programs often still won't work. The designer is left with the problem of how to find the remaining mistakes. The lists that follow may be of some help. We have attempted to categorize the types of errors that you may encounter. However, you must remember that a certain kind of error will not necessarily be limited to just one kind of program. The groupings we have arrived at may make it faster for you to pinpoint the error. But if you don't find the error within the category in which it seems most likely to occur, look under all the other categories.

ERRORS LIKELY TO BE FOUND IN CERTAIN PARTS OF A PROGRAM

The Initialization Section

- **Failure to initialize variables such as counters, pointers, sums, indexes, and so on.** Do not assume that the registers, memory locations, or condition codes

necessarily contain zero before they are used. Also make sure that you initialize the correct part of a register. For example, if you are going to use register D0 as an 8-bit counter for a DBRA loop, it is necessary to clear the entire low-order word of D0 since this instruction always operates on the entire 16-bit word.
- **Failure to follow through correctly in trivial cases.** It is usually here where you must decide what to do if there is nothing for the program to do (no data present, no entries in a list, and so on). Do not assume that such cases will never occur unless the program specifically eliminates them.
- **Accidental initializations.** Make sure that no jump or branch instructions transfer control back to the initialization section.

Loops

- **Updating counters, pointers, or indexes in the wrong place or not at all.** Be sure that there are no paths through a loop that either skip or repeat the updating function. Be especially careful when you deal with nested loops, and remember that counters for inner loops must be reinitialized each time they are entered.
- **Confusing postincrement and predecrement operations.** Remember that postincrement increments the address register after using its contents, while predecrement decrements the address register before using its contents. Also remember that it is the "size" of the instruction that determines the amount of the increment or decrement. A long word instruction increments or decrements by 4, a word instruction by 2 and a byte instruction by 1. Did you correctly specify the size?
- **Confusing the use of the DBcc instruction.** The condition specified is the condition that makes the program exit the loop, rather than remaining in the loop by taking the branch. Remember that if the condition is not met, the processor will decrement the counter and test for counter contents exactly equal to -1: the test is not for less than zero. Also remember that if you don't compensate for the -1 (rather than the zero) that is tested for, the loop will be executed one more time than you had expected.
- **Inverting the logic of a conditional jump such as using branch on carry set when you meant branch on carry clear.** Remember that compare and subtraction instructions perform the operations *destination* (second operand) $-$ *source* (first operand), and set the Carry and Zero flags as follows:

    Zero flag (Z) = 1 if destination $\neq$ source
    Zero flag (C) = 0 if destination $>$ source
    Carry flag (C) = 1 if destination $<$ source

    Note that the Carry flag is cleared if destination = source.
- **Changing condition codes before using them or failure to change them.** Remember that the MOVE instruction affects all the condition codes except the Extend (X) flag. Operations using address registers as a destination do not affect the condition codes with the exception of the CMPA instruction. Also refer back to the precautions given with Program 9-2b concerning testing of flags that may have been set as a result of more than one instruction.

Subroutines and Macros

- **Ignoring the effects of subroutines and macros.** Subroutine calls and references to macros typically result in the execution of many instructions. These instructions will almost always change the condition code register (CCR) and may change the contents of other registers and memory locations as well. Be sure that you know all the effects of any subroutine or macro you use. Also note the importance of documenting subroutines and macros so that users can determine their effect without examining a long listing.
- **Forgetting that the stack is used in subroutine linkages.** The JSR and BSR instructions save the return address in the hardware stack on top of any parameter you may have placed there. The RTS instruction simply transfers control to the address at the top of the current stack (user or supervisor). If you have not carefully managed the stack, the processor could end up at a completely unexpected location.
- **Using the wrong return instruction.** RTS does not restore condition codes, RTR does. Note that no subroutine calling instructions automatically store the contents of the condition codes; you must explicitly accomplish this function. Remember that RTR fetches the condition codes before it restores the program counter; thus, the sequence

    MOVE.W SR,-(A7)
    BSR SUBR

    will not work in conjunction with an RTR instruction. Instead, if you want to save the contents of the condition codes, you must do it at the beginning of the subroutine to which control is transferred.
- **Failure to restore previously saved registers.** This is a very common error. Be sure that you restore the correct number of registers and to the correct locations. Use the MOVEM.L instruction and store on the stack. Remember that if you are moving 16-bit words from memory to address registers, they will be sign-extended to 32 bits, and this may result in problems.
- **Using Link and Unlink instructions improperly.** Don't change the "link-register" during execution of the subroutine. For example, if you use LINK A6,#-16 at the beginning of a subroutine, then A6 must have exactly the same value when you execute the UNLK A6 instruction. Otherwise the stack will go out of phase and the result will probably be disastrous to your system. Also remember that the displacement is interpreted as a two's complement integer; if you have a stack that grows downward (as the system stack does) you have to specify a negative displacement with the link instruction. The displacement must also always be an even number since the stack is organized on a word boundary.

General Processing Sections

- **Reversing order of operands.** Remember that MOVE D1,D2 moves the contents of D1 to D2. (This is the opposite of the way the Z8000 and 8086 work.) Also remember that SUB src,dst and CMP src,dst perform the operation

dst - src. The DIV src,Dn instruction performs the operation Dn ÷ src (and stores the result in Dn).
- **Confusing addressing modes**
  - **Data versus addresses** (immediate and absolute). Remember that MOVE.W #$2000,D0 loads register D0 with the number 2000_{16}, whereas MOVE.W $2000,D0 loads register D0 with the contents of memory locations 2000_{16} and 2001_{16}.
  - **Address register direct and indirect.** Remember that CLR.L A0 loads register A0 with zeros, whereas CLR.L (A0) loads the memory word pointed to by A0 with zeros.
  - **Forgetting that addressing modes operate differently on jump instructions than on other instructions.** Jump instructions (JMP or JSR) are executed as if one level of indirection had been removed. For example, JMP $1000 loads 1000_{16} into the program counter, whereas MOVE $1000,A0 loads the contents of memory location 1000_{16} into register D0.
- **Ignoring the fact that certain instructions only operate in one size format**
  Examples: DBcc subtracts 1 from the low-order 16 bits of the specified data register.
  MOVEQ affects all 32 bits of the specified data register.
  MOVE ea,−(A7) and MOVE (A7)+,ea must always be performed on a word boundary (even address).
  MOVE to CCR is a word instruction but only the low-order byte of the status register is affected.
  DIVS and DIVU affect all 32 bits of the destination data register but use only 16 bits of the source. The same is true of MULS and MULU.
  When an address register is used as a destination, the entire register is affected regardless of what size you specify. If the source operand is specified as a word, it is sign-extended to 32 bits in the address register.
- **Forgetting that the MC68000 sign-extends your 16-bit addresses.** This may cause trouble if you work in the memory space between 32K and 64K (addresses 8000_{16} through $FFFF_{16}$). Also be careful when you load immediate values into an address register and when you use the absolute short addressing mode. In both of these cases, strange results can be obtained if the size is word and if the MSB of the word is a 1: the automatic sign-extension will propagate 1's through the most significant 16 bits of the long word address.
- **Forgetting the details of sign extension of data.** MOVEQ treats the operand as a signed value and extends the sign. ADDQ and SUBQ work only with positive numbers. MOVEM sign extends to 32 bits when moving words from memory registers.
- **Using the shift instructions improperly.** Remember the difference between arithmetic shifts, logical shifts, and rotates. They will all affect the condition codes even if they are operating on data in a memory location. If you specify that a shift count is to be found in a data register, remember that the count is interpreted modulo 64.

- **Confusing 8, 16, and 32-bit quantities.** Remember that the processor doesn't keep track of whether the variable you stored in a register was an 8-, 16-, or 32-bit value. You must specify the size in each instruction. Here are some size-related points to keep in mind:
    - A byte can hold two BCD numbers and the BCD instructions (ABCD, SBCD) are byte-sized.
    - A 16-bit word occupies two bytes and therefore "two addresses in memory." In other words, a 16-bit word stored in memory location 1000_{16} occupies location 1001_{16} also.
    - A long word (32 bits) occupies 4 bytes; this may be a common source of errors if you are used to 8-bit microprocessors.
- **Ignoring the limitations of read-only memory.** Obviously, instructions that both read from and write to memory locations make little sense when applied to an address occupied by a read-only memory (ROM) device. A sorting program that has been given data located in ROM will run forever!
- **Using the wrong register.** The MC68000 has a large number of data and address registers. While this is one of the sources of the power and flexibility of the processor, it demands that you very carefully keep track of what you put where. Note the specifications for two data registers may differ by only one character (e.g. D1, D2). The same is true of address and data registers (e.g. A1, D1). Typing errors are easy to make and often difficult to find.
- **Confusing BCD, binary, hexadecimal, and decimal numbers.** In the BCD representation, each decimal digit is coded separately into binary, using four binary digits (0 or 1). In hexadecimal representation, four binary digits are grouped together and represented with a hex digit (0 through F). For example, the decimal number 54_{10} is equal to 110110_2 in binary, 36_{16} in hexadecimal, and 54_{16} in the standard BCD representation.
- **Forgetting to transfer control past sections of the program that should not be executed.** Remember that the processor proceeds sequentially unless you tell it to do otherwise. You may need some unconditional branches to avoid routines that should not be executed.
- **Confusing the stack and its pointers.** The contents of the stack are always addressed with one of the indirect modes and the stack pointer is addressed using register direct mode.
- **Confusing the bit positions in the bit operate instructions.** Bits are numbered from 31 down through zero. The least significant bit is zero, bit 7 is the most significant bit (MSB) in a byte, bit 15 is the MSB in a word, and bit 31 is the MSB in a long word.

String Manipulation Errors

- **Counting the length of an array incorrectly.** Remember that the addresses 1000_{16} through 1004_{16} include five (not four) memory locations. Thus, the number of elements in an array is *ending address − starting address* + 1.

- **Confusing numbers and characters.** Remember that the ASCII representation of a digit is not the same as the binary or BCD representation. For example, the ASCII representation of the number seven is 37_{16}; 07_{16} is the ASCII BELL character which rings the bell on a teletypewriter.
- **Forgetting that word operations don't work on odd addresses.** String operations are often byte-sized. Be careful if you are using word or long word operations to move strings or append characters to a string. For example, if register A4 holds the address of the current position within a string and you want to append the text "The End" to the string, the instruction sequence

    ```
    MOVE.L #"THE ", (A4)+
    MOVE.L # "END", (A4)+
    ```

    will cause an address error exception if A4 points to an odd address before execution of the first instruction.

Input/Output Errors

- **Ignoring the physical limitations of I/O and interface chips.** While we address interface chips as if they were memory locations, they may not behave like memory devices. Storing data in an input port seldom makes sense, nor does loading data from an output port unless the port is latched and buffered. Some I/O devices have two different registers (one read-only and one write-only) at the same address. The 6850 ACIA control and status registers are an example of this case. Be careful of instructions like shift, negate, and so on, which read from and then write back to the "same" location; they will produce strange errors with register combinations like those provided by the 6850.
- **Using incorrect bits in status and control registers.** The order of bits in these kinds of registers may appear to be random. Are you sure you used the right combination?
- **Misusing the MOVEP instruction.** Remember that MOVEP uses every other address, all even addresses or all odd addresses.
- **Forgetting to reset or initialize I/O devices.** For example, the 6850 ACIA requires a software reset sequence.

Assembler-Related Errors

The use of an assembler is the only practical way to convert source programs into object code, but it can introduce a few annoying errors. In particular,

- **Be careful of what your assembler may use as defaults. For example, the standard MC68000 assembler will make the following assumptions:**
    - *Default instruction size is word if no size is specified.* Remember that it is good programming style always to specify the size with every instruction, even though it is obviously not necessary with instructions where the size is word.

- **Unmarked numbers are assumed to be decimal.** If you want hexadecimal numbers, ASCII characters, and so on, you must explicitly specify such numbers.
- **The default addressing modes are register direct and absolute.** That is, A1 specifies address register A1, not the memory location pointed to by A1. The value $1000 will specify memory location 1000_{16}, and #$1000 will specify the number 1000_{16}.
- **Be careful with absolute short addresses.** If you have used the ORG directive, the assembler assumes that any reference to an absolute address can be achieved using the short absolute addressing form of the instruction. The processor will then sign-extend this address. You should note that this condition may be remedied with later versions of assemblers.
- **Remember that the assembler chooses the quick form of instructions where possible, regardless of whether you have specified the quick version.** Thus, ADD #2,D0 will cause the object code for the ADDQ instruction to be generated.
- **Watch for simple typing errors.** The register numbers are close to each other on the keyboard and no assembler can detect a typing error if the erroneous result is a legal instruction. Also, some assemblers get confused if you insert extra spaces where it didn't expect them, or if you accidentally use meaningless characters such as 1/2. In fact, the assembler may object to a minor error, but accept a totally illogical entry that its developer never considered.
- **Remember, the assembler can print a reassuring message like TOTAL ERRORS 0 even when the program is wrong.** All the message means is that the assembler found no errors according to its interpretations of the rules of the language. This does not exclude errors that produce legal instructions or that are beyond the assembler's comprehension. Most of all, it does not exclude logical errors that may be present in your program and does not necessarily mean that the program does what you intended.

Exception Processing

Exception processing can, from the trouble-shooter's point of view, be divided into two groups: interrupts, and all the other types of exceptions. This is because, in general, interrupts are controlled by external devices and therefore appear to occur at random occasions. Other kinds of exceptions, illegal instructions, address errors, and so on, are often possible to pinpoint a specific instruction or sequence. If your microcomputer doesn't have an exception processing software system, it will be most useful to write one that at least tells you which exception caused a trap (address error, bus error, and so on), and gives you the address where the trap occurred.

Some errors that may be found when you deal with exceptions of any kind are:
- **Forgetting the general facts about exceptions.** The processor is put in the supervisor state, and some information (usually the program counter and status register) is saved on the supervisor stack.
- **Using the wrong return instruction.** RTE and RTR are not the same, so you cannot be clever and use your subroutines just as they are, as part of exception

processing. RTE restores the entire status register while RTR restores just the condition code portion of the status register. RTE is a privileged instruction.
- **Causing multiple bus or addressing errors.** If the processor recognizes an address or bus error while it is processing a previous address or bus error, it will halt. For example, assume that you have an odd value in the supervisor stack pointer for some reason. You try to use the stack pointer with this odd address value and thereby cause an address trap. But the trap handler also uses the supervisor stack and this causes a new address error which will then halt the processor.

Interrupt-Driven Programs

Interrupt-driven programs are particularly difficult to debug, since errors may show up only when an interrupt occurs at a particular time. If, for example, the program enables the interrupts a few instructions too early, an error will appear only if an interrupt occurs while the processor is executing those few instructions. In fact, you can usually assume that sporadic or randomly occuring errors are caused by the interrupt system.[2,3]

Since the MC68000 has an interrupt priority mask in the status register, it may be possible to mask off some of the interrupts and pinpoint the error. Sometimes a breakpoint placed at the start of the interrupt routine may give you a hint as to the cause of the problem, although this may be impossible in real-time systems. Another approach is to save the return addresses every time you get an interrupt, and in this way you may locate the section of the system that causes the problem.

Here are some typical errors in interrupt-driven programs:

- **Incorrect value of the interrupt priority level.** When the processor is reset, it sets its interrupt priority mask to level 7. Upon acknowledging an interrupt, the priority mask is set to the level of the interrupt being acknowledged. RTE will restore the status register, and thus the interrupt priority level, as it was before the interrupt occurred. Make sure that no path through a program fails to set the interrupt priority level to its desired value.
- **Allowing interrupts on a certain level before the system is ready to handle it.** System parameters such as condition codes, flags, pointers, and counters must be initialized first. A checklist might give some help here.
- **Forgetting to store and restore registers.** Interrupts are much like subroutines. Use the same precautions when storing and restoring registers or allocating space on the stack.
- **Forgetting that the interrupt leaves the old program counter and status register contents on the stack whether you use them or not.**
- **Forgetting to clear the source of the interrupt before exiting from the service routine.** For example, if the interrupt comes from a PIA, the interrupt service routine must read the PIA's data register in order to clear the interrupt flag. The read operation is necessary even if the interrupt is from an output device or a real-time clock; otherwise, the interrupt will remain active and will be recognized again as soon as the processor reenables interrupts on this level.

- **Failing to disable certain interrupts during multiword transfers and other critical sequences.** For example, assume that you have a real-time clock with six digits stored in six consecutive bytes of memory. If the clock contains 115959 and you are reading the digits from memory one at a time without disabling the interrupt that updates the clock, here is what could happen. If a clock-updating interrupt occurs after you have read the second digit, it will cause the four last digits to be 0000 and you will think the time is 110000. Such an error may be hard to find because it occurs so seldom and because some very special coincidences are required to create the error. Another area where you must be very cautious of interrupts is in delay routines.
- **Failing to reenable the interrupt after executing a routine that requires interrupts to be disabled.**
- **Ignoring the possibility that the interrupt routine may get reentered.** An interrupt routine might have to be reentered just like a subroutine (see Chapter 11).

A list of possible errors can be endless and the purpose of the preceding list is to give you some ideas as to where you might start looking for errors. Unfortunately, no one has found the algorithm which describes how to be one hundred percent sure that you have found all errors; you may be left with errors no matter how systematic you are. Sometimes the following approach may be your best bet: turn off the computer, have a beer, and let your brain rest. Perhaps let the problem sit overnight or have someone with a fresh viewpoint look at it. Often, when you are explaining a problem to someone else, you will see the answer yourself.

PROGRAM EXAMPLES

19-1. DEBUGGING A CODE CONVERSION PROGRAM

The purpose of this program is to convert a decimal number in memory location DIGIT to a 7-segment code in memory location CODE. The program should blank the display if DIGIT does not contain a decimal number. This appears to be a simple task and we start off with the flowchart shown in Figure 19-8. Our first coding attempt looks like this:

Initial Program: (from flowchart in Figure 19-8)

```
*
*BCD TO SEVEN SEGMENT DISPLAY CONVERSION
*
*INPUT--BCD NUMBER IN DIGIT
*OUTPUT--BIT PATTERN FOR SEVEN SEGMENT DISPLAY IN CODE
*
        DATA    EQU     $8000
        PROGRAM EQU     $4200

                ORG     DATA

        DIGIT   DS.B    1
        CODE    DS.B    1
```

```
SSEG       DC.B      $3F,$06,$5B,$4F,$66
           DC.B      $6D,$7F,$07,$7F

BCD_7SEG   MOVEA.W   SSEG,A0           GET BASE ADDRESS OF TABLE
           MOVE      DIGIT,D0          GET DIGIT TO CONVERT
           CMP.B     #9,D0             IF GREATER THEN 9
           BCS.S     DONE                 THEN DONE

           EXT.W     D0                ELSE MAKE LOOK LIKE A WORD
           MOVE.B    0(A0,D0),D1          GET CODE FROM TABLE

           MOVE.B    D0,CODE

DONE       RTS
```

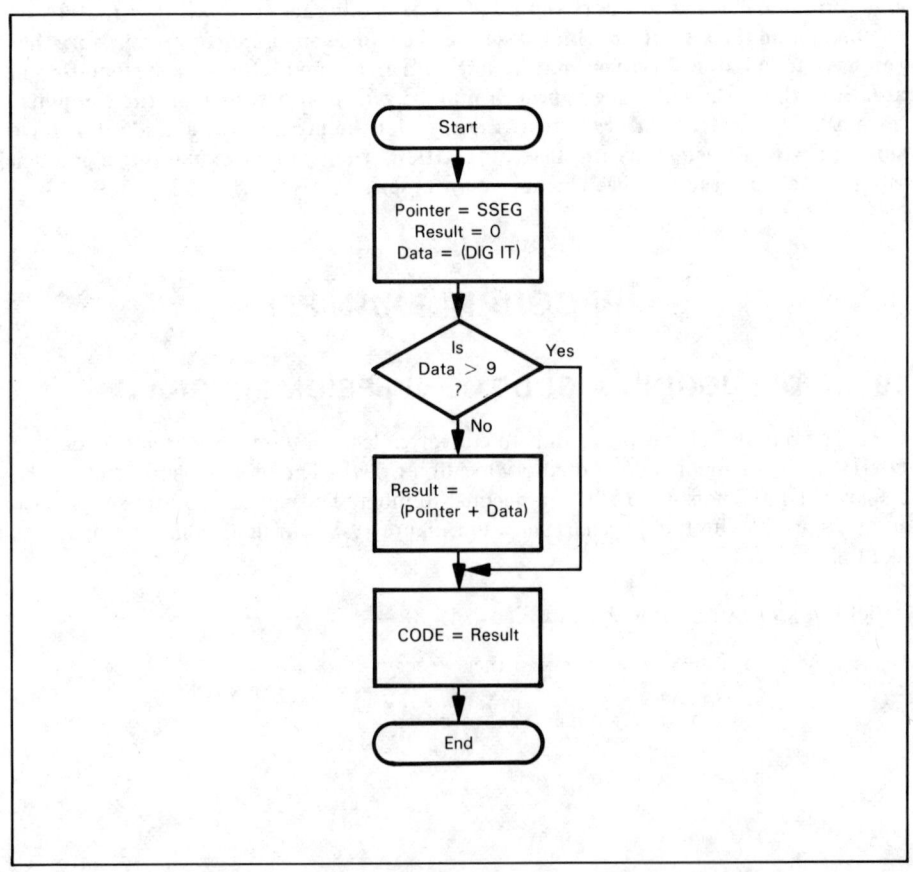

Figure 19-8. Flowchart of Decimal to Seven-Segment Conversion

Using the Checklist

Let us use the checklist we described earlier in this chapter to evaluate this program.

1. Every element of the design in the program? No! We forgot the section that clears the display if the data was not a decimal digit.
2. Initialization? Okay.
3. Conditional branches correct? No! Branch on carry set (BCS) will not handle the equality case correctly. (Try it!). BHI.S DONE is the correct instruction.
4. No loops.
5. Equality cases? Yes, they are now handled correctly.
6. Trivial cases? Yes, (DIGIT) = 0 is handled in the same way as other digits.(Since zero is just another digit in this example, this isn't really a trivial case.)

We also forgot to specify the suffix for the second MOVE instruction. Our second version of the program looks like this:

Second program:
```
DATA        EQU      $8000
PROGRAM     EQU      $4200

            ORG      DATA

DIGIT       DS.B     1
CODE        DS.B     1
SSEG        DC.B     $3F,$06,$5B,$4F,$66
            DC.B     $6D,$7F,$07,$7F

BCD_7SEG    MOVEA.W  SSEG,A0           GET BASE ADDRESS OF TABLE

            MOVEQ    #0,D1
            MOVE.B   DIGIT,D0          GET DIGIT TO CONVERT
            CMP.B    #9,D0             IF GREATER THEN 9
            BHI.S    DONE                 THEN DONE

            EXT.W    D0                ELSE MAKE LOOK LIKE A WORD
            MOVE.B   0(A0,D0.W),D1     GET CODE FROM TABLE

            MOVE.B   D0,CODE
DONE        RTS
```

The hand check did not uncover any errors in this version.

Assembling

The next step is to key in the program and assemble it.

Third Program:
```
00008000       DATA      EQU      $8000
00004200       PROGRAM   EQU      $4200

00008000                 ORG      DATA
```

```
008000 00000001          DIGIT   DS.B    1
008001 00000001          CODE    DS.B    1
008002 3F                SSEG    DC.B    $3F,$06,$5B,$4F,$66
008007 6D                        DC.B    $6D,$7F,$07,$7F

       00004200                  ORG     PROGRAM

004200 307900008002  BCD_7SEG    MOVEA.W  SSEG,A0         GET BASE ADDRESS OF TABLE
004206 7200                      MOVEQ    #0,D1
004208 103900008000              MOVE.B   DIGIT,D0        GET DIGIT TO CONVERT
00420E 0C000009                  CMP.B    #9,D0           IF GREATER THEN 9
004212 620C                      BHI.S    DONE               THEN DONE

004214 4880                      EXT.W    D0              ELSE MAKE LOOK LIKE A WORD
004216 12300000                  MOVE.B   0(A0,D0.W),D1      GET CODE FROM TABLE

00421A 13C000008001              MOVE.B   D0,CODE

004220 4E75          DONE        RTS

                                 END      BCD_7SEG
```

Single-Step

It is now time to single-step through this program (this can be done quickly because it's a short program). If you have the ability to specify which registers to display after each step, choose PC, D0, D1, SR, and A0.

We chose the following test data for the trials:

    0   The smallest decimal digit
    9   The lagest decimal digit
   10   A boundary case
   6B   A randomly selected case

For the first trial, we place zero in memory location DIGIT. After executing the first instruction, MOVE.W SSEG,A0 we find the value $3F06_{16}$ in register A0. That doesn't sound familiar; we expected to have 8000_{16} in A0. The first thing to check here is whether we selected the correct addressing mode. In this case, the answer is no; we confused the immediate and absolute addressing modes. Replace SSEG with #SSEG and try again. This time, we find $FFFF8000_{16}$ in register A0. Again, not the expected result. However, all of the F's must have come from sign-extension (provided that A0 contained zero when we first started). We have specified a word address to be loaded into A0 and the most significant bit in the word is 1. When this address is sign-extended, it produces all ones (FFFF) in the most significant word of the register. The solution is to specify the long word form of the MOVEA instruction. All of this trouble has showed us that the correct first instruction is MOVEA.L #SSEG,A0. (Once again, this is a weakness in the version of the assembler we are using and will probably be handled by later assemblers.)

After correcting this problem, we continue single-stepping through the program. Everything seems to work fine. The branch is not taken and we get $3F_{16}$ as we had expected in register D1. But when we check memory position CODE, we find the BCD digit which we used as the input test data, zero. Something is wrong. To find the problem, ask the question: which instruction(s) affects memory location CODE. In this case it is the last instruction: MOVE D0,CODE. What do we have in register D0? The BCD code. Where is the 7-segment code? In register D1. Aha! It appears that we have a typing error. We change D0,CODE to D1,CODE and make another try. This time we find $3F_{16}$ in memory location CODE. The program now looks like this:

Fourth Program:

```
            00008000       DATA      EQU      $8000
            00004200       PROGRAM   EQU      $4200

            00008000                 ORG      DATA

008000 00000001             DIGIT    DS.B     1
008001 00000001             CODE     DS.B     1
008002 3F                   SSEG     DC.B     $3F,$06,$5B,$4F,$66
008007 6D                            DC.B     $6D,$7F,$07,$7F

            00004200                 ORG      PROGRAM

004200 207C00008002 BCD_7SEG MOVEA.L #SSEG,A0         GET BASE ADDRESS OF TABLE
004206 7200                  MOVEQ   #0,D1
004208 103900008000          MOVE.B  DIGIT,D0         GET DIGIT TO CONVERT
00420E 0C000009              CMP.B   #9,D0            IF GREATER THEN 9
004212 620C                  BHI.S   DONE               THEN DONE
004214 4880                  EXT.W   D0               ELSE MAKE LOOK LIKE A WORD
004216 12300000              MOVE.B  0(A0,D0.W),D1      GET CODE FROM TABLE

00421A 13C100008001          MOVE.B  D1,CODE

004220 4E75         DONE     RTS

                             END     BCD_7SEG
```

Run Test

This time we run the entire program with the second test value, 9. A check of memory location CODE shows that it does not contain $7D_{16}$, which is the last value in the 7-segment code table. The input test value 9 should cause the program to follow the same path as for the value 0. To see what has happened, we make another single-step pass through the program. Everything works fine until we reach the MOVE.B 0(A0,D0.W),D1 instruction. We expected $7D_{16}$ to be loaded into D1 but this was not the case. A memory dump of the table and its environment shows that the value we get comes from the byte immediately following the 7-segment table. Did we miss an entry in the table? We have nine bytes in the table. The values 0 through 9 require ...ten bytes! A check shows that we forgot the last entry, $6F_{16}$, for the digit 9. After adding this value to the table the run test works with both 0 and 9.

The test result after the two last runs were

Digit	Code
10	6F
6B	6F

The code has not been changed since we tested with the digit equal to 9. Both of the values are invalid data so the error can probably be found in the neighborhood of the branch. To what location does the branch transfer control? Aha!, directly to the RTS instruction! We must execute the MOVE D1,CODE instruction and store the cleared results. The label DONE should be moved up one statement.

Exhaustive Test

Since the program is simple, it can be tested for all the decimal digits. The results are

Digit	Code
0	3F
1	06
2	5B
3	4F
4	66
5	6D
6	7F
7	07
8	7F
9	6F

The result for number 6 is wrong; it should be 7D. Since everything else seems to be correct, the error is almost surely in the table. Entry 6 in the table had been typed incorrectly.

Final Program:

```
*
*BCD TO SEVEN SEGMENT DISPLAY CONVERSION
*
*INPUT--BCD NUMBER 0-9 IN LOCATION DIGIT
*OUTPUT--BIT PATTERN FOR SEVEN SEGMENT DISPLAY
*         IN LOCATION CODE. DISPLAY CLEARED IF
*         DIGIT OUT OF RANGE
*
DATA        EQU     $8000
PROGRAM     EQU     $4200

            ORG     DATA

DIGIT       DS.B    1
CODE        DS.B    1
SSEG        DC.B    $3F,$06,$5B,$4F,$66
            DC.B    $6D,$7D,$07,$7F,$6F

            ORG     PROGRAM

BCD_7SEG    MOVEA.L #SSEG,A0        GET BASE ADDRESS OF TABLE
            MOVEQ   #0,D1
            MOVE.B  DIGIT,D0        GET DIGIT TO CONVERT
            CMP.B   #9,D0           IF GREATER THEN 9
            BHI.S   DONE              THEN DONE
            EXT.W   D0              ELSE MAKE LOOK LIKE A WORD
            MOVE.B  0(A0,D0.W),D1     GET CODE FROM TABLE
FINI        MOVE.B  D1,CODE
            RTS
            END     BCD_7SEG
```

Notice that we have also improved the comments.

Summary of Errors Discovered

The errors that we found in this example are typical of the ones that MC68000 assembly language programmers should expect. They include:

1. Failing to initialize registers or memory locations.
2. Inverting the logic on conditional branches.
3. Misalignment of data when dealing with byte values (although the assembler will usually tell you that something is wrong in this case).
4. Confusing the immediate and absolute addressing modes (i.e., data and addresses).
5. Forgetting when sign-extension occurs and when it does not (especially when dealing with addresses).
6. Failing to keep track of which register is used for what, or typing the wrong digit for a register number.
7. Copying lists of numbers, characters, or instructions incorrectly.
8. Branching to the wrong place.

19-2. DEBUGGING A SORT PROGRAM

This program sorts a list of unsigned 16-bit numbers into decreasing order. The address of the beginning of the list is in memory location LISTADDR and the first byte in the list contains the length of the list.

Initial Program: (from flowchart in Figure 19-9)

```
        00006000      DATA     EQU    $6000
        00004000      PROGRAM  EQU    $4000

        00006000               ORG    DATA

006000  00000004      LISTADDR DS.L   1                    ADDRESS OF START OF LIST

        00004000               ORG    PROGRAM

004000  22786000      BUB_SORT MOVEA.L LISTADDR,A1          GET START OF LIST
004004  7200                   MOVEQ  #0,D1
004006  1219                   MOVE.B (A1)+,D1              GET LENGTH OF LIST

004008  5341                   SUBQ   #1,D1                 N ENTRIES REQUIRES N-1 COMPA

00400A  45E90002               LEA    2(A1),A2              GET ADDRESS TO SECOND ELEMEN
00400E  08820000               BCLR.B #0,D2                 CLEAR INTERCHANGE FLAG

004012  B549          NEXT     CMPM.W (A1)+,(A2)+           IF (A1) <= (A2)
004014  6506                   BCS.S  NSWITCH               THEN TEST NEXT PAIR IF ANY

004016  3611                   MOVE.W (A1),D3               ELSE INTERCHANGE THE
004018  3292                   MOVE.W (A2),(A1)             ADJACENT ENTRIES
00401A  3483                   MOVE.W D3,(A2)

00401C  51C9FFF4      NSWITCH  DBRA   D1,NEXT

004020  08020000               BTST.B #0,D2                 INTERCHANGE DURING THIS PASS
004024  66EC                   BNE    NEXT                  IF YES, START NEW PASS

004026  4E75          DONE     RTS                          ELSE DONE

                               END    BUB_SORT
```

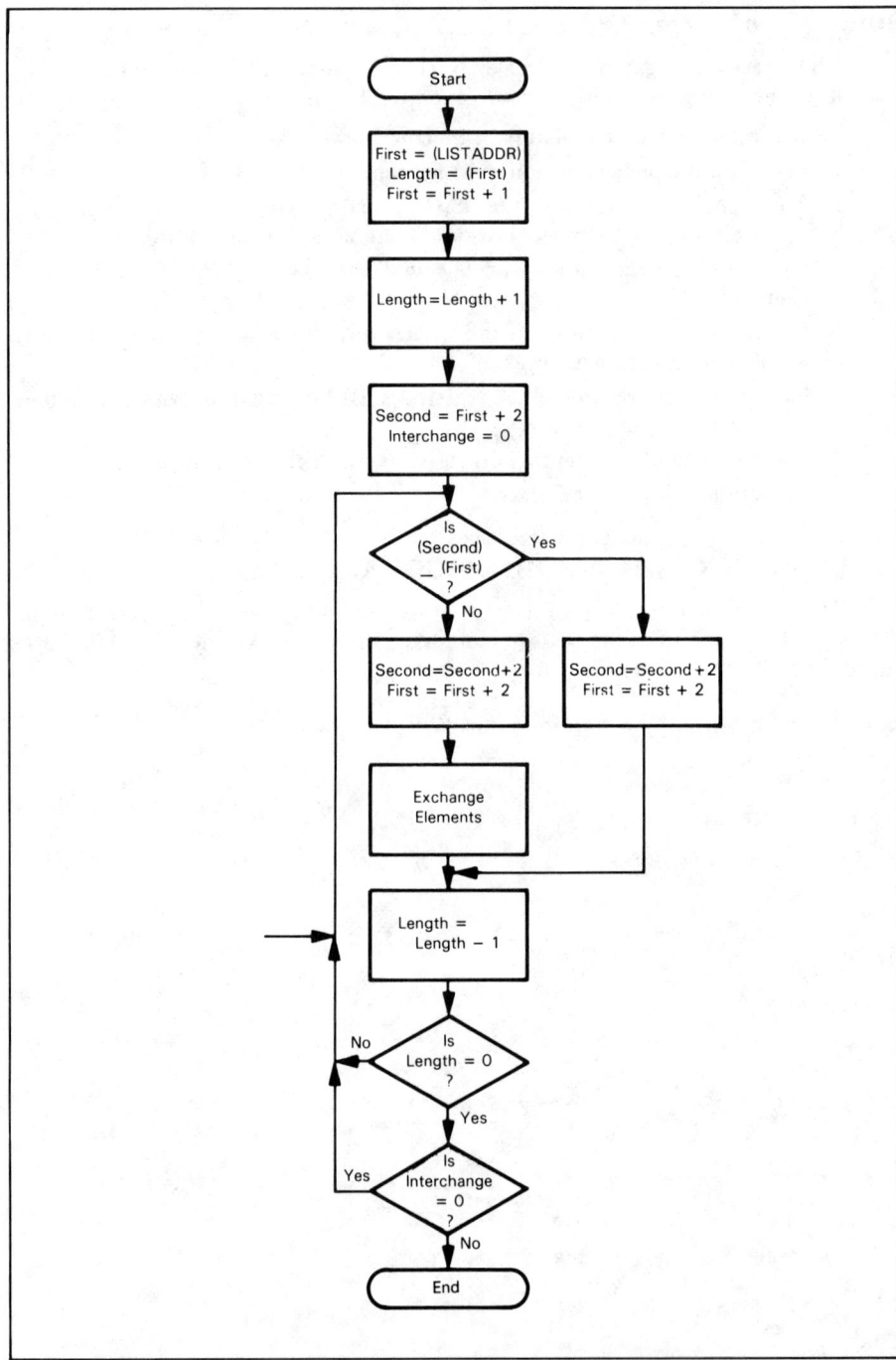

Figure 19-9. Flowchart of a Sort Program

Initial Hand Check

A hand check shows us that all of the blocks in the flowchart have been implemented and the registers used in the loop have been initialized. **We must examine two conditional branches carefully.** The branch in the inner loop BCS.S NSWITCH must be taken if the second entry is less than or equal to the first entry. The operation peformed is (A2) − (A1). If (A2)≠(A1), the Carry flag will be set because of the borrow. The equality condition (A2) = (A1) will not set the Carry flag but will set the Zero flag. The BCS instruction will not handle the equality case correctly; we must use BLS instead.

The second condition branch is BNE NEXT which is supposed to force another pass through the loop if an interchange occurred. We clear the interchange flag before the inner loop so a set flag means interchange and BNE will work fine here.

The next thing to check is the loop. Let us test the first iteration by hand. We assume that memory location LISTADDR contains 5000_{16}. The initialization section — the first six instructions — causes the following result:

```
A1 = 5001
A2 = 5003
D1 = count
D2 bit#0 = 0
```

The effect of the loop instructions is as follows:

```
NEXT      CMPM.W   (A1)+,(A2)+        (5001) - (5003) AND AUTOINCREMENT
          BLS.S    NSWITCH

          MOVE.W   (A1),D3            D3 := (5003)
          MOVE.W   (A2),(A1)          (5003) := (5005)
          MOVE.W   D3,(A2)            (5005) := (5003)

NSWITCH   DBRA     D1,NEXT            COUNT := COUNT - 1
```

There is something weird here. The contents of memory locations 5001 and 5003 were compared and then location 5005 somehow got involved in the interchange. Clearly, we forgot that the CMPM instruction autoincremented both A1 and A2. Let's try this code for the loop:

```
NEXT      CMPM.W   (A1)+,(A2)+        IF (A1) >= (A2)
          BLS.S    NSWITCH            THEN TEST NEXT PAIR IF ANY

          MOVE.W   -(A1),D3           ELSE INTERCHANGE THE
          MOVE.W   -(A2),(A1)+        ADJACENT ENTRIES
          MOVE.W   D3,(A2)+

NSWITCH   DBRA     D1,NEXT
```

A new check shows us that this code performs what we want.

Now let us check the last iteration. Suppose we have three elements:

```
(5000) = 03
(5001) = 2015
(5003) = 1B11
(5005) = 000A
```

This is what happens. After the first iteration:

```
D1 = 02
A1 = 5003
A2 = 5005
```

DBRA subtracts 1 from D1 and branches to NEXT.
After the second iteration:

$$D1 = 1$$
$$A1 = 5005$$
$$A2 = 5007$$

Now A2 points beyond the list and things should stop here. But when DBRA subtracts 1 from D1, the result becomes 0 and DBRA tests for −1. The branch will be taken and the loop executes one more time — one time too many. We must adjust D1 by subtracting 1 from it before we enter the loop.

The next checkpoint in our list is the equality cases. We checked what happened with two equal entries when we discussed the conditional branches, and that is the only equality case that exists in this program.

Checking Trivial Cases

What happens in the trivial cases? First, which are the trivial cases — zero entries in the list? Yes, but another trivial case is when there is only one entry in the list — it doesn't make much sense to try to sort a single element. Remember that trivial cases are not only zero entries, zero objects, and so on. What happens if we have one entry? The answer is that the program tries to sort 64K of memory (if there is read-only memory in this area, the program will run forever). A few instructions added to handle trivial cases will save you from a lot of trouble and they can usually be positioned outside of the loop so that they don't increase the execution time very much. The BLS.S DONE instruction is the only one required in our program to handle the trivial cases. The program now looks like this:

```
                 00006000        DATA     EQU      $6000
                 00004000        PROGRAM  EQU      $4000

                 00006000                 ORG      DATA

006000 00000004                  LISTADDR DS.L     1                    ADDRESS OF START OF LIST

                 00004000                 ORG      PROGRAM

004000 22786000                  BUB_SORT MOVEA.L  LISTADDR,A1          GET START OF LIST
004004 7200                               MOVEQ    #0,D1
004006 1219                               MOVE.B   (A1)+,D1             GET LENGTH OF LIST

004008 5341                               SUBQ     #1,D1                N ENTRIES REQUIRES N-1 COMPAR
00400A 631E                               BLS.S    DONE                 IF 0 OR 1 ENTRY THEN DONE

00400C 45E90002                           LEA      2(A1),A2             GET ADDRESS TO SECOND ELEMENT
004010 08820000                           BCLR.B   #0,D2                CLEAR INTERCHANGE FLAG
004014 5341                               SUBQ.W   #1,D1                ADJUST FOR DBCC

004016 B549            NEXT               CMPM.W   (A1)+,(A2)+          IF (A1) <= (A2)
004018 6506                               BCS.S    NSWITCH              THEN TEST NEXT PAIR IF ANY

00401A 3621                               MOVE.W   -(A1),D3             ELSE INTERCHANGE THE
00401C 32E2                               MOVE.W   -(A2),(A1)+          ADJACENT ENTRIES
00401E 34C3                               MOVE.W   D3,(A2)+

004020 51C9FFF4        NSWITCH            DBRA     D1,NEXT

004024 08020000                           BTST.B   #0,D2                INTERCHANGE DURING THIS PASS
004028 66EC                               BNE      NEXT                 IF YES, START NEW PASS

00402A 4E75            DONE               RTS                           ELSE DONE

                                          END      BUB_SORT
```

Run Test with Breakpoints

Now it is time to check the program on a computer or on a simulator. A simple set of test data is:

```
(6000) = 00005000    Address of array
(5000) = 02          Length of array
(5001) = 0100
(5003) = 0A00        Array to be stored
```

This set consists of two elements in the wrong order. The program should require two passes. The first pass should exchange the elements, producing:

```
(5001) = 0A00
(5003) = 0100

D2b#0 = 1            Interchange flag
```

The second pass should just find the elements already in the proper (descending) order and produce:

```
D2bit#0 = 0          Interchange flag
```

This program is too long for single-stepping, so we will use breakpoints instead. Each breakpoint will halt the computer and print contents of key registers. We will use four breakpoints and we position them as follows:

1. After SUBQ.W #1,D1 to check the initialization.
2. After CMPM.W (A1)+,(A2)+ to check the comparison and the branch.
3. After MOVE.W D3,(A2)+ to check the interchange.
4. After BTST.B #0,D2 to check the completion of a pass through the list.

Assuming that our trace facility allows us to display just the contents of those registers we select, we select registers PC, D1, D2, A1, A2, and the condition codes of the status register.

After the first breakpoint these are our results:

```
PC = 004016
CCR = 04
D1 = 0000
D2 bit#0 = 0
```

These are all correct, so the program is performing the initialization properly in this case.

When we start up our program again, we get a trap. (At this point the less intrepid travelers of the marvelous world of computer programming simply throw up their hands in dismay and consternation and cry, "Damn this noise!") The trap handler tells us that it is an address error and the instruction code that caused it was B549 (the program counter is not reliable in this case). This instruction code is the CMPM.W (A1)+,A2+ instruction. The size is word. A1 contains 5001, and A3 contains 5003 — both odd values! The list length is a byte value and this causes A1 and A3 to get odd values. This is a serious problem and the solution is far from trivial.

One solution is to rewrite the program so that it reads byte by byte instead but that is a lot of unnecessary work. A second alternative is to realign the entire list so that the words are on even boundaries. A third and simpler (for us) alternative is to decide that the first entry in the list (the length) should be a word. This alternative means that we only have to change the suffix after the MOVE instruction that obtains the length. But be careful. This is a change in the "specifications" and it may not fit with other parts of your system. However, in this case we assume that it is possible to make this change and the third instruction of the program is changed to:

MOVE. W (A1)+,D1

Note that this error would not have been discovered if the list had started in memory location 4FFF. Why?

Notice also that our program does not have any comments at the beginning to tell users how to specify the location and length of the list.

We must change the list to look like this before we can start our second trial:

(5000) = 0002
(5002) = 0100
(5004) = 0A00

This time the initialization gives us the same results, and after the second breakpoint these are the results:

PC = 004018
CCR = 00
D1 = 0000
D2 bit #0 = 0
A1 = 005004
A2 = 005006

These are the correct results, and we proceed to the third breakpoint:

PC = 004020
CCR = 00
D1 = 00
D2 bit #0 = 0
A1 = 005004
A2 = 005006

A check of memory locations shows:

(5002) = 0A00
(5004) = 0100

Exactly what we expected. We proceed to the fourth breakpoint:

PC = 004028
CCR = 04
D1 = FFFF
D2 bit #0 = 0
A1 = 005004
A2 = 005006

Something is wrong. The bit that should indicate that an interchange occurred is still 0. A quick look in the loop-de-loop shows that no instruction ever changes this bit. The solution is to insert BSET #0,D2 after MOVE.W D3,(A2)+.

At this point in the debugging procedure, the easiest thing to do is simply to set the interchange bit ourselves and proceed with the second pass. The next breakpoint we reach is the one at address 4016 following the SUBQ.W #1,D1 instruction:

PC = 004016
SR = 00
D1 = FFFF
D2 bit #0 = 1
A1 = 005004
A2 = 005006

There is still something wrong: the registers are not reinitialized. For this pass, we must be sure that we branch all the way to the start of the program to reinitialize.

We change BNE NEXT to BNE BUB SORT and this time everything works correctly.

Final Program:

```
         00006000   DATA      EQU     $6000
         00004000   PROGRAM   EQU     $4000

         00006000             ORG     DATA

006000 ·00000004   LISTADDR  DS.L    1                ADDRESS OF START OF LIST

         00004000             ORG     PROGRAM

004000 22786000   BUB_SORT  MOVEA.L LISTADDR,A1      GET START OF LIST
004004 7200                  MOVEQ   #0,D1
004006 3219                  MOVE.W  (A1)+,D1         GET LENGTH OF LIST

004008 5341                  SUBQ    #1,D1            N ENTRIES REQUIRES N-1 COMPARES
00400A 6322                  BLS.S   DONE             IF <= 0  THEN DONE

00400C 45E90002              LEA     2(A1),A2         GET ADDRESS TO SECOND ELEMENT
004010 08820000              BCLR.B  #0,D2            CLEAR INTERCHANGE FLAG
004014 5341                  SUBQ.W  #1,D1            ADJUST COUNTER FOR DBCC

004016 B549        NEXT      CMPM.W  (A1)+,(A2)+      IF (A1) <= (A2)
004018 630A                  BLS.S   NSWITCH          THEN TEST NEXT PAIR IF ANY

00401A 3621                  MOVE.W  -(A1),D3         ELSE INTERCHANGE THE
00401C 32E2                  MOVE.W  -(A2),(A1)+      ADJACENT ENTRIES
00401E 34C3                  MOVE.W  D3,(A2)+

004020 08C20000              BSET.B  #0,D2            SET INTERCHANGE FLAG

004024 51C9FFF0   NSWITCH   DBRA    D1,NEXT

004028 08020000              BTST.B  #0,D2            INTERCHANGE DURING THIS PASS ?
00402C 66D2                  BNE     BUB_SORT         IF YES, START NEW PASS

00402E 4E75        DONE      RTS                      ELSE DONE

                             END     BUB_SORT
```

This program still needs some comments at the start for documentation.

Other Test Cases

Clearly, we cannot test all possible cases for this program. Some other simple test cases we could use for debugging are:

1. No elements in list

    (6000) = 00005000
    (5000) = 0000

2. One element in list:

    (6000) = 00005000
    (5000) = 0001

3. A "random case" with two equal elements:

```
(6000) = 00008200
(8200) = 0004        Number of elements in list
(8202) = 8345
(8204) = 0001        Array to be stored
(8206) = 0001
(8208) = 4657
```

Summary of Errors Discovered

With this program, we have become acquainted with some other errors which you certainly will encounter in your career as an MC68000 programmer. They included:

1. **Specifying the wrong condition in conditional branches** (again, but this is a very common error).
2. **Forgetting the effects of autoincrements/autodecrements or forgetting the values of pointers.**
3. **Forgetting that DBcc tests for −1 or incorrectly calculating the length of an array** (length = end-start + 1).
4. **Failure to handle trivial cases and equality cases or perhaps even missing some of the trivial cases.**
5. **Trying to address words and long words at odd addresses.** This is very easy to do with poorly defined data structures that require a mixture of byte and word instructions.
6. **Forgetting to set and/or reset flags.**
7. **Forgetting to reinitialize the inner loops in nested structures.**

REFERENCES

1. For more information about logic analyzers, see:

   Brock, G. "Logic-State Analyzers Seek Out Microprocessor-System Faults," *EDN,* January 5, 1980, pp. 137-40.

   Lorentzen, R. "Logic Analyzers Finish What Development Systems Start," *Electronic Design,* March 29, 1980, pp. 81-85.

   Marshall, J. "Digital Analysis Instruments," *EDN,* January 20, 1980, pp. 141-43.

   Ogdin, C.A. "Setting up a Microcomputer Design Laboratory," *Mini-Micro Systems,* May 1979, pp. 87-94.

   Spector, I.H., and Muething, R. "Logic Analyzer Deploys Its Full Strength," *Electronic Design,* March 29, 1980, pp. 177-214.

2. Weller, W.J. *Assembly Level Programming for Small Computers.* Lexington, Mass.: Lexington Books, 1975, Chapter 23.
3. Baldridge, R.L. "Interrupts Add Power, Complexity to Microcomputer System Design," *EDN,* August 5, 1977, pp. 67-73.

20
Testing

Program testing[1] **is closely related to program debugging. We must test the program on the data that we used to debug it; for example,**

- **Trivial cases** such as no data or a single statement
- **Special cases** that the program singles out for some reason
- **Simple cases** that exercise particular parts of the program

For the decimal to seven-segment conversion program in Chapter 19, these cases cover all possible situations. The test data consists of:

- The numbers 0 through 9
- The boundary case 10
- The random case $6B_{16}$

The program does not distinguish any other cases. **Here debugging and testing are virtually the same.**

In the sorting program, the problem is more difficult. The number of elements could range from 0 to 255, and each of the elements could lie anywhere in that range. The number of possible cases is therefore enormous. Furthermore, the program is moderately complex. How do we select test data that will give us a degree of confidence in that program? **Here testing requires some design decisions.** The testing problem is particularly difficult if the program depends on sequences of real-time data. How do we select the data, generate it, and present it to the microcomputer in a realistic manner?

TESTING AIDS

Most of the tools mentioned earlier for debugging are helpful in testing also. Logic or microprocessor analyzers can help check the hardware; simulators[2] can help check the software. Other tools can also be of assistance:

1. **I/O simulations** that can simulate many devices from a single input and a single output device.
2. **In-circuit emulators** that allow you to attach the prototype to a development system or control panel and test it.[3]
3. **ROM simulators** that can be changed like RAM but otherwise behave like the ROM or PROM that will be used in the final system.
4. **Real-time operating systems** that can provide inputs or interrupts at specific times (or perhaps randomly) and mark the occurrence of outputs. Real-time breakpoints and traces may also be included.
5. **Emulations** (often on microprogrammable computers) that may provide real-time execution speed and programmable I/O.[4]
6. **Interfaces** that allow another computer to control the I/O system and test the microcomputer program.
7. **Testing programs** that check each branch in a program for logical errors.
8. **Test generation programs** that can generate random data or other distributions.

Formal testing theorems exist, but are only practical for verifying short programs. You must be careful that the test equipment does not invalidate the test by modifying the environment. Often test equipment may buffer, latch, or condition input and output signals. The actual system may not do this and may therefore behave differently.

Furthermore, extra software in the test environment may use some of the memory space or part of the interrupt system. It may also provide error recovery and other features that will not exist in the final system. A software test bed must be just as realistic as a hardware test bed since software failure can be just as critical as hardware failure.

Emulations and simulations are, of course, never precise. They are usually adequate for checking logic, but can seldom help test interfaces or timing. On the other hand, real-time test equipment does not provide much of an overview of the program logic and may affect the interfacing and timing.

SELECTING TEST DATA[5]

Few real programs can be checked for all cases. The designer must choose a sample set that is in some sense representative.

Structured Testing

Testing should, of course, be part of the total development procedure. **Top-down design and structured programming provide for testing as part of the design. This is called structured testing. Each module within a structured program should be checked separately. **Testing, as well as design, should be modular, structured, and top-down.**

Special Cases

But that leaves the question of selecting test data for a module. The designer must first list all special cases that a program recognizes. These may include:

- Trivial cases
- Equality cases
- Special situations

The test data should include all of these.

Forming Classes of Data

You must next identify each class of data that statements within the program may distinguish. These may include:

- Positive or negative numbers
- Numbers above or below a particular threshold
- Data that does or does not include a particular sequence or character
- Data that is or is not present at a particular time

Be careful; **each two-way decision doubles the number of classes** since you must test both paths. Thus three conditional branches will result in $2 \times 2 \times 2 = 8$ classes if the computer always executes each branch. **Limiting the size of test sets is another important reason to keep modules short and general.**

Selecting Data from Classes

You must now separate the classes according to whether the program produces a different result for each entry in the class (as in a table) or produces the same result for each entry (such as a warning that a parameter is above a threshold). In the discrete case, one may include each element if the total number is small or sample if the number is large. The sample should include all boundary cases and at least one case selected randomly. Random number tables are available in books, and random number generators are part of most computer facilities.[6]

You must be careful of distinctions that may not be obvious. For example, the MC68000 microprocessor will regard an 8-bit unsigned number greater than 127 as negative; you must consider this when using the branch instructions that depend on the Negative (Sign) flag.

EXAMPLES

20-1. TESTING A SORT PROGRAM

The special cases here are obvious:

- No elements in the array
- **One element,** magnitude may be selected randomly

The other special case to be considered is one in which elements are equal.

There may be some problem here with signs and data length. Note that the array itself must contain fewer than 256 elements.

We could check to see if the sign of the number of elements has any effect by choosing half the test cases with elements between 128 and 255 and half with elements between 2 and 127. We should choose the magnitudes of the elements randomly to avoid unconscious bias which might favor small numbers, decimal (rather than hexadecimal) digits, or regular patterns.

20-2. TESTING AN ARITHMETIC PROGRAM

Here we will presume that a prior validity check has ensured that the number has the right length and consists of valid digits. Since the program makes no other distinctions, test data should be selected randomly. Here a random number table or random number generator will prove ideal; the range of the random numbers is 0 to 255 for each byte in each number.

RULES FOR TESTING

Sensible design simplifies testing. The following rules can help:

1. **Eliminate trivial cases early** without introducing unnecessary distinctions.
2. **Avoid special cases,** since they increase debugging and testing time.
3. **Perform validity or error checks on the data before it is processed.**
4. **Avoid inadvertent distinctions,** particularly in handling signed numbers or in using instructions that are intended to handle signed numbers.
5. **Check boundary cases by hand.** Be sure to define what should happen in these es.
6. **Emphasize generality.** Each distinction and separate routine leads to more testing.
7. **Use top-down design and modular programming to modularize testing.**

CONCLUSIONS

Debugging and testing are the stepchildren of the software development process. Most projects leave far too little time for them and most textbooks neglect them. But designers and managers often find that these stages are the most expensive and time-consuming. Progress may be difficult to measure or produce. Debugging and testing microprocessor software is particularly difficult because the powerful hardware and software tools that can be used on larger computers are seldom available for microcomputers.

The designer should plan debugging and testing carefully. We recommend the following guidelines:

1. **Try to write programs that are easy to debug and test.** Modular programming, structured programming, and top-down design are useful techniques.
2. **Prepare a debugging and testing plan as part of the problem definition.** Decide early what data you must generate and what equipment you will need.
3. **Debug and test each module using top-down design.**
4. **Debug each module's logic systematically.** Use checklists, breakpoints, and the single-step mode. If the program logic is complex, consider using the software simulator.
5. **Check each module's timing systematically if this timing is a problem.** An oscilloscope can solve many problems if you plan the test properly. If the timing is complex, consider using a logic or microprocessor analyzer.
6. **Be sure that the test data is representative.** Watch for any classes of data that the program may distinguish. Include all special and trivial cases.
7. **If the program handles each element differently or the number of cases is large, select the test data randomly.**
8. **Document all tests.** If errors are found later, you will not have to repeat tests you have already run.

REFERENCES

1. G. J. Myers. *The Art of Software Testing,* Wiley, New York, 1979.

   R. C. Tausworthe. *Standardized Development of Computer Software,* Prentice-Hall, Englewood Cliffs, N.J., Vol. 1, 1977, Chapter 9; Vol. 2, 1979, Chapters 14 and 15.

   E. Yourdon. *Techniques of Program Structure and Design,* Prentice-Hall, Englewood Cliffs, N.J., 1975, Chapter 7.

2. F. J. Langley. "Simulating Modular Microcomputers," *Simulation,* May 1979, pp. 141-54.

   L. A. Leventhal. "Design Tools for Multiprocessor Systems," *Digital Design,* October 1979, pp. 24-26.

   F. I. Parke et al. "An Introduction to the N.mPc Design Environment," *Proceedings of the 1979 Design Automation Conference,* San Diego, Ca., pp. 513-19.

3. R. Francis and R. Teitzel. "Realtime Analyzer Aids Hardware/Software Integration," *Computer Design,* January 1980, pp. 140-50.
4. H. R. Burris. "Time-Scaled Emulations of the 8080 Microprocessor," *Proceedings of the 1977 National Computer Conference,* pp. 937-46.
5. R. A. DeMillo et al. "Hints on Test Data Selection: Help for the Practicing Programmer," *Computer,* April, 1978, pp. 34-41.

   W. F. Dalton. "Design Microcomputer Software," *Electronics,* January 19, 1978, pp. 97-101.
6. R. D. Grappel and J. Hemenway. "EDN Software Tutorial: Pseudorandom Generators," *EDN,* May 20, 1980, pp. 119-23.

   T. G. Lewis. *Distribution Sampling for Computer Simulation,* Lexington Books, Lexington, Mass., 1975.

   R. A. Mueller et al. "A Random Number Generator for Microprocessors," *Simulation,* April 1977, pp. 123-27.

V
MC68000 Instruction Set

Chapter 21 and Appendices A and B comprise a total reference for the MC68000 family.

DETAILED DESCRIPTIONS

Chapter 21 describes each instruction in detail. The descriptions are set in a template, as follows:

Instruction

The first line gives the standard instruction mnemonic and a one-line definition of the instruction.

Syntax

This section gives the standard assembly language syntax for the instruction. The order of the operands in two-operand instructions is source, then destination. For example, in the instruction

> MOVE.L   D0, D1

D0 is the source and D1 is the destination. In many instances, you can use any addressing mode for the operand(s). In these cases, we will use the term <ea> (for effective address) for the operand, and you may select any of the modes given.

In a few cases, the instruction is restricted to only one or two addressing modes. In these cases, we will give the addressing mode explicitly along with the syntax.

If the operation accepts can manipulate more than one size of data, we append an ".s" to the mnemonic, and list possible values for the size. This may be ".B" (for byte), ".W" (for word), or ".L" (for long). Not all sizes are available for all operands.

A few assemblers may not follow the syntax of "mnemonic src, dst" completely; consult your assembler's manual for verification.

Instruction Format

This section gives the bit format of the instruction word.

Condition Codes

This section lists the state of the condition codes of the status register following execution of the instruction.

363

Description

This section gives a full description of the instruction, including basic usage, any quirks associated with the instruction, and a few applications for the instruction.

Example

This section gives an example of the instruction: how it is assembled, the states of the source and destination before and after execution, and other information that may be useful for understanding the use of the instruction. While most instructions can use many different addressing modes, the example will usually use the simplest mode; that is, register direct.

APPENDICES

Appendices A and B give you a quick reference for the instruction mnemonics and op-codes for each instruction. Appendix A lists the instructions in alphabetical order according to mnemonic. Appendix B lists the instructions in numerical order according to op-code.

ABBREVIATIONS

In describing the instructions, addressing modes, operands, and so on, we will use some standard abbreviations to make the descriptions as concise as possible. You will recognize most of the abbreviations from other discussions throughout the earlier portions of the book.

GENERAL ABBREVIATIONS

An	Address register (n=0 to 7)
bd	Base displacement (8, 16, or 32 bits)
CCR	Condition code register
Dn	Data register (n=0 to 7)
dst	Destination
d8	8-bit displacement
d16	16-bit displacement
d32	32-bit displacement
<ea>	Effective address
od	Outer displacement (8, 16, or 32 bits)
PC	Program counter
src	Source
SP	Stack pointer
SR	Status register

Rn	Either data or address register (n=0 to 7)
xxx.L	32-bit address
xxx.W	16-bit address

ADDRESSING MODES

Dn	Data register direct
An	Address register direct
(An)	Address register indirect
(An)+	Address register indirect with post-increment
−(An)	Address register indirect with pre-decrement
(d16,An)	Address register indirect with 16-bit displacement
(d8,An,Xn)	Address register indirect with 8-bit displacement and index
(bd,An,Xn)	Address register indirect with 16- or 32-bit displacement and index
([bd,An,Xn],od)	Memory indirect preindexed
([bd,An],Xn,od)	Memory indirect postindexed
xxx.L	Absolute short
xxx.L	Absolute long
#<data>	Immediate
(d16,PC)	PC indirect with 16-bit displacement
(d8,PC,Xn)	PC indirect with 8-bit displacement and index
(bd,PC,Xn)	PC indirect with 16- or 32-bit displacement and index
[(bd,PC,Xn),od]	PC memory indirect preindexed
[(bd,PC),Xn,od]	PC memory indirect postindexed

INSTRUCTION ENCODING

The MC68000 instructions range from 1 to 11 words in length. The first word of the instruction contains the op-code as well as information on where to find the operand(s), in the form of two 3-bit fields (mode and register) per operand. A few instructions use a second word as part of the op-code. Depending on what the effective address of the operand(s) is, additional words may follow the instruction word(s).

Tables V-1, V-2, and V-3 summarize the effective address encoding. Look these over for a bit and then we will show you an example of how an assembler encodes an assembly instruction into its binary equivalent.

For our example, we will choose the instruction

        MOVE.L   D3,   ($10,A0,D0.W)

This tells the computer to move the long-word contents of D3 to the contents of the address formed by adding $10, A0, and the word value in the index register D0.

The first step is to get the op-code for the MOVE instruction from Chapter 21 or the

Table V-1. Addressing Mode Fields

```
 15 14 13 12 11 10  9  8  7  6  5  4  3  2  1  0
|     instruction op-code         |   mode  | register |
              single effective address format

 15 14 13 12 11 10  9  8  7  6  5  4  3  2  1  0
|D/A|  index   |W/L| scale | 0 |      displacement      |
       register
              extension word, brief format

 15 14 13 12 11 10  9  8  7  6  5  4  3  2  1  0
|D/A|  index   |W/L| scale | 1 |BS|IS| BD size | 0 | I/IS |
       register
|         base displacement (0, I, or 2 words)         |
|         outer displacement (0, 1, or 2 words)        |
         extension word(s), full format (68020 only)
```

register	Data or Address register (see Table V-2)
mode	Addressing mode (see Table V-2)
op-code	Instruction and possible mode/register information for second operand
displacement	signed 8-bit value
scale	index scaling factor (68020 only) 00 = 1X 01 = 2X 10 = 4X 11 = 8X
index register	Data or address register (000-111)
D/A	Index register type 0 Data register 1 Address register
I/IS	Index/Indirect Select (68020 only — see Table V-3)
BD size	Base displacement size (68020 only) 00 Reserved 01 Null displacement 10 Word displacement 11 Long displacement
IS	Index suppress (68020 only — see Table V-3)
BS	Base suppress (68020 only) 0 Evaluate and add base register 1 Suppress base register
W/L	Index register size 0 sign-extended word 1 signed long word

appendices. This gives us

15	14	13	12	11	10	9	8	7	6	5	4	3	2	1	0
0	0	Size		Destination						Source					
				Register			Mode			Mode			Register		

Size field: 01 = byte 11 = word 10 = long

Now refer to Table V-2 to get the mode/register fields for data register direct (000/011) and address register indirect with index (110/000). Filling this data in gives:

15	14	13	12	11	10	9	8	7	6	5	4	3	2	1	0
0	0	1	0	0	0	0	1	1	0	0	0	0	0	1	1

Table V-2. Mode/Register Encoding

Mode	Register	Addressing Operation
000	reg #	Data register direct
001	reg #	Address register direct
010	reg #	Address register indirect
011	reg #	Address register indirect with post-increment
100	reg #	Address register indirect with pre-decrement
101	reg #	Address register indirect with displacement
110	reg #	Address register memory indirect with index*
111	000	Absolute short
111	001	Absolute long
111	010	Program counter indirect with displacement
111	011	Program counter memory indirect with index*
111	100	Immediate data
111	101-111	Reserved

*68020 only

Table V-3. IS=I/S Addressing Mode Encoding (68020 Only)

IS	I/IS	Addressing Operation
0	000	Index, no memory indirect
0	001	Indirect pre-index with null outer displacement
0	010	Indirect pre-index with word outer displacement
0	011	Indirect pre-index with long outer displacement
0	100	Reserved
0	101	Indirect post-index with null outer displacement
0	110	Indirect post-index with word outer displacement
0	111	Indirect post-index with long outer displacement
1	000	No index, no memory indirect
1	001	No index, memory indirect with null outer displacement
1	010	No index, memory indirect with word outer displacement
1	011	No index, memory indirect with long outer displacement
1	100-111	Reserved

The source addressing mode (data register direct) is complete; the destination mode, howver, will require more information to be complete. Picking the correct type of extension word is straightforward and follows these rules:

1. For a simple displacement, immediate data, or absolute address, the extension word(s) is the value.
2. For indexing with an 8-bit displacement, the extension word is the brief format.
3. For memory indirection and for indexing with 16- or 32-bit displacement, the extension word is the full format. (This is only valid for the MC68020.)

Based on these rules, we generate the following instruction:

15	14	13	12	11	10	9	8	7	6	5	4	3	2	1	0
0	0	1	0	0	0	0	1	1	0	0	0	0	0	1	1
0	0	0	0	0	0	0	0	0	0	0	1	0	0	0	0

All instruction encodes work similarly to this example.

ASSEMBLER MNEMONICS AND OPTIMIZATIONS

In reviewing the list of instructions in the next chapter, you may become dismayed at the number of slightly different instructions and corresponding mnemonics. For example, there are four different binary add instructions, each differing only in the location or size of the operands. These are Add (ADD), Add Address (ADDA), Add Immediate (ADDI), and Add Quick (ADDQ).

Fortunately, most assemblers let you get away with the instruction ADD for all of these variations; the assembler attempts to decide which version is appropriate based on the operands involved. You should be aware, however, that each variation will decode into a different instruction, and that the machine won't let you get away with illegal operations (for example, a byte-sized ADDA instruction).

21
Descriptions of Individual MC68000 Instructions

ABCD — Add Binary Coded Decimal With Extend

Syntax:

  ABCD   Dn, Dm
  ABCD   −(An), −(Am)

Instruction Format:

15	14	13	12	11	10	9	8	7	6	5	4	3	2	1	0
1	1	0	0	Destination Register*			1	0	0	0	0	R/M	Source Register*		

R/M field: 0 = data register to data register   1 = memory to memory
*If R/M = 0, specifies a data register
 If R/M = 1, specifies an address register for the predecrement addressing mode

Condition Codes:

N	Undefined
Z	Cleared if result is non-zero, unchanged if zero
V	Undefined
C	Set if carry generated, cleared if no carry
X	Set if carry generated, cleared if no carry

Description:

This instruction adds the byte contents of the source operand, the value in the Extend (X) bit, and the byte destination, and stores the sum in the destination. The addition uses binary-coded decimal (BCD) arithmetic and affects only eight bits of data. Since the instruction includes the value in the Extend bit in calculating the sum, using the instruction with the address register indirect addressing mode gives you a quick method of implementing high-precision arithmetic.

Example:

If D0 is $43, D1 is $28, and the Extend bit is set, then after

    ABCD   D0, D1

D1 contains $71 and the Extend bit is clear.

ADD — Add Binary

Syntax:

    ADD.s   <ea>, Dn
    ADD.s   Dn, <ea>

where for dst=Dn, <ea> is

X	Dn	X	(d8,An,Xn)	X	#<data>
X	An	X	(bd,An,Xn)	X	(d16,PC)
X	(An)	X	([bd,An,Xn],od)	X	(d8,PC,Xn)
X	(An)+	X	([bd,An],Xn,od)	X	(bd,PC,Xn)
X	−(An)	X	xxx.L	X	[(bd,PC,Xn),od]
X	(d16,An)	X	xxx.L	X	[(bd,PC),Xn,od]

where for src=Dn, <ea> is

	Dn	X	(d8,An,Xn)	#<data>
	An	X	(bd,An,Xn)	(d16,PC)
X	(An)	X	([bd,An,Xn],od)	(d8,PC,Xn)
X	(An)+	X	([bd,An],Xn,od)	(bd,PC,Xn)
X	−(An)	X	xxx.L	[(bd,PC,Xn),od]
X	(d16,An)	X	xxx.L	[(bd,PC),Xn,od]

and where .s = .B, .W, or .L.

Instruction Format:

15	14	13	12	11	10	9	8	7	6	5	4	3	2	1	0
1	1	0	1	Data Register			Op-Mode			Effective Address				
										Mode			Register		

Op-Mode field:	Byte	Word	Long	Operation
	000	001	010	(<ea>)+(<Dn>) → <Dn>
	100	101	110	(<Dn>)+(<ea>) → <ea>

Condition Codes:

N	Set if result is negative, cleared otherwise
Z	Set if result is zero, cleared otherwise
V	Set if overflow is generated, cleared otherwise
C	Set if carry is generated, cleared otherwise
X	Set if carry is generated, cleared otherwise

Description:

This instruction adds the contents of the source operand to the contents of the destination operand and stores the sum in the destination. Note that at least one of the operands must be a data register.

Example:

If D0 contains $100 and the word at the address given by the label SUM contains $5480, then after the instruction

> ADD.W   SUM, D0

D0 contains $5580.

ADDA — Add Address

Syntax:

> ADDA.s   <ea>, An

where <ea> is

X	Dn	X	(d8,An,Xn)	X	#<data>
X	An	X	(bd,An,Xn)	X	(d16,PC)
X	(An)	X	([bd,An,Xn],od)	X	(d8,PC,Xn)
X	(An)+	X	([bd,An],Xn,od)	X	(bd,PC,Xn)
X	−(An)	X	xxx.L	X	[(bd,PC,Xn),od]
X	(d16,An)	X	xxx.L	X	[(bd,PC),Xn,od]

and where .s = .W or .L.

Instruction Format:

15	14	13	12	11	10	9	8	7	6	5	4	3	2	1	0
1	1	0	1	Address Register			Op-Mode			Effective Address			
										Mode			Register		

Op-Mode field:

Word	Long	Operation
011	111	(<ea>)+(<An>) → <An>

Condition Codes:

N	Unchanged
Z	Unchanged
V	Unchanged
C	Unchanged
X	Unchanged

Description:

This instruction adds the source operand to the value in an address register. Note that since it deals with addresses, the instruction permits only word and long-word operations.

Example:

If TABLE is a constant valued $00800000, and A0 contains $2000, then after the instruction

                    ADDA.L   #TABLE, A0

A0 contains the value $00802000.

ADDI — Add Immediate

Syntax:

ADDI.s   #<data>, <ea>

where <ea> is

X Dn	X (d8,An,Xn)	#<data>
An	X (bd,An,Xn)	(d16,PC)
X (An)	X ([bd,An,Xn],od)	(d8,PC,Xn)
X (An)+	X ([bd,An],Xn,od)	(bd,PC,Xn)
X −(An)	X xxx.L [(bd,PC,Xn),od]	
X (d16,An)	X xxx.L	[(bd,PC),Xn,od]

and where .s = .B, .W, or .L.

Instruction Format:

15	14	13	12	11	10	9	8	7	6	5	4	3	2	1	0
0	0	0	0	0	1	1	0	\multicolumn{2}{Size}	\multicolumn{6}{Effective Address}

| | | | | | | | | | | Mode | | | Register | | |

Size field: 00 = byte 01 = word 10 = long

Condition Codes:

    N Set if result is negative, cleared otherwise
    Z Set if result is zero, cleared otherwise
    V Set if an overflow is generated, cleared otherwise
    C Set if carry is generated, cleared otherwise
    X Set if carry is generated, cleared otherwise

Description:

This instruction adds the immediate data given as the source operand to the specified destination operand and stores the result in the destination. The number of bytes used for the immediate data matches the size attribute of the mnemonic, regardless of the actual size of the immediate data. That is, an ADDI.W will be followed by two bytes of operand data, and an ADDI.L will be followed by four bytes of operand data.

Example:

If D0 contains $1400050 and SUM is a pointer to a long-word variable, then

ADDI.I   #$804000, SUM

leaves the value $1C04050 in SUM.

ADDQ — Add Quick

Syntax:

ADDQ.S   #<data>, <ea>

where <ea> is

X Dn	X (d8,An,Xn)	#<data>
X An	X (bd,An,Xn)	(d16,PC)
X (An)	X ([bd,An,Xn],od)	(d8,PC,Xn)
X (An)+	X ([bd,An],Xn,od)	(bd,PC,Xn)
X −(An)	X xxx.L	[(bd,PC,Xn),od]
X (d16,An)	X xxx.L	[(bd,PC),Xn,od]

and where .S = .B, .W, or .L.

Instruction Format:

15	14	13	12	11	10	9	8	7	6	5	4	3	2	1	0
0	1	0	1	Data			0	Size		Effective Address					
										Mode			Register		

Data field: Three bits of immediate data, 0, 1-7 representing a range of 8, 1 to 7 respectively.
Size field: 00 = byte   01 = word   10 = long

Condition Codes:

- N   Set if result is negative, cleared otherwise
- Z   Set if result is zero, cleared otherwise
- V   Set if overflow is generated, cleared otherwise
- C   Set if carry is generated, cleared otherwise
- X   Set if carry is generated, cleared otherwise

Description:

This instruction adds the immediate data specified by the source to the data stored in the destination operand and stores the sum in the destination operand. This instruction differs from the ADDI instruction in that the immediate data is restricted to values 1-8. When assembled, the immediate data is part of the instruction word rather than the extension word(s).

Example:

If D4 contains the word value $1004, then after

ADDQ.W $4, D4

D4 contains $1008.

ADDX — Add Binary With Extend

Syntax:

ADDX.s   Dsrc, Ddst
ADDX.s   −(Asrc), −(Adst)

where .s = .B, .W, or .L.

Instruction Format:

15	14	13	12	11 10 9	8	7 6 5	4	3	2 1 0
1	1	0	1	Destination Register*	1	Size	0	0 R/M	Source Register*

Size field: 00 = byte   01 = word   10 = long
R/M field: 0 = data register to data register   1 = memory to memory
*If R/M = 0, specifies a data register
If R/M = 1, specifies an address register for the predecrement addressing mode.

Condition Codes:

    N   Undefined
    Z   Cleared if result is non zero, unchanged if zero
    V   Undefined
    C   Set if carry generated, cleared if no carry
    X   Set if carry generated, cleared if no carry

Description:

This instruction adds the contents of the source operand, the value in the Extend (X) bit, and the destination, and stores the sum in the destination. Since the instruction includes the value in the Extend bit in calculating the sum, you can use the instruction with the address register addressing mode to obtain a quick method of implementing high-precision arithmetic.

Example:

If the quad word (eight bytes) labeled Q0 contains $00140000 F000FFFF, and the quad word labeled Q1 contains $00000000 10000001, then after

```
            MOVEA.L    #Q0, A0
            MOVEA.L    #Q1, A1
            MOVE.W     #0, CCR
            ADDX.L     −(A1), −(A0)
            ADDX.L     −(A1), −(A0)
```

Q0 contains $00140001 00010000 and the Extend bit is clear.

AND — Logical AND

Syntax:

AND.s   <ea>, Dn
AND.s   Dn, <ea>

where for dst=Dn, <ea> is

X Dn	X (d8,An,Xn)	X #<data>	
An	X (bd,An,Xn)	X (d16,PC)	
X (An)	X ([bd,An,Xn],od)	X (d8,PC,Xn)	
X (An)+	X ([bd,An],Xn,od)	X (bd,PC,Xn)	
X -(An)	X xxx.L	X [(bd,PC,Xn),od]	
X (d16,An)	X xxx.L	X [(bd,PC),Xn,od]	

and where for src=Dn, <ea> is

Dn	X (d8,An,Xn)	#<data>	
An	X (bd,An,Xn)	(d16,PC)	
X (An)	X ([bd,An,Xn],od)	(d8,PC,Xn)	
X (An)+	X ([bd,An],Xn,od)	(bd,PC,Xn)	
X -(An)	X xxx.L	[(bd,PC,Xn),od]	
X (d16,An)	X xxx.L	[(bd,PC),Xn,od]	

and where .s = .B, .W, or .L.

Instruction Format:

15	14	13	12	11	10	9	8	7	6	5	4	3	2	1	0
1	1	0	0	\multicolumn{3}{c}{Data Register}	\multicolumn{3}{c}{Op-Mode}	\multicolumn{6}{c}{Effective Address}

| 1 | 1 | 0 | 0 | Data Register | Op-Mode | Mode | Register |

Op-Mode field:
	Byte	Word	Long	Operation
	000	001	010	(<ea>)∧(<Dn>) → <Dn>
	100	101	110	(<Dn>)∧(<ea>) → <ea>

Condition Codes:

- N Set if high-order bit of result is set, cleared otherwise
- Z Set if result is zero, cleared otherwise
- V Cleared
- C Cleared
- X Unaffected

Description:

This instruction performs a bitwise logical AND of the source and destination operands and stores the result in the destination. At least one of the operands must be in a data register.

Example:

If the word pointed to by FLAG_WORD contains $2376 and D0 contains $4A3C, then after

        AND.W   D0, FLAG_WORD

is evaluated as follows:

```
FLAG_WORD  = $2376 = 0010 0011 0111 0110
D0         = $4A3C = 0100 1010 0011 1100
FLAG_WORD  = $0234 = 0000 0010 0011 0100
```

leaving the value $0234 in FLAG_WORD.

ANDI—AND Immediate

Syntax:

    ANDI.s   #<data>, <ea>

where <ea> is

X Dn	X (d8,An,Xn)	#<data>
An	X (bd,An,Xn)	(d16,PC)
X An)	X ([bd,An,Xn],od)	(d8,PC,Xn)
X (An)+	X ([bd,An],Xn,od)	(bd,PC,Xn)
X -(An)	X xxx.L	[(bd,PC,Xn),od]
X (d16,An)	X xxx.L	[(bd,PC),Xn,od]

and where .s = .B, .W, or .L.

Instruction Format:

15	14	13	12	11	10	9	8	7	6	5	4	3	2	1	0
0	0	0	0	0	0	1	0	Size		Effective Address					
										Mode			Register		

Size field: 00 = byte 01 = word 10 = long

Condition Codes:

N	Set if high-order bit of result is set, cleared otherwise
Z	Set if result is zero, cleared otherwise
V	Cleared
C	Cleared
X	Unaffected

Description:

This instruction logically ANDs the immediate source the result in the destination.

Example:

If the constant long word MASK equals $FF007777 and D0 contains $80238001, then after

          ANDI.L   #MASK, D0

D0 contains $80000001 and the N flag is set.

ANDI to CCR — AND Immediate Data To the Condition Codes

Syntax:

    ANDI   #<data>, CCR

Instruction Format:

15	14	13	12	11	10	9	8	7	6	5	4	3	2	1	0
0	0	0	0	0	0	1	0	0	0	1	1	1	1	0	0
0	0	0	0	0	0	0	0	Byte Data							

Condition Codes:

N	ANDed with bit 3 of immediate data
Z	ANDed with bit 2 of immediate data
V	ANDed with bit 1 of immediate data
C	ANDed with bit 0 of immediate data
X	ANDed with bit 4 of immediate data

Description:

This instruction logically ANDs the immediate byte data with the condition code register and sets the flags appropriately. The instruction provides you with a means of selectively clearing one or more bits of the CCR.

Example:

If CCR contains $0B (N, V, and C flags set) and the constant CLR_C contains $FE, then after

        ANDI   #CLR_C, CCR

the CCR contains $0A (N and V flags set, the C bit has been cleared).

ANDI to SR—AND Immediate Data To the Status Register

(Privileged Instruction)

Syntax:

    ANDI   #<data>, SR

Instruction Format:

15	14	13	12	11	10	9	8	7	6	5	4	3	2	1	0
0	0	0	0	0	0	0	0	0	1	1	1	1	1	0	0
Word Data															

Condition Codes:

N	ANDed with bit 3 of immediate data
Z	ANDed with bit 2 of immediate data
V	ANDed with bit 1 of immediate data
C	ANDed with bit 0 of immediate data
X	ANDed with bit 4 of immediate data

Description:

This instruction logically ANDs the 16-bit immediate source data with the value from the status register (SR) and stores the result in the status register. Execution of this instruction allows your program to clear individual bits in the register. Note that the instruction is privileged; if you attempt to execute it from user mode, the processor will trap through the privilege-violation vector.

Example:

If the status register contains the value $2004 (indicating supervisor mode and N flag set), and the constant CLR__SUPER equals $DFFF, then

           ANDI   #CLR__SUPER, SR

leaves the value $0004 in the SR (clearing the supervisor bit and changing the processor mode to user mode).

ASL and ASR — Arithmetic Shift Left And Right

Syntax:

    ASL.s   Dn, Dm
    ASL.s   #<data>, Dn
    ASL   <ea>
    ASR.s   Dn, Dm
    ASR.s   #<data>, Dn
    ASR   <ea>

where <ea> is

	Dn	X	(d8,An,Xn)		#<data>
	An	X	(bd,An,Xn)		(d16,PC)
X	(An)	X	([bd,An,Xn],od)		(d8,PC,Xn)
X	(An)+	X	([bd,An],Xn,od)		(bd,PC,Xn)
X	-(An)	X	xxx.L		[(bd,PC,Xn),od]
X	(d16,An)	X	xxx.L		[(bd,PC),Xn,od]

and where .s = .B, .W, or .L.

Instruction Format:

                                                                    (Register)

15	14	13	12	11	10	9	8	7	6	5	4	3	2	1	0
1	1	1	0	Count/Register			dr	Size		I/R	0	0	Register		

                                                                     (Memory)

1	1	1	0	0	0	dr	1	1	Effective Address	
									Mode	Register

i/r: 0 = immediate shift count
       1 = register shift count
dr: 0 = right
       1 = left
Size field: 00 = byte   01 = word   10 = long
Count/Register: if i/r = 0, specifies shift count
                     if i/r = 1, specifies data register

Condition Codes:

- **N** Set if high-order bit of result is set, cleared otherwise
- **Z** Set if result is zero, cleared otherwise
- **V** Set if high-order bit changes during shift operation, cleared otherwise
- **C** Set according to last bit shifted out of operand
- **X** Set according to last bit shifted out of operand

Description:

These instructions shift the contents of the destination operand a specified number of times. The destination may be in a data register or in memory. When the destination is in a data register, you can specify the number of bits to shift either through immediate data (a value of 1-8) or through another data register (containing a Modulo 64 value of 0-63). If the destination is a memory location, the size of the shift is restricted to one bit, and in addition, the size of the operand must be word-sized.

The ASL instructions operate as follows:

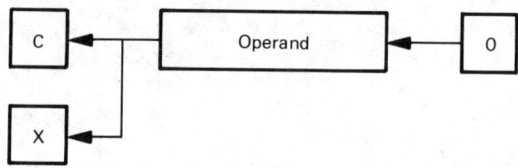

Note that the processor fills in the operand with zeros from the right side (bit 0) and drops the bits from the left side into the Carry (C) and Extend bits (X). For multiple bit shifts, these flags reflect the state of the final bit shifted out. If the sign of the operand ever changes, the processor sets the Overflow bit (V).

The ASR instruction operates as follows:

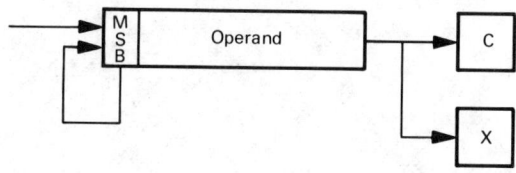

The processor replicates the state of the most significant bit. This means that a right-shifted operand will never change from negative to positive as the result of a shift. The bits falling out the right side of the operand end up in the Carry (C) and Extend (X) bits; for multiple bit shifts, these flags reflect the state of the final bit shifted out.

The difference between arithmetic shifts (ASR and ASL) and logical shifts (LSR and LSL) lies in the application for each. As the name implies, arithmetic shifts are useful in certain quick arithmetic functions. For example, a left shift by 2 bits is equivalent to a multiplication by 4; a right shift by 4 is equivalent to a division by 16. Because of their simplicity, the shifts operate faster than do the corresponding MUL or DIV instructions. To verify that the left shift operation (a multiply) hasn't overflowed its operand, the processor sets the V bit accordingly. To verify that the operand sign doesn't change on a right shift (a divide), the processor replicates the most significant bit.

The logical shift instructions are useful in manipulating bit masks and status-bit fields; in these applications, the sign or status of overflow is not important and can even lead to erroneous results.

Examples:

If D0 contains $0138 (312(10), then after

    ASL.W   #3, D0

D0 contains $09C0 (312(10) X 8 = 2496(10) = $09C0), and the C, X, and V bits are all clear.

If the word at the address of VAL1 is −120, then after

    ASR.W   VAL1

VAL1 contains −60.

B_{cc} — Branch

Syntax:

    B_{cc} displacement

Instruction Format:

15	14	13	12	11	10	9	8	7	6	5	4	3	2	1	0
0	1	1	0	\multicolumn{4}{c}{Condition}	\multicolumn{8}{c}{8-Bit Displacement}

| 16-Bit Displacement if 8-Bit Displacement = $00 |
| 32-Bit Displacement if 8-Bit Displacement = $FF |

Condition Codes:

    N   Unaffected
    Z   Unaffected
    V   Unaffected
    C   Unaffected
    X   Unaffected

Description:

This instruction tests a condition and then branches if that condition is true. If a branch is in order, the processor adds the two's complement displacement value to the program counter (PC). The displacement value can be an 8-bit value or a 16-bit value; on the MC68020, it can be a 32-bit value. The PC value used in evaluating the new address is the address of the instruction plus 2. The instruction can specify any one of 14 different conditions, as summarized in Table 21-1. The BRA instruction is a special case; the processor does no checking on the condition codes.

Table 22-1. B_{cc} Conditional Tests

Mnemonic(cc)	Condition	Condition Field	Test
HI	High	0010	$\overline{C} \wedge \overline{Z}$
LS	Low or same	0011	$C \vee Z$
CC	Carry clear	0100	$\overline{C}$
CS	Carry set	0101	C
NE	Not equal	0110	$\overline{Z}$
EQ	Equal	0111	Z
VC	Overflow clear	1000	$\overline{V}$
VS	Overflow set	1001	V
PL	Plus	1010	$\overline{N}$
MI	Minus	1011	N
GE	Greater or equal	1100	$(N \wedge V) \vee (\overline{N} \wedge \overline{V})$
LT	Less than	1101	$(N \wedge \overline{V}) \vee (\overline{N} \wedge V)$
GT	Greater than	1110	$(N \wedge V \wedge \overline{Z}) \vee (\overline{N} \wedge \overline{V} \wedge \overline{Z})$
LE	Less or equal	1111	$Z \vee (N \wedge \overline{V}) \vee (\overline{N} \wedge V)$

Normally, you specify the displacement as a label name. To calculate the numeric value of the displacement, the assembler subtracts the label value from the current instruction's address. You needn't provide a size for the instruction; the assembler will choose the appropriate size based on the size of the displacement. The displacement can be in either direction, jumping ahead of the current PC or behind it. You cannot, however, jump to the instruction immediately following the B_{cc} instruction.

Some documentation lists the B_{cc} instructions separately from the BRA instruction.

Example:

If the Carry bit is set, then

```
            BCS     NO_CLR
            CLR     VAL
NO_CLR:  ...
```

causes the processor to branch around the CLR instruction to the instruction at label NO_CLR.

BCHG — Test a Bit and Change

Syntax:

```
BCHG.s      Dn, <ea>
BCHG.s      #<data>, <ea>
```

where <ea> is

X	Dn	X	(d8,An,Xn)	#<data>
	An	X	(bd,An,Xn)	(d16,PC)
X	(An)	X	([bd,An,Xn],od)	(d8,PC,Xn)
X	(An)+	X	([bd,An],Xn,od)	(bd,PC,Xn)
X	−(An)	X	xxx.L	[(bd,PC,Xn),od]
X	(d16,An)	X	xxx.L	[(bd,PC),Xn,od]

and where .s =.B or .L (.L only valid when <ea>=Dn).

(Bit number in Dn)

15	14	13	12	11	10	9	8	7	6	5	4	3	2	1	0
0	0	0	0	\multicolumn{3}{c}{Data Register}			1	0	1	\multicolumn{2}{c}{Effective Address Mode}	\multicolumn{2}{c}{Register}

15	14	13	12	11	10	9	8	7	6	5	4	3	2	1	0
0	0	0	0	1	0	0	0	0	1	\multicolumn{2}{c}{Mode}	\multicolumn{2}{c}{Register}		

(Bit number is immediate)

Condition Codes:

N	Unaffected
Z	Set if bit tested is zero, cleared otherwise
V	Unaffected
C	Unaffected
X	Unaffected

Description:

This instruction tests a bit value, sets the Zero (Z) flag accordingly, and then changes it (that is, if it was a 0, it becomes a 1, or vice versa). The operand may be 32 bits in length and reside in a data register, or it may reside in memory as an 8-bit value.

You may choose one of two ways to specify the bit number; either through a data register or through immediate data. Bit numbers start with bit 0 as the least significant bit of the operand. For data register-resident operands, valid bit numbers range from 0-31; for memory-resident operands, valid bit numbers range from 0-7.

Example:

If the byte at label FLAGS contains $F1 (1111 0001), then after

                BCHG.B   #3, FLAGS

FLAGS contains the value $F9 (1111 1001), and the Z flag is cleared.

BCLR — Test a Bit and Clear

Syntax:

    BCLR.s   Dn, <ea>
    BCLR.s   #<data>, <ea>

where <ea> is

X	Dn	X	(d8,An,Xn)		#<data>
	An	X	(bd,An,Xn)		(d16,PC)
X	(An)	X	([bd,An,Xn],od)		(d8,PC,Xn)
X	(An)+	X	([bd,An],Xn,od)		(bd,PC,Xn)
X	−(An)	X	xxx.L		[(bd,PC,Xn),od]
X	(d16,An)	X	xxx.L		[(bd,PC),Xn,od]

and where .s = .B or .L (.L only where <ea>=Dn).

Instruction Format:

(Bit number in Dn)

15	14	13	12	11	10	9	8	7	6	5	4	3	2	1	0
0	0	0	0	Data Register			1	1	0	Effective Address					
										Mode			Register		

(Bit number immediate)

15	14	13	12	11	10	9	8	7	6	5	4	3	2	1	0
0	0	0	0	1	0	0	0	1	0	Effective					
										Address Mode			Register		

Condition Codes:

N	Unaffected
Z	Set if bit tested is zero, cleared otherwise
V	Unaffected
C	Unaffected
X	Unaffected

Description:

This instruction tests a bit value, sets the Zero flag (Z) accordingly, and then clears the bit. The operand can be 32 bits in length and reside in a data register or it may reside in memory as an 8-bit value.

You can choose one of two ways to specify the bit number: either through a data register or through immediate data. Bit numbers start with bit 0 as the least significant bit of the operand. For data register-resident operands, valid bit numbers range from 0-31; for memory-resident operands, valid bit numbers range from 0-7.

Example:

If D0 contains the value $12 (18(10), and D1 contains $104FF0EC (00010000 01001111 11110000 11101100), then after

    BCLR.L   D1, D0

D1 contains the value $104BF0EC (00010000 01001011 11110000 11101100), and the Z flag is set.

BFCHG — Test Bit Field and Change (MC68020 only)

Syntax:
    BFCHG   <ea>{offset:width}

where <ea> is

X	Dn	X	(d8,An,Xn)	#<data>
	An	X	(bd,An,Xn)	(d16,PC)

X (An)	X ([bd,An,Xn],od)	(d8,PC,Xn)
(An)+	X ([bd,An],Xn,od)	(bd,PC,Xn)
−(An)	X xxx.L	[(bd,PC,Xn),od]
X (d16,An)	X xxx.L	[(bd,PC),Xn,od]

Instruction Format:

15	14	13	12	11	10	9	8	7	6	5	4	3	2	1	0
0	1	1	0	1	0	1	0	1	1	\multicolumn{6}{c}{Effective Address}
										\multicolumn{3}{c}{Mode}	\multicolumn{3}{c}{Register}
0	0	0	0	\multicolumn{3}{c}{Do}	\multicolumn{3}{c}{Offset}	Dw	\multicolumn{5}{c}{Width}

Do: 0 = offset is immediate   Dw: 0 = width is immediate
1 = offset is data register   1 = width is data register

Condition Codes:

N   Set if high-order bit of field is set, cleared otherwise
Z   Set if bit field is zero, cleared otherwise
V   Always cleared
C   Always cleared
X   Unaffected

Description:

This instruction tests the contents of a bit field, sets the condition codes accordingly, and then logically NOTs the bit field contents. The operand may be in a data register or in memory. The field has an offset and a width, which you can specify either through immediate data or through data registers. If you specify the offset as immediate data, it can have values from 0-31. If you specify the offset in a data register, it can have values from -2^{31} through $2^{31}-1$. The width is a value between 1 and 32.

Note here that the bit order for bit fields differs from that of individual bits in that for bit fields, the most significant bit is bit number 1.

Example:

You have defined a long status word at the label STATUS. Within that word, the field comprising bit offsets 14-18 define a counter that you must negate before using. If the field contains the value 01110, then after

BFCHG   STATUS{14:5}

the field contains 10001 and the Negative (N) flag is set.

BFCLR — Test Bit Field and Clear
(MC68020 only)

Syntax:

BFCLR   <ea>{offset:width}

where <ea> is

X Dn	X (d8,An,Xn)	#<data>
An	X (bd,An,Xn)	(d16,PC)

X	(An)	X	([bd,An,Xn],od)		(d8,PC,Xn)
	(An)+	X	([bd,An],Xn,od)		(bd,PC,Xn)
	−(An)	X	xxx.L		[(bd,PC,Xn),od]
X	(d16,An)	X	xxx.L		[(bd,PC),Xn,od]

Instruction Format:

15	14	13	12	11	10	9	8	7	6	5	4	3	2	1	0
										\multicolumn{6}{c}{Effective Address}
1	1	1	0	1	1	0	0	1	1	\multicolumn{3}{c}{Mode}	\multicolumn{3}{c}{Register}
0	0	0	0	Do	\multicolumn{5}{c}{Offset}	Dw	\multicolumn{5}{c}{Width}

Do: 0 = offset is immediate Dw: 0 = width is immediate
1 = offset is data register   1 = width is data register

Condition Codes:

- **N**   Set if high order bit of field is set, cleared otherwise
- **Z**   Set if bit field is zero, cleared otherwise
- **V**   Always cleared
- **C**   Always cleared
- **X**   Unaffected

Description:

This instruction tests the contents of a bit field, sets the condition codes accordingly, and then clears the bit field contents. The operand may be in a data register or in memory. The field has an offset and a width, which you may specify either through immediate data or through data registers. If you specify the offset as immediate data, it can have values from 0-31. If you specify the offset in a data register, it can have values from -2^{31} through $2^{31}-1$. The width is a value between 1 and 32.

Note here that the bit order for bit fields differs from that of individual bits in that for bit fields, the most significant bit is bit number 1. This is discussed in further detail in Chapter 12.

Example:

You have defined several words of bit field data starting at the label FIELD_BASE. Within those fields, the 6-bit field beginning at offset +45(10) bits from the beginning contains the seconds count in the current time. If the current value is $23 (10111), and D0 contains the offset of 45, after the instruction

                BFCLR   FIELD_BASE{D0:6}

the field contains $000000 and no flags are set.

BFEXTS — Extract Bit Field Signed
(MC688020 only)

Syntax:

    BFEXTS   <ea>{offset:width}, Dn

where <ea> is

X	Dn	X	(d8,An,Xn)		#<data>
	An	X	(bd,An,Xn)	X	(d16,PC)

X	(An)	X	([bd,An,Xn],od)	X	(d8,PC,Xn)
	(An)+	X	([bd,An],Xn,od)	X	(bd,PC,Xn)
	−(An)	X	xxx.L	X	[bd,PC,Xn],od]
X	(d16,An)	X	xxx.L	X	[(bd,PC),Xn,od]

Instruction Format:

15	14	13	12	11	10	9	8	7	6	5	4	3	2	1	0
1	1	1	0	1	0	1	1	1	1	Effective Address					
										Mode			Register		
0	Register			Do		Offset				Dw			Width		

```
                      Do: 0 = offset is immediate
                          1 = offset is data register
                      Dw: 0 = width is immediate
                          1 = width is data register
```

Condition Codes:

- **N**   Set if high-order bit of field is set, cleared otherwise
- **Z**   Set if all bits are zero, cleared otherwise
- **V**   Always cleared
- **C**   Always cleared
- **X**   Unaffected

Description:

This instruction copies the contents of a bit field to a data register sign, extending the value to 32 bits. The operand may be in a data register or in memory. The field has an offset and a width, which you can specify either through immediate data or through data registers. If you specify the offset as immediate data, it can have values from 0-31. If you specify the offset in a data register, it can have values from -2^{31} through $2^{31}-1$. The width is a value between 1 and 32.

Note here that the bit order for bit fields differs from that of individual bits in that for bit fields, the most significant bit is bit number 1. This is discussed in further detail in Chapter 12.

Example:

You have defined a set of bit fields starting at COUNTERS, and a 12-bit counter lies at offset 108 bits from the start. If D0 contains 108, D1 contains 0, and the bit field contains −340, then after

                        BFEXTS   COUNTERS{D0:12}, D1

D1 contains −340 and the N flag is set.

BFEXTU — Extract Bit Field Unsigned

Syntax:

    BFEXTU   <ea>{offset:width}, Dn

where <ea> is

X	Dn	X	(d8,An,Xn)		#<data>
	An	X	(bd,An,Xn)	X	(d16,PC)
X	(An)	X	([bd,An,Xn],od)	X	(d8,PC,Xn)
	(An)+	X	([bd,An],Xn,od)	X	(bd,PC,Xn)

	-(An)	X	xxx.L	X	[(bd,PC,Xn),od]
X	(d16,An)	X	xxx.L	X	[(bd,PC),Xn,od]

Instruction Format:

15	14	13	12	11	10	9	8	7	6	5	4	3	2	1	0
1	1	1	0	1	0	0	1	1	1	Effective Address				
										Mode			Register		
0	Register			Do	Offset						Dw	Width			

Do: 0 = offset is immediate
     1 = offset is data register
Dw: 0 = width is immediate
     1 = width is data register

Condition Codes:

- N   Set if high-order bit of field is set, cleared otherwise
- Z   Set if all bits are zero, cleared otherwise
- V   Always cleared
- C   Always cleared
- X   Unaffected

Description:

This instruction copies the contents of a bit field to a data register, filling the unused bits of the register with zeros. The operand may be in a data register or in memory. The field has an offset and a width, which you can specify either through immediate data or through data registers. If you specify the offset as immediate data, it can have values from 0-31. If you specify the offset in a data register, it can have values from -2^{31} through $2^{31}-1$. The width is a value between 1 and 32.

The bit order for bit fields differs from that of individual bits in that for bit fields, the most significant bit is bit number 1. This is discussed in further detail in Chapter 12.

Example:

You have loaded an encoded long word into D0. At offset 10, a bit field starts that is 3 bits wide and represents the disk-drive status, currently valued at 101. After the instruction

                BFEXTU   D0{10:3}, D1

D1 contains 101 and the N flag is set.

BFFFO — Find First One in Bit Field

Syntax:

    BFFFO   <ea>{offset:width}, Dn

where <ea> is

X	Dn	X	(d8,An,Xn)		#<data>
	An	X	(bd,An,Xn)	X	(d16,PC)
X	(An)	X	([bd,An,Xn],od)	X	(d8,PC,Xn)
	(An)+	X	([bd,An],Xn,od)	X	(bd,PC,Xn)
	-(An)	X	xxx.L	X	[(bd,PC,Xn),od]
X	(d16,An)	X	xxx.L	X	[(bd,PC),Xn,od]

Instruction Format:

15	14	13	12	11	10	9	8	7	6	5	4	3	2	1	0
1	1	1	0	1	1	0	1	1	1	\multicolumn{4}{c} Effective Address			
1	1	1	0	1	1	0	1	1	1	Mode			Register		
0	\multicolumn{3}{c} Register			Do	\multicolumn{4}{c} Offset				Dw	\multicolumn{3}{c} Width		

Do: 0 = offset is immediate
     1 = offset is data register

Dw: 0 = width is immediate
     1 = width is data register

Condition Codes:

- **N**   Set if high-order bit of field is set, cleared otherwise
- **Z**   Set if all bits are zero, cleared otherwise
- **V**   Always cleared
- **C**   Always cleared
- **X**   Unaffected

Description:

This instruction searches the source bit field for the most significant bit that is set to 1. The processor places the bit offset (the original offset plus the offset to the first set bit) into the given data register. If the processor can't find a bit set to 1, it places the sum of the offset plus the width of the data register into the given data register. The instruction sets the condition codes based on the contents of the bit field, regardless of the result of the instruction.

The operand may be in a data register or in memory. The field has an offset and a width, which you can specify either through immediate data or through data registers. If you specify the offset as immediate data, it can have values from 0-31. If you specify the offset in a data register, it can have values from -2^{31} through $2^{31}-1$. The width is a value between 1 and 32.

Note here that the bit order for bit fields differs from that of individual bits in that for bit fields, the most significant bit is bit number 1. This is discussed in further detail in Chapter 12.

Example:

You have defined a set of 24-bit fields that represent a bit map for allocated space on a diskette (one bit field per track; each bit represents a sector). You want to find the first used sector on a track (that is, the first occurrence of a 1). If D0 contains the track number, currently 0, and BIT_MAP is the address of the bit map, then if the first available sector is sector 4,

                    BFFFO   BIT_MAP{D0:24}, D1

places a 4 into D1. No flags are set.

BFINS — Bit Field Insert

Syntax:

    BFINS   Dn, <ea>{offset:width}

where <ea> is

X	Dn	X	(d8,An,Xn)		#<data>
	An	X	(bd,An,Xn)		(d16,PC)

Descriptions of Individual MC68000 Instructions   **391**

	X	(An)		X	([bd,An,Xn],od)	(d8,PC,Xn)
		(An)+		X	([bd,An],Xn,od)	(bd,PC,Xn)
		−(An)		X	xxx.L	[(bd,PC,Xn),od]
	X	(d16,An)		X	xxx.L	[(bd,PC),Xn,od]

Instruction Format:

15	14	13	12	11	10	9	8	7	6	5	4	3	2	1	0
1	1	1	0	1	1	1	1	1	1	\multicolumn{4}{c	}{Effective Address}
										Mode			Register		
0	\multicolumn{3}{c	}{Register}	Do	\multicolumn{4}{c	}{Offset}	Dw	\multicolumn{4}{c	}{Width}

Do: 0 = offset is immediate
     1 = offset is data register
Dw: 0 = width is immediate
     1 = width is data register

Condition Codes:

N   Set if high-order bit of field is set, cleared otherwise
Z   Set if all bits are zero, cleared otherwise
V   Always cleared
C   Always cleared
X   Unaffected

Description:

This instruction inserts the bit field value in the specified source data register into the destination bit field and sets the flags based on the new bit field value. The operand can be in a data register or in memory. The field has an offset and a width, which you can specify either through immediate data or through data registers. If you specify the offset as immediate data, it can have values from 0-31. If you specify the offset in a data register, it can have values from -2^{31} through $2^{31}-1$. The width is a value between 1 and 32.

The bit order for bit fields differs from that of individual bits in that for bit fields, the most significant bit is bit number 1. This is discussed in further detail in Chapter 12.

Example:

If the first four bits of a communications message define the message type, and your message buffer begins at BUFF, then if D0 contains a 4, after

    BFINS   D0, BUFF{0:4}

the message class is set to 4 and no flags are set.

BFSET — Test Bit Field and Set

Syntax:

    BFSET   <ea>{offset:width}

where <ea> is

	X	Dn		X	(d8,An,Xn)	#<data>
		An		X	(bd,An,Xn)	(d16,PC)
	X	(An)		X	([bd,An,Xn],od)	(d8,PC,Xn)
		(An)+		X	([bd,An],Xn,od)	(bd,PC,Xn)
		−(An)		X	xxx.L	[(bd,PC,Xn),od]
	X	(d16,An)		X	xxx.L	[(bd,PC),Xn,od]

Instruction Format:

15	14	13	12	11	10	9	8	7	6	5	4	3	2	1	0
1	1	1	0	1	1	1	0	1	1	\multicolumn{2}{Efffective Address}				
1	1	1	0	1	1	1	0	1	1	Mode			Register		
0	0	0	0	Do	Offset					Dw	Width				

Condition Codes:

- N   Set if high-order bit of field is set, cleared otherwise
- Z   Set if all bits are zero, cleared otherwise
- V   Always cleared
- C   Always cleared
- X   Unaffected

Description:

This instruction tests the bit field data, sets the condition codes accordingly, and then sets the contents of the bit field to all 1s. The operand can be in a data register or in memory. The field has an offset and a width, which you may specify either through immediate data or through data registers. If you specify the offset as immediate data, it can have values from 0-31. If you specify the offset in a data register, it can have values from -2^{31} through $2^{31}-1$. The width is a value between 1 and 32.

Note here that the bit order for bit fields differs from that of individual bits in that for bit fields, the most significant bit is bit number 1.

Example:

FLAGS is the base address of a set of bit fields. At offset 39 is a 12-bit counter containing the value 34, which you want to initialize to −1. If you first load D0 with 39, then after

            BFSET   FLAGS{D0:12}

the bit field contains −1 (1111 1111 1111) and no condition flags are set.

BFTST — Test Bit Field

Syntax:

            BFTST   <ea>{offset:width}

where <ea> is

X	Dn	X	(d8,An,Xn)		#<data>
	An	X	(bd,An,Xn)	X	(d16,PC)
X	(An)	X	([bd,An,Xn],od)	X	(d8,PC,Xn)
	(An)+	X	([bd,An],Xn,od)	X	(bd,PC,Xn)
	−(An)	X	xxx.L	X	[(bd,PC,Xn),od]
X	(d16,An)	X	xxx.L	X	[(bd,PC),Xn,od]

Instruction Format:

15	14	13	12	11	10	9	8	7	6	5	4	3	2	1	0
1	1	1	0	1	0	0	0	1	1	\multicolumn{4}{c}{Effective Address}			
1	1	1	0	1	0	0	0	1	1	Mode			Register		
0	0	0	0	Do	\multicolumn{5}{c}{Offset}					Dw	\multicolumn{3}{c}{Width}		

Do: 0 = offset is immediate
1 = offset is data register
Dw: 0 = width is immediate
1 = width is data register

Condition Codes:

N   Set if high-order bit of field is set, cleared otherwise
Z   Set if all bits are zero, cleared otherwise
V   Always cleared
C   Always cleared
X   Unaffected

Description:

This instruction tests the contents of the specified bit field and sets the condition codes accordingly. The operand can be in a data register or in memory. The field has an offset and a width, which you may specify either through immediate data or through data registers. If you specify the offset as immediate data, it can have values from 0 to 31. If you specify the offset in a data register, it can have values from -2^{31} to $2^{31}-1$. The width is a value between 1 and 32.

Note here that the bit order for bit fields differs from that of individual bits in that for bit fields, the most significant bit is bit number 1. This is discussed in further detail in Chapter 12.

Example:

The 3-bit-wide bit field at offset 13 from the label BASE contains an encoded status value; the encoded value of 0 means that no status has been recorded. If its value is 101, then after

                 BFTST   BASE{13:3}

the N flag is set and the Z flag is cleared. The status value is unchanged.

BKPT — Breakpoint

Syntax:

     BKPT   #<data>

Instruction Format:

15	14	13	12	11	10	9	8	7	6	5	4	3	2	1	0
0	1	0	0	1	0	0	0	0	1	0	0	1	\multicolumn{3}{c}{Vector}		

Condition Codes:

N	Unaffected
Z	Unaffected
V	Unaffected
C	Unaffected
X	Unaffected

Description

This instruction signals external hardware that an illegal instruction has been executed. The execution of Breakpoint causes slightly different reactions on different processors:

- **MC68000 and MC68008** The processor considers this intruction to be just another illegal instruction and traps through the illegal instruction vector.
- **MC68010 and MC68012** The processor sends a special signal ("breakpoint cycle") out its bus lines to inform external hardware of the execution of an illegal instruction. The processor then traps through the illegal instruction vector.
- **MC68020** The processor sends a special signal ("breakpoint cycle") out from its bus lines to inform external hardware of the execution of an illegal instruction. The signal includes the immediate data given in the instruction. The external hardware may then provide the processor with a new instruction or it may force it to trap through the illegal instruction vector.

On the MC68000 and MC68008, the illegal instruction vector will always be at physical address $00000010. To catch the occurrence of an illegal instruction, the hardware simply monitors address and control bus lines for access to this address. On the later processors, this isn't possible, since they allow you to redefine the base address of the vector table through the vector base register (VBR). This instruction provides a means of signaling the hardware without relying on access to the illegal instruction vector.

Depending on your assembler and on the processor it is intended for, you may or may not have this instruction implemented.

Example:

After the MC68020 instruction

```
            BKPT        #3
```

the processor sends out a breakpoint cycle and then traps through vector number 4, the illegal instruction vector.

BSET — Test Bit and Set

Syntax:

```
BSET.s      Dn, <ea>
BSET.s      #data, <ea>
```

where <ea> is

X	Dn	X	(d8,An,Xn)		#<data>
	An	X	(bd,An,Xn)		(d16,PC)
X	(An)	X	([bd,An,Xn],od)		(d8,PC,Xn)
X	(An)+	X	([bd,An],Xn,od)		(bd,PC,Xn)

X	−(An)	X	xxx.L		[(bd,PC,Xn),od]
X	(d16,An)	X	xxx.L		[(bd,PC),Xn,od]

and where .s = .B or .L.

Instruction Format:

(Bit number in Dn)

15	14	13	12	11	10	9	8	7	6	5	4	3	2	1	0
0	0	0	0	Register			1	1	1	Effective Address					
										Mode			Register		

(Bit number is immediate)

15	14	13	12	11	10	9	8	7	6	5	4	3	2	1	0
0	0	0	0	1	0	0	0	1	1	Effective Address					
										Mode			Register		

Condition Codes:

- N   Unaffected
- Z   Set if tested bit is zero, cleared otherwise
- V   Unaffected
- C   Unaffected
- X   Unaffected

Description:

This instruction tests the state of a single bit in the operand, sets the Zero flag accordingly, and sets the bit's value to 1. You can specify the bit number either through a data register or through an immediate byte value. The operand can reside in a data register; in this case, the operand size is the full 32-bit width of the register. Those operands residing in memory can be byte-sized only.

You can use BSET to provide a "lock" mechanism for protecting common data in a multitasking system. Since two or more tasks may share the common data, and since any task may run at any time, one task could start manipulating the data before another has finished. This could lead to a corrupt database.

A standard means for providing protection is to define a lock flag. When this flag is set to true, the common data is in use; when false, your task can access the common data. Naturally, the first thing you'll need to do upon gaining access to the common data is to set the lock flag. The BSET flag is perfect for this since it tests and sets in the same instruction; it cannot be interrupted in between the time that it tests the flag and the time it sets the flag. (Reference the instruction BTST, which only tests the bit state.)

The instruction can be interrupted in the middle of its execution by a hardware bus request signal (different from peripheral interrupt), which can occur in a system that contains more than one CPU. If your system is such, you should use TAS or CAS instead of the BSET or BCLR. These instructions are indivisible even by a bus request.

Example:

Bit number 3 of the byte in memory at the label LOCKS may constitute the lock for a common data. The following piece of code will test for the lock condition:

```
BSET.B      #3, LOCKS
BNE         WAIT
```

If the bit was set (indicating lock), it remains set and the Z flag is cleared; the program branched to WAIT. If the bit was not set (indicating unlock), the instruction sets the bit (indicating lock), sets the Z flag, and falls through the BNE instruction.

BSR — Branch to Subroutine

Syntax:

BSR   <offset>

Instruction Format:

15	14	13	12	11	10	9	8	7	6	5	4	3	2	1	0
0	1	1	0	0	0	0	0	\multicolumn{8}{c	}{8-Bit Displacement}

| 16-Bit Displacement if 8-Bit Displacement = $00 |
| 32-Bit Displacement if 8-Bit Displacement = $FF |

Condition Codes:

N	Unaffected
Z	Unaffected
V	Unaffected
C	Unaffected
X	Unaffected

Description:

This instruction branches to the subroutine indicated by the offset value. Normally, this value is a program label that the assembler converts to an offset value. When this instruction is executed, the processor pushes the address of the instruction that follows the BSR instruction onto the stack. It then adds the value of the displacement to the PC (BSR instruction address plus 2) and begins execution at the new PC. Since the displacement is signed, the subroutine address may be ahead of or behind the current address.

This instruction differs from the JSR instruction in that the only addressing mode allowed is PC relative. This limitation is an advantage in that the processor can execute the instruction faster in this mode, and, in some cases, the instruction doesn't take up as much room as it would in other addressing modes.

Example:

If SUB1 is a label of a subroutine, then

```
BSR         SUB1
```

calls the subroutine SUB1.

BTST—Test Bit

Syntax:
BTST.s   Dn, <ea>
BTST.s   #data, <ea>

where <ea> is

X Dn	X (d8,An,Xn)	# <data>
An	X (Bd,An,Xn)	X (d16,PC)
X (An)	X ([bd,An,Xn],od)	X (d8,PC,Xn)
X (An)+	X ([bd,An],Xn,od)	X (bd,PC,Xn)
X −(An)	X xxx.L	X [(bd,PC,Xn),od]
X (d16,An)	X xxx.L	X [(bd,PC),Xn,od]

and where .s = .B or .L.

Instruction Format:

(Bit number in Dn)

15	14	13	12	11	10	9	8	7	6	5	4	3	2	1	0
0	0	0	0	\multicolumn{3}{c}{Register}	1	0	0	\multicolumn{6}{c}{Effective Address}

15	14	13	12	11	10	9	8	7	6	5	4	3	2	1	0
0	0	0	0	Register			1	0	0	Mode			Register		

(Bit number is immediate)

15	14	13	12	11	10	9	8	7	6	5	4	3	2	1	0
0	0	0	0	1	0	0	0	0	0	Mode			Register		

Condition Codes:

N	Unaffected
Z	Set if tested bit is zero, cleared otherwise
V	Unaffected
C	Unaffected
X	Unaffected

Description:
This instruction tests the state of a single bit in the operand and sets the Zero flag accordingly. The bit's value remains unchanged. You can specify the bit number either through a data register or through an immediate byte value. The operand can reside in a data register; in this case, the operand size is the full 32-bit width of the register. Those operands residing in memory can be byte-sized only.

Example:
In your application, several factors of a calculation may determine whether or not to print a value. As you test, if you find that you should print the value, you set a bit flag (bit 25) in data register D7. At the end of the loop, you test to see if you should print the value. With

the instructions

                  BTST.L   #25, D7
                  BNE   PRINT_SUM

if the bit is set, then the program branches to PRINT_SUM.

CALLM — Call Module (MC68020 Only)

Syntax:

    CALLM   #<data>, <ea>

where <ea> is

Dn	X (d8,An,Xn)	#<data>	
An	X (bd,An,Xn)	X (d16,PC)	
X (An)	X ([bd,An,Xn],od)	X (d8,PC,Xn)	
(An)+	X ([bd,An],Xn,od)	X (bd,PC,Xn)	
−(An)	X xxx.L	X [(bd,PC,Xn),od]	
X (d16,An)	X xxx.L	X [(bd,PC),Xn,od]	

Instruction Format:

15	14	13	12	11	10	9	8	7	6	5	4	3	2	1	0
										\multicolumn{6}{c}{Effective Address}						
0	0	0	0	0	1	1	0	1	1	\multicolumn{3}{c}{Mode}	\multicolumn{3}{c}{Register}			
0	0	0	0	0	0	0	0	\multicolumn{8}{c}{Argument Count}							

Condition Codes:

    N   Unaffected
    Z   Unaffected
    V   Unaffected
    C   Unaffected
    X   Unaffected

Description:

This instruction (MC68020 only) creates and files a module stack frame on the stack, loads the processor with the data provided by the module descriptor (in the effective address), and begins execution at the new address (as provided in the module descriptor). This instruction, when used in a system with the proper hardware configuration, provides a finer degree of memory access than is provided with the user/supervisor modes. The RTM instruction performs the opposite of this instruction: it restores a processor state from the stack frame.

By using several control lines, the processor can tell external hardware to use different locations for memory than it would use for normal program reads and writes. In this special memory, called "CPU space," certain locations define access-control hardware. When executed, this instruction compares the requested access level with that in the CPU space descriptors. If permission is granted, the processor continues with the instruction; if hardware says that permission is denied, the instruction traps through the format-error exception.

This instruction is used only in advanced systems that have the necessary hardware for granting or denying access. In your applications, you are unlikely to encounter it.

CAS — Compare and Swap (MC68020 only)

Syntax:

    CAS.s   Dc, Du, <ea>

where <ea> is

	Dn	X	(d8,An,Xn)	#<data>
	An	X	(bd,An,Xn)	(d16,PC)
X	(An)	X	([bd,An,Xn],od)	(d8,PC,Xn)
X	(An)+	X	([bd,An],Xn,od)	(bd,PC,Xn)
X	−(An)	X	xxx.L	[(bd,PC,Xn),od]
X	(d16,An)	X	xxx.L	[(bd,PC),Xn,od]

and where .s = .B, .W, or .L.

Instruction Format:

15	14	13	12	11	10	9	8	7	6	5	4	3	2	1	0
0	0	0	0	1	Size		0	1	1	Effective Address			
										Mode			Register		
0	0	0	0	0	0	0		Du			0	0	0	Dc	

Size field: 01 = byte   10 = word   11 = long

Condition Codes:

    N   Set if high-order bit of result is set, cleared otherwise
    Z   Set if result is zero, cleared otherwise
    V   Set if compare generates an overflow, cleared otherwise
    C   Set if compare generates a carry, cleared otherwise
    X   Unaffected

Description:

This instruction subtracts the value in the **"compare" data** register (labeled "Dc" in the preceding syntax) from the destination operand (<ea>), and sets the condition codes accordingly. If the Zero (Z) flag is set, the processor moves the value in the update register (labeled "Du" in the syntax) to the destination operand.

In a standard test and change instruction (such as BSET), the processor could be interrupted by a bus request in between the time it tests the operand (with a read cycle) and the time it sets the operand (with a write cycle). In a multiprocessor environment, another processor could potentially gain control of the bus in between cycles and change the value of the operand, thus corrupting its value. **The processor executes the CAS instruction using a** special type of bus cycle called a "read-modify-write" cycle; that action prevents another processor from interfering with the instruction while it does its compare and swap operation.

Example:
You have several CPUs in your system and have defined a queue in **"global" memory (all processors in the system have access to its data)**. The queue is first-in-first-out and uses linked lists (see Chapter 9). Since any processor can manipulate the queue and its pointers, you must provide some means of locking out other processors while your task inserts or deletes from the queue.

One method of doing this is to provide a "lock" byte that you can manipulate with the TAS instruction (which also uses a read-modify-write cycle). However, the CAS instruction is more applicable here, as is shown by the code segment that follows. In this example, HEAD is a memory value pointing to the first element in the queue, NEW_NODE is the address of a new queue element, and LINK is a constant defining the offset within a queue element that contains a pointer to the next element.

```
            MOVEA.L     NEWNODE, A0
            LEA         HEAD, A2
LOOP        MOVE.L      D0, (LINK,A0)
            MOVE.L      A0, D1
            CAS.L       D0, D1, (A2)
            BNE         LOOP
```

In this example, there are several tentative pointers prior to the CAS instruction: A0 and D1 point to the new node, D0 points to the current HEAD, and the LINK pointer in NEW_NODE points to the current HEAD. When the processor executes the CAS instruction, one of two conditions is true:

1. another processor may have changed the HEAD pointer
2. the HEAD pointer is the same

In the first case, the compare will fail, the swap won't take place, and the Z flag will be cleared, forcing a branch to the top. In the second case, the compare passes, so the pointer to NEW_NODE takes the place of HEAD and the Z flag is set, allowing the program to pass through the BNE instruction. While the swap takes place, the current processor has control of the bus, so that no other processor can modify the value of HEAD.

To remove an element from the queue, you would work to the end of the queue and swap the pointer to the last link with a local pointer, substituting the link with a NULL value.

CAS2 — Compare and Swap Two Values

Syntax:
    CAS2.s   Dc1:Dc2, Du1:Du2, (Rn1):(Rn2)
    where .s = .W or .L.

Instruction Format:

15	14	13	12	11	10	9	8	7	6	5	4	3	2	1	0
0	0	0	0	1	Size		0	1	1	1	1	1	1	0	0
D/A	Register 1			0	0	0	Du1			0	0	0	Dc1		
D/A	Register 2			0	0	0	Du2			0	0	0	Dc2		

Size field: 01 = byte 10 = word 11 = long

Condition Codes:

- **N** Set if high-order bit of result is set, cleared otherwise
- **Z** Set if result is zero, cleared otherwise
- **V** Set if compare generates an overflow, cleared otherwise
- **C** Set if compare generates a carry, cleared otherwise
- **X** Unaffected

Description:

This instruction subtracts the values in the compare data registers (labeled "Dc1" and "Dc2" in the syntax) from the two destination operands (pointed to by the registers labeled "Rn1" and "Rn2"), and sets the condition codes accordingly. If the Zero (Z) flag is set, the processor moves the values in the update register (labeled "Du1" and "Du2" in the syntax) to the destination operands. Note that in this unique case, data registers can function as address registers.

In a standard test and change instruction (such as BSET), the processor could be interrupted by a bus request in between the time it tests the operand with a read cycle and the time it sets the operand with a write cycle. In a multiprocessor environment, another processor could potentially gain control of the bus in between cycles and change the value of the operand, thus corrupting its value. The processor executes the CAS2 instruction using a special type of bus cycle called a read-modify-write cycle; this prevents another processor from interfering with the instruction while it does its compare and swap operation.

Example:

You have a multiprocessor system, in which you have defined a global first-in-first-out queue. You've implemented the queue using doubly linked lists and have a "get" pointer (indicating the next element to be removed) and a "put" pointer (indicating the last element queued). Since multiple processors have access to the queue, you must provide a means of protecting the get and put pointers while you manipulate them. You can do so by using the CAS2 instruction, since it lets you adjust two values at once.

In this example, PUT contains the address of the latest element, GET contains the address of the oldest element, and NEW contains the address of an element to add to the queue (after PUT). FORWARD and BACKWARD are constants that define the offset in the element structure where pointers ahead and behind are found.

```
              LEA            PUT, A0
              LEA            GET, A1
              MOVEA.L        NEW, A2
              MOVE.L         A2, D2
LOOP          MOVE.L         (A0), D0
              BEQ            EMPTY
              MOVE.L         D0, (FORWARD,A2)
              CLR.L          D1
              MOVE.L         D1, (BACKWARD,A2)
              LEA            (BACKWARD,A2), A1
              CAS2.L         D0:D1, D2:D0, (A0):(A1)
              BNE            LOOP
              BRA            DONE
EMPTY         MOVE.L         D0, (FORWARD,A2)
              MOVE.L         D0, (BACKWARD,A2)
              CAS2.L         D0:D0, D2:D2, (A0):(A1)
              BNE            LOOP
DONE          ...
```

In this example, prior to the CAS2 instruction, the pointers in the NEW element have been set up so that they point back to the current PUT and ahead to a null element. At the time of the CAS2, D0 points to the original PUT value, D1 points to a null element (value 0), D2 points to the NEW element, A0 contains PUT's address, and A1 contains a pointer to the BACKWARD pointer of the NEW element. When the processor executes the CAS2 instruction, if the PUT value hasn't changed, the NEW element is added to the list.

Note the special case when the list contains no elements (PUT is null); you load NEW's pointers with a null pointer and try to update GET and PUT.

CHK — Check Register Against Boundaries

Syntax:

    CHK.s   <ea>, Dn

    where <ea> is

X	Dn	X	(d8,An,Xn)	X	#<data>
	An	X	(bd,An,Xn)	X	(d16,PC)
X	(An)	X	([bd,An,Xn],od)	X	(d8,PC,Xn)
X	(An)+	X	([bd,An],Xn,od)	X	(bd,PC,Xn)
X	−(An)	X	xxx.L	X	[(bd,PC,Xn),od]
X	(d16,An)	X	xxx.L	X	[(bd,PC),Xn,od]

and where .s = .W or .L (.L for MC68020 only).

Instruction Format:

15	14	13	12	11	10	9	8	7	6	5	4	3	2	1	0
0	1	0	0	Data Register			Size		0	Effective Address					
										Mode			Register		

Size field: 10 = Long word (MC68020)
            11 = Word

Condition Codes:

    N   Set if Dn<0, cleared if Dn>source, undefined otherwise
    Z   Undefined

Descriptions of Individual MC68000 Instructions   403

V	Undefined
C	Undefined
X	Unaffected

Description:

This instruction compares the contents of a data register to the contents of the source operand. If the data register value is less than zero or greater than the source operand, the processor traps through exception vector 6 (offset $18) in the vector table. Naturally, you or the operating system should have defined a handler address at this vector. For a complete discussion of the sequences that occur during exception processing, refer to Chapter 14.

The long-word operand version of the instruction is valid only on the MC68020; the other processors only support the 16-bit operand.

Example:

This instruction is useful for maintaining array subscripts since you can subscript against an upper bounds before using it to fetch or store data. For example, you can define a byte array called TABLE that contains 100 entries, subcripted 0 to 99. If the word at the label TAB_SIZ contains the value 99, and D0 contains a potential subscript, then after

    CHK.W   TAB_SIZ, D0

if D0 contains a legitimate value, the program will continue normal execution. If the value is out of range, however, then the processor will trap through the CHK vector.

CHK2 — Check Register Against Bounds (MC68020 Only)

Syntax:

    CHK2.s   <ea>, Rn

where <ea> is

	Dn	X	(d8,An,Xn)		#<data>
	An	X	(bd,An,Xn)	X	(d16,PC)
X	(An)	X	([bd,An,Xn],od)	X	(d8,PC,Xn)
	(An)+	X	([bd,An],Xn,od)	X	(bd,PC,Xn)
X	−(An)	X	xxx.L	X	[(bd,PC,Xn),od]
X	(d16,An)	X	xxx.L	X	[(bd,PC),Xn,od]

and where .s = .B, .W, or .L.

Instruction Format:

15	14	13	12	11	10	9	8	7	6	5	4	3	2	1	0
0	0	0	0	0	Size		0	1	1	Effective Address					
										Mode			Register		
A/D	Register			1	0	0	0	0	0	0	0	0	0	0	0

Size field: 00 = byte 01 = word 10 = long

Condition Codes:

N	Undefined
Z	Set if Rn is equal to either boundary, cleared otherwise
V	Undefined
C	Set if Rn is out of bounds, cleared otherwise
X	Unaffected

Description:

This instruction compares a value in a data or address register against signed upper and lower boundaries. The bounds reside in memory; the lower boundary is at the address specified in the instruction; the upper boundary is at that address plus the operand size (that is, +1 for byte, +2 for word, and +4 for long word).

If the comparison falls in the range specified, the processor continues normal execution. If the comparison fails, then the processor begins exception processing using the CHK/CHK2 exception vector (vector number 6 at offset $18). (Refer to Chapter 14 for further information on exception processing sequences.)

Refer to the CMP2 instruction for a bounds test that does not generate an exception for out-of-bounds conditions.

Example:

In your application, you have defined an array of 100 elements with subscripts ranging from −50-49. If the two bytes at TAB_RANGE contain −50 and 49, respectively, and D0 contains a 100, then

        CHK2.B   TAB_RANGE, D0

causes a trap through the CHK/CHK2 exception vector.

CLR — Clear an Operand

Syntax:

    CLR.s   <ea>

where <ea> is

X	Dn	X	(d8,An,Xn)		#<data>
	An	X	(bd,An,Xn)		(d16,PC)
X	(An)	X	([bd,An,Xn],od)		(d8,PC,Xn)
X	(An)+	X	([bd,An],Xn,od)		(bd,PC,Xn)
X	−(An)	X	xxx.L		[(bd,PC,Xn),od]
X	(d16,An)	X	xxx.L		[(bd,PC),Xn,od]

and where .s = .B, .W, or .L.

Instruction Format:

15	14	13	12	11	10	9	8	7	6	5	4	3	2	1	0
0	1	0	0	0	0	1	0	Size		Effective Address					
										Mode			Register		

Size field: 00 = byte   01 = word   10 = long

Condition Codes:

N	Cleared
Z	Set
V	Cleared
C	Cleared
X	Unaffected

Description:

This instruction moves a zero to the specified operand.

Example:

If D0 contains the value $5400200F, then after

                CLR.L   D0

D0 contains $00000000.

CMP — Compare

Syntax:

    CMP.s   <ea>, Dn

where <ea> is

X	Dn	X	(d8,An,Xn)	X	#<data>
X	An	X	(bd,An,Xn)	X	(d16,PC)
X	(An)	X	([bd,An,Xn],od)	X	(d8,PC,Xn)
X	(An)+	X	([bd,An],Xn,od)	X	(bd,PC,Xn)
X	−(An)	X	xxx.L	X	[(bd,PC,Xn),od]
X	(d16,An)	X	xxx.L	X	[(bd,PC),Xn,od]

and where .s = .B, .W, or .L.

Instruction Format:

15	14	13	12	11	10	9	8	7	6	5	4	3	2	1	0
1	0	1	1	Data Register			Op-Mode			Effective Address					
										Mode			Register		

Op-Mode field: **Byte**   **Word**   **Long**   **Operation**
                         000   001   010   (<Dn>)−(<ea>)

Condition Codes:

N	Set if Dn−source, cleared otherwise
Z	Set if Dn−source, cleared otherwise
V	Set if Dn−source operation generates an overflow, cleared otherwise
C	Set if Dn−source operation requires a borrow, cleared otherwise
X	Unaffected

Description:

This instruction subtracts the contents of the source operand from a data register and sets the condition codes appropriately. The result of the subtraction is thrown away. The order of the operands is not necessarily the same as the order of the comparison performed by the instruction; it compares the destination to the source, not vice versa.

Example:

If D0 contains a $700 and D1 contains a $600, then

```
        CMP.W       D0, D1
        BLT         LABEL1
```

causes a branch to LABEL1 (D1 is less than D0).

CMPA — Compare Addresses

Syntax:

CMPA.s   <ea>, An

where <ea> is

X Dn	X (d8,An,Xn)	X #<data>
X An	X (bd,An,Xn)	X (d16,PC)
X (An)	X ([bd,An,Xn],od)	X (d8,PC,Xn)
X (An)+	X ([bd,An],Xn,od)	X (bd,PC,Xn)
X −(An)	X xxx.L	X [(bd,PC,Xn),od]
X (d16,An)	X xxx.L	X [(bd,PC),Xn,od]

and where .s = .W or .L.

Instruction Format:

15	14	13	12	11	10	9	8	7	6	5	4	3	2	1	0
1	0	1	1	Data Register			Op-Mode			Effective Address				
											Mode			Register		

Op-Mode field: Word   Long   Operation
                  011   111   (<An> − (<ea>))

Condition Codes:

N   Set if An − source, cleared otherwise
Z   Set if An − source, cleared otherwise
V   Set if An − source operation generates an overflow, cleared otherwise
C   Set if An − source operation requires a borrow, cleared otherwise
X   Unaffected

Description:

This instruction subtracts the source operand from the given address register and sets the condition codes accordingly. The result of the subtraction is thrown away. The order of the operands is not necessarily the same as the order in which the instruction makes its comparison; it compares the address register to the source operand, not vice versa.

Example:

If you are working through a TABLE that is $100 bytes long, using A0 as a pointer into the table, then

        CMPA.L   #TABLE+$100, A0
        BNE   MORE

will cause a branch to the label MORE until the two values are equal.

CMPI — Compare Immediate

Syntax:

    CMPI.s   #<data>, <ea>

where <ea> is

X Dn	X (d8,An,Xn)	#<data>
An	X (bd,An,Xn)	X (d16,PC)
X (An)	X ([bd,An,Xn],od)	X (d8,PC,Xn)
X (An)+	X ([bd,An],Xn,od)	X (bd,PC,Xn)
X -(An)	X xxx.L	X [(bd,PC,Xn),od]
X (d16,An)	X xxx.L	X [(bd,PC),Xn,od]

and where .s = .B, .W, or .L.

Instruction Format:

15	14	13	12	11	10	9	8	7	6	5	4	3	2	1	0
0	0	0	0	1	1	0	0	\multicolumn{2}{c}{Size}	\multicolumn{6}{c}{Effective Address}

| | | | | | | | | | | Mode | | | Register | | |

Size field: 00 = byte 01 = word 10 = long

Condition Codes:

    N   Set if <ea> < data, cleared otherwise
    Z   Set if <ea> = data, cleared otherwise
    V   Set if <ea> - data operation generates an overflow, cleared otherwise
    C   Set if <ea> - data operation requires a borrow, cleared otherwise
    X   Unaffected

Description:

This instruction subtracts the immediate source data from the destination operand and sets the condition codes accordingly. The result of the subtraction is thrown away. The order of the operands is not necessarily the same as the order in which the instruction performs the comparison; it compares the second operand to the first, not vice versa.

Example:

The value defined by the constant HIVAL defines the maximum value for the long variable at the label COUNTS. If COUNTS has exceeded HIVAL, then after

                    CMPI.L   #HIVAL, COUNTS

the N, Z, V, and C flags are all clear.

CMPM — Compare Memory

Syntax:
　　CMPM.s　　(Asrc)+,(Adst)+

where .s = .B, .W, or .L.

Instruction Format:

15	14	13	12	11	10	9	8	7	6	5	4	3	2	1	0
1	0	1	1	Destination Register			1	Size		0	0	1	Source Register		

Size field: 00 = byte　01 = word　10 = long

Condition Codes:
- **N**　Set if (Adst) < (Asrc), cleared otherwise
- **Z**　Set if (Adst) = (Asrc), cleared otherwise
- **V**　Set if (Adst) − (Asrc) operation generates an overflow, cleared otherwise
- **C**　Set if (Adst) − (Asrc) operation requires a borrow, cleared otherwise
- **X**　Unaffected

Description:
This instruction subtracts the value pointed to by Asrc from the value pointed to by Adst and sets the condition codes accordingly. The result of the subtraction is thrown away. After performing the operation, both address registers are incremented according to the size of the operation.

The order of the operands is not necessarily obvious for a comparison; it compares the second operand to the first, not vice versa.

Example:
You need to compare two strings in memory for equality. If A0 and A1 both point to strings, then

　　　　　CMPM.B　　(A0)+, (A1)+

compares the byte pointed to by A0 to the one pointed to by A1. If they are equal, the Z flag is set; otherwise, the Z flag is cleared. You might follow this instruction with a conditional branch (B_{cc}) or a decrement/test/branch (DB_{cc}) instruction.

CMP2 — Compare Register Against Bounds
(MC68020 only)

Syntax:
　　CMP2.s　　　<ea>, Rn

where <ea> is

	Dn	X	(d8,An,Xn)		#<data>
	An	X	(bd,An,Xn)	X	(d16,PC)
X	(An)	X	([bd,An,Xn],od)	X	(d8,PC,Xn)
	(An)+	X	([bd,An],Xn,od)	X	(bd,PC,Xn)
	−(An)	X	xxx.L	X	[(bd,PC),Xn,od]
X	(d16,An)	X	xxx.L	X	[(bd,PC),Xn,od]

and where .s = .B, .W, and .L .

Instruction Format:

15	14	13	12	11	10	9	8	7	6	5	4	3	2	1	0
0	0	0	0	0	Size		0	1	1	\multicolumn{6}{c}{Effective Address}
										Mode			Register		
A/D	\multicolumn{3}{c}{Register}	0	0	0	0	0	0	0	0	0	0	0	0

Size field: 00 = byte 01 = word 10 = long

Condition Codes:

N	Undefined
Z	Set if Rn is equal to either boundary, cleared
V	Undefined
C	Set if Rn is out of bounds, cleared otherwise
X	Unaffected

Description:

This instruction compares a value in a data or address register against signed upper and lower boundaries. The bounds reside in memory; the lower boundary is at the address specified in the instruction; the upper boundary is at that address plus the operand size (that is, +1 for a byte, +2 for a word, or +4 for a long word).

This instruction is analogous to the CHK2 instruction except that it does not cause an exception if the register value is out of bounds.

Example:

Your application reads in a number of entries from the user. You must verify that each entry is valid by comparing them to valid ranges. If D0 contains a user-entered value and REC_RANGE points to a range for that value, then

        CMP2   REC_RANGE, D0

verifies that the entry is in range. If the value is in range, the C flag is clear; if it is out of range, the C flag is set.

DB_{cc} — Test, Decrement, and Branch

Syntax:

    DB_{cc} Dn, displacement

Instruction Format:

15	14	13	12	11	10	9	8	7	6	5	4	3	2	1	0
0	1	0	1	Condition					1	1	0	0	1	Data Register		

Condition Codes:
- N   Unaffected
- Z   Unaffected
- V   Unaffected
- C   Unaffected
- X   Unaffected

Description:

This instruction tests the condition codes to see if they match a given condition. If they do match, the instruction is complete and the program continues with the next instruction. If that condition is not met, the processor decrements the given data register. If its new value is -1, then the instruction is complete and the program continues to the next instruction. If the value is something other than -1, the processor adds the 16-bit displacement value to the program counter and begins execution at the new address. The conditions possible are shown in Table 21-2.

Normally, you will specify the displacement value in terms of a statement label. The assembler then calculates the appropriate signed displacement (positive or negative) and inserts it into the instruction extension word.

Note the difference between the B_{cc} and DB_{cc} instructions; for B_{cc}, the branch is taken when the condition is true; for DB_{cc}, the branch will never be taken when the condition is true. For a further discussion of this instruction, refer to Chapter 6.

Table 21-2. DB_{cc} Conditional Tests

Mnemonics(cc)	Condition	Condition Field	Test
T	True	0000	1
F	False	0001	0
HI	High	0010	$\overline{C} \cdot \overline{Z}$
LS	Low or same	0011	$C \vee Z$
CC	Carry clear	0100	$\overline{C}$
CS	Carry set	0101	C
NE	Not equal	0110	$\overline{Z}$
EQ	Equal	0111	Z
VC	Overflow clear	1000	$\overline{V}$
VS	Overflow set	1001	V
PL	Plus	1010	$\overline{N}$
MI	Minus	1011	N
GE	Greater or equal	1100	$(N \cdot V) \vee (\overline{N} \cdot \overline{V})$
LT	Less than	1101	$(N \cdot \overline{V}) \vee (\overline{N} \cdot V)$
GT	Greater than	1110	$(N \cdot V \cdot \overline{Z}) \vee (\overline{N} \cdot \overline{V} \cdot \overline{Z})$
LE	Less or equal	1111	$Z \vee (N \cdot \overline{V}) \vee (\overline{N} \cdot V)$

Example:

A0 and A1 contain pointers to text strings, and D0 contains the maximum length of each string minus 1. The instructions

```
LOOP    CMPM.B   (A0)+, (A1)+
        DBNE     D0, LOOP
```

repetitively test the equality of each character of the strings. As long as they are equal and D0 is not equal to -1, the processor will keep looping. When a difference is found (the NE condition is true), or when D0 has been decremented to -1, the test fails and the execution proceeds sequentially.

DIVS/DIVSL — Signed Divide

Syntax:

DIVS.W	<ea>, Dn	
DIVS.L	<ea>, Dq	(MC68020 only)
DIVS.L	<ea>, Dr:Dq	(MC68020 only)
DIVSL.L	<ea>, Dr:Dq	(MC68020 only)

where <ea> is

X	Dn	X	(d8,An,Xn)	X	#<data>
	An	X	(bd,An,Xn)	X	(d16,PC)
X	(An)	X	([bd,An,Xn],od)	X	(d8,PC,Xn)
X	(An)+	X	([bd,An],Xn,od)	X	(bd,PC,Xn)
X	-(An)	X	xxx.L	X	[(bd,PC,Xn),od]
X	(d16,An)	X	xxx.L	X	[(bd,PC),Xn,od]

Instruction Format:

(Long)

15	14	13	12	11	10	9	8	7	6	5	4	3	2	1	0
0	1	0	0	1	1	0	0	0	1	Effective Address: Mode			Register		
0	Dq			1	Size	0	0	0	0	0	0	0		Dr	

Size field: 0 = Long word dividend
1 = Quad word dividend

(Word)

15	14	13	12	11	10	9	8	7	6	5	4	3	2	1	0
1	0	0	0	Register				1	1	1	Effective Address: Mode / Register				

Condition Codes:

- **N**   Set if quotient is negative, cleared otherwise; undefined if overflow or divide by zero.
- **Z**   Set if quotient is zero, cleared otherwise; undefined if overflow or divide by zero.
- **V**   Set if division overflow, cleared otherwise
- **C**   Always cleared
- **X**   Unaffected

Description:

These instructions divide the destination operand by the source and store the result in the destination. The processor considers the sign of the source and destination when computing the answer. The word division instruction is available on all processors; the long division instructions are available only on the MC68020.

The DIVS.W instruction works as follows: the processor divides the 32-bit dividend (in the destination register) by the 16-bit divisor. It then stores the 16-bit remainder of the division in bits 16-31 of the destination register and stores the 16-bit quotient in bits 0-15 of the destination register.

In the first long-word form (DIVS.L <ea>,Dq), the processor divides the 32-bit dividend (from the destination register) by the 32-bit source operand. It then stores the 32-bit quotient in the destination register, discarding the remainder.

In the second long-word form (DIVS.L <ea>,Dr:Dq), the processor operates on a 64-bit dividend contained in a destination register pair: the first register (Dr) containing the most significant long word, and the second (Dq) containing the least significant long word. It divides this "quad word" by the 32-bit source operand, storing the 32-bit remainder in the first register (Dr) and the 32-bit quotient in the second (Dq).

In the third long-word form, (DIVSL.L <ea>,Dr:Dq), the processor divides a 32-bit long word (from the Dq register) by the 32-bit source operand, storing the 32-bit remainder in the first register (Dr) and the 32-bit quotient in the second (Dq). The original value in Dr is discarded.

For the modes supporting register pairs, you can select any of the data registers; they needn't be adjacent or in numerical order.

The division can cause two error conditions. A division by zero causes a trap through vector number 5 (offset $14) in the exception table. If the quotient of the division is too big to fit into the destination, the Overflow flag is set.

Example:

If D0 contains 677, then after

```
            DIVS.W      #25, D0
```

the high word of D0 contains 2 (the remainder) and the low word of D0 contains 27 (the quotient).

DIVU/DIVUL — Unsigned Divide

Syntax:

```
DIVU.W          <ea>, Dn
DIVU.L          <ea>, Dq         (MC68020 only)
DIVU.L          <ea>, Dr:Dq      (MC68020 only)
DIVUL.L         <ea>, Dr:Dq      (MC68020 only
```

where <ea> is

X	Dn	X	(d8,An,Xn)	X	#<data>
	An	X	(bd,An,Xn)	X	(d16,PC)
X	(An)	X	([bd,An,Xn],od)	X	(d8,PC,Xn)
X	(An)+	X	([bd,An],Xn,od)	X	(bd,PC,Xn)
X	−(An)	X	xxx.L	X	[(bd,PC,Xn),od]
X	(d16,An)	X	xxx.L	X	[(bd,PC),Xn,od]

Descriptions of Individual MC68000 Instructions 413

Instruction Format:

15	14	13	12	11	10	9	8	7	6	5	4	3	2	1	0
0	1	0	0	1	1	0	0	0	1	\multicolumn{2}{c}{Effective Address}				

15	14	13	12	11	10	9	8	7	6	5	4	3	2	1	0
0	1	0	0	1	1	0	0	0	1	Mode			Register		
0	Dq			0	Size	0	0	0	0	0	0	0	Dr		

(Long)

15	14	13	12	11	10	9	8	7	6	5	4	3	2	1	0
1	0	0	0	Register			0	1	1	Effective Address					
										Mode			Register		

Condition Codes:

N Set if quotient is negative, cleared otherwise; undefined if overflow or divide by zero

Z Set if quotient is zero, cleared otherwise; undefined if overflow or divide by zero

V Set if division overflow, cleared otherwise

C Always cleared

X Unaffected

Description:

These instructions divide the destination operand by the source and store the result in the destination. The processor ignores the sign of the source and destination when computing the answer. The word-division instruction is available on all processors; the long-division instructions are available only on the MC68020.

The DIVU.W instruction works as follows: the processor divides the 32-bit dividend (in the destination register) by the 16-bit divisor. It then stores the 16-bit remainder of the division in bits 16-31 of the destination register and stores the 16-bit quotient in bits 0-15 of the destination register.

In the first long-word form (DIVU.L <ea>,Dq), the processor divides the 32-bit dividend (from the destination register) by the 32-bit source operand. It then stores the 32-bit quotient in the destination register, discarding the remainder.

In the second long-word form (DIVU.L<ea>,Dr:Dq), the processor operates on a 64-bit dividend contained in a destination register pair: the first register (Dr) containing the most significant long word, and the second (Dq) containing the least significant long word. It divides this "quad word" by the 32-bit source operand, storing the 32-bit remainder in the first register (Dr) and the 32-bit quotient in the second (Dq).

In the third long-word form, (DIVUL.L <ea>,Dr:Dq), the processor divides a 32-bit long word (from the Dq register) by the 32-bit source operand, storing the 32-bit remainder in the first register (Dr) and the 32-bit quotient in the second (Dq). The original value in Dr is discarded.

For the modes supporting register pairs, you can select any of the data registers; they needn't be adjacent or in numerical order.

The division can cause two error conditions. A division by zero causes a trap through vector number 5 (offset $14) in the exception table. If the quotient of the division is too big to fit into the destination, the Overflow flag is set.

Example:

If register D0 contains 240122005, D4 contains 235, and the long word at the label DIVISOR contains 3504, then after

        DIVUL.L   DIVISOR, D4:D0

D4 contains 3397 (the remainder) and D0 contains 68527 (the quotient).

EOR — Exclusive OR

Syntax:

    EOR.s   Dn, <ea>

where <ea> is

X Dn	X (d8,An,Xn)	#<data>
An	X (bd,An,Xn)	(d16,PC)
X (An)	X ([bd,An,Xn],od)	(d8,PC,Xn)
X (An)+	X ([bd,An],Xn,od)	(bd,PC,Xn)
X −(An)	X xxx.L	[(bd,PC,Xn),od]
X (d16,An)	X xxx.L	[(bd,PC),Xn,od]

and where .s = .B, .W, or .L.

Instruction Format:

15	14	13	12	11	10	9	8	7	6	5	4	3	2	1	0
1	0	1	1	Data Register			Op-Mode			Effective Address				
										Mode			Register		

Op-Mode field: **Byte**   **Word**   **Long**   **Operation**
                      100   101   110   (<ea>) ⊕ (<Dn>) → <ea>

Condition Codes:

N	Set if high-order bit of result is set, cleared otherwise
Z	Set if result is zero, cleared otherwise
V	Cleared
C	Cleared
X	Unaffected

Description:

This instruction performs a bitwise Exclusive OR of the contents of a data register with the contents of the destination operand and stores the results in the destination. EOR is commonly used to calculate checksums in communications messages.

Example:

If D0 contains $E3 and A3 points to a byte containing $A0, then

        EOR.B   D0, (A3)

moves the value $43 into (A3). This is calculated as

D0	= $E3	= 11100011
(A3)	= $A0	= 10100000
(A3)	= $43	= 01000011

EORI — Exclusive OR Immediate

Syntax:

    EORI.s   #<data>, <ea>

where <ea> is

X	Dn	X	(d8,An,Xn)		#<data>
	An	X	(bd,An,Xn)		(d16,PC)
X	(An)	X	([bd,An,Xn],od)		(d8,PC,Xn)
X	(An)+	X	([bd,An],Xn,od)		(bd,PC,Xn)
X	−(An)	X	xxx.L		[(bd,PC,Xn),od]
X	(d16,An)	X	xxx.L		[(bd,PC),Xn,od]

and where .s = .B, .W, or .L.

Instruction Format:

15	14	13	12	11	10	9	8	7	6	5	4	3	2	1	0
0	0	0	0	1	0	1	0	\multicolumn{2}{	c	}{Size}	\multicolumn{6}{	c	}{Effective Address}

| | | | | | | | | | | Mode | | | Register | | |

Size field: 00 = byte   01 = word   10 = long

Condition Codes:

    N   Set if high-order bit of result is set, cleared otherwise
    Z   Set if result is zero, cleared otherwise
    V   Cleared
    C   Cleared
    X   Unaffected

Description:

This instruction exclusively ORs the immediate data to the destination operand, storing the result in the destination.

Example:

If D0 contains $5522, then

                 EOR.W   #$B31C, D0

moves the value $E63E into D0.

EORI to CCR — Exclusive OR Immediate Data To the Condition Codes

Syntax:

    EORI   #<data>, CCR

Instruction Format:

15	14	13	12	11	10	9	8	7	6	5	4	3	2	1	0
0	0	0	0	1	0	1	0	0	0	1	1	1	1	0	0
0	0	0	0	0	0	0	0	\multicolumn{8}{c}{Byte Data}							

15	14	13	12	11	10	9	8	7	6	5	4	3	2	1	0
0	0	0	0	1	0	1	0	0	0	1	1	1	1	0	0
0	0	0	0	0	0	0	0	Byte Data							

Condition Codes:

- **N**   Changed if bit 3 of immediate data is 1, otherwise unaffected
- **Z**   Changed if bit 2 of immediate data is 1, otherwise unaffected
- **V**   Changed if bit 1 of immediate data is 1, otherwise unaffected
- **C**   Changed if bit 0 of immediate data is 1, otherwise unaffected
- **X**   Changed if bit 4 of immediate data is 1, otherwise unaffected

Description:

This instruction exclusively ORs the immediate data with the condition code register. The immediate data is limited to a single byte, and only bits 0-4 are defined.

Example:

If the Z flag is set and all others are clear, then

                EORI   #7, CCR

clears the Z flag and sets the V and C flags.

EORI to SR — Exclusive OR Immediate Data To Status Register (Privileged)

Syntax:

    EORI   #<data>, SR

Instruction Format:

15	14	13	12	11	10	9	8	7	6	5	4	3	2	1	0
0	0	0	0	1	0	1	0	0	1	1	1	1	1	0	0
Word Data															

Condition Codes:

- **N**   Changed if bit 3 of immediate data is 1, otherwise unaffected
- **Z**   Changed if bit 2 of immediate data is 1, otherwise unaffected

Descriptions of Individual MC68000 Instructions **417**

V	Changed if bit 1 of immediate data is 1, otherwise unaffected
C	Changed if bit 0 of immediate data is 1, otherwise unaffected
X	Changed if bit 4 of immediate data is 1, otherwise unaffected

Description:

This instruction exclusively ORs the immediate data with the status register and stores the result in the status register. The instruction is privileged and will cause an exception if it is executed in user mode.

Example:

If, on the MC68000, the Z flag is set and all other flags are clear, the supervisor bit is set, trace mode is off, and the interrupt mask is 0, then after

        EORI   #A000, SR

enables trace mode, changes from supervisor to user mode, and leaves the condition codes unchanged.

EXG — Exchange Registers

Syntax:

    EXG   Rx, Ry

Instruction Format:

15	14	13	12	11	10	9	8	7	6	5	4	3	2	1	0
1	1	0	0	Register			1	Opcode				Register			

Opcode: 01000 = exchange data registers
            01001 = exchange address registers
            10001 = exchange data and address registers

Condition Codes:

N	Unaffected
Z	Unaffected
V	Unaffected
C	Unaffected
X	Unaffected

Description:

This instruction exchanges the long-word values of two registers. You can swap two data registers, two address registers, or a data register and address register.

Example:

If D0 contains $10004030 and D3 contains $FFFF0000, then after

        EXG   D0, D3

D0 contains $FFFF0000 and D3 contains $10004030.

EXT/EXTB — Sign Extend

Syntax:

    EXT.s   Dn
    EXTB.L   Dn   (MC68020 only)

    where .s = .W or .L.

Instruction Format:

15	14	13	12	11	10	9	8	7	6	5	4	3	2	1	0
0	1	0	0	1	0	0	Type			0	0	0	Data Register		

Type field: 010=Extend Word   011=Extend Long   111=Extend Byte Long - (MC68020)

Condition Codes:

    N   Set if result is negative, cleared otherwise
    Z   Set if result is zero, cleared otherwise
    V   Cleared
    C   Cleared
    X   Unaffected

Description:

This instruction sign extends the value in the data register. The word-sized version (EXT.W) of the instruction extends the sign of a byte value into bits 8-15. The long-word version (EXT.L) of the instruction extends the sign of a word value into bits 16-31. A second long-word version (EXTB.L) extends the sign of a byte value into bits 8-31. This latter instruction is valid only on the MC68020, while the former instructions are available on all processors.

Example:

If D0 contains a $000000FF, then after

                    EXT.W   D0

D0 contains a $0000FFFF.

ILLEGAL — Take Illegal Instruction Trap

Syntax:

    ILLEGAL

Instruction Format:

15	14	13	12	11	10	9	8	7	6	5	4	3	2	1	0
0	1	0	0	1	0	1	0	1	1	1	1	1	1	0	0

Condition Codes:

N	Unaffected
Z	Unaffected
V	Unaffected
C	Unaffected
X	Unaffected

Description:

This instruction causes the processor to trap through the illegal instruction exception vector (vector 4, offset $10). While many bit patterns are illegal instructions, Motorola guarantees that this instruction will always be illegal in all future extensions of the instruction set.

Example:

ILLEGAL

The processor traps through exception table vector number 4.

JMP — Jump

Syntax:

    JMP   <ea>

where <ea> is

	Dn	X	(d8,An,Xn)		#<data>
	An	X	(bd,An,Xn)	X	(d16,PC)
X	(An)	X	([bd,An,Xn],od)	X	(d8,PC,Xn)
	(An)+	X	([bd,An],Xn,od)	X	(bd,PC,Xn)
	−(An)	X	xxx.L	X	[(bd,PC,Xn),od]
X	(d16,An)	X	xxx.L	X	[(bd,PC),Xn,od]

Instruction Format:

15	14	13	12	11	10	9	8	7	6	5	4	3	2	1	0
0	1	0	0	1	1	1	0	1	1	\multicolumn{3}{c}{Effective Address Mode}			\multicolumn{3}{c}{Register}		

15	14	13	12	11	10	9	8	7	6	5	4	3	2	1	0
0	1	0	0	1	1	1	0	1	1	\multicolumn{6}{c}{Effective Address}					
										\multicolumn{3}{c}{Mode}			\multicolumn{3}{c}{Register}		

Condition Codes:

N	Unaffected
Z	Unaffected
V	Unaffected
C	Unaffected
X	Unaffected

Description:

This instruction loads the program counter with the value specified by the effective address and begins execution at the new address.

Example:

If FUNC1 is the label of a segment of your program, then

                JMP   FUNC1

transfers control of the program to the instruction at FUNC1.

JSR — Jump to Subroutine

Syntax:

    JSR   <ea>

where <ea> is

	Dn	X	(d8,An,Xn)		#<data>
	An	X	(bd,An,Xn)	X	(d16,PC)
X	(An)	X	([bd,An,Xn],od)	X	(d8,PC,Xn)
	(An)+	X	([bd,An],Xn,od)	X	(bd,PC,Xn)
	−(An)	X	xxx.L	X	[(bd,PC,Xn),od]
X	(d16,An)	X	xxx.L	X	[(bd,PC),Xn,od]

Instruction Format:

15	14	13	12	11	10	9	8	7	6	5	4	3	2	1	0
0	1	0	0	1	1	1	0	1	0	\multicolumn{3}{c}{Effective Address Mode}			\multicolumn{3}{c}{Register}		

Condition Codes:

    N   Unaffected
    Z   Unaffected
    V   Unaffected
    C   Unaffected
    X   Unaffected

Description:

This instruction pushes the address of the instruction immediately following the JSR instruction onto the current stack. The processor then loads the PC with the given effective address and begins execution at the new address.

This instruction differs from the BSR in that it provides many more addressing modes for the new PC address than does the BSR instruction, which supports only relative branches.

Example:

If FUNC__1 is the label of a subroutine, then

                JSR   FUNC__1

calls the subroutine starting at FUNC__1.

LEA — Load Effective Address

Syntax:

LEA   <ea>, An

where <ea> is

	Dn	X	(d8,An,Xn)		#<data>
	An	X	(bd,An,Xn)	X	(d16,PC)
X	(An)	X	([bd,An,Xn],od)	X	(d8,PC,Xn)
	(An)+	X	([bd,An],Xn,od)	X	(bd,PC,Xn)
	−(An)	X	xxx.L	X	[(bd,PC,Xn),od]
X	(d16,An)	X	xxx.L	X	[(bd,PC),Xn,od]

Instruction Format:

15	14	13	12	11	10	9	8	7	6	5	4	3	2	1	0
0	1	0	0	Address Register			1	1	1	Effective Address			
										Mode			Register		

Condition Codes:

N	Unaffected
Z	Unaffected
V	Unaffected
C	Unaffected
X	Unaffected

Description:

This instruction calculates the value of the effective address and loads that value into the given address register. Since the calculation happens at execution time, this instruction helps you write position-independent code.

Example:

If your program is loaded at run time so that the label TABLE_1 is located at $1200, then the instruction

             LEA   (TABLE_1,PC), A0

uses PC relative addressing with a displacement to calculate the effective address of $1200; the result is loaded into A0.

LINK — Link and Allocate Space

Syntax:

LINK   An, #<data>

Instruction Format:

(Word)

15	14	13	12	11	10	9	8	7	6	5	4	3	2	1	0
0	1	0	0	1	1	1	0	0	1	0	1	0	Register		

(Long)

| 0 | 1 | 0 | 0 | 1 | 0 | 0 | 0 | 0 | 0 | 0 | 0 | 1 | Register |||

Condition Codes:

N	Unaffected
Z	Unaffected
V	Unaffected
C	Unaffected
X	Unaffected

Description:

This instruction pushes the contents of the specified address register onto the stack, loads the new value of the stack pointer into the address register, and, finally, adds the signed immediate data to the stack pointer. All MC68000 processors support 16-bit immediate values. The MC68020 also supports 32-bit values. The UNLNK instruction performs the reverse of the LINK instruction.

Note that since the stack grows downward, you should use negative numbers to allocate fresh space on the stack. You should not modify the address register between the LINK and UNLNK instruction. Finally, note that A7 serves as the stack pointer, so you should not use A7 as the frame pointer.

This instruction creates a "stack frame" in the stack memory. You can use the stack frame area for anything you need: temporary storage, buffers, and so on. Typically, compilers (for example, many C-language compilers) create a stack frame upon entry to functions and subroutines. They use this stack frame for storing local variables; this way, the local data is dynamically allocated and can be returned to free space (back to the stack) when the subroutine terminates.

Example:

In the illustration that follows, procedure A calls procedure B. At this time, the return address back to procedure B is on the top of the stack, as shown in Figure 21-1a. The first instruction of procedure B is

            LINK   A6, #<−10>

After executing this instruction, 10 bytes of the stack are allocated as procedure B's stack frame. A6 points to the start of that frame; SP points to the end of the frame. At this time, procedure B may use those 10 bytes of its frame for local variables, temporaries, and anything else for which it might need dynamic storage. This state is shown in Figure 21-1b.

At the end of procedure B, just before the RTS statement, procedure B executes a

            UNLNK   A6

This moves the contents of A6 into the stack pointer (thus deallocating procedure B's local data). It then pulls the original value of A6 from the stack. At this point, the stack points to the return address to procedure A (as shown by Figure 21-1c).

Note that procedure B could have called other procedures (or it could even call itself recursively). The called procedures would LINK and allocate their own stack frames just as procedure B did. Since A6 is saved on the stack, each LINK builds successive stack frames that UNLNK can unwind in order.

We used A6 as our frame pointer; you may use any address register except A7. Good programming practice, however, dictates that you be consistent in your stack frame pointer selection.

LSL/LSR — Logical Shift

Syntax:

```
LSL.s      Dx, Dy
LSL.s      #<data>, Dy
LSL        <ea>
LSR.s      Dx, Dy
LSR.s      #<data>, Dy
LSR        <ea>
```

where <ea> is

	Dn		(d8,An,Xn)	#<data>
	An	X	(bd,An,Xn)	(d16,PC)
X	(An)	X	([bd,An,Xn],od)	(d8,PC,Xn)
X	(An)+	X	([bd,An],Xn,od)	(bd,PC,Xn)
X	−(An)	X	xxx.L	[(bd,PC,Xn),od]
X	(d16,An)	X	xxx.L	[(bd,PC),Xn,od]

and where .s = .B, .W, or .L.

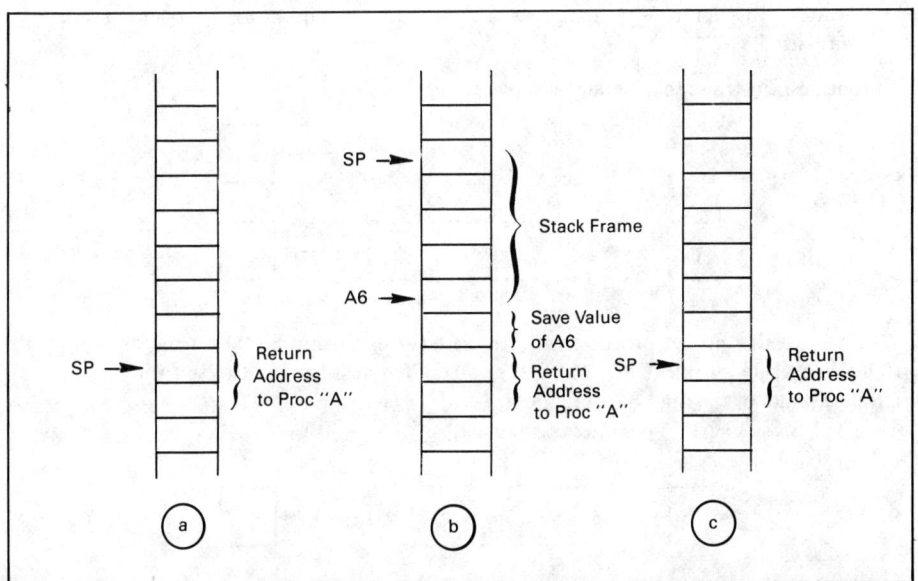

Figure 21-1. LINK Instruction Execution Sequence

Instruction Format:

(Register)

15	14	13	12	11	10	9	8	7	6	5	4	3	2	1	0
1	1	1	0	Count/Register			dr	Size		i/r	0	1	Register		

(Memory)

1	1	1	0	0	0	1	dr	1	1	Effective Address	
										Mode	Register

i/r field: 0 = immediate shift count
 1 = register shift count
d/r field: 0 = right 1 = left
Size field: 00 = byte 01 = word 10 = long
Count/Register field: if i/r = 0, specifies shift count
 if i/r = 1, specifies data register

Condition Codes:

N   Set if high-order bit of result is set, cleared otherwise
Z   Set if result is zero, cleared otherwise
V   Always cleared
C   Set according to last bit shifted out of operand, cleared for zero shift count
X   Set according to last bit shifted out of operand, cleared for zero shift count

Description:

These instructions shift the contents of the operand a specified number of times. The destination can be in a data register or in memory. When the destination is in a data register, you can specify the number of bits to shift either through immediate data (a value of 1-8) or through another data register (a value from 0-63). If the destination is a memory location, this shift is restricted to one bit, and in addition, the operand must be word-sized.

The LSL instructions operate as shown:

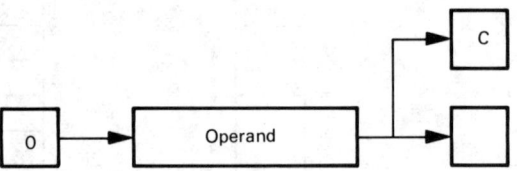

Note that the processor fills zeros into the least significant bit (bit 0) and drops the bits from the left side into the Carry (C) and Extend (X) flags. For multiple bit shifts, these bits reflect the state of the final bit shifted out.

The LSR instruction operates as shown:

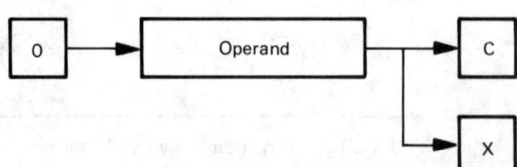

Descriptions of Individual MC68000 Instructions 425

Note that the processor fills zeros into the most significant bit and drops the bits from the right side into the Carry (C) and Extend (X) flags. For multiple bit shifts, these bits reflect the state of the final bit shifted out.

The difference between these instructions and their arithmetic shift counterparts (ASL and ASR) lies in their applications. Logical shifts are useful in manipulating masks and bit fields; in these shifts, the sign is not replicated. Arithmetic shifts are useful in integer arithmetic, where the sign is important; in these shifts, the sign is replicated and the Overflow (V) flag has meaning.

Examples:

If D0 contains $8138, then

            LSR.W   #3, D0

stores a value of $1027 into D0 and clears the C and X flags.

MOVE — Move Data

Syntax:

    MOVE.s   <ea1>, <ea2>

where <ea1> is

X	Dn	X	(d8,An,Xn)	X	#<data>
X	An	X	(bd,An,Xn)	X	(d16,PC)
X	(An)	X	([bd,An,Xn],od)	X	(d8,PC,Xn)
X	(An)+	X	([bd,An],Xn,od)	X	(bd,PC,Xn)
X	−(An)	X	xxx.L	X	[(bd,PC,Xn),od]
X	(d16,An)	X	xxx.L	X	[(bd,PC),Xn,od]

and where <ea2> is

X	Dn	X	(d8,An,Xn)		#<data>
	An	X	(bd,An,Xn)		(d16,PC)
	(An)	X	([bd,An,Xn],od)		(d8,PC,Xn)
X	(An)+	X	([bd,An],Xn,od)		(bd,PC,Xn)
X	−(An)	X	xxx.L		[(bd,PC,Xn),od]
X	(d16,An)	X	xxx.L		[(bd,PC),Xn,od]

and where .s = .B, .W, or .L.

Instruction Format:

15	14	13	12	11	10	9	8	7	6	5	4	3	2	1	0
0	0	Size		Destination						Source					
				Register			Mode			Mode			Register		

Size field: 01 = byte 10 = long 11 = word

Condition Codes:

N	Set if high-order bit of result is set, cleared otherwise
Z	Set if result is zero, cleared otherwise
V	Always cleared
C	Always cleared
X	Unaffected

Description:

This instruction moves the contents of the source operand to the destination operand. The processor examines the data as it moves it and sets the condition codes accordingly. If the source <ea> is an address register, you are limited to word and long-word movements. Also, movements to data registers affect only as many bits as are indicated by the size; the sign is not extended.

Example:

If D0 contains $1234 and A0 contains the address $200010, then

                MOVE.W   D0, (A0)+

moves $1234 to address $200010 and increments A0 to $200012.

MOVEA — Move to Address Register

Syntax:

MOVEA.s   <ea>, An

where <ea> is

X Dn	X (d8,An,Xn)	X #<data>
X An	X (bd,An,Xn)	X (d16,PC)
X (An)	X ([bd,An,Xn],od)	X (d8,PC,Xn)
X (An)+	X ([bd,An],Xn,od)	X (bd,PC,Xn)
X −(An)	X xxx.L	X [(bd,PC,Xn),od]
X (d16,An)	X xxx.L	X [(bd,PC),Xn,od]

and where .s = .W or .L.

Instruction Format:

0	0	Size	Destination Register	0	0	1	Source Mode	Register

Size: 10 = long   11 = word

Condition Codes:

N	Unaffected
Z	Unaffected
V	Unaffected
C	Unaffected
X	Unaffected

Description:

This instruction moves a word or long word from the effective address into an address register. The instruction affects the entire address register; the processor sign extends word-sized operands before loading them into the register.

This instruction differs from the general MOVE instruction only in its size and its effect on the condition codes. Many assemblers will let you get away with using the MOVE mnemonic with "An" as the destination; the assemblers assume you mean MOVEA and fill in the correct opcode.

Example:

The label TABLE contains the address of a database table. After

       MOVEA.L   #TABLE, A0

A0 points to TABLE.

MOVE From CCR — Move From Condition Code Register

Syntax:

  MOVE   CCR, <ea>

  where <ea> is

X	Dn	X	(d8,An,Xn)		#<data>
	An	X	(bd,An,Xn)		(d16,PC)
X	(An)	X	([bd,An,Xn],od)		(d8,PC,Xn)
X	(An)+	X	([bd,An],Xn,od)		(bd,PC,Xn)
X	−(An)	X	xxx.L		[(bd,PC,Xn),od]
X	(d16,An)	X	xxx.L		[(bd,PC),Xn,od]

Instruction Format:

15	14	13	12	11	10	9	8	7	6	5	4	3	2	1	0
0	1	0	0	0	0	1	0	1	1	\multicolumn{6}{c}{Effective Address}

| | | | | | | | | | | Mode | | | Register | | |

Condition Codes:

  N Unaffected
  Z Unaffected
  V Unaffected
  C Unaffected
  X Unaffected

Description:

This instruction moves the contents of the condition codes into the specified effective address. Note that although the instruction is sized as a word operation, only the lower byte contains the condition-code information; the upper byte is all zeros.

Example:

If the N and Z flags are set and the V, C, and X flags are clear, and STATUS is a label to a word in memory, then after

       MOVE   CCR, STATUS

STATUS contains $000C.

MOVE to CCR — Move to the Condition Code Registers

Syntax:

    MOVE   <ea>, CCR

where <ea> is

X Dn	X (d8,An,Xn)	X #<data>
An	X (bd,An,Xn)	X (d16,PC)
X (An)	X ([bd,An,Xn],od)	X (d8,PC,Xn)
X (An)+	X ([bd,An],Xn,od)	X (bd,PC,Xn)
X −(An)	X xxx.L	X [(bd,PC,Xn),od]
X (d16,An)	X xxx.L	X [(bd,PC),Xn,od]

Instruction Format:

15	14	13	12	11	10	9	8	7	6	5	4	3	2	1	0
										Effective Address					
0	1	0	0	0	0	0	1	1	1	Mode			Register		

Condition Codes:

    N   Set same as bit 3 of source
    Z   Set same as bit 2 of source
    V   Set same as bit 1 of source
    C   Set same as bit 0 of source
    X   Set same as bit 4 of source

Description:

This instruction moves the source operand to the condition-code register. Although the source operand is word-sized, only the five least significant bits of the CCR are affected; the rest are ignored.

Example:

If NEW_CCR contains the word value $001F, then after

                MOVE   NEW_CCR, CCR

all of the condition code flags are set to 1.

MOVE From SR — Move From the Status Register

Syntax:

    MOVE   SR, <ea>

where <ea> is

X Dn	X (d8,An,Xn)	#<data>
An	X (bd,An,Xn)	(d16,PC)
X (An)	X ([bd,An,Xn],od)	(d8,PC,Xn)
X (An)+	X ([bd,An],Xn,od)	(bd,PC,Xn)
X −(An)	X xxx.L	[(bd,PC,Xn),od]
X (d16,An)	X xxx.L	[(bd,PC),Xn,od]

Instruction Format:

15	14	13	12	11	10	9	8	7	6	5	4	3	2	1	0
0	1	0	0	0	0	0	0	1	1	\multicolumn{6}{c	}{Effective Address}

| | | | | | | | | | | Mode | | | Register | | |

Condition Codes:

N	Unaffected
Z	Unaffected
V	Unaffected
C	Unaffected
X	Unaffected

Description:

This instruction copies the contents of the status register to the destination location. On the MC68010, MC68012, and MC68020, this instruction is privileged and will cause an exception if executed while in user mode.

Example:

If on the MC68000, the status register indicates that in supervisor mode, the interrupt mask = 101, and the Z flag is set, then after

                      MOVE   SR, D0

D0 contains $2504.

MOVE to SR — Move to the Status Register (Privileged)

Syntax:

MOVE <ea>, SR

where <ea> is

X	Dn	X	(d8,An,Xn)	X	#<data>
	An	X	(bd,An,Xn)	X	(d16,PC)
X	(An)	X	([bd,An,Xn],od)	X	(d8,PC,Xn)
X	(An)+	X	([bd,An],Xn,od)	X	(bd,PC,Xn)
X	−(An)	X	xxx.L	X	[(bd,PC,Xn),od]
X	(d16,An)	X	xxx.L	X	[(bd,PC),Xn,od]

Instruction Format:

15	14	13	12	11	10	9	8	7	6	5	4	3	2	1	0
0	1	0	0	0	1	1	0	1	1	\multicolumn{6}{c	}{Effective Address}

| | | | | | | | | | | Mode | | | Register | | |

Condition Codes:

    N Set same as bit 3 of source
    Z Set same as bit 2 of source

V	Set same as bit 1 of source
C	Set same as bit 0 of source
X	Set same as bit 4 of source

Description:

This instruction moves the contents of the source-operand word to the status register. This instruction is privileged and will cause an exception if your program attempts to execute it from the user mode.

Example:

If on the MC68000, the constant NEW_SR is defined as $0001, then after

        MOVE   NEW_SR, SR

the status register indicates no trace, user mode, interrupt mask 0, and the Carry bit is set.

MOVE USP — Move to/From the User Stack Pointer (Privileged)

Syntax:

    MOVE   USP, An
    MOVE   An, USP

Instruction Format:

15	14	13	12	11	10	9	8	7	6	5	4	3	2	1	0
0	1	0	0	1	1	1	0	0	1	1	0	d	Register		

d: 0 = move to USP
   1 = move from USP

Condition Codes:

N	Unaffected
Z	Unaffected
V	Unaffected
C	Unaffected
X	Unaffected

Description:

These instructions move the 32-bit contents of the user stack pointer (A7) to or from an address register. This instruction is privileged; attempting to execute it from a user-mode program will cause an exception.

Recall that the MC68000 processors have separate user and supervisor stacks (in fact, the MC68020 has two supervisor stacks). One means of implementing a call to an operating-system function is to load the parameters onto the stack and execute a TRAP instruction. Since the processor is then in supervisor mode but the calling parameters are on the user-mode stack, this instruction provides the supervisor with a means of accessing the user's data (from the user stack).

Example:

If the user stack contains the address $00002000, then after

                MOVE   USP, A0

A0 contains $00002000.

MOVEC — Move To/From Control Register
(MC68010, MC68012, MC68020) (Privileged)

Syntax:

    MOVEC   Rc, Rn
    MOVEC   Rn, Rc

where Rc is

SFC	source function code register
DFC	destination function code register
USP	user stack pointer
VBR	vector base register
CAAR	cache address register
MSP	master stack pointer
ISP	interrupt stack pointer

Instruction Format:

15	14	13	12	11	10	9	8	7	6	5	4	3	2	1	0
0	1	0	0	1	1	1	0	0	1	1	1	1	0	1	dr
A/D	Register			Control Register											

dr field: 0 = control register to general register
          1 = general register to control register

Control Register field: $000 = SFC $801 = VBR
                             $001 = DFC $802 = CAAR (MC68020)
                             $002 = CACR (MC68020) $803 = MSP (MC68020)
                             $800 = USP $804 = ISP (MC68020)

Condition Codes:

N	Unaffected
Z	Unaffected
V	Unaffected
C	Unaffected
X	Unaffected

Description:

This instruction copies the contents of the specified control register (Rc) to a general purpose register (Rn). This is a privileged instruction; attempting its execution from user mode will bring about exception processing. Note that this instruction is available only on the MC68010, MC68012, and MC68020, and that not all control registers are defined on all of these processors. (Consult Chapter 3 for a description of the control registers available on the various processors.)

Example:

If the vector-base register contains $00800000, then after

                MOVEC   VBR, A0

A0 contains $00800000.

MOVEM — Move Multiple

Syntax:

    MOVEM.s   #<data>, <ea>
    MOVEM.s   <ea>, #<data>

where <ea> is

Dn	(d8,An,Xn)	#<data>
An	(bd,An,Xn)	(d16,PC)
(An)	([bd,An,Xn],od)	(d8,PC,Xn)
(An)+	([bd,An],Xn,od)	(bd,PC,Xn)
−(An)	xxx.L	[(bd,PC,Xn),od]
(d16,An)	xxx.L	[(bd,PC),Xn,od]

where .s = .W or .L.

Instruction Format:

15	14	13	12	11	10	9	8	7	6	5	4	3	2	1	0
0	1	0	0	d	1	0	0	1	Size	\multicolumn{2}{Effective Address}				

| 0 | 1 | 0 | 0 | d | 1 | 0 | 0 | 1 | Size | Mode | | | Register | | |

Size field: 0 = word 1 = long
       d: 0 = move to memory
          1 = move to registers

Bit mask for memory and (An)+
Bit mask for −(An)

A7	A6	A5	A4	A3	A2	A1	A0	D7	D6	D5	D4	D3	D2	D1	D0

D0	D1	D2	D3	D4	D5	D6	D7	A0	A1	A2	A3	A4	A5	A6	A7

Condition Codes:

N	Unaffected
Z	Unaffected
V	Unaffected
C	Unaffected
X	Unaffected

Description:

These instructions move the selected registers to or from consecutive memory locations. You select which registers to use by setting bits in the immediate data mask word as shown. The processor stores or fetches the data from least significant bit to most significant bit. The bit definition of the mask word depends on the addressing mode used.

- If you specify the memory address with postincrement mode (for movement from memory only), the least significant bit of the mask is D0.
- If you specify the memory address with predecrement mode (for movement to memory only), the least significant bit of the mask is A7.

- If you specify the memory address using any of the other modes (for movement in either direction), the least significant bit of the mask is D0, as it was for postincrement.

Note that most assemblers provide shorthand notation for specifying which registers to use. A common notation uses the hyphen (-) to indicate a range of registers; for example, A1-A5 builds a mask for using A1, A2, A3, A4, and A5. The slash (/) indicates an OR of single registers; for example, D0/D1/A0/A1 builds a mask for using D0, D1, A0, and A1. These notations are not standard, however, so you should consult your assembler's user manual for specific details.

Example:

If A6 contains a $1000, then after

        MOVEM.L   D0/D1/A0/A1, −(A6)

address $1004 holds the contents of D0, $1008 holds D1, $100C holds A0, $1010 holds A1, and A6 contains $1010. Later in your program you can restore the values of those saved registers with

        MOVEM.L   (A6)+, D0/D1/A0/A1

MOVEP — Move Peripheral Data

Syntax:

    MOVEP.s   Dn, (disp, An)
    MOVEP.s   (disp, An)

where .s = .W or .L.

Instruction Format:

15	14	13	12	11	10	9	8	7	6	5	4	3	2	1	0
0	0	0	0	\multicolumn{3}{Data Register}			\multicolumn{3}{Op-Mode}			0	0	1	\multicolumn{3}{Address Register}		

Op-Mode field: 100 = transfer word from memory to register
                101 = transfer long from memory to register
                110 = transfer word from register to memory
                111 = transfer long from register to memory

Condition Codes:

N	Unaffected
Z	Unaffected
V	Unaffected
C	Unaffected
X	Unaffected

Description:

This instruction moves data between a data register and alternate bytes of memory. This instruction simplifies the movement of data between the processor and certain older 8-bit devices, whose registers lie on alternate bytes of memory (all odd or all even). One operand must be a data register, the other an address specified by address indirect with displacement. The operation transfers the high-order byte of the register first and the low-order byte of the register last.

Example:

If D0 contains $4304, A0 has a value of $800000, which is the base address of a peripheral's control registers. A word-count register (word-sized) lies at the bytes at offsets 4 and 6. After

                            MOVEP.W   D0, (4,A0)

the word count register contains $4304 ($800004 contains $43 and $800006 contains $04).

MOVEQ — Move Quick

Syntax:

    MOVEQ   #<data>, Dn

Instruction Format:

15	14	13	12	11	10	9	8	7	6	5	4	3	2	1	0
0	1	1	1	\multicolumn{3}{c}{Data Register}			0	\multicolumn{6}{c}{Data}					

Data field: Data is sign extended to a long operand and all 32 bits are transferred to the data register.

Condition Codes:

    N   Set if high-order bit of result is set, cleared otherwise
    Z   Set if result is zero, cleared otherwise
    V   Cleared
    C   Cleared
    X   Unaffected

Description:

This instruction moves a signed 8-bit immediate value into a data register. The processor extends the sign of the value through all 32 bits of the register.

Example:

After the instruction,

                            MOVEQ   #-1, D0

D0 contains the long-word value -1 ($FFFFFFFF) and the N flag is set.

MOVES — Move Address Space (Privileged)
(MC68010, MC68012, MC68020)

Syntax:

    MOVES.s   Rn, <ea>
    MOVES.s   <ea>, Rn

where <ea> is

	Dn	X	(d8,An,Xn)	#<data>
	An	X	(bd,An,Xn)	(d16,PC)
X	(An)	X	([bd,An,Xn],od)	(d8,PC,Xn)
X	(An)+	X	([bd,An],Xn,od)	(bd,PC,Xn)
X	−(An)	X	xxx.L	[(bd,PC,Xn),od]
X	(d16,An)	X	xxx.L	[(bd,PC),Xn,od]

and .s = .B, .W, or .L.

Instruction Format:

15	14	13	12	11	10	9	8	7	6	5	4	3	2	1	0
0	0	0	0	1	1	1	0	\multicolumn{2}{c}{Size}	\multicolumn{4}{c}{Effective Address}			
										\multicolumn{2}{c}{Mode}	\multicolumn{2}{c}{Register}		
A/D	\multicolumn{3}{c}{Register}	dr	0	0	0	0	0	0	0	0	0	0	0

dr field: 0 = EA to register
         1 = register to EA

Condition Codes:

N	Unaffected
Z	Unaffected
V	Unaffected
C	Unaffected
X	Unaffected

Description:

This instruction moves data between a register and memory. Unlike the normal MOVE instruction, this instruction sends external hardware the contents of a function-code register as well as the address of the operand. The instruction is privileged; if it is executed in user mode, an exception results. Since the MC68000 and MC68008 do not have the function-code registers, these processors do not implement this instruction.

As we discussed in Chapter 2, whenever the processor accesses memory, it sends the memory controller some information about the requested access. The information may be for an instruction or for data, and it may be for a user program or a supervisor program. Also, the request may be in a special area called "CPU space." For reads from memory, the processor uses the value in the source function code (SFC) register; for writes to memory, the processor uses the value in the destination function code (DFC) register.

A memory management unit (MMU) "maps" program-supplied logical addresses into physical addresses. This mapping simplifies programming in a multitasking environment since each task thinks it starts at address $00000000 (for example). Prior to executing a particular task, the operating system loads the MMU with data telling how to map the logical addresses to physical addresses.

The operating system (in supervisor mode) has its own set of MMU mapping registers separate from the user-mode registers. This keeps a user task from accidentally (or otherwise) accessing vital operating system data and code. The MMU distinguishes between user and supervisor accesses by the data on the function-code lines.

In servicing user requests, the operating system must be able to get at the user's data. On the MC68000 and MC68008, the system can copy part of the user's MMU to its own MMU and thus access the data. With the MC68010, MC68012, and the MC68020, the method is simpler; the system can load the function-code registers with the appropriate user-mode code. A subsequent MOVES instruction thus instructs the MMU to map to user address space instead of supervisor space.

Another encoding of the function codes implies CPU space. In this case, the MMU can access yet another portion of memory. You can use CPU space in several ways, but primarily you would use it for communicating with some peripheral devices.

Note that MOVES is the only instruction that uses the data in the function-code registers.

Example:

A user program can request system services (on some operating systems) by pushing request parameters onto the user stack and then executing a TRAP. Since executing the TRAP puts the processor into supervisor mode, which has its own stack pointer, the supervisor routine must have some means of getting at the data on the user stack. The following code (located in the service routine) will do this:

```
MOVE     USP, A0
MOVEC    #1, SFC
MOVES.L  (A0), D0
```

This code segment fetches the user's stack pointer and puts it into A0. The program then loads the source function code register with 1, which signifies user data space access. The MOVES instruction then loads D0 with the long-word value from the user stack.

MULS — Signed Multiply

Syntax:

MULS.W	<ea>, Dn	
MULS.L	<ea>, Dn	(MC68020 only)
MULS.L	<ea>, Dh:Dl	(MC68020 only)

where <ea> is

X	Dn	X	(d8,An,Xn)	X	#<data>
	An	X	(bd,An,Xn)	X	(d16,PC)
X	(An)	X	([bd,An,Xn],od)	X	(d8,PC,Xn)
X	(An)+	X	([bd,An],Xn,od)	X	(bd,PC,Xn)
X	−(An)	X	xxx.L	X	[(bd,PC,Xn),od]
X	(d16,An)	X	xxx.L	X	[(bd,PC),Xn,od]

Descriptions of Individual MC68000 Instructions 437

Instruction Format:

15	14	13	12	11	10	9	8	7	6	5	4	3	2	1	0	
1	1	0	0	\multicolumn{3}{Register}			1	1	1	\multicolumn{3}{Effective Address Mode}			\multicolumn{3}{Register}			(Word)

15	14	13	12	11	10	9	8	7	6	5	4	3	2	1	0	
0	1	0	0	1	1	0	0	0	0	Effective Address Mode			Register			(Long)
0	Dl			1	Size	0	0	0	0	0	0	0	Dh			

Size Field: 0 = 32-bit product
1 = 64-bit product

Condition Codes:

- **N**   Set if high-order bit of result is set, cleared otherwise
- **Z**   Set if result is zero, cleared otherwise
- **V**   Set if operation causes overflow of destination register, cleared otherwise
- **C**   Cleared
- **X**   Unaffected

Description:

These instructions multiply the two signed operands together, storing the signed result in the destination. The first instruction (MULS.W) is available on all processors and multiplies the 16-bit source and the low 16 bits of the destination data register together, producing a 32-bit product in the data register.

The other two instruction forms are available only on the MC68020. The first long form (with the single destination register) multiplies the 32-bit signed source with the 32-bit signed destination and yields a 32-bit product in the destination register. The second form multiplies the 32-bit signed source with the 32-bit signed destination from Dl and stores the 64-bit product in the Dh:Dl register pair. The most significant long word is in Dh, with the least significant long word in Dl.

For the first long-word format (long-word product), you should check the status of the Overflow (V) flag after the operation to verify the legitimacy of the result. With the other two formats, overflow will never occur.

Example:

If D0 contains −2500 and D1 contains 19400, then after

                MULS   D1, D0

D0 contains −48500000.

MULU — Multiply Unsigned

Syntax:

MULU.W	<ea>, Dn	
MULU.L	<ea>, Dn	(MC68020 only)
MULU.L	<ea>, Dh:Dl	(MC68020 only)

where <ea> is

X	Dn	X	(d8,An,Xn)	X	#<data>
	An	X	(bd,An,Xn)	X	(d16,PC)
X	(An)	X	([bd,An,Xn],od)	X	(d8,PC,Xn)
X	(An)+	X	([bd,An],Xn,od)	X	(bd,PC,Xn)
X	−(An)	X	xxx.L	X	[(bd,PC,Xn),od]
X	(d16,An)	X	xxx.L	X	[(bd,PC),Xn,od]

Instruction Format:

(Word)

15	14	13	12	11	10	9	8	7	6	5	4	3	2	1	0
1	1	0	0	Register			0	1	1	Effective Address					
										Mode			Register		

(Long)

0	1	0	0	1	1	0	0	0	0	Effective Address					
										Mode			Register		
0	Dl			0	Size	0	0	0	0	0	0	0	Dh		

Size field: 0 = 32-bit product
             1 = 64-bit product

Condition Codes:

N	Set if high-order bit of result is set, cleared otherwise
Z	Set if result is zero, cleared otherwise
V	Set if operation causes overflow of the destination register, cleared otherwise
C	Cleared
X	Unaffected

Description:

These instructions multiply the two unsigned operands together, storing the unsigned result in the destination. The first instruction (MULU.W) is available on all processors and multiplies the 16-bit source and the low 16 bits of the destination data register together, producing a 32-bit product in the data register.

The other two instruction forms are available only on the MC68020. The first long form (with the single destination register) multiplies the 32-bit unsigned source with the 32-bit unsigned destination and yields a 32-bit product in the destination register. The second form multiplies the 32-bit unsigned source with the 32-bit unsigned destination from Dl and stores the 64-bit product in the Dh:Dl register pair. The most significant long word is in Dh, with the least significant long word in Dl.

For the first long-word format (long word product), you should check the status of the

Descriptions of Individual MC68000 Instructions **439**

Overflow (V) flag after the operation to verify the legitimacy of the result. With the other two formats, overflow will never occur.

Example:

If D0 contains 32500 and D1 contains 49401, then after

                MULS   D1, D0

D0 contains 1608782500.

NBCD — Negate Decimal With Extend

Syntax:

NBCD   <ea>

where <ea> is

X Dn	X (d8,An,Xn)	#<data>
An	X (bd,An,Xn)	(d16,PC)
X (An)	X ([bd,An,Xn],od)	(d8,PC,Xn)
X (An)+	X ([bd,An],Xn,od)	(bd,PC,Xn)
X −(An)	X xxx.L	[(bd,PC,Xn),od]
X (d16,An)	X xxx.L	[(bd,PC),Xn,od]

Instruction Format:

15	14	13	12	11	10	9	8	7	6	5	4	3	2	1	0
0	1	0	0	1	0	0	1	1		Effective Address					

(bits 5-0: Effective Address — Mode (5-3), Register (2-0))

Condition Codes:

N	Undefined
Z	Set if result is zero, cleared otherwise
V	Undefined
C	Set if a borrow was required, cleared otherwise
X	Set if a borrow was required, cleared otherwise

Description:

This instruction subtracts the destination and the Extend flag (X) from 0 and stores the result back in the destination. The operation uses binary-coded decimal (BCD) arithmetic. (For more information on BCD arithmetic, refer to Chapter 8.)

Example:

If A2 points to a byte in memory containing the value $27, and the Extend flag is set, then after

                NBCD   (A2)

the byte contains 72 and the Carry (C) bit is set.

NEG — Negate

Syntax:

    NEG.s   <ea>

    where <ea> is

X	Dn	X	(d8,An,Xn)		#<data>
	An	X	(bd,An,Xn)		(d16,PC)
X	(An)	X	([bd,An,Xn],od)		(d8,PC,Xn)
X	(An)+	X	([bd,An],Xn,od)		(bd,PC,Xn)
X	−(An)	X	xxx.L		[(bd,PC,Xn),od]
X	(d16,An)	X	xxx.L		[(bd,PC),Xn,od]

    and where .s = .B, .W, or .L.

Instruction Format:

15	14	13	12	11	10	9	8	7	6	5	4	3	2	1	0
0	1	0	0	0	1	0	0	Size		Mode			Register		

(bits 5–3 = Mode, bits 2–0 = Register, together forming Effective Address)

Size field: 00 = byte   01 = word   10 = long

Condition Codes:

    N   Set if high-order bit of result is set, cleared otherwise
    Z   Set if result is zero, cleared otherwise
    V   Set if operation generates an overflow, cleared otherwise
    C   Set if result is nonzero, cleared if result is zero
    X   Set if result is nonzero, cleared if result is zero

Description:

    This instruction subtracts the operand from zero and replaces the difference into the operand. Note that this operation forms the two's complement of the original operand value.

Example:

    If the low-order byte in D0 contains $3A, then after

                NEG.B   D0

    D0 contains $C6 and the N, C, and X bits are set.

NEGX — Negate With Extend

Syntax:

    NEGX.s   <ea>

    where <ea> is

X	Dn	X	(d8,An,Xn)		#<data>
	An	X	(bd,An,Xn)		(d16,PC)
X	(An)	X	([bd,An,Xn],od)		(d8,PC,Xn)
X	(An)+	X	([bd,An],Xn,od)		(bd,PC,Xn)

X	−(An)	X	xxx.L		[(bd,PC,Xn),od]
X	(d16,An)	X	xxx.L		[(bd,PC),Xn,od]

and where .s = .B, .W, or .L.

Instruction Format:

15	14	13	12	11	10	9	8	7	6	5	4	3	2	1	0
										\multicolumn{4}{c}{Effective Address}
0	1	0	0	0	0	0	0	\multicolumn{2}{c}{Size}	\multicolumn{2}{c}{Mode}	\multicolumn{2}{c}{Register}

Size field: 00 = byte 01 = word 10 = long

Condition Codes:

- N   Set if high-order bit of result is set, cleared otherwise
- Z   Set if result is zero, cleared otherwise
- V   Set if the operation generates an overflow, cleared otherwise
- C   Set if a borrow is required, cleared otherwise
- X   Set if a borrow is required, cleared otherwise

Description:

This instruction subtracts the operand and the Extend flag (X) from zero and replaces the difference into the operand. (Refer to Chapter 8 for a discussion of multiprecision arithmetic.)

Example:

If the long word pointed to by A0 contains $01023032 and the Extend bit is clear, then after

$$\text{NEGX.L} \quad (A0)$$

the value at A0 is $FEFDCFCE, and the N, C, and X bits are set.

NOP — No Operation

Syntax:

NOP

Instruction Format:

15	14	13	12	11	10	9	8	7	6	5	4	3	2	1	0
0	1	0	0	1	1	1	0	0	1	1	1	0	0	0	1

Condition Codes:

- N   Unaffected
- Z   Unaffected
- V   Unaffected

C   Unaffected
X   Unaffected

Description:

This instruction performs no meaningful work except to consume a machine cycle. You can use NOP in cases where you need a slight delay (for example, for hardware to catch up) or in debugging to replace a questionable instruction.

NOT — Logical Complement

Syntax:

NOT.s   <ea>

where <ea> is

X Dn	X (d8,An,Xn)	#<data>
An	X (bd,An,Xn)	(d16,PC)
X (An)	X ([bd,An,Xn],od)	(d8,PC,Xn)
X (An)+	X ([bd,An],Xn,od)	(bd,PC,Xn)
X −(An)	X xxx.L	[(bd,PC,Xn),od]
X (d16,An)	X xxx.L	[(bd,PC),Xn,od]

and where .s = .B, .W, or .L.

Instruction Format:

15	14	13	12	11	10	9	8	7	6	5	4	3	2	1	0
										Effective Address				
0	1	0	0	0	1	1	0	Size		Mode			Register		

Size field: 00 = byte 01 = word 10 = long

Condition Codes:

N   Set if high-order bit of result is set, cleared otherwise
Z   Set if result is zero, cleared otherwise
V   Cleared
C   Cleared
X   Unaffected

Description:

This instruction performs a bitwise complement of the operand. This entails the replacement of each 1 in the operand with a 0 and each 0 with a 1.

Example:

If the long word at VAL1 contains $1F004209, then after

          NOT.L   VAL1

VAL1 contains $E0FFBDF6 and the N flag is set.

OR — Inclusive Logical OR

Syntax:

    OR.s   <ea>, Dn
    OR.s   Dn, <ea>

where for dst = Dn, <ea> is

X	Dn	X	(d8,An,Xn)	X	#<data>
	An	X	(bd,An,Xn)	X	(d16,PC)
X	(An)	X	([bd,An,Xn],od)	X	(d8,PC,Xn)
X	(An)+	X	([bd,An],Xn,od)	X	(bd,PC,Xn)
X	−(An)	X	xxx.L	X	[(bd,PC,Xn),od]
X	(d16,An)	X	xxx.L	X	[(bd,PC),Xn,od]

and where for src = Dn, <ea> is

	Dn	X	(d8,An,Xn)		#<data>
	An	X	(bd,An,Xn)		(d16,PC)
X	(An)	X	([bd,An,Xn],od)		(d8,PC,Xn)
X	(An)+	X	([bd,An],Xn,od)		(bd,PC,Xn)
X	−(An)	X	xxx.L		[(bd,PC,Xn),od]
X	(d16,An)	X	xxx.L		[(bd,PC),Xn,od]

and where .s = .B, .W, or .L.

Instruction Format:

15	14	13	12	11	10	9	8	7	6	5	4	3	2	1	0
1	0	0	0	Data Register			Op-Mode			Effective Address					
										Mode			Register		

Op-Mode field:

	Byte	Word	Long	Operation
	000	001	010	(<ea>)∨(<Dn>) → <Dn>
	100	101	110	(<Dn>)∨(<ea>) → <ea>

Condition Codes:

    N   Set if high-order bit of result is set, cleared otherwise
    Z   Set if result is zero, cleared otherwise
    V   Cleared
    C   Cleared
    X   Unaffected

Description:

This instruction performs a bitwise logical OR of the contents of the source operand with the contents of the destination operand and stores the result in the destination. OR is a common logical instruction and is most often used to set one or more bits to 1.

Example:

If D3 contains $1007 and D7 contains $0FF0, then after

                OR.W   D3, D7

D7 contains $1FF7. This is calculated as

```
D3 = $1007 = 0001000000000111
D7 = $0FF0 = 0000111111110000
D7 = $1FF7 = 0001111111110111
```

ORI — Inclusive OR Immediate

Syntax:

ORI.s   #<data>, <ea>

where <ea> is

X Dn	X (d8,An,Xn)	#<data>
An	X (bd,An,Xn)	(d16,PC)
X (An)	X ([bd,An,Xn],od)	(d8,PC,Xn)
X (An)+	X ([bd,An],Xn,od)	(bd,PC,Xn)
X −(An)	X xxx.L	[(bd,PC,Xn),od]
X (d16,An)	X xxx.L	[(bd,PC),Xn,od]

and where .s = .B, .W, or .L.

Instruction Format:

15	14	13	12	11	10	9	8	7	6	5	4	3	2	1	0
0	0	0	0	0	0	0	0	Size		Effective Address					
										Mode			Register		

Size field: 00 = byte   01 = word   10 = long

Condition Codes:

N   Set if high-order bit of result is set, cleared otherwise
Z   Set if result is zero, cleared otherwise
V   Cleared
C   Cleared
X   Unaffected

Description:

This instruction is used to OR the immediate data to the destination operand; storing the result is stored in the destination.

Example:

If the long word at the label FLAGS contains $8F77F010, then after

                 ORI   #10000001, FLAGS

FLAGS contains $8F77F011 and the N flag is set.

ORI to CCR—Inclusive OR Immediate
To Condition Codes

Syntax:

    ORI   #<data>, CCR

Instruction Format:

15	14	13	12	11	10	9	8	7	6	5	4	3	2	1	0
0	0	0	0	0	0	0	0	0	0	1	1	1	1	0	0
0	0	0	0	0	0	0	0	\multicolumn{8}{c}{Byte Data}

15	14	13	12	11	10	9	8	7	6	5	4	3	2	1	0
0	0	0	0	0	0	0	0	\multicolumn{8}{c|}{Byte Data}							

Condition Codes:

N	Takes value of bit 3 of immediate data
Z	Takes value of bit 3 of immediate data
V	Takes value of bit 3 of immediate data
C	Takes value of bit 3 of immediate data
X	Takes value of bit 3 of immediate data

Description:

    This instruction logically ORs the condition codes with the immediate data.

Example:

    If the N flag is set and all others are clear, then after

                ORI   #$1F, CCR

all of the flags are set.

OR to SR—Inclusive OR Immediate
To Status Register (Privileged)

Syntax:

    ORI   #<data>, SR

Instruction Format:

15	14	13	12	11	10	9	8	7	6	5	4	3	2	1	0
0	0	0	0	0	0	1	0	0	1	1	1	1	1	0	0
\multicolumn{16}{c}{Word Data}															

Condition Codes:

N	Takes value of bit 3 of immediate data
Z	Takes value of bit 3 of immediate data

V   Takes value of bit 3 of immediate data
C   Takes value of bit 3 of immediate data
X   Takes value of bit 3 of immediate data

Description:

This instruction logically ORs the immediate data with the data in the status register (SR). Note that this is a privileged instruction; your attempt to execute it from a user-mode program will cause exception processing through the privilege violation vector.

Example:

If the supervisor bit is set, the Z flag is set, and the interrupt mask is 000, then after

ORI   #$0700, SR

the status register contains $2704 (supervisor bit set, interrupt mask is 111, and the Z flag is set).

PACK — Pack BCD (MC68020 only)

Syntax:

PACK   −(An), −(Ay), #<data>
PACK   Dn, Dm, #<data>

Instruction Format:

15	14	13	12	11	10	9	8	7	6	5	4	3	2	1	0
1	0	0	0	Destination Register*			1	0	1	0	0	R/M	Source Register*		
16-Bit Extension:Adjustment																

R/M field: 0 = data register to data register
          1 = memory to memory
*If R/M = 0, specifies a data register
 If R/M = 1, specifies an address register for the predecrement addressing mode.

Condition Codes:

N   Unaffected
Z   Unaffected
V   Unaffected
C   Unaffected
X   Unaffected

Description:

This instruction converts two bytes of data into a single byte of packed binary-coded decimal data. The instruction adds the immediate word data to the two bytes and moves bits 11-8 and 3-0 to bits 7-0 of the destination. Note that the source is two bytes long while the destination is a single byte; as a result, when using the address register mode, the processor decrements the source by two but decrements the result by one.

With this instruction, you can convert a string of ASCII or EBCDIC data into a packed decimal string for manipulation with the various BCD instructions. To unpack the BCD string back into an ASCII string, use the UNPCK instruction.

Example:

If D0 contains the word $3539 (which is ASCII for "59"), then after

      PACK   D0, D1, #0

D1 contains the byte $59.

PEA — Push Effective Address

Syntax:

 PEA   <ea>

where <ea> is

	Dn	X	(d8,An,Xn)		#<data>
	An	X	(bd,An,Xn)	X	(d16,PC)
X	(An)	X	([bd,An,Xn],od)	X	(d8,PC,Xn)
	(An)+	X	([bd,An],Xn,od)	X	(bd,PC,Xn)
	−(An)	X	xxx.L	X	[(bd,PC,Xn),od]
X	(d16,An)	X	xxx.L	X	[(bd,PC),Xn,od]

Instruction Format:

15	14	13	12	11	10	9	8	7	6	5	4	3	2	1	0
0	1	0	0	1	0	0	0	0	1	\multicolumn{3}{c}{Effective Address}			

| | | | | | | | | | | Mode | | | Register | | |

Condition Codes:

 N Unaffected
 Z Unaffected
 V Unaffected
 C Unaffected
 X Unaffected

Description:

This instruction calculates an absolute address based on the given effective address and pushes that 32-bit value onto the stack. Note that the value put on the stack is an address, not the value at that address.

This instruction is used to evaluate addresses that may be unknown at assembly time, as would be the case with position-independent code (code that uses no absolute addresses). Refer also to the instruction LEA.

Example:

Your assembler has determined that the label VAL1 is $126 bytes away from the extension word following this PEA instruction:

```
                    PEA         (VAL1,PC)
```

At run time, this instruction is located at address $1000. The processor computes the absolute address of VAL1 as $1126 and pushes this value (as $00001126) onto the stack.

RESET — Reset External Devices
(Privileged)

Syntax:
```
RESET
```

Instruction Format:

15	14	13	12	11	10	9	8	7	6	5	4	3	2	1	0
0	1	0	0	1	1	1	0	0	1	1	1	0	1	0	0

Condition Codes:

N	Unaffected
Z	Unaffected
V	Unaffected
C	Unaffected
X	Unaffected

Description:
This instruction tells the processor to raise its output signal RESET, notifying external devices to reset themselves to their initial states. Nothing significant happens to the processor, and it continues with the next instruction. This instruction is privileged; if you attempt to execute it from a user-mode instruction, it will cause exception processing.

Example:
Following
```
                    RESET
```
all external devices reset their internal state.

ROL/ROR — Rotate

Syntax:
```
ROR.s       Dn, Dm
ROR.s       #<data>, Dn
ROR         <ea>
ROL.s       TDn, Dm
ROL.s       #<data>, Dn
ROL         <ea>
```

Descriptions of Individual MC68000 Instructions **449**

where <ea> is

Dn	X (d8,An,Xn)	#<data>
An	X (bd,An,Xn)	(d16,PC)
X (An)	X ([bd,An,Xn],od)	(d8,PC,Xn)
X (An)+	X ([bd,An],Xn,od)	(bd,PC,Xn)
X −(An)	X xxx.L	[(bd,PC,Xn),od]
X (d16,An)	X xxx.L	[(bd,PC),Xn,od]

and where .s is .B, .W, or .L.

Instruction Format:

(Register)

15	14	13	12	11	10	9	8	7	6	5	4	3	2	1	0
1	1	1	0	Count/Register			dr	Size		i/r	1	1	Register		

(Memory)

1	1	1	0	0	1	1	dr	1	1	Effective Address	
										Mode	Register

Count/Register field: if i/r = 0, immdediate data
if i/r = 1, data register
dr field: 0 = right 1 = left
Size field: 00 = byte 01 = word 10 = long

Condition Codes:

N   Set if high-order bit of result is set, cleared otherwise
Z   Set if result is zero, cleared otherwise
V   Cleared
C   Set if last bit rotated out of operand was set, cleared otherwise
X   Unaffected

Description:

This instruction rotates the bits of the operand either left or right. When the operand is a register, you can specify the number of bits to rotate through an immediate value (1-8) or through another data register (value 0-63). For operands in memory, you are restricted to a rotate of one bit; memory operands are restricted to 16-bit values, also.

For the ROL instruction, the processor shifts the bits to the left. As bits leave the high-order bit, the processor moves them into both the low-order bit and the Carry bit. This is illustrated as follows:

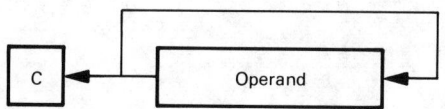

For the ROR instruction, the processor shifts the bits to the right. As bits leave the low-order bit, the processor moves them into the high-order bit as well as the Carry bit. This is illustrated on the next page.

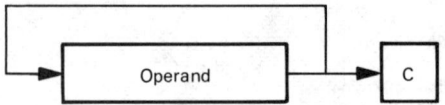

Example:

If the low-order byte of D0 contains $A7, then after

                  ROL   #3, D0

D0 contains $3D and the C bit is set.

ROXL/ROXR — Rotate With Extend

Syntax:

ROXR.s	Dn, Dm
ROXR.s	#<data>, Dn
ROXR	<ea>
ROXL.s	Dn, Dm
ROXL.s	#<data>, Dn
ROXL	<ea>

where <ea> is

	Dn	X	(d8,An,Xn)		#<data>
	An	X	(bd,An,Xn)		(d16,PC)
X	(An)	X	([bd,An,Xn],od)		(d8,PC,Xn)
X	(An)+	X	([bd,An],Xn,od)		(bd,PC,Xn)
X	−(An)	X	xxx.L		[(bd,PC,Xn),od]
X	(d16,An)	X	xxx.L		[(bd,PC),Xn,od]

and where .s is .B, .W or .L.

Instruction Format:

(Register)

15	14	13	12	11	10	9	8	7	6	5	4	3	2	1	0
1	1	1	0	Count/Register			dr	Size		i/r	1	0	Register		

(Memory)

15	14	13	12	11	10	9	8	7	6	5	4	3	2	1	0
1	1	1	0	0	1	0	dr	1	1	Effective Address					
										Mode			Register		

Count/Register field: if i/r is 0, immediate data
                      if i/r is 1, data register
dr field: 0 = right 1 = left
Size field: 00 = byte 01 = word 10 = Long

Condition Codes:

    N   Set if high-order bit of result is set, cleared otherwise
    Z   Set if result is zero, cleared otherwise
    V   Cleared

C   Set if last bit rotated out of operand was set, cleared otherwise; set to the value of X for a rotate of zero
X   Set if last bit rotated out of operand was set, cleared otherwise; unaffected for a rotate of zero

Description:

These instructions rotate the bits of the operand either left or right. When the operand is in a register, you can specify the number of bits to rotate through an immediate value (1-8) or through another data register (value 0-63). For operands in memory, you are restricted to a rotate of one bit; memory operands are restricted to 16-bit values, also.

These instructions differ from the ROL and ROR instructions in that they include the Extend (X) flag in the Rotate operation and can thus be used as part of multiprecision rotates (involving operands longer than 32 bits).

The ROXR instruction shifts the bits of the operand to the right. As bits leave the least significant bit, the processor moves them into both the Carry (C) and X flags. The processor moves the previous contents of the X flag into the most significant bit of the operand. This is illustrated as follows:

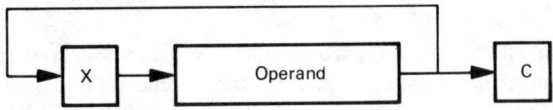

The ROXL instruction shifts the bits of the operand to the left. The processor moves the X flag into the least significant bit of the operand and moves the bit shifted out of the most significant bit into both the X and C flags. This is illustrated as follows:

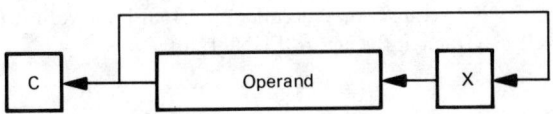

Example:

You have a four-word datum in memory, pointed to by A0, which you want to rotate one bit to the left. The following instructions will perform this function:

```
            ANDI.B      #0F, CCR        ; clear extend flag
            ROXL.W      (A0)            ; rotate the 4 words
            ROXL.W      (2,A0)
            ROXL.W      (4,A0)
            ROXL.W      (6,A0)
            BCC         NOWRAP          ; rotate msb to lsb?
            BSET.W      #0, (A0)        ; if so, then set lsb
NOWRAP:
```

RTD — Return and Deallocate Parameters
(MC68010, MC68012, MC68020)

Syntax:

    RTD   #<data>

Instruction Format:

15	14	13	12	11	10	9	8	7	6	5	4	3	2	1	0
0	1	0	0	1	1	1	0	0	1	1	1	0	0	0	0

Condition Codes:

N	Unaffected
Z	Unaffected
V	Unaffected
C	Unaffected
X	Unaffected

Description:

This instruction pulls the long word from the stack and moves it into the program counter. After this is done, the processor addresses the sign-extended 16-bit immediate data to the stack pointer. This instruction provides a handy means of returning from a subroutine that required arguments passed on the stack. Note that there is no JSR or BSR instruction that automatically pushes parameters onto the stack prior to the call. You must do this manually with the MOVE instruction.

This instruction is not available on the MC68000 and MC68008.

Example:

If a subroutine FUNC1 requires that its caller push four long words to the stack prior to the JSR FUNC1 call, then at the end of FUNC1, after

                    RTD   #$10

the function returns control to its caller and removes the four long words from the stack.

RTE — Return From Exception
(Privileged)

Syntax:

    RTE

Instruction Format:

15	14	13	12	11	10	9	8	7	6	5	4	3	2	1	0
0	1	0	0	1	1	1	0	0	1	1	1	0	1	1	1

Condition Codes:

N	Set according to stacked status word
Z	Set according to stacked status word
V	Set according to stacked status word
C	Set according to stacked status word
X	Set according to stacked status word

Description:

This instruction restores the state of the processor at the completion of an exception handler routine by pulling the stack frame from the supervisor stack. As a minimum, the status register and program counter are on the stack. Other data may also be present and removed by this instruction: the contents of the stack as well as internal processor states dictate how much data to remove. (Refer to Chapter 14 for details on stack frame contents.)

Note that this instruction is privileged; if you attempt to execute it from a user-mode program, the processor will trap through the privilege violation vector.

Example:

At the end of an interrupt exception handler on the MC68020, the instruction

    RTE

pulls a format $0 stack frame from the supervisor stack, restoring the former status register (SR) and program counter (PC).

RTM — Return from Module

Syntax:
    RTM Rn

Instruction Format:

15	14	13	12	11	10	9	8	7	6	5	4	3	2	1	0
0	0	0	0	0	1	1	0	1	1	0	0	D/A	Register		

Condition Codes:

N	Set according to stacked status word
Z	Set according to stacked status word
V	Set according to stacked status word
C	Set according to stacked status word
X	Set according to stacked status word

Description:

This instruction loads a previously saved module state from the top of the stack. The processor state (program counter, status word, and so on) come from the stacked data.

This instruction is the complement of the CALLM instruction.

Since this instruction is uncommon and requires external hardware, we will not go into further detail about it.

RTR — Return and Restore Condition Codes

Syntax:
RTR

Instruction Format:

15	14	13	12	11	10	9	8	7	6	5	4	3	2	1	0
0	1	0	0	1	1	1	0	0	1	1	1	0	0	1	1

Condition Codes:
- N   Set according to value from stack
- Z   Set according to value from stack
- V   Set according to value from stack
- C   Set according to value from stack
- X   Set according to value from stack

Description:
This instruction pulls a word from the stack and moves the five least significant bits into the condition-code register. It then pulls the long word from the stack and moves it into the program counter. Program execution continues at the new PC.

This instruction (not privileged) functions similarly to the RTE instruction (privileged), except that RTR ignores the high byte of the stacked word while RTE restores the entire status register.

The MC68000 processors don't have a special call subroutine instruction for automatically saving the condition code registers. Subroutines that use the RTR instruction should explicitly save the condition codes upon entry with the instruction MOVE CCR,−(SP).

Example:
The function SUB1 promises not to disturb the condition codes. To achieve this, it will execute:

```
SUB1:   MOVE    CCR,−(SP)   ; save CCR
          .                 ; ← body of subroutine
          .
          .
        RTR                 ; return and restore CCR
```

RTS — Return From Subroutine

Syntax:
RTS

Instruction Format:

15	14	13	12	11	10	9	8	7	6	5	4	3	2	1	0
0	1	0	0	1	1	1	0	0	1	1	1	0	1	0	1

Condition Codes:

N	Unaffected
Z	Unaffected
V	Unaffected
C	Unaffected
X	Unaffected

Description:

This instruction pulls the long word from the stack and moves it into the program counter. Program execution continues at the new program counter. This instruction is the complement to the JSR and BSR instructions.

Example:

If the instruction at address $20000 was JSR SUB1, then at the end of SUB1 after

                            RTS

the value $20004 is pulled from the stack, and program execution continues at that address.

SBCD — Subtract BCD With Extend

Syntax:

    SBCD   Dn, Dm
    SBCD   −(An), −(Am)

Instruction Format:

15	14	13	12	11	10	9	8	7	6	5	4	3	2	1	0
0	1	0	0	1	1	1	0	0	1	1	1	0	0	1	0

Condition Codes:

N	Undefined
Z	Unchanged if result is zero, cleared otherwise
V	Undefined
C	Set if a borrow was generated, cleared otherwise
X	Set if a borrow was generated, cleared otherwise

Description:

This instruction subtracts both the contents of the source operand and the value of the Extend (X) flag from the contents of the destination operand. The subtraction is performed using binary-coded decimal (BCD) arithmetic. The operands must either both be data registers or both be found in memory using address register indirect with predecrement. The size of the operation is restricted to a single byte; however, since the X flag is utilized, you can use several consecutive SBCD instructions to implement multiprecision BCD arithmetic.

Example:

If D5 contains $57 (BCD value 57), D3 contains $43 (BCD value 43), and X is set, after

        SBCD   D3, D5

D5 contains $13.

S_{cc} — Set According to Condition

Syntax:

    S_{cc} <ea>

where <ea> is

X	Dn	X	(d8,An,Xn)		#<data>
	An	X	(bd,An,Xn)		(d16,PC)
X	(An)	X	([bd,An,Xn],od)		(d8,PC,Xn)
X	(An)+	X	([bd,An],Xn,od)		(bd,PC,Xn)
X	−(An)	X	xxx.L		[(bd,PC,Xn),od]
X	(d16,An)	X	xxx.L		[(bd,PC),Xn,od]

Instruction Format:

15	14	13	12	11	10	9	8	7	6	5	4	3	2	1	0
0	1	0	1	\multicolumn{5}{c}{Condition}	1	1	\multicolumn{3}{c}{Mode}	\multicolumn{3}{c}{Register}

(Effective Address: Mode | Register)

Condition Codes:

    N   Unaffected
    Z   Unaffected
    V   Unaffected
    C   Unaffected
    X   Unaffected

Description:

This instruction tests the state of the specified condition. If the condition is true, the processor sets the byte at <ea> to all ones; if the condition is false, the processor sets the byte to all zeros. The conditions are listed in Table 21-3.

Example:

If the Carry and Zero flags are set, then after

    SLS   LOW_VAL

the byte at LOW_VAL is true (all ones).

Table 21-3. CC Conditional Tests

Mnemonic(cc)	Condition	Condition Field	Test
T	True	0000	1
F	False	0001	0
HI	High	0010	$\overline{C} \wedge \overline{Z}$
LS	Low or same	0011	$C \vee Z$
CC	Carry clear	0100	$\overline{C}$
CS	Carry set	0101	C
NE	Not equal	0110	$\overline{Z}$
EQ	Equal	0111	Z
VC	Overflow clear	1000	$\overline{V}$
VS	Overflow set	1001	V
PL	Plus	1010	$\overline{N}$
MI	Minus	1001	N
GE	Greater or equal	1100	$(N \wedge V) \vee (\overline{N} \wedge \overline{V})$
LT	Less than	1101	$(N \wedge \overline{V}) \vee (\overline{N} \wedge V)$
GT	Greater than	1110	$(N \wedge V \wedge \overline{Z}) \vee (\overline{N} \wedge \overline{V} \wedge \overline{Z})$
LE	Less or equal	1111	$Z \vee (N \wedge \overline{V}) \vee (\overline{N} \wedge V)$

STOP—Load Status Register and Stop
(Privileged)

Syntax:
STOP   #<data>

Instruction Format:

15	14	13	12	11	10	9	8	7	6	5	4	3	2	1	0
0	1	0	0	1	1	1	0	0	1	1	1	0	0	1	0

Condition Codes:

- N   Set according to immediate data
- Z   Set according to immediate data
- V   Set according to immediate data
- C   Set according to immediate data
- X   Set according to immediate data

Description:

This instruction loads the 16-bit immediate data into the status register and stops instruction execution. The processor will not resume execution until it receives an interrupt of high enough priority or else an external reset. Note that if the trace bit is set when the instruction begins, the processor will process the exception rather than stop.

This is a privileged instruction; if you attempt to execute this instruction from a user-mode program, exception processing will result.

Example:

After the instruction

                 STOP   #$300

the processor stops execution. An interrupt at priority 4 or higher will restart the processor.

SUB — Subtract Binary

Syntax:

    SUB.s   <ea>, Dn
    SUB.s   Dn, <ea>

where for dst = Dn <ea> is

X	Dn	X	(d8,An,Xn)	X	#<data>
X	An	X	(bd,An,Xn)	X	(d16,PC)
X	(An)	X	([bd,An,Xn],od)	X	(d8,PC,Xn)
X	(An)+	X	([bd,An],Xn,od)	X	(bd,PC,Xn)
X	-(An)	X	xxx.L	X	[(bd,PC,Xn),od]
X	(d16,An)	X	xxx.L	X	[(bd,PC),Xn,od]

and where for src = Dn <ea> is

	Dn	X	(d8,An,Xn)	#<data>
	An	X	(bd,An,Xn)	(d16,PC)
X	(An)	X	([bd,An,Xn],od)	(d8,PC,Xn)
X	(An)+	X	([bd,An],Xn,od)	(bd,PC,Xn)
X	-(An)	X	xxx.L	[(bd,PC,Xn),od]
X	(d16,An)	X	xxx.L	[(bd,PC),Xn,od]

and .s = .B, .W, or .L.

Instruction Format:

15	14	13	12	11	10	9	8	7	6	5	4	3	2	1	0
1	0	0	1	Data Register			Op-Mode			Effective Address					
										Mode			Register		

Op-Mode field:	Byte	Word	Long	Operation
	000	001	010	(<ea>) - (<Dn>) → <Dn>
	100	101	110	(<Dn>) - (<ea>) → <ea>

Condition Codes:

- N   Set if high-order bit of result is set, cleared otherwise
- Z   Set if result is zero, cleared otherwise
- V   Set if an overflow is generated, cleared otherwise
- C   Set if a borrow is generated, cleared otherwise
- X   Set if a borrow is generated, cleared otherwise

Description:

This instruction subtracts the source operand from the destination operand and stores the result in the destination. At least one of the operands must be a data register. Note that when the source is an address register, you can only subtract word and long-word values; in all other modes, you can subtract byte, word, and long word values.

Example:

If D0 contains $2300 and the word at the label BALANCE contains $2500, then after

                 SUB.W   D0, BALANCE

BALANCE contains $200.

SUBA — Subtract Address

Syntax:

    SUBA.s   <ea>, An

where <ea> is

X Dn	X (d8,An,Xn)	X #<data>
X An	X (bd,An,Xn)	X (d16,PC)
X (An)	X ([bd,An,Xn],od)	X (d8,PC,Xn)
X (An)+	X ([bd,An],Xn,od)	X (bd,PC,Xn)
X −(An)	X xxx.L	X [(bd,PC,Xn),od]
X (d16,An)	X xxx.L	X [(bd,PC),Xn,od]

and where .s = .W or .L.

Instruction Format:

15	14	13	12	11	10	9	8	7	6	5	4	3	2	1	0
1	0	0	1	\multicolumn{3}{c}{Data Register}			\multicolumn{3}{c}{Op-Mode}			\multicolumn{6}{c}{Effective Address}

				Data Register			Op-Mode			Effective Address					
1	0	0	1							Mode			Register		

Op-Mode field: Word   Long   Operation
                                011   111   (<ea>) − (<An>) → <An>

Condition Codes:

    N   Unaffected
    Z   Unaffected
    V   Unaffected
    C   Unaffected
    X   Unaffected

Description:

This instruction subtracts a word or long-word operand from the value in an address register. The result in the address register is always 32 bits long; the processor sign extends 16-bit operands to 32 bits before performing the subtraction.

Example:

If A0 contains $20000 and REC__SIZ is a constant defined as $220, then after

                SUB.W   REC__SIZ, A0

A0 contains $1FDE0.

SUBI — Subtract Immediate

Syntax:

    SUBI.s   #<data>, <ea>

where <ea> is

X Dn	X (d8,An,Xn)	#<data>
An	X (bd,An,Xn)	(d16,PC)

X	(An)	X	([bd,An,Xn],od)		(d8,PC,Xn)
X	(An)+	X	([bd,An],Xn,od)		(bd,PC,Xn)
X	−(An)	X	xxx.L		[(bd,PC,Xn),od]
X	(d16,An)	X	xxx.L		[(bd,PC),Xn,od]

and where .s = .B, .W, or .L.

Instruction Format:

15	14	13	12	11	10	9	8	7	6	5	4	3	2	1	0
0	0	0	0	1	0	0		Size		Effective Address					
										Mode			Register		

Size field: 00 = byte   01 = word   10 = long

Condition Codes:

- N   Set if high-order bit of result is set, cleared otherwise
- Z   Set if result is zero, cleared otherwise
- V   Set if an overflow is generated, cleared otherwise
- C   Set if a borrow is required, cleared otherwise
- X   Set if a borrow is required, cleared otherwise

Description:

This instruction subtracts the immediate data from the destination operand and stores the difference in the destination. The size of the operation matches the size of the immediate data.

Example:

If A0 points to a long word containing the value $12340000, then after

    SUBI.L   #1, (A0)

the word at A0 contains $1233FFFF.

SUBQ — Subtract Quick

Syntax:

    SUBQ.s   #<data>, <ea>

where <ea> is

X	Dn	X	(d8,An,Xn)		#<data>
X	An	X	(bd,An,Xn)		(d16,PC)
X	(An)	X	([bd,An,Xn],od)		(d8,PC,Xn)
X	(An)+	X	([bd,An],Xn,od)		(bd,PC,Xn)
X	−(An)	X	xxx.L		[(bd,PC,Xn),od]
X	(d16,An)	X	xxx.L		[(bd,PC),Xn,od]

where .s = .B, .W, or .L.

Instruction Format:

15	14	13	12	11	10	9	8	7	6	5	4	3	2	1	0
0	1	0	1	\multicolumn{3}{c}{Data}	1	\multicolumn{2}{c}{Size}	\multicolumn{4}{c}{Effective Address}			

Effective Address: Mode | Register

Data field: Three bits of immediate data, 0, 1-7 representing a range of 8, 1 to 7 respectively.
Size field: 00 = byte 01 = word 10 = long

Condition Codes:

N Set if high-order bit of result is set, cleared otherwise
Z Set if result is zero, cleared otherwise
V Set if an overflow is generated, cleared otherwise
C Set if a borrow is required, cleared otherwise
X Set if a borrow is required, cleared otherwise

Description:

This instruction subtracts the immediate data from the destination operand. Unlike SUBI, the value of the immediate data is 1-8 and is part of the instruction word rather than an extension word. When the destination is an address register, the entire register is used, regardless of the operation size.

Example:

If D0 contains $400, then after

                SUBQ.W   #4, D0

D0 contains $3FC.

SUBX — Subtract With Extend

Syntax:

SUBX.s   Dn, Dm
SUBX.s   −(An), −(Am)

where .s = .B, .W, or .L

Instruction Format:

15	14	13	12	11	10	9	8	7	6	5	4	3	2	1	0
1	0	0	1	\multicolumn{3}{c}{Destination Register*}	1	\multicolumn{2}{c}{Size}	0	0	R/M	\multicolumn{3}{c}{Source Register*}

Size field: 00 = byte 01 = word 10 = long
R/M field: 0 = data register to data register 1 = memory to memory
*If R/M = 0, specifies a data register
 If R/M = 1, specifies an address register for the predecrement addressing mode.

Condition Codes:

N	Set if high-order bit of result is set, cleared otherwise
Z	Unchanged if the result is zero, cleared otherwise
V	Set if an overflow is generated, cleared otherwise
C	Set if a borrow was generated, cleared otherwise
X	Set if a borrow was generated, cleared otherwise

Description:

This instruction subtracts both the contents of the source operand and the value or the Extend (X) flag from the contents of the destination operand. The operands must either both be data registers or both be found in memory using address register indirect with predecrement.

Example:

If D0 contains $2000300, D1 contains $4000300, and the Extend bit is set, then after

        SUBX   D0, D1

D1 contains $1FFFFFF.

SWAP — Swap Register Halves

Syntax:
    SWAP   Dn

Instruction Format:

15	14	13	12	11	10	9	8	7	6	5	4	3	2	1	0
0	1	0	0	1	0	0	0	0	1	0	0	0	Data Register		

Condition Codes:

N	Set if bit 31 of result is set, cleared otherwise
Z	Set if result is zero, cleared otherwise
V	Cleared
C	Cleared
X	Unaffected

Description:

This instruction swaps the high- and low-order 16-bit values in the given data register.

Example:

If D0 contains $12345678, then after

        SWAP   D0

D0 contains $56781234.

TAS — Indivisible Test and Set

Syntax:
TAS   <ea>

where <ea> is

X Dn	X (d8,An,Xn)	#<data>
An	X (bd,An,Xn)	(d16,PC)
X (An)	X ([bd,An,Xn],od)	(d8,PC,Xn)
X (An)+	X ([bd,An],Xn,od)	(bd,PC,Xn)
X −(An)	X xxx.L	[(bd,PC,Xn),od]
X (d16,An)	X xxx.L	[(bd,PC),Xn,od]

Instruction Format:

15	14	13	12	11	10	9	8	7	6	5	4	3	2	1	0
0	1	0	0	1	0	1	0	1	1	\multicolumn{3}{c}{Mode}	\multicolumn{3}{c}{Register}

(Bits 5–0: Effective Address — Mode / Register)

Condition Codes:
- **N** Set if high-order bit of result is set, cleared otherwise
- **Z** Set if result is zero, cleared otherwise
- **V** Cleared
- **C** Cleared
- **X** Unaffected

Description:
This instruction tests the byte-sized operand, sets the N and Z flags appropriately, and then sets the high-order bit (bit 7) of the operand to 1. The processor uses a read-modify-write bus cycle; this means that, in a multiprocessor system, no other processor can gain control of the bus in between the time that your processor tests the operand and the time it sets the operand. This instruction is useful for locking data commons and device accesses in multiprocessor systems.

Example:
If the byte at the label LOCK contains $80, then after

TAS   LOCK

LOCK still contains $80 and the N flag is set.

TRAP — Trap Through Exception Table

Syntax:
TRAP   #<vector>

Instruction Format:

15	14	13	12	11	10	9	8	7	6	5	4	3	2	1	0
0	1	0	0	1	1	1	0	0	1	0	0	\multicolumn{4}{c}{Vector}

Condition Codes:

N	Unaffected
Z	Unaffected
V	Unaffected
C	Unaffected
X	Unaffected

Description:

This instruction pushes the program counter (pointing at the instruction following TRAP) followed by the status register. It then moves the long word from the exception table vector requested by the immediate data. Table 14-1 shows the vector table entries associated with the TRAP instruction.

Note that after the TRAP is executed, the processor is operating in supervisor mode.

Example:

After the following instruction,

```
            TRAP       #3
```

the processor begins execution at the address specified by trap vector 3 (exception vector 35, offset $8C in the vector table).

TRAP$_{cc}$ — Trap on Condition
(MC68020 only)

Syntax:

TRAP$_{cc}$
TRAP$_{cc}$ #<data>

Attribute size: word, long

Instruction Format:

15	14	13	12	11	10	9	8	7	6	5	4	3	2	1	0
0	1	0	1	Condition				1	1	1	1	1	Mode		
Operand															

Mode field: 010 = word operand 011 = Long word operand 100 = no operand

Condition Codes:

N	Unaffected
Z	Unaffected

V   Unaffected
C   Unaffected
X   Unaffected

Description:

This instruction tests the specified condition and if true, it traps through exception vector 7 (offset $1C). If the condition is false, the program continues execution normally. The conditions possible are shown in Table 21-4.

The instruction may optionally specify a word or long word of immediate data; this data has no significance to the processor, and can be used for any purpose. The exception handler can access this data as an offset to the stacked program counter. (The stacked program counter is the address of the next instruction, not the immediate data.)

This instruction is available only on the MC68020.

Example:

If the Carry bit is set, then after

TRAPCS

the processor begins exception processing.

Table 21-4. Trap$_{cc}$ Conditional Tests

Mnemonic(cc)	Condition	Condition Field	Test
HI	High	0010	$\overline{C} \wedge \overline{Z}$
LS	Low or same	0011	$C \vee Z$
CC	Carry clear	0100	$\overline{C}$
CS	Carry set	0101	C
NE	Not equal	0110	$\overline{Z}$
EQ	Equal	0111	Z
VC	Overflow clear	1000	$\overline{V}$
VS	Overflow set	1001	V
PL	Plus	1010	$\overline{N}$
MI	Minus	1011	N
GE	Greater or equal	1100	$(N \wedge V) \vee (\overline{N} \wedge \overline{V})$
LT	Less than	1101	$(N \wedge \overline{V}) \vee (\overline{N} \wedge V)$
GT	Greater than	1110	$(N \wedge V \wedge \overline{Z}) \vee (\overline{N} \wedge \overline{V} \wedge \overline{Z})$
LE	Less or equal	1111	$Z \vee (N \wedge \overline{V}) \vee (\overline{N} \wedge V)$
F	Never true	0001	0
T	Always true	0000	1

TRAPV — Trap on Overflow

Syntax:

    TRAPV

Instruction Format:

15	14	13	12	11	10	9	8	7	6	5	4	3	2	1	0
0	1	0	0	1	1	1	0	0	1	1	1	0	1	1	0

Condition Codes:

    N   Unaffected
    Z   Unaffected
    V   Unaffected
    C   Unaffected
    X   Unaffected

Description:

This instruction tests the state of the Overflow (V) flag and traps through exception table vector 7 (offset $1C) if the flag is set. If the V flag is clear, program execution continues normally.

Example:

If the V flag is set, then after

    TRAPV

the processor begins exception processing.

TST — Test an Operand

Syntax:

    TST.s   <ea>

where <ea> is

X Dn	X (d8,An,Xn)	#<data>
An	X (bd,An,Xn)	X (d16,PC)
X (An)	X ([bd,An,Xn],od)	X (d8,PC,Xn)
X (An)+	X ([bd,An],Xn,od)	X (bd,PC,Xn)
X −(An)	X xxx.L	X [(bd,PC,Xn),od]
X (d16,An)	X xxx.L	X [(bd,PC),Xn,od]

and where .s = .B, .W, or .L.

Instruction Format:

15	14	13	12	11	10	9	8	7	6	5	4	3	2	1	0
0	1	0	0	1	0	1	0	\multicolumn{2}{c}{Size}	\multicolumn{6}{c}{Effective Address}

15	14	13	12	11	10	9	8	7	6	5	4	3	2	1	0
0	1	0	0	1	0	1	0	Size		Mode			Register		

Size field: 00 = byte   01 = word   10 = long

Descriptions of Individual MC68000 Instructions   **467**

Condition Codes:

N	Set if high-order bit of operand is set, cleared otherwise
Z	Set if operand is zero, cleared otherwise
V	Cleared
C	Cleared
X	Unaffected

Description:

This instruction tests the operand and sets the Negative (N) and Zero (Z) bits accordingly. The operand remains unchanged.

Example:

If the long word contained in D0 is $00000000, then after

                TST.L   D0

the Z flag is set.

UNLK — Unlink and Deallocate Stack

Syntax:

    UNLK   An

Instruction Format:

15	14	13	12	11	10	9	8	7	6	5	4	3	2	1	0
0	1	0	0	1	1	1	0	0	1	0	1	1	\multicolumn{3}{l	}{Address Register}

Condition Codes:

N	Unaffected
Z	Unaffected
V	Unaffected
C	Unaffected
X	Unaffected

Description:

This instruction loads the stack pointer with the long word stored in the given address register. A long word at the new stack pointer is then pulled and stored in the same address register. When executed, this instruction removes the frame created by the LINK instruction. Refer to that instruction for a more detailed discussion and example.

UNPK — Unpack BCD (MC68020 only)

Syntax:

    UNPK   −(An), −(Am), #<data>
    UNPK   Dn, Dm, #<data>

Instruction Format:

15	14	13	12	11 10 9	8	7	6	5	4	3	2 1 0
1	0	0	0	Destination Register*	1	1	0	0	0	R/M	Source Register*

R/M field: 0 = data register to data register
            1 = memory to memory
*If R/M = 0, specifies a data register
If R/M = 1, specifies an address register for the predecrement addressing mode.

Condition Codes:

N	Unaffected
Z	Unaffected
V	Unaffected
C	Unaffected
X	Unaffected

Description:

This instruction unpacks a byte of data containing two BCD digits into two bytes of data. It then adds the adjustment to the two-byte result. This instruction is unusual in that its source is a single byte but its destination is a two-byte value.

UNPK allows you to convert a BCD value into separate bytes, and, with the adjustment, into ASCII or EBCDIC notations. This instruction is the complement of the PACK instruction and is implemented only on the MC68020.

Example:

If the byte pointed to by A0 (after decrement) contains $45, then after

    UNPK   −(A0), −(A1), #$30

A1 points to a word containing $3435 (ASCII for "45").

VI
Appendices

The following pages summarize the MC68000 instruction set. Appendix A lists the instructions and op-codes alphabetically. Appendix B lists the instructions numerically by op-code.

A
Alphabetic Listing of Instructions

Mnemonic	Description	Opcode
ABCD	Add decimal with extend	1100 xxx1 0000 xxxx
ADD	Add	1101 xxxx xxxx xxxx
ADDA	Add address	1101 xxxx xxxx xxxx
ADDI	Add immediate	0000 0110 xxxx xxxx
ADDQ	Add quick	0101 xxx0 xxxx xxxx
ADDX	Add extended	1101 xxx1 xx00 xxxx
AND	AND logical	1100 xxxx xxxx xxxx
ANDI	AND immediate	0000 0010 xxxx xxxx
ANDI	AND immediate to CCR	0000 0010 0011 1100
ANDI	AND immediate to SR	0000 0010 0111 1100
ASL	Arithmetic shift left	1110 xxx1 xxx0 0xxx
ASR	Arithmetic shift right	1110 xxx0 xxx0 0xxx
B$_{cc}$	Branch	0110 xxxx xxxx xxxx
BCHG	Test bit and change	0000 xxx1 01xx xxxx
BCLR	Test bit and clear	0000 0001 10xx xxxx
BFCHG	Test bit field and change	1110 1010 11xx xxxx 0000 xxxx xxxx xxxx
BFCLR	Test bit field and clear	1110 1100 11xx xxxx 0000 xxxx xxxx xxxx
BFEXTS	Extract signed bit field	1110 1011 11xx xxxx 0xxx xxxx xxxx xxxx
BFEXTU	Extract unsigned bit field	1110 1001 11xx xxxx 0xxx xxxx xxxx xxxx
BFFFO	Find first one in bit field	1110 1101 11xx xxxx 0xxx xxxx xxxx xxxx
BFINS	Insert bit field	1110 1111 11xx xxxx 0xxx xxxx xxxx xxxx
BFSET	Set bit field	1110 1110 11xx xxxx 0000 xxxx xxxx xxxx
BFTST	Test bit field	1110 1000 11xx xxxx 0000 xxxx xxxx xxxx
BKPT	Breakpoint	0100 1000 0100 1xxx

Mnemonic	Description	Opcode
BSET	Test bit and set	0000 xxx1 11xx xxxx
BSR	Branch to subroutine	0110 0001 xxxx xxxx
BTST	Test bit	0000 xxx1 00xx xxxx
CALLM	Call module	0000 0110 11xx xxxx
CAS	Compare and swap one operand	0000 1xx0 11xx xxxx 0000 000x xx00 0xxx
CAS2	Compare and swap two operands	0000 1xx0 1111 1100 xxxx 000x xx00 0xxx xxxx 000x xx00 0xxx
CHK	Check against bounds	0100 xxxx xxxx xxxx
CHK2	Check against two bounds	0000 0xx0 11xx xxxx xxxx 1000 0000 0000
CLR	Clear operand	0100 0010 xxxx xxxx
CMP	Compare	1011 xxxx xxxx xxxx
CMP2	Compare against two bounds	0000 0xx0 11xx xxxx xxxx 0000 0000 0000
CMPA	Compare address	1011 xxxx xxxx xxxx
CMPI	Compare immediate	0000 1100 xxxx xxxx
CMPM	Compare memory	1011 xxx1 xx00 1xxx
DBcc	Test, decrement and branch	0101 xxxx 1100 1xxx
DIVS	Signed divide	1000 xxx1 11xx xxxx
DIVSL	Long signed divide	0100 1100 01xx xxxx 0xxx 1x00 0000 0xxx
DIVU	Unsigned divide	1000 xxx0 11xx xxxx
DIVUL	Long unsigned divide	0100 1100 01xx xxxx 0xxx 0x00 0000 0xxx
EOR	Exclusive OR	1011 xxxx xxxx xxxx
EORI	Exclusive OR immediate	0000 1010 xxxx xxxx
EORI	Exclusive OR immediate to CCR	0000 1010 0011 1100
EORI	Exclusive OR immediate to SR	0000 1010 0111 1100
EXG	Exchange registers	1100 xxx1 xxxx xxxx
EXT	Extend sign	0100 1000 xx00 0xxx
EXTB	Extend sign of byte to long	0100 1001 xx00 0xxx
ILLEGAL	Illegal instruction	0100 1010 1111 1100
JMP	Jump	0100 1110 11xx xxxx
JSR	Jump to subroutine	0100 1110 10xx xxxx
LEA	Load effective address	0100 xxx1 11xx xxxx
LINK	Link and allocate	0100 1x10 010x xxxx
LSL	Logical shift left	1110 xxx1 xxxx xxxx
LSR	Logical shift right	1110 xxx0 xxxx xxxx
MOVE	Move data	00xx xxxx xxxx xxxx
MOVE	Move from CCR	0100 0010 11xx xxxx
MOVE	Move from SR	0100 0000 11xx xxxx
MOVE	Move to CCR	0100 0100 11xx xxxx
MOVE	Move to SR	0100 0110 11xx xxxx
MOVE	Move user stack pointer	0100 1110 0110 xxxx
MOVEA	Move address	00xx xxx0 0xxx xxxx
MOVEC	Move control register	0100 1110 0111 101x xxxx xxxx xxxx xxxx
MOVEM	Move multiple registers	0100 1x00 1xxx xxxx
MOVEP	Move peripheral	0000 xxxx xx00 1xxx
MOVEQ	Move quick	0111 xxx0 xxxx xxxx
MOVES	Move address space	0000 1110 xxxx xxxx xxxx x000 0000 0000
MULS	Signed multiply	1100 xxx1 11xx xxxx
MULSL	Long signed multiply	0100 1100 00xx xxxx 0xxx 1x00 0000 0xxx
MULU	Unsigned multiply	1100 xxx0 11xx xxxx
MULUL	Long unsigned multiply	0100 1100 00xx xxxx 0xxx 0x00 0000 0xxx
NBCD	Negate decimal with extend	0100 1000 00xx xxxx
NEG	Negate	0100 0100 xxxx xxxx
NEGX	Negate with extend	0100 0000 xxxx xxxx
NOP	No operation	0100 1110 0111 0001
NOT	Logical complement	0100 0110 xxxx xxxx
OR	Inclusive OR	1000 xxxx xxxx xxxx
ORI	Inclusive OR immediate	0000 0000 xxxx xxxx
ORI	Inclusive OR immediate to CCR	0000 0000 0011 1100
ORI	Inclusive OR immediate to SR	0000 0000 0111 1100

Mnemonic	Description	Opcode
PACK	Pack to BCD	1000 xxx1 0100 xxxx
PEA	Push effective address	0100 1000 01xx xxxx
RESET	Reset external devices	0100 1110 0111 0000
ROL	Rotate left	1110 xxx1 xxxx xxxx
ROLX	Rotate left with extend	1110 xxx1 xxxx xxxx
ROR	Rotate right	1110 xxx0 xxxx xxxx
RORX	Rotate right with extend	1110 xxx0 xxxx xxxx
RTD	Return and deallocate	0100 1110 0111 0100
RTE	Return from exception	0100 1110 0111 0011
RTM	Return from module	0000 0110 1100 xxxx
RTR	Return and restore CCR	0100 1110 0111 0111
RTS	Return from subroutine	0100 1110 0111 0101
SBCD	Subtract decimal with extend	1000 xxx1 0000 xxxx
Scc	Set according to codes	0101 xxxx 11xx xxxx
STOP	Load SR and stop processor	0100 1110 0111 0010
SUB	Subtract	1001 xxxx xxxx xxxx
SUBA	Subtract address	1001 xxxx xxxx xxxx
SUBI	Subtract immediate	0000 0100 xxxx xxxx
SUBQ	Subtract quick	0101 xxx1 xxxx xxxx
SUBX	Subtract with extend	1001 xxx1 xx00 xxxx
SWAP	Swap register halves	0100 1000 0100 0xxx
TAS	Test and set operand	0100 1010 11xx xxxx
TRAP	Trap through vector table	0100 1110 0100 xxxx
TRAPcc	Trap on condition	0101 xxxx 1111 1xxx
TRAPV	Trap on overflow	0100 1110 0111 0110
TST	Test operand	0100 1010 xxxx xxxx
UNLK	Unlink stack	0100 1110 0101 1xxx
UNPK	Unpack BCD	1000 xxx1 1000 xxxx

B
Numeric Listing of Instructions

Mnemonic	Description	Opcode
ORI	Inclusive OR immediate to CCR	0000 0000 0011 1100
ORI	Inclusive OR immediate to SR	0000 0000 0111 1100
ORI	Inclusive OR immediate	0000 0000 xxxx xxxx
BCLR	Test bit and clear	0000 0001 10xx xxxx
ANDI	AND immediate to CCR	0000 0010 0011 1100
ANDI	AND immediate to SR	0000 0010 0111 1100
ANDI	AND immediate	0000 0010 xxxx xxxx
SUBI	Subtract immediate	0000 0100 xxxx xxxx
RTM	Return from module	0000 0110 1100 xxxx
CALLM	Call module	0000 0110 11xx xxxx
ADDI	Add immediate	0000 0110 xxxx xxxx
CMP2	Compare against two bounds	0000 0xx0 11xx xxxx xxxx 0000 0000 0000
CHK2	Check against two bounds	0000 0xx0 11xx xxxx xxxx 1000 0000 0000
EORI	Exclusive OR immediate to CCR	0000 1010 0011 1100
EORI	Exclusive OR immediate to SR	0000 1010 0111 1100
EORI	Exclusive OR immediate	0000 1010 xxxx xxxx
CMPI	Compare immediate	0000 1100 xxxx xxxx
MOVES	Move address space	0000 1110 xxxx xxxx xxxx x000 0000 0000
CAS2	Compare and swap two operands	0000 1xx0 1111 1100 xxxx 000x xx00 0xxx xxxx 000x xx00 0xxx
CAS	Compare and swap one operand	0000 1xx0 11xx xxxx 0000 000x xx00 0xxx
BTST	Test bit	0000 xxx1 00xx xxxx

Mnemonic	Description	Opcode
BCHG	Test bit and change	0000 xxx1 01xx xxxx
BSET	Test bit and set	0000 xxx1 11xx xxxx
MOVEP	Move peripheral	0000 xxxx xx00 1xxx
MOVEA	Move address	00xx xxx0 0xxx xxxx
MOVE	Move data	00xx xxxx xxxx xxxx
MOVE	Move from SR	0100 0000 11xx xxxx
NEGX	Negate with extend	0100 0000 xxxx xxxx
MOVE	Move from CCR	0100 0010 11xx xxxx
CLR	Clear operand	0100 0010 xxxx xxxx
MOVE	Move to CCR	0100 0100 11xx xxxx
NEG	Negate	0100 0100 xxxx xxxx
MOVE	Move to SR	0100 0110 11xx xxxx
NOT	Logical complement	0100 0110 xxxx xxxx
NBCD	Negate decimal with extend	0100 1000 00xx xxxx
SWAP	Swap register halves	0100 1000 0100 0xxx
BKPT	Breakpoint	0100 1000 0100 1xxx
PEA	Push effective address	0100 1000 01xx xxxx
EXT	Extend sign	0100 1000 xx00 0xxx
EXTB	Extend sign of byte to long	0100 1001 xx00 0xxx
ILLEGAL	Illegal instruction	0100 1010 1111 1100
TAS	Test and set operand	0100 1010 11xx xxxx
TST	Test operand	0100 1010 xxxx xxxx
MULUL	Long unsigned multiply	0100 1100 00xx xxxx 0xxx 0x00 0000 0xxx
MULSL	Long signed multiply	0100 1100 00xx xxxx 0xxx 1x00 0000 0xxx
DIVUL	Long unsigned divide	0100 1100 01xx xxxx 0xxx 0x00 0000 0xxx
DIVSL	Long signed divide	0100 1100 01xx xxxx 0xxx 1x00 0000 0xxx
TRAP	Trap through vector table	0100 1110 0100 xxxx
UNLK	Unlink stack	0100 1110 0101 1xxx
MOVE	Move user stack pointer	0100 1110 0110 xxxx
RESET	Reset external devices	0100 1110 0111 0000
NOP	No operation	0100 1110 0111 0001
STOP	Load SR and stop processor	0100 1110 0111 0010
RTE	Return from exception	0100 1110 0111 0011
RTD	Return and deallocate	0100 1110 0111 0100
RTS	Return from subroutine	0100 1110 0111 0101
TRAPV	Trap on overflow	0100 1110 0111 0110
RTR	Return and restore CCR	0100 1110 0111 0111
MOVEC	Move control register	0100 1110 0111 101x xxxx xxxx xxxx xxxx
JSR	Jump to subroutine	0100 1110 10xx xxxx
JMP	Jump	0100 1110 11xx xxxx
MOVEM	Move multiple registers	0100 1x00 1xxx xxxx
LINK	Link and allocate	0100 1x10 010x xxxx
LSL	Logical shift left	1110 xxx1 xxxx xxxx
LEA	Load effective address	0100 xxx1 11xx xxxx
CHK	Check against bounds	0100 xxxx xxxx xxxx
ADDQ	Add quick	0101 xxx0 xxxx xxxx
SUBQ	Subtract quick	0101 xxx1 xxxx xxxx
DBcc	Test, decrement and branch	0101 xxxx 1100 1xxx
TRAPcc	Trap on condition	0101 xxxx 1111 1xxx
Scc	Set according to codes	0101 xxxx 11xx xxxx
BSR	Branch to subroutine	0110 0001 xxxx xxxx
Bcc	Branch	0110 xxxx xxxx xxxx
MOVEQ	Move quick	0111 xxx0 xxxx xxxx
DIVU	Unsigned divide	1000 xxx0 11xx xxxx
SBCD	Subtract decimal with extend	1000 xxx1 0000 xxxx
PACK	Pack to BCD	1000 xxx1 0100 xxxx
UNPK	Unpack BCD	1000 xxx1 1000 xxxx

Mnemonic	Description	Opcode
DIVS	Signed divide	1000 xxx1 11xx xxxx
OR	Inclusive OR	1000 xxxx xxxx xxxx
SUBX	Subtract with extend	1001 xxx1 xx00 xxxx
SUB	Subtract	1001 xxxx xxxx xxxx
SUBA	Subtract address	1001 xxxx xxxx xxxx
CMPM	Compare memory	1011 xxx1 xx00 1xxx
CMPA	Compare address	1011 xxxx xxxx xxxx
EOR	Exclusive OR	1011 xxxx xxxx xxxx
CMP	Compare	1011 xxxx xxxx xxxx
MULU	Unsigned multiply	1100 xxx0 11xx xxxx
ABCD	Add decimal with extend	1100 xxx1 0000 xxxx
MULS	Signed multiply	1100 xxx1 11xx xxxx
EXG	Exchange registers	1100 xxx1 xxxx xxxx
AND	AND logical	1100 xxxx xxxx xxxx
ADDX	Add extended	1101 xxx1 xx00 xxxx
ADD	Add	1101 xxxx xxxx xxxx
ADDA	Add address	1101 xxxx xxxx xxxx
BFTST	Test bit field	1110 1000 11xx xxxx 0000 xxxx xxxx xxxx
BFEXTU	Extract unsigned bit field	1110 1001 11xx xxxx 0xxx xxxx xxxx xxxx
BFCHG	Test bit field and change	1110 1010 11xx xxxx 0000 xxxx xxxx xxxx
BFEXTS	Extract signed bit field	1110 1011 11xx xxxx 0xxx xxxx xxxx xxxx
BFCLR	Test bit field and clear	1110 1100 11xx xxxx 0000 xxxx xxxx xxxx
BFFFO	Find first one in bit field	1110 1101 11xx xxxx 0xxx xxxx xxxx xxxx
BFSET	Set bit field	1110 1110 11xx xxxx 0000 xxxx xxxx xxxx
BFINS	Insert bit field	1110 1111 11xx xxxx 0xxx xxxx xxxx xxxx
ASR	Arithmetic shift right	1110 xxx0 xxx0 0xxx
LSR	Logical shift right	1110 xxx0 xxxx xxxx
ROR	Rotate right	1110 xxx0 xxxx xxxx
RORX	Rotate right with extend	1110 xxx0 xxxx xxxx
ASL	Arithmetic shift left	1110 xxx1 xxx0 0xxx
ROL	Rotate left	1110 xxx1 xxxx xxxx
ROLX	Rotate left with extend	1110 xxx1 xxxx xxxx

Index

A

A-line instructions, 216
ABCD, 371
Absolute addressing, 39
ADD, 372
Add instructions
    address, 373
    binary, 372
    binary coded decimal, 371
    immediate, 374
    quick, 375
    with extend, 376
ADDA, 373
ADDI, 374
Addition, 62, 68, 77, 81, 132, 134, 135, 185
ADDQ, 375
Address errors, 217, 228
Address register direct addressing, 38
Address register indirect addressing, 40
    with displacement, 42
    with displacement and index, 44
    with postincrement, 42
Address register indirect with predecrement, 41
Address registers, 19, 21
Addressing modes, 36
ADDX, 376
Alternate function code registers, 26
ALU (arithmetic logic unit), 19
AND, 376
And instructions
    immediate, 377
    to the condition codes, 378
    to the status register, 379
ANDI, 377
    to CCR, 378
    to SR, 379

Arithmetic shift, 380
Arrays, 75
    multidimensional, 138
ASCII, 95
ASL, 380
ASR, 380
Assembler mnemonics, 369
Assemblers, 4
    errors, 340
    function, 9
    types, 10
Assembly language
    advantages, 6
    applications, 8
    format, 10
Autovectoring, 219, 235

B

Baudot, 95
Bcc, 382
BCD (binary coded decimal)
    instructions, 34
BCHG, 383
BCLR, 384
BFCHG, 384
BFCLR, 386
BFEXTS, 387
BFEXTU, 388
BFFFO, 389
BFINS, 390
BFSET, 391
BFTST, 392
Binary digits, 4
Bit field instructions, 33, 197
    extraction, 387, 388
    insert, 390
    scan, 389
    test, 392

Bit field instructions, *continued*
    test and change, 385
    test and set, 391
    test clear, 386
Bit manipulation instructions, 32, 108
Bit test instructions
    test, 397
    test and change, 383
    test and clear, 384
    test and set, 394
Bits, 4
BKPT, 393
Boolean arithmetic instructions, 31
Branch, 382
Branch to subroutine, 396
Breakpoint Instruction, 393
Breakpoints, 218
    debugging, 324
    inserting, 324
    precautions, 335
    setting and clearing, 324
BSET, 394
BSR, 396
BTST, 397
Bubble sort, 162
Bus errors, 220, 229
Buses, 19, 201
Byte disassembly, 65

C

CAAR (cache address register), 28
Cache control, 27
CACR (cache control register), 28
Call module, 398
Call-by-name, 176
Call-by-value, 176
CALLM, 398
Carry bit, 23
CAS, 399
CAS2, 400
Case structure, 292
CCR (condition code register), 23
Check bounds, 402, 403
Checklist, 334
CHK, 402
CHK2, 403

Clear, 404
CLR, 404
CMP, 405
CMP2, 408
CMPA, 406
CMPI, 407
CMPM, 408
Coding, 259
Comments, 15, 54, 312
Communication devices, 202
Compare instructions
    address, 406
    binary, 405
    bounds, 408
    compare and swap, 399, 400
    immediate, 407
    memory, 408
Comparison, 66, 86
Complement, 442
Conditional assembly, 14
Constant definition, 12
Conversion
    ASCII to decimal, 122
    BCD to decimal, 124
    binary to ASCII, 127
    decimal to seven-segment, 119
    hexadecimal to ASCII, 118, 179, 182
Coprocessor control instructions, 36
CPU (central processing unit), 19
CPU support peripherals, 203
CPU-peripheral interface, 203
Cross assemblers, 10

D

Data definition, 12
Data movement, 30, 59, 425
Data register direct addressing, 38
Data registers, 19, 21
Data space, 224
Data structures, 160, 306
DBcc, 409
DC (define constant data), 55, 122
Debugging, 259, 323
Decimal precision, 135
Device controllers, 203

Direct addressing, 37
Directives, 10, 12, 55
Divide, signed, 411
Divide, unsigned, 412
Division, 143
DIVS, 411
DIVSL, 411
DIVU, 412
DIVUL, 412
DMA (direct memory access), 206, 208
Do-until structure, 291
Do-while structure, 291
Documentation, 260, 311
    importance of, 322
Documentation package, 321
DS (define storage), 56

E

EBCDIC, 95
Effective address, 36, 76, 365, 421, 447
END (end of program), 56
EOR, 414
EORI, 415
EORI to CCR, 416
EORI to SR, 416
EQU (equate), 56
Errors
    assembler, 340
    exception processing, 341
    handling, 262
    initialization, 335
    input/output, 339
    looping, 336
    processing, 337
    string manipulation, 339
Example format, 53
Exception initialization, 236
Exception priorities, 214, 229
Exception processing, 211, 232, 233, 234
Exception processing sequences, 213
Exception types, 213, 228
Exception vector table, 211, 230
Exceptions, 225
Exchange registers, 417

Exclusive or instructions
    binary, 414
    immediate, 415
    to the condition codes, 416
    to the status register, 416
EXG, 417
Expressions, 55
EXT, 418
EXTB, 418
Extend bit, 23
External definition, 13

F

F-line instructions, 216
Factorials, 69, 187
File inclusion, 14
Flags, clearing and setting, 133
Flowcharting, 276
    advantages, 276
    as documentation, 318
    disadvantages, 276
    examples, 278
Format error, 218

H

Hashing, 149
High-level languages, 3
    advantages, 6
    applications, 7
    disadvantages, 6
Human factors, 263

I

If-then-else structure, 290
ILLEGAL, 418
Illegal instructions, 215, 228, 418
Immediate addressing, 39
Implicit addressing, 37
Information hiding, 288
Inputs/Outputs in design, 261, 262
Instruction set, 30
    alphabetic order, 471
    encoding, 365
    format, 363
    numeric order, 475
Instruction traps, 215

Integer arithmetic instructions, 31
Interrupt enabling and disabling, 227
Interrupt mask bits, 23
Interrupt system characteristics, 226
Interrupts, 206, 219, 225, 227, 229

J

JMP, 419
JSR, 420
Jump, 419
Jump table, 165
Jump to subroutine, 420

L

Labels, 11, 54
Library routines, 320
LIFO (last-in, first-out), 22
LINK, 421
Link and allocate space, 421
Linkers, 10
Listing control directives, 14
Lists
    doubly-linked, 158
    entry, 147
    linked, 156
    searching, 150
Load effective address, 421
Logic analyzer, 333
Logical and, 376
Loops, 75
LSL, 423
LSR, 423

M

Machine architecture, 19
Machine language, 4
Macro assemblers, 10
Macros, 13
Maintenance, 260
Maintenance manual, 322
Master bit, 26
Memory
    access sizes, 28
    arrangement, 28
    byte ordering, 28
Memory dump, 330
Memory indirect addressing, 47, 196
Memory indirect post indexed, 47

Memory indirect preindexed, 48
Memory maps, 319
MMU (memory management unit), 220
Mnemonics, 4, 11, 54
Modes of operation, 227
Modular programming, 285
    advantages, 285
    disadvantages, 285
    examples, 286
    principles, 286
MOVE, 425
    from CCR, 427
    from SR, 428
    to CCR, 428
    to SR, 429
MOVEA, 426
MOVEC, 431
MOVEM, 432
MOVEP, 433
MOVEQ, 434
MOVES, 434
MOVE USP, 430
Move instructions
    address space, 434
    from condition codes, 427
    from status register, 428
    multiple registers, 432
    peripheral data, 433
    quick, 434
    to address register, 426
    to condition codes, 428
    to status register, 429
    to/from control register, 431
    to/from user stack pointer, 430
MULS, 436
Multiplication, 138, 139
Multiply, signed, 436
Multiply, unsigned, 438
Multiprecision arithmetic, 131
Multiprocessor control instructions, 36
MULU, 438

N

NBCD, 439
NEG, 440
Negate, 440
Negate binary coded decimal, 439

Negative bit, 23
NEGX, 440
No operation, 441
NOP, 441
Normalization, 90
NOT, 442
Notation, 54

O

Object code, 10
Off-line storage, 202
On-line memory, 201
One's complement, 61
Operands, 9, 12
Operator interaction, 263
OR, 443
OR to CCR, 445
OR to SR, 445
Or instructions
  immediate, 444
  to condition codes, 445
  to status register, 445
ORG (origin), 56
ORI, 444
Overflow bit, 23

P

PACK, 446
Pack binary coded decimal, 446
Parameter lists, 173, 319
Parity, 106
PC (program counter), 22
PEA, 447
Peripherals, 19, 201
Polled I/O, 206, 226
Position independent code, 39, 177
Priorities, 23, 226
Privilege violations, 20, 228
Privileged instructions, 20, 228
Problem definition, 259, 261
Processing section, 262
Program control instructions, 34
Program counter indirect with displacement, 45
Program counter indirect with displacement and index, 46
Program counter memory indirect postindexed, 49

Program counter memory indirect preindexed, 50
Program design, 259
Program development, 15
Program format, 57
Program logic manual, 322
Program sections, 13
Program space, 224
Push effective address, 447

Q

Queues, 156

R

Radices, 4, 55
RAM (random access memory), 19, 201
Read-modify-write cycle, 400, 463
Real time clock, 245
Redesign, 260
Register dump, 326
Register indirect addressing, 40
Reset exception, 222, 229
Reset external devices, 448
RESET instruction, 448
Return and deallocate, 452
Return and restore condition codes, 454
Return from exception, 452
Return from module, 453
Return from subroutine, 454
ROL, 448
ROM (read only memory), 201
ROR, 448
Rotate, 448, 450
ROXL, 450
ROXR, 450
RTD, 452
RTE, 452
RTM, 453
RTR, 454
RTS, 454
Running the program, 57

S

SBCD, 455
Scaled indices, 195
Scaling, 44
Scc, 456
Self-documenting programs, 311

Set according to condition codes, 456
Shift, 423
Shift and rotate instructions, 32, 64, 381, 448, 450
Sign extension, 21, 418
Single stepping, 329
Software development stages, 257
Software simulation, 332
Sorting, 161
Source code, 9
SRAM (static random access memory), 201
Stack frames, 214
Stack pointer, 25, 27
Stacks, 22, 160, 421
Standard documentation forms, 321
Status register, 23, 26
Status/control registers, 19, 204
STOP, 457
Stop execution, 457
Storage devices, 201
Strings, 95
    comparison, 109
    length, 97
    search, 102
    substitution, 103
Structured programming, 289
    advantages, 293
    as documentation, 318
    disadvantages, 294
    examples, 293, 295
    rules, 300
Structured testing, 358
SUB, 458
SUBA, 459
SUBI, 459, 460
Subroutines, 173
    recursive, 178
    reentrant, 177
    relocatable, 177
Subtraction instructions
    address, 459
    binary, 458
    binary coded decimal, 455
    immediate, 459
    quick, 460
    with extend, 461
SUBX, 461

Supervisor bit, 23
Supervisor mode, 20
SWAP, 462
Swap register halves, 462
System control instructions, 35

T

Table lookup, 121
Tables, 147
TAS, 463
Test, decrement and branch, 409
Test operand, 466
Test and set, 463
Testing, 260, 357
    aids, 358
    data, 358
    rules, 360
    structured methods, 358
Top down design, 301
    disadvantages, 301
    examples, 302
Totaling, 84
Trace bit, 23, 26
Tracing, 218, 329
TRAP, 463
Trap on condition, 464
Trap on overflow, 466
Trap through exception table, 463
TRAPcc, 464
TRAPV, 466
TST, 466

U

Unimplemented instructions, 215, 228
Unlink and deallocate stack, 467
UNLK, 467
Unpack binary coded decimal, 467
UNPK, 467
User mode, 20
User's guide, 322

V

Vector base register, 26
Vector table, 212, 230
Vectoring, 226
Virtual Memory, 220

Z

Zero bit, 23

Other related Osborne/McGraw-Hill titles include:

68000 Microprocessor Handbook
Second Edition
by William Cramer and Gerry Kane

For serious programmers and hardware designers, this is a complete handbook to the 68000 microprocessor family. In this revised, expanded edition, all of the 68000 chips, including the 68008, 68010, 68012, and 68020, are examined. You'll find in-depth coverage of addressing modes, signal conventions, instruction sets, exception processing logic, as well as timing and bus operations. If you're designing software for the Macintosh,™ Atari® ST, Commodore Amiga,™ Tandy® 6000, AT&T UNIX™ PC, or other 68000 computers, this handbook is an invaluable resource for all your programming queries.

$14.95p
0-07-881205-4, 176 pp., 7⅜ x 9¼

Mastering the Macintosh™ Toolbox
by David B. Peatroy and DATATECH Publications

With *Mastering the Macintosh™ Toolbox*, experienced programmers can access the storehouse of programming routines found in the Mac's special Toolbox. These routines enable you to include the unique features of the Apple® Macintosh™ computer in a variety of software applications. You'll learn to use Macintosh™ Pascal to call up Toolbox routines for programming graphics, icons, windows, menus, the cursor, and the mouse. A compendium of powerful programming tools, *Mastering the Macintosh™ Toolbox* lets you take full advantage of the Macintosh computer.

$16.95p
0-07-881203-8, 208 pp., 7⅜ x 9¼

80386/80286 Assembly Language Programming
by William H. Murray and Chris Pappas

This comprehensive guide enables serious programmers to take full advantage of the unique design of the 80386 and 80286 microprocessors found in the IBM® PC AT, COMPAQ® Desk Pro 286, TANDY 6000,® and other major computer systems. Instructions for programming the 8087/80287/80387 coprocessor are also included. The authors carefully detail the use of assembler pseudo-ops; macros, procedures, and libraries; and testing and debugging techniques. You'll also find instructions for interacting with high-level languages such as BASIC, Pascal, and FORTRAN. Many practical programming examples show beginners how to implement assembly language, while experienced programmers have an invaluable reference to the 80386 and 80286 instruction set.

$19.95p
0-07-881217-8, 400 pp., 6⅜ x 9¼

65816/65802 Assembly Language Programming
Michael Fischer

This addition to the Osborne/McGraw-Hill ALP series is a complete handbook to assembly language programming with the 65816 and 65802 microprocessors. Serious programmers will find complete coverage of the 65816 and 65802 chip series. Assemblers, instruction sets, arithmetic operations, loops, and code conversion are presented. You'll also learn about sorting and searching, subroutines, I/O and interrupts, debugging and testing. Michael Fischer, a columnist for *Bay Area Computer Currents* and director of the San Francisco Apple Core User Group, provides you with concise, comprehensive information. *65816/65802 Assembly Language Programming* fulfills the need for both a tutorial and a lasting reference.

$19.95p
0-07-881235-6, 450 pp., 6⅜ x 9¼

The 8086 Book
by Russell Rector and George Alexy

"...is far superior to any other book about the 8086." (Dr. Dobbs Journal)

Anyone using, designing, or simply interested in an 8086-based system will be delighted by this book's scope and authority. As the 16-bit microprocessor gains wider inclusion in small computers, this book becomes invaluable as a reference tool which covers the timing, architecture and design of the 8086, as well as optimal programming techniques, interfacing, special features and more.

$18.95p
0-07-931029-X, 624 pp., 6½ x 9¼

C Made Easy
by Herbert Schildt

With Osborne/McGraw-Hill's popular "Made Easy" format, you can learn C programming in no time. Start with the fundamentals and work through the text at your own speed. Schildt begins with general concepts, then introduces functions, libraries, and disk input/

output, and finally advanced concepts affecting the C programming environment and UNIX™ operating system. Each chapter covers commands that you can learn to use immediately in the hands-on exercises that follow. If you already know BASIC, you'll find that Schildt's C equivalents will shorten your learning time. *C Made Easy* is a step-by-step tutorial for all beginning C programmers.

$18.95p
0-07-881178-3, 350 pp., 7³⁄₈ x 9¹⁄₄

Advanced C
by Herbert Schildt

Herbert Schildt, author of *C Made Easy*, now shows experienced C programmers how to develop advanced skills. You'll find thorough coverage of important C programming topics including operating system interfacing, compressed data formats, dynamic allocation, linked lists, binary trees, and porting. Schildt also discusses sorting and searching, stacks, queues, encryption, simulations, debugging techniques, and converting Pascal and BASIC programs for use with C. A complete handbook, *Advanced C* is both a teaching guide and a lasting resource.

$19.95p
0-07-881208-9, 350 pp., 7³⁄₈ x 9¹⁄₄

The C Library
by Kris Jamsa

Design and implement more effective programs with the wealth of programming tools that are offered in *The C Library*. Experienced C programmers will find over 125 carefully structured routines ranging from macros to actual UNIX™ utilities. There are tools for string manipulation, pointers, input/output, array manipulation, recursion, sorting algorithms, and file manipulation. In addition, Jamsa provides several C routines that have previously been available only through expensive software packages. Build your skills by taking routines introduced in early chapters and using them to develop advanced programs covered later in the text. A complete resource, *The C Library* belongs on the shelf of every C programmer.

$18.95p
0-07-881110-4, 220 pp., 7³⁄₈ x 9¹⁄₄

Using Turbo Pascal™
by Steve Wood

Maximize your advanced programming skills with *Using Turbo Pascal*™ by Steve Wood. Wood, a programmer for Precision Logic Systems, thoroughly covers Turbo Pascal, including version 3.0, for the experienced programmer. The book discusses program design and Pascal's syntax requirements, develops a useful application of the program, and gives an overview of some of the advanced utilities and features available with Turbo Pascal.

$19.95p
0-07-881148-1, 350 pp., 6¹⁄₂ x 9¹⁄₄

Advanced Turbo Pascal®: Programming & Techniques
Herbert Schildt

For instruction and reference, *Advanced Turbo Pascal*® is an invaluable resource. This highlevel guide benefits experienced Turbo Pascal® users who want to build their programming skills. Every standalone chapter presents a complete programming topic: sorting and searching; stacks, queues, linked lists, and binary trees; dynamic allocation using pointers; and operating-system interfacing. You'll also examine statistics, encryption and compressed data formats, random numbers and simulations, expression parsers, converting C and BASIC to Pascal, efficiency, porting and debugging.

$18.95p
0-07-881220-8, 350 pp., 7³⁄₈ x 9¹⁄₄

Turbo Pascal® Library
Kris Jamsa and Steven Nameroff

This library of programming tools enables Turbo Pascal® users to write more effective programs that take full advantage of Borland's best-selling compiler. In this varied collection there are utility routines for Pascal macros as well as routines for string and array manipulation, records, pointers, and pipes. You'll also find I/O routines and a discussion of sorting that covers bubble, shell, and quick-sort algorithms. In addition, the authors provide routines for the Turbo Toolbox® and the new Turbo Graphix® package. *Turbo Pascal® Library* complements two other Osborne tutorials, *Using Turbo Pascal*® and *Advanced Turbo Pascal*® **and provides programmers with an excellent resource of practical tools.**

$18.95p
0-07-881238-0, 300 pp., 7³⁄₈ x 9¹⁄₄

A User Guide to the UNIX™ System (2nd Edition)
by Dr. Rebecca Thomas and Jean Yates

Now the best-selling *User Guide to the UNIX*™ *System* has been revised and expanded to cover applications of the UNIX™ operating system for Bell Laboratories' New System V and Berkeley UNIX. Twelve extensive tutorials take you from initial log on to advanced program control and input/output procedures. You'll find special emphasis given to word processing and to the most commonly used UNIX system commands. Error messages are fully explained, and a System Administration appendix tells you how to oversee the system's operation. Whether you're already familiar with UNIX or just getting acquainted, this fully illustrated guide makes an excellent reference tool.

$18.95p
0-07-881109-0, 520 pp., 7½ x 9¼

Advanced Programmer's Guide to UNIX™ System V
by Rebecca Thomas, Ph.D., Lawrence R. Rogers, and Jean L. Yates

C programmers who already know UNIX™ fundamentals can use this guide to write more effective programs with the software tools in UNIX System V. Thomas and Yates, two renowned names in the computer industry and the authors of *A User Guide to the UNIX™ System*, lend their expertise to help you develop sophisticated skills. This book explains and illustrates the use of the Bourne and C shells, text editors, the C compiler, library archives, utilities, subroutines, and system calls. You'll also learn about the new interprocess communication features, which are important in designing commercial applications software.

$21.95p
0-07-881211-9, 560 pp., 7⅜ x 9¼

The Practical Guide to Local Area Networks, Covers IBM® & Compatible Computers
Rowland Archer

You can gamble your company's money on a local area network...or you can read this book first. Deciding which local area network is right or you doesn't have to be a difficult process. With *The Practical Guide to Local Area Networks*, you'll be prepared to evaluate and select the LAN that's best for your business needs. LAN specialist Rowland Archer guides you through the process of planning your LAN installation, pointing out the advantages and potential pitfalls every step of the way. Archer then applies the criteria he has developed to five of the most popular LANs available for the IBM® PC and compatible computers: IBM® PC Network, 3Com Ethernet,® Corvus Omninet,® Orchid PCnet,® and Novell NetWare.™ With Archer's advice and insights in *The Practical Guide to Local Area Networks*, you, too, can become a LAN expert.

$21.95p
0-07-881190-2, 250 pp., 6½ x 9¼

Micro-to-Mainframe Links
by Ronald F. Kopeck

Here's a book that sorts out all the complex issues involved in linking microcomputers to mainframes for sophisticated, high-powered applications. With *Micro-to-Mainframe Links*, data processing and communications professionals can fully understand the major considerations behind PC-to-mainframe integration. A concise, detailed text thoroughly explains the planning and evaluation process used in determining how PC-to-mainframe linking fits into your office environment. Data transfer, security, and use of existing networks are also discussed. You'll find out about link products and the real and hidden costs of linking, as well as maintenance and service. And you'll learn about monitoring, the safe ways to begin the PC-to-mainframe link by establishing and evaluating tests and measurements. Kopeck, a widely-known consultant and editor of *Micro-to-Mainframe Link News*, draws on his extensive knowledge of this field to bring you the most comprehensive coverage possible.

$18.95p
0-07-881228-3, 300 pp., 7⅜ x 9¼

Available at fine bookstores and computer stores everywhere.

For a complimentary catalog of all our current publications contact: Osborne/McGraw-Hill, 2600 Tenth Street, Berkeley, CA 94710

Phone inquiries may be made using our toll-free number. Call 800-227-0900 or 800-772-2531 (in California). TWX 910-366-7277.

Prices subject to change without notice.

The manuscript for this book was prepared and submitted to Osborne **McGraw-Hill** in electronic form. The Acquisitions Editor for this project was Jon Erickson and the Project Editor was Lyn Cordell.

Text design uses Times Roman for text body and Univers bold for display.

Cover art by Yashi Okita. Cover supplier is Phoenix Color Corp. Cover Stock, 50 lb. Glatfelter. Book printed and bound by R. R. Donnelly & Sons Company, Crawfordsville, Indiana.